COMMUNICATIONS AND POWER
IN MEDIEVAL EUROPE

———

THE CAROLINGIAN AND OTTONIAN CENTURIES

COMMUNICATIONS AND POWER
IN MEDIEVAL EUROPE

THE CAROLINGIAN AND OTTONIAN CENTURIES

KARL LEYSER

EDITED BY
TIMOTHY REUTER

THE HAMBLEDON PRESS
LONDON   AND   RIO GRANDE

Published by The Hambledon Press 1994

102 Gloucester Avenue, London NW1 8HX (U.K.)

P.O. Box 162, Rio Grande, Ohio 45674 (U.S.A.)

ISBN 1 85285 013 2

A description of this book is available from
the British Library and from the Library of Congress

Typeset by York House Typographic Ltd
Printed on acid-free paper and bound in Great
Britain by Cambridge University Press

Contents

Preface   vii

Acknowledgements   ix

Abbreviations   xi

1   Concepts of Europe in the Early and High Middle Ages   1

2   Three Historians   19

3   Early Medieval Warfare   29

4   Early Medieval Canon Law and the Beginning of Knighthood   51

5   The Ottonians and Wessex   73

6   The Anglo-Saxons 'At Home'   105

7   Liudprand of Cremona: Preacher and Homilist   111

8   Ends and Means in Liudprand of Cremona   125

9   *Theophanu Divina Gratia Imperatrix Augusta*: Western and Eastern Emperorship in the Later Tenth Century   143

10   987: The Ottonian Connection   165

11   Maternal Kin in Early Medieval Germany   181

12   Ritual, Ceremony and Gesture: Ottonian Germany   189

13   The Ascent of Latin Europe   215

Index   233

Preface

At the time of Karl Leyser's death on 27 May 1992, 'ambushed by a stroke', to quote the obituary he himself wrote for Bruce McFarlane, he was preparing a second collection of his articles for publication as a sequel to his *Medieval Germany and its Neighbours, 900-1250* (London: Hambledon Press, 1982), under the title *Communications and Power: the European Experience, 900-1200*. He also had several other articles in hand intended for separate publication. Henrietta Leyser, Martin Sheppard and I decided to expand the collection as originally planned to include all of his articles, published or unpublished, which had not appeared in the earlier collection. The present volume and its companion, *Communications and Power in Medieval Europe: The Gregorian Revolution and Beyond* (London: Hambledon Press, 1994), are the result of that decision. After considering various other possibilities, we settled for an arrangement of the essays in rough chronological order, with a dividing-line between this volume and its companion at around the year 1000.

Though the two collections are only in a limited sense a substitute for any of the various books Karl is known to have planned, the essays they contain nevertheless form a remarkably coherent whole. More will be said of this in the preface to the companion volume; here it is sufficient to describe what has been done in preparing the two collections. A number of essays existed only as typescripts for lecture delivery (most of his scholarly work began life as lectures delivered to seminars or conferences) or as barely legible manuscripts awaiting dictation to the typist. In these cases there was no scholarly apparatus apart from an occasional scribbled reference in the margin of the text, though in some cases there were equally illegible notes taken from his reading of primary sources. There was not only the problem of deciphering Karl's hand – he habitually drafted using a soft pencil on narrow-lined foolscap, which has not made life easier for his editor – but also, in those cases where a German as well as an English text has survived, of conflating the two versions without distorting his intentions. The pieces left unpublished at Karl's death would not have been published in precisely the form offered here had he lived longer: there are omissions, silences, and occasionally weaknesses in the argument. But all of them contain so much of interest and of value that it would have been a pity to omit them on the grounds that they are less than perfect; readers should judge them by the insights they contain rather than by their deficiencies, and reserve their criticisms for the editor. There is no doubt also that Karl would have provided his usual footnotes, rich in interesting asides and citations from unexpected sources, and also that he would have taken the opportunity provided by resetting to revise the published essays as well as bring their apparatus up to date. For the essays published under Karl's own eye editorial intervention in the text has been confined to such things as uniformity of spelling, punctuation and capitalisation, and in the footnotes to formal consistency and occasional bibliographical additions, especially where new editions of sources have appeared since the date of original publication. The texts previously unpublished have been copy-edited respectfully but firmly and have also been provided with a fairly full scholarly apparatus: occasionally this has the function of an editorial comment or gloss. In all cases the status of the text offered is indicated at the beginning of the essay, and for those pieces already published the original pagination is embedded in the running text in square brackets, so that references to the originals may be checked more easily. Those essays which I have prepared for separate publication since Karl's death have all had some additions and corrections made in the course of preparing them for publication in this volume and its companion; hence it is the versions given here which should for preference be cited in future scholarly writing.

A number of Karl's and my colleagues and friends have given generous help with references to primary and secondary sources and in clearing up problems of interpretation and transcription, and I should here like to thank Gerd Althoff, Donald Bullough, Jinty Nelson, Bernd Schneidmüller, Jonathan Shepard and Martina Stratmann for their help with the essays in this volume, though they are not responsible for my remaining errors. My thanks are also due to the library staff of the Monumenta Germaniae Historica for their assistance, to the president, Horst Fuhrmann, for his encouragement, and to Martin Sheppard of the Hambledon Press, not least for his toleration of editorial indecisiveness and of revised deadlines. Above all I must thank Henrietta Leyser, for constant encouragement, for help with transcriptions and with references, and most of all for giving me the opportunity to spend so many hours following the thought-processes and intuitions of a remarkable and sensitive medieval historian. I hope that others will learn as much from reading the two collections as I have done in preparing them for publication.

Timothy Reuter   Munich, August 1993

Acknowledgments

The editor and the publishers are most grateful to the original publishers for permission to reprint essays here.

1   *Past and Present*, 137 (1992), pp. 25-47. World Copyright: The Past and Present Society, Corpus Christi College, Oxford, England.

2   (a) This is published here for the first time; (b) and (c) are taken from *The Blackwell's Dictionary of Historians*, ed. J. Cannon (Oxford: Basil Blackwell, 1988), pp. 408-10; 450-1.

3   *The Battle of Maldon*, ed. Janet Cooper (London: The Hambledon Press, 1993), pp. 87-108.

4   *Institutionen, Kultur und Gesellschaft im Mittelalter. Festschrift für Josef Fleckenstein zu seinem 65. Geburtstag*, ed. Lutz Fenske, Werner Rösener and Thomas Zotz (Sigmaringen: Jan Thorbecke Verlag, 1984), pp. 549-66.

5   First published in German as 'Die Ottonen und Wessex', *Frühmittelalterliche Studien* 17 (1983), pp. 73-97 (Walter de Gruyter Verlag).

6   *Anglo-Saxon Studies in Archaeology and History*, 2, ed. D. Brown, J. Campbell and S.C. Hawkes (British Archaeological Reports, British Series 92, Oxford: B.A.R., 1981), pp. 237-42.

7   *The Bible in the Medieval World: Essays in Memory of Beryl Smalley*, ed. D. Wood and K. Walsh (Studies in Church History, Subsidia 4, Oxford: Blackwells, 1985), pp. 43-60.

8   *Byzantium and the West, c. 850 – c. 1200: Proceedings of the XVIII Spring Symposium of Byzantine Studies, Oxford, 30 March – 1 April 1984*, ed. J.D. Howard-Johnston (Amsterdam: A.M. Hakkert, 1988), pp. 119-43.

9   This is published here for the first time.

10 This is published here for the first time.

11 *Past and Present*, 49 (1970), pp. 126-34. World Copyright: The Past and Present Society, Corpus Christi College, Oxford, England.

12   This is published here for the first time. A German version is to appear in
      Frühmittelalterliche Studien 27 (1993).

13   First published as *The Ascent of Latin Europe: An Inaugural Lecture
      Delivered before the University of Oxford on 7 November 1984*, Oxford:
      Clarendon Press, 1986, pp. 28.

Abbreviations

Adalbert, *Continuation*	See under Regino, *Chronicon*
Adam of Bremen, *Gesta*	*Magistri Adami Bremensis Gesta Hammaburgensis Ecclesiae Pontificum*, ed. B Schmeidler (MGH SRG 1, Hanover, 1917)
Adémar of Chabannes, *Chronicon*	Adémar de Chabannes, *Chronique*, ed. J. Chavanon (Collection de textes pour servir à l'étude et à l'enseignement de l'hisoire 20, Paris, 1897)
Annales Bertiniani	*Les Annales de Saint-Bertin*, ed. F. Grat and others (Paris, 1964)
Annales ESC	*Annales. Economies, Sociétés, Civilisations*
Annales Fuldenses	*Annales Fuldenses sive Annales regni Francorum orientalis*, ed. F. Kurze (MGH SRG 7, Hanover, 1891)
Annales Regni Francorum	*Annales regni Francorum inde ab a. 741 usque ad a. 829, que dicuntur Annales Laurissenses Maiores et Einhardi*, 2nd edn by F. Kurze (MGH SRG 6, Hanover, 1895)
AQDG	Ausgewählte Quellen zur Deutschen Geschichte des Mittelalters (Freiherr-vom-Stein-Gedächtnis-Ausgabe)
Bernhardi, *Lothar III.*	W. Bernhardi, *Lothar von Supplinburg* (Jahrbücher der Deutschen Geschichte 15, Leipzig, 1879)

Bernhardi, *Konrad III.*	W. Bernhardi, *Konrad III.* (Jahrbücher der Deutschen Geschichte 16, Leipzig, 1883)
Böhmer-Appelt	J.F. Böhmer, *Regesta Imperii III: Salisches Haus, 1. Teil, 1. Abt.: Die Regesten des Kaiserreiches unter Konrad II. (1024-1039)*, revised by H. Appelt (Graz, 1951)
Böhmer-Baaken	J.F. Böhmer, *Regesta Imperii IV: Ältere Staufer, 3. Abt.: Die Regesten des Kaiserreiches unter Heinrich VI., 1165(1190)-1197*, revised by G. Baaken (Cologne, 1972)
Böhmer-Graff	J.F. Böhmer, *Regesta Imperii II: Sächsisches Haus, 919-1024, 4. Abt.: Die Regesten des Kaiserreiches unter Heinrich II., 1002-1024*, revised by T. Graff (Vienna, 1971)
Böhmer-Mikoletzky	J.F. Böhmer, *Regesta Imperii II: Sächsisches Haus, 919-1024, 2. Abt.: Die Regesten des Kaiserreiches unter Otto II., 955(973)-983*, revised by H.L. Mikoletzky (Graz, 1950)
Bömer-Ottenthal	J.F. Bömer, *Regesta Imperii II: Sächsisches Haus, 919-1024, 1. Lieferung*, revised by E. von Ottenthal (Innsbruck, 1893)
Bömer-Uhlirz	J.F. Bömer, *Regesta Imperii II: Sächsisches Haus, 919-1024, 3. Abt: Die Regesten des Kaiserreiches unter Otto III., 980(983)-1002*, revised by M. Uhlirz (Graz, 1956)
Bömer-Zimmermann	J.F. Bömer, *Regesta Imperii II: Sächsische Zeit, 5. Abt.: Papstregesten 911-1024*, revised by H. Zimmermann (Vienna, 1969)

Bresslau, *Konrad II.*	H. Bresslau, *Jahrbücher des Deutschen Reiches unter Konrad II.*, 2 vols. (Jahrbücher der Deutschen Geschichte 12, Leipzig, 1879-84)
Brun, *Saxonicum Bellum*	*Brunos Buch vom Sachsenkrieg*, ed. H.-E. Lohmann (MGH Deutsches Mittelalter 2, Leipzig 1937)
D(D)	Diploma(ta). The reference is by convention to the initial of the ruler's name, his number and that of the edition in the Diplomata series of the MGH; thus D H II 10 is no. 10 in the edition of Henry II's diplomata.
DA	*Deutsches Archiv für Erforschung des Mittelalters*
Dümmler, *Ostfränkisches Reich*	E. Dümmler, *Geschichte des ostfränkischen Reiches*, 3 vols., 2nd edn (Jahrbücher der Deutschen Geschichte 7, Leipzig 1887-88),
EHR	*The English Historical Review*
Einhard, *Vita Karoli*	Einhardi Vita Karoli Magni, 6th edn by O. Holder-Egger (MGH SRG 25, Hanover, 1911)
Ermold, *Carmen*	Ermold le Noire, *Poème sur Louis le Pieux et Épitres au Roi Pepin*, ed. E. Faral (Les Classiques de l'histoire de France au moyen âge 14, Paris, 1964)
Flodoard, *Annales*	*Les Annales de Flodoard*, ed. P. Lauer (Collection de texts pour servir à l'étude et à l'enseignement de l'hisoire 39, Paris, 1905)
Gesta Francorum	Anonymous, *Gesta Francorum et aliorum Hierosolimitanorum*, ed. R. Hill (Nelson's Medieval Texts, Edinburgh, 1962)

Hirsch-Papst-Bresslau, *Heinrich II.* — S. Hirsch, H. Pabst and H. Bresslau, *Jahrbücher des Deutschen Reiches unter Heinrich II.*, 3 vols. (Jahrbücher der Deutschen Geschichte 11, Leipzig 1862-75)

HZ — *Historische Zeitschrift*

JEccH — *Journal of Ecclesiastical History*

Köpke-Dümler, *Otto der Große* — R. Köpke and E. Dümmler, *Kaiser Otto der Große* (Jahrbücher der Deutschen Geschichte 9, Leipzig, 1876)

Lampert of Hersfeld, *Annales* — *Lamperti monachi Hersfeldensis Opera*, ed. O. Holder-Egger (MGH SRG 38, Havover, 1894)

Leyser, *Rule and Conflict* — K.J. Leyser, *Rule and Conflict in an Early Medieval Society: Ottonian Saxony* (London, 1979)

Leyser, *The Gregorian Revolution* — K.J. Leyser, *Communications and Power in Medieval Europe: The Gregorian Revolution and Beyond* (London, 1994)

Leyser, *Medieval Germany* — K.J. Leyser, *Medieval Germany and its Neighbours, 911-1250* (London, 1982)

Liudprand, *Antapodosis* — *Liudprandi Opera* ed. J. Becker,

Liudprand, *Historia Ottonis* — 3rd edn (MGH SRG 40,

Liuprand, *Legatio* — Hanover, 1915)

Meyer von Knonau, *Heinrich IV.* — G. Meyer von Knonau, *Jahrbücher des Deutschen Reiches unter Heinrich IV. und Heinrich V.*, 7 vols. (Jahrbücher der Deutshcen Geschichte 14, Leipzig, 1980-1909), vols. 1-5.

Meyer von Knonau, *Heinrich V.* — G. Meyer von Knonau, *Jahrbücher des Deutschen Reiches unter Heinrich IV. und Heinrich V.*, 7 vols. (Jahrbücher der Deutschen Geschichte 14, Leipzig, 1890-1909), vols. 6-7.

MGH — *Monumenta Germaniae Historica*, with subseries:

BDK — *Die Briefe der Deutschen Kaiserzeit*

Capit. — *Capitularia regum Francorum*

Conc.	*Concilia*
Deutsches Mittelalter	
Epp.	*Epistolae in Quart*
Epp. Sel.	*Epistolae Selectae*
LdL	*Libelli de Lite*
Poetae	*Poetae Latini Medii Aevi*
SRG NS	*Scriptores rerum Germanicarum, nova series*
SRG	*Scriptores rerum Germanicarum in usum scholarum*
SS	*Scriptores in Folio*
MIÖG, MÖIG	*Mitteilungen des Instituts für Österreichische Geschichtsforschung* [1921-44: *des Österreichischen Instituts für Geschichtsforschung*]
NA	*Neues Archiv der Gesellschaft für ältere deutsche Geschichtskunde*
Nithard, *Historiae*	Nithard, *Histoire des Fils de Louis le Pieux*, ed. P. Lauer (Les Classique de l'histoire de France au moyen âge 7, Paris, 1926)
Notker, *Gesta Karoli*	Notker the Stammerer, *Gesta Karoli Magni Imperatoris*, ed. H.F. Haefele (MGH SRG NS 12, revised edn, Munich 1980).
Ordericus Vitalis, *Historia Ecclesiastica*	Ordericus Vitalis, *Historia Ecclesiastica*, ed. M. Chibnall, 6 vols. (Oxford Medieval Texts, 1969-80)
Regino, *Chronicon*	*Reginonis Abbatis Prumiensis Chronicon cum continuatione Treverensi*, ed. F. Kurze (MGH SRG 50, Hanover, 1890)
RHC	Académie des Inscriptions et Belles-Lettres, *Recueil des Historiens des Croisades, série II: Historiens Occidentaux*, 5 vols. (Paris, 1844-95)
Richer, *Historiae*	Richer, *Histoire de France*, ed. R. Latouche, 2 vols. (Les Classiques de l'histoire de France au moyen âge 12 and 17, Paris, 1930-37)

Rodulfus Glaber, *Historiae*

Rodulfi Glabri Historiarum Libri Quinque ed. J. France (Oxford Medieval Texts, Oxford 1989)

Rolls Series

Rerum Britanniarum Medii Aevi Scriptores, 99 vols. (London, 1858-96)

Ruotger, *Vita Brunonis*

Ruotgeri Vita Brunonis Archiepiscopi Coloniensis, ed. I. Ott (MGH SRG NS 10, Weimar, 1951)

Settimane

Settimane di studio del Ćentro italiano di studi sull'alto medioevo

Simson, *Ludwig der Fromme*

B. Simson, *Jahrbücher des Fränkischen Reiches unter Ludwig dem Frommen*, 2 vols. (Jahrbücher der Deutschen Geschichte 6, Leipzig, 1874-76)

Steindorff, *Heinrich III.*

E. Steindorff, *Jahrbücher des Deutschen Reiches unter Heinrich III.*, 2 vols. (Jahrbücher der Deutschen Geschichte 13, Leipzig 1874)

Thietmar, *Chronicon*

Thietmari Merseburgensis Episcopi Chronicon, ed. R. Holtzmann (MGH SRG NS 9, Berlin, 1935)

TRHS

Transactions of the Royal Historical Society

Uhlirz, *Otto III*

M. Uhlirz, *Jahrbücher des Deutschen Reiches unter Otto II. und Otto III.*, 2: *Otto III., 983-1002* (Jahrbücher der Deutschen Geschichte 10/2, Berlin, 1954)

Vorträge und Forschungen

Vorträge und Forschungen herausgegeben vom Konstanzer Arbeitskreis für mittelalteriche Geschichte

Waitz, *Heinrich I.*

G. Waitz, *Jahrbücher des Deutschen Reichs unter König Heinrich I.* (Jahrbücher der Deutschen Geschichte 8, Leipzig, 1885)

Wattenbach-Holtzmann-Schmale	W. Wattenbach, *Deutschlands Geschichtsquellen im Mittelalter: Die Zeit der Sachsen und Salier*, revised by R. Holtzmann, new edn by F.-J. Schmale, 3 vols. (Darmstadt, 1967-71)
Wattenbach-Levison-Löwe	W. Wattenbach, *Deutschlands Geschichtsquellen im Mittelalter: Vorzeit und Karolinger*, revised by W. Levison and H. Löwe, 6 continuously paginated fascicles (Weimar, 1952-90)
Wattenbach-Schmale	W. Wattenbach, *Deutschlands Geschichtsquellen im Mittelalter: Die Zeit der Staufer*, new edn by F.-J. Schmale, vol. 1 (Darmstadt, 1976)
Widukind, *Res gestae Saxonicae*	*Widukindi Corbeiensis rerum gestarum Saxonicarum libri III*, 3rd edn by H.E. Lohmann and P. Hirsch (MGH SRG 60, Hanover, 1935)
William of Malmesbury, *Gesta Regum*	*Willelmi Malmesbiriensis monachi De gestis regum Anglorum libri quinque; Historiae Novellae libri tres*, ed. W. Stubbs, 2 vols. (Rolls Series 90, London, 1887-89)

1

Concepts of Europe in the Early and High Middle Ages

Like so much else, Bede, Fredegarius and the Carolingian savants inherited their ideas of Europe from late antiquity, above all from the luminaries who conveyed the substance of this disintegrating world to their eager and anxiously waiting disciples in the eighth and ninth centuries and eventually to the high middle ages altogether. Both the mythology and cosmology in which Europe emerged as one of the constituent parts of the world intrigued and exercised the imaginations of the Carolingian court circles they reached and, it could be said, poured into their lavish poetry up to the very end of the ninth century. Most of this, if not all, resounded again in the festive notes struck by Ottonian historiography and panegyric to celebrate the triumphs of the tenth-century Saxon rulers and their following. They too wanted to be seen and measured by European scales. Among their writers one at least, Liudprand of Cremona, nursed truly continental [26] cultural perspectives, and it is tempting almost to call him the first European.[1]

The three pillars of wisdom – and this is not meant ironically – through whom the early and high middle ages received the traditions to bolster their sense of European belonging, thus giving a past to their refashioned political and military present, were St Augustine, Isidore of Seville and above all the late fourth- and early fifth-century Christian world historian, Orosius. Theirs, however, was a messy inheritance. The ancient world had fostered a myth of

* First published posthumously in *Past and Present*, 137 (1992), pp. 25-47. World Copyright: The Past and Present Society, Corpus Christi College, Oxford, England. A few additions and corrections have been made to the footnotes.

[1] J. Fischer, *Oriens-Occidens-Europa: Begriff und Gedanke 'Europa' in der späten Antike und im frühen Mittelalter* (Veröffentlichungen des Instituts für Europäische Geschichte in Mainz 15, Wiesbaden, 1957), has sought to survey systematically how the term Europe was used from the fifth to the end of the eleventh century when he oddly thought it became extinct for the time being. See also D. Hay, *Europe: The Emergence of an Idea* (Edinburgh, 1957; 2nd edn New York, 1968). In all fairness I start off by acknowledging indebtedness to Fischer's exposé, which suffers, however, from being too detached from the sorts of pressures that shaped and changed the concept and its traditions. Valuable is T. Schieder, 'Vorwort zum Gesamtwerk', in *Handbuch der Europäischen Geschichte*, 1: *Europa im Wandel von der Antike zum Mittelalter*, ed. T. Schieffer (Stuttgart, 1976), pp. 1-21.

Europe, the story of Zeus' desire aroused by the sight of the daughter of King Agenor picking flowers, abducting her in the shape of a bull over the waters to Crete (which later counted as part of Europe) and, once again a man, begetting three sons by her. Returned to earthly converse Europe married the king of Crete, Asterios, and brought up her three sons.[2] Of our three transmitters, St Augustine and Isidore of Seville marshal this story, the former only to write wryly of the public shows and games to which it gave rise. They were staged to placate false deities and furnish occasions for popular holidays.[3] The Europa theme belonged to a polite education, the urbane bearing of elevated social milieux and those who danced attendance on them. Bishops in the world of late Roman antiquity had to master its language and conventions in order to convert it. Their medieval successors did the same.

Side by side with this myth and stemming from it Europe had come to be seen also as a region, designating at first Thrace – the Greek mainland, but not the Peloponnese – but then growing [27] ever larger northwards and westwards as travellers ventured inland and mariners sailed round the Pillars of Hercules and discovered the Atlantic coasts and Britain, gradually forcing their knowledge on reluctant geographers. Whether the *orbis terrarum* was tripartite or made up of only two segments, Africa and Europe rather than Asia and Europe counting as one, had remained for a long time in dispute. But a universe made of three parts, Asia, Europe and Africa, became the shared view of our three authorities. There was more dispute about the frontiers between them, especially that between Europe and Asia. While the River Phasis flowing into the Black Sea from the east was often mentioned, by Orosius' time and for centuries later the River Don, the Sea of Azoff and – much harder to trace – what were called the Riphean Mountains counted as the boundaries between the two continents.[4]

Western and central European literati, above all historians, thus inherited and took over this geographically and cosmologically orientated understanding of Europe. Richer of St Rémi in the later tenth century began his history of France with a brief account of the tripartite earth, *orbis plaga*, as the cosmographers explained it, and here he leaned wholly on Orosius. Africa and Europe he envisaged surrounded by ocean. The Mediterranean, *mare nostrum*, severed them from one another.[5] Otto of Freising begins the first book of his world history, the *Chronica* or *History of the Two Cities*, with a brief account of the known human habitat, just as Orosius had done in the opening

[2] Escher, 'Europe', *Paulys Real-Encyclopädie der Classischen Altertumswissenschaft*, ed. G. Wissowa and others, 81 vols. (Stuttgart, 1893-1978), vol. 6 pt. 1, cols. 1291-2.

[3] Augustine, *De Civitate Dei* XVIII 12, ed. B. Dombart and A. Kalb with some emendations (Corpus Christianorum series Latina 48, Turnhout, 1955), pp. 602-3 and Isidore of Seville, *Etymologiarum sive Originum libri XX* XIV 4, ed. W.M. Lindsay, 2 vols. (Oxford, 1911), vol. 2, no pagination.

[4] Orosius, *Historiarum adversum Paganos Libri VII* I 2, ed. C. Zangemeister (Corpus Scriptorum Ecclesiasticorum Latinorum 5, Vienna, 1882), p. 10.

[5] Richer, *Historiae* I 1, p. 6. The term *mare nostrum* is Orosius's, loc. cit. (n.4).

sentences of his *Adversus paganos libri* VII, and he quotes Orosius verbatim. He ends the chapter by directing his readers to consult Orosius if they want to know about the provinces of the continents, their exact situation and regions.[6] Here it is worth noting that Europe was thought to be much larger than Africa. Both together could not equal Asia. The assumed smallness of Africa explained why [28] it and Europe were regarded by some as a single unit, just one part of the cosmos.

In Richer there is a small but startling overtone sounded in the citation of Orosius. Richer spoke of 'that part of the earth which is commodious to men' when he introduced the tripartite division.[7] He thus introduced a criterion not to be found in his source, habitability. Europe here already has an economy. It served above all to introduce Gaul, 'White Gaul', as the country where his civilised affections lay. Europe makes more than a fleeting appearance in Lombard texts of the late seventh and eighth centuries. A Master Stephanus (*c.* 698) praised the exalted origins of the Lombard royal house in the confines of Europe and then turned to their king, Aripert (653-62), the pious and Catholic ruler who had extirpated Arian heresy among his people and so made the Christian faith grow.[8] If the Franks had migrated from Asia into Europe, the Lombards, in their reflections on the past, cultivated their own European origins. Their historian, Paul the Deacon (*ob.* 787) had a larger vision of these antecedents in the migrations of German tribes, and he saw Germany as the homeland of all the *gentes* that had afflicted Europe. The Lombards, even if they came from an island he called Scandinavia, were none the less a Germanic people. He even purported to know the cause of their migration: they became too numerous so that they could no longer all live together. Some had to migrate.[9] It seems as if Paul would not regard the original homes of these *gentes*, their barbaric hinterland, as part of Europe. By implication, a degree of civilisation was already attached to the European name.

Already in seventh-century hagiography Europe could furnish a topos for boastful grandiloquence. In the *Life of St Gertrude* we read 'Who is there living in Europe who does not know the loftiness of her forbears, their names and habitats and the places they owned?', as there were a European public to discuss such matters.[10] This raises more generally the question of the milieu [29] in which some familiarity with the concept of Europe was at home, whether mythological or as one of the constituent parts of the known world. The clerical literati, historians and poets, in whose works references to Europe have here been searched for and traced, were for the most part a small élite

---

[6] Otto of Freising, *Chronica sive Historia de Duabus Civitatibus* I 1, ed. A. Hofmeister (MGH SRG 45, Hanover, 1912), pp. 36-8.

[7] Richer, *Historiae* I 1, p. 6: 'orbis itaque plaga, quae mortalibus sese commodam praebet'.

[8] *Rhythmi Aevi Merovingici et Carolini* no. cxlv, *MGH Poetae* 4/2, p. 728.

[9] Paul the Deacon, *Historia Langobardorum* I 2, *MGH Scriptores rerum Langobardicarum et Italicarum saec. VI-IX* 1, pp. 48-9.

[10] *Vita Sanctae Geretrudis* prologue, *MGH Scriptores rerum Merovingicarum* 2, p. 454 (in both the A- and the B-version).

drawn from the ranks of a larger élite, the clerical order as such. They often belonged to the ambience of rulers, and in this way the idea of the continents and of Europe's distinctive quality as one of them might be imparted also to the lay aristocracy. Not many of them had sat in schoolrooms, though a clerical tutor at home could have imparted not only an element of literacy but also geographical, historical and other knowledge. To be aware of itself and its roles, duties, rank and privileges, the aristocracy of any *gens* needed to know about its past and cultivate it, and this could not be done without some elementary geographical framework and knowledge.[11] Itineracy, moreover, was the lot of emperors and kings, and hence also of their lay warrior entourages. Europe could come to mean something to a lay noble who had accompanied a Carolingian or Ottonian royal overlord all the way to Rome and back. Such knowledge could be communicated also to their fellows who had stayed at home.

It is to the author so tantalisingly identified with Fredegarius and his *Chronicae* that we must turn for the most fertile and enduring myth of Frankish beginnings and their European bearings. Here is, for the first time, the story of the Franks' Trojan origins. Priamus was their first king. Part of them migrated to Macedonia, where they became the staunchest warriors. Not only Troy and its ruler, but the Macedonians Philip and Alexander, were unblushingly enlisted as Frankish royal forbears and cited to exemplify early Frankish prowess. A second host of Franks – for peoples were then seen first and foremost as warriors and armies – followed a king named Francio whom they had elected, and he directed them from Asia into Europe and settled them between the Rhine and the Danube. For a time they were subject to the 'Consul Pompey'. Then, however, they concluded friendship with the Saxons, rebelled, and shook off his domination. Thereafter no people up to the present day (the early eighth [30] century) had been able to vanquish the Franks. They built another Troy on the Rhine; it may have been Xanten.[12] All this is flourishing fiction handed down over many generations. In St Martin, moreover, the Franks possessed and boasted of a patron saint of European stature. Thanks to

---

[11] P. Riché, *Education et culture dans l'Occident barbare, 6e-8e siècles* (Paris, 1962), p. 273, thought it probable, however, that most Frankish aristocrats received a minimum of instruction. R. McKitterick, *The Carolingians and the Written Word* (Cambridge, 1989), pp. 211-70, ch. 6, especially p. 227, agrees.

[12] *Fredegarii et aliorum Chronica* II 4-6, *MGH Scriptores rerum Merovingicarum* 2, pp. 45-6. On Xanten see J.M. Wallace-Hadrill, 'Fredegar and the History of France', in idem, *The Long-Haired Kings and other Essays in Merovingian History* (London, 1962), pp. 71-94, here p. 82. Wallace-Hadrill also discusses the question of single or multiple authorship of Fredegar's text; for more recent discussion see *Quellen zur Geschichte des 7. und 8. Jahrhundert*, ed. H. Wolfram, A. Kustering and H. Haupt (AQDG 4a, Darmstadt, 1982), pp. 9-13.

him Europe could be said to have a saint no less eminent and potent than those of Asia and Africa.[13]

At the same time the Occident, Latin Christendom, would not rest content with King Priamus and a merely pagan account of origins in the story of the daughter of King Agenor, even if she was countenanced a little by Isidore of Seville and also, albeit with disdain, by St Augustine. It needed also a biblical one and found it in the descent of the sons of Noah. Already in Isidore of Seville they were the founders of towns and regions in Europe, Asia and Africa.[14] The whole human race must be descended from them and they, Shem, Ham and Japheth therefore divided the world between them. Europe was Japheth's share, and his numerous offspring and their descendants in turn were the ancestors of all the greater European peoples: Franks, Latins, Alemans and Britons, to name but some. Nennius' *Historia Brittonum* is a very specific source here, and enshrines seventh-century traditions.[15]

Yet what gave shape, relevance and duration to the notion of Europe from the early seventh century onwards was Rome, or rather the Roman Church and its head, the papacy. The addresses of two letters by St Columba, to Pope Gregory I and Pope Boniface IV respectively, deserve to be quoted in full: 'To the holy lord and father in Christ, the most beautiful ornament of the Roman Church, to the most august, as it were, ornament [31] of all languishing Europe, the egregious look-out, expert in the knowledge of divine casualty, I, lowly Columba, send salutation in Christ.' The rhetorical contrast between wilting Europe and its spiritual head, bathed in light and clothed in imperial epitheta, reveals a new cultural landscape, however rugged and as yet fitful. The questions Columba raised – the date of Easter, simony, and monks leaving the communities where they had made their vows – called for authoritative answers, and this on a European plane. The letter he addressed to Pope Boniface IV opened on an even more histrionic note: 'To the most beauteous head of all churches in the whole of Europe, the dear pope, the exalted prelate, pastor of pastors, the most reverend overseer: the humblest to the highest, the least to the greatest, the rustic to the polished, the short of speech to the most eloquent, the last to the first, the stranger to the native, the poor to the mighty – strange to say and novelty – the exiguous bird Columba ventures to write to Father Boniface'.[16] Once again the missive is full of urgent and outspoken injunctions and warnings, but more clearly still than in the earlier letter the pope is seen to be the head of a European body of churches. In the early

---

[13] So Sulpicius Severus, his biographer. See Fischer, *Oriens-Occidens-Europa* (as n. 1), p. 42. For poetic echoes of this theme in the Carolingian period see *Alcuini Carmina*, no. xc, strophe xxi, *MGH Poetae* 1, p. 316; Radbod, *In Translatione Sancti Martini Sequentia, MGH Poetae* 4/1, p. 165b.

[14] Isidore, *Etymologiae* (as n. 3), IX 2.

[15] F. Lot, *Nennius et l'Historia Brittonum: Étude critique* (Bibliothèque de l'École des Hautes Études 263, Paris, 1934), pp. 160-1.

[16] Columba, *Epistolae*, nos. 1 and 5, *MGH Epp.* 3, pp. 156, 170; Fischer, *Oriens-Occidens-Europa* (as n. 1), pp. 47-8.

seventh century this meant above all the northern shores of the Mediterranean world, and north of the Alps mainly Merovingian Gaul and the Rhineland which counted as part of it. Certain classical continuities, but also the possibility of expansion, were latent in this European circumscription of the papacy.

The ascent of the Carolingians, who built their authority and power, first mayoral and then regal, on the resumption of fiercely aggressive policies towards the Merovingian kingdom's neighbours and unwilling subject peoples, soon dwarfed all previous scales and dimensions of Frankish rule. Einhard, quoting from the inscription on Charlemagne's tomb, wrote of him that he had nobly enhanced the kingdom of the Franks so that it was now nearly twice as large as the already great and mighty Reich he had taken over from his father Pippin, the first Carolingian king. Einhard then proceeded to recite the emperor's conquests: Aquitaine, Gascony, the Pyrenees, northern Spain up to the Ebro, Italy from Aosta to lower Calabria, Saxony, Pannonia, Dacia, Istria, Dalmatia and Liburnia (adjoining Istria and Carniola). He, [32] Charlemagne, also made a whole host of wild and barbarian peoples tributary, and here Einhard cited a number of Slav tribes in Germany, east of the Rhine up to the Vistula and between the Danube and the sea.[17] Whatever Einhard's exaggerations – and there were some – the conquests and the ill-assorted ensemble of regions and peoples brought under Frankish clientage cried aloud for a common designation and vehicle for summary comprehension. For Einhard the *regnum Francorum* was the be-all and end-all of his world. Yet other literati, letter-writers and poets of Charlemagne's and his successors' courts and environments found such a designation in Europe. If references to it in Merovingian writings had been sparse, they became plentiful from the later eighth century onwards. In the homily Cathwulf addressed to Charlemagne around 775, the author, after reminding the king of his successes and good fortune – like the timely death of his brother and rival Karlmann, the flight of the Lombard host, the bloodless seizure of Pavia with all its treasures, and the first visit to Rome – exhorted the king to show gratitude to God 'because he has raised you to the honour of the kingdom of Europe's (*regni Europae*) glory.'[18] Even greater divine gifts than all these would follow if the king honoured God and his churches. Cathwulf almost certainly did not wish Europe to be understood as a single kingdom when he used this term. He meant that Charlemagne had been exalted to wield rule in all Europe.

In 775 the Frankish king was still far from the full overthrow of the Saxons, nor had he yet ventured to strike at Arab strongholds in northern Spain. In 790, when writing to his erstwhile master Colcu in Northumbria, Alcuin also somewhat exaggerated Charlemagne's successes. By God's mercy, he wrote, his holy church in the parts of Europe had peace and was growing and flourishing, and he stated that the Old Saxons and the Frisians had, at Charlemagne's insistence, be it by gifts or by threats, been converted.[19] Yet

---

[17] Einhard, *Vita Karoli* cc. 15, 31, pp. 17-18 and 35-6 (the funerary inscription).
[18] *Epistolae variorum...* no. 7, *MGH Epp.* 4, pp. 502-5.
[19] Alcuin, *Epistolae* no. 7, *MGH Epp.* 4, p. 32.

this was far from being the end of Saxon resistance, and from 794 onwards hosts still marched year after year into Saxony to complete the work of conquest and to cope with risings. The letter all the same conveyed something of Charlemagne's [33] European-wide commitments: the year before he had marched against the Slavs, the Greeks had sent a fleet to Italy, and the Avars had threatened both Italy and Bavaria. The offensive in Spain was progressing under Charlemagne's counts and *missi*, and here the writer paused to deplore the Saracens' domination of Africa and over most of Asia, thus duly linking Europe with the other constituent parts of the world. A letter to a disciple about numbers is didactically illustrated by, among other examples, the division of the earth into three parts: Europe, Africa and India, in all of which God was to be worshipped with faith, hope and charity.[20]

Alcuin was and remained a schoolmaster. When the news of the sack of Lindisfarne by the Vikings and the expulsion of Bishop Higbald reached him, he wrote a letter of consolation, but it was again full of warnings and injunctions. Higbald must correct any shortcomings in his own ways to regain the help of his patron saints. There must be no vainglory in dress, no drunkenness. To have the protection of their saints, the bishop and his people must walk in their ways. Higbald was also advised not to be overwhelmed by dismay. God chastised those whom he loved, and perhaps he castigated the bishop more because he loved him more. There followed a history lesson. Jerusalem had perished in flames; Rome, where apostles and martyrs abounded, was devastated by pagans, but by God's own mercy soon recovered. Nearly all Europe – and these writers were fond of their 'nearly' – was emptied and devastated by the swords of the Goths and Huns, but now, thanks to God, it shone with churches, like the heavens with stars, and in them the holy offices throve.[21] The letter cannot have given much comfort and cheer to Higbald, but it is noteworthy that Europe could be seen by Alcuin as having a history, a past and a present to which he felt he belonged. He shared this awareness and grasp of the European past with Paul the Deacon, as we have seen.

If Britain is excepted, if it belonged to Europe only marginally if at all – and this despite Alcuin – then Charlemagne's empire covered nearly all of it and his court, increasingly stationary at Aachen, became for a time its centre. The men of letters had already before 800 spoken of the Reich as an *imperium Christianum*. The fact that Pope Leo III, unsafe in Rome, had had to [34] come all the way to Paderborn to meet the protector he needed in order to be reinstated and defended against his accusers only enhanced the European stature Charlemagne already possessed and gave it a new political and ecclesiastical clout. It is in the magnification of just these events in the poem *Karolus magnus et Leo papa* that the person of Charlemagne itself attracted the most glowing European epithets. Here he is the head of the world, the venerable apex of Europe

---

[20] Ibid. no. 81, p. 124.
[21] Ibid. no. 20, p. 57.

ruling his second Rome, Aachen, that was rising in new splendour. Here also, and this twice, he was called Europe's lighthouse and finally *rex, pater Europe* before Leo, the highest earthly pastor.[22] Europe is here the geographical and spiritual setting of that world order which alone counted, the Christian one, centred on Charlemagne, his religious and secular following at court and in the bishoprics, monasteries and the lands of the *regna* under his lordship. That he should have attempted to shape this society, police it and harness it to common tasks, without of course destroying its ethnic identities and pasts, was the first attempt of its kind since Roman imperial times. It was a European attempt all the more since it embraced peoples and areas that had remained outside the Roman frontiers, as the Poeta Saxo later pointed out.[23] His Europe, moreover, was no longer merely Mediterranean and Gallic; it was moving eastwards and further north. The emperorship of 800 only enhanced and underlined ideas already current during the 790s.

The eulogists of Louis the Pious clung to this European mantle which they inherited from Charlemagne's poets and flatterers. One indeed, Theodulf of Orléans, had been a member of the old emperor's circle. Disgraced and banished under his successor he pleaded in verse with his friends to intervene on his behalf. In his poem, the *Battle of the Birds*, Europe is the *opimus ager*, the best and most nourishing soil for every species of flying creature.[24] Another victim of Louis the Pious's displeasure, Ermoldus Nigellus, [35] sought to regain favour more directly with a poem setting out and praising the deeds and achievements of the emperor up to date (826). The *elegiacum carmen, In honorem Hludowici Christianissimi caesaris augusti*, whatever its faults, is a masterly narrative poem that depicts the routines, feasts and great occasions of Louis the Pious's court all the more vividly in that its author yearned to return and take part again at least in the doings of the *palatium* of his patron, Pippin of Aquitaine. He knew also where power lay in that hotbed of intrigues and rancours around the emperor's person of which he himself had become the victim. Europe necessarily figured in his grandiose attempt to please. In describing Louis's meeting with the pope, Stephen IV, in 816, Ermold addresses him: 'You, pious emperor, have the kingdoms of Europe (*Europae regna*) in your powerful grip.'[25] The echo of Cathwulf's letter is very striking. Europe also clinched a rhetorical climax Ermold created to describe Louis the Pious's host for the Breton campaign of August-September 818. He had

---

[22] *Karolus Magnus et Leo Papa* lines 92-3 (apex), 12 and 169 (lighthouse), 529 (father of Europe), *MGH Poetae* 1, pp. 368, 366 and 370, 379; there is a less widely available new edition by H. Beumann, F. Brunhölzl and W. Winkelmann, *Karolus Magnus et Leo Papa: Ein Paderborner Epos vom Jahre 799* (Paderborn, 1966). On the events leading up to Leo III's journey to Paderborn see P. Classen, *Karl der Große, das Papsttum und Byzanz*, 3rd edn by H. Fuhrmann and C. Märtl (Beiträge zur Geschichte und Quellenkunde des Mitelalers 9, Sigmaringen, 1986), pp. 42-57

[23] Poeta Saxo, *Annalium de gestis Caroli magni imperatoris libri quinque*, Book V, lines 651-2, *MGH Poetae* 4/1, p. 70: 'Quorum Romani nomina nescierunt'.

[24] Theodulf of Orléans, *Carmina* no. lxxii line 202, *MGH Poetae* 1, p. 568.

[25] Ermold, *Carmen*, line 923, p. 72.

summoned contingents from all over the Reich and ordered them to assemble at a place Ermold mistakenly thought to have been Vannes. It is interesting also that he called the gathering a *placitum*. The emperor had summoned the Franks and the peoples subject to them. There were Suabians, Saxons, Thuringians and Burgundians. 'I forbear', Ermold continued, 'to cite all the peoples and tribes of Europe that had come to fight the Breton prince.'[26] Ermoldus wanted the largest stage for his flatteries. In an earlier letter addressed to King Pippin, he exhorted him to obey his father always, 'whose faith, uprightedness, wisdom and fame were known in all Europe and Asia.'[27]

Poets like Walafrid Strabo and Sedulius Scottus, when hailing patrons or high-ranking friends and well-wishers less exalted than kings, still plucked the Europe-string to play their tunes of flattery and ingratiation. The fact that Carolingian kings like Charles the Bald and Louis the German ruled over smaller realms than their father and grandfather had done did not discourage the poets from endowing them with European epitheta and horizons, if only through their descent from Charlemagne. When Sedulius [36] addressed Charles the Bald his grandfather was *Europae princeps, imperiale decus* ('ruler of Europe, imperial glory'), [28] and he repeated these lines in a later piece and more aptly. Charlemagne was a Caesar, renowned in the whole world and again *Europae princeps, imperiale decus*.[29] Europe was made to rejoice or to grieve when either good fortune or death struck the Carolingian house. The birth of Lothar's son Charles by Ermengarde, his first wife, in 845, was greeted in a joyful poem: he was a 'bright new star, the glory of the world, the hope of Rome', and this new star shone for the peoples of Europe.[30] He did not live beyond his eighteenth year. Sedulius Scottus was no less assiduous in paying his court to Louis the German. He too was likened to a star that brightened Europe.[31] Hrabanus Maurus, Louis's erstwhile opponent, spoke in a letter to the king of his good name which was spread in all the provinces of Germany and Gaul, and of his praises which were being sung aloud in nearly (again the rhetorical *paene*) all parts of Europe.[32] In an equally encomiastic letter sent by Abbot Ermenrich of Ellwangen to Abbot Grimald, Louis the German's arch-chaplain, it is not just Grimald who is lauded, but even more his master Louis, 'our beloved king'. Louis likened to the pleasantest of rivers flowing from the foremost springs of all Europe. Even though he now rules over a more limited realm, that is, his share of the divided Frankish Reich, by his virtue he outshines Hercules, who had lorded it over the centaurs, and by his skill Ulysses. Ask the Slavs (against whom Louis had warred on the whole not

---

[26] Ibid. lines 1510-20, p. 116.
[27] Ermold, *Epistola II*, lines 189-90, p. 230.
[28] Sedulius Scottus, *Carmina* II 14, line 8, *MGH Poetae* 3, p. 182.
[29] Ibid. II 28, lines 1-2, p. 193.
[30] Ibid. II 23, lines 6-7, p. 189.
[31] Ibid. II 30, lines 27-8, p. 195.
[32] Hrabanus Maurus, *Epistolae* no. 37, *MGH Epp.* 5, p. 472.

unsuccessfully) and you will not marvel at my notice of him.[33] The death of Bertha, Lothar II's daughter, who had been married to Margrave Adalbert II of Tuscany, in 925, evoked an epitaph reminiscent of greater days: 'Now Europe sighs, now grieves all Francia, Corsica, Sardina, Greece and Italy'; yet she was not the only Carolingian Bertha for whom the epitaph might have been composed.[34] [37]

From these examples – and there are a good many others not cited here – one conclusion about ninth-century users of the term 'Europe' forces itself upon the reader of so much occasional Carolingian poetry and schooled letter-writing. Europe had become more than anything else a topos of panegyric, a cultural emblem rather than a solid, firm geographical and ethnic concept. It was flaunted liberally and with much repetition in the context of flattery and praise when addressing the great. The European scale and comparative were to hand and readily exchanged among the literati, and these ninth-century savants and men of letters were also aware of that tripartite world of which Europe was one constituent element. They even paraded their knowledge of the classical mythology of the continent in their verses. They knew that Europe, daughter of Agenor, had been ravished by Zeus who took her to Greece, and that she had given her name to the *patria*.[35] In a cosmographic poem of unknown, late eighth-century origin, Europe as a whole has become a homeland, and the author set about describing it country by country and people by people beginning with Scythia and the Maeotic Swamps (southern Russia and the Sea of Azoff). Towards the north the Don girdled it; this was the correct tradition. The whole account has a strongly Frankish ring, though the Saxons too are cited as an 'agile', hard and warlike people. In Gallia Belgica between Rhine and Seine the royal demesne and the princely warriors who came from there were lauded.[36]

The final note in this genre of Carolingian narrative historical poetry was struck by the Poeta Saxo of the late ninth century who set Einhard's *Life of Charlemagne* and the reworked Frankish royal annals to verse, though these were not his sole annalistic source. He did not disguise either the intensity, duration or the ferocity of Charlemagne's wars to overcome the Saxons, but observed with pride that it was done with enormous effort and sweat and to 'drag us away from the cult of demons the [38] peoples of all Europe had to be

---

[33] Ermanrich of Ellwangen, *Epistola ad Grimaldum abbatem, MGH Epp.* 5, p. 536.

[34] *Epitaphium Berthae* lines 23-4, *MGH Poetae* 4/3, p. 1008. For other Carolingian Berthas see K.F. Werner, 'Die Nachkommen Karls des Grossen bis um das Jahr 1000 (1.-8 Generation)', in *Karl der Große: Lebenswerk und Nachleben*, 4: *Das Nachleben*, ed. W. Braunfels and P.E. Schramm (Düsseldorf, 1967), pp. 402-82 and table, especially pp. 444 (daughter of Charlemagne), 449 (daughter of Lothar I), 451 (daughter of Louis the German), table (generation V a27, daughter of Berengar I).

[35] *Rhythmi Aevi Merovingici et Carolini* no. xxxix, *MGH Poetae* 4/2, p. 552.

[36] *Uersus de Asia et de uniuersi mundi rota*, strophes 15 (Europe/Agenor), 16-17 (boundaries), 23 (Saxons), 25 (Gallia Belgica), in *Itineraria et alia geographica*, 2 vols. (Corpus Christianorum series Latina 175-6, Turnhout, 1965), vol. 1, pp. 445, 446, 448, 449.

mobilised and called to arms'.[37] But his was not a lone voice. When Notker the Stammerer addressed himself to a failing Carolingian, Charles III, in his nostalgic *Gesta Karoli* (composed around 887), he once again struck the Carolingian-Frankish-European chords with all their self-assertive grandiloquence. Despite recent failures and humiliations at the hands of the Vikings this theme flourished, reminding men of better days and spurring them on to renewed efforts. Nearly all Europe had assembled round Charles after his triumph over the Avars. All Europe was recruited and hence had a share in one of the emperor's greatest works, building the bridge over the Rhine at Mainz.[38] It was a joint and immensely well-ordered and well-organised effort by which Notker perhaps wished to imply that such a European-wide enterprise would now be quite impossible. Hārūn al-Rashîd's envoys, moreover, were invited by Charlemagne to partake of his banquet, where the foremost man of all Francia and Europe would dine.[39] Europe here was but an enlarged Francia. To relieve the dearth of the Lybians, so Notker narrated, Charles dispatched grain, wine and even oil, the riches of Europe.[40] A clear awareness of Europe with its advantages and potential as against north Africa seems to underline these proud reminiscences. The Lybians even become tributaries. Some faint recollection of the presents the embassy from Fustat may have offered in 801 perhaps underlay these tales.[41]

The breakup of Carolingian rule was, like its growth by conquest, seen in a European framework and as a European phenomenon. The Fulda Annals in a famous passage report under the year 888 that while the new (and illegitimate) Carolingian, Arnulf, received the homages of Bavarians, Eastern Franks, Saxons, Thuringians and Slavs at Regensburg and dwelt there for a long time, 'many kinglets sprang up in Europe', which is then more or less equated with the Carolingian realm of the sick, deserted and abandoned Charles III. The annalist then enumerates arrogations and attempted arrogations in Italy, upper Burgundy, Provence [39] and northern France.[42] Regino of Prüm, when he described the same events, also reflected on them. All the kingdoms which had obeyed Charles III fell away from their mutual connections and set about raising kings from their own midst (*viscera*). This caused great wars, for there were plenty of Frankish princes capable of ruling, yet they chanced to be so nearly equal to one another that they would not deign to bow to their peers.[43] Regino described the new kings and their kingdoms like the Fulda annalist, but he saw them only in an all-Frankish setting.

These Frankish-European horizons and eulogies were matched by similar Byzantine ones. Writing from Naples, Eugenius Vulgarius sought to ingratiate

[37] Poeta Saxo (as n. 23) V lines 29-32, p. 56.
[38] Notker, *Gesta Karoli* I 30, pp. 40-1.
[39] Ibid. II 8, p. 60
[40] Ibid. II 9, p. 63.
[41] As suggested by Haefele in Notker, *Gesta Karoli*, p. 63 n. 3.
[42] *Annales Fuldenses*, p. 116.
[43] Regino of Prüm, *Chronicon*, p. 129.

himself with the emperor Leo VI in verse. He described him as vanquishing Europe and overthrowing Africa, thus fulfilling an emperor's perennial task of subduing the barbarian world. He was the *rerum dominus*, whatever the reality of his Bulgarian wars with their defeats and costly tactics of buying off this formidable enemy may have been.[44] For the Byzantines, however, Europe could never gain the significance it came to have for their Carolingian western rivals and adversaries. The European provinces of their empire were but a part, and that not the richest part, of a whole which had its centre of gravity in Asia Minor. True, there were European cities of the greatest cultural and religious importance, like Thessalonika and Adrianople, but in the ranking of the themes and the desirability and salaries of these commands those of Asia had precedence for the most part and counted for more even than Macedonia and Thrace, even though the first was the home of the reigning dynasty from the later ninth century onwards.[45]

However trivial and occasional the contexts of all the panegyrical ninth-century verse that has been surveyed here may have been, its authors and their courtly audience felt themselves to be Europeans. They were the owners of a literary tradition which carried weight precisely because it was shared, an erudite *lingua* [40] *franca*. It was a common possession which crossed new, and as yet very unstable, regnal frontiers and ethnic boundaries, part of a culture that began to distinguish and bear the hallmark of Latin Christianity. More self-consciously than anyone, however, the papacy gave body, action and reality to this awareness. Despite its vicissitudes in Rome it never ceased to pronounce itself the head and foremost authority in the western church, indeed the church as a whole. An an institution, therefore, it came to be less dependent on its political fortunes in Rome than on its rising precedence and the awe which its privileges inspired among often hard-pressed petitioners from everywhere, not only Francia. A letter of Pope Leo IV (d. 858) to the patriarch of Constantinople of *c.* 853 shows him vaunting a European-wide jurisdiction in all its undefined amplitude. The patriarch Ignatius (847-58) had sent a pallium to the pope, as a token, no doubt, of fraternal and collegial amity. The gift was firmly refused, not without a note of deliberate condescension. No doubt, Leo caused to be written, the present was kindly meant; but as the Roman Church was clearly the head and mistress of all churches it was not its custom to accept a *pallium* from elsewhere (the *aliunde* was distinctly offensive), but rather to bestow it on those on whom it was to be conferred all over Europe (*per totam Europam*). For this reason the pope asked the patriarch not to take it ill that he sent the gift back to its donor. The text stressed first of all the fullness of papal discretion to honour subject prelates in this way.[46] The use of the term Europe, moreover, opened up the widest perspectives for papal supremacy. It

---

[44] *Eugenii Vulgarii Sylloga* no. xviii, *MGH Poetae* 4/1, p. 425.

[45] See in general *Costantino Porfirogenito de Thematibus*, ed. A. Pertusi (Studi e testi 160, Vatican City, 1952), and W. Treadgold, *The Byzantine Recovery, 780-842* (Stanford, 1988), pp. 14-17, 337-41.

[46] *Epistolae selectae Leonis IV* no. 41, *MGH Epp.* 5, p. 607.

could extend eastwards as well as westwards, and so marked the patriarch of Constantinople clearly as less than equal to the bishop of Rome. Yet could it also entail a narrowing, a curtailment of the European dimension, if it was coterminous with the reach of papal privileges and favours? Were the provinces of Byzantium part of papal Europe? It is perhaps characteristic that Leo's successor, Nicholas I, evaded such questions of frontiers by speaking principally of Orient and Occident.[47]

European consciousness in the Carolingian ninth century was not only an urbane, literary self-indulgence. It gained a sterner complexion and urgency with the catastrophes that began to [41] threaten the Carolingian world, the movements of the Vikings and their shattering blows and devastations in the heartlands of erstwhile Carolingian well-being. Underlying the poetry, the *belles-lettres*, and the courtly converse of the élite, and essential for the formation of a sense of Europe, had been the many decades of internal peace which the heartlands of the Reich, west Francia, east Francia and Italy, had enjoyed for almost sixty years under Charlemagne and Louis the Pious. It was a unique experience in the early medieval Occident, which in itself buttressed the European horizons of the men of letters and their audience. When this peace broke down, thanks to the relentless fraternal feuds of the Carolingian family, their respective followers and the greater nobles as well as the attacks of the Vikings, the crisis also had a profound impact on the European *mentalité* that animated the articulate few. The Vikings were an inner-European phenomenon. They came from a north that had hitherto scarcely counted. Their unwelcome visitations gave, however, a new inflexion to the meaning of Europe in the historiography of the struggling Frankish kingdoms. They crystalised the notion of Europe and associated it with a degree of civilisation, goods and values that had to be defended against enemies, occasionally described as barbarians.[48] Europe was, and wanted to be seen as, Christian. The Vikings were not.

Such a conception of Europe, a continent threatened and on the defensive, became even more pressing when the enemies were strangers from the Eurasian steppes, different in aspect, bearing and basic equipment from the settled inhabitants and the warriors of central and western Europe. Horseborne nomads and archers, the Magyars struck deep and often into east Francia, west Francia, Burgundy and Italy so that they could be perceived

---

[47] For example Pope Nicholas I, *Epistolae* nos. 46, 87, 88, 107, *MGH Epp.* 6, pp. 325, 452, 475, 620.
[48] For Vikings as barbarians see e.g. Sedulius Scottus, *Carmina* (as n. 28) II 15, lines 5-6, p. 183; Johannes Scottus, *Carmina* III 6, *MGH Poetae* 3, p. 541; *Annales Bertiniani*, p. 31 (the famous passage on the *Rus'* coming from Byzantium through Francia in 839). For the eastern Franks it was rather the Slavs who were barbarians, as can be seen from Notker, *Gesta Karoli* I 30 and II 12, pp. 17, 70, 74 and *Annales Fuldenses, s.a.* 840, p. 30. The antithesis of Europe and barbarism is also offered by Eugenius Vulgarius in the poem cited in n. 44.

clearly as a menace to all Europe.[49] Liudprand of Cremona accused King [42] Arnulf, the illegitimate Carolingian (*ob.* 899) of allying with the Hungarians to destroy the Moravian principality and cast down its ruler, Sviatopluk. He deplored Arnulf's blind ambition. Thanks to the Magyars, the overthrow of a wretched little man – he underestimated Sviatopluk – brought ruin to the whole of Europe.[50] The *Antapodosis*, where Liudprand looked back on the Magyar raids after they had at last been defeated by Otto I at the Lech in 955, was in fact conceived as a history of Europe even though Liudprand was well aware that he had realised only part of his design.[51] It was a commissioned work. Liudprand wrote it at the behest of a Spanish bishop *in partibus infidelium*, who had come to Frankfurt as the envoy of the caliph, Abd ar-Rahman III. Recemund, the bishop of Elvira, had asked him to set down the deeds of the emperors and kings of all Europe – and here Byzantium clearly belonged since there was as yet no Ottonian emperor. From this, the introduction to the *Antapodosis*, it is evident that Liudprand had a vision of Europe as a whole and could present to his readers at least some of the forces, be they *basileis*, kings, princes, their women, warriors, servants and resources who were at work shaping its future.[52] The vision became large and vivid when he described in much detail, for instance, the events in 944-5 which brought about the downfall of the Lecapenoi in the Great Palace of Constantinople which he still regarded as the centre of the Christian universe.[53] Stephen and Constantine Lecapenus found that they had gained nothing by overthrowing their father. Their attempt to do away with the legitimist Macedonian *basileus*, Constantine Porphyrogenitus, ended with their own banishment, imprisonment and death. According to Liudprand, not only Europe but also Asia and Africa, that is to say the whole known world, rejoiced in their downfall and the arrival and now unquestioned authority of Constantine.[54]

No other western writer was so well informed about Byzantium [43] as Liudprand, who here described a Byzantine *coup d'état,* seemingly from oral sources, in such detail that he must be counted among the prime sources for the palace revolution. With him we have also reached the beginnings of Ottonian historiography. The Saxon royal house built up an *imperium* by waging wars to achieve and to secure their kingship in east Francia and Lotharingia and to reward their warriors as kings must. This meant campaigning in west Francia

---

[49] The best summaries of the Hungarian raids are G. Fasoli, *Le incurzioni ungare in Europa nel secolo 10.* (Florence, 1945) and S. de Vajay, *Der Eintritt des ungarischen Stammesbundes in die europäischen Geschichte, 862-933* (Mainz, 1968); see also K.J. Leyser, 'The Battle at the Lech, 955. A Study in Tenth-Century Warfare', *History*, 50 (1965), pp. 1-25 (Leyser, *Medieval Germany*, pp. 43-67).

[50] Liudprand, *Antapodosis* I 13, p. 15.

[51] Ibid. title and I 1, pp. 1 and 4, for Recemund's request for a history of the whole of Europe and Liudprand's response that he had only covered a part of it.

[52] The background to the work's composition is discussed in K.J. Leyser, 'Ends and Means in Liudprand of Cremona', below pp. 125ff.

[53] Liudprand, *Antapodosis* V 20-2, pp. 141-4.

[54] Ibid. V 2, p. 144.

and Italy, relentless and incessant fighting above all to dominate and exploit the Slavonic peoples to the east of the rivers Elbe and Saale.[55] But before they could gain a lasting ascendancy they had to perform the European task of defeating the Magyar raiders whose great expeditions left almost none of the important cultural regions and economic strongholds of the centre, west and south unscathed. Widukind of Corvey told his readers and not least of all his hoped-for patroness, Otto I's daughter Mathilda, what a terrible threat they had been. The very sight of the Hungarians, their dress and bearing were horrendous for their victims. Widukind justified his detailed description because Mathilda must know from what kind of enemies her grandfather, Henry I and her father, had liberated nearly all Europe (he could not deny that they still resided in Pannonia).[56] Commenting on the battle at the Lech he remarked that no king for two hundred years had rejoiced in such a victory as Otto I had just won, perhaps alluding to Charles Martel's encounter with the Arabs near Poitiers in 732. Before the decisive onset, after a bad start to the battle, Otto I, according to Widukind, addressed and encouraged his warriors. He did this by extolling their superiority. It would be shameful for the lords of nearly all Europe – so he is made to describe his largely Bavarian, Aleman and Rhine-Frankish host – to give their hands to their enemies, that is promise to be subject to them.[57] Widukind of Corvey thus wanted the battle at the Lech to be seen as a European engagement, nor was he much mistaken in his assessment of what it [44] meant for the Reich, its neighbours and, not least of all, for the Liudolfing house itself.[58]

Its historiographers, Widukind and the Quedlinburg annalist, could henceforth clothe Ottonian rule in the same genre of European eulogies and grandiloquence as the Carolingian poets and historians had done, and do this regardless of the fact that the Ottonians did not seek to regain the fullness of Carolingian overlordship. Yet by and large their hegemony emerged, and their panegyrists were not slow in proclaiming and applauding it. Already to Widukind Henry I was *regum maximus Europae*.[59] In the preface to book two of the *Res gestae Saxonicae* Mathilda is called the rightful mistress of all Europe, though her father's power also reached into Africa and Asia.[60] This was probably no more than an allusion to Byzantine and perhaps 'Ummayad or even Fatimid embassies that had visited the Ottonian court in 956 with their exotic presents.[61] Widukind himself had mentioned them. It was an honour paid only to powerful and victorious kings. The Quedlinburg annals later

---

[55] Leyser, *Rule and Conflict*, especially pp. 109-12 on the structural military problems of the Ottonian rulers; T. Reuter, *Germany in the Early Middle Ages, c. 800-1056* (London, 1991), pp. 160-74, is a convenient survey.

[56] Widukind, *Res gestae Saxonicae* I 18-19, p. 29.

[57] Ibid. III 46, p. 127.

[58] Leyser, 'Battle at the Lech' (as n. 49), pp. 24-5 (pp. 66-7).

[59] Widukind, *Res gestae Saxonicae* I 41, p. 60.

[60] Widukind, *Res gestae Saxonicae* II prologue, p. 61.

[61] Widukind, *Res gestae Saxonicae* III 56, p. 135; see Köpke-Dümmler, *Otto der Große*, pp. 278-9.

unhesitatingly bestowed this European-dimension on the empress Theophanu and the young Otto III and his successor Henry II. In 991 Theophanu and Otto kept their Easter court with 'imperial glory' at Quedlinburg, where Margrave Hugo of Tuscany and Miesco of Poland had come with the other 'foremost men of Europe' in order to pay their respects and render obeisance to the imperial honour.[62] All brought their most precious possessions to offer as gifts and were themselves sent home with gifts in return. In 996 the Salian Gregory V, Otto III's kinsman, was enthroned as pope and on Ascension Day he consecrated Otto emperor 'to the plaudits of the people of nearly all Europe'.[63] In 1021 the Quedlinburg annalist again had all the leading men of Europe flock to Merseburg as well as envoys of diverse peoples, not specified, to pay their due respects to Henry II who had come there for his Easter court.[64] Next year Henry II's host, on its way back from Rome,[45] was struck by a plague, but the emperor escaped it. He had but few warriors in his company, but more met and joined him *en route* until Mother Europe sent him on his way back to Germany to hold a synod.[65] *Mater Europa*, the expression the annalist used, suggests sentiments of warmth, of belonging and the existence of common bonds, over and above tribal and local links and identities. Yet parallel passages are not readily at hand, and it is noteworthy also that in the great examples of late Ottonian imperial iconography Otto III and Henry II are attended by female figures, representing countries subject or partly subject to them: Italia, Roma, Gallia, Germania and Sclavina. Together these might be deemed to stand for Europe, but no figure of Europe herself appears in these paintings.[66] West Francia and Anglo-Saxon or Anglo-Danish England in the late tenth and early eleventh centuries lay outside and well beyond the reach of the Ottonian Reich, and Europe is unthinkable without them.

The Ottonians' concept of Europe was somewhat self-centred and remained so well into the eleventh century. The Niederalteich annals, whose compilatory section was put together not long before 1032 from older sources available to the annalist, give a fairly detailed account of the role of Duke Henry of Bavaria and Bishop Abraham of Freising's rising against Otto II in 974. Had it not been thwarted by the promptitude of Margrave Berthold of the northern march nearly all Europe might have been laid low and ruined by it.[67] It was not

---

[62] *Annales Quedlinburgenses, MGH SS* 3, p. 68.

[63] Ibid. p. 73.

[64] Ibid. p. 86

[65] Ibid. p. 88.

[66] There are a number of such illustrations, including one in a detached leaf now in Chantilly, one in the Trier *Registrum Gregorii* and one in the Gospel-Book of Otto III now in Munich. For further details and dating – the current consensus is that the first two date from the end of Otto II's reign and the beginning of Otto III's reign respectively, the third from late in Otto III's reign – see H. Mayr-Harting, *Ottonian Book Illumination: An Historical Study*, 2 vols. (London, 1991), vol. 1 pp. 159-62 with references to the specialist literature.

[67] *Annales Altahenses maiores*, ed. E. von Oefele (MGH SRG 4, Hanover, 1891), p. 12. Berthold held a march in the Frankish region of Bavaria around Schweinfurt, so the term 'northern' is explained by the annalist's Bavarian perspective.

Henry of Bavaria's last attempt to seize the kingship from the senior branch of the Ottonian house, but perhaps his alliance with Boleslas of Bohemia and Miesco of Poland presented an especially serious challenge to the order bequeathed by Otto I to his successor. Altogether the most lasting and profound change and development in the tenth and early eleventh centuries was the enlargement and the emergence [46] of a new east and south-eastern European world which from then on became a permanent, essential and articulate feature of its ethnic and political make-up and its Latin-Christian culture. By the early eleventh century Bohemia, Poland and Hungary were effective members of the European community of *regna*, the last two with kings and dukes that had their own links with Rome and did not depend on the *Reichskirche*. If Bohemia remained part of the Empire it none the less gained a very special place in it. What had been ethnic reservoirs became ordered polities that permanently stood between the west and the great spaces of Russia.[68]

Not all of Slavonic Europe had been so close to the nobility and social order of the Empire and the *regna* of France, England, northern Spain and, eventually, Sicily. Adam of Bremen, the great historian and ethnographer of the northern world, which he watched and knew from his vantage-point as church provost in Bremen, has left us a description of a flourishing if vigorously heathen town that had its own access to the centres of civilisation, like Constantinople. It lay by the mouth of the Oder, seven days' journey from the Elbe. Not only barbarians, but also Greeks dwelt in the vicinity of Jumne (probably to be identified with Wolin on the Baltic coast). Saxons lived there too, but had to keep their Christianity under wraps. The natives were pagans, but none the less well mannered and hospitable. Jumne was evidently a great emporium, a huge port of exchange, full of everything worthwhile produced in the north. Adam of Bremen thought it was the greatest city of Europe.[69] He wrote his great history of the church of Hamburg-Bremen from 1072 onwards, and this reveals the existence and vitality of a northern and Slavonic Europe not yet part of Latin Christianity, but wealthy, not uncivilized and in touch with the Mediterranean by its own means and commercial routes.

Post-Carolingian and post-Ottonian Europe thus consisted of a plurality of kingdoms, of which the empire was only the most prestigious, but in no way set over all the others or possessing [47] authority in the west and in Anglo-Saxon England. One of its most respected historians, the monk Rodulf Glaber, writing in Burgundy, has given us a fair portrait of this pluralism, of which he was conscious. The downfall of the Carolingians with their imperial habitus and the side-by-side of late Ottonians and Salians and Capetians seem to have

---

[68] See on this F. Dvornik, *The Making of Central and Eastern Europe*, 2nd edn (Gulf Breeze, Florida, 1974), and also J. Fried, *Otto III. und Boleslaw Chrobry: Das Widmungsbild des Aachener Evangeliars, der 'Akt von Gnesen' und das frühe polnische und ungarische Königtum* (Frankfurter historische Abhandlungen 30, Wiesbaden, 1989), on the crucial events of the year 1000.

[69] Adam of Bremen, *Gesta* II 22, p. 79.

given him deep satisfaction. He approved of the political structure of Europe as it had turned out, just as he approved of the European passion for pilgrimages to the east and to Jerusalem.[70] Latin Christianity and the Occident were moulded by this monastic culture no less than by the material development which in the eleventh century began here and there to gain momentum.

Moreover Europe, or the Occident, was in the later eleventh century on the threshold of a new surge of aggressive self-awareness. For some decades Latin Christianity had been divided and rent by the emergence of new powers like the Normans and the conflicts that harassed old ones, above all the empire. But none of these developments, least of all the arrival of the Normans, diminished European aggressiveness on the frontiers, be it in south Italy or in Spain. No very strong sense of Europe could perhaps emerge from these particularist and acquisitive enterprises, or from the conflicts of the Salians with their disaffected princes and the papacy. But with the preaching of the crusade,[71] which mobilised French, Provençal, Italian and German warriors as well, the Occident became a power both military and religious as well as intellectually self-possessed, a power which remained imposing and frightening until the cumulative losses of two world wars reduced both its power and its will to continue living in age-old habits and forced its inhabitants to share a new ethos of living together.

---

[70] Rodulfus Glaber, *Historiae* I preface, I i 4-5, I iv 16, and II i 1 (on the new European order), IV ii 18 (on pilgrimages to Jerusalem), pp. 1, 10, 30, 48-50, 198. Note, however, that Rodulfus does not talk explicitly of Europe but instead contrasts the 'Roman Empire' with 'distant and barbarous provinces' (I preface, p. 1). See also '987: the Ottonian Connection', below, pp. 178-9 with nn. 74ff.

[71] According to William of Malmesbury, Urban II himself claimed when preaching the crusade in 1095 that Europe was endangered by the Seljuk advance; see Hay, *Europe* (as n. 1), pp. 30-1, and for the development of the idea in the high and late middle ages now B. Karageorgos, 'Der Begriff Europa im Hoch- und Spätmittelalter', *DA*, 48 (1992), pp. 137-64.

2

Three Historians

(a) Nithard and his Rulers

Nithard was a singular author; there was no one really like him as a historian of events, a critic of motivation and a deeply disillusioned commentator on rulers and rulership. Not only had he played a prominent part in the wars over Louis the Pious's inheritance, he also combined in himself capacities and qualities that for centuries were to be divided and by their very division to define the societies of the tenth century and the high middle ages. Nithard was a lay *litteratus*, but in his case this did not only mean that he shared a certain learning with clerically and monastically educated men serving in the secular or regular church.[1] His *Histories* are the wry, gaunt, and, for the most part, melancholy story of a Carolingian predicament, the birth of a fourth son to Louis the Pious from a lawful and much-desired marriage when most of the Carolingian Reich and the emperorship itself had already been assigned to the oldest son of Louis's first union, with subordinate positions – Bavaria and Aquitaine – for his younger brothers, Louis and Pippin. As Nithard in one lapidary sentence phrased it: 'When Charles was born [in 823] his father did not know what to do for him since he had already divided the whole empire among the others.[2]

But it would be misleading to pursue only Nithard's relentless account of this elemental family predicament. Nithard was an orthodox man who believed in

* Of the three pieces here gathered, (a) is the previously unpublished typescript of a lecture given at a conference in Paris in 1989; the notes are editorial. The two short texts (b) and (c) are taken from *The Blackwell's Dictionary of Historians*, ed. J. Cannon (Oxford: Basil Blackwell, 1988), pp. 408-10 and 450-1 respectively; thanks are due to the editor and publishers for permission to republish here. Although the two short texts are somewhat different in form from the other essays in this collection, so many of these make extensive use of the writings of Widukind and Thietmar that it seemed helpful to include them here.

[1] For Nithard's education and career see the introduction of Lauer to Nithard, *Historiae*, pp. vi-xiv; M. Manitius, *Geschichte der lateinischen Literatur des Mittelalters*, 1 (Munich, 1911), pp. 657-60; Wattenbach-Levison-Löwe, pp. 353-7; J.L. Nelson, 'Public *Histories* and Private History in the Work of Nithard', in eadem, *Politics and Ritual in Early Medieval Europe* (London, 1986), pp. 195-237, especially pp. 196-8.

[2] Nithard, *Historia* I 3, p. 8: 'Karolo quidem nato, quoniam omne imperium inter reliquos filios pater diviserat, quid huic faceret, ignorabat'.

the divine direction of events, and yet to him the leading men were not only themselves responsible for what they did but they also had the power and the *virtus* to perceive the duties of their political and military inheritance in a way no other writer so searingly observes. All Nithard's rulers were measured against the tasks they had to fulfil and – this judgement transfused all four books of the *Histories* – all were found wanting, some more and some less, and this despite Nithard's own allegiance to Charles the Bald.[3]

To understand him, we must first of all be constantly aware that he was a Carolingian himself, a grandson of Charlemagne's, and by Charlemagne all his successors are judged and scaled, both at the beginning and the end of his blistering work. Nithard grew up hard by the emperor's palace, and he remembers the very hour of his death so as to authenticate the judgements that follow.[4] Charlemagne outshone all in every wisdom and virtue – there is no central quality as in Einhard – and it is the effect that mattered: 'To all men on earth he was terrible, lovable and admirable, and so he created an empire at once mighty and useful' (an old Frankish *utilitas* here).[5] Let us note that the *terror* came first in this recital of good rule, but in the next sentence it became but a moderate, albeit still very necessary *terror*, one that compelled Franks and 'barbarians', their subjects, to think of nothing but the *publica utilitas*, the public good.[6]

Here simultaneously is not only the persistent measurement for all Nithard's rulers, Charlemagne, but also the idea of a *publica utilitas* that underlay Nithard's judgement. In other words, Nithard as a historian was capable of appealing to political ideas as the court of highest instance before which the rulers whom he served or to whom he stood close must pass muster or face condemnation.[7] Nithard's complaints at all critical moments – e.g. Lothar's risings in 830 and 833, or the two half-brothers', Charles's and Louis's, conduct

---

[3]   Nithard's view of Lothar was consistently negative; for criticisms of other rulers for failing to live up to their duties see below, n. 8, and on Nithard's judgements on rulers, Nelson, 'Public Histories' (as n. 1), *passim*, and H. Patze '*Iustitia* bei Nithard', in *Festschrift für Hermann Heimpel zum 70, Geburtstag am 19, September 1971*, 3 vols. (Göttingen, 1973), vol. 3, pp. 147-65.

[4]   Nithard, *Historiae* I 1, p. 4, citing Einhard, *Vita Karoli* c. 30.

[5]   Ibid: 'Ut omnibus orbem inhabitantibus terribilis, amabilis pariterque et admirabilis videretur, ac per hoc omne imperium omnibus modis, ut cunctis manifeste claruit, honestum et utile effecit.'

[6]   Ibid.: 'Nam super omne . . . Francorum barbarorumque ferocia ac ferrea corda, quae nec Romana potentia domare valuit, hic solus moderato terrore ita repressit, ut nihil in imperio moliri, praeter quod publicae utilitati congruebat, manifeste auderent.' The *publica* or *communis utilitas* is an important concept for Nithard: see also ibid. II 6, pp. 52 and 52; II 8, p. 62; IV 6 and 7, p. 142. On the *res publica* in Frankish political thought see W. Wehlen, *Geschichtsschreibung und Staatsauffassung im Zeitalter Ludwigs des Frommen* (Historische Studien 418, Lübeck, 1970), pp. 33-56, and on Nithard pp. 61-78, 96-105; H.-W. Goetz, '*Regnum*: Zum politischen Denken der Karolingerzeit', *ZRGGA* 116 (1987), pp. 110-89, *passim*, especially pp. 130-1 on Nithard.

[7]   See here especially Patze, 'Iustitia' (as n. 3).

after Fontenoy – that the *res publica* received short measure at the hands of its rulers must therefore be taken seriously.[8] And for this reason also *res publica*, I venture to assert, meant something more to him than only the material base of kingship, the immediate resources at the disposal of Carolingian rulers, and was not merely a transmitted residure of Ciceronian coinage.[9] Pitched against the common good, the *publica utilitas* which Nithard, *laudator temporis acti*, linked so wholeheartedly with Charlemagne, was its opposite, *cupiditas*, meaning really the ambition and greed both of principals, like Lothar in 830 and 833, and of their followings.[10] It should also be noted that when the monk Guntbald sent to Louis (the German) in Bavaria and to Pippin in Aquitaine to bring about Louis the Pious's restoration in 830, both were promised enlargements of their meagre shares from the 817 settlement, and, Nithard tells us, they greedily obeyed their father's call.[11] In other words, their motives for the emperor's restoration were no different from those of Lothar for his overthrow. Nithard's grim story is enhanced still more by his equally sardonic comments on the monk Guntbald, who fancied himself as a *secundus a rege*, as if to replace Count Bernard, the chamberlain of the palace coup of 829.[12] Here we uncover another stark trait of Nithard's historical insight: the fictitious motive. Guntbald secretly sent his messages to Louis the German and Pippin under the guise of religion.[13] The phrase and the sham that lay behind it were to resurface only in the historiography of the eleventh century, in the *Annales* of Lampert of Hersfeld. The princes in 1076 gradually deserted Henry IV 'sub

---

[8]   Nithard, *Historiae* I 3, p. 12: 'Res autem publica, quoniam quisque cupiditate illectus sua querebat, cotidie deterius ibat'; I 4, p. 16: 'quoniam quisque eorum propria querebat, rem publicam penitus neglegebant'; III 2, p. 84: 'Re autem publica inconsultius quam oporteret omissa, quo quemque voluntas rapuit perfacile omissus abscessit.'

[9]   *Pace* J. Fried, 'Der karolingische Herrschaftsverband im 9. Jahrhundert zwischen "Kirche" und "Königshaus" ', *HZ*, 235 (1982), pp. 1-43; against an all too pessimistic view of Carolingian 'political theory' see also J.L. Nelson, 'Kingship and Empire', in *The Cambridge History of Medieval Political Thought, c. 350 – c. 1450*, ed. J.H. Burns (Cambridge, 1988), pp. 211-51, especially pp. 213-229.

[10]   See the passages cited above, n. 8, and also *Historiae* III 1 and 5, pp. 80 and 104, on refraining from *iniqua cupiditas*; IV 1, p. 118: 'quoties populum christianum perjurum sua cupiditate effecerit [Lothar]'; IV 2, p. 122: '[Saxons] supra modum cupidi'; IV 5, p. 136: 'sic quoque perjuria ceteraque facinora devitare, ni ceca cupiditas impediret' (in the negotiations about a *divisio regni* in the autumn of 842).

[11]   Ibid. I 3, p. 12: 'promittens, si in sua restitutione una cum his qui hoc cupiebant adesse voluissent, regnum utrisque se ampliare velle. Ac per hoc per facile cupideque paruere...

[12]   Ibid. I 3, p. 12: 'secundus in imperio esse volebat'; for the term see I 3, pp. 10 and 12, I 4, p. 16, and for related formulations in ninth-century sources H. Keller, 'Zur Struktur der Königsherrschaft im karolingischen und nachkarolingischen Italien: Der "consiliarius regis" in den italienischen Königsdiplomen des 9. und 10. Jahrhunderts', *Quellen und Forschungen aus italienischen Archiven und Bibliotheken* 46 (1967), pp. 123-223, here p. 137.

[13]   Nithard, *Historiae* I 3, p. 4: 'assumptoque Guntbaldo quodam monacho sub specie religionis in hoc negotio ad Pippinum Ludovicumque, filios eius, occulte direxit...' See also II 10, p. 74: before Fontenoy, Lothar claims to need time to consider Charles's and Louis's proposals, but 'Re autem vera Pippinus non venerat; illum hac dilatione expectare volebat.'

optentu religionis [under the guise of religion]' after Gregory VII had excommunicated him.[14]

Altogether Louis the Pious appears in a sorry light in Nithard's narrative.
He was the passive recipient of his own re-investiture with arms and the crown.
Repentant bishops and nobles imposed them on him.[15] Later Nithard seems to
belie this passivity. When in 839 the emperor easily put down his son's attempt
to seize all the east Frankish lands, Nithard has him triumphantly return to
Aachen. 'Wherever he went he was by divine aid victorious', but in the very
next phrase he speaks of Louis's old age and increasing decrepitude.[16] This
then became the springboard for the final intrigues of the reign, the attempt to
secure Charles's future with a vastly increased inheritance by making a deal
with Lothar, at the expense of Pippin II and Louis the German, and hoping
that this would endure after Louis the Pious's death.[17]

This at once raise the question of how Nithard saw the chief architect of the
whole conflict, the mother of his lord Charles, the man who had commissioned
the *Histories*.[18] It seems that he clearly disapproved of her influence over her
son. As Nithard judged the situation, it mattered vitally for Charles that he
should hold and cover the country north and south of the Seine valley right up
to the Loire. Judith, however, was in Aquitaine, and Charles twice heeded her
calls for help, thus leaving his base open to Lothar, who at once advanced and
pressed Charles's men to defect. Some of them did.[19] In 841, shortly before
Fontenoy, some of Charles's councillors proposed that he went to meet his
mother with the Aquitanians, but the majority advised that he should either
march against Lothar or await his coming on whatever ground he chose. If he
went elsewhere, especially south, this would be regarded as flight, so that
Lothar and his men would become bolder, and the vacillators, those who had
hitherto held back out of fear, would make plans to join him. 'Quod et evenit
[and this is what happened]', Nithard starkly concluded when the first option
prevailed and Charles went off to Châlons to meet his mother and the
Aquitanians with her.[20] Later, after the battle of Fontenoy had been fought
and won, Nithard's indignation rose again. When there was good news from

[14] Lampert, *Annales*, p. 264. However, more coded questionings of motive in the form of
officious denials can be found in other ninth-century writers; see for example the comments of
Annales Fuldenses s.a. 858 and 879, pp. 49-50 and 93 on the actions of Louis the German and Louis
the Younger.

[15] Nithard, *Historiae* I 4, p. 18: 'coronam et arma regi suo imponunt'.

[16] Nithard, *Historiae* I 6, p. 28: 'Post Aquis exultans rediit, quoniam, quocumque se verterat,
nutu divino victor erat. Veruntamen ingruente senili aetate et propter varias afflictiones poene
decrepita imminente...'

[17] Ibid. I 6-7, pp. 24/36; on the background see J.L. Nelson, *Charles the Bald* (London, 1992),
pp. 100-6.

[18] On the relationship between the first two books of the *Historiae*, explicitly addressed to
Charles, and the last two, aimed at a rather different audience, see Patze, '*Iustitia*' (as n. 3), pp.
158-63 and Nelson, 'Public *Histories*' (as n. 1), pp. 199-213.

[19] Nithard, *Historiae* II 3 and 9, pp. 42/44.

[20] Ibid. II 9, pp. 64/66.

everywhere, especially the south, Louis with his men marched back to the Rhine while Charles with his mother turned towards the Loire. Once again, in his judgement, the *res publica* fared worse than it should have done.[21]

Fontenoy, for all the bloodshed among Frankish warrior society and for all the booty, which the victors found to be so abundant that they persuaded themselves to forego a pursuit of Lothar's fugitive followers, emerges from Nithard's pen all the same as a battle from which Charles drew few immediate gains.[22] Even the loyalties of the Île-de-France remained uncertain. Lothar succeeded in collecting fresh forces and in stirring up a popular revolt in Saxony, and even if many of its nobles sided with Louis, it distracted them and forced them to concentrate on emergencies nearer home. It needed a second campaign by the half-brothers early in 842 to force Lothar to flee from Sinzig, abandon Aachen, the *sedes regni* still, and retreat as far as the Rhône valley with a much-shrunken following.[23]

Nithard's description of the two half-brothers, however conventional, is wholly secular, shaped by aristocratic norms and formalities. They were both of middle height, bold, munificent, prudent and eloquent as Carolingian princes should be;[24] but what mattered most to Nithard, who knew the ineluctable pressures they had to face from dissident followings, was their *unanimitas* and *concordia* when they met at Strasbourg early in 842. They slept and dined in the same house and asked of one another only things that were useful to both.[25] Later, Charles and Louis were often enough bitter and brutal enemies, exploiting one another's weaknesses and embarrassments.[26] This makes their shared meals, spectacles and games in Strasbourg all the more manifestations of a lived ideal of *fraternitas* as against Lothar's shifts and turns and with their respective followings taken into partnership by their mutual oaths. Here were perhaps manifestations, and that not only symbolic ones, of a

[21] Ibid. III 2, p. 84: 'Cumque adversa undique propulsa viderentur, ac spes prosperitatis cuique hinc inde faveret, Lodhuwicus cum suis Renum petiit, Karolus vero una cum matre Ligerim adiit. Res autem publica inconsultius, quam oporteret, omissa; quo quemque voluntas rapuit, perfacile omissus abscessit.'

[22] Ibid. III 1, pp. 80/82.

[23] Ibid. III 2-7 and IV 2 (Saxon uprising), pp. 82/114, 120/24. On the Stellinga uprising cf. T. Reuter, *The Annals of Fulda (Ninth-Century Histories, II)* (Manchester, 1992), p. 20 with n. 6.

[24] Nithard, *Historiae* III 6, p. 110. For other descriptions of Frankish rulers in similar semi-conventional style cf. Einhard, *Vita Karoli* c. 22, pp. 26-7; Thegan, *Vita Hludowici* c. 19, *MGH SS* 2, pp. 594-5.

[25] Nithard, *Historiae* III 6, p. 110. Cf. *Annales Fuldenses s.a.* 847, p. 36, *Annales Bertiniani s.a.* 841, pp. 37-8, and on the significance of such rituals of community J.L. Nelson, 'The Lord's Anointed and the People's Choice: Carolingian Royal Ritual', in *Rituals of Royalty, Power and Ceremonial in Traditional Societies*, ed. D. Cannadine and S. Price (Cambridge, 1987), pp. 137-180, especially pp. 166-72; G. Althoff, *Verwandte, Freunde und Getreue: Zum politischen Stellenwert der Gruppenbindungen im früheren Mittelalter* (Darmstadt, 1990), pp. 204-5; idem, *Amicitiae und Pacta: Bündnis, Einung, Politik und Gebetsgedenken im beginnenden 10. Jahrhundert* (Schriften der MGH 37, Hanover, 1992), pp. 29-30.

[26] These discords may be most conveniently followed in Nelson, *Charles the Bald* (as n. 17), especially pp. 170-3, 187-91, 219-25, 238-9.

res publica and a *publica utilitas* which Nithard elsewhere saw only neglected and ignored.[27]

If for the latter-day reader of Nithard's *Four Books of Histories* there emerges a hero, it was not the man for whom he wrote, Charles the Bald, but his half-brother, Louis the German. Louis had fared poorly in the 817 settlement and throughout Louis the Pious's reign he had been relegated and confined to Bavaria. From there however he broke loose time and again to draw all the east Frankish portions of the Frankish Reich – Alemannia, Thuringia, Saxony and east Francia – into his ambit.[28] Nithard silently accepted this enlargement of Louis's *regna*; for an adherent of division as he was there was no alternative.[29] What he tells us about Louis, however, conjures up his iron determination to remain in alliance and take risks to help his half-brother and so thwart Lothar's effort to achieve sole rule, an effort not immediately abandoned even after Fontenoy, an effort also, that, if we are to believe Nithard's glum phrases, would not have shied away from violence, treachery and probably blindings.[30] The Carolingians, unlike the Ottonians, did this to one another. To enlarge his hold and bring Alemannia, the Saxons, Thuringians and especially eastern Franks into his fidelity Louis had to overcome enemies, including the archbishop of Mainz.[31] He marched all the same with an army into western Francia and thus took much larger military risks than Charles. He also, at a critical moment, won the first success in the field warring against Lothar, when he defeated Adalbert, *dux Austrasiorum* as Nithard called him, whom Lothar had posed to observe and bar Louis after having chased him back to Bavaria as his father had done so often before.[32] Louis could now cross the Rhine. We read in Nithard of the heavy toll his march into west Francia took of his men and especially of his horses, and of the run-down condition of his army before Fontenoy. But they stuck it out all the same and roused Nithard to one of his rare passages of heroic rhetoric. Despite

---

[27] Nithard, *Historiae* III 5 (the Strasbourg oath-taking) and 6 (the public rituals of community), pp. 100/112, especially p. 110: 'tractabant tam pari consensu communia quam et privata; non quicquam aliud quilibet horum ab altero petebat, nisi quod utile ac congruum illi esse censebat'; cf. by contrast the passages cited above, n. 8.

[28] On the formation of the east Frankish kingdom in the 820s and 830s see H. Zatschek, 'Die Reichsteilungen unter Kaiser Ludwig dem Frommen: Studien zur Entstehung des ostfränkischen Reiches', *MÖIG* 49 (1935), pp. 185-224; W. Eggert, *Das ostfränkisch-deutsche Reich in der Auffassung seiner Zeitgenossen* (Forschungen zur mittelalterlichen Geschichte 21, Berlin, 1973), pp. 15-26, 231-45 (on the development of the terminology for the new kingdom); E. Ewig, 'Überlegungen zu den merowingischen und karolingischen Teilungen', in *Nascita dell'Europa ed Europa carolingia: un'equazione da verificare* (Settimane 27, Spoleto, 1981), pp. 225-60, esp. pp. 246-53. The discussion is summarised in T. Reuter, *Germany in the Early Middle Ages, c. 800-1056* (London, 1991), pp. 47-50.

[29] Though some criticism is expressed in *Historiae* I 8, p. 34: 'Lodhuwicus a Baioaria solito more egressus Alamanniam invasit cum quibusdam Toringis et Saxonibus sollicitatis.'

[30] Nithard, *Historiae* II 8, p. 64; II 10, p. 70; III 7, p. 112.

[31] Nithard, *Historiae* II 7, pp. 58/60.

[32] Ibid. II 7 and 9, pp. 58/60 and 66; for Louis the Pious and Louis the German see the literature cited above, n. 28.

their sorry plight Louis's men were anxious not to leave an unworthy memory to posterity, as they might should their lord not help his brother. If there was any risk of that they would rather suffer penury, or, if need be, death, than lose their unvanquished name and repute.[33] From Nithard's pages Louis emerges as the very founder of an east Frankish kingdom that was to become Germany. It was a *novum*, even more so than the togetherness of the west Frankish regions anchored in the treaty of Coulaines.[34]

We have encountered Nithard as a hard-faced historian with a down-to-earth secular intelligence who knew what stirred and drove his own *gens* and the Frankish nobility like the air he breathed. Of his own inner self and his religion he revealed little. It is characteristic of him that he did not use the story of the wondrous arrival of Charles the Bald's crown and royal ornaments from Aquitaine as a means to create a transcendant sacrality for his lord. True, it happened *divino nutu*, and yet it served only to raise and sustain morale.[35] In fact Nithard's rulers did not enjoy any kind of numinous status in his *Histories*. The distance between heaven and earth remained stark and unbridged. We are also far away from the ideal imperatives of Jonas of Orléans in his *De institutione regia* with its themes of equity and justice which were so hard to translate into the daily practice of governance.[36] Instead, certain very terrestrial Frankish topics constantly recur in Nithard's work, like spectres haunting him and his milieu. The foremost of these was that of loyalty. Nithard saw the struggle between Lothar and his brothers as an unceasing attempt to suborn loyalties, to wean supporters away from kinsmen and rivals by bribery and threats.[37] He himself suffered, for when he was sent to Lothar to negotiate and

---

[33] Nithard, *Historiae* III 10, p. 70: 'timentes, ne forte, si ab auxilio fratris frater deficeret, posteris suis indignam memoriam reliquissent; quod quidam ne facerent, elegerunt omni penuriae, etiam, si oporteret, morti potius subire quam nomen invictum amittere.' Compare II 4, p. 46, for similar comments on Charles's following in 840; and for an explanation of the favourable view of Louis taken especially in book IV see Nelson, 'Public *Histories*' (as n. 1), p. 223 and n. 118.

[34] *MGH Conc.* 3, no. 3, pp. 10-17. On Coulaines see P. Classen, 'Die Verträge von Verdun und von Coulaines 843 als Grundlagen des westfränkischen Reiches', *HZ*, 196 (1963), pp. 1-35, and modifying him E. Magnou-Nortier, *Foi et fidelité: Recherches sur l'évolution des liens personnels chez les Francs du VIIe au IXe siècle* (Toulouse, 1976), pp. 98-108; Nelson, *Charles the Bald* (as n.17), pp. 138-9; eadem, 'The Intellectual in Politics: Context, Content and Authorship in the Capitulary of Coulaines, November 843', in *Intellectual Life in the Middle Ages: Essays Presented to Margaret Gibson*, ed. L. Smith and B. Ward (London, 1992), pp. 1-14, esp. pp. 6-9; Althoff, *Amicitiae* (as n. 25) pp. 29-30.

[35] Nithard, *Historiae* II 8, pp. 60/62; for comment on the stage-management and symbolism of this episode see Nelson, *Charles the Bald* (as n. 17), pp. 113-14.

[36] Jonas of Orléans, *De institutione laicali*, Migne, *PL.*, 106, cols. 121-278; see I. Schröder, 'Zur Überlieferung von De institutione laicali des Jonas von Orleans', *DA*, 44 (1988), pp. 83-97. For the difficulties experienced by lay aristocrats in translating the admonitions of clerical moralists into practical action, see J.L. Nelson, 'The Quest for Peace in a Time of War', in *Träger und Instrumentarien des Friedens im frühen und hohen Mittelalter*, ed. J. Fried (Vorträge und Forschungen, Sigmaringen, forthcoming).

[37] For *sollicitare* in Nithard see I 2, 4 and 8, II 1, 2, 6 and 8, pp. 8, 14, 34, 38, 40, 58, 62. On 'soliciting' here and later in the Frankish fraternal disputes see Nelson, 'Public *Histories*' (as n. 1) p. 211 and n. 64; eadem, *Charles the Bald* (as n. 17), pp. 105-12.

refused to change sides, he lost *honores* which Louis the Pious had given him.[38] Lothar used and carried out such threats again and again, and we can learn from faint hints in Nithard's pages that Lothar's brother and half-brother did exactly the same.[39] The Carolingian fraternal conflicts were won and lost by the shifting interests and anxieties of followings. For the competing magnates and their struggles for *honores* Carolingian house-rivalries were essential. What is so strange and startling here is that we find bastard feudalism before feudalism, or rather that the beginnings and the formation of stable vassalic societies were as seamy and treacherous as their dissolution in the later middle ages. Nithard had his own vocabulary for this struggle to sway loyalties, notably the verb *sollicitare*, to tempt, rouse and incite, in this case defection. It had a classical past, as Caesar's *Bellum Gallicum* and *Bellum Civile* suggest, works which Nithard knew.[40] The act of 'soliciting' became itself the subject of intense negotiations between the chief contenders. Lothar must stop trying to suborn Charles's and Louis's men; he promises to and promptly breaks his engagement.[41]

To sum up: man of affairs and warrior, Nithard was also a historian of stark insight and power, one of the greatest the middle ages knew. His accounts of events during Louis the Pious's reign and after his death was moved by a deep indignation about the heedlessness with which the chief and most responsible actors, Carolingian rulers and their *primores*, not excluding his own lord, Charles, ignored their true duties and erred, pursuing only immediate personal aims. Not for nothing was his whole tale of woe framed by the memory of Charlemagne's time, both at the beginning and at the end.[42] The contrast drawn is deep and tragic. Nithard's main concern was the *res publica, utilitas* justice and loyalties. He was anxious to prove that his side, Charles and Louis the German had fought for *iustitia* when they pressed home division and opposed Lothar and unity.[43] But beyond that we can see in the mounting gloom of his prefaces the deeper fear that men of his stamp, fighting in different camps, were no longer able to control their world.[44]

---

[38] Nithard, *Historiae* II 2, p. 40. Nithard writes of himself in the third person. For comment see Nelson, 'Public *Histories*' (as n. 1), pp. 215-23.

[39] For such hints see e.g. *Historiae* III 3, p. 96: 'ni statutis aut stauendis concordia concurrat, quid cuique debatur armis decernant' (a threat directed primarily at Lothar, but also at his followers); III 4, p. 98: Charles 'minis atque blanditiis horum animos maximo labore compescere studuisset'. The phrase 'minis atque blanditiis' is characteristic both of Nithard's accounts of how kings won over support (see II 3, p. 44, II 7, p. 58) and of Carolingian historiography in general.

[40] For *sollicitare* in Caesar see e.g. *De Bello Gallico* III 8, V 2 and 6, VI 2, VII 43, 54, 63, 64; *De Bello Civile* II 33, III 21 and 22; for Nithard's use of the word see above, n. 37, and on his use of Caesar see the echoes assembled by M. Manitius, 'Zu deutschen Geschichtsquellen des 9. bis 12. Jahrhunderts', *NA*, 11 (1886), pp. 43-73, here pp. 69-70.

[41] Nithard, *Historiae* II 2, pp. 40/42 and II 3, pp. 44/46.

[42] Nithard, *Historiae* I 1 and IV 7, pp. 4, 144. See Patze, '*Iustitia*' (as n. 3), p. 163 on the structural effect of these references at the beginning and end of the work.

[43] On *iustitia* and the *res publica* see Patze, '*Iustitia*' (as n. 3) and the quotations in nn. 6 and 8.

[44] On the changes in tone in the prefaces see Nelson, 'Public *Histories*' (as n. 1), pp. 199, 211-12, and more generally eadem, 'Quest for Peace' (as n. 36).

(b) Widukind of Corvey

Most of what is known about Widukind's life and work is the little he chose to tell his readers: a monk of Corvey who entered the monastery when perhaps 15 years old, *c.* 940; he came from a ' noble family, quite likely the *stirps Widukindi*, the descendants of Charlemagne's foremost Saxon enemy. Mathilda, the wife of Henry I, was deemed to belong to this kin. The three books of his *Res Gestae Saxonicae* have the character of an epic and convey vividly the strains of tragic conflict within Saxon aristocratic society and its ruling family during the decades of their most rapid expansion and booty-laden triumphs. In the opening words of the *Res Gestae Saxonicae* Widukind informed his readers that he would now turn to the deeds of his princes, of his own kind and people, having first written about the triumphs of the warriors of the highest Emperor, God. The choice of words and images strike the note of all that follows: the wars of Henry I and the great crises of Otto I's reign.

Three versions of his work have been traced through the manuscripts. The second of these he dedicated to Otto I's twelve-year-old daughter Mathilda, abbess of Quedlinburg, in 968, without however setting aside his stem saga of the Saxon people's origins and land seizures from an earlier draft in which the Ottonians did not yet hold so special a place. The last and final version ends with the death of Otto I, his followers' lament, and their oaths to his son Otto II next day, 8 May 973. It is now thought that the first version had been concluded only a short while before the dedication rather than in 958. Widukind's prose is steeped in Sallust, and in his descriptions of the Liudolfings he owed something to Einhard's *Life of Charlemagne*, but his *Res* [451] *Gestae* do not quite breathe Einhard's secularity. At great crises and in desperate situations it was God who saved Otto I from his enemies and gave him victory against the odds, but Widukind also dwelt on the king's iron nerve and unshakable resolve. At the battle of the Lech (955) Otto is made to say to his men that they had divine protection, more *virtus* and far better weapons than their Magyar enemies. *Dilatatio inperii* was Widukind's theme but he also knew the risks. In this suspense between the known and the unknown, the natural and the supernatural shaping the historical process, lies Widukind's enduring literary strength. His work lived on and was received by later Saxon and east Frankish historians such as Thietmar, Frutolf and the Lotharingian Sigebert of Gembloux.

(c) Thietmar of Merseburg

Thietmar's *Chronicon*, written from 1012 onwards, at first sought to record only the fortunes of the see of Merseburg. Yet it soon [409] burst this modest frame and became a history of the Reich, its kings, its ruling circles (especially the Saxon aristocracy) and, last, but not least, a memoir of Thietmar himself. He belonged to this wealthy nobility, being the son of an east Saxon count, Siegfried, whose seat and family sanctuary lay at Walbeck on the Aller. Destined for the church as a boy, Thietmar enjoyed an excellent education at the Magdeburg cathedral school, and by the year 1000 was a beneficed member of the cathedral community. It was Archbishop Tagino of Magdeburg who in 1008/9 recommended him to Henry II for the vacant see of Merseburg.

Thietmar was a small, unsightly man but with an indefatigable memory and understanding for the situation about him, for his kin, their neighbours and rivals, and for the Saxon-Slav southeastern frontiers. He was a compulsive writer driven towards history and memoirs by a restless pastoral conscience. He felt deeply about the eternal welfare of those he commemorated in his pages. Full of self-reproach he hoped that his readers and successors would intercede for him. His *Chronicon* breaks off in 1018 but he was still dictating it to a scribe as he lay ill and dying. The manuscript at Dresden with many entries in his own hand survives in a facsimile edition, the original having suffered grieviously in 1945.

Thietmar's diction is complex, his style idiosyncratic – not to say crotchety – despite his classical learning, but this makes him all the more intimate and communicative long before historians sought such close relations with their readers. He divided his work into eight books and wrote programmatic verse prologues for some of them. The first he devoted to Henry I, the next to Otto the Great to whose times he looked back as a golden age. Books III and IV dealt with Otto's son and grandson and Thietmar excelled in describing the succession crises of 983-85 and 1002. From book V onwards he wrote ever more closely to events and he became well acquainted with Henry II, who often stayed at Merseburg. For the earlier tenth century Thietmar had used Widukind of Corvey as a source; for the later, up to 998, he drew on the Quedlinburg annals. His own experiences,[410] journeys, participation in the campaigns against Boleslas Chrobry of Poland, the promotions and deaths of archbishops of Magdeburg, the misdeeds of his cousin Werner, the Saxon nobles' outrages against their bishops, the feuds of the lower Rhine region and some news from further afield, like King Swein's plunder of England, dominate the later books. More than any other writer of the Ottonian ambit the bishop of Merseburg conveys a sense of place and occasion, the milieu of the ruling families and the parameters of their outlook and feelings. Throughout his mood is sombre, sometimes ironical, always profoundly religious. His work lived on and joined the mainstream of twelfth-century Saxon historiography.

3

Early Medieval Warfare

Clausewitz has told us that 'war is neither an art nor a science but a province of social life'.[1] This was still truer of the early middle ages than it was of his own age with its cumbersome mobilisations and its *Bürgerlichkeit* (the civil tenor of life) even in rural Prussia. In Widukind of Corvey, *bellum* and *inimicitia* are part of the life process itself, divinely guided and therefore all the more unquestioned. *Summa pax* was the outcome of successful war, and meant the enjoyment of power in the form of overlordship in all its manifestations, of exacting goods and services from the defeated and being able to dictate to them at will on what we would be tempted to call matters of policy.[2] Writers like Einhard, when they wished to describe the stirrings of resistance and rebellion among peoples whom the Franks had subdued, often expressed this with the words: they refused to do what they were bid, *imperata facere*.[3] And so ubiquitous were their campaigns, so much was the host the centre of action and the essential institution of dominance and social being, that these *imperata*, i.e. orders, were for the most part the duty to come to host, to march and fight with the Franks when told to do so.

War was thus a primary and perennial preoccupation of Carolingian and post-Carolingian society from the eighth to the early eleventh century. Few and far between were the years when there was no *expeditio* and the Frankish Royal Annals notice it with astonishment.[4] For instance the older version set

---

* First published posthumously in *The Battle of Maldon*, ed. Janet Cooper (London: Hambledon Press, 1993), pp. 87-108; thanks are due to the editor for permission to republish here. Minor alterations and additions have been made to footnotes, the text merely brought into line with the conventions of this volume.

[1]   K. von Clausewitz, *Vom Kriege* II 3, ed. W. Hahlweg (Bonn, 1952), p. 201: 'Wir sagen also, der Krieg gehört nicht in das Gebiet der Künste und Wissenschaften, sondern in das Gebiet des gesellschaftlichen Lebens.' The translation in *On War*, ed. M. Howard and P. Paret (Princeton, 1976), p. 149, is, unusually, rather imprecise.

[2]   For *summa pax* see Widukind, *Res gestae Saxonicae* I 14 and II 37, pp. 23 and 97.

[3]   Einhard, *Vita Karoli* c. 12, p. 15; cf. also ibid. c. 10, p. 13, on the Bretons: 'quae imperarentur se facturos polliceri coacti sunt'.

[4]   Philippe Contamine, *La Guerre au moyen âge* (Nouvelle Clio 24, Paris, 1980), pp. 98-9 noted these entries but not the reasons behind them.

down under the year 792: 'In this year no host went out [*iter exercitale*]'.[5] The reason for this may have been merely the magnitude of the preparations for the war against the Avars: a ship bridge across the Danube which could be put together and opened at will seems to have absorbed all attention and resources. Next year an even larger public work, the attempt to link the Rhine with the Danube, mobilised and engrossed huge labour reserves.[6] Charlemagne then sent out no expeditions, but his Reich itself was attacked by Islamic raiders in Septimania and the Saxons hacked down a column of Frankish troops which had marched through Frisia, by the River Weser.[7] In his later years Charles himself often stayed at Aachen throughout, leaving it only to hunt in the Ardennes. He no longer led all expeditions personally, but they were all the same sent out annually, although they did not always call for levying the whole and by now very cumbersome and unwieldy military potential of the Reich.[8]

War was also the heart of the matter of the nascent Ottonian Reich. We do not possess for the Ottonian rulers a work like the *Annales regni Francorum*, unless we take Adalbert's continuation of Regino of Prüm's *Chronicon* as being one. But the Frankish annals read like an order of battle and marching table of the Frankish Reich as Adalbert does not; nor was this his intention.[9] Yet we can piece together evidence for almost ceaseless campaigning under the first Liudolfing king, Henry I. To begin with he had to struggle to be received and recognised in the south. There were constant campaigns in Lotharingia and encounters with the Magyars, and the nine years' peace with them did not mean that warfare rested. On the contrary it opened the chance of taking the offensive against the Slavs, a chance that was ruthlessly taken, and this not only in order to train Saxon warriors in the arts of equestrian combat.[10] It is also characteristic that when Otto I is described by Flodoard as dwelling in peace and leisure ('in pace et otio degens') under the year 956, that is to say the year after the military triumphs over the Magyars and the coalition of Slav peoples, he still despatched his son Liudolf with an army to Italy to

---

[5] *Annales Regni Francorum*, p. 92. The E-version transfers this account to 790, ibid., p. 87.

[6] Ibid., 92 and 94 (original version), 93 (E-version). On the *fossa Carolina* and its failure see H.H. Hofmann, 'Fossa Carolina', in *Karl der Große: Lebenswerk und Nachleben, 1: Persönlichkeit und Geschichte*, ed. H. Beumann (Düsseldorf, 1965), pp. 437-53.

[7] *Annales regni Francorum*, p. 95.

[8] For the campaigns and the army-raising techniques see F.L. Ganshof, *Frankish Institutions under Charlemagne*, trans. B. Lyon (Providence, RI, 1968), pp. 59-68 and T. Reuter, 'The End of Carolingian Military Expansion', in *Charlemagne's Heir: New Perspectives on the Reign of Louis the Pious*, ed. P. Godman and R. Collins (Oxford, 1990), pp. 391-405.

[9] Adalbert, *Continuatio*, pp. 154-79. On Adalbert as a historian see M. Lintzel, 'Erzbischof Adalbert von Magdeburg als Geschichtsschreiber', in idem, *Ausgewählte Schriften*, 2 vols. (Berlin, 1961), vol. 2, pp. 399-406 (first published 1939); K. Hauck, 'Erzbischof Adalbert von Magdeburg als Geschichtsschreiber', in *Festschrift für Walter Schlesinger*, ed. Helmut Beumann (Cologne, 1974), vol. 2, pp. 276-344.

[10] For the *histoire événementielle* see Waitz, *Heinrich I.*, pp. 34-149, for the Saxon 'new model army' cf. Widukind, *Res gestae Saxonicae* I 35, pp. 48-51 with K.J. Leyser, 'Henry I and the Beginnings of the Saxon Empire', in idem, *Medieval Germany*, pp. 11-42.

crush King Berengar who had raised and restored his effective regime again.[11] Under the year 957 and 959 we read monotonously: *rex iterum Sclavos invasit*, i.e. he campaigned himself, but 958 was not a year of peace either. According to Flodoard Otto warred against the Slavs again, this time for the additional reason that a smouldering inner-Saxon feud, the unrelenting hostility of the younger Wichmann, echoed and enlisted a clientèle among the Wends.[12]

We must all the same ask the question: how endemic was the state of war in the Ottonian Reich? On the frontiers warfare rarely ceased and there was an awful lot of frontier to the east, north and southeast. In Flodoards's France, moreover, not a year passed without some campaigning: Carolingians, Robertians, the house of Vermandois and others were fighting and already in the tenth century much of this warfare focused on and was about castles.[13] We do not have to wait until the coming of the stone keep in the eleventh for this to be so. In the Reich we have Magyar invasions and the great wars about the kingship. Otto I, almost immediately after his coronation, launched a campaign against the Slav Redarii, even though he had a recent defeat at the hands of the Bohemians to avenge. It was almost as if his kingship was on trial, as if he had to show his warriors that he possessed the mettle for what was a ruler's unceasing and essential task.[14] Next year, in 937, he had to face his first Hungarian invasion, followed shortly afterwards by the internal unrest and warfare which then continued with climaxes and pauses until 941, when his brother Henry at last submitted. More Slav and Lotharingian embroilments followed as well as the large campaign in France in 946.[15] But even here there are some years to account for when we do not hear of any fighting and its accompanying devastations, *depopulatio*, and plundering.[16] Some inland regions like southern Suabia may have been relatively quiescent during the later years of Otto's rule, after Liudolf's rising and the crisis of the battle at the

[11] Adalbert, *Continuatio*, pp. 168-9.

[12] Adalbert, *Continuatio s.a.* 957 and 959, p. 169; Flodoard, *Annales s.a.* 958, p. 146; Widukind, *Res Gestae Saxonicae* III 60, p. 136 (on Wichmann and his Slav clientèle).

[13] See e.g. Flodoard, *Annales s.a.* 949, pp. 121-8: in his description of the campaigning which followed the decisions of the synod of Ingelheim in the disputed Rheims election, he mentions the siege or capture of fortifications at Pierrepont-en-Laonnois, Omont, Laon, Mareuil, Coucy and Châtillon-sur-Marne. On castle-building in tenth-century France see B.S. Bachrach, 'Early Medieval Fortification in the "West" of France: A Revised Technical Vocabulary', *Technology and Culture*, 16 (1975), pp. 531-69; G. Fournier, *Le Château dans la France médiévale: essai de sociologie monumentale* (Paris, 1978), pp. 38-59; Kelly DeVries, *Medieval Military Technology* (Peterborough, Ontario, 1992), pp. 213-18.

[14] Widukind, *Res gestae Saxonicae* II 3 (defeat by Bohemians) and 4 (campaign against the Slavs), pp. 68-70, 70-1. II 4 opens: 'Rex autem audito huiuscemodi nuntio minime turbatur, sed divina virtute roboratus cum omni exercitu intrat terminos barbarorum ad refrenandam eorum saevitiam.' The *barbari* can be identified as the Redarii from a contemporary diploma of Otto I's: ibid., p. 70 n. 4.

[15] For the events of these years see Köpke-Dümmler, *Otto der Große*, pp. 1-154.

[16] B. Scherff, *Studien zum Heer der Ottonen und der ersten Salier* (Bonn, 1985), p. 11, reckons 941, 942, 944, 945 and 947 as years without campaigns, with a gap then until 971.

Lech in 955. Unlike the east Saxons the Suabians were not committed to constant dangerous and aggressive, albeit profitable, frontier warfare. Some of their nobles later campaigned with the emperor's host in Italy, but except for Duke Burchard's expedition against King Berengar's son Adalbert in 965, not very many.[17] Does that mean that this and other regions enjoyed long periods of peace? A somewhat later passage in Thietmar of Merseburg suggests that it might have been so. Under the year 1008 he reported the outbreak of trouble in Trier where the see had fallen vacant. The community elected a youth well below the canonical age who happened to be the brother of the Empress Cunigunde and had served the deceased archbishop, Liudolf, as a *capellanus*. They thought this would please the king, Henry II, but he preferred and raised one of his own former chaplains who was also Archbishop Willigis of Mainz's provost and chamberlain. The troublesome Luxemburg kin of Cunigunde took this ill and the men of Trier now fortified the archiepiscopal palace to hold it against the king. Thietmar added: a region that had hitherto been peaceful was now tormented by arson, the habitual concomitant of most early medieval warfare. These men paid for their transgressions in the same coin. They in turn suffered depredation.[18]

Our central theme must be to find out how the needs and predicaments of late Carolingian and post-Carolingian societies shaped and determined belligerency but also how the technicalities of warfare, its ways and means, in turn imposed on societies and moulded their structures, values and make-up. In all this we must not see the institutions of the church as an antithesis to the rise and development of the military strata we encounter in the empire, west Francia and England. On the contrary, in the time-span here under review, that is to say from the mid-ninth to the early eleventh century, a process of mobilisation and militarisation inescapably became part also of the church's experience. It was not, nor did it want to be, the passive and helpless sufferer of violence at the hands of either external or internal foes. Vikings, Saracens and Magyars were known to be pagans and unbelievers; the internal ones, the 'bad Christians', *mali Christiani*, were usually mentioned in the same breath as

---

[17] For Burchard's expedition see Adalbert, *Continuatio*, p. 176. Gerhard, *Vita Oudalrici episcopi Augustensis* c. 28, *MGH SS* 4, 416, says of Ulrich of Augsburg's Suabian nephews that they frequently fought in Italy for the emperor.

[18] Thietmar, *Chronicon* VI 35, pp. 316/318; cf. especially p. 316: 'Palas a Trevirensibus contra regem firmatur ac terra haec hactenus pacifica crebis concremacionibus quatitur'. On the other hand the *Gesta Treverorum* c. 29, *MGH SS* 8, 169 talk of the 'monasteria urbis, rapina comprovincialium praediis exhaustis' on the accession of Archbishop Egbert in 979, and Ruotger, *Vita Brunonis* c. 25, p. 26, talks of Brun of Cologne's peacekeeping activities around Trier and in Alsace. It may simply be that the grass seemed greener to Thietmar on the other side of the hill (for his own troubles and those of his fellow bishops in Saxony see *Chronicon* VIII 23-8, pp. 520/26).

the heathen assailants.[19] The *gladius materialis*, the wherewithal to coerce and punish the wicked, was desperately needed by churchmen and exalted in their prayers, so that those who wielded it should be able to perform their function, which was to protect churches as well as the weak and the helpless for whom the higher clergy claimed to speak at the same time as they did for their own order and privileges. To attract protection, to direct the correction of the wicked, the great prelates of the ninth and tenth centuries, men like Hincmar, Brun of Cologne and Willigis of Mainz sought to set examples, to exalt kings and at the same time to temper their conduct.[20] More difficult still, they and their like tried in what was for centuries an uphill struggle to persuade, cajole and bribe lay nobles – men who could only hope to acquire surplus wealth swiftly by acts of war – to respect the possessions of churches and monasteries.

Much early medieval warfare was merely an extension and enlargement of feuds, themselves endemic in the aristocratic societies of Latin Europe; more was ethnocentric, like the defence of settlements, wealth and authority against heathen attackers. But by far the most part was about rule and lordship, contesting for them against rivals who were often if not always kinsmen. Underlying all types of war, however, was a simple quest for wealth in all its forms, booty, treasure held by enemy kings, labour services, manufacturing corvées and, last but not least, tribute. Nowhere was this so clearly the case as in the Saxon wars against the Slavonic tribes settled between the Saale and the Elbe, the Sorbs, and against those to the east of the Elbe north of its junction with the Saale, like the Wilzi, Redarii, Hevelli and Abodrites. Tribute in all its forms was the means by which the Saxon kings maintained their *milites* on a permanent war footing and in turn the most usual employment for these *milites* was war against Slav tribes, meaning their containment and subjection, the occupation and garrisoning of some of their lands and areas of settlement, and the exaction of tribute. This was the normal occupation of the warriors of Ottonian east Saxony, the gathering in of the renders in kind and in cash by which they themselves were maintained.[21] Compared with this the occasional

---

[19] Cf. *Annales Fuldenses s.a.* 857, pp. 49-50; Regino, *Chronicon, s.a.* 883, p. 121: 'tantaque rapina et violentia ab his in regno fit, ut inter horum et Nortmannorum malitiam nil differret, preter quod a cedibus et incendiis abstinerent'. Berengar I's diplomata for Novara (911) and Padua (915), ed. L. Schiapparelli, *I diplomi de Berengario I* (Fonti per la storia d'Italia 35, Rome, 1903), pp. 209 no. 76 and 266 no. 101 talk of the 'persecutione Paganorum atque malorum Christianorum virorum' and of the 'Paganorum malorumque Christianorum debacchationem' respectively. See also H. Fichtenau, *Lebensordnungen des 10. Jahrhunderts*, 2 vols paginated as one (Stuttgart, 1974), pp. 501, 561; English translation by P. Geary as *Living in the Tenth Century* (Chicago, 1991), pp. 383, 430.

[20] See in general on these developments C. Erdmann, *Die Entstehung des Kreuzzugsgedankens* (Stuttgart, 1935), English as *The Origins of the Idea of Crusade*, trans. M.W. Baldwin and W. Goffart (Philadelphia, 1977); F. Prinz, *Klerus und Krieg im frühen Mittelalter* (Monographien zur Geschichte des frühen Mittelalters 2, Stuttgart, 1971); J.M. Wallace-Hadrill, *Early Germanic Kingship in England and on the Continent* (Oxford, 1971); J. Flori, *L'Idéologie du glaive* (Geneva, 1983).

[21] K.J. Leyser, 'Ottonian Government', in idem, *Medieval Germany*, pp. 88-90.

Italian expedition were less important, demanded fewer men, albeit sometimes for long periods, and brought fewer, though more sophisticated, spoils.
But here too the collection of riches – rare liquid resources, artefacts and silks –
was an essential if unavowed objective. Beside, even above this must be set the
zealous and competitive acquisition of relics by fair means or foul. These, the
pignora sanctorum, the warrants of the saints, were not the least desired things
that attracted Saxon bishops and lay warriors to these long-distance military
enterprises.[22]

Timothy Reuter, in his admirable article on 'Plunder and Tribute in the
Carolingian Empire', has set out some of the more lucrative occasions in the
ninth century when great riches fell into the hands of victorious armies.[23] The
question that must conversely be raised, however, is: why did kings, lay
princes, bishops and abbots take their own treasures and most precious
valuables with them on campaigns at all, and keep on doing so, moreover, not
only in the tenth but also in the eleventh century? At the battle of Flarchheim
in January 1080 the Saxons under their king, Rudolf of Rheinfelden and Otto
of Northeim won another victory over Henry IV and his invading host. His
retreating men came too close to the Wartburg and were suddenly attacked
from there while they rested and hoped to refresh themselves. The assailants
not only drove away the tired Henrician troops, but also seized everything they
had: besides horses and arms, golden and silver plate, pepper – very much a
form of treasure – other spices, mantles and precious vestments. The patriarch
of Aquileia was one of those who suffered loss. We owe this information to the
Saxon historian of the great war against Henry IV, Brun of Merseburg.[24] In the
battle by the River Elster on 15 October 1080 where Rudolf of Rheinfelden
fell, the victory all the same remained with the Saxons. Once more they owed it
mostly to Otto of Northeim, who succeeded in storming the Henrician camp –
with a force of *pedites*, let us note. Otto also succeeded in preventing his men
from plundering before they had dealt with the unbeaten detachment of one of
Henry's commanders, Henry of Laach, the count palatine of Lotharingia.
When Henry and his men had been driven away across the river, where many
drowned, Otto invited his troops to seize the hard-earned spoils of their *virtus*
at last. They found many good things: precious tents, the chests of bishops full
of sacred vestments and plate, gold and silverware for daily use, thin bars of
silver and gold, a large amount of minted money, a great many excellent
horses, arms of all kinds, changes of clothes and priceless garments – or to put
it briefly, whatever the (arch)bishops of Cologne, and Trier and fourteen
others had brought with them, whatever Duke Frederick (the first Hohenstaufen duke of Suabia) and Count Henry 'and other very rich men had brought

---

[22] E. Dupré-Theseider, 'La grande rapina dei corpi Santi dell'Italia al tempo di Ottone I', in
Festschrift für Percy Ernst Schramm (Wiesbaden, 1964), vol. 2, pp. 420-32; T. Reuter, *Germany in
the Early Middle Ages, c. 800-1056* (London, 1991), pp. 271-2.

[23] 'Plunder and Tribute in the Carolingian Empire', *TRHS*, fifth series 35 (1985), pp. 75-94.

[24] Brun, *Bellum Saxonicum* c. 117, pp. 109-11.

along, our men seized and triumphantly returned to their camp'.[25] Of course, many of the articles named were needed on campaign and in action, and some of the bishops' gilt cups and vestments must have been chalices and robes for the celebration of mass. But much else which they and the lay princes had with them could not have been urgently needed, and much might have been more simple and less valuable than in fact it was. Why then this display and luxury? Why did bishops and high lay nobles prefer to carry their treasures about with them rather than leave them behind in their *palatia* or fortified dwellings at home? It is of course possible that there too they lived itinerant rather than stationary lives, moving from estate to estate, not unlike their kings travelling ceaselessly with their insignia and chapels.[26] It could also be that security was not necessarily maintained more easily when the lords and owners of treasures and precious objects were away. Wives could not always effectively control households and some of their household officers travelled with great men, prelates and lay princes in war too.[27] It could also be – and this is where I look for the answer to the question – that all these precious possessions were needed to express and maintain rank and standing in situations and crises where they might be threatened, as could happen in war. A bishop could only be himself if he had the vestments and costly trappings of his exalted station with him and on him.[28] We know of lay princes wearing their golden chains and *armillae*, wristlets, as badges of rank by which they could be instantly recognised and casting them off in a hurry to disguise their standing or as a sign of surrender.[29] Ostentatious display and boasting were essential ingredients of warfare. A great man always had to proclaim his lordship visibly for the eyes of his followers, his peers and rivals.[30] He also needed to have the means to reward good service there and then.

---

[25] Ibid. c. 122, pp. 114.17.

[26] On the itineracy of eleventh-century bishops see P. Johanek, 'Die Erzbischöfe von Hamburg-Bremen und ihre Kirche im Reich der Salierzeit', in *Die Salier und das Reich*, 2: *Die Reichskirche in der Salierzeit*, ed. S. Weinfurter and F. M. Siefarth (Sigmaringen, 1991), pp. 92-4, and also the comments by Leyser, 'Ottonian Government' (as n. 21), pp. 94-9, on the restricted opportunities for long-distance travelling available to magnates.

[27] For the difficulties encountered by women defending castles see e.g. *Vita Balderici episcopi Leodiensis* c. 22, *MGH SS* 4, 732, though one could also adduce successes or at least honourable failures, e.g. Thietmar, *Chronicon* V 39, p. 264 (defence of Schweinfurt against Henry II by Henry of Schweinfurt's mother Eila); Alpert of Metz, *De diversitate temporum* II 13, ed. H. van Rij and A.S. Abulafia (Amsterdam, 1980), p. 70 (Adela of Elten's defence of Upladen).

[28] Fichtenau, *Lebensordnungen* (as n. 19), p. 95 (English translation, pp. 66-7).

[29] See the references to *armillae* and *torques* in Widukind, *Res gestae Saxonicae* I 26, II 1 (here as royal ornaments) and II 11, pp. 38, 66, 77. In the last passage Thangmar, Otto I's rebellious brother, after being cornered and forced to take refuge in a church, removed his *armis cum torque aurea* and laid them on the altar, presumably as a sign of surrender. Liudprand, *Antapodosis* II 62, p. 65, describes how Adalbert of Ivrea stripped himself of his *apparatus* when surrounded by the Magyars and disguised himself as a simple *miles*. On armbands as signs of authority in general see P.E. Schramm, *Herrschaftszeichen*, 3 vols (Schriften der MGH 13, Stuttgart 1953-55) vol. 1, pp. 177-8, 184-7, vol. 2, pp. 538-53.

[30] See the remarks and examples in Fichtenau, *Lebensordnungen* (as n. 19), pp. 74-95 (English translation, pp. 50-67).

The bonds which ordinarily bound men to their lords gave some cohesion in strange surroundings to fluid and malleable, because in part inarticulate, societies. They were therefore needed *a fortiori* in war. Roman armies had known fixed and long-standing formations, structured sub-units: there were cohorts, maniples and centuries and legions had headquarters with staffs and emblems.[31] Ninth-century Carolingian armies marched and fought in detachments called *scarae* but sometimes the word was used to describe the operations of a single striking force.[32] Tenth-century historians, like Widukind of Corvey and Thietmar after him, avidly fell back on and used the term *legio* to describe the composition of their own Saxon hosts and of armies in general. The huge force which invaded France in 946 was made up of thirty-two; at the Lech in 955 there fought only eight.[33] A count Thietmar boasted in 915 that he had come with thirty legions when he reported to Henry I who was in a tight spot and faced an attack by King Conrad I who had marched up and besieged him at Grone (near Göttingen) with a sizeable host.[34] Widukind thus used *legio* to give some indication of an army's size, and Thietmar followed him in this. His legions were the major units of a host, which operated either on their own or in concert. Since he did not give figures their strength cannot easily be assessed from his text and it will no doubt have varied; yet to judge from the context and the scope of the operations he described it should be measured in a few hundreds rather than thousands.[35] Widukind, though not Thietmar, also knew and occasionally liked to use the word *legatus* in the sense of commander. At the battle of Lenzen, fought in 929 against a massive coalition of Slavs, King Henry I oddly had not come to take charge himself but gave the command to two *legati*, Bernard and Thietmar. We do not know how many 'legions' they had with them.[36]

This raises the problems of command. There were no formal structures of command. When Count Bernard was in difficulties and could not make any more headway he asked his colleague, *collega*, to come to his aid. Count Thietmar, it appears, had fifty mounted men who then brought the decision.[37]

[31] See A.R. Neumann, 'Exercitus', *Der Kleine Pauly*, 5 vols. (Stuttgart, 1967), vol. 2, pp. 479-82; G. Webster, *The Roman Imperial Army in the First and Second Centuries*, 3rd edn (London 1985).

[32] J.F. Niermeyer, *Mediae Latinitatis Lexicon Minus* (Amsterdam, 1954-76), pp. 943-4, *s.v. scara, scarire, scaritus*; Ganshof, *Frankish Institutions* (as n. 8), pp. 64, 68. The range of meaning of the term can be seen in *Annales Bertiniani*, pp. 88, 125, 151, 152, 180, 181, 242, 246.

[33] Widukind, *Res gestae Saxonicae* III 2 and 44, pp. 105, 124. The army of 946 is described as a 'magnus valde exercitus'.

[34] Ibid. I 24, p. 37.

[35] Thietmar, *Chronicon*, p. 608 (index, *s.v.*). On these units of organisation see K.J. Leyser, 'The Battle at the Lech, 955: a Study in Medieval Warfare', *Medieval Germany*, pp. 58-9.

[36] Widukind, *Res gestae Saxonicae*, I 36, p. 52; elsewhere he uses the word exclusively in the sense 'ambassador, legate, messenger'.

[37] Ibid.; cf. Scherff, *Studien* (as n. 16), pp. 13-16. For references to difficulties resulting from jealousies and divided command in Carolingian armies see *Annales Regni Francorum s.a.* 782, pp. 61, 63 (E-version); *Annales Fuldenses s.a.* 849, pp. 38-9; Region, *Chronicon s.a.* 890, pp. 135-6 (here a Breton campaign against the Vikings).

Before a great action men swore to help one another, not only here in the battle against the Slavs, but also in 955 at the Lech against the Magyars.[38] These were *bella publica* against a common enemy, which for the time being over-rode the latent and overt enmities and feuds among the warriors assembled in the host. The oath was really a promise not to use the occasion for getting rid of an enemy by leaving him unsupported at a critical moment. This happened among the Italians at the Brenta in 899, according to Liudprand of Cremona's vivid account of the action, where rival contingents hoped that the Hungarians would do their dirty work for them.[39] And even when there was no doubt about who was in charge there might be unsanctioned and even prohibited action by individual noble warriors in search of distinction and as a challenge to an envied rival and leader, as happened on Otto I's first campaign in 936. Otto had just raised Hermann Billung to be *princeps militiae*, to take command in this campaign against the Slav Redarii. Hermann's brother Wichmann and other princes were not pleased, and Wichmann left the host in dudgeon.[40] Under Carolingian usages this was an offence for which Duke Tassilo of Bavaria was eventually tried and ruined.[41] Otto does not seem to have been able to punish recalcitrants then, and was glad when Wichmann later came to terms with him again. Hermann Billung managed well and won his first engagement but this only roused more envy and rivalry. Widukind tells us that one Ekkard son of Liudolf – almost certainly Ottonian kin – collected some of the best warriors from the whole host and so formed a band. With them he crossed the bog dividing the Saxons from the Slavs – against Otto's express orders. With his volunteers Ekkard attacked the Redarian fortress, but he was quickly surrounded and perished with all his companions in the attempt to outdo Hermann Billung. Eighteen young men fell.[42] Nor was this the only instance of indiscipline in the quest for distinction and its rewards. There were others, Thietmar mentioned one Thiedbern whom he called *miles egregius*. He had recently received four fortresses on the River Mulde as a fief (*beneficium*). In 1005 he took part in Henry II's campaign against Boleslas Chrobry. The host suffered much on the march but reached the River Spree, where Thiedbern learned the enemy lay in waiting and was doing harm from an ambush. To win praise for himself he secretly assembled the best of his mates

[38] Widukind, *Res gestae Saxonicae* I 36 (933) and III 44 (955), pp. 52, 124.

[39] Liudprand, *Antapodosis* II 15, pp. 44-5. For the problem in Carolingian armies see the complaint by Charlemagne in a late capitulary, *MGH Capit.* 1, p. 161, no. 71, c.2: 'Quae causae efficiunt, ut unus alteri adiutorium praestare nolit, sive in marcha sive in exercitu ubi aliquid utilitatis defensione patriae facere debet'.

[40] Widukind, *Res gestae Saxonicae* II 4, p. 70.

[41] P. Classen, 'Bayern und die politischen Mächte im Zeitalter Karls des Großen und Tassilos III.', in *Ausgewählte Aufsätze von Peter Classen*, ed. J. Fleckenstein and others (Sigmaringen, 1983), pp. 242-4.

[42] Widukind, *Res gestae Saxonicae* II 4, p. 71. The only evidence for Ekkard's kinship with the Ottonians is his father's name Liudolf, but in the context this seems a strong pointer, in spite of the objections raised by R. Schölkopf, *Die sächsischen Grafen (919-1024)* (Studien und Vorarbeiten zum Historischen Atlas Niedersachsens 22, Göttingen, 1957), p. 106.

(*consocii*) and tried to intercept the Poles by stealth (*dolo*). They retreated into a thicket of felled trees, giving cover, and from there began to fire with archery on the Saxon warriors who were following them, their usual method of defence. Thiedbern was killed together with three named 'knights' of Bishop Arnulf of Halberstadt.[43] Again the quest for distinction, the initiative of gathering friends and companions for a deed of daring outside the current norms of attachment and service and again the mournful result.

Altogether it was difficult for commanders of the late ninth, tenth and early eleventh centuries to concert operations so as to achieve effective co-operation between allied and friendly hosts fighting the same enemy. Here is another example from Henry II's wars against the Polish duke, Boleslas Chrobry, in 1015. Boleslas had defaulted on his promise to join Henry II on his *expeditio Romana* where Henry hoped for and gained his imperial coronation. Not only had Boleslas defaulted, he was also suspected of having tried to intrigue against the king in Lombardy.[44] Thietmar again is our chief source and the bishop of Merseburg, close to an ever-threatened frontier, knew about war and took part as was his duty.[45] More than one army advanced eastwards but they could not bring about a junction: the duke of Bohemia and a Bavarian force were meant to join the emperor but failed to do so. Further north Duke Bernard Billung advanced towards the Oder with a force made up of bishops, counts and heathen Liutizi. Each of these contingents operated quite success-fully on their respective fronts, capturing prisoners and seizing spoils the enemy had looted first. Henry's own force was thus too small to achieve anything decisive and he retreated. On the way back the Poles hiding in a forest attacked the Saxon column of march, roaring three times; the ritual should be noted. In the end their assault, once again backed by heavy arrow fire, was successful and they inflicted severe casualties. Margrave Gero, Count Folkmar and two hundred of the best 'knights' were killed and stripped.[46] This failure to concert operations was not unusual, though it could be managed, as Charlemagne had succeeded in doing when he trapped Duke Tassilo or Bavaria with forces advancing from the west, the north and the south.[47] On the whole poor communications favoured those who possessed interior lines. The Bouvines campaign of 1214, where John's operations and attempted advance from the south proved a fiasco, may serve as another and later example.

It was not uncharacteristic of Henry II's setbacks that even his enemy, when he heard of noble casualties, is said to have been sorry, and in this case

[43] Thietmar, *Chronicon* VI 22, p. 300. Compare also the disastrous results of rivalries at the battle of the Sündtal in 782 (*Annales regni Francorum*, cited above, n. 37).

[44] Thietmar, *Chronicon* VI 92, VII 4 and 9, pp. 384, 402 and 408.

[45] For the following campaign see Thietmar, *Chronicon* VII 16-22, pp. 414-22.

[46] Ibid. VII 21, p. 422.

[47] *Annales regni Francorum s.a.* 787, p. 78; see also the account of the campaigns against the Avars, ibid. *s.a.* 791, p. 88, and for later successful campaigns with divided forces *Annales Fuldenses s.a.* 869, 882, 895-6, pp. 69 (Carloman and Charles), pp. 107-8 (Charles III) and 127 (Arnulf), and Uhlirz, *Otto III.,* vol. 2, pp. 152, 159, 468-70 (campaign against Brandenburg in 992).

Boleslas made no difficulties about returning the bodies of the fallen men of note for burial in their family sanctuaries. Henry II himself wanted to turn back to retrieve the bodies of Margrave Gero and Count Folkmar but he was persuaded to send Bishop Eid of Meissen instead for this task.[48] The incident highlights a deep-rooted feature of early medieval warfare: the enormous importance and the central role of leaders in holding together the little universes of their followings and so, by their collaboration, giving some coherence and solidarity to hosts in the fissiparous and segmented societies from which most of them sprang. The royal presence, of course, did this even more.[49] Leaders, when present, had a charismatic task in their hosts even if they were themselves unable to wield effective command. A Breton duke, though mortally ill, had himself placed on a stretcher before the *acies* of his men because they demanded his presence.[50] For this reason the historians from the ninth to eleventh century always mentioned the death and losses of commanders. Even in the tight narrative economy of Einhard's *Life of Charlemagne* we are not only told of the three great men who fell in the Spanish expedition of 778 – Eggihard, Anselm and, need I say, Hruodlandus - we are also given their positions in the Frankish hierarchy: the first had been in charge of the king's table and the second count palatine, while Roland was margrave of the Breton march.[51] Later Einhard mentioned in particular the *proceres Francorum* who succumbed in the most ambitious, far-flung and profitable of Charlemagne's military enterprises, the Avar war. Here, he wrote, only two of the foremost Franks perished: Eric, duke of Friuli and Gerald, the *praefectus Baioariae*, of the close kin of Hildegard, Charlemagne's most important wife.[52] The very circumstances of their death are given in detail and the habit of recording such exalted casualties can be traced in most of the ninth and tenth-century annals, chronicles and histories.[53] Their deaths in action could be catastrophic to morale and totally disrupt campaigns. When Count Robert, ancestor of the Capetians, and Duke Ramnulf were killed by the Northmen in 866, the Frankish army abandoned its operations and

[48] Thietmar, *Chronicon* VII 22, p. 422 (Eid of Meissen). For Boleslas's regrets see the Thiedbern episode, ibid. VI 22, p. 302; however, on the occasion referred to above Eid found Boleslas 'multum de pernicie nostra gaudenti'.

[49] Demonstrated negatively by *Annales Fuldenses s.a.* 872, pp. 74-6: Louis the German 'misit Thuringios et Saxones contra Sclavos Marahenses, qui, quoniam regem secum non habebant et inter se concordes esse nolebant, idcirco hostibus terga verterunt et plurimis suorum amissis turpiter redierunt; ita ut quidam comites in illa expeditione fugientes a mulierculis illius regionis verberati et de equis in terram fustibus deiecti referantur'.

[50] Regino, *Chronicon, s.a.* 875, p. 109. Cf. also Bede, *Historia Ecclesiastica* III 18, ed. B. Colgrave and R.A.B. Mynors (Oxford, 1969), p. 268, for the story of Sigeberht of East Anglia, brought out of a monastery to lead his men in battle.

[51] Einhard, *Vita Karoli* c. 9, p. 12.

[52] Ibid. c. 13, p. 16.

[53] See, for example, the accounts of the disastrous battle fought by Charles the Bald's men against Pippin of Aquitaine in 844, *Annales Fuldenses*, pp. 34-5 and *Annales Bertiniani*, pp. 46-7, or the long list of the Saxon magnates who fell at the battle against the Northmen in *Annales Fuldenses s.a.* 880, p. 94.

everyone went home, thus enabling the Northmen, who had been cornered, to return triumphantly to their ships.[54] Something similar happened in 885 when Duke Ragenold fell.[55] All went home sadly, having accomplished nothing of any use.

It is quite clear that these losses created dangerous and worrying gaps in the structure of authority, always precarious in societies in which so much depended on military success. In the *Battle of Maldon* the loss of the leader at once led to flights and desertions.[56] The fate of followers (vassals and warriors) who had lost their lord and commander was unenviable: their loyalties and their futures were now in peril.[57] There is a good story in Thietmar of Merseburg and in Alpert of Metz to illustrate this and it leads us into an underworld of gang warfare and revenges which makes it more than doubtful whether the silence of chroniclers, the absence of news about wars and feuds for years on end, really meant that there was peace in a given area. In this case we are well informed because the feud between Count Balderich and Count Wichmann in the extreme west of Saxony, the border-land between Saxony and lower Lotharingia, became a *cause célèbre*.[58] The driving force behind this upheaval was a Saxon noblewoman, Adela of Elten, who might be described as the Lady Macbeth of the lower Rhine. To fight out her cause and claims on part of her paternal inheritance she married Balderich, about whose origins there were some doubts. She needed him to be represented in the comital courts of the region, where unlike Anglo-Saxon ladies she had no right to plead herself.[59] Between her and her husband and Count Wichmann there was a long-running feud, with petty skirmishes around fortresses. In the end Balderich and Wichmann were reconciled, and exchanged hospitality and presents. When it came to Count Wichmann's being entertained by Balderich and Adela in their residence at Upladen, a plot was hatched against his life, according to Alpert, by Adela. Wichmann, after he had left Upladen, was killed by a serf a short distance away – his own warriors had been delayed on purpose, but Balderich was about and did not avenge the killing.[60] First on the scene,

---

[54] Regino, *Chronicon s.a.* 867, pp. 92-3.

[55] *Annales Vedastini*, ed. B. von Simson (MGH SRG 12, Hanover, 1909), pp. 57. For an early eleventh-century example see Adémar, *Chronicon* III 70, p. 195.

[56] 'The Battle of Maldon' lines 185-201, *The Battle of Maldon A.D. 991*, ed. D. Scragg (Oxford, 1991), pp. 24/26.

[57] See *Vita Balderici episcopi Leodiensis* c. 21, *MGH SS* 4, 732. The point is missed by Rosemary Woolf, 'The Ideal of Men Dying with their Lord in *Germania* and in *The Battle of Maldon*', *Anglo-Saxon England*, 5 (1976), pp. 63-81, at pp. 65-6.

[58] The contemporary accounts of the feud and its consequences are in Thietmar, *Chronicon* VII 47-8, VIII 7 and 18, pp. 456-8, 502, 514, and Alpert, *De Diversitate Temporum* (as n. 27) I 1-4 and II 1-13, 14-18, pp. 8-14, 42-70, 74-8; see also Hirsch-Papst-Bresslau, *Heinrich II.*, vol. 2, pp. 345-54 and vol. 3, pp. 310-15, and F.W. Oediger, 'Adelas Kampf um Elten (996-1002)', in idem, *Vom Leben am Niederrhein: Aufsätze aus dem Bereich des alten Erzbistums Köln* (Düsseldorf, 1973), pp. 217-35.

[59] On this aspect see Oediger, 'Adelas Kampf' (as n. 58).

[60] Alpert, *De Diversitate Temporum* II 12, p. 66; cf. also Thietmar, *Chronicon* VII 47, p. 456, for Balderich's role.

according to Thietmar – Alpert differs – was Bishop Dietrich of Münster, who saw to the dead man's obsequies and caused him to be buried in the nunnery of Vreden at the frontier into Saxony. He also began organising revenge. Next arrived Duke Bernard Billung, a kinsman of the deceased who now became both guardian of his small son and another avenger. He also, so Thietmar tells us, comforted (*solatur*) the now helpless *milites* of Count Wichmann, as much as he could, and this is no isolated instance.[61] When Margrave Gero was laid to rest in his house's monastery at Nienburg, Archbishop Gero of Magdeburg consoled and reassured not only his wife and heir but also his grieving friends, knights and vassals.[62]

The deaths of great personages in combat could turn military success into failure. When Rudolf of Rheinfelden met Henry IV in pitched battle by the River Elster on 15 October 1080, Henry suffered a sharp defeat but his enemy Rudolf died of his wounds in the mêlée and this gave Henry's cause a great boost, especially as Rudolf lost the right hand with which he had sworn fealty to the Salian king.[63] In 1075 Henry in turn had won a great victory over the Saxon rebels, but their princes had for the most part got away from the battle, while he had lost several eminent men, as hostile chroniclers reported with much *schadenfreude*.[64]

It can be shown, and I hope to have done so in my article 'Early Medieval Canon Law and the Beginnings of Knighthood', that long before chivalry had been built into the ethos of warfare there was already an honour of arms, a notion that certain crimes and outrages were incompatible with bearing arms and the *cingulum militare*.[65] It is thus possible to speak of an increasing aristocratisation of warfare, a process aided by the growing importance of the mounted warrior with hauberk, helmet and sword, trained for close-quarter action.[66] But it would be quite wrong to think of fighting in this period as a particularly chivalrous or magnanimous pursuit. In the first place there were a great many spoiling operations and devastations, warfare *ad facinus tantum non ad imperium* as Widukind once described it when a close kinsman and enemy of Hermann Billung raided across the Saxon frontier with his Slav warband.[67]

---

[61] Thietmar, *Chronicon* VII 48, pp. 456, 458.

[62] Ibid. VII 22, p. 424.

[63] Frutolf, *Chronicon universale*, MGH SS 6, 204; *Vita Heinrici IV imperatoris* c. 4, ed. W. Eberhard (MGH SRG 58, Hanover, 1899), p. 19. Meyer von Knonau, *Heinrich IV.*, vol. 3, pp. 644-52, gives further references.

[64] Brun, *Bellum Saxonicum* cc. 46-7, p. 45; see Meyer von Knonau, *Heinrich IV.*, vol. 2, pp. 879-80 for further references.

[65] 'Early Medieval Canon Law and the Beginnings of Knighthood', below, pp. 51-71. See now also J.L. Nelson, 'Ninth-century Knighthood: the Evidence of Nithard', *Studies in Medieval History Presented to R. Allen Brown*, ed. C. Harper-Bill, C.J. Holdsworth and J.L. Nelson (Woodbridge, 1989), pp. 255-66.

[66] Leyser, 'Henry I' (as n. 10); Contamine, *La Guerre* (as n. 4), pp. 108-11.

[67] Widukind, *Res gestae Saxonicae* III 52, p. 131.

Moreover *dolus* and *astutia*, craft and cunning, were admired qualities in a commander. Widukind of Corvey extolled Margrave Gero, who overcame the *dolus* of the Slavs with cunning of his own, cunning and brutality to boot, in that he is reported to have caused to be killed nearly thirty of their princes after inviting them to a great feast and making them drunk with wine.[68] Later in Widukind's account Gero is again praised for his many skills and plans. When the Ottonian host was in an extremely difficult situation in their 955 campaign against the Abodrites, he encouraged one of their chieftains to boast himself into a false sense of security. He then crossed the swamp dividing the hosts by a flanking march in which his own Slav clients, the Ruani, acted as guides. The trick worked to perfection.[69] Even at Fontenoy in 841 which the victors wanted to have regarded as trial by battle, a *judicium Dei*, Charles the Bald and Louis the German seem to have been able to seize an important feature overlooking Lothar's camp on the morning of 25 June, when battle was to be joined at a fixed hour. Against this it might be said that Lothar too had manoeuvred for advantage by keeping negotiations open until Pippin of Aquitaine had marched up and joined him.[70] The point could be clinched by recalling that the *Battle of Maldon* poet did not think it wisdom but foolhardy pride in Earl Byrhtnoth to have allowed the Danes access to the ford.[71]

If war was waged with cunning in the early middle ages, it was nevertheless swathed in rituals and of these one of the most important was boasting. Christians and their heathen enemies shared this, and boasts evidently crossed camps. The Magyars in 955 contended that unless the earth split open or heaven collapsed on top of them they could not be defeated.[72] The Vikings habitually jeered at Frankish hosts and once in a while their mockery is even recorded.[73] Duke Eberhard of Francia, sent by his brother King Conrad I to battle it out with the Saxons under Duke Henry, the future king, is in Widukind's account made to advance to the Eresburg and, such was his arrogance, to be worried above all lest the Saxons should not dare to show

---

[68] Ibid. II 20, p. 84; for a similar incident in the dealings between Bavarians and Magyars in the early tenth century see the evidence assembled by K. Reindel, *Die bayerischen Luitpoldinger, 893-989: Sammlung und Erläuterung der Quellen* (Quellen und Erörterungen zur bayerischen Geschichte, neue Folge 11, Munich, 1953), pp. 51-2 no. 36.

[69] Widukind, *Res gestae Saxonicae* III 54-5, pp. 133-5.

[70] See J.L. Nelson, *Charles the Bald* (London, 1992), pp. 115-20, and eadem, 'Public *Histories* and Private History in the Work of Nithard', *Speculum*, 60 (1985), pp. 251-93, here pp. 207f., with a discussion of F. Pietzcker, 'Die Schlacht bei Fontenoy', *Zeitschrift der Savigny-Stiftung für Rechtsgeschichte, Germanistische Abteilung* 81 (1964), pp. 318-42, who argues that Charles and Louis broke the rules at Fontenoy by making a surprise attack before the agreed time.

[71] 'The Battle of Maldon' (as n. 56) line 89, p. 20.

[72] Adalbert, *Continuatio*, p. 168.

[73] *Annales Vedastini* (as n. 55) *s.a.* 885, pp. 56-7: 'Francosque qui venerant ex regno Karlomanni irrisere Dani: "Ut quid ad nos venistis? Non fuit necesse. Nos scimus, qui estis, et vultis, ut ad vos redeamus; quod faciemus" '; Regino, *Chronicon s.a.* 891, p. 137: 'Illi . . . cachinnis et exprobrationibus agmina lacessunt, ingeminantes cum insultatione et derisu, ut memorarentur Guliae [the reference is not clear] turpisque fugae caedisque patratae, post modicum similia passuri.' Note also Godafrid's boasts in 810, Einhard, *Vita Karoli* c. 14, p. 17.

themselves outside the walls so that he could fight them. The words were no sooner out of his mouth when lo and behold the Saxons met him a mile outside the fortress. The Saxon historian thus not only turned the boast round but capped it as well, though in doing so he almost certainly retained and conveyed a tradition. The Saxons did such slaughter among the Franks that the mimes declaimed: where was there a hell big enough that it would have room for so many dead?[74] That any of them might be saved does not seem to have occurred to them, but then war was deemed to be a sinful occupation and killing in battle even when fighting for lord or king in a just cause had to be atoned for by penance.[75] Here the church's change in attitudes, not least of all Gregory VII's offer of *absolutio peccatorum* to the sincere *fideles Sancti Petri* fighting for the cause in Germany, was a startling development.[76] Widukind concluded his story with his own scathing comment: 'Eberhard, the king's brother, was freed from the fear that the Saxons might be absent; for he had seen them present and went away shamefully, having been put to flight by them'.[77] For Widukind, Eberhard's want of *fortuna et mores*, which later made him unfit him to succeed his brother in kingship, stemmed from this defeat.[78]

In the very next line he reveals the gravity of warfare and the seriousness of its outcome for all those concerned. When the king, Conrad I, heard that his brother had fought badly, 'male pugnatum a fratre', he gathered the whole strength of the Franks to seek out Henry to be revenged.[79] Widukind's phrase is echoed by others, who speak of the 'rash battle', the *pugna incauta*, the *certamen non utile*,[80] as well as relating the careless and imprudent behaviour of individual fighters and great warriors, like Count Robert the Strong, who perished because he rushed at the enemy in haste, only half-armed and protected.[81]

---

[74] Widukind, *Res gestae Saxonicae* I 23, p. 36. Compare also his account of the exchange of boasts and insults between Otto I and Hugh the Great at the outset of the campaign of 946, III 2, pp. 104-5. For a further discussion of boasting rituals see 'Ritual, Ceremony and Gesture', below, pp. 205-6.

[75] Though some distinction might be made between killing in general and killing to defend oneself or one's kin. See Nelson, 'Ninth-century Knighthood' (as n. 65), p. 257, and most recently R. Kottje, *Die Tötung im Kriege: Ein moralisches und rechtliches Problem im frühen Mittelalter* (Beiträge zur Friedensethik 11, Barsbüttel 1991).

[76] Gregory VII, *Registrum* VII 14a, p. 486; on the background to this see Leyser, 'On the Eve of the First European Revolution', *The Gregorian Revolution and Beyond*, p. 14.

[77] Widukind, *Res gestae Saxonicae* I 23, p. 36.

[78] Ibid. I 25, p. 38.

[79] Ibid. I 24, p. 36.

[80] For Widukind's own usage see ibid. III 19 (Otto I blames Eckbert for losing a battle, *incautum certamen*) and 72-3 (the Byzantines lose a battle in southern Italy, with the combination of *minus caute* and *a suis male pugnatum*), pp. 114, 149. Cf. also *Annales regni Francorum s.a.* 782 (E-version), p. 63: 'male etiam pugnatam est'; *Annales Fuldenses s.a.* 884 (Regensburg continuation), p. 112, 'contra illos incaute venerunt; sed tamen pugnam certaminis iniere non utile, nam ad illos victora concessit'; Regino, *Chronicon s.a.* 890: 'Quos cum ultra, quam oporteret, inprovide persequeretur, ab ipsis extinguitur, ignarus quia vincere bonum est, supervincere bonum non est; periculosa est enim desperatio.'

[81] See above at n. 54.

There are certain features of early medieval warfare which must impress any reader of narrative sources such as the *Annals of Saint-Bertin* and the *Annals of Fulda* and Regino of Prüm's *Chronicle*. The armed encounter in all its forms, whether it was the relatively rare pitched battle or the swift skirmish, was by no means the only or even the principal risk run by the warrior. The hazards of the march to and from the theatre of operations might be quite as taxing. Severe rains or the outbreak of disease among horses and men could and often did prove calamitous.[82] Sometimes the annalists recorded the safe return of a host from a campaign even if it had not achieved anything very notable; its safe return alone was deemed to be a success worth mentioning. In 869 Louis the German's sons took the field against the Sorbs in one expedition and against the Moravians in another, while he himself fell ill and sent a third force against a Moravian prince called Rastiz. In the final entry for the year in the *Annals of Fulda* Meginhard noted with great satisfaction that the sons had done well everywhere and that they came back triumphantly without damage to any of their warriors.[83] In 872 Meginhard reported a Bohemian campaign from which the host, after ruining the enemy countryside, returned unharmed. Yet another contingent came back with great difficulty.[84] Disease, of course, was a problem on the march, where armies traversed unfamiliar ground and had to live off unfamiliar foods and drink. In 867 the Emperor Louis II wanted to strike at Benevento and sought help from his brother Lothar II. The fighting went well (*feliciter*) but Lothar's forces suffered severely from illnesses caused by the climate: dysentery and diarrhoea were rampant and many died. Many also, Regino reported, died from the bites of spiders. He saw in these events not only a manifestation of divine wrath against the divorce-raddled King Lothar but against all his kingdom. The very existence of Lotharingia, Regino opined, was no longer pleasing to God.[85]

Disease was above all an ever-present threat during sieges. Under the year 873, Regino described Charles the Bald's siege of the Northmen in Angers. The Franks and the Bretons used new machines, we are told, and the Bretons threatened to divert the river-bed of the Maine. The Northmen were frightened and, as ever, worried about being able to return to their ships. They offered the king a sum of money to be allowed free egress from his kingdom and Charles, in Regino's view greedily and shamefully, agreed.[86] One can see Charles's point of view: the chance for once to receive cash from the Northmen rather than having to pay it out. But Regino also revealed that the large besieging host was afflicted by hunger and pestilence. This happened all too often and was one of the more respectable reasons why Charles III in 882, at

---

[82] *Annales regni Francorum s.a.* 810, p. 132 (cattle plague); *Annales Fuldenses s.a.* 882, 896, pp. 108, 127.

[83] *Annales Fuldenses*, pp. 68-70. On the theory of Meginhard of Fulda's authorship of this section of the annals, assumed above, see Wattenbach-Levison-Löwe, vol. 6, p. 682.

[84] *Annales Fuldenses*, p. 76.

[85] Regino, *Chronicon*, pp. 93-4.

[86] Ibid., pp. 105-7.

the siege of a Viking army enclosed at Asselt, came to terms when he, so it was thought, might have forced the Vikings to surrender.[87] They too were beset by illness. Hygiene in camp and hygiene discipline were most likely poor among the Franks so that disease spread early and fast. It was probably better among the Vikings.

We have mentioned famine, and problems of supply for men and horses all too often dominated and shaped military operations in the early middle ages as they had done before and were to do later. Reading Caesar's *Bellum Gallicum* and the *Bellum Civile* one is struck by the all-importance of corn supplies for his troops – and also good water. They ate meat only in an emergency, with good grace, it is true, but looking forward to the harvest coming soon.[88] This preference seems to have been inherited by the Byzantines. Here too hard tack was the standard ration.[89] In the Latin west, however, meat became essential. Carolingian armies marched off with cattle on the hoof.[90] Bishop Werner of Strasbourg, setting off in 1028 with his household on an embassy to Constantinople, from where he wanted to go on to a pilgrimage to Jerusalem, had a large train of horses, cattle, sheep and pigs according to Wipo.[91] A cattle plague could spell disaster to a campaign and was, so the Poeta Saxo averred, worse than an enemy raid.[92] The heavier equipment, the development of mounted warfare with swords, helmets, shields and hauberks, may have prescribed a diet with greater protein weight. The image of western war is traceable also in Nicephorus Phocas's taunts as related by Liudprand of Cremona. The emperor slated the Latins' heavy shields and gear as unserviceable and scoffed at their gluttony, their *gastrimargia*, which would in his estimate – and he knew about war – render the Ottonian *milites* useless.[93] That the food and the heavy equipment hung together was not among Liudprand's replies but it is hinted at in other sources, for example by Widukind when he described the hardships which the Slavs could endure more easily than their Saxon enemies. These

[87] *Annales Fuldenses*, pp. 98-9 (Mainz version; hostile) and 108-9 (Regensburg version; more sympathetic).

[88] Demonstrated most clearly by the numerous occurrences of *frumentum* and its derivatives in the same phrase as *pabulum* and its derivatives; see e.g. *Bellum Galicum* 1.16.2-3, 7.16.3, 7.64.2, 7.74.2; *Bellum Civile* 1.48.7, 1.61.7, 1.78.1, 1.84.1, 3.43.3.

[89] C.W. Oman, *A History of the Art of War in the Middle Ages, 1: 378-1278*, 2nd edn (London, 1924), p. 109, referring to Leo the Wise's *Tactica*: each group of infantry was to be accompanied by a cart carrying biscuit.

[90] Ganshof, *Frankish Institutions* (as n. 8), p. 67. For a wide-ranging survey of the role of animals in warfare at this time see B.S. Bachrach, 'Animals and Warfare in Early Medieval Europe', *L'uomo di fronte al mondo animale nell'alto medioevo* (Settimane 31, Spoleto, 1985), pp. 707-64.

[91] Wipo, *Gesta Chuonradi* c. 22, in *Wiponis Opera* ed. H. Bresslau (MGH SRG 61, Hanover, 1915), pp. 41-2, at p. 41.

[92] Poeta Saxo, *Annalium de gestis Caroli magni imperatoris libri quinque* Book IV, lines 238-9, *MGH Poetae* 4/1, p. 51: 'Nam sevior omni/Hoste nefanda lues pecudum genus omne peremit.'

[93] Liudprand, *Legatio* c. 11, p. 182.

must have included diet.[94] We hear also of the terrible damage Saxon warriors did on the lands and to the buildings of their own people. The Thietmar of Merseburg has left a self-reproachful account of the 1010 campaign against Boleslas where he described the wreckage and arson wrought by a Saxon host on the lands of their own margrave, Gero. The king, Henry II, did nothing either to stop or to punish it. Only Gero's slaves were spared and not carried away.[95] The huge requirements of Latin warriors, French and German in particular, are reflected also in a story of the anonymous *Gesta Francorum* about a reputed conversation between Kherboga, the emir of Mosul, and his mother: 'Do Bohemund and Tancred not eat 2000 cows and 4000 pigs at a single meal?'[96] Their huge consumption of meat was part of the Latins' self-awareness, here caricatured by being seen through the enemy's eyes. A similarly massive reliance on meat is brought home to us by the Annalista Saxo, who wrote in the middle of the twelfth century, not without pride, that Otto I's household and following needed 1000 pigs and sheep, 10 cartloads of wine, 10 of beer, 1000 malters of grain, 8 head of cattle, every day, not to mention 'chicken, piglets, fish, eggs, vegetables and more, as is found in writing'.[97]

Since horses were fast becoming the chief *dramatis personae* of Western warfare, it is worth asking how they were fed and maintained on campaigns, often far away from their home grounds and pastures. Foraging inevitably became an essential and perennial occupation of warriors and their commanders. It was always a risky operation because it meant temporary dispersal. More than once armies were caught at this critical moment. In 936 an Ottonian force – it was the famous gangsters' warband, the *legio Mesaburiorum* – had just won a victory over the Bohemians and were now foraging and plundering when a counter-attack caught and destroyed them.[98] At Andernach in 876, Louis the Younger, the east Frankish king, had manoeuvred with skill against Charles the Bald, who had invaded his kingdom to deprive him of rule and sight by a surprise attack. Louis had placed himself at Andernach, a fortified stronghold, but only part of his force was at hand when the superior west Frankish forces were drawing near, the rest, perhaps most of them, had gone to forage.

The battle of Andernach is one of the best documented encounters of the ninth century. The *Annals of Fulda*, Regino, Hincmar and the *Annals of Saint-Vasst* reported it, the first three with many details.[99] It was unusual rather than

[94] Widukind, *Res gestae Saxonicae* II 20, p. 84: 'Est namque huiuscemodi genus hominum durum et laboris patiens, victu levissimo assuetum, et quod nostris gravis oneris esse solet, Sclavi pro quadam voluptate ducunt.'

[95] Thietmar, *Chronicon* VI 56, p. 344.

[96] *Gesta Francorum* IX, p. 56.

[97] *Annalista Saxo* s.a. 968, *MGH SS* 6, 622.

[98] Widukind, *Res gestae Saxonicae* II 3, pp. 67-9.

[99] *Annales Fuldenses*, pp. 87-9; *Annales Bertiniani*, pp. 207-10; Regino, *Chronicon*, pp. 111-12; *Annales Vedastini* (as n. 55), p. 41.

typical. Charles the Bald sought to achieve his surprise by marching all night and over difficult ground. The effort miscarried and the fatigue of his men probably brought about their defeat next morning. Louis the Younger was able to break into their too closely packed formation to win a crushing victory with plenty of prisoners and spoils for his host even though his Saxon contingent failed and broke. Louis seems to have reckoned that action might be joined for once in darkness so that he ordered his warriors to wear white clothes so as to be able to recognise one another in a mêlée.[100] Charles and his host, in headlong retreat, were hampered by their own baggage trains and it appears that among his camp-followers were merchants selling shields. They too cluttered up the narrow route of retreat and whatever they carried likewise fell into the victors' hands.[101]

Early medieval warfare was by no means unsophisticated and its primary and underlying concern with goods and services is reflected in the style of military operations. The disruption of enemy supplies and the destruction of resources needed to sustain fighting abilities were stratagems familiar to heathen and Christians alike. In his savage campaigns against the Moravians the east Frankish king Arnulf sought to urge and induce the Bulgars in the south not to sell them any salt.[102] Early in 891 the Northmen again moved their fleet from Brittany to Lotharingia. The host Arnulf sent against them was outmanoeuvred by the Vikings, who crossed the Meuse by Liège and began to operate in the Franks' and Bavarians' rear. They spread in the woods and moors near the palace at Aachen, killing whomever they met and, having gained control of the Frankish lines of communication, they were able to seize carts and other vehicles carrying supplies to the Christian host;[103] that there were such convoys and logistic support behind a late-ninth-century east Frankish force is revealed by this incident. Set against the débâcle of the spring of 891, the battle at the Dyle in the autumn of the same year makes a startling contrast, but it is noteworthy that Arnolf's victory in no way ended the menace of the Great Host. The fleet to which the Northmen wanted to return – few of them managed it – remained unharmed and there were such large forces on it that next year they could once again strike deep into the Rhineland, with devastating results. The battle thus brought surprisingly little relief to the stricken countryside of lower Lotharingia.[104]

In the ninth and for part of the tenth century the Northmen were the most frequent external enemies of the west, though in the Reich the Magyars outdid them in the tenth. Much has been written about their ships but scholars have not, to my mind, paid enough attention to their techniques of land warfare.

---

[100] *Annales Fuldenses*, p. 88.

[101] *Annales Bertiniani*, p. 209; the *Annales Fuldenses* attribute the immobility of the western Franks to divine intervention.

[102] *Annales Fuldenses s.a.* 892, p. 121.

[103] Regino, *Chronicon*, p. 136.

[104] For the battle of the Dyle see ibid., pp. 137-8 and *Annales Fuldenses*, pp. 119-21; the raiding into Lotharingia next year is reported by Regino, *Chronicon*, p. 138.

Peter Sawyer in his *The Age of the Vikings* called their depredations an extension of normal dark age activity, and Michael Wallace-Hadrill did not altogether disagree with this.[105] What had been overlooked here is their peculiar style of waging war on land and the special difficulties this imposed on Frankish hosts even if, as happened in the early 880s, they had begun to combat them more successfully than before.[106] The Northmen had by then mastered some of the arts of equestrian mounted warfare, but they also possessed some very special skills of their own. They could and frequently did use ground which Frankish armies always avoided if possible. They massed, hid and then emerged from woods. We saw this above in the operations round Aachen early in 891. It happened quite frequently, and Latin sources mentioned the *invia*, the trackless regions the Northmen traversed.[107] Once when the Franks did venture into a wood to attack them they managed to disperse in it so swiftly that the attackers gained nothing.[108] More important still was the Northmen's habit of retreating into a stone building, a church, a house or, on one occasion, the palace of Nymwegen, and turning it into a fortress from which they could burst forth at their chosen time when it looked as if they were at bay.[109] Now and again they attacked at night.[110] Above all they had the capacity, the tools and the skills to erect quick and effective field fortifications, dykes fortified by stakes, palisades and advanced ditches. Time and again their enemies were hampered by these works.[111] The great count Henry, one of their most ubiquitous assailants and admired everywhere as a great warrior,

[105]Peter Sawyer, *The Age of the Vikings*, 2nd edn (London, 1971), p. 30; J.M. Wallace-Hadrill, 'The Vikings in Francia', *Early Medieval History* (Oxford, 1975), p. 222: 'the difference between a Frankish count in revolt against his king and laying waste the countryside, and a Viking whose depredations were not dissimilar in effect, was best expressed as a difference in religion', P. Sawyer, *Kings and Vikings* (London, 1982), pp. 94-7, restates with some qualification the case for not overestimating the extent of Viking depredation.

[106]For example the successful battles fought against the Vikings at Thiméon in 880 and at Saucourt in 881; the defence of the Rhineland mounted by the Babenberger general Henry and Archbishop Liutprand of Mainz in the early 880s; the successful defence of Paris against heavy odds in 885-6. See W. Vogel, *Die Normannen und das fränkische Reich bis zur Gründung der Normandie (799-911)* (Heidelberg, 1906), pp. 268, 271-2, 294-311, 338-47.

[107]See *Annales Vedastini* (as n. 55) *s.a.* 891, p. 69: 'per invia loca parant redire ad castra' and ibid. *s.a.* 890 and 898, pp. 68 ('loci incommoditatem') and 80 ('Normanni more solito loca inoportuna tenentes rediere ad naves'); Regino, *Chronicon s.a.* 892, p. 138: 'Normanni . . . nequaquam ausi sunt se committere planioribus atque campestribus locis, sed silvas semper tenentes'.

[108]Regino, *Chronicon s.a.* 891, p. 136: 'hostilem expeditionem a tergo relinquentes in silvis et paludibus Aquis palatio contiguis disperguntur'.

[109]For examples see A. d'Haenens, *Les Invasions normandes en Belgique au IXe siècle* (Louvain, 1967), p. 99; Oman, *Art of War* (as n. 89), p. 75.

[110]Wallace-Hadrill, 'Vikings in Francia' (as n. 105), pp. 220-1, cites their attacks on Bordeaux in 848 and Chartres in 859; note also the attacks on Noyon in 859, *Annales Bertiniani*, p. 81 and on Stavelot, *Miracula S. Remacli* II 1, *MGH SS* 15, 439.

[111] For example at Angers in 873, where Regino, *Chronicon*, p. 106, reports that they took over the town, whose inhabitants had fled, and immediately put its defences in order; ibid. *s.a.* 891, p. 137: 'ligno et terrae congerie more solito se communiunt'.

came to grief when he rode into what might today be described as a tank-trap. As he tried to get out, momentarily helpless and at a severe disadvantage, he was slain.[112]

The Northmen were also masters of the surprise attack. At Saucourt in 881, they retreated, as so often, into a vill. Frankish and Ottonian armies were, as we have seen, vulnerable in the moment of victory, when everyone was busy with his own concerns, be it looting, tending wounds, refreshing himself or seeing to his horses' needs. At Saucourt the Northmen suddenly sallied forth again and killed at least one hundred men; had it not been for Louis III's presence of mind, they might have turned defeat into victory. The Saint-Vaast annalist put the sudden setback down to the Franks' impiety, giving to themselves rather than to God the glory of their success.[113]

Like their opponents, the Northmen saw themselves and wanted to be seen as aristocratic warriors. Early in 882 they entered Prüm and for three days made it the base of their plundering raids on the neighbourhood. A large host of foot-soldiers approached, recruited from the villages and fields, approached. When the Vikings saw that they were faced by an armed *ignobile vulgus* whose members knew nothing of military usage, i.e. were not men of war, they rushed upon them and slaughtered them like cattle, so Regino reports.[114] The Christian aristocracy on the whole disapproved of such self-help by the underprivileged.[115] Yet the Northmen were also capable of socially subversive warfare and knew both in England and on the Continent how to hit their enemies where it hurt most. Abbo in his *Bellum Parisiacum* describes them as enslaving free men (whom they then sold) and freeing slaves, making them lords.[116]

We must draw conclusions. Offensive war was in the ninth and tenth century the most convenient and effective way to acquire a modicum of surplus wealth, to wrest that wealth from an opponent and his subjects. It was also the basis of incipient political power. Poland began with Miesco's paid warband. *Dilatatio imperii*, the enlargement of empire, was deemed to be a worthy aim, and at the frontiers of *Christianitas* war gained additional stature when it was directed against infidels and pagans, long before the beginnings of papally blessed holy militarism.[117] A man's standing was usually assessed by his record as a warrior.

---

[112] Regino, *Chronicon s.a.* 887, pp. 125-6.

[113] *Annales Vedastini* (as n. 55), p. 50.

[114] Regino, *Chronicon*, p. 118.

[115] *Annales Bertiniani s.a.* 859, p. 80, report the suppression of a west Frankish peasants' self-help league by their own magnates; see on this passage Nelson, *Charles the Bald* (as n. 70), p. 194.

[116] Abbo, *Le Siège de Paris par les Normands* book 1, lines 184-5, ed. H. Waquet (Paris, 1942), p. 30.

[117] Cf. Widukind, *Res gestae Saxonicae* I 33, p. 45: 'dilatandum imperium'. For the Christian legitimisation of war against the pagans see the references given by Nelson, 'Ninth-century Knighthood' (as n. 65), p. 259 and, for an early example taken from a text frequently cited here, *Annales Fuldenses s.a.* 882, p. 99: Charles III issued orders that 'quisque de suo exercitu in defensione sanctae aecclesiae zelo Dei commotus aliquem de Nordmannis... occidit, aut eum iugulare aut ei oculos eruere'. For papal blessing of militarism see above, n. 76.

There were not many aristocratic lay civilians, in northern Europe at least, or at any rate they were not praised as such. Stephen of Blois had to suffer a volley of abuse from a kinsman of Bohemund in the presence of the emperor Alexis Comnenos: 'Never have I heard of any knightly deed he performed'.[118] In Widukind men are sometimes praised in terms borrowed from Sallust. Counts Siegfried and Henry, both forbears of Thietmar of Merseburg, were *domi militiaque optimi*, at home and in the field outstanding, i.e. in the governance of their own homes, families and following and in the *militia* which began as soon as they left home.[119] Not all *militia* thus entailed instant violence. Nobles and their armed followings went to assemblies, often called *exercitus*,[120] and went home again. They may not have used their arms but the threat was always there. It is possible that there were islands of peace, even prolonged peace but it was an armed peace, disrupted in any case by virulent bloodfeuds. The very term *militia secularis* must teach us how deeply rooted, quintessential and inescapable war was in the societies, the economies, the politics and the world-picture itself of early medieval Europe. To return to Clausewitz: in the early middle ages, one is tempted to say, policy was a continuation of war by other means – life gift-giving, bribery and suborning loyalties – rather than his way round.[121]

---

[118] *Gesta Francorum* IX, p. 64.

[119] Widukind, *Res gestae Saxonicae* I 25, II 33, III 44 and 51, pp. 38, 94, 124, 131; cf. also Thietmar, *Chronicon* IV 10 and V 4, pp. 150, 226. Even bishops might be described in such phrases; Ruotger, *Vita Brunonis* c. 25, p. 26, or the epitaph on Dietrich I of Metz, SS 4, 483: 'Hic consobrinus caesaris inclity/ Haerebat illi militiae et domi.'

[120] E.g. in *Annales Fuldenses s.a.* 872 and 894 (though there a real army is involved), pp. 75, 124; Widukind, *Res gestae Saxonicae*, I 26 (the election of Henry I) and III 16, pp. 39, 112. See also Leyser, 'Early Medieval Canon Law', below, p. 62.

[121] Clausewitz, *On War* (as n. 1) I 24 and VIII 6, pp. 86, 605: 'a continuation of political activity by other means' and 'a continuation of political intercourse with the admixture of other means'.

4

Early Medieval Canon Law and the Beginnings of Knighthood

For the development of knighthood the later eleventh and early twelfth centuries are widely thought to have been the crucial and most formative moment.[1] Its chief characteristic was a new brotherhood in arms which bound together men of high birth, great wealth and assured positions with much more modest warriors, often their vassals, with whom they came to share increasingly certain fundamental values and rituals. A modern simile might be that of an officers' mess, where there is a common bond between all members, regardless of rank. It would indeed be unwise were the most junior second lieutenant to presume on this and occupy habitually his colonel's favourite

* First published in *Institutionen, Kultur und Gesellschaft im Mittelalter. Festschrift für Josef Fleckenstein zu seinem 65. Geburtstag*, ed. Lutz Fenske, Werner Rösener and Thomas Zotz (Sigmaringen: Jan Thorbecke Verlag, 1984), pp. 549-66. Thanks are due to the publishers and editors for permission to reproduce here. The author's own corrections to the text have been inserted; a few bibliographical additions have been made to the footnotes, mostly to give references to more recent editions of texts.

[1]   Our honorand, to whom the following pages are gratefully offered and dedicated, is himself one of the foremost guides in any attempt to explore the manifold roots of chivalry. Of his authoritative contributions to this topic I cite here: J. Fleckenstein, 'Die Entstehung des niederen Adels und das Rittertum', in *Herrschaft und Stand*, ed. J. Fleckenstein (Veröffentlichungen des Max-Planck-Instituts für Geschichte 51, Göttingen, 1977), pp. 17-39 and idem, 'Adel und Kriegertum und ihre Wandlung im Karolingerreich', in *Nascita dell'Europa carolingia: un'equazione da verificare* (Settimane 27, Spoleto, 1981), pp. 67-100. In embarking upon this paper I was much encouraged by a question he raises in his indispensable study: 'Zum Problem der Abschließung des Ritterstandes', in *Historische Forschungen für Walter Schlesinger*, ed. H. Beumann (Cologne, 1975), p. 262 and n. 58: what did the idea of the *ordo militaris* owe to antique models? Only a modest, half-way step towards answering it is attempted here. For the importance of the later eleventh and early twelfth century see the papers of S. Painter, F.L. Ganshof and A. Borst, in *Das Rittertum im Mittelalter*, ed. A. Borst (Wege der Forschung 349, Darmstadt, 1976) and now G. Althoff, 'Nunc fiant Christi milites, qui dudum extiterunt raptores. Zur Entstehung von Rittertum und Ritterethos', *Saeculum*, 32 (1981), pp. 317-33. See also R.C. Smail, *Crusading Warfare (1097-1193)* (Cambridge Studies in Medieval Life and Thought, new series 3, Cambridge, 1956), pp. 106ff. For the military aristocracy of England and its equipment and weaponry from *c*. 900 to 1066 see N.P. Brooks, 'Arms, Status and Warfare in Late-Saxon England', in *Ethelred the Unready*, ed. D. Hill (British Archaeological Reports, British Series 59, Oxford, 1978), pp. 81-103.

armchair but the community of attitudes and of status is there none the less. In the late eleventh and early twelfth century the church's novel uses of warfare and marked advances of military techniques in mounted combat calling for enhanced skills, training and standardisation, combined to bring about a new ethos, a collective sense of their own worth and also a judgement of conduct among both, the great and the rank and file. The gulf that divided them in the earlier middle ages began to narrow. Evidence of that gulf is still plentiful and suggests the relatively low status of mere *milites*. When Gregory VII wanted to rouse his flagging and tired followers to take greater risks and expose themselves more in the struggle for the church's *libertas* he reminded them more than once of the *milites seculares*. [550] 'Think, think, dear brethren, how many of them give themselves to death every day for their lords, kept only by a paltry wage'.[2] He seems to have thought of the humblest category of mounted warriors, the *miles gregarius* who had only his equipment and his maintenance. A much-discussed legend on the Bayeaux Tapestry prompts the same observation: 'Here Bishop Odo with his man comforts the *pueri*' – it was when things were going badly and there had been a near-panic.[3] One meaning of the word *puer* has for the most part been ignored by scholars interpreting this passage, namely 'servant', 'slave'. Under medieval descriptions of age *pueritia* ended at fourteen years. The mounted men depicted on the tapestry here were older than that. Armed gangs of servants, *pueri*, were familiar enough in Merovingian warfare.

Let us look now at the other side of the coin, the evidence for the common attitudes, the shared values and judgements that bound together high and low in the military society of the twelfth century. A good example that comes to mind is the scathing condemnation of the conduct of Stephen of Blois in the pages of the anonymous knight who wrote the *Gesta Francorum*.[4] It was admittedly given voice by a half-brother of Bohemund who is reported to be with the emperor Alexis Comnenos at Philomelium. Guy, when he heard the news of the crusading army's grim situation in Antioch through Stephen, who had left the host, burst into violent abuse of the count of Blois: 'Perhaps you believe this imprudent old knight. Never have I heard of any deed of knighthood he performed. He has baled out shamefully and disgracefully like a scoundrel and a wretch.' For an obscure *miles* to propagate such judgements on a prince's military conduct speaks volumes. Moreover his work spread and was much the most-copied treatise on the first crusade.

Two questions arise. How did this solidarity, these common attitudes and conventions, shared between great men and their *milites*, come into being? Secondly, what were the presuppositions of this development, above all how does the status of the warrior appear in the sources of the ninth, tenth and early

---

[2]   Gregory VII, *Registrum* IX 21, p. 602 and see also *The Epistolae Vagantes of Pope Gregory VII* no. 54, ed. and trans. by H.E.J. Cowdrey (Oxford Medieval Texts, Oxford 1972), p. 132.

[3]   *The Bayeux Tapestry*, general editor Sir Frank Stenton (London, 1957), Pl. 68 and pp. 175, 180.

[4]   *Gesta Francorum* IX, p. 65.

eleventh centuries before we stumble upon the characteristic ensemble of cultural, military and social attributes that went to make knighthood? There are sources throwing light on this problem which have not been consulted and explored enough and it is hoped to make a beginning with their exploration here. However, the first of these questions will not be altogether ignored either and we must in any case ask how novel and distinctive the values and conventions of chivalry really were and what roots they had in the military societies of the Carolingian, Anglo-Saxon and Ottonian worlds.

Georges Duby in a celebrated and much-cited article has taught us that the word *miles* increasingly replaced the use of *nobilis* in eleventh-century French charters to describe the status of donors and witnesses.[5] In a later study he showed conclusively with a sample from southern Burgundy that the *milites* of the later eleventh century were the descendants of a few wealthy clans [551] of the later tenth so that a homogeneous aristocracy emerges which wanted to be identified with *militia* and saw its good birth adequately expressed by this term.[6] Duby was well aware that this development was not uniform and that in other regions, for instance the Namurois, studied by Genicot, and in Gueldres, explored by van Winter, chivalry and nobility remained socially distinct, knights as a stratum standing below the nobility.[7] In the empire, on the whole, he concluded his article on the origins of knighthood, older Carolingian political structures survived as did the distinction between knights and princes, the only possessors of complete freedom, the only men really deemed noble.[8]

That this ignores the free nobility of the Reich, the non-princely aristocracy who were not and avoided becoming *ministeriales* stands to reason. Yet more important for our topic are the not at all infrequent references to great nobles as *milites* in the centuries before the advent of chivalry, before the rituals specifically associated with knighthood gained currency. When Thietmar of Merseburg mentioned two of his ancestors who fell at the battle of Lenzen in 929, he calls them *milites optimi genere clarissimi* and *miles* here did not mean vassal.[9] At another place he condemned or at least shook his head over Oda, the daughter of Margrave Dietrich of the northern march who had been a nun at Kalbe but then married Duke Miesco of Poland. 'She spurned', he wrote, 'the celestial bridegroom and preferred to him a *vir militaris*.[10] Already in Widukind of Corvey a member of the Stade comital family is one of a group of *milites* who disapproved of their leader's, Duke Hermann Billung's decision

[5] G. Duby, 'Les Origines de la chevalerie', cited here from his *Hommes et structures du moyen âge* (Paris, 1973), pp. 325-41.

[6] G. Duby, 'Lignage, noblesse et chevalerie au XIIe siècle dans la règion mâconnaise: Úne révision', in *Hommes et structures* (as n. 5), pp. 395-422. For a critical appraisal see O.G. Oexle, below, n. 17.

[7] Duby, 'Les Origines' (as n. 5), p. 329f.; L. Genicot, *L'Économie rurale namuroise au bas moyen âge, 1199-1429*, 2 vols. (Namur, 1943-60) and J.M. van Winter, *Ministerialiteit en ridderschap in Gelre en Zutphen* (Groningen, 1962).

[8] Duby 'Les Origines' (as n. 5), p. 340.

[9] Thietmar, *Chronicon* I 10, p. 16.

[10] Ibid. IV 57, p. 196.

not to risk battle with the Slavs in 955. He is called at the same time *bellator acerrimus*.[11] Widukind also liked to use the word *commilitones* for the companions-in-arms of great nobles and members of the Ottonian house like Thangmar, Otto I's half-brother and Henry, his brother. This, as I have shown elsewhere, implied both their nobility and a certain camaraderie amongst the warriors of the Saxon tenth century.[12] This in turn even suggests shared values across whatever social distances which set off the great from their military following.

To find out what these were we must take note of another characteristic feature of early medieval warfare which has found expression in certain turns of phrase not infrequently employed by writers describing armed encounters. The *primores* and the *principes* in the ninth, tenth and eleventh centuries were not only expected to command their mounted hosts, they also [552] had to expose themselves and fight in person. At least their historians praise them when they took part in combat. Conversely cowardice of any kind was derided and slated. Of Otto I in the battle at the Lech Widukind wrote *fortissimi militis...ac optimi imperatoris officium gerens*, as he turned his horse towards the enemy.[13] The phrase came, like so many others, from Sallust but we find it used again, not only in Germany but also in England. Lampert of Hersfeld dwelt lovingly on Otto of Northeim's valour and generalship at the battle by the Unstrut on 9 June 1075 where the Saxons suffered a serious defeat. He was everywhere, always at the most threatened point, now fighting now exhorting laggards. Lampert's account culminates once more in Sallust's phrase: *Strenue profecto et egregii militis et optimi ducis officio fungebatur*.[14] When we turn to England, Florence of Worcester applied the citation to Edmund Ironside at the battle of Sherston in 1016 and he also wrote of Harold's personal combats at Hastings.[15] William of Malmesbury again quite clearly applied the Sallustian topos with its antithesis, *munus imperatorium, militis officium* to the English king.[16] Dukes and kings were meant to lead from the front as far as possible though their mere presence gave cohesion and might lend charisma to their hosts.

War could serve many ends to societies as much addicted to it as were those of early medieval Europe. It could be a means to preserve a given social fabric and yet also become, if its demands exceeded the manpower resources of an élite, a leveller and open doors for successful participants. Both these features illuminate the styles of fighting current in the west. The mounted warrior, the

[11] Widukind, *Res gestae Saxonicae* III 52, p. 131. That *miles* = *bellator* designated men like Count Siegfried and much humbler warriors in tenth-century Saxony, all fighting on horseback, is not insignificant. See next note.

[12] Ibid. II 11, 15, 33, pp. 75, 80, 94 and K.J. Leyser, 'Henry I and the Beginnings of the Saxon Empire', *EHR*, 83 (1968), pp. 30f. (Leyser, *Medieval Germany*, pp. 40f.).

[13] Widukind, *Res gestae Saxonicae* III 46, pp. 127f.

[14] Lampert, *Annales s.a.* 1075, pp. 219f.

[15] *Florentii Wigorniensis Monachi Chronicon ex Chronicis*, ed. B. Thorpe (English Historical Society, London, 1848), vol. 1, p. 175: 'strenui militis et boni imperatoris oficia simul exequebatur', and also p. 227.

[16] William of Malmesbury, *Gesta Regum* III 243, vol. 2, p. 303.

miles armatus, was now the backbone of effective belligerency. His monopoly, ascendancy and social eminence was enshrined in the teaching of the three orders, studied so profusely, in the utterances of Adalbero of Laon, Abbo of Fleury and Gerard, bishop of Cambrai.[17] The foremost representatives of this warring stratum were recognisable at once by their gear, their gold ornaments and jewels, their fine equipment and superior mounts. An unwarlike north Italian count who wanted to disguise himself in a military emergency, a Hungarian surprise attack, threw away his belt, his golden armrings (*armillae*) and precious gear and so passed himself off as a humble *miles* ransomed for a trifling sum by one of his own vassals.[18] Even as spoils these precious hallmarks of high rank were exclusive and jealously guarded. There is a story in Thietmar which shows how dangerous it was for the rank and file, or the ignoble, even to touch, let alone pocket the war-gear of a great *dux*. Some Slav auxiliaries [553] seem to have been the first to find the body of Conrad the Red, Otto I's son-in-law who was killed by a Hungarian arrow at the battle of the Lech in 955. They took some of his accoutrements and brought them home to their native village where they were concealed for many years. Eventually Otto I heard of this from a Slav chieftain who stood close to him and the villagers were compelled to fight judicial duels, always weighted against them. They lost, forfeiting their lives as well as their spoils. Thietmar did not quite know why they suffered but that they ever dared to harbour and conceal these possessions seemed enough of a reason.[19]

If any one piece of equipment became emblematic and summed up aristocratic military status it was a warrior's belt, the *cingulum militare*. We hear quite a lot about precious belts in narrative and documentary sources of the early middle ages. In a letter addressed to King Edward the Elder, the writer, perhaps a *dux* Ordlaf, recited the crimes of a man called Helmstan.[20] The first of them was that he had stolen a belt. It was a grave matter because a precious belt denoted a man's rank, his status. We hear much of costly belts given by Louis the Pious to his court nobles at Easter as against the Frisian cloaks bestowed on lesser men. Grooms, bakers and cooks received woollen and

---

[17] G. Duby, *Les Trois ordres ou l'imaginaire du féodalisme* (Paris, 1978). I have used the English translation: *The Three Orders: Feudal Society Imagined*, trans. by A. Goldhammer (Chicago, 1980), and see J. Le Goff, 'Les Trois fonctions indo-européennes, l'historien et l'Europe féodale', *Annales ESC*, 34 (1979), pp. 1187-1215 and O.G. Oexle, 'Die funktionale Dreiteilung der Gesellschaft bei Adalbero von Laon', *Frühmittelalterliche Studien*, 12 (1978), pp. 1-54; 'Die Wirklichkeit und das Wissen: Ein Blick auf das sozialgeschichtliche Œuvre von Georges Duby', *HZ*, 232 (1981), pp. 61-91; 'Tria genera hominum. Zur Geschichte eines Deutungsschemas der sozialen Wirklichkeit in Antike und Mittelalter', in *Institutionen, Kultur und Gesellschaft im Mittelalter: Festschrift für Josef Fleckenstein zu seinem 65. Geburtstag*, ed. L. Fenske, W. Rösener and T. Zotz (Sigmaringen: Jan Thorbecke Verlag, 1984), pp. 483-500, for a critical appraisal.

[18] Liudprand, *Antapodosis* II 62, p. 65.

[19] Thietmar, *Chronicon* II 38, p. 86. Compare this incident with the rumour reported by Flodoard, *Annales*, pp. 73f., that Duke Giselbert of Lotharingia's body was not found in 939 because the fishermen who had taken his *spolia* concealed it. He had drowned in the Rhine.

[20] F.E. Harmer (ed.), *Select English Historical Documents of the Ninth and Tenth Centuries*, no. 18 (Cambridge, 1914), pp. 30-2, 60-3, 114-116.

linen garments and short swords.[21] When the Emperor Lothar's son, Louis, went with his uncle, Bishop Drogo, to Rome in 844, Pope Sergius II anointed him and, so the St Bertin Annals recorded, decorated him with a belt.[22] The act of *Wehrhaftmachung* consisted of girding the young man with a belt and we hear of it in the case of Louis the Pious himself. His anonymous biographer described it succinctly: Louis joined his father at Regensburg in 791 and because he had reached the threshold of adolescence (fourteen) he was girded with a sword.[23] The same biographer reported that in the autumn of 837 Louis summoned an assembly at Quierzy where he first of all girded Charles with arms, i.e. a sword, before crowning him as king in the presence of his half-brother Pippin of Aquitaine.[24] There is no doubt that the act of arming him was a solemnity which here served as the indispensable first step to furnish him with a kingship in one of the heartlands of the Frankish Reich. We hear of belts in Anglo-Saxon wills, for instance that of the Aetheling Aethelstan (1014), eldest son of Aethelred II, who bequeathed to Christ Church Canterbury not only rich lands but also 'the sword with the silver hilt which Wulfric made and the gold belt and armlet which Wulfric made'.[25]

That belts with costly fittings to hang swords were deemed to be ornaments of secular exaltation appears from another passage in the Anonymous's *Life* of Louis the Pious. He [554] concluded a chapter on the emperor's monastic and other ecclesiastical reforms and his patronage of Benedict of Aniane with the report: 'Then at last the bishops and clerks began to give up belts with golden baldrics and jewelled knives, exquisite garments and boots with spurs. Louis thought it a monstrosity that men of the clerical order should aspire to these emblems of worldly glory.'[26] What matters here is that most of the items mentioned were martial. The ecclesiastical legislation of the ninth century forcefully endorsed these sentiments in forbidding clerks to wear clothes other than those of their order. In the east Frankish kingdom this culminated in the massive promulgation of Decreta at the council of Tribur in 895. There we read, as was laid down already in c. 7 of the council of Chalcedon in 451, that clerks once they had taken up and been deputed to their clergy 'neque ad militiam neque ad aliquam veniant dignitatem mundanam'.[27] What matters here is that the ancient canon made sense to the bishops of Arnulf's kingdom. Already *militia* – and it can only mean the profession of arms here – was a secular dignity, if not the secular dignity par excellence. The division of society

---

[21] Notker, *Gesta Karoli* II 21, pp. 91f. On belts see also P.E. Schramm and F. Mütherich, *Denkmale der deutschen Könige und Kaiser*, 1: *Ein Beitrag zur Herrschergeschichte von Karl dem Großen bis Friedrich II., 768-1250*, 2nd edn (Veröffentlichungen des Zentralinstituts für Kunstgeschichte in München 2, Munich, 1981), pp. 93 (Ermoldus Nigellus) and 142, no. 70 (Otto II).

[22] *Annales Bertiniani s.a.* 844, p. 46.

[23] Anonymous ('Astronomer'), *Vita Hludowici imperatoris* c. 6, ed. R. Rau (ADGQ 5, Darmstadt, 1955), p. 266.

[24] Ibid. c. 59, p. 366.

[25] *Anglo-Saxon Wills*, ed. D. Whitelock (Cambridge, 1930), no. 20, p. 56.

[26] Anonymous, *Vita Hludowici* (as n. 23) c. 28, p. 302.

[27] *MGH Capit.*, vol. 2, pp. 228f., c. 27.

into the three orders is implied and taken for granted in this and much other Carolingian church legislation. We must ask why certain writers of the later tenth and early eleventh century specifically remarked on it rather than whether they perceived the social order in any very new way.[28]

Awareness of it, not only as between clergy and warrior nobility but also as between the latter and the peasantry, appears in the literature of the ninth century now and again. There is a strange, and perhaps not enough noticed story, in Paschasius Radbertus' *Epitaphium Arsenii*, written sometime in 837/ 38 and completed *c.* 853.[29] Its hero, Charlemagne's cousin Wala spent his childhood at the king's court 'bound to liberal pursuits' when the king, to test his character, thrust him out and had him placed under open arrest under one of the great who had the task of humiliating him so that he should learn to cope with adversity. One day he was made to take out and drive two oxen and a cart when he met a *ruricola*, a countryman, girded with a belt and arms. Wala addressed him and asked him whether he was willing to exchange his poor and ill-made weapons for his – he still seems to have borne some despite his oxen and cart. The rustic could hardly believe the offer but agreed.[30] Wala reflected that the cheap weapons fitted his cart since he now did not follow the *militia saeculi* but the pursuits of common life. Peasants were as yet not disarmed but the sense of what was appropriate for each class and its tasks appears clearly in this episode as it did in Louis the Pious's choice of Easter gifts for the various ranks of his attendants. It is revealing also in that noble education did not normally include such tests of character and much more likely it seems that Wala had in fact, or was suspected of having, tampered in Pippin the Hunchback's conspiracy of 792 and suffered temporary banishment and disgrace.[31] [555]

There is a whole body of evidence which throws light on military status in Frankish and post-Frankish society. It is enshrined in the ecclesiastical and mixed legislation of the Carolingian ninth century and here the terms *miliciae cingulum, cingulum militare* stand for the sum total of the warrior's profession. For certain grave crimes the Carolingian church prescribed that the offender lost the hallmarks of his military standing and that standing itself, either in part or wholly to the end of his days while doing penance. At the council of Mainz in 847 which met under the presidency of Hrabanus Maurus, it was laid down that the slayer of a priest must expiate his misdeed for twelve years. If he denied it he must, if a freeman, offer an oath with twelve others. If he was a serf he had to go the ordeal with twelve glowing hot ploughshares. A convicted

---

[28] See above, n. 17. The ninth-century awareness of the tripartite order in the writings of Alfred and Haimo of Auxerre needs stressing; see most recently E. Ortigues, 'Haymon d'Auxerre, théoricien des trois ordres', in *L'École carolingienne d'Auxerre de Murethach à Rémi, 830-908: Entretiens d'Auxerre 1989*, ed. D. Iogna-Prat, C. Jeudy, G. Lobrichon (Paris, 1991), pp. 181-227.

[29] Paschasius Radbertus, *Epitaphium Arsenii* I, ed. E. Dümmler (Abhandlungen der königlichen Akademie der Wissenschaften zu Berlin, Berlin, 1900), pp. 28-9.

[30] Ibid. p. 29. Radbert's text is, perhaps deliberately, obscure here. At first sight it would seem that he meant Wala exchanged oxen and cart for the peasant's arms but then Wala's reflections suggest that he still had the cart.

[31] L. Weinrich, *Wala: Graf, Mönch und Rebell* (Historische Studien 386, Lübeck 1963), pp. 16f.

culprit shall lay down his *miliciae cingulum* to the end of his days and lose his marriage. The last but one of these provisions can only have applied to the freeman.[32] In chapter 20 of the council's acts it was laid down that parricides must neither assume the belt of 'knighthood' nor contract marriage. 'The sacred canons don't allow it'.[33] These rulings found their place also in Hraban's *Poenitentiale*.

At a synod held in Pavia in 850 it was provided that anyone deprived of communion, excluded from holy places and subject to public penance for his crimes, must not use the belt of secular *militia*, nor administer any kind of public function.[34] At a council held in Worms in 868 canon c. 26 prescribed that he who killed a priest intentionally shall eat no meat, should not take up arms or travel on horseback but go everywhere on foot.[35] After ten years of this regime he should be allowed to ride again and may receive communion but in all other matters the observance was to remain as before, i.e. he remained disarmed. Patricides and matricides, c. 30 decreed, shall not eat meat, bear or take arms (here clearly: if they had not yet been girded) except against pagans. The ninth century with its Viking raids speaks here and fighting the heathen could thus, if it did not count as a redeeming work, at least save the offender from the penance of losing armed status altogether. Yet even so such men could not ride so that they must have served as footsoldiers against the Northmen or Slavs. For a noble warrior this too was a stigma. The bishops had powers to increase or lessen the duration of this penance. A widely current later provision which was however attributed to a council at Thionville in 821, dealt again with the violators of clerks. Here it was decreed that if someone killed a bishop, not by accident but with intent, he shall not eat meat or drink wine all the days of his life, lay down the *cingulum militare* and remain without hope of marriage forever.[36] [556]

We must note that besides expressions like *cingulum militare deponere* the Carolingian ordinancies also used phrases such as *arma non sumere, arma non gerere* and *arma deponere* to denote the suspension or total loss of military

---

[32] *MGH Conc.* 3, no. 14, p. 182, c. 24. For what follows see H.E. Feine, *Kirchliche Rechtsgeschichte: Die katholische Kirche*, 4th edn (Cologne, 1964), pp. 120ff, C. de Clercq, *La Législation religieuse Franque de Clovis à Charlemagne, 507-814* (Louvain, 1936) and C. de Clercq, *La Législation religieuse Franque, 2: De Louis le Pieux à la fin du IXe siècle* (Antwerp, 1958) and B. Poschmann, *Die abendländische Kirchenbuße im frühen Mittelalter* (Breslauer Studien zur historischen Theologie, 16, Breslau, 1930). The Carolingian churchmen of the ninth century sought to uphold and to retain the performance of public penance for open, notorious and grave misdeeds.

[33] *MGH Conc.* 3, no. 14, p. 171, and see Hrabanus Maurus, *Epistolae* no. 32, c. 11, *MGH Epp.* 5, p. 463.

[34] *MGH Conc.* 3, no. 23, pp. 225-6.

[35] J.D. Mansi, *Sacrorum Conciliorum Nova et Amplissima Collectio*, vol. 15 (Venice, 1770), col. 874, c. 26. On the council of Worms in 868 see W. Hartmann, *Das Konzil von Worms 868. Überlieferung und Bedeutung* (Abhandlungen der Akademie der Wissenschaften in Göttingen, phil.-hist. Klasse, dritte Folge, no. 105, Göttingen, 1977).

[36] *Concilium et Capitulare de Clericorum Percussoribus* c. 4, *MGH Capit.* 1, p. 361 and p. 362, c. 5.

standing. Both the assumption of arms and laying them down were thus already, and quite clearly, rites of passage, not confined only to royal princes of whose festivities on being belted we read now and again in the narrative sources. The third of the *Capitula pro lege habenda* which were announced at a great assembly of bishops and lay magnates at Worms in August 829, inveighed against men who deserted or killed their wives in order to marry another woman. The culprit was to lay down his arms and perform public penance. Here the sanctions are particularly striking. The counts should arrest such men if they proved contumacious and keep them in irons until their case could be brought to the emperor's notice.[37] Enforcement was not left to anathemas alone. Archbishop Hincmar would remember and cite this chapter verbatim in his tract against Lothar's treatment of Thietberga.[38] We shall find the Worms *capitulum* applied also in another case.[39]

The frequent combination: loss of military standing and of marriage which we meet in these canons and capitulii is arresting. These were evidently seen as the foremost amenities and attributes of secular life which the penitent must forfeit to earn forgiveness. The whole body of this legislation was received in full, not without its internal inconsistencies into the canonical collections of the early middle ages, especially the two greatest pre-Gregorian works, Regino of Prüm's *Libri duo de synodalibus causis et disciplinis ecclesiasticis* of the early tenth century and Bishop Burchard of Worm's *Decretum* of the early eleventh. Regino cited the council of Mainz where parricides were forbidden to take up arms or marry. He recorded the constitutions against the slayers of priests and men who killed their wives to marry others.[40] Where provisions contradicted one another, some allowing offenders to bear arms against pagans and to keep their wives, others forbidding all weapons and marriage, he did not comment on these discrepancies.

In Burchard's *Decretum* we find the chapter attributed to the assembly at Thionville which dealt with the killing of a bishop. An archbishop of Mainz, according to Burchard, called on the princes to laud the sentence.[41] Again, lay enforcements had to be ensured. Here also a letter of Pope Nicholas I (858-67) to Bishop Ratold of Strasbourg is cited. It dealt with a case of matricide and the culprit, a certain Diothar, was named by the pope and is recorded by Burchard. Among many other penances he must not bear arms except against

---

[37] *MGH Capit.* 2, pp. 18f., c. 3.

[38] Hincmar of Rheims, *De Divortio Lotharii Regis et Theutbergae Reginae*, responsio 5 c. 4, ed. L. Böhringer (MGH Conc. 4, Suppl. 1, Hanover, 1992), pp. 137-8.

[39] See below, at n. 57.

[40] Regino of Prüm, *Libri duo de synodalibus causis et disciplinis ecclesiasticis* II 27, 28, 29, 42, 43, 75, ed. F.W.H. Wasserschleben (Leipzig, 1840), pp. 224, 225, 230, 231, 243. On Regino's *Libri duo* see H. Fuhrmann, *Einfluß und Verbreitung der pseudoisidorischen Fälschungen*, 3 vols. (Schriften der MGH 24, Stuttgart, 1972-74), vol. 2, pp. 435ff. and the article by R. Pokorny in *History of Medieval Canon Law*, ed. W. Hartmann and K. Pennington (forthcoming).

[41] Burchard of Worms, *Decretum* VI 5 and 6, Migne, *PL* 140, col. 766, 767. On Burchard's *Decretum* see Fuhrmann, *Einfluß* (as n. 40), vol. 2, pp. 442ff.

pagans nor ride horses. He might keep his lawful wife lest he fall to fornication.[42] The judgement of Paulinus of Aquilea (787-802) on Aistulf, a Lombard who had murdered his wife and afterwards charged [557] her with adultery on the testimony of a criminal, was sterner. If Aistulf did not submit to a gruelling regime of penitence in a monastery, the course recommended, he must perform even harsher public penance throughout his life in the world: he must forego wine, beer and meat always except on Easter and Christmas Day. He should repent on bread, water and salt and persist in fasts, vigils and alms-giving. He might never be girt with arms again nor conduct a plea. He should not have a wife, nor a concubine nor any other sexual intercourse. He must not presume to have baths or attend 'joyful banquets' (*convivia laetantium*) and receive communion only at the very end of life. Burchard received and amplified this text and in the *Decretum* the culprit also had to forego riding.[43] The bishop of Worms prescribed exactly the same regime for those who had killed their lords or had been privy to their being killed: either monastic confinement altogether or loss of arms and abandonment of all secular, especially legal, business among many other mortifications.[44]

It is quite clear that we are dealing here with nobles and important men rather than humbler criminals. The amenities foregone point to the loss of an aristocratic way of life. The penitent remaining in the world did not lose his rank altogether but it was hollowed out and stripped of quintessential features. From the point of view of military status the frequent link between the abandonment of arms and horsemanship is worth noting. Together they now circumscribed the warrior. In Book XVII of his *Decretum* Burchard also set out the penalties for incest. Their relevance will become apparent later: the penitent must never bear arms again, kiss anyone and receive only the viaticum.[45]

The canons of the Carolingian councils, the capitularies, Regino and Burchard have been surveyed in some detail on the subject of forfeiting the *cingulum militare*. What can they tell us about the evolving military society of the ninth centuries? To answer this question we must first look for the sources of the Carolingian legislators, men like Theodulf of Orléans, Hrabanus and Hincmar. Here as elsewhere the Carolingian scholars and ecclesiastical states-men fell back on the prescriptions of the church in the later Roman Empire and on snatches of late-Roman law but here as elsewhere they adapted what they borrowed to their needs and uses. In late-Roman legal texts the *cingulum* was mentioned not infrequently and it simply denoted a badge of rank, a function that bestowed on its holder a certain standing but not necessarily only a military one. It could mean any civil office and service in the imperial

---

[42] Burchard, *Decretum* (as n. 41) VI 46, cols. 776f., and Pope Nicholas I, *Epistolae* no. 139, *MGH Epp.* 6, pp. 658f.

[43] Burchard, *Decretum* (as n. 41) VI 40, cols. 774f., and Paulinus of Aquileia, *Epistolae* no. 16, *MGH Epp.* 2, pp. 520ff.

[44] Burchard, *Decretum* (as n. 41) XIX 5, col. 954.

[45] Burchard, *Decretum* (as n. 41) XVII 8, cols. 920f.

household. In this sense it was used also by late Roman and early Merovingian churchmen. In the rulings of Pope Siricius, a contemporary of the emperor Theodosius I, and of Pope Leo the Great the return of a penitent to the *cingulum militare* and a new marriage or the return of men vowed to the religious life and entering the clergy, to their former ways, were severely condemned.[46] Sixth-century Merovingian church councils endorsed these principles and they find their place in the great canonistic [558] collection, the *Vetus Gallica*.[47] The councils also proclaimed that incestuous unions were to preclude men from serving in the *militia palatii* or act in the courts.[48] We seem to be watching the birth of a moral order and the way it was to be policed for a thousand years, the church striving to enlarge its authority over conduct with far-reaching secular consequences.

J. Flori, in his study, 'Les origines de l'adoubement chevaleresque' held that the *cingulum militare* in our ninth-century sources echoed the classical sense and simply stood for public life. In the Carolingian age, he declared, the terms *cingulum militare* as well as *militia* meant any public function, be it secular or ecclesiastical rather than just armed and military service.[49] There are good reasons to question this interpretation. Sometimes the Carolingian conciliar constitutions distinguished between a *cingulum militare* and other secular dignities. The synod of Pavia (c. 12) set out in some detail from what functions criminals deprived of communion and denied entry to holy places, were to be excluded: they could not use the belt of secular *militia* or administer any public office, since they could not go to assemblies, greet men or judge their cases while they were subjects to the divine sentence. They might take care of their

---

[46] For Pope Siricius see Migne, *PL* 13, cols. 1137 c. 5, 1158f., 1165. For Leo the Great see Migne *PL* 54, col. 1206, Inquisitio XII and Migne, *PL* 56, col 356A. In general see B. Porschmann, *Die abendländische Kirchenbuße im Ausgang des christlichen Altertums* (Münchner Studien zur historischen Theologie 7, Munich, 1928), pp. 23, 24, 58ff., 100, 119. For the *cingulum* in the Codex Justinianus see Codex VII.38.1 and XII.17.3.

[47] H. Mordek, *Kirchenrecht und Reform im Frankenreich. Die Collectio Vetus Gallica, die älteste systematische Kanonessammlung des Frañnkischen Gallien. Studien und Edition* (Beiträge zur Geschichte und Quellenkunde des Mittelalters 1, Sigmaringen, 1975), p. 350 (Leo the Great), p. 525 (Council of Chalcedon, c. vii).

[48] *Concilium Clippiacense* (626-7) c. 10. For the wider meaning of *cingulum* see ibid., c. 18: 'in quolibet gradu vel cingulo constitutus', in *Concilia Galliae A. 511-A. 695*, ed. C. de Clercq (Corpus Christianorum series latina 148, Turnhout, 1963), pp. 293ff. For *militae cingulum* in the sense of even the clerical vocation see *Concilium Claremontanum* (535) c. 13, ibid., p. 108 and cf. *Concilium Matisconense* (581-3) c. 11, ibid., p. 225, where we read *abiecto religionis cingulo* for the same provision. A penitent's return to the *cingulum militiae saecularis* barred him from admission to the ranks of the clergy. See *Concilium Thelense* (418) c. 3 in *Concilia Africae, A. 345-A. 525*, ed. C. Munier (Corpus Christianorum series latina 149, Turnhout, 1974), p. 61.

[49] J. Flori, 'Les Origines de l'adoubement chevaleresque: Études des remises d'armes et du vocabulaire qui les exprime dans les sources historiques latines jusqu'au début du XIIIe siécle', *Traditio*, 35 (1979), pp. 216ff, and see H. Keller, 'Militia, Vasallität und frühes Rittertum im Spiegel oberitalienischer miles-Belege des 10. und 11 Jahrhunderts', *Quellen und Forschungen aus italienischen Archiven und Bibliotheken*, 62 (1982), pp. 98-102. For further literature on the topic see 'Early Medieval Warfare', above, p. 33 with n. 20 and 'Ritual, Ceremony and Gesture', below, p. 190 with n. 8.

domestic concerns unless their crimes forbade even that. If there is any ambiguity in the phrase *nullo militiae secularis uti cingulo* there is none in the equally often used terms: *arma deponere, arma non sumere, arma non gerere nisi contra paganos*. They make it clear that we are dealing with the habitus of fighting men. The laity at the council of Tribur in 895 would have no difficulty in distinguishing *militia* from other worldly dignity. Even if the laying down of the *cingulum militare* entailed all the secular preoccupations of a noble, the stressmark rested undoubtedly on his tasks as a warrior.[50]

Flori is right in so far as the *exercitus*, the host, was itself the most important political and public institution of many early medieval societies. It could be the seat of judgement and the agent of decision-making. Thus we meet it in Thegan's *Life* of Louis the Pious (c. 6) where [559] Charlemagne summoned his son to come to him with all the *exercitus*, bishops, abbots, dukes, counts and their deputies (*locopositi*) in order to make him his associate in the emperorship.[51] We meet it again in Saxony where the Franks had sought to prohibit ancient stem assemblies because they regarded them as likely centres of disaffection, subversion and rebellion. In Widukind of Corvey the *exercitus* was the political society in action. Berengar II and his son Adalbert submitted and swore fealty to Otto I at Augsburg *coram omni exercitu*.[52] Archbishop Frederick of Mainz incurred the anger of almost the entire host in 953 when Duke Henry of Bavaria accused him of siding with his brother's and his own enemies.[53] In Widukind again, at least half a man's life was lived in the host. More than once he described great nobles as *domi militiaque optimi*, another classical phrase used to describe the horizons of the tenth century.[54]

We must now ask the question whether men were really deprived of their *cingulum militare* and reduced to lasting, abject penance, ceasing to be participating members of their *exercitus* and *conventus* as the canons envisaged. That temporary loss of military status was not uncommon can be gleaned from the Relatio of the bishops addressed to Louis the Pious at Worms in 829. We read, under the heading of 'what must be announced to the people', that those deprived of communion and liable to public penance, banished also from *castra militaria*, must on no account act as godfathers.[55] *Castra militaria* could here stand for all public functions and not only military ones. There are

---

[50] It should be noted however that Abbo of Fleury in his *Collectio Canonum* c. 51, Migne, *PL* 139, col. 506 interpreted Luke 3:14 to refer not only to *militia armata*, 'sed quisque militae suae cingulo utitur, dignitatis suae miles ascribitur'. This could mean *milites, protectores* and *rectores* i.e. holders of judicial offices, even if they needed armed power for their exercise. Abbo, the scholar, evidently knew the late classical usus of the term *militiae cingulum*. For c. 12 of the synod of Pavia see above, n. 34.

[51] Thegan, *Vita Hludowici imperatoris* c. 6, ed. R.Rau (as n. 23), p. 218.

[52] In August 952: Widukind, *Res gestae Saxonicae* III 11, p. 110.

[53] Ibid. III 16, p. 112.

[54] Ibid. II 33 (Duke Conrad) and III 51 (Counts Henry and Siegfried of the Stade comital *stirps*) pp. 94, 131.

[55] *MGH Capit.* 2, p. 39, c. 35.

indeed examples of the church's prescriptions being applied and enforced.[56] At the council of Mainz in 852 where Archbishop Hrabanus presided over the episcopate and abbots from the entire east Frankish kingdom, a certain Albgis was by common decision condemned to do full penance under the canons: four years on bread, water, vegetables and herbs, except at the chief feasts; then four more years of fasting on bread and water on three days a week. He must lay down the *cingulum militare* and remain all his life without marriage. By the king's command – this the bishops had no power to do – he was to be sent into exile. His crime had been to abduct another's wife publicly, to take her to the frontiers of the Reich into the as yet callow Christianity of the Moravians and there, by his adultery, he brought the church into disrepute.[57] There can be little doubt that Albgis was judged under clause 3 of the *Capitula pro lege habenda*, put forward at Worms in 829.[58] A certain Batto, who had killed five men, was to do penance for the whole of his life and to forego marriage though nothing was said about the *cingulum*. A cousin of the loathed Count Bernard, the chamberlain Count Odo, had [560] his arms taken away and was forced into exile as one implicated in the grave charges made against Bernard and the Empress Judith.[59]

Yet much the most important victim of the *statuta canonum* in the ninth century was Louis the Pious himself. The proceedings to reduce him to a state of penitential disablement in 833 bear out the church's legislation in every detail. His son, the Emperor Lothar, had now taken charge, the Empress Judith had been deported and Louis himself was to be turned into an abject penitent since he had not, or not yet, become a monk, as the defectors hoped he would. In the bishops' *relatio* about the penance which the emperor promised at Compiègne Louis is accused of having angered God and scandalised the church. A mission is sent to him with a *cartula* of his offences, a *summa reatum*. They included sacrilege, homicide, violence against his brothers, the death of his nephew Bernard, perjury – oaths he had compelled men to swear – and useless wars where they committed crimes. Louis was even blamed for the recent events of his own betrayal. He had become impossible as a ruler and a man and must make amends. After having confessed, made his profession of penance and returned the *cartula* to the bishops, they placed it on the altar of St Médard, Soissons. Then he laid down the *cingulum militare* and according to the record of Bishop Agobard of Lyons, he himself flung his arms

---

[56] See above, nn. 42, 43, for the cases of Diothar and Aistulf. There were others. See the letter of Pope Benedict III to Bishop Salomon I of Constance about the penance of a fratricide (855-58). Here the culprit, who had sought absolution at Rome, received milder treatment. He was allowed to keep his wife and walk about armed. *Acta Pontificum Romanorum Inedita*, vol. 3, ed. J. von Pflugk-Harttung (Tübingen, 1886), no. 4, p. 4.

[57] *MGH Conc.* 3, no. 26, pp. 248-9, c. 11.

[58] See above, n. 37.

[59] Anonymous, *Vita Hludowici* (as n. 23) c. 45: 'armis ablatis exilio deportatus', p. 336. He was restored but killed in action against Lothar's supporters in 834. Bernard's brother suffered more brutal treatment and was blinded.

on to the base of the altar.[60] Then he took off the *habitus saeculi* and had himself clad in a penitent's garb by the bishops. It is the next sentence of the *relatio* which matters: 'so that no one after such and so great a penance should ever again revert to the *militia secularis*'.[61] The canonical ruling seems oddly out of place in the text. It was the hoped-for outcome of the ritual and Louis bowed to it in so far that he had the bishops revest him with his royal *ornatus* and his arms at Saint-Denis on March 1, in 834. This due, formal and solemn reconciliation ended his status as a penitent.[62]

At the synod of Hohenaltheim in 916 the Suabian lord Erchanger and his associates were accused of trying to lay hands on the *christus Domini*, their lord and king and to seize their bishop, Salomon of Constance. They were to leave secular life, lay down their arms and also enter a monastery to do rigorous penance all their lives. The synod imposed similar atonements on perjurors and those who broke their oaths to the king. Here, too, laying down arms went hand in hand with being confined to a monastery.[63] The canons of Hohenaltheim seem to aggravate the conditions of forfeiting armed status and of penance but they echo all the same the conciliar legislation of the preceeding century. There was no assurance that even in a monastery men like Erchanger and his followers would accept their changed condition.

More revealing still are the accusations hurled against the Salian king, Henry IV, by his Saxon enemies and the penalties which according to the Saxon bishops and lords he must incur. [561] On 24 August 1073 the archbishop of Mainz, Siegfried, and envoys of Archbishop Anno of Cologne met the Saxons in revolt at Corvey in order to pacify them on the king's behalf. Lampert of Hersfeld is our source for the rebels' charges. Besides the grievances and injuries which had been at least in part the causes of the rising, they alleged other and graver matters, shameful deeds Henry was said to have committed against his friends, his wife, Bertha of Turin, his sister, the abbess of Quedlin-burg and others close to him. If these crimes were judged by ecclesiastical laws, the Saxons asserted, Henry must be condemned to lose his marriage, the *miliciae cingulum* and all secular usage – how much more therefore the kingship.[64] Here then we find a direct citation of the familiar Carolingian

---

[60] *Agobardi cartula de poenitentia ab imperatore acta, MGH Capit.* 2, pp. 56f.

[61] *Episcoporum de poenitentia quam Hludowicus imperator professus est relatio Compendiensis, MGH Capit.* 2, no. 197, pp. 51-5, here especially p. 55.

[62] See Louis the Pious's own letter to Abbot Hilduin of St Denis: 'cingulumque militare iudicio atque auctoritate episcopali resumpsimus' *MGH Epp.* 5, p. 327 and see Simson, *Ludwig der Fromme*, vol. 2, pp. 90f.

[63] *Synodus Altheimensis* (916) cc. 21, 22, 23, *MGH Conc.* 6/1, pp. 28-31. On the synod of Hohenaltheim see Fuhrmann, *Einfluß und Verbreitung* (as in n. 40), vol. 2, p. 313 and n. 47 with further literature, and on the sources for these chapters idem, 'Die Synode von Hohenaltheim (916) – quellenkundlich betrachtet', *DA*, 43 (1987), pp. 440-68, especially pp. 448-52.

[64] Lampert, *Annales s.a.* 1073, p. 162 and see Meyer von Knonau, *Heinrich IV.*, vol. 2, pp. 270-2. For a careful discussion of Henry IV's conduct see L. Fenske, *Adelsopposition und kirchliche Reformbewegung im östlichen Sachsen* (Veröffentlichungen des Max-Planck-Instituts für Geschichte, 47, Göttingen, 1977), pp. 118ff.

canonistic precepts. The Saxons desperately needed a case to repudiate Henry IV lawfully. As yet Gregory VII had not furnished them with a valid sanction and it is clear why his sentences later were so welcome. The uncouth charges levelled at Henry IV such as incest with his sister, the abbess, and grotesque marital misconduct, have always been puzzling and very difficult to understand and all the same they were widely disseminated. Not only Lampert but also Brun in his *Book of the Saxon War* and Manegold of Lautenbach uttered these filthy accusation.[65] The last-named included that of incest. Gregory VII, in some of his letters, also hints at dark deeds widely rumoured abroad.[66] In Lampert's account of Henry's meeting with Gregory at Canossa the pope is made to say that the princes of the Reich had charged him with crimes that called for his suspension from all government, communion and every secular usage to the end of his life.[67] In the light of the canons these, on the face of it somewhat preposterous accusations and slanders can be explained and indeed begin to make sense. If the canons were applied Henry IV would be made impossible as a ruler and a man. He could be set aside as Lothar and his followers had tried to set aside Louis the Pious. Here too preposterous charges had filled the air, not least of all that of misconduct between Count Bernard and the empress for which Bernard fled and his kinsman, as we saw, was exiled and deprived of his arms.

The canons of the Carolingian church, as recorded and marshalled by Regino and Burchard, had thus become part of a living body of law. Here they served to enable a group of disaffected prelates and east Saxon princes to set aside their king. Much has been written about a Germanic right of resistance which is thought to have manifested itself in the Saxon rising but here it was not this shadowy and elusive right but the church's sanctions which struck at the root of military status and *a fortiori* kingship.[68] Until Gregory VII excommunicated and deposed Henry IV and the Saxon revolt regained its stance this was an indispensable weapon in the Saxons' armoury to justify and propagate their cause against the king. [562]

Our last example comes from the pages of Sugar's *Life* of Louis VI. In this case the culprit was Thomas of Marle, accused of countless crimes and devastations at a council held at Beauvais in December 1114, not least of all that he had protected the commune in Laon and the murderers of Bishop Gaudry. A papal legate, Cardinal Cuno of Palestrina, presided. Thomas was placed under a general anathema and, although absent, unbelted: *cingulum militare ei...decingit.* By the judgement of all he was deposed from every

[65] Brun, *Bellum Saxonicum* cc. 6-9, pp. 16-18 and Manegold, *Liber ad Gebehardum*, c. 29, ed. K. Francke, *MGH LdL* 1, p. 363.

[66] *Epistolae Vagantes* (as n. 2) no. 14, p. 38.

[67] Lampert, *Annales s.a.* 1077, p. 296.

[68] F. Kern, *Gottesgnadentum und Widerstandsrecht im früheren Mittelalter*, 2nd edn by R. Buchner (Darmstadt, 1954), pp. 168ff. and especially p. 170, n. 367 where he commented on Lampert's account of the meeting at Corvey: 'Hier ist zweifellos der Einfluß Gregors VII zu spüren'. This seems a little *ex post facto*.

worldly honour as a criminal and infamous enemy of Christianity.[69] Here then the canonistic precepts we have seen so vigorously promulgated in the assemblies and councils of the ninth century strike at a twelfth-century culprit when chivalry had, so to say, come of age. Their relevance for the possession enjoyment of the honours of military status, is obvious. The idea that infamous conduct thrust a man out of the society of his princely, noble and knightly companions sprang at least in part from this legislation which must have lent it force and authority. It has sometimes been thought that the church was slow and reluctant to give its blessing to the new secular values of fighting and the attitudes of the knightly caste. Many years ago Carl Erdmann showed that this is mistaken and that we find the blessing of arms and the injunction to use them against pagans and for the aid of the weak already in the tenth century.[70] It has been shown here how much ecclesiastical sanctions had mattered throughout the ninth and later, when it came to deciding when and why military status and the honour of arms must be suspended and relinquished. The church could at no time remain indifferent to the hierarchies of armed secular power and not seek to influence and shape their conduct.

There were of course other ways in which military standing could be forfeited, ways wholly subject to lay judgement. In Frederick Barbarossa's constitution against arsonists of 1186 it was the *judex provincialis*, the *Landrichter*, who deprived the sons of priests, deacons and rustics of the *cingulum militiae* they had assumed.[71] We read in William of Malmesbury that when Harold lay dead on the field of Hastings, a knight slashed at his hip with his sword. The Conqueror expelled him from the *militia* because he had done a shameful and ignominious deed.[72] Thangmar, the half-brother of Otto I, was described by Widukind of Corvey as an astute and experienced warrior but, while on the whole honourable, he lacked a sense of shame and restraint: *inter arma honesta minus pudicitia usus*.[73] Widukind had earlier reported the excesses and outrages of Thangmar and his warband in the rising against Otto's kingship. Lastly we must not overlook a strange story in Hincmar's annals where a Carolingian disarmed himself in a fit of madness or diabolical

---

[69] Suger, *Vie de Louis le Gros* c. 23, ed. A. Molinier (Collection de textes pour servir à l'étude et à l'enseignement de l'histoire 4, Paris, 1887), pp. 81f., and see H. Hoffmann, *Gottesfriede und Treuga Dei* (Schriften der MGH 20, Stuttgart, 1964), pp. 210f.

[70] C. Erdmann, *Die Entstehung des Kreuzzugsgedankens* (Stuttgart, 1935), pp. 51-85 (English as *The Origins of the Idea of Crusade*, trans. M.W. Baldwin and W. Goffart (Philadelphia, 1977), pp. 57-94). A fine example is that of Count Ansfried, which Erdmann, however, thought to have been exceptional (p. 80, n. 78, English pp. 89f. n. 78). Ansfried on being made bishop of Utrecht placed his sword on the altar saying: 'Hactenus hoc honorem terrenum obtinui et hostes pauperum Christi et viduarum expuli'. See Alpertus of Metz, *De diversitate temporum* I 12, in *Alpertus van Metz Gebeurtenissen van deze tijd & Een fragment over bisschop Diederik van Metz*, ed. H. van Rij and A.S. Abulafia (Amsterdam, 1980), p. 26.

[71] *MGH Const.* 1, no. 318, c. 20, pp. 451f. The disarming and exile of Count Odo of Orleans in 830 should perhaps be recalled here (see above n. 59). It defies classification.

[72] William of Malmesbury, *Gesta Regum* III 243, vol. 2, p. 303.

[73] Widukind, *Res gestae Saxonicae* II 11, p. 76, and cf. pp. 74f.

possession. It was the son of Louis the German, Charles, who in [563] 873, at a *curia* held at Frankfurt, suddenly rose to say that he wished to give up secular life, that he would have no further intercourse with his wife, loosened his sword which he then allowed to fall to the ground and was about to undo his belt.[74] Behind the scene and the story lies one of the many plots or rumoured plots of wishing to seize power at the expense of an ageing father and the punishment in store for those who tried. The bishops became Charles's psychiatric helpers. The reference to the wife and the visits to the holy places of the martyrs' shrines place this incident half within and half without the parameter we have explored.

What can be deduced about military status and society from the canons, capitularies and literature of the ninth century we have surveyed? First and foremost, it seems, that they addressed themselves to an aristocratic, military caste and prescribed for it the profession of arms. There were no civilians in this lay nobility. A non-belligerent lay noble was a monster just like an armed priest. Both of course existed but the former caused much embarrassment, rather more than the latter. We find him now and again in the sources, like the Italian *comes imbellis* who threw away his gear, the Hugh Timidus of Thegan's *Life* of Louis the Pious, the Saxon and Thuringian counts who behaved so ill on an expedition against the Slavs that women were reported to have belaboured them, the son also of a lower Rhenish count in the early eleventh century who needed a deputy and stand-in, since he could neither fight not act in other spheres.[75] The conception of the society of the three orders imposed its tyranny and reflected the rise of barriers. What we do not know is exactly where the boundary-line ran between those enjoying military status and honours and those who did not. It is well known that early medieval warfare had not yet become the exclusive province of the nobility. Anybody who had and wore a sword needed a belt to carry it. The man who wanted to clear himself of a charge of priest-slaying by offering an oath is described as a *liber* in the council of Mainz's canon.[76] *Liber* was and remained a notoriously flexible term but its use here does not necessarily mean that the boundary was generously drawn and that the barriers remained low. A story from Notker's *Gesta Karoli* may be cited to illustrate this. Two men of illegitimate and servile birth who had come from the gynaeceum at Colmar wished to be in Charlemagne's following. Both had proved themselves as brave warriors but the emperor

---

[74] *Annales Bertiniani* (as n. 22) *s.a.* 873, p. 191 and see Dümmler, *Ostfränkisches Reich*, vol. 2, pp. 352-5. For a noblemans's belt slipping in public and his sword falling to the ground as an ill omen foretelling the end of his *militia* see *Ex Sigehardi Miraculis S. Maximini* c. 16, *MGH SS* 4, p. 234 and K.J. Leyser, 'The Tenth-Century Condition', in Leyser, *Medieval Germany*, pp. 6f.

[75] Liudprand, *Antapodosis* II 62, p. 65; on Count Hugh see Thegan, *Vita Hludowici* (as in n. 51) cc. 28, 55, pp. 232, 248. Thegan all the same accused him of disloyalty. On his remiss conduct in command see Anonymous, *Vita Hludowici* (as in n. 23) c. 41, p. 326 and *Annales regni Francorum s.a.* 827, pp. 173f. Next year Balderic, *dux* in Friuli, was accused of cowardice (ibid. p. 174). On the counts fisticuffed by women see *Annales Fuldenses s.a.* 872, pp. 75f. On the lower Rhenish count unable to act see Alpertus of Metz, *De diversitate temporum* (as in n. 70) II 1, 5, 8, pp. 42, 50-6.

[76] Cf. above, pp. 57-8 and n. 32.

ordered them to serve in his chamber. They resented it and preferred death in action.[77]

A later age might have found room for them in the ranks of the *ministeriales* but the laws of supply and demand governed warfare at all times. For those who shared in the style of [564] equestrian combat now dominant, even if they were not of the most eminent birth, military operations offered opportunities for distinction, for success, rewards and enhanced social standing. The following of almost any great man was nicely graded. It included well-born men with prospects: wealth and inheritances to come, or already theirs, and less well-born ones and also the lesser kinsmen of *potentes*. Yet in battle, close-quarter action *in acie*, these distinctions in rank might not always tell. War is no respector of persons. Even a king could be struck down by a *miles gregarius* as William Rufus once was.[78] It is worthwhile to remember this feature of warfare: the pell-mell of action which could blot out differences of rank and birth for a brief moment and allow the normally less privileged to emerge victoriously from an encounter with a *potens*. We do not know who maimed and mortally wounded Rudolf of Rheinfelden at the battle by the Elster on 15 October 1080.[79] The Saxon *vir militaris* Hosed who killed a Slav prince at the Recknitz in 955 is another case in point.[80] He became famous and was duly rewarded. Rufus again was all *magnanimitas* towards the *miles* who nearly killed him. This too then was a timeless characteristic of warfare which could raise men both in the tenth and later eleventh century. Differences in the quality of equipment used by the great men and their followers could be enormous but where there was as much standardisation as we can see on the Bayeux Tapestry, the relative chances of an obscure individual mounted warrior to distinguish himself increased.

For the formation of knighthood and the beginnings of an international knightly society it is also worth remembering the sheer scale of warfare in western, central and southern Europe during the last third of the eleventh century. Military enterprises of hitherto undreamt-of scope were mounted from northern France, coupled with new and more effective methods of equestrian combat: the Norman conquest and occupation of England, the rapid expansion of Norman lordship in southern Italy and Sicily, the stepping up of aggressive operations in Spain. All this was followed by the largest and

[77] Notker, *Gesta Karoli* II 4, p. 52.

[78] William of Malmesbury, *Gesta Regum* IV 309, vol. 2, pp. 364f.

[79] Meyer von Knonau, *Heinrich IV.*, vol. 3, p. 339 and Excurs III, pp. 644-52: According to the older Landulf of Milan, one of Henry IV's *milites* killed him, according to Boso he was lethally wounded by his own men failing to recognise him. The very discrepancy of these reports is significant.

[80] Widukind, *Res gestae Saxonicae* III 55, pp. 134f., and see Leyser, 'Henry I' (as n. 12), p. 14 (p. 24).

most far-flung operation ever attempted by post-Carolingian armies, the first crusade. At the same time warfare intensified and cut more deeply than ever before into German society. The conflict between Henry IV and his enemies, the *fideles Sancti Petri*, was fought out on a scale that rapidly outgrew all existing dimensions. After 1077 there were campaigns every year with at least one pitched battle and sometimes even two, so that William of Malmesbury could write of Henry IV that he had fought *in acie* no less than sixty-two times.[81] Even if the momentum of action slackened somewhat after 1090, the mobilisation of mounted military manpower which had sustained the fighting in the Reich for so many years, now fuelled local warfare between the *fideles Sancti Petri* and Henry's men or just feuding groups of nobles.

Not until the fourteenth century did Europe as a whole experience a volume of military activity surpassing that of the later eleventh. The intensification of warfare, as we have said, [565] went hand in hand with dramatic developments in the methods, techniques and equipment for fighting on horseback.[82] More men capable of being trained in these techniques were needed and somehow found. It is not contended that war always at once enhanced the social standing of the mounted participants though it can sometimes be shown that it did. Fulcher of Chartres tells us of *armigeri* promoted to knighthood but also of horsemen not deemed to be knights.[83] Yet these too might have to be promoted in a military emergency, of which there were plenty in the Latin kingdom, to raise their fighting spirit and pay. The refinements of chivalry, on the other hand, could well have been accomplished in a more peaceful and courtly setting. It was perhaps also fortunate for the rising prestige, standing and numbers of mounted fighting men that the growth in the scale of equestrian warfare preceeded, if only by a little, the equally important developments of siege technology and the new demands now made upon the skills of experts in siegecraft. Had this not been so, the *milites* might well have had to share their rewards and renown much more than they did with engineers and foremen. In Outremer the Genoese saw to it in any case that their know-how commanded its price in cash and esteem. Sieges indeed, by their very nature, could aid the entry of very humble men into the charmed circle of higher armed status. The

[81] William of Malmesbury, *Gesta Regum* III 289, vol. 2, pp. 343f.

[82] On these developments of method see D.J.A. Ross, 'L'Originalité de "Turoldus": le maniement de la lance', *Cahiers de civilisation médiévale*, 6 (1963), pp. 127-38. I am indebted to Dr Maurice Keen of Balliol College for this reference. See also R. Allen Brown, 'The Battle of Hastings', *Anglo-Norman Studies*, 3 (1980), pp. 12ff.

[83] Fulcher of Chartres, *Historia Hierosolymitana (1095-1127)* II xi 2, and III xxxi 7, ed. H. Hagenmeyer (Heidelberg, 1913), pp. 408 and 726 for an *armiger* knighted by the count of Tripoli. For the *equitantes* who were not knights see ibid., II xxxii 3, p. 496, and Smail, *Crusading Warfare* (as in n. 1), p. 109 (but he thought *armigeri* normally did not fight at all).

story of the *strator* scaling the Red Tower of Tortona in 1155, whom Frederick Barbarossa wanted to honour with the *cingulum militare*, is often cited. There is a similar story about Henry IV's operations outside the Leonine City in 1083 when a baker and a *camerlengus* of the *familia* of Thedald and the church of Milan achieved a break-in for the host, according to the older Landulf's *Historia Mediolanensis*. *Novi milites* he called the two men and Henry rewarded them with gold and silver.[84] They seem to resemble a little the artisan-*milites* of communal Italy whom Otto of Freising apprehended and denounced so much.[85]

The expansion in the scale of mounted combat during the later eleventh century sprang almost wholly from the heartlands of what had been Carolingian and Ottonian Europe: France, Suabia, Saxony, Bavaria, the Rhine and Main Valleys and northern Italy. It is here also that the canons of the ninth-century councils weighed most effectively on military status. The legislation we have surveyed and its impact must be regarded as part of that Christianisation of warfare which historians have so often associated with quite different phenomena: the peace movement, the patient persuasion and education of the lay nobility by Cluny, the crusade [565] itself.[86] The Carolingian councils and their canons made an early and very important contribution to the idea that bearing arms was a dignity which imposed obligations and was therefore incompatible with certain forms of reprehensible, sinful conduct, particularly grave and almost inexpiable crimes. The church's own militarisation and increased participation in Carolingian warfare during the ninth century must have helped to propagate the conciliar legislation bearing on the loss of the *cingulum militare*.[87] It was not just a voice from outside when aristocratic bishops and abbots shared the experience of campaigning and fell side by side with lay nobles fighting against Northmen and Slavs. The *ignobile vulgus* was by no means yet without weapons but the honour of arms had become the hallmark

---

[84] Otto of Freising and Rahewin, *Gesta Frederici imperatoris* II 25, ed. F.- J. Schmale (AQDG 17, Darmstadt, 1965), p. 326. For the assault on the Leonine City see Landulf, *Historia Mediolanensis* III 32, *MGH SS* 8, p. 99 and Meyer von Knonau, *Heinrich IV.*, vol. 3, pp. 474ff. According to the *Vita Heinrici IV. imperatoris* c. 6, ed. W. Eberhard (MGH SRG 58, Hanover, 1899), p. 23 it was a *scutarius* who scaled an unguarded spot on the walls. See also H. Keller, 'Militia' (as in n. 49), p. 67. Advances in siege technology are now analysed and discussed by R. Rogers, *Latin Siege Warfare in the Twelfth Century* (Oxford, 1992); I should like to thank him for permission to consult this work in its earlier thesis form.

[85] Otto of Freising, *Gesta Frederici* (as in n. 83) II 14, p. 308.

[86] See Althoff, 'Nunc fiant' (as in n. 1) and Duby, *The Three Orders* (as in n. 17), pp. 134ff. on the peace of God, but cf. pp. 26f., where the canons on penitence, including loss of armed status and marriage, were to be applied to peace-breakers.

[87] F. Prinz, *Klerus und Krieg im früheren Mittelalter* (Monographien zur Geschichte des Mittelalters 2, Stuttgart, 1971), especially chapters 3 and 4.

and was already the hereditary possession primarily of nobles.[88] It must be seen descending downwards, on being shared most widely by lesser men, rather than spreading upwards.[89] How it could be forfeited is no less relevant for the beginnings of knighthood than how it might be acquired.

[88] The term 'honour of arms' that has been used here frequently is fully authenticated by the sources of the tenth and eleventh centuries. It was part of their reality and cannot be dismissed as a historians' import. We have met it in Widukind (see n. 73) and in Alpert of Metz when he described Ansfried's tranformation from count to bishop (see n. 70). We find it above all in the following superb passage from the *Life* of Count Burchard the Venerable, written in 1058. Count Burchard, now a monk, is made to reply to his fellow-monks who were taken aback by his humble services as a novice: 'Si, inquit, cum militari honore sublimatus essem atque, ut dicitis, militum stipatus agmine, comitatus dignitate fulgerem, mortali regi lucerne indigenti cereum manu anteferebam, quanto magis nunc immortali imperatori debeo servire atque ante ipsum candelabra ardentia manibus cum exhibitione humilitatis reverenter ferre': *Vie de Bouchard le Vénérable Comte de Vendôme... par Eudes de Saint-Maur* c. 11, ed. C. Bourel de la Roncière (Collection de textes pour servir à l'étude et à l'enseignement de l'histoire 13, Paris, 1892), p. 29.

[89] As against J.M. van Winter, 'Cingulum Militiae. Schwertleite en miles-terminologie als spiegel van veranderend menselijk gedrag', *Tijdschrift voor Rechtsgeschiedenis*, 44 (1976), pp. 47-8.

5

The Ottonians and Wessex

Anglo-Saxon England in the tenth century presents more similarities with the world of the Reich than at any other time of their respective histories.[1] It had a regnal structure with a partially ethnic basis and it knew the predominance or at least hegemony of one kingdom, Wessex and its society, over all the others, largely because it gave them their kings. The continental Saxons enjoyed similar advantages thanks to the east Frankish kingship of their leading family, the Liudolfings. The rulers of Wessex in the tenth century acquired an *imperium* which did not so much imitate the Ottonians as develop like forms of overlordship even ahead of them. They gathered the relics of warlike saints and Christian emperors, St Maurice and Constantine, even a little before the Liudolfings began to do so or at much the same time as Henry I gained the

---

[*] First published in German as 'Die Ottonen und Wessex', *Frühmittelalterliche Studien* 17 (1983), pp. 73-97. Thanks are due to the editors and to Walter de Gruyter Verlag for permission to publish this version. The present text is based primarily on an incomplete and unfootnoted typescript in English, which made some rearrangements of the German text and added some new material, and secondarily on the published German version of 1983. The apparatus is based on that of the German version, with updating to take account of new literature and editions, and editorial additions for the new portions of the English typescript.

[1] There is no comprehensive study of the relations between the Reich and England in the tenth century. The observations of J. Campbell, 'England, France, Flanders and Germany: Some Comparisons and Connections', in *Ethelred the Unready: Papers from the Millenary Conference*, ed. D. Hill (British Archaeological Reports: British Series 59, Oxford 1978), pp. 255-70, are very suggestive. On the continental connections of the Anglo-Saxon monastic reform movement see *Tenth-Century Studies: Essays in Commemoration of the Millenium of the Council of Winchester and Regularis Concordia*, ed. D. Parsons (London, 1975), with the contributions by D.A. Bullough, 'The Continental Background of the Reform', pp. 20-36 (revised in idem, *Carolingian Renewal: Sources and Heritage* (Manchester, 1992), pp. 272-96) and H. Taylor, 'Tenth-Century Church Building in England and on the Continent', pp. 141-68; P. Wormald, 'Æthelwold and his Continental Counterparts: Contact, Comparison, Contrast', in *Bishop Æthelwold: His Career and Influence*, ed. B. Yorke (Woodbridge, 1988), pp. 13-42. The recent survey by V. Ortenberg, *England and the Continent in the Tenth and Eleventh Centuries: Cultural, Spiritual and Artistic Exchanges* (Oxford, 1992), pp. 41-94, contains a mass of material which should be used with caution.

Holy Lance.[2] Between the Anglo-Saxons and the Old Saxons a sentiment of common descent was alive. We find it in a letter of St Boniface, addressed to his countrymen *c.* 738 asking them to pray for the conversion of their continental brethren.[3] 'Have pity on them', he wrote, 'because as they themselves are wont to say "we are of the same flesh and blood." ' A similar mood inhabits the letter which Ealdorman Æthelweard sent to his kinswoman, Mathilda, the daughter of Liudolf of Suabia (*ob.* 957), and abbess of Essen (*ob.* 1011). In this, written in 980 or a trifle after, Æthelweard not only reminds his cousin of their common descent from King Æthelwulf, King Alfred's father but also of an earlier letter he had addressed to her where he recalled their *commune genus* and the migration of the Anglo-Saxons from the continent. The chronicle which followed and which he dedicated to Mathilda *coactus propinquitatis amore*, bore out and enlarged upon this sense of community.[4] Occasionally Æthelweard alluded to victories which the Old Saxons had won over 'barbarians', meaning Vikings, defending their coasts and fighting under King Arnulf at the battle of the Dyle in 891.[5] If we look upon Æthelweard's *Chronicon* as an anthology rather than a complete analogue of a version of the *Anglo-Saxon Chronicle*, these incidents matter.

We find a remnant of this sense of common descent and interests in a text as late as the *Leges Edwardi Confessoris*. 'When the Saxons from Germany come they should be received in the kingdom like our own sworn brethren and like our own citizens. For they sprang erstwhile from the blood of the *Angli*, that is to say from Engern, a place and region in Saxony, and the English from their blood; they are made one people, one kind.'[6] Conversely, when the Salian king Henry IV wanted to mount an expedition of revenge and punishment against his Saxon opponents he tried to enlist the aid of that other enemy of the Saxons, William the Conqueror.[7]

---

[2] William of Malmesbury, *Gesta Regum* II 135, vol. 1, pp. 149ff. The critical observations by M. Lapidge, 'Some Latin Poems as Evidence for the Reign of Athelstan', *Anglo-Saxon England*, 9 (1981), pp. 61-98, are confined to the style of the verses on Athelstan quoted by William. Lapidge does not doubt (ibid., p. 71) that William used sources now lost for his account of Athelstan. For a banner of St Maurice and a sword of Constantine presented to Athelstan by Duke Hugh the Great in 926 see K.J. Leyser, 'The Tenth Century in Byzantine-Western Relationships', in Leyser, *Medieval Germany*, pp. 116-17.

[3] *S. Bonifatii et Lullii Epistolae* no. 46, ed. M. Tangl (MGH Epp. sel. 1, Berlin, 1916), p. 75.

[4] *The Chronicle of Æthelweard*, ed. A. Campbell (Nelson's Medieval Texts, Edinburgh, 1962), pp. 1f. See E. van Houts, 'Women and the Writing of History in the Early Middle Ages: the Case of Abbess Matilda of Essen and Æthelweard', *Early Medieval History*, 1 (1992), pp. 53-68, especially pp. 63-5.

[5] *Aethelweard* (as n. 4), pp. 45, 48.

[6] *Leges Edwardi Confessoris*, 32 C la, *Die Gesetze der Angelsachsen*, ed. F. Liebermann (Halle, 1903), vol. 1, p. 658. On Anglo-Saxon ideas of the *gens Anglorum* see P. Wormald, 'Bede, the *Bretwaldas* and the Origins of the *Gens Anglorum*', in *Ideal and Reality in Frankish and Anglo-Saxon Society: Studies Presented to J.M. Wallace-Hadrill*, ed. P. Wormald (Oxford, 1983), pp. 99-129, especially pp. 121-9.

[7] Brun, *Bellum Saxonicum*, p. 38.

How did this sense of common bonds express itself? Even before the Old Saxons advanced to kingship in the Reich, in quite a few ways. The English share in the Saxon mission was enshrined in the traditions of ecclesiastical centres like Bremen and much was owed to Utrecht, the stronghold of St Willibrord's and St Boniface's disciples, with its enduring links with England. The great biblical epic, the *Heliand*, must be seen as stemming from Anglo-Saxon roots, not least of all the opening which took over the miracle of Caedmon's inspiration in Bede. In the Alfredian Orosius translation Old Saxony is geographically a key area. Old Saxon successes against Danish raiders were recorded carefully in the *Anglo-Saxon Chronicle*, Aethelweard's source and also by Asser.[8] John the Old Saxon served King Alfred but it must be remembered that he had already left his stemland before he came to England. In the *Translatio sancti Alexandri*, as is well known, the continental Saxons appear as migrants from Britannia, perhaps a faint echo of the reverse migration known from other sources.[9] Relations with England could not be paramount for the ninth-century continental Saxons, because for better or for worse they had to learn to live with their conquerors, the Franks. Against the sense of brotherhood in the letter of St Boniface ring the ominous words of Einhard:[10] 'the long Franco-Saxon wars ended on conditions proposed by Charlemagne and accepted by the Saxons. They abandoned the cult of demons, received the sacraments of the Christian faith and joined the Franks to become one people with them [*unus cum eis populus efficerentur*]'. These sentiments glossed mass deportations but they were echoed in late ninth-century Saxony itself by the Poeta Saxo and more cautiously by Widukind of Corvey, where the Saxons became, thanks to Charlemagne's wisdom, brothers of the Franks and *quasi* ('as if') one people through the Christian faith.[11] It was the religious and material culture of the Franks, their institutions like comital office, the new family links between leading Saxon and Frankish nobles, the translation of saints from Francia and Rome to the new bishoprics and abbeys of Saxony, the defence of very long and dangerous frontiers against powerful Slav peoples and Danes, usually with Frankish help, which made up the main themes of Saxon history in the ninth century.

Slowly, and not without frequent setbacks, the Saxon aristocracy and their followers acquired the military capacity to fight wars of aggression on their own along these frontiers and to exploit the economies of the Slav tribes. It is idle to speculate whether they learned the art of mobile defence based on fortresses, which in turn were built by new and heavy labour services imposed

---

[8] On John the Old Saxon see *Asser's Life of King Alfred* c. 78, 94, 95-8, ed. W.H. Stevenson (Oxford, 1904), pp. 63, 81ff. and now Lapidge, 'Latin poems' (as n. 2), pp. 72-83.

[9] B. Krusch, *Die Übertragungen des Hl. Alexander von Rom nach Wildeshausen 851: Das älteste niedersächsische Geschichtsdenkmal* (Nachrichten von der Gesellschaft der Wissenschaft zu Göttingen, Phil.-Hist. Kl., Fachgr. 2., Berlin, 1933), no. 4, p. 423.

[10] Einhard, *Vita Karoli* c. 7, p. 10

[11] Widukind, *Res gestae Saxonicae* I 15, p. 25; see on this 'From Saxon Freedoms to the Freedom of Saxony', *The Gregorian Revolution and Beyond*, p. 52.

on the rural population, from Alfredian Wessex or from west Frankish and Rhenish models.[12] The central event and the starting point for any study of the Ottonians' relations with Anglo-Saxon England in the tenth century is Otto I's marriage to Edith, daughter of Edward the Elder and Aelflaed, his second wife, late in 929-30. Edith was the half-sister of Athelstan, who received the Liudolfing overtures and concluded the alliance.[13] Its importance is reflected in the relatively eloquent sources on both sides: the *Anglo-Saxon Chronicle*, Aethelweard and the later deposits of lost materials in Florence of Worcester and William of Malmesbury,[14] as well as the foremost continental writers, the Saxons' Widukind of Corvey, Hrotsvitha of Gandersheim, the Quedlinburg annalist and Thietmar of Merseburg but also Liudprand of Cremona and Adalbert, the continuator of Regino of Prüm, as well as the author of the first *Passio* of St Ursula, all dwelt on this match.[15] Let us see what they had to say.

In the late summer of 929 a Saxon host won a shattering victory over the principal Slav tribe of the north, the Redarii, at Lenzen. Two ancestors of Thietmar of Merseburg fell in the battle. The king was not present himself, and the decision had been brought about by fifty mounted *milites* launched on the Slavs' flank.[16] The joy of the recent victory, Widukind wrote, was enhanced by the royal wedding which was celebrated at this time with much largesse. For the king gave to his son Otto as his bride the daughter of Edmund – here Widukind got it wrong – the sister (really half-sister) of Athelstan, who bore him a son, Liudolf and a daughter who married Conrad, *Francorum dux*, Widukind called him to describe his eminence.[17] Hrotsvitha is much fuller.[18] She knew among other things that the bride's mother was a woman of much nobler ancestry than the mother of Athelstan, and is thus really the earliest witness to what later were to be widely circulated stories about Athelstan's

---

[12] K.J. Leyser, review of K.-U. Jäschke, *Burgenbau und Landesverteidigung um 900: Überlegungen zu Beispielen aus Deutschland, Frankreich und England* (Sigmaringen, 1975), *EHR*, 92 (1977), pp. 125-6.

[13] On this marriage see K. Hauck, 'Geblütsheiligkeit', in *Liber Floridus: Mittellateinische Studien Paul Lehmann . . . gewidmet*, ed. B. Bischoff and S. Brechter (St Ottilien, 1950), pp. 187-240, here pp. 190f.

[14] *The Anglo-Saxon Chronicle*, ed. and trans. by D. Whitelock in idem (ed). *English Historical Documents*, 1: *c. 500-1042*, 2nd edn (London, 1979), p. 218; *Æthelweard* (as n. 4), p. 2; 'Florence' of Worcester, *Chronicon ex Chronicis*, ed. B. Thorpe (London, 1848), vol. 1, p. 132; William of Malmesbury, *Gesta Regum* II 112 and 126, pp. 117, 137.

[15] Widukind, *Res gestae Saxonicae* I 37, p. 54; Hrotsvitha, *Gesta Ottonis*, verses 66-124, in *Hrotsvithae Opera*, ed. P. Winterfield (MGH SRG 34, Hanover, 1902), pp. 206-8; *Annales Quedlinburgenses s.a.* 929, MGH SS 3, p. 54; Thietmar, *Chronicon* II 1, p. 38; Liudprand, *Antapodosis* IV 17, p. 114; Adalbert, *Continuatio*, p. 158; W. Levison, 'Das Werden der Ursula-Legende', *Bonner Jahrbücher* 132 (1928), pp. 1-164 (also published separately, Cologne, 1928, with same pagination), here p. 144. For further sources see Waitz, *Heinrich I.*, pp. 133-5 and Böhmer-Ottenthal, no. 23h.

[16] Thietmar, *Chronicon* I 10, pp. 14/16.

[17] Widukind, *Res gestae Saxonicae* I 36-7, pp. 51-4; for the genealogy see *Handbook of British Chronology*, ed. E.B. Fryde, D.E. Greenway, S. Porter and I. Roy, 3rd edn (Royal Historical Society Guides and Handbooks 2, London, 1986), pp. 24-5.

[18] Hrotsvitha, *Gesta Ottonis* (as n. 15), verses 70-124.

origins.[19] Here too the initiative is made to lie with Henry, who decided on and chose a worthy spouse for his oldest son by Mathilda, Otto, 'the future king'. Let us leave the *vaticinium post eventum* aside for a moment and look at the Ottonian house's situation. Otto, born in 912, had now reached the age of seventeen. He was of age and *sui juris*. Only a short time before, in 928, a captive Slav noblewoman had given him a son called William, a name not normally at home in the Liudolfing family; he was to join the church and rise to be archbishop of Mainz. Hrotsvitha unfolds for us tellingly the wholly new orientation, the most essential feature of Henry's quest for a bride for his son. He did not want to find her in his own kingdom. The Carolingians in the second half of the ninth century intermarried not exclusively but for the most part with their own nobility. The first royal wedding of the Ottonians very deliberately and consciously broke with this practice and according to modern commentators became an example henceforth followed by all the kings and emperors who had been born and bred for the succession.[20] Only those who reached kingship unexpectedly, usually later in life and of mature years, like Henry II, married to the Luxemburger Cunigunde, and Conrad II, married to Gisela, the daughter of a duke of Suabia but also the granddaughter of a Burgundian king, did not wholly conform to the practice of espousing princesses from outside the Reich. What then lay behind Henry I's decision to send envoys to Athelstan to sue for the hand of one of his sisters or half-sisters then living under his *mund*?

Saxon kingship in east Francia was a very recent phenomenon in 929 and by no means yet taken for granted by the leading nobles of the other *gentes* and their numerous followings, Franks, Suabians, Bavarians and from 925 Lotharingians as well. They were bound to think that it was novel, not to say fortuitous, something that might prove to be of brief duration. The *Vita* of Radbod, bishop of Utrecht, who died in 917, written in the second half of the tenth century, said as much.[21] A contemporary panegyric of Duke Arnulf of Bavaria found in the fragment of a chronicle accidentally preserved in a St Emmeram manuscript dismissed the Saxon Henry with scorn.[22] The novelty of Liudolfing kingship is also well-illustrated by a much-quoted passage in the *Continuatio* of Regino of Prüm. It occurs under the year 931 but fits much better into Henry's itinerary in 930. 'In this year', we read, 'the king was called by Eberhard and the other counts and bishops of Francia and everyone honoured him in their houses and in the seats of their churches with banquets

---

[19] William of Malmesbury, *Gesta Regum* II 131, 139, vol. 1, pp. 141-2, 155-7; see S. Keynes, 'England, 900-1016', in *The New Cambridge Medieval History*, 3: *900-1024*, ed. T. Reuter (Cambridge, forthcoming).

[20] K. Schmid, 'Neue Quellen zum Verständnis des Adels im zehnten Jahrhundert', in *Königswahl und Thronfolge in ottonisch-frühdeutscher Zeit*, ed. E. Hlawitschka (Wege der Forschung 178, Darmstadt, 1971), pp. 404ff. and idem, 'Die Thronfolge Ottos des Großen', ibid., pp. 447ff.

[21] *Vita Radbodi episcopi Traiectenisis, MGH SS* 15/1, pp. 568-71.

[22] *Fragmentum de Arnulfo duce Bavariae, MGH SS* 17, p. 570: 'ubi nullus parentum suorum nec tantum gressum pedis habere visus est'.

and presents as became a king'.[23] Later the *servitia* of bishops, the mainte-
nance of the itinerant king *en route*, would be taken for granted. Under Henry
I they needed a special demonstration. The invitations from the lay princes,
Duke Eberhard and the counts, were and remained altogether exceptional.
The kings later had no right to the hospitality of their great lay nobles and
rarely stayed with them.[24]

Through Otto's marriage with the Anglo-Saxon royal princess the Liudolfings came to share in and to manifest a Saxon kingship that was, unlike theirs,
very old indeed, as old as that of the Franks and sanctified too by warriors who
had died for the faith. Hrotsvitha laid the greatest stress on Edith's descent
from the martyr king St Oswald, whose praises, she wrote, were sung by all the
world.[25] There had been no Frankish king resembling him, largely because
there was no Frankish Bede. The marriage with Edith did not just break with a
tradition that east Frankish kings married daughters of their own high aristocracy. By choosing an Anglo-Saxon royal princess the Liudolfings produced a
historical warranty for their own Saxon kingship which made it much more
authentic and explicit. This is also how Widukind saw it. The princess and later
queen embodied and brought with her two family qualities: *sancta religio* and
regalis potentia.[26] In this way the Liudolfings were able to give their kingship a
past hitherto undreamt of, and so also a new dimension for the future. We shall
see how much they valued this. Their regality now no longer needed a special
justification, though Widukind later provided that too.[27] The marriage thus
enhanced Ottonian rule outside Saxony, and it widened the distance between
them and their erstwhile Saxon peers within. It was perhaps not accidental or a
mere coincidence that celebrations began on Henry I's great journey through
the Reich in 929-30, most probably in Francia and the Rhineland. He may have
shown off his son and his son's bride to the Frankish nobles even before the
couple feasted in Saxony.

Hrotsvitha's concern with Edith's descent from St Oswald is echoed strikingly in Old Saxon calendars in which the Northumbrian king's day and
martyrdom, on 5 August, were widely commemorated, not least of all in Essen
where Ealdorman Æthelweard's correspondent, Mathilda, Edith's granddaughter, ruled. Here we find St Oswald in a tenth-century sacramentary, now

[23] Adalbert, *Continuatio s.a.* 931, pp. 158f. and Schmid, 'Thronfolge' (as n. 20), pp. 455, 460.

[24] C. Brühl, *Fodrum, Gistum, Servitium Regis*, 2 vols. (Kölner Historische Abhandlungen 17,
Cologne, 1968), vol. 1, pp. 179-80.

[25] Hrotsvitha, *Gesta Ottonis* (as n. 15), verses 94-7, p. 207.

[26] Widukind, *Res gestae Saxonicae* II 41, pp. 99f. wrote in his obituary for Edith: 'Haec nata ex
gente Anglorum non minus sancta religione quam regali potentia pollentium stirpe claruit'.

[27] H. Beumann, *Widukind von Korvei: Untersuchunger zur Geschichtsschreibung und Ideen
geschichte des zehnten Jahrhunderts* (Abhandlungen zur Corveyer Geschichtsschreibung 3, Weimar, 1950), pp. 244ff.

in the University Library at Düsseldorf.[28] Here too the continental Saxons sought to become part of an older tradition. They had been Christians for at the most 130 years, whereas their Anglo-Saxon fellows had been so ever since the seventh century, and this again was an association worth seeking. We may compare the reverence for the holy Anglo-Saxon warrior king with the faintly ironic commentary on the devotees of another insular saint, the Irish St Columba, who had preached in Scotland. It is found in a Corvey sacramentary of the late tenth century and is probably one of the oldest Irish jokes: 'The devotees of this confessor also claim that he never, or at least hardly ever told a lie' is entered in the calendar here.[29]

We have yet another source for Henry I's bridal mission for his son. It comes from a wholly unexpected quarter, the prologue of the first *Passio* of St Ursula and her companions, a cult which established itself and flourished above all in Cologne. The prologue was addressed to Archbishop Gero (969-76), a Saxon and nephew of the great margrave of the same name and it belongs perhaps to the later years of his pontificate, though this is far from certain. The dedicatory letter recalls an embassy of Otto I to England headed by a Count Hoolf who was to win for Otto, already called *magnus* and *imperator*, 'a bride from the noblest lineage of that people, the king's daughter, which he did', and the author added: 'I speak of something known to nearly all'. It was in England and allegedly through St Dunstan that the envoy first heard the story of the holy virgins of Cologne, their leader St Ursula and their *passio*. The prologue mistimes events, bristles with errors and improbabilities and yet may record important details of both dynastic and religious traffic between England and the Reich.[30]

929 was a critical year for the Ottonians. On 16 September Henry I, at Quedlinburg, 'ordered his house' and made a grant of dower to his wife, Mathilda. It included five fortified royal residences in Saxony with all their appurtenances and Otto I's consent is prominently recorded in the diploma which had a legislative tone in its context.[31] By this time the Anglo-Saxon wedding negotiations were well advanced and a favourable reply must have reached Henry I, an embassy from Wessex was on its way or had already arrived escorting or followed shortly afterwards by the bride. Henry I had already provided for his queen in 927, but these arrangements needed amplification now that Mathilda was about to have a rival in the Ottonian family and

---

[28] MS D 2, fol. 15. St Oswald is absent from the calendars of the Essen sacramentaries, MS D 1 and MS D 3; on these books see the references given in Van Houts, 'Women and the Writing of History' (as n. 4), p. 60, nn. 32-3. His feast-day (5 August) was noted in that of Borghorst, where Edith's obit was also recorded in the calendar of feasts; see G. Althoff, *Das Necrolog von Borghorst: Edition und Untersuchung* (Westfälische Gedenkbücher und Nekrologien 1, Münster, 1978), pp. 30, 121. His feast was also entered in the necrologies of Schildesche and Stederburg.

[29] Munich, Staatsbibliothek, MS clm 10077, fo. 221v: 'eodem die sancti columbe confessoris qui in ibernia genitus scociam predicavit adfirmant etiam cultores eius nunquam aut rarissime se mentitum fore.'

[30] Levison, 'Werden der Ursula-Legende' (as n. 15), pp. 142-57, and commentary pp. 58-90.

[31] D H I 20.

would no longer enjoy exclusive ascendancy among its womenfolk. Here we come to the most important feature of Otto's wedding. It has to be pieced together from quite a different and of late all too fashionable batch of sources, the *Libri Memoriales* of St Gallen, Reichenau and Pfäfers. Here Karl Schmid has drawn attention to some unmistakably royal entries which must belong to the end of 929 or the year 930. We know that Henry I spent Christmas 929 at Strasbourg and the entries must have been made shortly afterwards during a visit to the two great abbeys by the Lake of Constance. They are more or less contemporary, and in the Reichenau entry we find King Henry, Queen Mathilda and then Otto, and he alone – as against his brothers Henry and Brun, the other sons of Mathilda – is also called *rex*.[32] It suggests that he and only he in the Ottonian house was intended to succeed to the kingship, or at least that his father wished him to. This was probably both the *conditio sine qua non* and the purpose of his marriage to the Anglo-Saxon royal princess. The alliance singled him out as the Liudolfing most clearly qualified to be the future king. The royal marriage and the succession buttressed one another.

Serious objections have been raised to this interpretation of the Reichenau *Liber Memorialis* entry. It has been argued that if the monks called Otto *rex* that was their own business, their *Privatsache*.[33] Yet it is questionable whether they would have dared to describe Otto alone as king among Henry and Mathilda's sons if they did not at least know of the reigning ruler's declared wishes and plans. Karl Schmid also drew attention to a late and rather dubious chronicle source, the Lausanne annals, which inform us that Otto was actually crowned and sacred king at Mainz in 930.[34] Even without this it is fairly clear what intentions and aspirations lay behind the royal wedding and the great perambulation of the Reich in 929/30 but it is not at all clear how far it was as yet possible to bring these plans for the succession to fruition. Historians have called the years 929/30 the climax of Henry I's reign, but was it really so, before his victory over the Magyars in 933 and his renowned campaign against the Danes in 934?[35] In 930 the king's prestige and standing may not yet have been adequate to gain the indispensable consent of the great for Otto's kingship and so turn the Liudolfings into a real *stirps regia*. It was only with the succession secure that they could be said to have become just that; the contrast with Hugh Capet's successful elevation of his son Robert in 987 is striking. The Lausanne

[32] Schmid, 'Neue Quellen' (as n. 20), pp. 392, 405ff.; idem, 'Thronfolge' (as n. 20), pp. 449f.

[33] Hartmut Hoffmann, 'Zur Geschichte Ottos des Großen', *DA* 28 (1972), pp. 42-73, here p. 44.

[34] Schmid, 'Neue Quellen' (as n. 20), p. 410. See now E. Hlawitschka, 'Die Ottonen-Einträge der Lausanner Annalen', in *Roma Renascens: Beiträge zur Spätantike und Rezeptionsgeschichte. Ilona Opelt von ihren Freunden und Schülern zum 9.7.1988 in Verehrung gewidmet*, ed. M. Wissemann (Frankfurt, 1988), pp. 125-48, especially pp. 128-31.

[35] Schmid, 'Thronfolge' (as n. 20), pp. 460ff. and E. Hlawitschka, 'Die verwandtschaftlichen Verbindungen zwischen dem hochburgundischen und dem niederburgundischen Könighaus: Zugleich ein Beitrag zur Geschichte Burgunds in der ersten Hälfte des zehnten Jahrhunderts', in *Grundwissenschaften und Geschichte: Festschrift für Peter Acht*, ed. W. Schlögl and P. Herde (Münchener Historische Studien, Abteilung Geschichtliche Hilfswissenschaften 15, Kallmünz, 1976), pp. 28-57, here p. 57.

annal stands by itself and the silence of the Saxon writers, Liudprand and Adalbert, the continuator of Regino, perhaps means that if Otto's promotion was already planned for 930 it did not come off, despite the honours and attentions paid to Henry and his family *en route*. Adalbert's famous account of Henry's festive reception in Francia may thus conceal failure rather than announce success. This view gains some support from a diploma which Henry I bestowed on the canons of the church of St Mary at Aachen confirming their revenues.[36] In 930 the king stayed and kept Whitsun at Aachen. That he should have visited Charlemagne's seat at this moment is in itself very significant. The diploma cited the great western dukes as sponsors, Giselbert of Lotharingia and Eberhard of Franconia, though they were only termed *comites*, but Otto who must have been there, let alone his bride, were not mentioned. It seems then that these leading men were not yet ready to see Otto associated with his father in royal acts or even as their equal and would not yet commit themselves to him as their future king despite his Anglo-Saxon bride.

The St Gallen and Reichenau *Libri Memoriales* also contain direct evidence of the Wessex embassy's movements in the Reich. There is in the St Gallen *Liber* a very large entry headed by King Athelstan, followed by Archbishop Wulfhelm and eight other bishops as well as two abbots. Bishop Coenwald of Worcester, who led the legation, appears near the end with perhaps two of his lay-noble companions. At Reichenau only Athelstan, Archbishop Wulfhelm and one Wignand were commended to the prayers of the community. The St Gallen *Liber*, however, contains another entry which recorded the date of the Wessex embassy's visit, October 15, that they stayed for four days and took part in the feast of the abbey's patron saint. Bishop Coenwald brought with him rich presents of silver and, we learn, he had the task of distributing these among the monasteries all over Germany.[37] In this way Wessex, its king, episcopate and lay nobles were given wide publicity in the Reich. Verses were written in Athelstan's honour and addressed to him from Francia.[38]

Hrotsvitha waxed lyrical over the riches and treasures which came with the bride whom Bishop Coenwald perhaps escorted to Saxony. These were valuable resources for Henry I, who needed them for his expensive military policies. They may even have helped him to pay the tributes due to the Hungarians which gave Saxony an essential breathing space and freedom from raids. Edith too was personally well-furnished with treasures so that she could

---

[36] D H I 23; K. Hauck, 'Die Ottonen und Aachen, 876 bis 936', in *Karl der Große: Lebenswerk und Nachleben*, 4: *Das Nachleben*, ed. W. Braunfels und P.E. Schramm (Düsseldorf, 1967), pp. 39-53.

[37] Schmid, 'Neue Quellen' (as n. 20), pp. 400f.; G. Althoff, *Amicitiae und Pacta: Bündnis, Einung, Politik und Gebetsgedenken im beginnenden 10. Jahrhundert* (Schriften der MGH 37, Hanover, 1992), pp. 124-7.

[38] W.H. Stevenson, 'A Latin Poem addressed to King Athelstan', *EHR*, 26 (1911), pp. 482-7. See against this now Lapidge, 'Some Latin Poems' (as n. 2), pp. 83-93. For a context for these and for the mss. discussed in nn. 40ff. see also M. Wood, 'The Making of King Aethelstan's Empire: an English Charlemagne', in *Ideal and Reality* (as n. 6), pp. 250-72.

display her royal origins in her new home.[39] One of the Anglo-Saxon gifts Hrotsvitha herself may have seen and admired. It was a manuscript with an ivory binding which either Bishop Coenwald, Henry or Otto I gave to Gandersheim. It still lay there in the eleventh century, for we find an entry from the time of Abbess Sophia, Otto II's daughter (1002-39) which listed the estates and tithes of the foundation. Bishop Bernward of Hildesheim confirmed them at the time of the abbey church's dedication on 5 January 1007.[40] The entry cannot have been ordered much later. The manuscript is a Carolingian evangeliary, written and painted at Metz round the year 860. On folio 169 there appears an entry in an Anglo-Saxon hand of the tenth century: 'eadgifu regina aethelstan rex angulsaxonum et mercianorum'. Eadgifu is often thought to have been the king's half-sister, the wife of the Carolingian Charles the Simple who with her son Louis had taken refuge in Wessex. Yet she could also have been Edward the Elder's third wife, also called Eadgifu, Aethelstan's stepmother. The purpose of the entry was once again commemoration. The two people mentioned were to be prayed for.[41]

We can be sure that Henry I's envoys to England in 929, Count Hoolf and his companions, had not gone there empty-handed. One of the gifts from the Liudolfings to Athelstan has survived, this too a late-Carolingian evangeliary which came from and may have been created at Lobbes in the diocese of Liège.[42] Here too we find an inscription in an Anglo-Saxon hand on fol. 23: 'ODDA REX MIHTHILD MATER REGIS'. It is noteworthy that she was not called *regina* but simply the king's mother. This suggests sometime between 936 and 939 as the date of the gift, when the Anglo-Saxon scribe was most likely to have the status of the two persons to be commemorated described to him in this style. Athelstan gave this book, with its four paintings of the evangelists, to Christ Church, Canterbury, where it still was in the twelfth century.[43] In the announcement of the donation he called himself 'Anglorum basileos et curagulus totius Bryttannie', as if he consciously wanted to place

---

[39] Hrotsvitha, *Gesta Ottonis* (as n. 15) verses 107-11, p. 207.

[40] Coburg, Landesbibliothek, MS 1 (so-called Gandersheim Gospels). See P.E. Schramm and F. Mütherich, *Denkmale der deutschen Könige und Kaiser*, 1: *Ein Beitrag zur Herrschergeschichte von Karl dem Großen bis Friedrich II., 768-1250*, 2nd edn (Veröffentlichungen des Zentralinstituts für Kunstgeschichte in München 2, Munich, 1981), pp. 139-40, no. 63; S. Keynes, 'King Athelstan's Books', in *Learning and Literature in Anglo-Saxon England; Studies Presented to Peter Clemoes on the Occasion of his Sixty-Fifth Birthday*, ed. M. Lapidge and H. Gneuss (Cambridge, 1985), pp. 143-201, here p. 189 with n. 217, for references.

[41] Keynes, 'Athelstan's Books' (as n. 40), pp. 189-93, discusses the entry and possible explanations of its origin and purpose.

[42] London, British Library, MS Cotton Tiberius A II (from Christ Church, Canterbury); see Schramm and Mütherich, *Denkmale* (as n. 40), p. 140 no. 64; Keynes, 'Athelstan's Books' (as n. 40), p. 147 and n. 24; H. Hoffmann, *Buchkunst und Königtum im ottonischen und frühsalischen Reich*, 2 vols. (Schriften der MGH 30, Stuttgart, 1986), pp. 9-10.

[43] Ibid., pp. 147-53; Keynes suggests dates of 936 × 968 (or 962) for the inscription, but *mater regis* may imply a date early in Otto's reign, when Mathilda was estranged from Otto (see below at n. 82ff.).

himself above his Saxon brother-in-law.[44] That Athelstan gathered and possessed manuscripts is well-known; Otto I too had some in his treasure and received a dedication. As yet, however, he did not dispose of a scriptorium, let alone a court school where he could have commissioned a luxury manuscript, and even the one he sent to Athelstan the latter caused to be sumptuously bound and further embellished with gold paint. The Wessex ruler was in a better case, as the book he gave to the St Cuthbert community showed, but he too preferred to fall back on the Carolingian past when he wanted to make a memorable and solemn gift of the sacred texts to Otto. Perhaps there was no time to commission something fresh.[45]

To exchange gifts and to be seen receiving them was of enormous importance for the rulers of the late- and post-Carolingian kingdoms. Presents testified to their lordship and without them it counted for little in the eyes of their own followers and could barely hope to last. The arrival of costly and rare objects from abroad and far away was indispensable for the exercise of the royal function of patronage and largesse. In the early middle ages these movements of rarities, exotic animals, dogs, precious materials, choice weapons, artefacts, luxury manuscripts and, not least of all, relics, between rulers were not just by-products and epiphenomena of diplomacy but part of its very essence and substance. Not for nothing had Hrotsvitha called England *terram sat deliciosam*.[46]

We must now turn to what may seem to us a strange and archaic feature of the alliance between Wessex and the Old Saxons. For Athelstan had not only sent Edith to Henry I, he sent two girls. A sister or half-sister, called Ælfgifu, accompanied Edith so that Otto should be able to choose.[47] There were precedents for this. In 819 Louis the Pious had picked his second wife Judith, the daughter of Count Welf, from a large number of noble girls summoned to Aachen for the purpose.[48] Otto chose Edith – at first sight, Hrotsvitha assures us – but the outcome could not be known beforehand. This may explain why the name of neither girl appears in the Anglo-Saxon *Liber Memorialis* entries at Reichenau and St Gallen but it is not a wholly convincing explanation for

[44] Ibid., pp. 149-50.

[45] Ibid., pp. 146-53, 170-9 (London, British Library, MS Cotton Otho B IX, a continental manuscript given to St Cuthbert's), 180 (Cambridge, Corpus Christi College, MS 183): 'the only [book donated by Athelstan] wholly written in England during his reign'. On the absence of court book production in Otto I's pre-imperial period see Hoffmann, *Buchkunst* (as n. 42), pp. 8-11, and H. Mayr-Harting, *Ottonian Book Illumination: An Historical Study*, 1: *Themes* (London, 1991), pp. 36-43.

[46] Hrotsvitha, *Gesta Ottonis* (as n. 15) verse 75, p. 206. On the diplomatic function of gift-giving see K.J. Leyser, 'The Tenth Century in Byzantine-Western Relationships', in idem, *Medieval Germany*, pp. 103-37, here pp. 114-17; Wood, 'Aethelstan's Empire' (as n. 38) pp. 265-7; Hannig, '*Ars Donandi*', below, n. 113.

[47] Hrotsvitha, *Gesta Ottonis* (as n. 15), verses 112-20, pp. 207f.

[48] E. Ward, 'Caesar's Wife: The Career of the Empress Judith, 819-829', in *Charlemagne's Heir: New Perspectives on the Reign of Louis the Pious*, ed. P. Godman and R. Collins (Oxford, 1986), pp. 205-27, here pp. 207-8.

their omission. The name of an Odgiva (?Ælfgifu) stands together with King Athelstan, King Edmund and Archbishop Oda (942-58) in a later Pfäfers entry.[49] It is equally remarkable that Edith did not figure in the Liudolfing family entries associated with Henry I's journey into southern Suabia after his Christmas court at Strasbourg in 929 where, as we saw, Otto once occurs as *rex* and the kin of Mathilda stood out prominently. It is possible that the marriage had not yet taken place and conceivable that Mathilda's jealousy of her new rival in the Liudolfing house was already making itself felt but these are conjectures.

Ælfgifu, according to Æthelweard, was married to a certain king 'by the Alps'; in William of Malmesbury's *Gesta Regum* he had become a mere duke.[50] His identity has been a scholar's headache for generations. R.L. Poole and others who followed him thought he was Conrad of Burgundy, the son of Rudolf II (*ob.* 937), the king Juranian Burgundy, who began his long shadowy reign under Ottonian sponsorship in 937 as a 'filius parvus'.[51] His English wife would then have been more than ten years older than him, and if his first wife Adelana is to be identified with Edward the Elder's daughter Ælfgifu, then her daughter Gisela, the wife of Henry the Wrangler, would have been half a west Saxon by descent and have considerably strengthened Ottonian-Insular links. There are no hints of this in the sources, however, and who Ælfgifu's husband was has recently been established with about as much certainty as can be hoped for, short of the discovery of new evidence. According to Eduard Hlawitschka, Ælfgifu married Louis, whom from three references we know to have been a brother of Rudolf II. A son of this union with the significant name Henry appears prominently in 943 and 961 in a Burgundian *placitum* and in two diplomata among those present at the transactions recorded.[52] It was by no means usual to give sons the name of a sister's father-in-law, but how else can the 'Heinricus filius Ludowici' in the Burgundian *placitum* be explained?[53] Louis was the son and the brother of a king, but we find him described only as a count and the same is true for his son Henry. Yet to the Anglo-Saxons he was an *ætheling*, the member of a *stirps regia* and a royal prince who might, if his brother lacked offspring, or if the great preferred him, succeed to the kingship

---

[49] Keynes, 'Athelstan's Books' (as n. 40), p. 201, discusses the entry and associates it tentatively with a visit to Rome by Archbishop Oda; he identifies Odgiva with Edmund's mother.

[50] *Aethelweard* (as n. 4), p. 2; William of Malmesbury, *Gesta Regum* II 112, 126, 135, vol. 1, pp. 117, 137, 149.

[51] R.L. Poole, 'The Alpine Son-In-Law of Edward the Elder', in *Studies in Chronology and History*, ed. A.L. Poole (Oxford, 1934), pp. 115-22. According to a diploma of Conrad's of 963 his first wife was called Adelana: *Die Urkunden der Burgundischen Rudolfinger*, ed. T. Schieffer and H.E. Mayer (MGH Die Urkunden der Burgundischen Rudolfinger, Munich, 1977), no. 38. The term 'filius parvus' is taken from Flodoard, *Annales s.a.* 937, p. 68.

[52] Hlawitschka, 'Verwandschaftliche Verbindungen' (as n. 35), pp. 50-7.

[53] On contemporary naming customs in princely houses see M. Mitterauer, 'Zur Nachbenennung nach Lebenden und Toten in Fürstenhäusern des Frühmittelalters', in *Gesellschaftsgeschichte. Festschrift für Karl Bosl zum 80. Geburtstag*, ed. F. Seibt (Munich, 1988), pp. 386-99.

itself.[54] We hear nothing of other descendants from this match and exact knowledge of it faded with time. Perhaps it was known that it had not been a brilliant one. Ealdorman Æthelweard in his letter to Mathilda of Essen confessed that he did not know exactly whom Ælfgifu had married and he asked his kinswoman, the abbess, to tell him since, he opined, she had better means of coming by this information than he had – a further indication, incidentally, that Conrad was not the bridegroom, since he was hardly a complete unknown.[55] What matters is that the marriage came about under Ottonian patronage and could be used at once to extend Ottonian influence into the Burgundian royal house. We know that Otto I had sway over Conrad, Rudolf II's successor, before the young Burgundian ruler set up on his own from about 942 onwards, still however under Otto's protection. The resumption of east Frankish preponderance in the Juranian kingdom, which went back to the days of King Arnulf of Carinthia in the late ninth-century, was thus an additional boon of the Anglo-Saxon connection, which established an in-law relationship between the Liudolfings and the Welf Rudolfings, as they were called, and opened up around 935 the lands between Jura and Alps with the Rhône valley and the Alpine passes to Ottonian influence even before Otto's second marriage with Adelheid, the Burgundian king's daughter, intensified the links.

For the remaining years of Henry I's reign, from 930 to 936, we hear nothing of either Otto or Edith. It is assumed that they resided in Magdeburg, her dower, but this cannot be proved. They do not appear as sponsors on Henry I's diplomata, where Mathilda occurs at least three times.[56] This is not without significance. In the opening section of Book II of his *Res gestae Saxonicae* Widukind wrote:[57] 'Now that the *pater patriae*, the greatest and best of kings, Henry had died [2 July 936] the whole people of the Franks and Saxons elected his son Otto who had already been designated by his father a while ago [*iam olim designatum*']. This becomes a much more understandable phrase, Karl Schmid reasoned, if the designation of Otto took place in 929 or 930 at the time of and closely linked with his marriage to Edith rather than if it happened only 936 at an assembly held at Erfurt when Henry I was already rather ill. There, if we may believe Widukind, he distributed his lands and treasures among his sons.[58] As for Otto, he placed him over his brothers and the whole of the *imperium Francorum*. Whether *olim* refers to this, as Hartmut Hoffmann suggests it might, there can be no doubt all the same that the decisions of the Erfurt assembly were not sudden and unexpected.[59] We must not think, however, that Otto I's future was therefore assured. He was by no means home

---

[54] D. Dumville, 'The Aetheling: a Study in Anglo-Saxon Constitutional History', *Anglo-Saxon England*, 8 (1980), pp. 1-33.

[55] *Æthelweard* (as n. 4), p. 2.

[56] See below at n. 74.

[57] Widukind, *Res gestae Saxonicae* II 1, p. 63.

[58] Schmid, 'Thronfolge' (as n. 20), pp. 426-39.

[59] Hoffmann, 'Zur Geschichte' (as n. 33), pp. 45-57.

and dry yet. In the first place designation by itself could not determine the succession unless it met with acceptance and a ready response from the great and their followings and we do not know who took part at Erfurt other than Saxons and Thuringians. By 936, moreover, Otto's position had if anything deteriorated, both within his own family and among the Saxon nobility. His younger brother Henry's claims were now much more formidable, for Henry had by then come of age and was capable of action, of commanding a following and being trusted by it to fulfil expectations of advancement and profit. Above all Henry I's wife, Mathilda, the mother of the two Liudolfing princes, favoured her younger as against her elder son.

Why? Was this only a maternal whim? Here we must turn once again to Otto's wife, the Wessex royal princess Edith. Edith came from a much nobler *stirps* than did Mathilda.[60] Her family and ancestry were regal. Mathilda's descent was thought to go back, prominently enough, to Charlemagne's great enemy, the Saxon *dux* Widukind.[61] Mathilda had become regal only quite recently, thanks to her husband's fortune. Yet her queenly status may have suffered from Henry I's notorious refusal to be blessed and anointed by the archbishop of Mainz.[62] Whatever good reasons this refusal may have had in 918, they looked far less good with the passage of time. The church's historiography reckoned it to have been a grave fault in Henry, a sin, to decline the anointing offered by Archbishop Heriger.[63] True, the chief sources recording these criticisms belong to the later tenth and early eleventh century, Gerhard's *Life* of St Ulrich of Augsburg and Thietmar of Merseburg's *Chronicon*, but it is quite possible that already in Henry I's later years when he had entered into much closer relations with the episcopate and there was once again a court clergy, the rejection of anointing was felt to be an embarrassment.[64] It was precisely the planned expedition to Rome which was meant to compensate for this, though illness prevented Henry from carrying this out.[65] The refusal of unction meant also that Mathilda cannot have undergone the church's coronation and unction rituals. The blemish, the defect in title was hers too, another reason for her to resent Otto's wife. Not for nothing did

---

[60] But Edith cannot be called a 'born queen', *pace* Schmid, 'Neue Quellen' (as n.20), p. 413, n. 71; see P. Stafford, 'The King's Wife in Wessex, 800-1066', *Past and Present*, 91 (1981), pp. 3-27.

[61] K. Schmid, 'Die Nachfahren Widukinds', *Deutsches Archiv*, 20 (1964), pp. 1-47, here pp. 11ff.

[62] P.E. Schramm, 'Der Ablauf der deutschen Königsweihe nach dem "Mainzer Ordo"', *Kaiser, Könige und Päpste: Gesammelte Aufsätze zur Geschichte des Mittelalters*, 4 vols. in 5 (Stuttgart, 1969), vol. 3, pp. 59-,107, here pp. 79-80, noted that Henry's refusal of unction excluded Mathilda from coronation. From the extensive literature on Henry's refusal we shall here cite only E. Karpf, 'Königserhebung ohne Salbung: Zur politischen Bedeutung von Heinrichs I. ungewöhnlichem Verzicht in Fritzlar (919)', *Hessisches Jahrbuch für Landesgeschichte*, 34 (1984), pp. 1-24.

[63] Gerhard, *Vita S. Oudalrici episcopi* c. 3, *MGH SS* 4, p. 389; Thietmar, *Chronicon* I 8, pp. 12f.

[64] J. Fleckenstein, *Die Hofkapelle der deutschen Könige*, 2: *Die Hofkapelle im Rahmen der ottonisch-salischen Reichskirche* (Schriften der MGH 16/2, Stuttgart, 1966), pp. 3-16.

[65] Widukind, *Res gestae Saxonicae* I 40, p. 59.

Widukind and the two *Vitae* dwell so much on Mathilda's regality, not for nothing were they so anxious to drive it home.

This of course raises the important question whether Edith was crowned and anointed with her husband in 936 at Aachen in the celebrated ritual described in so much detail by Widukind of Corvey. It is not an easy question to answer since Widukind did not mention her with a single word at this point. Thietmar, however, did. He wrote that she was consecrated by Otto's orders sometime after his own sacering: 'Confortatus in Deo tunc et in regno', and the twelfth-century *Annalista Saxo* repeated this under the year 936.[66] It was obviously a separate ceremony, and for this there were very good west Frankish Carolingian precedents, not least of all the case of Charles the Bald's daughter Judith who in 856 was married to Edith's and Aethelweard's joint ancestor, King Aethelwulf of Wessex, Alfred's father. For this ceremony we even possess an *ordo*, one of the earlist of its kind.[67] Historians have thought that Thietmar only applied a consecration ritual to Edith retrospectively.[68] When he wrote, it had become customary for queens to be crowned and blessed. Yet we find *formulae* for the coronation of a queen in the Mainz *ordo* of c. 960. Moreover, it has been overlooked that Thietmar returned to the theme of Edith's sacering. He has a formal obit notice for her, following Widukind, and there he underlined her inauguration once more when he wrote that she died in the eleventh year of her *ordinatio*.[69] Whatever role Edith played at Aachen on 7 August 936 or shortly afterwards – and I am inclined to think that she was sacred – her mother-in-law was not there to watch it and her absence was deliberate. She remained in Saxony, where on the thirtieth day of her husband's death she took important steps for the foundation of a congregation of nuns at Quedlinburg, her dower, furnished them with what they needed in food and clothing out of her *proprietas* with her son's consent, and 'confirmed her act in writing', according to Thietmar's autograph report.[70] By this time Otto had left for the west. When later in the year he himself uttered a diploma on 13 September for the new foundation over Henry I's grave, the context did not mention Mathilda as sponsor at all although she had the endowment and

[66] Thietmar, *Chronicon* II 1, p. 38; *Annalista Saxo, MGH SS* 7, p. 600.

[67] P.E. Schramm, *Der König von Frankreich: Das Wesen der Monarchie vom 9. zum 16. Jahrhundert* (Darmstadt, 1960), pp. 21f. There is a rich recent literature on Judith: see P. Stafford, 'Charles the Bald, Judith and England', in *Charles the Bald: Court and Kingdom*, 2nd edn by M.T. Gibson and J.L. Nelson (British Archaeological Reports: International Series 101, Aldershot, 1990), pp. 139-53 and S.F. Wemple, *Women in Frankish Society: Marriage and the Cloister, 500 to 900* (Philadelphia, 1981), pp. 84, 245f., with further bibliography.

[68] Schramm, 'Ablauf' (as n. 62), p. 80. According to him Adelheid was also not crowned, but that does not take into account her time as Italian queen between 947 and 950. If she was not sacred before her consecration and unction in 962 then that would make the assumption that Edith was anointed more difficult.

[69] Thietmar, *Chronicon* II 3, p. 42. Widukind, *Res gestae Saxonicae* II 41, p. 100, also conceded her a 'regni consortia'.

[70] Thietmar, *Chronicon* I 21, pp. 26f. On the significance of the thirtieth day see H. Herold, 'Der Dreissigste und die rechtsgeschichtliche Bedeutung des Totengedächtnisses', *Zeitschrift für Schweizerisches Recht*, neue Folge 57 (1937), Heft 6.

welfare of Quedlinburg at heart more than anyone else.[71] This again more than hints at rifts in the royal family.

That Mathilda favoured her younger son Henry rather than Otto for the succession is affirmed by several sources: her later *Vita* and Thietmar.[72] One of her reasons for this may have been that he was as yet unmarried, which would have meant that his mother retained much influence, not least of all over his choice of a future queen. Given the exalted status of the Anglo-Saxon princess, the demands and claims made on Henry's behalf – and Mathilda was not alone in pressing them – gain a new significance. Henry and his supporters argued that he, as against Otto, was born in the purple, 'in regali aula natus', that is after Henry I had become king and this idea, in part a Byzantine import, challenged the wish and designation of Henry I.[73] Now, to borrow a Byzantine notion of kingly rank, *porphyrogenesis*, has in itself always seemed a learned gloss to try to explain and justify Henry's conduct. Yet if it set off against Otto I's royal marriage, his new connection with the Anglo-Saxon *stirps regia*, it gains a new meaning and importance. It was the one and only argument that could be mustered to prefer Henry as future king to Otto and his royal wife. As kingship in east Francia now had to be passed on undivided it would be dangerous to undervalue the idea of purple-born status in Henry's defiance of his brother's title.

Our view that there was rivalry between Mathilda and Edith is supported by the evidence of their sponsorship of royal grants. These are usually mentioned in diplomata but some royal gifts could be made without any intervention. It has already been pointed out that in Henry I's lifetime Otto and Edith did not intervene at all except for Otto's necessary consent to the diploma settling the affairs of the Liudolfing house, while Mathilda occurs three times, twice at least very properly in gifts to Westfalian nunneries.[74] After Otto I's accession Mathilda's name vanishes from the diplomata with one exception, a grant to Quedlinburg in 937, until Queen Edith's death on 26 January 946. Then, only three days later, Mathilda's name reappears for the first time in many years on a gift to Quedlinburg, not indeed as sponsor but as a spiritual beneficiary of the elemosynary grant which was also *pro anima dilectissimae coniugis nostre*. Here she was called ostentiously *nostra domina*.[75] She did not intervene in the habitual sense of the word before 954, when the gift, again to Quedlinburg, was funded out of her own dowry.[76] While she lived, Edith had sponsored six

---

[71] D O I 1.

[72] Thietmar, *Chronicon* I 21, p. 28; *Vita Mahthildis reginae (posterior)* c. 6, *MGH SS* 4, p. 287.

[73] M. Lintzel, 'Heinricus natus in aula regali', in idem, *Ausgewählte Schriften*, 2 vols. (Berlin, 1961), vol. 2, pp. 276-82.

[74] DD H I 13 and 41 (Herford), 24 (St Maximin, Trier), 38 (Neuenheerse); the Liudolfing house-diploma is D H I 20.

[75] D O I 18 and 75, this last really not so much an intervention as a donation 'in elemosina domni genitoris nostri Heinrici regis nostraeque dominae ac matris reginae Mahthildae'.

[76] D O I 172.

grants out of sixty-nine, always in conjunction with someone else, not infrequently her son Liudolf.[77] Once, in 942, Otto gave land *pro remedio animae
dilectissimae coniugis nostrae Aedigidis et pro salute filii nostri Liudolfi*,
suggesting faintly that they had been ill or that she had suffered a miscarriage.[78]
Edith's interventions were not numerous – one in every eleven diplomata – set
against Mathilda's almost total exclusion they reinforce the impression that her
coming had brought new tensions to an already troubled family.

Ill-will between mothers-in-law and daughters-in-law can in any case be
found in several generations of the Ottonian house; we may think here of the
difficulties between Adelheid and Theophanu, and it does not seem that
Mathilda had particularly good relations with Otto's second wife, the Burgundian Adelheid. When Adelheid suggested a match between her daughter
Emma by her first marriage to King Lothar of Italy and Mathilda's grandson
Henry the Wrangler, the old queen ruled it out. It would not be a lucky
match.[79] The two *Vitae Mathildis* make it very clear that Mathilda's personal
preferences belonged to and remained with her son Henry and with Henry's
son Henry. Her partiality may have been another reason for the alliance
between and rebellion by Liudolf and Conrad the Red, Otto I's son-in-law.
Neither of her two biographers as much as mentioned Otto's and Edith's
offspring, that is Liudolf and Liudgard, by name. Their histories and memory
were cultivated widely elsewhere, by Hrotsvitha, Adalbert, Liudprand and
Thietmar among others.[80] When Liudolf fell out with his uncle Henry, over his
father's second match, Widukind pointedly observed that he was vulnerable
because he now lacked maternal support; Henry thus exploited Liudolf's
endangered position as the stepson of the new Queen Adelheid, and Liudolf's
grandmother did not relent.[81]

Yet our argument is seemingly contradicted by stories from the *Lives* of
Mathilda, both the earlier *Vita*, dating from the beginning of Otto II's reign,
and the later one, which belongs to the early months of Henry II's accession
and struggle for his kingship. In both these *Vitae* we read that there was indeed
a manifest and glaring estrangement between Otto I (and also his brother
Henry) on one side and the dowager queen on the other. Her lavishness and
expenditure of treasure were regarded as a serious drain on royal resources.

---

[77] D O I 3 for Corvey (with Liudolf), D O I 6, D O I 7 (with Liudolf), D O I 13, D O I 24, D O I
69 (with Liudolf). Most of her interventions fell in the earliest years of Otto's reign. In D O I 6
Edith appeared together with Duke Giselbert of Lotharingia in a donation for Bishop Balderic of
Utrecht in 936.

[78] D O I 50 for St Michael's, Fallersleben.

[79] *Vita Mahthildis* (as n. 72) c. 20, p. 296.

[80] W. Glocker, *Die Verwandten der Ottonen und ihre Bedeutung in der Politik: Studien zur
Familienpolitik und zur Genealogie des sächsischen Kaiserhauses* (Dissertationen zur mittelalterlichen Geschichte 5, Cologne, 1989), pp. 101-19, gives full references; on Liudgard see also below at
n. 127ff.

[81] Widukind, *Res gestae Saxonicae* III 10, p. 110: 'Heinricus autem sciens adulescentem
maternis destitutum suffragiis, contemptui coepit eum habere'. Cf. also Hrotsvitha, *Gesta Ottonis*
(as n. 15) verse 419: 'Acriter orbatum dimittebat Liudulfum'.

Mathilda's servants were attacked and mugged when they carried gifts to churches, and the dowager herself had to abandon the lands which Henry I had given her by his house-order of 929. She returned to her own family lands in Engern in the west where she was free to continue her religious patronage.[82] One can see here how much Otto I's resources and authority in Saxony were concentrated and poised on Ostfalia. After some years of rift and enmity, because things ceased to go well for Otto – here the *Vitae* alluded to the desperate struggles of his regime between 937 and 941 – it was, according to the older biographer, Edith who approached the king and admonished him to make peace with his mother and restore her to her dower. In the later *Vita* a group of bishops and princes went to Edith and asked her to intervene, which she did.[83] It is difficult to determine whether this reconciliation happened some years or only shortly before Edith's death. It took place at Grone, where Otto can be found staying early in December 941.[84] According to the earlier *Vita*, good feeling and charity between mother and sons lasted a good while before Edith died. But if Mathilda received her dower lands again, even as early as 941, she did not, as we have noted, reappear in royal diplomata, even for Quedlinburg before 29 January 946.[85] This in itself suggests that the restoration of peace and goodwill within the closer Liudolfing family group had its limits. Edith's later magnanimity towards Mathilda does not exclude earlier tensions between them, and in any case to have placed the dowager under an obligation was in itself a sign of patronage and superiority. Her intervention suggests also that she herself had been one of the causes of the quarrel.[86]

Edith lived with Otto through the most dangerous years of his reign when he had to fight for his kingship against enemies in Francia, Bavaria and Lotharingia no less than rivals in his own family with their native followers. He was in critical and at times almost desperate situations when it seemed, as Widukind put it, that Saxon rule in the Reich was no longer possible.[87] We do not usually know how queens fared during months of internal warfare, plundering and sieges but there is one stray notice about Edith in Adalbert of St Maximin's *Continuation* of Regino of Prüm's *Chronicle*. Adalbert reported the intense and relentless fighting for the year 939: Otto's siege of Breisach on the upper Rhine while Saxony was being raided by Dukes Giselbert and Eberhard, and then their deaths at Andernach. During all this marching, counter-marching, fighting and siege-warfare, Adalbert tells us, the queen settled in the relative

---

[82] *Vita Mahthildis reginae antiquior* c. 8, *MGH SS* 10, pp. 577-8; *Vita Mahthildis* (as n. 72) c. 11, pp. 290-1. On Mathilda and her lives see P. Corbet, *Les Saints ottoniens: Sainteté dynastique, sainteté royal et sainteté féminine autour de l'an Mil* (Beihefte der Francia 15, Sigmaringen, 1986), especially pp. 30-40, 155-234.

[83] *Vita Mahthildis antiquior* (as n. 82) c. 9, p. 578; *Vita Mahthildis* (as n. 72) c. 12, pp. 291f.

[84] Böhmer-Ottenthal, no. 101a.

[85] See above at n. 75f.

[86] Schmid, 'Neue Quellen' (as n. 20), pp. 413f. n. 71 makes this quite clear, though it is not until 936 that one can speak of 'two queens in the Reich'.

[87] Widukind, *Res gestae Saxonicae* II 24, p. 87: 'nec ultra spes erat regnandi Saxones'.

security of Lorsch Abbey.[88] Later Henry IV, in similar circumstances, left his wife Bertha at Hersfeld. A well-known story about Otto I, which we owe to Liudprand of Cremona, gains a fresh poignancy from this not much noticed chronicle entry. During the siege of Breisach, desertions of bishops and lay nobles began to empty Otto's camp. His chances looked poor and it was dangerous to be caught on the wrong side. A count with a formidable vassalage wanted to explicit the king's plight and sell his aid dearly by demanding the abbey of Lorsch from him as a fief. Liudprand records the story to tell his readers of Otto's unshakable resolve and divinely willed superiority over his opponents, however hard they pressed him. The count received a very rough answer and was told on the authority of Matthew 7:6 that one must not give what is holy to dogs.[89] His demand may have seemed all the more insolent, insulting and intolerable, and so have aroused Otto's much-feared anger, because the queen was sheltering in the abbey. Did Adalbert perhaps know something of the story, since he notes Edith's stay at the monastery?[90] Liudprand's anecdote gains a little in credibility from the stray chronicle notice.

Hrotsvitha has left the fullest lament for Edith's early death. It spoke of her maternal care for her subjects, which she preferred to giving strict orders as a *dominatrix*, yet we are also told that the people heeded her commands. She was the *domna regalis*.[91] We are left in no doubt that she was mourned and that her queenly functions had been real. There were *signa*, miracles, after her death. Even in her piety there appears, precisely because it resembled that of her mother-in-law Mathilda, a certain element of rivalry.[92] According to Thietmar, she fulfilled the role which so often fell to the lot of wives of the great in the tenth century: the duty of intercession. 'All things harmful that happened to him [Otto I] publicly or secretly, he evaded by the grace of divine mercy and the intercession of his very holy wife Edith.'[93] It meant making amends by prayer and almsgiving as well as pleading for those who were in trouble. Above all Thietmar and later Magdeburg tradition credited Edith

---

[88] Adalbert, *Continuatio s.a.* 939, p. 161: 'Interim dum haec, quae prediximus, aguntur, domna Edgid regina Lauresham monasterio commmoratur.'

[89] Liudprand, *Antapodosis* IV 28, pp. 123f.

[90] See especially K. Hauck, 'Erzbischof Adalbert von Magdeburg als Geschichtsschreiber', in *Festschrift für Walter Schlesinger*, 2 vols., ed. H. Beumann (Cologne, 1974), pp. 276-353, here pp. 293-4, 328-9 who convincingly shows that Adalbert wrote after Liudprand.

[91] Hrotsvitha, *Gesta Ottonis* (as n. 15) verses 395-415, pp. 215-16; see also ibid. verse 597, p. 221; the precise phrase *domna regalis* has not been located within the corpus of Hrotsvitha's works. On Edith's sanctity see Corbet, *Saints ottoniens* (as n. 82), pp. 46-50.

[92] *Vita Mahthildis* (as n. 72) c. 19, p. 296 and *Annalista Saxo, MGH SS* 6, p. 600, as well as *Annales Palidenses, MGH SS* 16, p. 62.

[93] Thietmar, *Chronicon* II 3, p. 40; on the mediatory role of queens in the Ottonian and Salian Reich see G. Althoff, 'Königsherrschaft und Konfliktbewältigung im 10. und 11. Jahrhundert', *Frühmittelalterliche Studien*, 23 (1989), pp. 265-90 and T. Reuter, 'Unruhestiftung, Fehde, Rebellion, Widerstand: Gewalt und Frieden in der Politik der Salierzeit', in *Die Salier und das Reich*, 3: *Gesellschaftlicher und ideengeschichtlicher Wandel im Reich der Salier*, ed. S. Weinfurter (Sigmaringen, 1991), pp. 297-325.

with the initiative in the foundation of the monastery which later became the archbishopric. As Magdeburg had been her dowry we may believe that she did more than merely consent to the endowment. According to the Magdeburg annals the relics of Innocentius were sent by King Rudolf of Burgundy to Otto and his queen jointly, a hint not only of her influence but also of the family connection.[94]

Edith had certainly brought a Wessex following to her new home in Saxony, though we cannot find any trace of it in the narrative sources or among the clerks at the Ottonian court, unlike the men who came to the Reich with Henry I's daughter, Mathilda, the wife of the Salian Henry V.[95] According to a later and very dubious source a kinsman and 'chancellor' named Thorketel conducted Edith across the sea and the journey went up the Rhine to Cologne.[96] Yet whoever accompanied her, her presence in Saxony might furnish a possible focus for the exiled and might make her a protectress whose patronage was worth gaining. What this meant is well illustrated by the *Life* of St Dunstan by 'B', which according to some was in fact written by an Old Saxon or at least by someone with connections and experience in the Reich, who had perhaps studied for a time under the Saxon bishop Evrachar, a disciple of Brun of Cologne's, in Liège.[97] Dunstan, he relates, had powerful enemies at the court of King Edmund, who successfully engineered his expulsion and deprivation. Then we read in the *Vita* the story of Edmund's narrow escape from death in the Cheddar Gorge: how his horse nearly plunged down a precipice. But the king in the last moment confessed his offence again the holy man and was saved so that he could make amends. Yet the *Vita*, perhaps not unwittingly,

---

[94] Thietmar, *Chronicon* II 3, p. 40: 'Cuius instinctu Magadaburgiensem aedificare coepit civitatem', he wrote somewhat confusingly. In the *Annales Magdeburgenses* we read: 'Eodem tempore praedictus rex instinctu et petitione coniugis suae Edith reginae abbaciam regalem intra urbem Magdeburg fundavit', *MGH SS* 16, p. 143 where we also find: 'Cuius corpus Rodoulfus rex Burgundionum ei ac reginae transmissum, regium immo divinum munus donavit', that is the relics of St Innocent. See on this also D O I 14 (21 September 937), the foundation of the house at Magdeburg: 'Ob memoriam patris nostri et pro remedio ipsius animae nostrique et coniugis nostrae, cuius et praedictus locus dos fuit', and compare D O I 15 (27 September 937). Mathilda is conspicuously not named in the 'pro remedio'-passus.
[95] Hrotsvitha, *Gesta Ottonis* (as n.15) verses 109f.: 'Praedictam sociis domnam comitantibus aptis/ Trans mare percerte summo direxit honore'. For Henry V's treatment of Mathilda's entourage see K.J. Leyser, 'England and the Empire in the Early Twelfth Century', in idem, *Medieval Germany*, p. 195.
[96] *Historia monasterii Croylandensis Ingulpho adscripta*, a paragraph in *MGH SS* 10, p. 460. See also above at n. 37.
[97] *Vita Sancti Dunstani auctore B.*, in *Memorials of St Dunstan, Archbishop of Canterbury*, ed. W. Stubbs (Rolls Series 63, London, 1874), pp. 3-52. On 'B' see his letter ibid., pp. 385-8 and Stubbs' introduction, pp. xxxiiff. According to A. Gransden, *Historical Writing in England c. 550– c. 1307* (London, 1974), p. 78, he was a Flemish monk or cleric; according to M. Lapidge, 'The Hermeneutic Style in Tenth-Century Anglo-Latin Literature', *Anglo-Saxon England*, 4 (1975), pp. 67-111, here p. 81 and n. 2 he was an Englishman, a case made more fully in idem, 'B. and the *Vita S. Dunstani*', in idem, *Anglo-Latin Literature, 900-1066* (London, 1992), pp. 279-91, especially pp. 281-7, where it is argued that B. wrote in exile at Liège and hoped by so doing to be able to return to England.

gives us a glimpse of another and far less miraculous reason for Dunstan's restoration to favour and indeed his advance to the abbacy over the royal sanctuary at Glastonbury. There were at this time important visitors at Edmund's court, envoys from the *regnum oriens*, that is the east Frankish kingdom and its ruler Otto I.[98] To them Dunstan turned in his distress, and they promised him all the amenities of their kingdom if he came with them as an exile. The date must be 943 or a little earlier, the year when Dunstan entered upon his charge. Edith was then alive and Otto I's queen. The Saxon king had just given proof that he could have the better of his enemies and his alliance was, as we shall see, needed by Edmund. Edith and Otto as the protectors of disaffected and malcontent refugees from the Wessex court and Edmund's regime were dangerous. This was one of the consequences and risks of prestigious princely marriages abroad, a reason perhaps why Charlemagne angrily refused to allow one of his daughters to marry Offa's son.[99]

The Ottonian match of 930 had another important bearing on the Reich's relationships with its neighbours. It brought the Liudolfings into a whole network of connections and with one stroke gave them an international standing, we could say, in the newly forming post-Carolingian order. In the ninth century, great princely families had measured themselves against one another by their links and affinity with the Carolingian *stirps*. Some, like the Liudolfings, had such links and remembered them. Others, their rivals, had not. The Carolingians were still there in the tenth century but they no longer constituted the sole hard currency and standard of comparison. Athelstan's other half-sisters were married to Charles III (the 'Simple'), Duke Hugh the Great, the Capetian, and, allegedly, an Aquitanian *dux*, whose identification has caused as much difficulty as the husband of the Aelfgifu who had been sent with Edith to Germany.[100] Edith's sisters and half-sisters thus gave her Saxon father-in-law and his family a hitherto undreamed-of place and wide affinities among the leading princes of western Europe, partly even before the marriages of Otto I's two sisters did so, beginning with Gerberga's match with Giselbert of Lotharingia in 929. Wessex in the early tenth century thus became the pivot of western and central European alliances.[101]

How important their Wessex connections were to the Ottonians can be seen not only from the embassies that trafficked to and fro between England and the Reich in the 940s but also from the consternation and distress caused by Edith's relatively early death. No source reveals its cause; it was sudden and seemingly unexpected. The wives of the Ottonian rulers with this one exception outlived their husbands. The news reached the king while he was out

[98] *Vita Sancti Dunstani auctore B.* (as n. 97) c. 13, p. 23 and Stubbs' introduction, pp. xvif.

[99] J.M. Wallace-Hadrill, 'Charlemagne and England', in idem, *Early Medieval History* (Oxford, 1975), pp. 155-80, here pp. 161-2.

[100] The various hypothetical identifications, none satisfactory, are discussed by Poole, 'Alpine Son-In-Law' (as n. 51), p. 117 n. 2 and Keynes, 'Athelstan's Books' (as n. 40), p. 191 n. 232.

[101] Leyser, 'Byzantine-Western Relationships' (as n. 46).

trying to refresh himself a little with hunting.[102] It is remarkable how frequently we find husbands and wives in the early middle ages separated from one another at the great crises of their life together. Once again the *Life* of St Dunstan by 'B' gives us some shadowy but startling evidence of Otto's plans after his bereavement. It comes from a vision of Dunstan's in 946 shortly before the murder of King Edmund at Pucklechurch on May 26. He again saw an envoy from the *regnum oriens* with a large *rotulus*, who talked to him in a Saxon voice and mentioned that he had certain secrets to discuss with the king, 'quaedam nuptialis verbi secreta', in other words he had come to arrange another marriage alliance now that Edith had died.[103] When his coming had been announced to the king and the envoy was to be brought to his presence he could not be found anywhere, and on the same day Edmund was slain. Our evidence hangs by a slender thread, especially as in one manuscript of the *Vita* we read *nuntialis* instead of *nuptialis*, though this makes very little sense. It is quite possible that Otto and his circle wanted to renew the alliance and once again strengthen it by a marriage. Nothing came of this after Edmund's murder but in 949 we find Wessex envoys from the new King Eadred arriving in Aachen for Easter where Gerberga, now the wife of the west Frankish king Louis IV d'Outremer, met her brother Otto I to seek help against domestic enemies, especially the Capetian Duke Hugh the Great.[104] The latter too was now Otto's brother-in-law. About the purpose of this embassy we are not informed, but it is worth remembering that Otto had not yet remarried.

For some years at least the alliance between the Ottonians and the kings of Wessex had, in fact, a quasi-political content and this, ironically, was the fate and well-being of the Carolingian ruler of France. Louis d'Outremer's father had ended his days as the prisoner of his enemy, Herbert of Vermandois, in 929 but his Anglo-Saxon wife and his son had taken refuge in England. When the west Frankish princes wished to restore him in 937, Athelstan demanded oaths and guarantees from them, especially from the *dux Francorum*, Hugh. Two years later he sent a fleet to help Louis d'Outremer. It ravaged the coast by Ponthieu and the estuary of the Somme 'and did none of the business for which it had come', as Flodoard dryly observed.[105] Some years later, when the Carolingians had become a prisoner first of the Normans and then of Duke Hugh the Great, only Anglo-Saxon and Ottonian pressures can be said to have saved him from the fate of his father and preserved for him a viable powerbase. This was the *casus foederis* for Otto and Edmund in the spring of 946, when Gerberga begged desperately for help from both of them.[106] The death of Edmund and Eadred's precarious position in Northumbria shifted the main

---

[102]Thietmar, *Chronicon* II 4, p. 42.

[103]*Vita Sancti Dunstani auctore B*. (as n. 97) c. 33, pp. 45f. and p. xvii of Stubbs' introduction.

[104]Flodoard, *Annales*, p. 122 und Richer, *Historiae*, vol. 1, p. 274.

[105]Flodoard, *Annales s.a.* 937, 939, pp. 68-9, 73 (the quotation in the text).

[106]Ibid *s.a.* 946, pp. 101f. and Richer, *Historiae* II 49 and 50, vol. 1, pp. 207-10. P. Lauer, *Le Règne de Louis IV d'Outre-Mer* (Bibliothèque de l'École des Hautes Études 127, Paris, 1900), pp. 139ff., 144ff.

burden of intervention on behalf of the west Frankish Carolingian on to Otto's and Saxon shoulders.

The Flodoard passage mentioning the Anglo-Saxon embassy to Aachen in 949 and its echo in Richer's *History* is the last continental source I can find for Wessex diplomatic traffic to the Ottonian Reich.[107] There are no references or reports of English ambassadors in any of the later Ottonian sources, for example the Quedlinburg annals, which took such pleasure in reciting all the foreign missions that arrived to offer their respects, treasures and gifts to Otto III and Henry II. But they confined themselves largely to generalities, and we do not know whether there were Anglo-Saxons among the visitors from all Europe in 919 or 1021.[108] In the latter year it is doubtful, for Cnut's and Henry's interests in Sclavinia clashed, and it was Conrad II who was the first to get on friendly terms with the northern ruler.[109] Thietmar of Merseburg not infrequently heard news from England: he knew in a garbled way of St Ælfheah's martyrdom, of the ravages of Swein Forkbeard and the regime of Cnut; he even mentioned 'a certain place' called London, *urbem quandam nomine Lundunam*; and he cited an Anglo-Saxon informant, named Sewald, for the Danes' maltreatment of the archbishop, whom like the writer of the St Ursula *passio* he mistook for St Dunstan.[110] Yet there is no evidence that his informant had come as an envoy on an official mission to Saxony. He may have been a refugee.

The English sources are a little more expansive, at any rate for Edgar's reign. Here the arrival of foreign embassies to honour the king with precious gifts is part of a well-established canon to sing the praises of a great ruler and extol his prestige. In Florence of Worcester we read that the kings of many peoples honoured him out of fear of him or because of affection for his wisdom, *strenuitas* and generosity. The emperor Otto I 'who had his aunt as wife', is the only one designated by name. He sent presents and concluded a treaty of peace with him.[111] Closer and richer information comes from Byrhtferth's *Vita Oswaldi*. Here we read that Edgar sent an abbot Aetherius and a thegn Wulfmaer to the emperor and that they brought back even more wonderful gifts than they had taken as well as a *pactum pacis*.[112] What are we to understand by this phrase? It meant almost certainly that the partners to the agreement bound themselves to treat one another's *fideles* and subjects, for instance merchants, benevolently and perhaps also on engagement not to

[107]Levison, 'Werden der Ursula-Legende' (as n. 15), p. 144.

[108]*Annales Quedlinburgenses, MGH SS* 3, pp. 68, 86.

[109]Bresslau, *Konrad II.*, vol. 1, pp. 101-4.

[110]Thietmar, *Chronicon* VII 36, 37, 39, 40-3, VIII 7, pp. 442, 444, 446-50, 502. Thietmar also knew about Danegeld: ibid. VII 36, p. 442. For Dunstan see ibid. VII 42, p. 448 and Levison, 'Werden der Ursula-Legende' (as n. 15), p. 144.

[111]Ibid.

[112]*Vita Sancti Oswaldi auctore anonymo* c. 4, in *The Historians of the Church of York and its Archbishops*, ed. J. Raine, 3 vols. (Rolls Series 71, London, 1879), vol. 1, p. 435. On the oldest *Vita* see Gransden, *Historical Writing* (as n. 97), pp. 8, 80-7; M. Lapidge, 'Byrhthferth and the Vita s. Ecgwini', *Medieval Studies*, 41 (1979), pp. 331-53, here pp. 333, 341-2.

favour and help on another's enemies should these seek refuge at the contracting party's court. In the *Vita Oswaldi* too, Edgar's relations with the emperor form a category apart; they are not included under the foreign embassy topos. Here the show of respect emanated from Edgar, and we do not hear of an imperial return embassy. That the English king's envoys came back with even more valuable presents than they had taken seems to gloss over this defect.[113]

Can Edgar's embassy to the emperor be dated? The thegn Wulfmaer received a grant from the king in 973, and the mission is reported in the *Vita Oswaldi* just before the account of Oswald's journey to Rome in 972 to receive the pallium for his new archiepiscopal dignity.[114] That was more than a routine visit and according to Eadmer's *Life of Oswald* he also went to Rome to discuss *negotia regni* with the pope.[115] Let us also note from the tenth-century *Vita* that Oswald, just like Bishop Coenwald of Worcester in 929, scattered wealth lavishly en route: huge amounts of silver pennies were given away in charity at churches, abbeys, *civitates* and castles. The tenth-century English kings deliberately flaunted their wealth and so propagated their standing in Europe here, for it is unlikely that Oswald spent his own in this way.[116] There then follows in the *Vita* the account of Edgar's great royal ritual, the coronation and unction at Bath in Whitsun 973.[117] We can also narrow the date of the embassy to the emperor by some of Oswald's monastic appointments in the *Vita*.[118] Everything points to the autumn of 972, when Otto I had at last returned northwards after nearly six years in Italy, staying at St Gallen, the Reichenau, then Ingelheim where a synod was held, and at Frankfurt on his way.[119] If the embassy from England reached him there it would explain why the English are missing from the catalogue of the throng of envoys which waited upon Otto I and Otto II early in 973 in Saxony, at Magdeburg where they kept Palm Sunday, at Quedlinburg, the customary venue for Easter, and at Merseburg where they spent Ascension Day. According to Widukind, the Quedlinburg and the Altaich annals, there were Romans, Greeks, Beneventans, Italians, Hungarians, Danes, Slavs, Bulgars and Russians *cum magnis muneribus*. At

---

[113] J. Hannig, 'Ars donandi: Zur Ökonomie des Schenkens im früheren Mittelalter', in *Armut, Liebe, Ehre: Studien zur historischen Kulturforschung*, ed. R. van Dülmen (Frankfurt, 1988), pp. 11-37, shows that this would in fact imply inferiority; see also K.J. Leyser, 'The German Aristocracy from the Ninth to the Twelfth Centuries', in idem, *Medieval Germany*, p. 180.

[114] Wulfmaer's grant: P. Sawyer, *Anglo-Saxon Charters. An Annotated List and Bibliography* (Royal Historical Society Guides and Handbooks 8, London, 1968), no. 793. The text is in *Cartularium Saxonicum*, ed. W. de Gray Birch, 3 vols. (London, 1893), vol. 3, pp. 605f. no. 1291.

[115] *Vita Sancti Oswaldi* (as n. 112) c. 4, pp. 435-6; Eadmer, *Vita Sancti Oswaldi Eboracensis Episcopi et Confessoris* c. 22, in *Historians of the Church of York* (as n. 112) vol. 2, p. 27.

[116] *Vita sancti Oswaldi* (as n. 112), c. 4, pp. 435-6; for Coenwald see above n. 37.

[117] *Vita Sancti Oswaldi* (as n. 112) c. 4, pp. 436-8. On Edgar's coronation and unction in Bath at Whitsun 973 see J. L. Nelson, 'Inauguration Rituals', in *Early Medieval Kingship*, ed. P. Sawyer and I. Wood (Leeds, 1977), pp. 50-71, here pp. 63-70.

[118] *Vita Sancti Oswaldi* (as n. 112) c. 4, p. 435: 'Eodem tempore mira direxit munera Imperatori'. On Oswald's reforming measures and appointments see E. John, 'St Oswald and the Church of Worcester', in idem, *Orbis Britanniae and other Studies* (Leicester, 1966), pp. 234-48.

[119] Köpke-Dümmler, *Otto der Große*, pp. 488-93, 497f.

Merseburg there were also north African envoys from the Fatimid cali-phate.[120] Only the English are missing from the Ottonian sources. Was this merely because they had already called in the autumn of 972?

The account of their embassy in the *Vita Oswaldi* also precedes, as we have noted, the solemn, elaborate and by no means easily understood report of Edgar's coronation and anointing at Bath at Whitsun 973. This again is significant.[121] The Wessex embassy to Otto I and Otto II must be seen, like Oswald's journey, as a preparation for the Bath solemnities. Edgar's corona-tion had very distance imperial overtones. His was an *imperium* in England, and he wanted to be seen as an equal of the Ottonians in ritual no less than in the exercise of overlordship. The envoys may have come to inform themselves about imperial styles and ceremonial or to confirm that their own were of equal standing. Oswald, the thegn Wulfmær and Abbot Aetherius (whom I have not succeeded in identifying) must have heard about the coronation and anointing of Theophanu, Otto II's Byzantine bride, by Pope John XIII in Rome at Easter 972 and we know that Edgar's second wife, Ælfthryth, the mother of Æthelred II, received the *benedictio* and, to go by later evidence, the full ritual of coronation and anointing in 973.[122] She was the first native Anglo-Saxon queen to do so. The silence of the Ottonian writers about the English envoys of the *BASILEUS totius Albionis*, when so many other embassies are proudly recited, may conceal an element of displeasure about the rivalry and *imitatio imperii* to be enacted in Bath.[123]

Originally the English connection had attracted the Ottonians and furnished them with a valuable authentication of their own very recent kinship. By now, however, the orientation of the Saxon Reich had changed. Anglo-Saxon perspectives were replaced by the Burgundian-Italian ones of Otto I's second wife Adelheid, and also by the dialogue with Byzantium and the vast ethnic welter and economic pull of Sclavinia, Kievan Russia and the Bulgars. At the same time the Old Saxons had made more than good, and the imperial connection, as it had now become, rang very agreeably and genially in the ears of the Anglo-Saxon chroniclers and biographers wishing to sing the praises of

---

[120] Böhmer-Ottenthal, nos. 562d and 567a.

[121] As suggested in Böhmer-Zimmermann, no. 505.

[122] For Theophanu see '*Theophanu Imperatrix*', below, p. 158; for Ælfthryth and Anglo-Saxon queenship see P. Stafford, *Queens, Concubines and Dowagers: The King's Wife in the Early Middle Ages* (London, 1983), pp. 127-33 and her bibliographical postscript, 'Judith' (as n. 67), pp. 152-3; J.L. Nelson, 'The Second English Ordo', in eadem, *Politics and Ritual in Early Medieval Europe* (London, 1986), pp. 361-74, here pp. 367, 372-4, accepts possible influence, but argues that Wessex may already have known the sacering of queens in the early tenth century. The *Vita Sancti Oswaldi* (as n. 112) c. 4, pp. 436-8 is difficult to interpret here. A much later witness is the letter to Eadmer, *Memorials of St Dunstan* (as n. 97) no. 36, pp. 422ff. The writer, Nicholas, was a monk in Worcester. He referred to the *auctoritas* 'tam cronicarum quam carminum, quae ea tempestate a doctis patria lingua composita de his noscuntur'.

[123] On the titles see H. Kleinschmidt, *Untersuchungen über das englische Königtum im 10. Jahrhundert* (Göttinger Bausteine zur Geschichtswissenschaft 49, Göttingen, 1979), pp. 33-105, especially p. 41 for examples of the title given above.

Edgar. They now sought the imperial touch, the evidence and manifestations of contact on equal terms.

There remains Ealdorman Æthelweard. There is something strangely one-sided in his address to Mathilda of Essen. He said nothing about the other descendants of Edith, her daughter Liudgard, her son Liudolf and above all Mathilda's brother, Otto who became duke of both Suabia and Bavaria under the emperor Otto II. Otto was the donor, or with his sister the joint donor, of one of Essen's magnificent processional crosses, the choicest of the monastery's treasures. Here Florence of Worcester and the Abingdon version of the *Chronicle* were more eloquent.[124] Florence mentioned Liudolf's tomb in St Alban at Mainz, and the Abingdon *Chronicle* not only gave a tempered account of the battle of Cotrone in 982, where Otto II's army was almost destroyed by Saracens of Sicily – in the Abingdon version it was an Ottonian victory – but it also reported Duke Otto's early death in the same year. 'He was the son of the *aetheling* Liudolf and this Liudolf was the son of Otto the Elder by the daughter of King Edward', so the chronicler wrote. According to one scholar it was Æthelweard who furnished and directed this part of the *Chronicle* and he would have Mathilda stand behind this report.[125] It is not impossible, though Æthelweard had asked for different information. Duke Otto left no descendants and as far as is known had not yet married when the exertions of the disastrous south Italian campaign killed him at Lucca. The male descent from Edith seems to have ended with him. Mathilda, abbess of Essen, outlived her brother for nearly thirty years, like so many sisters in religion. Æthelweard may of course have talked about Liudolf and Otto in those parts of his correspondence with his kinswoman which he mentions but which has not come down to us.[126]

Even stranger is the absence of any reference to Liudgard in the Anglo-Saxon sources. She died in 953. We know very little about the marriages of tenth-century women, but in this case we are told that her union with Conrad the Red and her life were unhappy.[127] Once, it is reported, a certain Cono boasted of illicit intercourse with her, and the slander had to be refuted by the wager of a judicial duel. Whatever Liudgard's personal life and fate, she was the ancestress of the Salian house which is thus linked to Edith and has a partly Anglo-Saxon origin. Yet, strange to say, there are no echoes or awareness of

---

[124] *Florentii Wigorniensis Chronicon* (as n. 14), pp 136 (Liudolf's death and burial), 147 (battle with the Saracens, death of Duke Otto and his descent from Edward the Elder); cf. *Anglo-Saxon Chronicle* (as n. 14), pp. 232f. and n. 1; L. Whitbread, 'Æthelweard and the Anglo-Saxon Chronicle', *EHR*, 74 (1959), pp. 577-89.

[125] Whitbread, 'Æthelweard' (as n. 124), pp. 579, 583-4.

[126] *Aethelweard* (as n. 4), p. 1, mentioned in his prologue a letter from Mathilda which he had received and an earlier letter to her which he had written; for a discussion see Van Houts, 'Women and the Writing of History' (as n. 4), pp. 63-4.

[127] Köpke-Dümmler, *Otto der Große*, p. 228 and n. 4.

this in the eleventh-century imperial sources.[128] The reason for this may have been that the venerable royal house of Wessex had now been laid low and lived scattered in exile, at least those members of it who had escaped Cnut. Besides, a new and more recent marriage connection between the rulers of England and the Salians now commanded all the attention of the Reich's historians, the alliance between Cnut's and Emma's daughter Gunnhilde and Conrad II's son and successor Henry III in 1036.[129] Edward the Confessor's accession in 1043 was graced by an embassy with presents from Henry. His *Vita* recorded this as coming from an emperor of the Romans although Henry had not yet been crowned. Yet the biographer's explanation of this honour is the recent match: 'He had married the sister [really half-sister] of the same King Edward'.[130] The Salian also enjoyed the help of Edward the Confessor's fleet in his war against Count Baldwin of Flanders in 1049.[131] Edward took station with his ships at Sandwich while Henry invaded and laid waste part of Baldwin's lordships. Henry III in turn proved himself as an ally and as a friend of Edward's in 1054 when Bishop Ealdred of Worcester was sent to Cologne, where he spent a whole year arranging for the return of Edmund Ironside's son from Hungary to England.[132] These connections may well have been founded on a sense of family relationship both recent and going back to a distant past.

We have by no means exhausted the subject of Anglo-Ottonian relationships. It had other dimensions which should be more than mentioned: monastic reform, manuscript illumination, architecture, trade and currency. It is now known that German, including Old-Saxon, moneyers struck coins and worked in English mints under Edgar.[133] Here attention is to be drawn to two hitherto not much noticed links, one from Edgar's time and on of around the turn of the century. Both the poem in the *Chronicle* and William of Malmesbury in the *Gesta Regum* record a tradition of blame, a grave flaw in Edgar's rule: that he favoured and entertained foreigners to excess.[134] The most characteristic and crisis-prone feature of the late Saxon polity was undoubtedly the presence of

---

[128]Perhaps because the circle of Conrad II chose to stress his maternal ancestry rather than his Ottonian descent through his father; cf. Wipo, *Gesta Chuonradi* c. 2, in *Wiponis Opera*, ed. H. Bresslau (MGH SRG 61, Hanover, 1915), pp. 15-16.

[129]Böhmer-Appelt, nos. 225c and 238c. Note her renaming as Cunigunde, by contrast with Edith, whose name was in fact a testimony to her desired origins.

[130]*The Life of King Edward the Confessor who Rests at Westminster* c. 1, 2nd edn by F. Barlow (Oxford Medieval Texts, Oxford, 1992), p. 16.

[131]'Florence' of Worcester, *Chronicon* (as n. 14), p. 201; *The Anglo-Saxon Chronicle, 1041-1154* in *English Historical Documents*, 2: *1042-1189*, ed. D.C. Douglas and G.W. Greenaway, 2nd edn, (London, 1981), pp. 116f.

[132]F. Barlow, *Edward the Confessor* (London, 1970), pp. 214-17; G. Ronay, *The Lost King of England: The East European Adventures of Edward the Exile* (Woodbridge, 1989, pp. 125-35 (to be used with caution).

[133]O. von Feilitzen and C. Blunt, 'Personal Names in the Coinage of Edgar', in *England Before the Conquest: Studies in Primary Sources Presented to Dorothy Whitelock*, ed. P. Clemoes and K. Hughes (Cambridge, 1971), pp. 183-214, here pp. 208f.

[134]*The Anglo-Saxon Chronicle* (as n. 14) *s.a.* 959, p. 225; William of Malmesbury, *Gesta Regum* II 148, vol. 1, p. 165.

military and naval forces maintained by taxation close to the royal court. It appears to go back to Edgar, known somewhat misleadingly as the 'peaceable', who kept up an enormous fleet and seems to have retained in his service, his *familia*, to borrow William of Malmesbury's expression, large numbers of men from outside his kingdoms. His wealth and patronage attracted them and they included continental Saxons, not to mention also heathen Danes. William wrote that the Saxons' uncouth ferocity set a bad example to the natives.[135] From this passage in the *Gesta Regum* and the *Chronicle* it is quite clear that the men who came were warriors, nobles to whom the prospects of service with Edgar seemed better than their chances under the Ottonians or their margraves in eastern Saxony. We know that their *imperium* opened career opportunities and hopes of land and treasure in that feud-ridden society. For every 'in' there was an enemy and an 'out'. Migration and exile were common enough. Later we find Saxons in the service of the emperor Henry II's hard adversary, the Polish duke Boleslas Chrobry.[136] In the tenth century they were evidently attracted to the court and service of Edgar. The *pactum pacis* was thus not without its purpose and meaning.[137]

A second excursion into the unexpected leads us to a well-known, much discussed and often-cited legislative text, *IV Aethelred*, about the tolls due from the traders coming to London.[138] Its date is disputed but cannot vary much outside the late tenth and early eleventh century. Among the merchants who had to display their wares we find men from Rouen, Flanders, Ponthieu, *Francia* (perhaps the Île-de-France here) and then Huy, Liège and Nivelles in Lotharingia which was under Ottonian rule. Distinguished from them all and evidently enjoying a special and more privileged status were the *homines imperatoris* and we hear much about what they brought to London and also about the customary gifts they had to present at Christmas and Easter. These throw some light on what they marketed. They gave two lengths of grey cloth, one of brown, ten pounds of pepper, five pairs of gauntlets and two kegs of vinegar twice a year. What is arresting here but has so far not attracted any special comment are the twenty pounds of pepper. It seems a sizeable amount and suggests that this essential spice was brought in bulk to England by the men of the emperor, the merchants under his protection. At this point comparisons of scale and quantity might be of help. Pepper was a valuable commodity, almost a form of currency and treasure in the early middle ages.

---

[135]Ibid., p. 165.

[136]Saxon warriors marched with Boleslas Chrobry against Kiev in 1014 and 1018; according to Thietmar there were 300 such participants on the profitable expedition of 1018 and they ('nostrates') were feared by the natives. There were also Saxons permanently in Boleslas's service, for example Erich, who came to him after having committed a killing, was then captured by Henry II and fell in the course of the Russian expedition of 1018. Thietmar, *Chronicon* VI 91, VII 16, VIII 31-3, pp. 382, 418, 528-32.

[137]On the *pactum pacis* see above at n. 112.

[138]*IV Aethelred* 2, 8-10, in Liebermann, *Gesetze der Angelsachsen* (as n. 6), vol. 1, pp. 234f. On this text see P. Wormald, 'Aethelred the Lawmaker', in *Ethelred the Unready* (as n.1), pp. 47-80, here pp. 62f.

Bede mentioned it first of all among the precious possessions he keep in a coffer and was anxious to distribute on his death-bed.[139] St Boniface received a present of two pounds of pepper from a cardinal deacon.[140] About the year 1000, very close in other words to the date of *IV Aethelred*, rich Venetian merchants had to give one pound of pepper to the *magister camerae* of the royal court at Pavia once a year when they visited the city.[141] In London it later became policy to confine the German importers to the bulk trade. They had to sell pepper and other wares in quantities of no less than twenty-five pounds, so that the retail business should remain in native hands.[142]

Where in the Reich could all this pepper have come from? Fortunately there is a source which gives us a lead. It is the economic reconnaissance report of Ibrahim-ibn-Jacub who came from the Cordovan caliphate and travelled extensively in western Europe, the Ottonian Reich and Sclavania during the 960s and early 970s.[143] He even met Otto I and conversed with him, perhaps in Merseburg in 973 when some Bulgars whom he also mentions visited Otto's court. Ibrahim has left a very elaborate description of the city of Mainz and its market and he was particularly astonished by the variety of spices from the near east that could be bought there. He spoke of pepper in the first place and also of a rare Arab coin he found in circulation.[144] It would seem then that Mainz was a considerable emporium where imported spices, not least of all pepper, were marketed. It was certainly one of the principal toll stations in the Ottonian Reich where few enjoyed exemption. If we ask whence the pepper had come to Mainz, there is good evidence that it was carried through Venice. The Venetians traded extensively in spices in the tenth century as we saw from the dues they had to pay to the *magister camerae* of the palace at Pavia: pounds of pepper, cinnamon, ginger and galingale were the foremost commodities they owed. That they continued to sell these to German merchants can be inferred from a stray autograph entry in Thietmar of Merseburg's *Chronicon*. Four large Venetian ships loaded with spices were lost at sea in 1017. Would Thietmar have troubled to mention this if their cargo did not interest him and how had he heard ?[145] It can be shown, moreover, that Mainz merchants went to Venice in the tenth century and knew their way about there.[146] We also know that Magdeburg merchants traded with and may have visited England

[139]Letter from Cuthbert to Cuthwin on the death of Bede, *Venerabilis Baedae Historiam Ecclesiasticam...*, ed. C. Plummer, vol. 1 (Oxford, n.d.), p. clxiii.

[140]*Epistola* 62, ed. Tangl (as n. 3), p. 128; see also nos. 49 and 80, pp. 84, 189.

[141]*Instituta regalia et ministeria camerae regum Longobardorum et Honorantiae civitatis Papie* c. 5, *MGH SS* 30/2, 1453.

[142]*Libertas Londoniensis* 8, 2, in *Gesetze der Angelsachsen* (as n.6), vol. 1, p. 675 and *Liber Custumarum*, in *Monumenta Gildhallae Londoniensis*, ed. H.T. Riley, 4 vols. (Rolls Series 12, London, 1860) vol. 2 pt. 1, pp. 61f.

[143]A. Miquel, 'L'Europe occidentale dans la relation arabe d'Ibrâhîm b. Ya'qûb (Xe s.)', *Annales ESC*, 21 (1966), pp. 1048-64; Wattenbach-Holtzmann-Schmale, vol. 3, p. 14*.

[144]Miquel, 'Relation arabe' (as n. 143), pp. 1059f.

[145]Thietmar, *Chronicon* VII 76, p. 492 (an entry in Thietmar's own hand).

[146]Liudprand, *Antapodosis* VI 4 and 6, pp. 153f., 155.

because they, who were exempt from most tolls and customs elsewhere, had to pay at Thiel, the main exit port to England situated on the lower Lek. At least they brought their wares there, which the merchants of Thiel, the experts in the crossing, then conveyed over the North Sea.[147]

Let us attempt a conclusion. Anglo-Ottonian relations in the tenth century have more than one theme. They were complex and lay in several spheres which did not always intersect. For the Liudolfings the marriage alliance with the royal house of Wessex furnished a badly needed authentication of their own all too recent kingship in the east Frankish Reich. It was at the same time a confirmation and even a justification of a specially Saxon kingship. Even if the queen was not yet *consors regni* in Wessex itself, and did not as yet have a defined position in east Francia, Edith brought her exalted and holy descent with her to a society which carefully weighed up and esteemed cognatic as well as agnatic ancestry.[148] Otto must have been concerned to stress his wife's royal descent as much as possible; even if the marriage did not immediately and *ipso facto* secure his succession to the kingship it did much to raise his standing within his own house, among the Saxon nobility and in the Reich. The Liudolfing marriage into the royal family of Wessex gave Henry I important new family connections with the princely families of western Europe, even though the Carolingians were not at the time ruling in west Francia, and these links of *affinitas* may have made the marriage alliances of Otto's own sisters easier. All these things as well as the substantial treasures brought by the ambassadors and the bride herself fell to the Ottonians' advantage. For the house of Wessex the marriage was but an enlargement of its already formidable tradition and network of European connections. Yet it also reinforced a sense of kinship to which St Boniface had borne witness. It is also possible that Athelstan's connections with the Saxon kings were directed against the Danes; this at least is suggested by a dark and out-of-the-way passage in Ekkehard IV's *Casus sancti Galli*.[149] In the eleventh century under Cnut it was the future of the Scandinavian north and its conversion, questions of church organisation and of influence there, which dominated relations between the Empire and the Anglo-Saxon kingdom, which we can now no longer call in essence a kingdom of Wessex. The Ottonians were here dealing with a continental power. The last Liudolfing ruler, Henry II, lived to experience this dangerous development, though he could do little to direct its course. Thietmar's Anglo-Saxon informant may have been a refugee from Aethelred's England.

Edith's entry into the Ottonian family circle added to and intensified its tensions. Whether she wanted to or not she stood at the centre of the struggle for the kingship which filled Otto I's early years. Her presence may have made

---

[147]DD O II 112, 140; K.J. Leyser, 'Ottonian Government', *EHR*, 96 (1981), pp. 721-53, here pp. 739f. (Leyser, *Medieval Germany,* pp. 87-8).

[148]For the political role of Ottonian queens and the status of *consors regni/imperii* see 'Theophanu Imperatrix', below, pp. 158-60, with references. For the possible effects of Anglo-Saxon on continental queenship and vice versa see above at nn. 67, 122.

[149]Ekkehard, *Casus sancti Galli* c. 81, ed. H.F. Haefele (ADGQ 10, Darmstadt, 1980), p. 170.

it easier for Lotharingia, Frankish, Suabian and Bavarian dukes to bow to him but she may also have been the unwilling cause of Henry's murderous plots against his brother. For a number of years the alliance between the Ottonians and Wessex was of great importance in rescuing the west Frankish Carolingians from the oppressive preponderance of Hugh the Great and his allies and preserving a power-base for them. The marriage between Conrad, duke of Lotharingia, and Liudgard, Edith's daughter, also underlines this aspect of the alliance. The ambassadors from Wessex must have met not only Otto and his sister, the west Frankish queen Gerberga, in Aachen in 949, but also Conrad and probably Liudgard as well.[150] Yet later on the centre of gravity of Ottonian rule shifted and the Anglo-Saxon connection became less important as Otto's brother Brun, archbishop of Cologne and duke of Lotharingia, succeeded in bringing west Frankish affairs under control using Lotharingian resources alone. In Otto's last years it was the king of Wessex and Mercia, Edgar, who wanted to display his own imperial claims in a conscious appropriation of Ottonian practice. As we sought to show, it is probable that Edith shared the sacral dignity of her husband in coronation and unction, and this may have had an effect on the position of the Anglo-Saxon queen.

The *pax* and *amicitia* which made up the substance of most embassies reflected the very real risks of marriage alliances abroad. They provided domestic enemies with refuges and possible bases for a come-back. Exile was a common lot among the nobilities and princely families of early medieval Europe and its heroic literature. Not the least important feature of the Liudolfing-Wessex alliance lay in the exchange of gifts and the visible access of standing and renown which rulers conferred on one another and their ever-expectant followers by these exchanges. Nor must we ignore the arrival of the St Ursula cult at Cologne with its English connections; Cologne was almost the hub of Anglo-German relations throughout the middle ages. The vogue of the St Oswald cult in Saxon cloisters gave depth and dimension to Hrotsvitha's eagerness to welcome Edith as the descendant of the Northumbrian warrior king and martyr.

Much depended on the survival of relatives, as we can see from Aethelweard's letter to Mathilda. Edith's death twenty-seven years before her husband's and the death of her grandson Duke Otto without issue, the relative obscurity of the Salians after Conrad the Red's death at the battle of the Lech in 955 and Liudgard's in 953, no doubt also the troubles in England after Edgar's reign, meant that links which had once been close now weakened and thinned again. Historians tend to claim that there must have been much diplomatic traffic of which we have lost all trace; but embassies were an expensive business because of the inescapable exchange of gifts, and they often served to enhance prestige. Without explicit references in the sources their existence must remain unprovable and unproven. The Ottonian Reich's

---

[150]Conrad's presence is shown by D O I 110 (Aachen, 15 May 949); cf. n. 78.

horizons had also changed, although its later historians – Thietmar and the Quedlinburg annalist – never forgot what it is tempting to call its Anglo-Saxon beginnings, and there was Edith's tomb in St Maurice, Magdeburg, to recall them to later generations.

6

The Anglo-Saxons 'At Home'

When in 1819 Freiherr vom Stein set about founding the *Monumenta Germaniae Historica* the ideal before him was that every educated German should have the medieval sources of his country's history and former greatness on the shelves of his library. By the indirect route of rousing a new consciousness and awareness of their past he hope to foster in cultured Germans also a new zeal for the unity and solidarity which had been thwarted at the Congress of Vienna. Only a long and arduous process of historical education could bring about the changes in political structures that were needed to replace particularism with a larger, overriding sense of national identity and the institutions to match. Not the least painful and ironical obstacle in his way was that particularism itself lay so deeply embedded in the historical traditions of Germany and was one outcome of his great enterprise. As the present Director of the *Monumenta*, Professor Horst Fuhrmann, said in 1969 when he addressed a large audience of guests who had come to commemorate its 150th anniversary: 'What patriotic dilettantism had founded was taken over by pertinent expertise', the refined editorial skills, philological mastery and interpretative, critical knowledge which were the foundations of the German historical school.[1]

Yet not all the currents of Freiherr vom Stein's patriotic idealism were lost in the quicksands of scholarship. Most of the works he and his chosen collaborator and successor, G.H. Pertz, had to explore were in Latin and the educated Germans of their day could read and enjoy a Latin text, but translation followed closely on the heels of the *Monumenta's* editions, and so the sources could and did reach a much larger audience. Characteristically some of this matter-of-fact classical erudition has departed from the educated Germans of today so that the Freiherr-vom-Stein commemorative *Monumenta's* texts, oblige with German translations on the facing pages. Yet there remains a trace of proprietorship, of self-awareness, whether painful or proud, between the Germans and their major medieval historical writings.

* First published in *Anglo-Saxon Studies in Archaeology and History*, 2, ed. D. Brown, J. Campbell, S.C. Hawkes (British Archaeological Reports, British Series 92, Oxford: B.A.R., 1981), pp. 237-42. Thanks are due to the editor and publishers for permission to republish here.
[1] H. Fuhrmann, 'Die Sorge um den rechten Text', *DA*, 25 (1969), p. 13.

No institution with the authority, thoroughness and command of historical method of the *Monumenta* stood behind the publication of England's medieval historical sources. Here the Master of the Rolls, appointed by the government of the day, and the Deputy keeper of the Public Records, allocated editions to volunteers and bidders at so much a page. Among them we find Stubbs and Maitland [238] but also far less capable and reliable editors and some of the work for the Anglo-Saxon centuries has had to be done all over again. Yet this is true also for many of the *Monumenta's* early editions. The *Rolls Series* ran to 253 volumes and it was as Dom David Knowles put it, 'from the beginning an extraordinarily inexpert affair'.[2] The unique and still unexhausted wealth of record sources in England from the midtwelfth century onwards and the positivistic strain in the make-up of so many English medievalists brought it about that documentary evidence was rated much more highly than literary and narrative sources. Records were deemed to possess an objectivity and edictive value which chronicles and annals lacked. Not surprisingly they remained the less favoured, poor cousins of English medieval historical studies until relatively recently with the rise of the Nelson, and now Oxford, Medieval Texts. Historians were, and some of them still are, haunted by an obsession with 'bias' which often meant that the wrong questions were asked and answered.

The *English Historical Documents* series, inaugurated in 1953 under the general editorship of David Douglas, should be seen as another turning point in the treatment of the sources and this in two ways: the very catholicity, range and wealth of texts assembled and translated in these volumes enable students, whether scholars or beginners, to cross frontiers hitherto closed to them. Primary materials are made accessible which normally demand daunting philological skills and critical methodologies from their would-be users. The scholarship and editorial guidance offered in these volumes, moreover, almost begin to make up for the lack of academic, institutional care which had governed the history of the sources hitherto, outside the Public Record Office. Of no volume in the series is this truer than the first one, published in 1955, under the masterly editorship of Dorothy Whitelock and here brought up to date with recent work in a second edition, a huge treasury of every kind of evidence: narrative, charters, poetry, laws and letters, from 500 to 1042, all translated from the Latin, Anglo-Saxon and Scandinavian languages, occasionally also – but far too rarely – the Celtic ones.[3] What is more, the orchestra of all these voices from five and a half centuries of English history is conducted by the same virtuoso who marshalled the vast ensemble twenty-five years ago. If there are any preferences and preponderances at all, they have quite rightly been given to Bede and the *Anglo-Saxon Chronicle*, on which Professor Whitelock herself has done the lion's share of the exploratory, critical and interpretative work as well as rising to the defence of wrongly impugned texts, like Asser's *Life of Alfred*.

[2] M.D. Knowles, 'Great Historical Enterprises, IV: The Rolls Series', *TRHS*, fifth series, 11 (1961), p. 158.

[3] D. Whitelock (ed.), *English Historicla Documents*, 1: *c. 500-1042,* 2nd edn (London, 1979).

What the *Monumenta* and the *Geschichtschreiber der deutschen Vorzeit* have done in many volumes is here done for the Anglo-Saxons in one. True, we have an anthology, not a complete run of all the sources and we should note that nothing has been dropped from the first edition and nothing added to it either. Also the original tripartite division: secular narrative sources – are there any such things for the early middle ages? – charters and laws, and ecclesiastical sources, which include the letters, stands. Each one of these genres is introduced by the editress with authoritative experience and its pecularities and special problems are set out [239] with a careful discussion of recent controversies and advances. Not only this but also work which cannot be illustrated in an anthology of texts, new ground gained in archaeology, coinage, architecture and art, has been enfolded in Professor Whitelock's survery. A general introduction takes the reader through Anglo-Saxon history: the invasions and settlements, the early kingdoms, conversion, the Scandinavian asault, the empire of Wessex, of Cnut and the society and institutions in which Dr Whitelock would underscore stability and enduring traits rather than profound changes and transformations.

From the pages of this concentrated survey of events, rulers, institutions, ecclesiastical and lay, the reader is referred to the sources which illustrate these themes and so he can experience the evidence at first hand, albeit in translation. That is the innermost purpose of the collection. Occasionally we find that the source is arresting for quite different reasons than the points raised in the introduction. These unexpected boons are not the least enjoyable feature of this volume. For instance, that King Wulfhere of Mercia (657-74) had a residence at Thame is revealed in a very early charter for Chertsey which also tells us something about the port of London (no. 54). The will of Bishop Ælfwold of Crediton (997-1016) is interesting not just for the horse-breeding lands mentioned in it but for many other things like the bequest of a Hrabanus Maurus manuscript to a lay noble and the extraordinary store of weapons which the prelate owned (no. 122).

Now and again, it must be said, striking portions of text have been omitted. For instance Dr Whitelock cites some clauses from the report of the legates who visited England in 786. They held councils and issued injunction to the English bishops. Thus they ordered (c.10) that no priest should dare to celebrate mass with bare legs, i.e. not wearing long garments. There was to be bread for communion, not hard tack, nor were the celebrants to use an ox's horn as a chalice because it was of blood. One chapter of the legates' report (c.11) was a very treatise on kingship and the obedience kings owed to bishops. Unfortunately these passages, which throw a flood of light on the predicaments of the church in a rustic society and economy, have been left out and the part of the injunction cited (c. 10 again) is much less telling.[4]

In history, Lucien Febvre once said, unless you know what you are looking for, you won't find it. What then should the general reader look for in Anglo-

---

[4] Ibid., no. 191.

Saxon history? This is no otiose question, for the *English Historical Documents* series wants to reach him, the general reader, that undefinable *monstrum* and legislator on whose whims, hoped-for voracity and Cheshire cat smile all publishers depend. In a general preface, it is true, we are presented with other familiars: those who teach and study history. Of their enrichment by the series we have already spoken. There is still talk, though, of the reading public outside schools and universities who should be given the opportunity to check tendentiousness and partiality in interpreting the past by consulting the sources directly. This could be a tall order. It implies a faintly pragmatic view of historical studies, as if commonsense and ratiocination sufficed to make the sources comprehensible. We are still too close to the [240] analogy of a judicial process rather than the dawning of a new kind of understanding, a new insight into the ways early medieval societies thought, behaved and applied their norms and values. Here common sense and impartiality are not enough. Some of the reasoning from the dust-jacket has rubbed off on the volume. Since miracles and visions mattered to the early middle ages, the general reader should be given rather than denied them.

It is assumed also that the reading public has some kind of pre-existing, organic relationship with the past and this too begs a question. It is one of the disturbing symptoms of our cultural disarray and educational crisis that the past, whether rightly or wrongly understood, whether critically grasped or misconceived, is no longer shaping our cultural make-up and sense of identity enough. This is one of history's abiding and most essential tasks. Its enemies threaten to deprive us, the young especially, of cultural roots and a fundamental sense of orientation. Without them we are but computer fodder.

Let us return to the question: What should the general reader look for in Anglo-Saxon history? The Angles and Saxons who invaded the country now named after them, settled there, founded kingdoms and enlarged their possessions from the fifth to the tenth centuries, were the only peoples in northern Europe who developed practices of effective government outside the Carolingian Reich. Their kings were able to impose taxes and services on the basis of a rough but sound system of assessment which we encounter in Bede and the text known as the Tribal Hidage. They knew legislation, charters and it seems, adequate communications between royal and local governance. They were able to receive and to absorb ideas from the Carolingian empire and develop them in the later ninth and tenth centuries, precisely because they had ways and means of adaptable central and local controls already functioning. We may ask and wonder, why? The answer is twofold, positive and negative. The Franks in Gaul battened on Roman provincial administration, exploited and abused it and in the end allowed it to go to seed. The Anglo-Saxons imposed their lordship over a much longer period of struggle. The battle took longer to win. Their success and conquests were less spectacular and had to be secured by more effective and lasting internal disciplines and obligations. It could be objected that certain Germanic peoples on the continent faced similar problems and situations, for instance the Old Saxons in north Germany.

There, however, we cannot find any royal government nor legislation. The difference lay in the timely coming of Christianity, the immensely potent beginnings of a literary culture which did not spurn the use of the vernacular before long.

We tend to think that centralisation, bureaucracy, too much government and taxation are very recent troubles in our polity, quite novel English diseases, contrary to the mainstream of all the best historical traditions. The reverse is true. They are deep-seated and deeply rooted phenomena in English political society, part of its very birth. Throughout the tenth century the kings of Wessex, now rulers also of Mercia, East Anglia and intermittently, Northumbria, and their *witan*, sought to impose more uniform procedures in justice, the pursuit of thieves, local police [241] and to saddle lords with responsibilities for the behaviour of their men. Later Saxon England possessed the most impressive monetary system in western and central Europe, with frequent recalls of the currency and much royal control. Military and naval forces were levied and mobilised with a remarkable regularity and uniformity. No Christian kingdom outside Byzantium could be and was as relentlessly taxed as that ruled by Æthelred II and Cnut.

Let no one think that these achievements gave to later Saxon England greater stability and more safety than its continental neighbours enjoyed. On the contrary the system of formidable government, poised on burghs, and above all, of taxation based on a searching method of land assessment, made the English kingdom more dangerous, insecure and vulnerable because it was so tempting to foreign invaders and their professional military followings. Between 975, the death of Edgar, and 1066, the possession of the English kingship was more troubled and fought over than that of any other Latin European power. Mercenary troops and ships' crews dominated the commanding heights. It was to get rid of these janissaries that Edward the Confessor, in his brief moment of independence, abolished the *heregeld*, the key to the housecarls' stranglehold on the royal palace. Yet as he had no sons, the atmosphere of struggle, feuds and rancorous intrigues, so vividly depicted on the Bayeux Tapestry, brooded over his later years no less than his earlier ones.

The Confessor's reign lies outside the scope of our volume but even the casual reader must carry away with him an impression of ubiquitous written communications, of massive legislation and a steady dialogue between the king and his entourage, shires and burghs in the tenth and early eleventh century. The theme of a close-cropping, hard-taxing government, active and tangible even on the backs of remote and humble villagers, should not pass out of his sight. Professor Whitelock discusses documents like the Tribal Hidage and the Burghal Hidage and it is a little surprising that she has not included them in her anthology, given their central importance. It is strange also that the legislation of synods has not gained a larger place in the collection and not quite clear why the papal privilege, the solemn, formal papal act for a church, has not come through as a category next to the charters. Very generous bibliographies have been given throughout and it is usually stated where sources have been edited, published and discussed before so that it is surprising not to find Walter Holtzmann's *Papsturkunden in England* mentioned somewhere, nor the more recent but essential *Papstregesten 911-1024* compiled by Harald Zimmermann. Not only the general reader but also the scholar and student of history will miss an index of names and subjects which would make it easier to circumvent Lucien Febvre's warning. Lastly it is sad to have to record that a volume which was originally meant to be within the reach of the undergraduate's and certainly his teacher's purse, may now be too costly even for a library to acquire.

It would be, as it were, churlish and very remiss to end on a note of complaint rather than express gratitude and admiration for a second edition which surveys and sums up so much of the work on [242] Anglo-Saxon England during the last twenty-five years. Professor Whitelock has endowed the volume with all the things characteristic of her scholarship and achievement, her views on the *Chronicle*, that King Alfred was not the driving force behind it, that we must reckon with a royal writing office in the later Saxon period and that Æthelred II's reign, despite its calamities, was a golden age of historical, pastoral and homiletic literature. She opens the reader's eyes and leads him towards some of the most poignant and moving moments of her entire subject: the plight of the exile who had lost his lord in the poem, the *Wanderer*, the relationship between lord and followers in the *Battle of Maldon* and the poetry of the Viking enemy who recorded: 'Cnut, liberal with jewels, asked me if I would serve him as well as Olaf, the generous with rings. I said it became me to have but one lord at a time, and I meant my answer truthfully. Enough examples are given to every man.'[5]

---

[5] Ibid., no. 17.

7

Liudprand of Cremona: Preacher and Homilist

In the history of medieval Bible studies the tenth century in Beryl Smalley's own words brought a sudden interruption,† a dramatic pause, and any reader of her *magnum opus* must come away with the strong impression of a hiatus between the Carolingian commentators and the great teachers of the eleventh century, Fulbert of Chartres, Berengar of Tours, Drogo of Paris, and Lanfranc.[1] Strangely enough she did not mention Atto of Vercelli's elaborate and weighty *Expositio in Epistolas S. Pauli*, written not long after 940, which at least continued and used the massive labours of the ninth-century scholars. As Beryl saw this interlude, its foremost spirits turned away from literary studies towards liturgy, and the great abbots of Cluny in their sermons and meditations concentrated on the dramatic and emotional aspects of Scripture. Their method, as she put it, might be called exclamatory. The sermons of Abbot Odo of Cluny, of Atto of Vercelli and Rather of Verona which we possess seem to bear out these characteristics. They were addressed to clerical and monastic communities in a tone of forthright instruction. Sometimes they expounded their texts directly, more often they employed them to drive home a lesson or a moral. For instance, as death came about through the fault of a woman, the joy of the Resurrection was conveyed to the disciples through a woman, St Mary Magdalen, so that the original opprobrium was forever removed from the sex [44] (Odo).[2] The pre-pascal diet of *lactuca agrestis*, bitter herbs (Numbers 9:11), must change ill will in the heart and turn it to sighs, laments, and true peace

* First published in *The Bible in the Medieval World: Essays in Memory of Beryl Smalley*, ed. D. Wood and K. Walsh (Studies in Church History, Subsidia 4, Oxford: Blackwells, 1985), pp. 43-60; thanks are due to the editors and to the Ecclesiastical History Society and Basil Blackwell Ltd for permission to republish. A few additions have been made to the footnotes.

† In presenting this study in memory of Beryl Smalley I have ventured on what was in part new ground for me. I am very grateful to Professor Bernhard Bischoff for letting me have an advance copy of his edition of Liudprand's sermon. My indebtedness to his *apparatus criticus* will be obvious and is gladly acknowledged. I should like to thank no less Sir Richard Southern, Alexander Murray, and Henrietta and Conrad Leyser for their suggestions, advice and encouragement.

1 B. Smalley, *The Study of the Bible in the Middle Ages*, 3rd edn (Oxford, 1983), pp. 44-5.

2 Odo of Cluny, *Sermo* 2, Migne, *PL*, 133, col. 721. On Carolingian sermons and homilies see R. McKitterick, *The Frankish Church and Carolingian Reforms, 789-895* (London, 1977).

before the worshipper can partake of Easter fare (Rather).[3] A Whitsun sermon of Atto's is propounded in a shortened version lest the vulgar are bored, suggesting that it might have been addressed or translated to a lay crowd. Here the more merciful dispensations of Christ's laws are contrasted with the sternness of Mosaic dicta. For this very reason it became imperative not to lose time for penitence.[4]

Some of the foremost Ottonian bishops were renowned as preachers, and praised by the historians and biographers of the tenth and early eleventh centuries for their power of the word. Of Archbishop Frederick of Mainz (937-54). Widukind wrote that he was great in prayer and in the largesse of his alms but outstanding in his preaching, albeit a consistent enemy of Otto I.[5] Gerhard, St Udalrich of Augsburg's biographer, dwelt long and lovingly on the saint-bishop's *ammonitio* of clergy and people and on his regular visitations, *causa regendi, praedicandi et confirmandi*.[6] Ruotger did not omit to extol Archbishop Brun of Cologne (953-65) for his preaching of the word of God, and Thietmar of Merseburg praised Archbishop Willigis of Mainz (975-1011) above all for his *praedicatio*.[7] He was like a sun illuminating the hearts of laggards. On another occasion he mentioned that Archbishop Adalbert of Magdeburg (968-81) delivered an excellent sermon. Of his own Thietmar spoke modestly only in passing.[8] Otloh, the biographer of St Wolfgang, especially noted that his hero avoided intricate and sophistic expositions. By his simple, austere, and admirable mode [45] of address he drew enormous crowds of both sexes, and many of his hearers went away moved to tears.[9] The mideleventh-century *Vita* of Archbishop Heribert of Cologne (999-1021) described a Palm Sunday sermon of his when he harangued – the word often used is *disputare* – clergy and people on the ruinous disobedience of the first man and the hope of resurrection and glory.[10]

Of these eight bishops three came to be venerated as saints, and a fourth, Willigis, had an office composed in his honour in the twelfth century.[11] That they and others should have fulfilled their duty of preaching is not unexpected. Bishops were meant to preach, and it was felt to be desirable that priests should too. All the same, it may come as a surprise that Liudprand of Cremona's name must be added to this list of eminent and appealing tenth- and early eleventh-century homilists. Hitherto he has been known to us for two of the most vivid, not to say lurid, historical works of the Ottonian age, and a third, a justification of Otto I's doings at Rome – the *Antapodosis* begun in 958

[3]   Rather of Verona, *Sermo I de Pascha, Ratherii Veronensis Opera Minora*, ed. P.L.D. Reid (Corpus Christianorum Continuatio Mediaevalis 46, Turnout, 1976), pp. 41-3.

[4]   Atto of Vercelli, *Sermo* 12, Migne, *PL*, 134, cols. 849-50.

[5]   Widukind, *Res gestae Saxonicae* III 15, p. 112.

[6]   Gerhard, *Vita S. Oudalrici Episcopi*, c. 4 and 6, *MGH SS* 4, pp. 391, 394.

[7]   Ruotger, *Vita Brunonis* c. 33, pp. 33-4. For Willigis see Thietmar, *Chronicon* III 5, p. 102.

[8]   Thietmar, *Chronicon* III 1, pp. 96-8; for Thietmar's own preaching see ibid. VI 70, p. 360.

[9]   Otloh, *Vita Sancti Wolfgangi Episcopi* c. 19, *MGH SS* 4, p. 535.

[10] Lantbert, *Vita Sancti Heriberti Archiepiscopi* c. 9, *MGH SS* 4, p. 747.

[11] See *MGH SS* 15, pp. 742-3, 746-8.

and not yet finished in 962 –, the *Legatio*, his polemic about his embassy to Constantinople, written in 969, and the *Historia Ottonis* of 964-5. To these must now be added an Easter sermon composed sometime between 958 and 961. We owe its discovery to Bernhard Bischoff, who has edited the text from a renowned Freising manuscript which had once belonged to Bishop Abraham of Freising (957-94) and is now Clm 6426 of the State Library in Munich.[12]

Bishop Abraham was a great patron, who during his long but troubled pontificate commissioned and acquired an impressive number of *codices* for his cathedral. Clm 6426, however, with the Liudprand homily, occupied a very special place among them and was more intimately linked with its owner than all the others. It is a handbook, an episcopal *vade-mecum* [46] with blessings, essential and befitting *formulae*, but above all missionary aids in Slavonic, which Bishop Abraham needed for the arduous and urgent tasks that confronted him in the vast Carinthian temporalities of his see. In this remote Alpine bastion a large Slav population still awaited conversion. The gathering with Liudprand's text was joined to these important and unusual helps for the bishop's day-to-day use. That Liudprand's sermon should have found a place just here reveals how much Abraham must have valued it. There is, moreover, clear evidence that the Bishop of Freising cared also for Liudprand's historical writings, the *Antapodosis* and the *Historia Ottonis*, for he possessed both in another of his manuscripts, now Clm 6388, where his own hand has been detected.[13]

The sermon in Bishop Abraham's handbook is headed: ΟΜΙΛΕΙΑ ΤΟΥ ΛΙΟΥΤΖΙΟΥ ΤΟΥ ΙΤΑΛΙΚΟΥ διακόνου [homily of Liutsios the Italian deacon], thus unmistakably revealing its authorship, and Liudprand himself may have penned the Greek letters of the title. Bernhard Bischoff, moreover, has identified the Fulda-North-German hand of this, at one time folded, fascicule in the codex.[14] It has been suggested that Abraham acquired it perhaps at Corvey, where he was exiled after taking a prominent part in Henry the Wrangler's and his mother's, the Duchess Judith's, conspiracy against Otto II in 974.[15] We cannot be at all sure about this. Most likely Abraham knew Liudprand personally at the Ottonian court, both before and after his promotion to the see of Freising in 957. That Liudprand, after difficult beginnings, was able to join the clerical *familia* of Otto I, and serve him in his

[12] B. Bischoff, 'Eine Osterpredigt Liudprands von Cremona (um 960)', in idem, *Anecdota Novissima: Texte des vierten bis sechzehnten Jahrhunderts* (Quellen und Untersuchungen zur lateinischen Philologie des Mittelalters 7, Stuttgart, 1984), pp. 20-34. On the manuscript see also idem, 'Über gefaltete Hanschriften, vornehmlich hagiographischen Inhalts', in idem, *Mittelalterliche Studien*, vol. 1 (Stuttgart, 1966), pp. 93-100.

[13] N. Daniel, *Handschriften des zehnten Jahrhunderts aus der Freisinger Dombibliothek* (Münchener Beiträge zur Mediävistik und Renaissance-Forschung 11, Munich, 1973), pp. 105-6.

[14] Bischoff, 'Gefaltete Handschriften' (as n. 12), p. 93, and Daniel, *Handschriften* (as n. 13), p. 106.

[15] Daniel, *Handschriften* (as n. 13), pp. 79-87, especially p. 83.

chapel as a refugee from Italy, is known.[16] Whether Abraham too was one of Otto I's *capellani* has been much debated and remains uncertain, but it cannot by any means be ruled out.[17] As a bishop he attended Otto's *curia* at Regensburg in February 961, and he may even have heard Liudprand deliver his homily in some form, [47] which according to Bischoff should be dated between 958 and 961.[18] During these years Liudprand, as we know, was working on the *Antapodosis*, which of all his writings thus stands nearest to the homily. It is here that we must look for affinities between Liudprand the preacher and Liudprand the historian. Let us listen to what the future bishop of Cremona had to say to his audience and readers.

His themes were, as befitted the occasion, the central tenets of Christian belief, the Incarnation, the Redemption, and the Trinity. Liudprand however chose to cast his *exposé* of the articles of faith in the form of a vigorous dialectic. They were to be vindicated against the doubts and objections of a Hebrew. Liudprand in his homily thus reveals himself not only as a well-schooled theologian, but his sermon must also be seen as a forceful contribution to the continuous and troubled debate between the Church and Judaism at a time when that debate was as yet unaccompanied by wholesale massacres and plunder.[19]

Throughout, the Jew is called *infelix*, and once he is addressed in Greek as ὦ ἄπιστε [unbeliever] but Liudprand never becomes vehemently abusive. The Jew feared and refused to hear the Christian message. In the words of the Apostle James's letter (1:23) he listened to the message, but did not act upon it. Liudprand opens his sermon magnificently, not only with a ringing statement of the Creed, but also its dogmatic exposition. The Hebrew then enters the argument: If God is omnipotent, to which I agree, what need had he, the Uncreated, to become *creatura* to set free his creation.[20] By his might alone he could liberate man from the power of the apostate angel whom he had cast down. To this the preacher replies: 'You sin, for by proclaiming only God's power you deny his true justice. [48] If God had freed fallen man by his power alone and not also by reason where would his justice be by which the prophet had affirmed him to be the just judge?' Liudprand here followed Augustine,

[16] J. Fleckenstein, *Die Hofkapelle der deutschen Könige*, 2: *Die Hofkapelle im Rahmen der ottonisch-salischen Reichskirche* (Schriften der MGH 16, Stuttgart, 1966), pp. 46-50.

[17] Fleckenstein, *Hofkapelle* (as n. 16), pp. 45-6, but see also p. 216 n. 403, where he thought it very doubtful.

[18] Bishop Abraham's presence appears from Otto I's diploma for a clerk, Diotpert, dated Regensburg, 13 February 961 (D O I 221).

[19] On Christian-Jewish relations and exchanges in the tenth century see B. Blumenkranz, *Juifs et chrétiens dans le monde occidental, 430-1096* (Études juives 2, Paris, 1960). For a debate between Church and Synagogue, which the author dates in the middle of the tenth century, see his *Les Auteurs chrétiens latins du moyen age sur les juifs et le judaïsme* (Études juives 4, Paris, 1963), no. 188. See also F. Lotter, 'Zu den Anfängen deutsch-jüdischer Symbiose in frühottonischer Zeit', *Archiv für Kulturgeschichte*, 55 (1973), pp. 1-34, and especially now J.M. Wallace-Hadrill, *The Frankish Church* (Oxford, 1983), pp. 390-403.

[20] Bischoff, 'Osterpredigt' (as n.12), p. 24, lines 12-14.

De Trinitate, xiii, 13, but he did so with a vivacity all his own. By power, he averred, God could have coerced the proud angel to forego his pride, but the angel had wanted to make himself the equal of his creator by his own violation. Where there was a will to sin there must also be an ability to do so. God created the angels so that they should either of their own will enjoy eternal bliss or be punished by perpetual damnation. Wishing to refurbish the *ordo* which had been diminished by the lapse of the unclean spirits – and here Liudprand again followed Augustine – the Lord therefore created man *ex limo terrae* to punish the devil all the more by man's possible transition to his, the devil's former glory. The devil, touched by envy and in his hatred of the Creator, now sought to bring it about that man through an act of disobedience should not be able to reach the beatitude from which he, the fiend, had lapsed.[21]

The preacher then described Eve's temptation, the Fall, and its consequence, death.[22] And, O Hebrew, so that I anticipate your silent question', Liudprand continues, 'well did God allow man to be tempted when he foreknew that he would yield to temptation.'[23] Throughout, the idea of justice is profoundly linked with the ability to choose, to decide for better or for worse. Temptation and the chance to resist it was the permanent condition of mankind. Liudprand continues: God, grieving that man whom he had created, had been deceived by the devil's fraud wanted to free him from the jaws of due death not by power alone but by power joined to holy reason. If the opponent said, 'Why did God wish to liberate only man and not the fallen angel?' it was because the latter had sinned of his own malice, whereas man burdened by the weight of his flesh was incited by the serpent's insinuation, and so man alone was to be liberated by divine grace. And since the merit of no angel could suffice for the redemption of the whole world, God wanted to free man *per principium hoc est creatorem increatum*. That, Liudprand explained, was God's son.[24] [49]

This brings the preacher to the Trinity and the opponent's question, an often-voiced one in the Christian-Jewish debate: How can divinity without contagion and corruption adhere to the flesh? Good question, Liudprand replies, 'and unknown to yourself, O Hebrew, you have sent missiles by which you yourself will be injured'. He added that he was really forbidden to unfold the mysteries of the Lord to one who did not and would not believe 'yet shall I try as best as I can, to explain for the sake of the simplicity of certain believers.'[25] Human frailty cannot speak worthily about God. Our language cannot really describe him or compare him with anything, but – and here Liudprand continues to address the simple – only by comparison with visible things can we arrive at an understanding of invisible ones. Yet his discussion and analysis of the concepts of the 'word' and 'substance' here is far from

---

[21] Ibid., pp. 24-5, and notes 5 and 7 for Augustine's exposition.
[22] Ibid., pp. 25-6.
[23] Ibid., p. 26, lines 67-9.
[24] Ibid., p. 26, lines 85-90.
[25] Ibid., pp. 26-7, lines 95-106.

simple and unfolds, as Bischoff noted, Liudprand's schooling in the *artes*.[26] He then turns to the familiar simile of the sun, its fire, splendour, and heat. If there were three words, *sol, splendor,* and *calor*, theirs was not a diverse, but one and the same, substance, and since their nature, substance, and functioning were the same, we don't speak of three suns, three lights, and three heats, but one sun; yet so that when you name it you had not named the words heat or splendour but have understood the substance of the words to be one. The analogy with the Trinity is then drawn: Why should the Hebrew believe that God the Father, God the Son, and God the Holy Spirit were three gods and not one? When Abraham greeted the three angels he called upon one God. Again and again Liudprand appeals to the Old Testament as irrefragable evidence for the New. 'Hence Abraham, when he saw the angels, in three persons understood deity's one essence'.[27]

From this confident demonstration of the Trinity Liudprand comes to speak of the Incarnation. Only the Son was incarnated so that by this mystery he could free us from the devil's grip, not by power alone, but by just and true reason. Liudprand here approached the central drama of Easter. The devil did not believe that Christ was at once God and man, but trusting in his victory over the first man he sought to ensnare him by temptation. [50] Vanquished by our redeemer he thought that if he could encompass the death of him who was without sin, the whole world would be subject to him, since there is no one else without sin. In causing Christ to be crucified by the Jews, the devil sought to snatch what was forbidden, and so lost justly what he held and had acquired. Liudprand here returns to his earlier theme. 'Consider God's power joined to just, holy, and true reason'.[28] It was just that the devil by this act, his attempt to extinguish the man without sin and God on the cross and to drag him to the shadows of death, where he boasted he held the whole human race justly, should by the power of the immortal and just God rightly lose what he trusted he rightly possessed. Nor must it be believed, Liudprand continued, that Christ did an injury to the devil. Death fled when he saw life approach, whose onset he could not bear. 'This, O Hebrew, is why I exalt and wish to put forward a philosophical dilemma.' Dialecticians say that two opposites cannot be together *in eodem*. When one is there, the other must be absent. You cannot deny that God is life and the devil death. Since it is so, nay, because it is so, death prejudiced himself in having life come to him when he could not bear its presence. For this we Christians celebrate Easter.[29]

Liudprand here is heir to a long tradition, well affirmed in Carolingian writings, a tradition, moreover, which outlived him for more than a century: the idea that the devil by the first man's sin and lapse had acquired just rights

---

[26] Ibid., p. 22.
[27] Ibid., p. 28, lines 161-3.
[28] Ibid., p. 30, lines 204-6.
[29] Ibid., p. 30, lines 215-23.

over all mankind, which he forfeited only by his transgression against Christ.[30] Gilbert Crispin was to argue still in this vein, although the prologue of his *Dialogue* with the Jew from Mainz was addressed to St Anselm, who decisively broke with this haunting view.[31] It is noteworthy in Liudprand's sermon that he treated the devil's rights with studied ambiguity and reserve. In the critical passage, *que tenebat, iuste perdidit adquisita* could mean that it was just that he lost what he had [57] held, but it might also describe the devil's title, the same *iuste* covering both – the past and the state of mankind after Christ's sacrifice.[32] In what follows Liudprand spoke of rights which the devil boasted he had, and rights that he confidently thought he possessed, rather than rights which he did lawfully possess.[33] He wanted to show that divine power and divine justice had triumphed together through Christ's voluntary act followed by the harrowing of hell and the Resurrection.

Liudprand then turned to the yet unanswered question: How could immortal God adhere to corruptible and mortal man without compromising his nature? He answered it again with spiritual interpretations of Old Testament texts, Proverbs 9:1 and Psalms 8:5-8, as well as another appeal to the likeness of the sun. If the sun was not soiled by the filth its rays traversed, or divided by the tree it saw cut down, so let the Jews not wonder that immortal God could without detriment to himself take on the humanity he had come to liberate. Here Liudprand washes his hands of the Hebrew and does not want to 'litigate' with him any longer. He now comes to the most urgent part of his homily.[34]

In the last part of his sermon the preacher turns from soteriological teaching to pastoral practice. Having demonstrated how man had gained the chance of his own salvation, Liudprand now wishes to show how he might attain it and how he must strive for it. He strikes a new note of entreaty, and the homiletic here really begins. 'Therefore, dearest brethren – and this is the first time he refers to his audience again after opening words – because we celebrate Holy Easter, let us inwardly imitate what we are outwardly seen to have solemnised.'[35] Deeds must follow words. Easter is called a *transitus*. We keep it reverently if we leave behind vices and go over to virtues. The whole of this section is dominated by a telling reminder of divine judgement to come. The

---

[30] On this see J. Rivière, *Le Dogme de la rédemption au début du moyen âge* (Bibliothèque Thomiste 19, Paris, 1934), pp. 7-61, and above all R.W. Southern, *Saint Anselm and his Biographer: A Study of Monastic Life and Thought 1059 – c. 1130* (Cambridge, 1963), pp. 85-7, 93-7.

[31] *Gisleberti Crispini Disputatio Iudei et Christiani et Anonymi Auctoris Disputationis Iudei et Christiani Continuatio*, ed. B. Blumenkranz (Stromata Patristica et Mediaevalia 3, Utrecht, 1956), p. 50, and now in *The Works of Gilbert Crispin, Abbot of Westminster*, ed. A.S. Abulafia and G.R. Evans (Auctores Britannici Medii Aevi 8, London, 1986), pp. 34-5; see also Southern, *Anselm* (as n.30), pp. 90-1.

[32] Bischoff, 'Osterpredigt' (as n. 12), p. 30, lines 204-5.

[33] Ibid., '...ad mortis tenebras in quibus se iuste humanum genus gloriabatur habere . . . ab immortalis et iusti Dei potentia iuste perderet, quod se iuste possedisse confideret.'

[34] Ibid., pp. 30-1, line 233, ω απιστε.

[35] Ibid., p. 32, lines 270-1.

wicked sometimes forsook their misdeeds because they feared earthly rulers and the death-penalty of the body, but for the sake of immortal God, the king of kings who can punish body and soul eternally, they gave up [52] nothing. Earthly execution can often be avoided by bribes, influence, or the expectation of making amends, but eternal torments can be averted only by one's own good works in this life. He who has no oil for his lamp at the end, that is, good works in his conscience, will not be able to borrow it. Liudprand is here the brilliant stylist both his admirers and his critics have acknowledged. His image, from Matthew 25, then leads him to quote St Paul, II Corinthians, 6:2: *Ecce nunc tempus acceptabile, ecce nunc dies salutis.*[36] Now is the time, let us now prove ourselves as God's ministers. Liudprand is here clearly haranguing his own *ordo*, his fellow clerks, whose task it is to preach God's mercy, but who must also avow that he is just a judge. Through us, his unworthy servants, Christ continues to act and to declare how eternal reward might be gained and eternal condemnation escaped. He knew also that we could not ascend to heaven by our own goodness, and therefore he sought to prepare a ladder for us by which if we wish it we can fly there.

We are not left long in suspense about what constituted this ladder. God did not wish some to be poor and others to be rich from any want of power. He mercifully wanted there to be poor in this life for the salvation of the rich, so that the rich could by the love of charity make them partners of their wealth, and so themselves partake with them in eternal bliss.[37] Liudprand seems to think that the poor had a much better chance of salvation. Every one of us must consider the plight of the wretched and the disabled and set it against his own relative good health and prosperity. It might all have been the other way about. Charity was therefore the greatest and most acceptable sacrifice we can offer to God. Liudprand here vastly enhances the urgency and effect of his discourse by breaking into dialogue, between himself and his audience, between them and God. 'What are we doing for God by which we might earn these things, namely wealth and good health? Nothing, I say. What could we do? Nothing better than what we have learned by his grace: love God and love your neighbour. But you say, "I do love my neighbour". "How", speaks God, "do you love your neighbour whom you don't visit when he is ill and don't [53] hear when he cries to you for help". Our behaviour, my brethren, is detestable.'[38] At this point Liudprand appealed pungently to one of the strongest and most important social bonds his world knew: *familiaritas*. When we see the *familiares* of the kings and princes of this life, we receive them with great honour and beg them to accept the gifts to press upon them again and again, even if they don't want them. We offer them not trash, but things we ourselves value. Now the poor were the *familiares* of Our Lord Jesus Christ, but not only do we not give them presents, but we don't deign to look at them, and if we respond

---

[36] Ibid., p. 32, lines 293-5.
[37] Ibid., p. 33, lines 307-10.
[38] Ibid., p. 33, lines 318-27.

to their cries and afflictions, we don't do it in person: and the paltry things we offer them we send not by an honoured but by some low servant.[39] Liudprand then grimly depicts the retribution that awaited those who behaved like this. Here he recited Abraham's words to the rich man in the torments of hell.[40] The homily ends with a dialogue between a bishop, whose locked barns are full of freshly harvested grain, and one of the *clerici* of the audience. Some bishops preferred to throw away old and rotting grain which might yet help to relieve distress rather than distribute it. 'If it is like this, my brethren, I don't defend myself nor anyone else who does such things, but denounce him vehemently and deem him, though alive, to be already dead.' The exhortation rises once more to a shrill climax: It won't help you to share the torments of false bishops. Their 'woe, woe' is of no use to your 'woe', and companionship in suffering does not relieve the pain of burning.[41] May he who was made man for our sake avert it from us. Liudprand then concludes by returning to the theme of Easter.

There is no doubt that his sermon was addressed to relatively well-to-do and privileged clerks such as he was himself. Judging by the final, imaginary dialogue between one such member of his audience and a bishop, it is at least possible that he, Liudprand, was already marked out for promotion to an Italian see, a bishop-designate as it were, when he wrote and perhaps delivered his sermon. Otto I's expedition to Italy, where Liudprand of course [54] accompanied and served him, assembled in August 961, but had been planned at least since Christmas 960. Easter in 961 fell on 7 April, but we do not know where the king kept it. He was on his way to Saxony. In the last sentences of his homily Liudprand appears to identify himself with the erring prelate who preferred to throw away spoiling victuals rather than distribute them. He himself is one of the scribes to whom he alluded through Matthew, 25:3 where it is enjoined that one should do what they say but not follow their deeds. The humility – and modesty – *topos* would fit in all the better if Liudprand was about to rise above the ranks of his fellow clerks. Whether the future bishop of Cremona referred to an actual famine, specific events or persons in his homily must remain uncertain. The St Gallen *Annals* reported a hard year, widespread dearth, and many deaths through shortages under the date 959-60.[42]

As an exponent of dogma Liudprand can bear comparison with his foremost Italian colleagues of whom we possess Easter sermons, Atto of Vercelli and Rather of Verona. His vividness and dialogue are distinctive and all his own. They may have come across better than Rather's more profound but morose spirits. Atto too could be vivid and to the point as well as brief, and his vision of contemporary Italian society was acute, but Liudprand in his homily harnessed his insights more forcefully to his immediate purpose. As for so many of his

---

[39] Ibid., p. 33, lines 327-35. On *familiaritas* see Leyser, *Medieval Germany*, pp. 75, 94 and especially 99-100.

[40] Luke 16:25.

[41] 'Osterpredigt', p. 34, lines 345-6, 354-6.

[42] *Annales Sangallenses Maiores s.a.* 959 (960), *MGH SS* 1, p. 79.

clerical contemporaries, charity was above all a means of salvation.[43] He was nothing if not self centred: the poor were there to enable the rich to earn their way to heaven. The deep division between the well-off, privileged, and relatively secure higher clergy and the *vulgus* is evident in what he wrote about the *familiares* of the great, and in his effort to present the poor as the *familiares* of Christ who might possess influence in the highest court and tribunal of them all. It was an effective image to drive home and so temper the rigours of the social cleavage.

The question must now be asked where Liudprand's homily stands in relation to his historical works, above all whether his personality as a writer, already complex enough, has become even [55] more bewildering and full of contradictions now. Here we shall look solely at the *Antapodosis* and not at the *Historia Ottonis* and the *Legatio*. Both these were *livres d'occasion*, while in conception and in composition the *Antapodosis* overlapped the date of the sermon, as has already been noted. For the question here raised it is for many reasons the more relevant text. Now with very few exceptions, modern scholars have portrayed Liudprand as a brilliant, albeit vain, subjective, entertaining, not to say scabrous and risqué, writer. Robert Holtzmann commented many years ago that his theological schooling stood far below that of Atto of Vercelli, and he also remarked on his vanity and conceit towards Byzantium's ruling circles. In the *Antapodosis*, he thought, the polemic pushed aside the initially didactic and edifying purposes.[44] Helmut Beumann reflected on Liudprand's subtlety and ambivalence. He was too clever by far.[45] Auerbach, who examined Liudprand's style, slated him more severely: courtier and diplomat, he was an ecclesiastic only in name. His literary talent was considerable but superficial, journalistic and anecdotic. As a man he thought him vain, vengeful, and indiscreet.[46]

Liudprand's editor for the *Scriptores Rerum Germanicarum* in the *Monumenta*, Joseph Becker, laid the foundations for all this censure. He too felt that Liudprand belonged only outwardly to the clerical *ordo*, and while he did not wish away the many theological utterances in his historical works, he thought that they were a mere varnish rather than signs of inner piety. Liudprand was vain, self-pleasing, and fond of lascivious and piquant tales. He wanted to entertain and, it is true, to edify. Becker thus saw that Liudprand in his histories wished to show the hand of God at work rewarding good and punishing evil, yet at the same time he remarked on his passionate and temperamental make-up. He was the most personal of early medieval

---

[43] On tenth-century almsgiving see K.J. Leyser, 'The German Aristocracy from the Ninth to the Early Twelfth Century: a Social and Cultural Sketch', *Past and Present*, 41 (1968), p. 26 (Leyser, *Medieval Germany*, p. 162).

[44] Wattenbach-Holtzmann-Schmale, vol. 1, p. 320.

[45] H. Beumann, 'Der Schriftsteller und seine Kritiker im frühen Mittelalter', *Studium Generale*, 12 (1959), pp. 502-4, also in idem, *Wissenschaft vom Mittelalter* (Cologne, 1972), pp. 21-4.

[46] E. Auerbach, *Literary Language and its Public in Late Latin Antiquity and in the Middle Ages* trans. R. Manheim (London, 1965), p. 153.

writers.[47] Only Karl Hauck guarded himself, and [56] warned his readers against these judgements, and saw in Liudprand one of the earliest propagators of a divinely willed and legitimated royal and imperial rule for Otto I.[48] It is possible to go further still and to insist on Liudprand's urgent and unremitting homiletic purposes throughout the *Antapodosis*. Here too he at times preached, and interpreted critical moments and events in Otto I's struggles for his kingship with the help of biblical example and precept. Only through the sacred texts could Otto's survival and victories in these critical years, especially 939, be explained. There was no other way. Let us follow him.

The *Antapodosis* is a parallel history of kings and princes 'of part of Europe' from the late ninth to the mid tenth century. It had at one moment wanted to be more ambitious, a history of the whole of Europe, but even so Liudprand's design was formidable, and has no match in the historical writings of the tenth century.[49] It was addressed to and professedly written at the request of Bishop Recemund of Elvira, a servant of the Umyad Caliph of Cordoba. Liudprand had met him as Abd ar-Rahman III's envoy at Frankfurt in 956. The proem of the book not only describes its purposes, but also its method. Liudprand's *neniae* must be regarded as the modest self-deprecation required of an author in Carolingian and post-Carolingian convention, and if he wished to divert, it was a *utilis comediarum risus* that justified his stories.[50] The stressmark lies on *utilis*. He would speak of the deeds of enervate kings and effeminate rulers only to unfold their just divine repression. Above all, Liudprand throughout the *Antapodosis* is the sworn enemy of all wheeling and dealing between Christian rulers and the attackers and invaders of contemporary Christendom, Saracens and Magyars.

Bernhard Bischoff has pointed out certain linguistic affinities between the sermon and the *Book of Revenge*. Liudprand was fond [57] of Graecisms, and one at least is used conspicuously in both works, *amphibologia*, meaning ambiguity.[51] He has also drawn attention to the use of dialogue in the *Antapodosis* no less than in the homily to enliven the narrative. Moreover, Liudprand, in the midst of relating calamities like the Saracen onslaught on southern Italy, pauses in his story to insert a whole chapter, very like his sermon, rehearsing for his readers the Saviour's beneficence, his providence, his sacrifice, and his constant wish for man's good. If, for the time being, he castigates us because we do not respond to his blessings, he then again re-animates the Christian

---

[47] *Liudprandi Opera*, ed. Becker, pp. xiii-xiv, xvii, xx.

[48] K. Hauck, 'Erzbischof Adalbert von Magdeburg als Geschichtsschreiber', in *Festschrift für Walter Schlesinger*, 2 vols., ed. H. Beumann (Mitteldeutsche Forschungen 74, Cologne, 1974), vol. 2, pp. 298-305.

[49] Liudprand, *Antapodosis*, title and I 1, pp. 1, 4.

[50] On Liudprand's encounter with Recemund see Becker's introduction, pp. viii-ix. For 'utilis comoediarum risus' see *Antapodosis* I 1, p. 4, and Beumann, *Wissenschaft* (as n. 45), p. 24.

[51] 'Osterpredigt' (as n. 12), pp. 22 and 28 line 162; Liudprand, *Antapodosis* III 47, p. 99; further IV 12, p. 111 and also IV 26, p. 120, an important example, not indexed.

spirit of resistance, so that the Saracens should not mock and say, 'Where is their God?'[52] Despite all the embroilments, the interplay of war, intrigue, ambition and license, which he describes without embellishment in the *Antapodosis*, Liudprand wanted to make it quite clear that divine guidance and not chance governed human affairs.

Nowhere did he demonstrate this so effectively as when he dwelt on Otto I's, to him, miraculous victory over his enemies in the war waged against his disaffected brother, Henry, and Duke Giselbert of Lotharingia in 939. Otto had marched to the lower Rhine from Saxony, and some of his mounted men had already crossed it near Xanten when Henry and Giselbert, with superior forces, advanced upon the detachment now stationed on the left bank by Birten. There was no time nor shipping to come to their aid, an Otto met the crisis by praying in front of the Holy Lance with the nails of the Cross, which accompanied him on his journeys. There was nothing else he could do. His men on the far side, however, were victorious against the odds, and according to Liudprand suffered no casualties. Widukind, who also gave a good account of the battle, made it clear that Otto lost men and there were many wounded. In his narrative too the king prayed, but it was a *ruse de guerre* which won the encounter.[53]

In the *Antapodosis* Liudprand not only narrated at length how Otto's father, Henry I, had acquired the Holy Lance, but he also [58] wrote what can only be described as a sermon, a homily, to explain and magnify Otto's unexpected success. Purposefully he digressed to present the victory of the few over the many as the work of divine providence, whereby God wished to make known to wavering men, and indeed to Otto himself, how dear he was to him. At first sight it may seem strange that in order to do so Liudprand resorted to John, 20:25-28, the story of doubting Thomas. He himself in his pulsing prose entered into a dialogue with the Apostle. It is also evident that Liudprand mastered the interpretation of the text resting on St Augustine and Gregory the Great. Heretics, Manicheans, who did not believe Christ to have risen in the body, were refuted by it, and above all Thomas's doubts were not accidental, but part of the economy of divine providence. By them the faith of the many was confirmed and strengthened. It was just this idea Liudprand applied to Otto I's victory at Birten. Not Otto's faith, but that of the weaker brethren, those who believed only in superior numbers, human prowess, or chance, was enhanced by the victory through prayer. Men must be roused by it to place their hopes in God, and also learn that Otto, their king, belonged to

---

[52] Liudprand, *Antapodosis* II 46, p. 58
[53] Ibid. IV 24, pp. 117-18; Widukind II 17, pp. 82-3, and see Köpke-Dümmler, *Otto der Große*, pp. 82-4, and Hauck, 'Erzbischof Adalbert' (as n. 48), p. 304

the elect.[54] Loyalty as a religious duty could hardly have been propagated more forcefully.

Liudprand continued in this vein, and the next events in Otto's struggle against his formidable rivals, Henry, the Frankish Duke Eberhard, and Giselbert, are transposed into a further homily. Otto here overcame not only his visible but also invisible enemies, his own passions and temptation. God sometimes allowed sinners to worst their adversaries, but it was given only to a few to uphold unshakeable strength of spirit, not to be elated by success or broken by adversity. This stoic equanimity, which Einhard had set forth as one of Charlemagne's qualities, is here Christianised and becomes a form of piety.[55] The fight at Birten had settled nothing, and when, [59] later in the year, Otto with a Saxon host surrounded the fortress of Breisach his situation changed for the worse. His camp began to empty through desertions, and he was short of warriors. When a count with a sizeable following sought to exploit his situation and press for the grant of the abbey of Lorsch as the price for continued service, Liudprand had the king reply: *Nolite sanctum dare canibus*, and not only this, but even expound the passage thus: although the learned teach that it must be understood spiritually, I reckon that I am giving the holy to the dogs if I grant the lands of monasteries, which pious men gave to those warring for God, i.e., monks, to those fighting in the *saeculum*.[56] The count collapsed. Liudprand crowns his homily with the observation that the devil, having seen that he could not harm Otto by mobilising so many enemies against him, prompted the count to ask for the saints' patrimony so that the king might incur God's wrath. 'But because he could not do this we shall now set forth how the pious prince grew in stature because of his constancy in this temptation, God fighting for him.' Liudprand finally interpreted the decisive battle at Andernach, in which Eberhard and Giselbert lost their lives, by Psalms, 80:15. Because he, Otto, walked in the Lord's ways, the Lord laid his hands upon his persecutors.[57]

Here, then, Otto's survival and eventual victory was the outcome of biblical precept observed, temptation resisted. Liudprand wanted to show not only why rebellion against such a ruler was in itself sinful, but also that resistance to temptation worked and could be seen to lead to triumph. The preacher in him was no stranger to the historian. This does not mean that we have explained him in full. His macabre tales and obsessions still pose serious problems. Once we find him use in a very light-hearted, not to say shameless, way a biblical

---

[54] Liudprand, *Antapodiosis* IV 26, pp. 120-2. On the medieval interpretation of John 20:24-29 and its history see U. Pflugk, 'Die Geschichte vom ungläubigen Thomas (Johannes 20, 24-29) in der Auslegung der Kirche von den Anfängen bis zur Mitte des sechzehnten Jahrhunderts' (unpublished Ph.D. thesis, Hamburg, 1965), especially pp. 116, 126, 141. He does not comment on Liudprand's use of the story, though, and leaves a notable gap between the ninth and the twelfth century in his survey. I am greatly indebted to Alexander Murray for enabling me to read this work.

[55] Liudprand, *Antapodosis* IV 28, p. 123, and cf. Einhard, *Vita Karoli* c. 7 and 8, pp. 10-11.

[56] Liudprand, *Antapodosis* IV 27 and 28, pp. 122-4.

[57] Ibid. IV 29, pp. 124-5.

image which his sermon had employed as a solemn appeal, the story of Lazarus blessed and *dives* in torment. In the sermon this had served as a dire warning. In *Antapodosis* it became the witty plea by which Liudprand elicited a further gift from the emperor Constantine Porphyrogenitus in the course of his first embassy to the Byzantine court (949-50). He had already been given one, as was customary, when the emperor made him attend [60] the annual pay parade of the higher dignitaries. Liudprand saw the spectacle, the display of enormous wealth and, at the same time, ceremonial orderliness, but when Constantine had him asked through the logothete how he liked it, he replied that it would please him very much if it was of any use to him, just as Lazarus' blessed ease in heaven would have pleased the parching rich man in hell if it had profited him in any way. Because this could not happen, how, I pray, could it please?[58] Here, then, Liudprand turned the parable on its head, nor could he forbear telling the story. Yet for all his cheek, underlying his writings is a passionate concern to tell his readers and listeners that it was not chance, but divine direction, *ratio*, justice, and judgement that governed their lives and awaited them often enough here, and certainly in the next world.

Liudprand's arguments have been surveyed but shortened here. In his sermon he often liked to pause, to draw out, enlarge, and glitter with rhetorical flourishes like beats on a tympanum. Where, then, finally, does he stand as an expositor of scriptures? His method too might be called 'exclamatory', and he certainly had a strong sense for the dramatic and emotional features of his texts, to return to Beryl Smalley's characterisation of the tenth century. It would, however, be mistaken to regard this period altogether as one of stagnation in the history of medieval Bible studies. The Carolingian legacy here as elsewhere was huge and very much alive, calling for great effort and cultivation. With preachers like Atto, Rather, Odo of Cluny, Ælfric, and now Liudprand, it would seem that that effort was made, and it must not be thought that the eleventh-century scholars started with *tabula rasa*.

---

[58] Ibid. VI 10, p. 158

8

Ends and Means in Liudprand of Cremona

It is possible and indeed tempting to see the whole of the tenth century through the eyes of a few quintessential writers, to find it personified and characterised in all its richness and variety, its fertile diversities no less than its Latin Christian unities, in the pages of Widukind of Corvey, Thietmar of Merseburg, Flodoard, Richer and more still than any of these, in Liudprand of Cremona. For Italy as the centre of a Mediterranean axis and the hub of a northern world he is our chief spokesman, not least of all because he himself was conscious of this situation and cast himself in the role of a European historian. He is also the representative of a vigorous, legally literate and articulate urban life which began to gather momentum, autonomy and above all wealth under the blanket of its alien, immigré, neither wholly absorbed not yet wholly unabsorbed ruling class, the Carolingian high aristocracy. To even the most purist Byzantinist Liudprand of Cremona is and must be an arresting and inescapable figure. To understand his writings and his aims as the self-conscious portrayer of divine justice visiting the doings of enervate kings, as the agent and apologist of Otto I's dealings with the papacy and lastly as the irate pamphleteer against Nicephorus Phocas's Byzantium, we must first of all locate him socially.[1] Where should we place his family and connections? [120]

---

* First published in *Byzantium and the West, c. 850-c. 1200: Proceedings of the XVIII Spring Symposium of Byzantine Studies, Oxford, 30 March – 1 April 1984*, ed. J.D. Howard-Johnston (Amsterdam, 1988), pp. 119-43. Thanks are due to the editor and the publisher, Adolf M. Hakkert, for permission to republish here. A few additions and corrections have been made to the footnotes.

[1] A specific survey and characterisation of tenth-century historiography is not readily to hand. On Liudprand of Cremona see above all his editor J. Becker, *Liudprandi Opera* (MGH SRG 41, Hanover, 1915), pp. vii-xxiii; M. Manitius, *Geschichte der lateinischen Literatur des Mittelalters*, vol. 2 (Munich, 1923), pp. 166-75; Wattenbach-Holtzmann-Schmale, vol. 1, pp. 318-21 and vol. 3, pp. 102*-3*. More recently see J.N. Sutherland, 'The Idea of Revenge in Lombard Society in the Eighth and Tenth Centuries: The Cases of Paul the Deacon and Liudprand of Cremona', *Speculum*, 50 (1975), pp. 391-410; J. Koder and T. Weber, *Liutprand von Cremona in Konstantinopel: Untersuchungen zum griechischen Sprachschatz und zu realienkundlichen Aussagen in seinen Werken* (Byzantina Vindobonensia 13, Vienna, 1980); M. Rentschler, *Liudprand von Cremona: Eine Studie zum ost-westlichen Kulturgefälle im Mittelalter* (Frankfurter Wissenschafliche Beiträge, Kulturwissenschaftliche Reihe 14, Frankfurt, 1981) – often questionable; and now J.N.

They belonged to the royal *familiaritas*, the *palatium* of Pavia, the men who controlled the sophisticated, slippery and at the same time profitable levers of government under a succession of royal adventurers from the north, eventually the Ottonians and Salians. Their views, attitudes and interests did not always coincide with those of their masters, nor did Liudprand, for all his devotion to Otto I and his family, strike all the right notes in the *Legatio*, as we shall see. The future envoy to Constantinople came from an influential, local family. His *parentes* gained for him, not without much outlay of cash, the post of a confidential secretary to Margrave Berengar, the controlling power after the fall and departure of King Hugh whom Liudprand had served from boyhood onwards.[2] His relations with Byzantium were in fact hereditary. Both his stepfather and his father had been on embassies to the East, the one in 941, the other in 927.[3] Liudprand himself was to go on them at least three times, most probably four: in 949 when he acted emissary for Berengar, in 960 when his mission for Otto I seems to have been halted on the island of Paxos and he described himself as a prisoner, in 968/69, the mission which is recorded in the *Legatio* and lastly, if the *Translatio Sancti Hymerii* is to be believed, in 971 when he was one of two bishops who accompanied Archbishop Gero of Cologne to the court of John I Tzimisces to escort a long-hoped-for bride for Otto II and her treasures back to Italy. From this journey, according to the *Translatio*, he never returned to Cremona again. He is thought to have died, though [121], on Italian soil. Whether he wanted to or not – and the *Translatio* has it that he was forced to go – his expertise and speaking knowledge of Greek were indispensable. Of late the *Translatio S. Hymerii* has come to be regarded as a better source than it was in Becker's and Max Manitius's day.[4]

Girolamo Arnaldi thought that Liudprand came of merchant stock but it seems unlikely.[5] This is not to underrate the roles and functions of merchants in tenth-century diplomacy. Liudprand himself has described how he met Otto I's envoy to Byzantium, Liutfrid, in Venice before 25 August 949, the day of their joint departure, and Liutfrid was a very rich Mainz merchant.[6] John of

---

Sutherland, *Liudprand of Cremona, Bishop, Diplomat, Historian: Studies of the Man and his Age* (Spoleto, 1988 completed 1977 and published posthumously).

[2] Liudprand, *Antapodosis* IV 1, p. 104 and V 30, p. 149: 'secretorum eius conscium ac epistolarum constituunt signatorem'.

[3] Liudprand, *Antapodosis* III 22-4, pp. 82-3, his father's embassy. For his stepfather's see ibid. V 14 and 15, pp. 137-9 and further R. Hiestand, *Byzanz und das Regnum Italicum im 10. Jahrhundert* (Zürich, 1964), pp. 154f., 181ff.

[4] For 960 see Liudprand, *Antapodosis* III 1, p. 74. For the embassy of 971 see the *Translatio S. Hymerii, MGH SS* 3, p. 266, n. 23; Becker, *Liudprandi Opera* (as n. 1), p. xii; Manitius, *Geschichte* (as n. 1), pp. 171f. Already Köpke-Dümmler, *Otto der Große*, p. 478 n. 3 were inclined to accept the report of the *Translatio*. For a more recent endorsement of the *Translatio* as a contemporary source and of Liudprand's last visit to Constantinople in 971 see W. Ohnsorge, 'Die Heirat Ottos II. mit der Byzantinerin Theophano', *Braunschweigisches Jahrbuch*, 54 (1973), p. 39 and n. 69.

[5] 'Liutprando e la storiografia contemporanea nell'Italia centro-settentrionale', in *La Storiografia Altomedievale* (Settimane 17, Spoleto, 1970), pp. 517f.

[6] Liudprand, *Antapodosis* VI 4, pp. 153f and Arnaldi, 'Liutprando' (as n. 5), p. 518.

Gorze's embassy to Cordoba in 953 relied heavily on the services of experienced Verdun merchants and the relief mission which had to be sent to
extricate John from Cordoba was conducted and manned by a Verdun trader.[7]
But while Liudprand treated Otto I's envoy with respect, elsewhere he talks of
merchants with an air of distance, not to say disdain. The Venetians and
Amalfitans earned their livelihood by selling 'us' Byzantine purple-dyed
cloaks, he reported himself saying to the imperial authorities, and he bitterly
resented that his purchases of purple mantles should be treated like the
merchants'.[8] He was of course a bishop by then but his voice became one of
scorn in [122] *Legatio*, c. 9 when he belittled the onlookers who lined the route of
the emperor Nicephorus Phocas's procession. The crowd which gathered
along the way from the palace to Hagia Sophia was made up of traders and
ignoble persons, he wrote.[9] From this it would appear that Liudprand sprang
from a family of urban nobles with hereditary palace connections. He thought
himself a cut above merchants and is anxious to let us know that he was by birth
a man of rank as well as substance. In the first chapter of Book III of the
Antapodosis he explains to his mandatory, Bishop Recemund of Elvira, the
strange title he had chosen for his work: it was to be one of retribution against
Berengar, now king of Italy, and his wife Willa with whom he had fallen out
and broken so that he fled northwards to the Ottonian court where he was able
to enter the services of Otto I's chapel. He would repay Berengar and Willa for
their lies, their plunder and the impieties they had committed against his,
Liudprand's house, his *cognatio* and his *familia*. Let us weigh his words
carefully. He spoke of his house as if he had now become the head of it – we do
not know when his stepfather or his mother died. He had a *cognatio* and a
familia which meant men who served him, unfree and free, for their keep and
perhaps their prospects, and all this well before he had become a bishop.[10]

Diplomacy in the tenth century may well have been a rewarding if dangerous
occupation. We know from Liudprand that his father rendered valuable
services to the emperor Romanus Lecapenus and was richly repaid for them.
He had apparently been assaulted by Slav rebels near Thessalonica but the
attack must have been beaten off and some of the leading assailants were
captured. He himself could present them to the emperor.[11] It could well be that
not only the standing but also the wealth of Liudprand's family owed something to these occasions. His own experience in 949 can serve as an illustration.
Liudprand in the *Antapodosis* is very bitter about Berengar's meanness. The
costs of the embassy were borne by his stepfather – it must be remembered that
Berengar was not [123] yet king – and Liudprand himself (or rather his stepfather)

[7]   *Vita Iohannis Gorziensis*, cc. 116, 117, 130, 134, *MGH SS* 4, pp. 370, 375, 376 and see also
Arnaldi, 'Liutprando' (as n. 5), p. 518.
[8]   Liudprand, *Legatio* c. 55, p. 205.
[9]   Ibid. c. 9, p. 180.
[10]   Liudprand, *Antapodosis* III 1, p. 74.
[11]   Ibid. III 24, p. 83.

had to provide the indispensable gifts to present to Constantine Porphyrogenitus. Berengar had only furnished him with a letter. He has told us what he
offered: nine hauberks, seven shields with gilded bosses, two silver-gilt cups,
swords, lances, spits and four eunuch slaves.[12] Constantine not only honoured
him with a relatively early second audience at which he himself conversed with
the envoy which was unusual. Dinner followed and afterwards the emperor
also gave him and his followers a great gift.[13] But this was not all. In the week
before Palm Sunday Liudprand, no doubt to impress him, was invited to watch
the annual payment of their ρογαι to the *rector domus*, the commander-in-
chief and the admiral, followed by the highest-ranking dignitaries, the *magis-
troi* and *patrikioi*, then the *protospatharioi* and many others. Liudprand saw
the 'pay-parade' and noted, as he was meant to, particularly its dignity and
orderliness. Asked what he thought of it by Constantine but through the
logothete, Liudprand had the wit, not to say effrontery, to reply that it would
please him very well if it were of any use to him, just the rich man parching in
hell would have been pleased by Lazarus's ease if it had given him any relief
but since this did not happen, how could it please him? Constantine took this
well and gave the ambassador a great court dress and a pound of gold.[14]
Altogether Liudprand may have gone home scarcely any poorer than when he
arrived with his presents. In the *Antapodosis*, in sum, he can be seen as
something of a client of the Macedonian dynasty, a clientage which echoed and
had resonance still in the *Legatio*.

Hitherto Liudprand has been known to us through three works to which a
few papal privileges, exchanges, *placita*, a diploma and a letter of Otto I's,
where he appears, can be added: the *Antapodosis* which he began to write in
958 and had not yet finished in 962 when Otto I had been crowned emperor by
Pope John XII, the *Historia Ottonis* which he wrote in 964/65 cutting out
abruptly with the [124] degradation of Pope Benedict V as an *invasor*, then
finally the *Relatio de Legatione Constantinopolitana*.[15] This, in the form of a
letter addressed to Otto I, his son and fellow-emperor, Otto II, and Adelheid,
the *Augusta*, must have been written in 969 shortly after Liudprand's return to

---

[12] Ibid. VI 3, 6, pp. 153, 155f.

[13] Ibid. VI 7, p. 156: 'magnoque post convivium me meosque asseculas munere donavit'.

[14] Ibid. VI 10, pp. 157f. for Liudprand's thorough description of the occasion.

[15] For the papal privileges see H. Zimmermann (ed.), *Papsturkunden 896-1046* (Österreichische Akademie der Wissenschaften, Philosophisch-Historische Klasse, Denkschriften 174,
Vienna, 1984), nos. 179, 185, 186, 187 (a *spurium* for Meissen), 197, all 967 × 969. For Liudprand's
participation in a royal judgement at Ravenna in April 967, see C. Manaresi, *I placiti del 'Regnum
Italiae'*, vol. 2 pt. 1 (Fonti per la storia d'Italia 96/1, Rome, 1957) no. 155, p. 51, and also no. 156,
p. 56, of 12 June 967, at Monte Veltraio, where he subscribed: 'Hliuto episcopus interfui'. He
intervened on behalf of the Patriarch Rodald of Aquileia in Otto I's diploma of 29 April 967 (D O I
341). For his prominent role as Otto I's representative at a synod in Milan in 969 see *I placiti*, no.
206, pp. 242-4. In 970 he also presided over a plea together with Count Heccico 'comes vassus et
missus imperialis' at Ferrara. See *I placiti*, no. 164, pp. 97-9. The last two can serve as evidence to
show that Liudprand remained high in the esteem and confidence of Otto I after his embassy to
Constantinople in 968.

Italy from Corfu where we hear of him by his own account early in January with strident complaints about further delays and extortion. The *Legatio*, as we have it, also breaks off unfinished. It may well rest on notes Liudprand made en route and it must be distinguished from any written report he may have submitted to the Ottonians on his return.

To these three *opera* must now be added a fourth. It has long been known that Bishop Abraham of Freising (955-993/4) possessed a copy of the *Antapodosis* and the *Historia Ottonis*. Italian peculiarities have been traced in this Freising manuscript (now at Munich, clm 6388), an important branch in the transmission of the text which became one of the channels of its early propagation.[16] [125] Bishop Abraham of Freising had however an even more famous codex, now clm 6426, his handbook as a bishop with homilies, including one by Rather of Verona, canonistic snippets, *formulae*, blessings and Old Slavonic texts which had a part to play in the missionary efforts of the see of Freising in Carinthia.[17] Here, also, there is a homily by Liudprand, an Easter sermon. We owe its discovery to Bernhard Bischoff who has now edited it. He can show that the fascicule with the sermon was handled by Liudprand himself who gave it its superscription in Greek.[18] Bischoff dated the sermon about the year 960, a difficult time because we know that Liudprand was then employed on a mission eastwards and suffered arrest in Paxos but this may have happened in summer so that there was room for the homily before he departed.[19] As he calls himself a deacon it must fall into the time before his promotion to the episcopate but from internal evidence it could have been written and delivered when it was imminent and expected. In his sermon Liudprand reveals himself as a schooled theologian and a dialectician. The Trinity is triumphantly vindicated against a Hebrew whose arguments are taken to task one by one. This leads him to expound the Incarnation and to extol Easter as the victory of life over death. However deeds must follow words. Liudprand above all exhorts his brethren, fellow clerks, to works of charity. It is here that we can once again locate him socially and recognise his own situation in his vivid images: if we meet the *familiares* of kings and princes

[16] On Bishop Abraham of Freising see K. Becher in *Neue Deutsche Biographie*, vol. 1 (Berlin, 1953), p. 21 and K.J. Leyser, 'Liudprand of Cremona, Preacher and Homilist', above, pp. 111-24. On Munich, Staatsbibliothek, MS clm. 6388 see N. Daniel, *Handschriften des zehnten Jahrhunderts aus der Freisinger Dombibliothek* (Münchener Beiträge zur Mediävistik und Renaissance-Forschung 11, Munich, 1973), pp. 105-6 and J. Koder, 'Liudprand von Cremona und die griechische Sprache' in J. Koder and T. Weber, *Liudprand* (as in n. 1), pp. 62-5.

[17] On this manuscript see B. Bischoff, 'Über gefaltete Hanschriften, vornehmlich hagiographischen Inhalts', in idem, *Mittelalterliche Studien* 1 (Stuttgart, 1966), pp. 93-100 and Daniel, *Hanschriften* (as n. 16), pp. 114ff.

[18] B. Bischoff, 'Eine Osterpredigt Liudprands von Cremona (um 960)', in idem, *Anecdota Novissima: Texte des vierten bis sechzehnten Jahrhunderts* (Quellen und Untersuchungen zur Lateinischen Philologie des Mittelalters 7, Stuttgart, 1984), pp. 20-34.

[19] For Liudprand's mission halted on Paxos see Liudprand, *Antapodosis* III 1, p. 74 and K.J. Leyser, 'The Tenth Century in Byzantine-Western Relationships', in *Relations Between East and West in the Middle Ages*, ed. D. Baker (Edinburgh, 1973), p. 30 and n. 7 (Leyser, *Medieval Germany*, p. 104).

we receive them with great honour and offer them precious [126] gifts even if they protest. The poor are the *familiares* of our Lord, Christ, but we offer them little or nothing.[20]

In its vivacity and social forcefulness the sermon is very much the authentic and familiar voice of Liudprand. What light does this newcomer throw on the works we know? Here we must above all look at the *Antapodosis* and leave aside for the moment the *Historia Ottonis* and the *Legatio*. Not only were sermon and *Antapodosis* conceived in temporal closeness to one another, the *Book of Retribution* is also much less of a *livre d'occasion* than were both the *History* and the *Embassy*. Here the sermon only strengthens an impression that can already be gained without it: it is Liudprand's seriousness and homiletic urgency throughout. He will not countenance any accommodation and self-interested cow-bargaining between Christians and their heathen attackers, Saracens, and Magyars alike. Those who engaged in such practices for their own ends like the nobles of Provence, the emperor Arnulf and later, Hugh of Arles, king of Italy, who allowed the Saracens of Fraxinetum to survive in order to block the Alpine passes for him, all incurred the just penalties of God's wrath. The emperor Arnulf was in the end eaten by worms.[21] Liudprand has often been regarded as a light-hearted, scurrilous writer, only too anxious to entertain, revelling in sexual anecdote and without a larger or [127] deeper message.[22] That does him scant justice. In the very opening of the *Antapodosis* he has told us that the minds of academicians, peripatetics and stoics, tired if they were not refreshed again by the 'utilis comoediarum risus' and the enjoyable histories of heroic deeds. If this is true of the execrable pagans, if we read of Pompey, Hannibal, Hasdrubal and Scipio Africanus, which is noxious, why should the deeds of their Christian equals be ignored, and – he adds by implication – the 'utilis comoediarum risus'

---

[20] Bischoff, 'Osterpredigt' (as n. 18), pp. 21-2 and Leyser, 'Liudprand of Cremona', above, pp. 118-20.

[21] For Liudprand's condemnation of the Emperor Arnulf, whom he accused of opening the Magyars' way into western Europe, see Liudprand, *Antapodosis* I 13, pp. 15-16. He blamed him also for outrages committed by his men during the invasion of Italy in 896, ibid. I 33, pp. 25-6. For Arnulf's death see ibid. I 36, p. 27. Here Liudprand did not want to be sure whether Arnulf suffered on earth and eternally for his crime of letting in the Magyars or whether his horrible illness atoned for this. For Liudprand's censure of Hugh of Arles's *foedus* with the Saracens of Fraxinetum see ibid. V 17, p. 139. It too was followed by divine retribution: ibid. V 31, p. 149. However, while Liudprand denounced Romanos Lecapenos for giving himself and one of his sons precedence over Costantine VII as *basileis* (ibid. III 37, p. 91), he did not animadvert on him for allegedly inviting the African Saracens to help him subdue rebellious Byzantine provinces in southern Italy (ibid. II 45, pp. 57f.).

[22] For these judgements on Liudprand see Leyser, 'Liudprand of Cremona', above, pp. 120-1. More recently J.N. Sutherland in his articles, 'The Idea of Revenge' (as n. 1) and 'The Mission to Constantinople in 968 and Liudprand of Cemona', *Traditio*, 31 (1975), pp. 55-81, did not join his chorus of dismissal but he concluded all the same: 'Liudprand was neither a profound thinker nor a specially religious man' ('Idea of Revenge', p. 408) and (to my mind a sad misjudgement): 'The *Antapodosis* shows few signs of a well-developed sense of God, his nature and power, or his purpose in creating the world' (ibid).

not also be harnessed to the exposure of vice, sloth or merit, here for didactic purposes? This is what in the sequel he does.[23]

Liudprand the Byzantinist must be placed into a larger setting. The very ample space assigned to Byzantium in the historical landscape of the *Antapodosis* can only be understood if we are aware of what Liudprand had in mind when he planned and wrote it. Here we must turn to the dedication of the *Antapodosis*. It was addressed to and its very composition had been prompted by Recemund, bishop of Elvira, in Spain under the rule of the Umayyad Caliph Abd ar-Rahman III.[24] Liudprand had escaped from Italy and at first his exile seems to have been far from easy. He may not have found at once a ready welcome in the Ottonian entourage and until 955 Otto was engaged in almost continuous warfare. Of Charlemagne Einhard had written that he loved [128] foreigners and spared no trouble and expense to entertain and keep them at his court.[25] Widukind of Corvey who followed Einhard's *topoi* and used his words so skilfully in presenting Otto I to his readers did not repeat this, like other Einhard passages, when he wrote of the Saxon king. Perhaps Otto I did not like foreigners, but it was inevitable with his growing prestige that they should flock to his court and seek his protection and goodwill. He also had uses for their services, not least of all Liudprand's. Liudprand met Recemund of Elvira at Otto's February *curia* in Frankfurt in 956.[26] He had come there as the envoy of Abd ar-Rahman III to find a way out of a quandary. Three years before Otto had sent a mission to Cordoba headed by none other than John of Gorze. They came with presents and the usual letter but here the trouble lay. The letter's contents were known in Cordoba before the ambassadors presented them.[27] They contained a few commonplaces aimed at the *perfidia* of the caliph which could only be regarded as blasphemy of the Islamic faith. The penalty for this was death and not even the diplomatic immunity of the envoys could have shielded them from this fate if Otto I's missive, drafted under the auspices of his brother Brun, the *archicapellanus*, had been read aloud and interpreted to the caliph's court. He himself was compromised if he connived at and knowingly counte-nanced such utterances. The two great empires, Cordoba and Byzantium at the western and eastern ends of the Mediterranean both feared diplomatic surprises and maintained what might be called a diplomatic early warning system. That Otto I chose two reforming monks, like John and his companion Garamannus for the embassy to Cordoba was in itself very significant. These men were already *perfecti* and dead to the world, ready, if need be to face

[23] Liudprand, *Antapodosis* I 1, pp. 3-5.

[24] On Recemund of Elvira see *Le Liber Ordinum en usage dans l'église wisigothique et mozarabe d'Espagne du cinquième au onzième siècle*, ed. D. Marius Férotin (Monumenta Ecclesiae Liturgica 5, Paris, 1904), pp. xxxiii-xxxv. See also H. Florez, *España Sagrada*, vol. 12 (Madrid, 1754), pp. 171-4 and E. Lévi-Provençal, *Histoire de l'Espagne Musulmane*, 2: *Le Califat umaiyade de Cordoue*, 2nd edn (Paris, 1950), pp. 139, 148-9, 161-2 and vol. 3, pp. 222-3 and pp. 239f.

[25] Einhard, *Vita Karoli*, c. 21, p. 26.

[26] Köpke-Dümler, *Otto der Große*, pp. 277-80 and Böhmer-Ottenthal, no. 241a.

[27] *Vita Iohannis Gorziensis* (as n. 7) cc. 119, 120, p. 371.

martyrdom. The real point of this mission was not so much the Saracen raiders' nest at Fraxinetum, only nominally [129] under the caliph's jurisdiction, but a kind of religious reconnaissance. In the *Vita Iohannis Gorziensis* by John of St Arnulf the last twenty-two chapters dealt with this Cordoban mission and the true villains in it were not Abd ar-Rahman and his court but the local Christians, the Mozarabs with their compromises, their assimilative practices, their anxiety not to give offence to their Moslem overlords.[28]

Recemund of Elvira had been a well-educated, bilingual, lay court official, a secretary who redacted petitions and drafted their answers since all traffic into and out of the palace had to be in writing. The object of his mission was to persuade Otto I to redraft the letter which his envoys had to present to the caliph. John of Gorze had remained deaf to all proposals to suppress the original letter and offer the presents only. Recemund had volunteered for the counter-embassy after he had ascertained that it would not be dangerous. The bishopric of Elvira was his immediate reward.[29] That an envoy from Cordoba and Liudprand, the political refugee from the Italian kingdom could meet and make one another's acquaintance under Otto I's patronage says much for the new stature and eminence of the Saxon Reich. At his February court in Frankfurt Otto I also received ambassadors from Byzantium, Rome and other parts of the world, including 'Saracens', perhaps from Ifriqiya. They all came to congratulate him on his recent victories over Magyars and Slavs and to honour him with the exotic, costly presents that were almost the purpose of these exchanges.[30]

Recemund of Elvira, the Cordoban diplomat and Liudprand of a Pavese family, no doubt landed, but urban in upbringing and outlook, had much in common. They were the servants of princes with sophisticated courts, in Liudprand's case those of Hugh of Arles and Berengar II. They were *litterati* and men of talent. Recemund too was an author and part of the famous Cordoban [130] Calendar with its survey of crop cultivations, one of our principal sources for the economy of Moslem Spain, is linked with him. Their Mediterranean likeness cannot be overlooked. It was Recemund who asked for a history with the 'deeds of the emperors and kings of the whole of Europe'.[31] That Liudprand did not offer his first major literary work to his Ottonian patrons and protectors but to a bishop *in partibus infidelium* is at first sight very surprising indeed, but I hope to show that in doing so he did not act against the wishes of his Liudolfing benefactors. The *Antapodosis* is a parallel history of Italy, the east-Frankish kingdom and Byzantium, roughly from the late ninth

---

[28] Ibid. cc. 122, 123, p. 372.

[29] Ibid. cc. 128, 129, pp. 374-5.

[30] Widukind, *Res gestae Saxonicae* III 56, p. 135.

[31] For Recemund's share in the calendar see Férotin, *Liber Ordinum* (as n. 24), pp. xxxiii-xxxv, and especially R. Dozy, *Le Calendrier de Cordoue*, new edn and French trans. by Ch. Pellat (Medieval Iberian Peninsula Texts and Studies 1, Leiden, 1961). For Liudprand's programme in the *Antapodosis* cf. I 1, p. 4: 'totius Europae... imperatorum regumque facta' with the well-attested heading: 'Regum atque principum partis Europae', p. 1.

to the mid-tenth century. It is remarkable how little notice Liudprand took of western *Francia* and Anglo-Saxon England. The deeds of emperors and kings are presented in a rough, sometimes very rough, chronological order and despite his switch to the theme of being even with Berengar II and his wife Willa, Liudprand adhered to a certain scheme. There is no doubt however that the pivot of his for the most part Mediterranean world as far as it belonged to *Christianitas* was Byzantium. Liudprand treated the empire readily as the *caput* of the Christian universe as he skirted along his story: Rome, Italy, east Francia and the Burgundian kingdom with Provence being the other *regna* and principalities he kept under review all through. They are seen as parts of a larger whole, Europe, presided over by Constantinople, and Liudprand looked upon the Hungarian attacks and the depredations of the Saracens of Fraxinetum and southern Italy as a compound threat to this whole. Now the inscription to Recemund of Elvira, the Spanish bishop *in partibus*, is not forgotten throughout the six books of the *Antapodosis*. He is addressed at least twelve times in the text. Some scholars e.g. Martin Lintzel, thought that this was a mere literary [131] fiction and therefore of no special importance. It seems to me to be, on the contrary, decisive for understanding the *Antapodosis* and its massive Byzantine component.[32]

At this point it is necessary to glance briefly once more at the last twenty-two chapters of the *Life* of John of Gorze with their harsh criticism of the Mozarabs' temporising attitudes, the temptation to succumb to the attractions of Islamic urban culture only half resisted, the spread of syncretistic practices like refusing to eat pork and practising circumcision. In the ninth century this process of erosion had been checked and resisted by a spate of notoriously deliberate martyrdoms. By openly and publicly attacking Islam the Christian 'activists' forced the Moslem authorities in al-Andalus to persecute and so again harden the boundaries between the ruling and the ruled communities.[33] It seems that the challenge to assimilative and culturally fusing Christian urban society or at least its wealthier cells, now no longer came from within but from without. The author of the Lotharingian monk's *Life* told his readers that the Latins in Cordoba needed to be reminded of their duties as Christians. Their culture and their pleasure were suspect and wrong.

[32] M. Lintzel, *Studien über Liudprand von Cremona* (Historische Studien 233, Berlin, 1933), p. 53 reprinted in idem, *Ausgewählte Schriften*, 2 vols. (Berlin, 1961), vol. 2, p. 382. The places in the *Antapodosis* where Recemund is directly addressed or referred to are: I 1, pp. 3-4; I 2 p. 5 (Fraxinetum); I 11, p. 13 (the vigilance of the Emperor Leo the Wise); I 30, p. 24 (re-ordinations); I 44, p. 31 (in praise of King Lambert, *ob*. 898); III 1, p. 73 (explaining *antapódosis*); III 3 , p. 75 (the burning of Pavia in 924); IV, 1, p. 104 (Liudprand henceforth a participant of what he relates); IV 6, p. 105 (on Manasses of Arles); IV 24, p. 117 (Otto I's victory at Birten); IV 28, p. 123 (Otto resists temptation); V 2, p. 131 (the battle of Simancas); V 19, p. 141 (a reference to Cordoba).

[33] On these persecutions see F.R. Franke, 'Die freiwilligen Märtyrer von Cordoba und das Verhältnis der Mozaraber zum Islam', *Spanische Forschungen der Görresgesellschaft* Erste Reihe, 13 (1958), pp. 1-170 and E. Colbert, *The Martyrs of Cordoba (850-59): A Study of the Sources* (The Catholic University of America, Studies in Mediaeval History, New Series 17, Washington D.C., 1962).

Now Liudprand in the *Antapodosis*, in a less ascetic manner, had exactly the same message for the Spanish Christians or at least for one of their leading lights, an influential man whom he had come to know. Recemund of Elvira is addressed as one who had perforce to [132] live among infidels. He must therefore be kept in touch and instructed. He must know what went on inside *Christianitas* and above all where its righteous interests and those of the Saracens and other enemies clashed. Recemund is asked to commemorate in his prayers the Pavese who were burned to death on 12 March 924, 'hora tertia' when the Hungarians assaulted the city and set it on fire.[34] When Liudprand mentioned a battle (at Simancas) fought on 19 July (939) where Abd ar-Rahman III suffered a sharp defeat at the hands of King Ramiro II of Leon, the bishop is meant to sympathise with the victors and not with his worsted master.[35] It is not for nothing that the very first topic of the *Antapodosis* was the Hispano-Arabic colony at Fraxinetum and the terrible damage it had inflicted on Provence and the Alpine regions. The *Vita Iohannis Gorziensis* and the *Antapodosis* had something startling in common despite their profoundly differing origins. John of Gorze's biographer dwelt above all on his hero's *constantia* when under duress in Cordoba and on his aggressive, not to say dangerously impolitic behaviour, especially towards the anxious Mozarabic dignitaries, the leading members of the Christian community in al-Andalus. The manners and the habitus of the caliph were described up to a point in a tone of distance and an affected lack of curiosity. John remains a monk throughout. He would not wear the right clothes when the time for the long-awaited reception audience at last came, no court dress. The caliph is made to be impressed by this. He had sent John ten pounds in coins to acquire robes and the envoy had given it all to the poor. Abd ar-Rahman in the end agreed to receive him in his black habit, saying he would see him even if he wore a sack.[36] To the biographer this irony served as proof for John's observance of the Rule at all times.

Behind the *Vita Iohannis* and the *Antapodosis* lay a hardening of attitudes which accompanied success. They hardened because [133] Europe had until recently suffered too much from Norse, Saracens and Magyars not to be harsh and intolerant in its responses. It is this mood which shaped the pages of Liudprand no less than the biography of John of Gorze. Other texts, like Hrotsvitha of Gandersheim's *Pelagius*, a poem in honour of one of the latest Christian martyrs in al-Andalus (d. 925) who rejected both conversion and homosexuality, strengthen the sense of a new aggressiveness.[37] It expressed itself in a profound distaste for everything associated with the enemies of

---

[34] Liudprand, *Antapodosis* III 3, p. 75.

[35] On the battle of Simancas, which was fought on 1 August 939, see R. Collins, *Early Medieval Spain: Unity in Diversity, 400-1000* (London, 1983), pp. 197, 241 and Lévi-Provençal, *Histoire* (as n.24), pp. 56-62.

[36] *Vita Iohannis Gorziensis* (as n. 27) c. 131, p. 375.

[37] *Hrotsvithae Opera*, ed. P. von Winterfeld (MGH SRG 34, Berlin, 1965), pp. 52-62 and *Hrotsvithae Opera*, ed. H. Homeyer (Paderborn, 1970), pp. 123-46.

Christianity. What matters here is that in Liudprand Byzantium is, like the west, surrounded by ferocious *gentes* and some of their enemies, like Magyars, Northmen and Saracens, they shared. Even though Otto I is, in Book IV of the *Antapodosis*, called 'nunc imperator', the problem of the two emperorships does not cloud the pages of the *Antapodosis*.[38]

We do not know whether Recemund of Elvira ever received a *Widmungsexemplar* of the work especially written for him. We should assume he did rather than not even thought it lacked a formal conclusion and a Spanish branch of its transmission has barely been hinted at. The *Antapodosis* had an important literary afterlife and spread in Lotharingia, Bavaria and Austria, not apparently in Italy. Writers like Sigebert of Gembloux and Frutolf of Michelsberg used and valued it.[39] It has been suggested that the Ottonians may not have felt slighted that the *Antapodosis* in which they were after all referred to almost always in a panegyric tone, was addressed to Recemund of Elvira rather than one of them, say the literate Empress Adelheid with her own interests in Italy. The letter John of Gorze had to take to Cordoba was the Saxon king's rejoinder to the caliph's own matter of course Islamic self-assertion. Its Christian counterthrust was, as we saw, deliberate. To extricate the [134] ambassador it had to be suppressed but a historiographical survey of Christian Europe's sufferings and then its growing strength and solidarity sent to a Christian servant of the Umayyads, made readily the same point, albeit in a more roundabout way. The destruction of Fraxinetum remained high on Otto I's programme as late as 968 when Liudprand was in Constantinople and the showdown with the Greeks in southern Italy had taken a menacing turn.[40]

To it and the *Legatio* we must now turn. Liudprand was in Constantinople only from 4 June to 2 October 968. For an embassy over such distances this was in the tenth century not an exceptionally long time. John of Gorze had been detained in Cordoba for three years and the envoys Abd ar-Rahman III had previously sent to Otto I spent no less time involuntarily in Germany. The caliph's principal ambassador, a bishop, had died.[41] The general prospects for Liudprand's mission were poor after Otto I's setback and retreat from Bari in March 968.[42] Without a fleet he could not take it but he had found allies in the

---

[38] Liudprand, *Antapodosis* VI 4, p. 153.

[39] For the spread of Liudprand's *Antapodosis* see the introduction of Becker's edition, p. xxxii-xxxiv and J. Becker, *Textgeschichte Liudprands von Cremona* (Quellen und Untersuchungen zur lateinischen Philologie des Mittelalters, 3/2 Munich, 1908), pp. 39-46 and also Manitius, *Geschichte* (as n. 1), p. 174.

[40] For this see Otto I's letter of 968 in Widukind, *Res Gestae Saxonicae* III 70, p. 147, announcing his intention to return home via Fraxinetum and to destroy the Saracens there.

[41] *Vita Iohannis Gorziensis* (as n. 27) c. 115, p. 370.

[42] For the situation on the eve of Liudprand's embassy see Köpke-Dümmler, *Otto der Große*, pp. 346f., Böhmer-Ottenthal, nos. 468b, 468c and R. Hotzmann, *Geschichte der sächsischen Kaiserzeit* (Munich, 1943), pp. 217-18. On Liudprand's mission, besides the literature cited above n. 1, see Lintzel, *Liudprand* (as n. 32), pp. 370-84, Sutherland, 'Mission' (as n. 22) and P. Lamma, 'Il problema dei due imperi e dell'Italia meridionale nel giudizio delle fonti letterarie dei secoli IX e X' in *Atti del 3 Congresso Internazionale di Studi sull'Alto Medioevo* (Spoleto, 1959), especially pp. 229-46.

south and could continue to threaten the Greeks there. Even so, it must be remembered that Liudprand received a chrysobull and it is quite possible that the exchanges between him and his interlocutors were nothing like as shrill and heated as the *Legatio* suggests.[43] If Nicephorus Phocas denied Otto the *basileus Francorum* title which we find twice in Cedrenus, he certainly did not break all bridges with Liudprand.[44] Nor must we [135] believe, as some scholars suggest, that the bishop of Cremona lacked all diplomatic skills.[45] We don't know. Diplomacy is only the setting, not the substance of the *Legatio*. It does not tell us what Liudprand could or could not offer. Occasionally the text allows us to see that what the bishop of Cremona purported to say and what he did say differed. This is particularly the case after the arrival of Pope John XIII's letters and envoys where the *imperator Graecorum* title gave of course deep offence. Liudprand withdrew here at once and did his best to pacify the Greeks by promising the correct address next time: 'Romanorum imperatores et Augusti'.[46]

The *Legatio* is clearly a call to war and offers the justification for such a war with a call to judgement on Nicephorus and his patriarch. It sought to win over opinion for more hostilities in Liudprand's own ambience, the Italian great and their *familiares*. They were to be informed, disillusioned and re-educated about the Greeks. The libel set the tone for Otto I's military operations of 969 which at Bovino suffered a bad setback with the capture of Count Pandulf of Capua, his chief ally, and later, at Ascoli, achieved a brutal success.[47] In the *Legatio* Liudprand tendered advice to the two Ottos which reflects the momentarily close relations with Pope John XIII. When he addressed them as *imperatores Romanorum* however, we know that Otto I, in his diplomata, remained firmly 'imperator augustus' and no more. He treated this advice and its manifestations with reserve. The murder of Nicephorus in December 969 and the accession of John Tzimisces did his work for him shortly afterwards. So much for the course of events.

The most arresting feature of Liudprand's vision of Constantinople and the imperial court in the *Legatio*, that which strikes us most [136] and must have struck his contemporary audience at once were the details, the minute observations, comments and outbursts. Liudprand was a glutton for the taste, the feel and the smell of everything he came across in Constantinople and he succeeded in conveying this to his readers. The food, the sauces, the wine, the clothes worn at processions, the Greeks' headgear, all these received the closest attention in

---

[43] For Liudprand's chrysobull see Liudprand, *Legatio*, c. 56, p. 206.

[44] W. Ohnsorge, 'Die Anerkennung des Kaisertums Ottos I. durch Byzanz', *Byzantinische Zeitschrift*, 54 (1961), pp. 28-52, especially pp. 29-32, reprinted in idem, *Konstantinopel und der Okzident* (Darmstadt, 1966), pp. 176-207, especially pp. 178-81.

[45] E.g. Rentschler, *Liudprand* (as in n. 1), p. 56.

[46] Liudprand, *Legatio*, cc. 47, 51, 53, pp. 200f., 202-3.

[47] On the 969 campaign in southern Italy see Köpke-Dümmler, *Otto der Große*, pp. 460-5, 468f., and see also Vera von Falkenhausen, *Untersuchungen über die byzantinischen Herrschaft in Süditalien vom 9, bis ins 11. Jahrhundert* (Schriften zur Geistesgeschichte des östlichen Europa 1, Wiesbaden, 1967), pp. 47-51, 83.

the *Legatio*, much more still than they had done in the *Antapodosis*.[48] They do not all carry the allegorical overtones of the wild asses he saw in Nicephorus's parks. What were Liudprand's purposes? Whey does he tell us so much about these things, grateful though we are to possess them? Travellers' books were rare in the Latin west of the tenth century, much rarer than among the Arabs. We have the Alfredian reports of Ohthere's and Wulfstan's journeys added to the Orosius translation and we have again that other *Legatio* of the tenth century already discussed here, the last twenty-two chapters of the *Life of John of Gorze*.[49] We should be doing an injustice to the *legatio*-part of the *Vita Iohannis* if we failed to see it as the splendid source it is for the Verdun slave trade, the routes it used, the entry formalities at the frontier between Christian and Moslem Spain between Barcelona and Tortosa. Despite the deliberate austerity of the text, it does in the end devote a paragraph to the *apparatus* of the solemn, formal reception which echoes Arab accounts of the arrival of an embassy sent by Constantine Porphyrogenitus: the files of soldiers lining the route, both foot and horse, the mock combats staged by various bodies of troops all of different armament, men on mules and Moors who were posted [137] there to frighten the ambassadors and apparently did, the precious carpets and hangings, all these descriptions are not so unlike the scenes narrated by Liudprand; at least the genres are comparable.[50]

For Constantinople, however, Liudprand seems to stand on his own. His *Legatio* as a polemic has none of the solemnity of the great ninth-century controversy between the emperors Louis II and Basil I enshrined in Louis's letter of 871 with its hard-strained arguments to justify the Carolingian *imperiale nomen*.[51] These problems were there in 968 but they do not hold the centre of the stage in Liudprand's harangue and not even the fluctuating allegiances of the south Italian Lombard princes seem to dominate the exchanges between Nicephorus and Otto's envoy all the time.[52]

[48] T. Weber, 'Essen und Trinken in Konstantinopel des 10. Jahrhunderts nach den Berichten Liudprands von Cremona', in Koder and Weber, *Liudprand* (as n. 1), pp. 73-99.

[49] For these travel reports see *The Old English Orosius*, ed. J. Bately (Early English Text Society, Supplementary Series, London, 1980), p. 1xxif., 13-18 and *Anglo-Saxon Prose*, ed. and trans. M. Swanton (London, 1975), pp. 32-7.

[50] *Vita Iohannis Gorziensis* (as n. 27), cc. 117, 118, pp. 370-1 for John's journey, and cc. 132, 133, pp. 375-6 for the receptioin by the caliph. The embassy sent by Constantine VII to Cordoba is described in Lévi-Provençal, *Histoire* (as n. 24), pp. 151-3, and see A.A. Vasiliev, *Byzance et les Arabes*, 2:1 *La Dynastie Macédonienne (867-950)*, ed. M. Canard (Corpus Bruxellense Historiae Byzantinae 2/1, Brussels 1960), pp. 323-31 and 2/2 (Brussels, 1950), pp. 276-81, a translation of the text of Maqqari, citing Ibn Hayyan.

[51] Louis II's letter is in *MGH Epp.* 7, pp. 385-94; it is discussed by F. Dölger, 'Europas Gestalung im Spiegel der fränkisch-byzantinischen Auseinandersetzung des 9. Jahrhunderts', in idem, *Byzanz und die europäische Staatenwelt* (Darmstadt, 1964), pp. 311ff., 336ff. and by W. Ohnsorge, 'Die Entwicklung der Kaiseridee im 9. Jahrhundert und Süditalien', in idem, *Abendland und Byzanz* (Darmstadt, 1958), pp. 219-26 and idem, *Das Zweikaiserproblem im früheren Mittelalter* (Hildesheim, 1947), pp. 40-5; see also Lamma, 'Problema' (as n. 41), pp. 181ff.

[52] They are, however, one of the *Legatio's* most persistent themes, as Lamma, 'Problema' (as n. 41), has shown.

Liudprand's techniques in denigration here deserves some attention. You may recall his slighting remarks about the old and torn clothes worn by many of the *optimates* in Nicephorus's Whitsun procession from the Palace to Hagia Sophia. He wrote that they must have had these clothes from their great grandfathers and even then they were not new.[53] The rhetorical exaggeration is brilliant. Now the Byzantine aristocracy was fluid enough, there were plenty of *novi homines* and *arrivistes*. For a Byzantine noble it may well have been a cause of honour and pride to be seen wearing now and again [138] an ancestral garb at these festive functions. It could even be a demonstration of opposition. New robes and court dress were distributed lavishly every year as Liudprand himself has described in *Antapodosis* so that the wearing of old clothes must have been deliberate. Liudprand may have known this too but chose to ignore it in order to gain his effect and depict the grand ceremonial as a threadbare occasion. Here not only Nicephorus but the whole of his court, his *optimates*, were being slated.

To find out what Liudprand intended we must in fact consult another text, only to discover to our surprise that the bishop of Cremona did not stand alone, that he followed in fact, one could almost say, a tradition. Some of the things he tells us had been told before and seen together they reveal which features of the Byzantine polity, which rituals and procedures struck western observers, mainly ambassadors, most and clashed most severely with their own ruling habitat. To the best of my knowledge Byzantinists have not used the incidents in Notker of St Gallen's *Gesta Karoli* very much, above all systematically, though stray references have made here and there to compare them with Liudprand's *Legatio*.[54]

Notker wrote his *Gesta Karoli* in the 880s nearer the end rather than the beginning of the reign of the unfortunate Charles III who had encouraged him to set down his tales. Notker's source for Charlemagne's embassies and wars must have been Adalbert, the father of one of his fellow-monks and his *nutritor*, a great warrior-noble with much experience. We can thus locate the Frankish lay circles who possessed some knowledge of the eastern empire and its court. The first surprising discovery the Byzantinist makes when looking at Notker is one about communications. He furnishes clear evidence that the land-route between Byzantium and the east [139] Frankish kingdom was open and passable. Notker credited Charlemagne with having opened the route by victories over Slavs, Avars and Bulgars.[55] From what he said it can be deduced

---

[53] Liudprand, *Legatio*, c. 9, p. 181.

[54] Notker, *Gesta Karoli*. They have been referred to by Weber, 'Essen und Trinken' (as n. 47), p. 89 and n. 90 and by Becker in his edition of the *Legatio*, c. 63, p. 210 n. 3. On the *Gesta Karoli* see H. Löwe, 'Das Karlsbuch Notkers von St. Gallen und sein zeitgeschichtlicher Hintergrund', in H. Löwe, *Von Cassiodor zu Dante: Ausgewählte Aufsätze zur Geschichtsschreibung und politischen Ideenwelt des Mittelalters* (Berlin, 1973), pp. 123ff.; J.M. Wallace-Hadrill, *The Frankish Church* (Oxford, 1983), pp. 333ff. and H.-W. Goetz, *Strukturen der spätkarolingischen Epoche im Spiegel der Vorstellungen eines zeitgenössischen Mönchs: Eine Interpretation der 'Gesta Karoli' Notkers von Sankt Gallen* (Bonn, 1981).

[55] Notker, *Gesta Karoli* I 27, pp. 37f.

that the overland journey in the later ninth century, until the Magyars came, was possible and by no means unusual. The real reasons for this were the temporary pacification of the Bulgars and the rise of the Grand Moravian principality, perhaps also the great, competitive, missionary enterprises from Byzantium, Rome and east Francia in this region.

One parallel to Liudprand offers itself readily in the *Gesta*. You will recall (*Legatio*, c. 63) his bitter words about Greek bishops when, on his way back, he had a poor reception from the one in Leucas. He had not found a single hospitable bishop in all Greece, he complained.[56] There is a story to match this in the *Gesta*. A Carolingian embassy to Byzantium arrived in the autumn and Charles's *legatus* was made to stay with a bishop who imposed a regime of dearth and abstinence and was much given to fasting and prayer. Next spring he presented his charge to the *basileus*, here called *rex*. The emperor asked him how he found the bishop and the envoy replied: he, your bishop, is a most holy man in as far as it is possible to be so without God. The emperor was naturally shocked and asked how could anyone be holy without God. The envoy is made to reply: 'Scriptum est Deus caritas est', of which he has none.[57]

It seems to have been frequent Greek practice to break up the cohesion of foreign embassies by separating their members from one another. It is vouched for in Menander Protector and Liudprand mentions it too.[58] For instance at his first dinner at Nicephorus's [140] table where he complains at being seated only fifteenth, his *comites*, he writes, were not even allowed to dine in the same building.[59] At most of his interviews, it appears, his *leones*, his military (and clerical) following, were left behind in his quarters. Exactly the same practice is hinted at in the *Gesta Karoli* (II,6) where the various members of Charlemagne's mission were divided from one another.[60] We must understand how disconcerting this was to westerners. Their entire lives were lived in *Hausgenossenschaft* and *familiaritas*, the close association of kinsmen, followers and servants under the same roof. This is no less true of a bishop than a layman and some of Liudprand's irritation, even some of his *gaffes* might be explained by his being unable to consult his following, and from finding himself isolated from his *leones* as he called them. Confronted by the unexpected the Latins sought shelter by going into a huddle.

---

[56] Liudprand, *Legatio* c. 63, pp. 210-11.

[57] Notker, *Gesta Karoli* II 6, p. 53.

[58] *Excerpta de legationibus gentium e Menandro*, 6, in *Excerpta de Legationibus*, i. ed. C. de Boor (Berlin, 1903), pp. 447f. The separation of foreign emissaries from one another was not invariable Byzantine custom, e.g. Liudprand, *Antapodosis* VI 7, p. 156 (see above n. 13) when Liudprand and his following were, it seems, all invited together to the imperial banquet but it could be, and often was, used to disconcert them.

[59] For Liudprand's isolation from his staff and following see Liudprand, *Legatio*, c. 11, p. 181. Elsewhere he speaks usually in the first person, e.g. ibid. cc. 15 19, 21, 25-9, pp. 183, 185, 186f., 188-90. The plural 'invitaremur' (ibid. c. 19, p. 185) refers to Liudprand and the Bulgarian envoys. Altogether Liudprand had twenty-five men in his company (ibid. c. 34, p. 193), including five knights (ibid. c. 24, p. 188) and four Greek guards had been attached to him (c. 34, p. 193).

[60] Notker, *Gesta Karoli* II 6, pp. 53, 55.

Yet by far the most important and profound difference of political styles between east and west, also Cordoba and the west, lay in the all-embracing ritual and formality, the elaboration and matchless ubiquity of Byzantine court ceremonial.[61] It is not that the Carolingian and Ottonian courts knew no ritual, solemnities and formalities but they were intermittent and punctuated a routine of close companionship and *familiaritas*. It would also be mistaken to think that this western ritual only embraced crown-wearings. A [141] careful reading of e.g. Ermoldus Nigellus suggests that there was more. But the Ottonian court and society developed such occasions only slowly and they rejected Otto III's attempts to innovate here.[62]

Liudprand of course knew of this profound difference and was prepared for it as he prides himself in the *Antapodosis*. Not for him to be surprised by the artificial singing birds in the tree, the mechanical roar of the lions, the sudden elevation of the *basileus* at the reception audience.[63] Yet the helplessness of the Latins faced by this unremitting ceremonial is well exposed in a tale of the *Gesta Karoli* where an attempt is made to ape and so ridicule Byzantine procedures. Notker seems to allude to a traceable embassy of Charlemagne's, that of Bishop Heito of Basle and Count Hugh of Tours in 811. Once again they were dragged hither and thither, ill-treated and 'per diversissima loca divisi'. On their return they persuaded Charlemagne to make an example of the Byzantine counter-embassy, to make their journey unpleasant for them and their arrival even more so. The latter took the form of taking the Greeks from one Carolingian household officer to the next: first the constable, then the count palatine, then the butler (*magister mensae*) and finally the chamberlain. Each of these officers is represented as sitting in dignity surrounded by his attendants and minions and each time the envoys mistook him for Charlemagne himself only to be abused by their guides and pushed on. When they [142] finally came to Charlemagne he is characteristically shown standing at a

---

[61] On Byzantine court ceremonial and its expressive range see above all O. Treitinger, *Die oströmische Kaiser- und Reichsidee nach ihrer Gestaltung im höfischen Zeremoniell* (Jena, 1938), pp. 1-6 and pp. 197-202, on receptions. See also the introductory remarks to A. Vogt (ed.), *Constantin VII Porphyrogénète: Le livre des cérémonies, Commentaire* vol. 1 (Collection Byzantine, Paris, 1935), pp. xviii-xxxiii. Ceremonial are also the purposes and setting of the *Kletorologion* of Philotheos, ed. J.B. Bury in his *The Imperial Administrative System in The Ninth Century* (The British Academy Supplemental Papers 1, London, 1911).

[62] Ermold, *Carmen*, verse 684, p. 54: 'Hic cadit ante pedes, vestigia basiat alma' (Einhard before Charlemagne in 813) and cf. lines 173, 213, 582, pp. 18, 20, 46. Solemnities of the court, processions and well-ordered meals played their part in the baptism of King Heriold and his Danes in 826. See Ermold, *Carmen*, pp. 166ff. Otto III's attempts to manifest his kingship in new ways and so change its character, e.g. by dining alone and creating a new palace hierarchy, were widely criticised. See Thietmar, *Chronicon* IV 47, pp. 184f. For other sources and comment see P.E. Schramm, *Kaiser, Rom und Renovatio*, vol. 1, 2nd edn (Darmstadt, 1957), p. 148 and n. 2; Leyser, 'Tenth Century' (as n. 19), p. 44 (Leyser, *Medieval Germany*, p. 118); idem, *Rule and Conflict*, p. 103 and n. 29; '*Theophanu Imperatrix*', below, p. 164.

[63] Liudprand, *Antapodosis* VI 5, p. 155: 'Nulla admiratione commotus, quoniam quidem ex his omnibus eos qui bene noverant fueram percontatus'.

window surrounded by his family rather than alone on a throne.[64] This by no means exhausts the parallels to Liudprand in Notker. Even the notorious fish-sauce, the fish dipped in *pigmenta* is there.[65] Throughout the west the Greeks were reputed to be cunning and astute. In the *Gesta Karoli* the Carolingian envoy is made to outwit them. In Widukind of Corvey they won their victory at Bovino by trickery.[66] Liudprand is anxious to convince his Italian audience that they were a match for the Byzantines in war, no less than in other dealings.

What conclusions can be drawn from these analogies between the *Legatio* and the stories of the *Gesta*? It would be rash to say that all western envoys nursed the sentiments we encounter in these two so different works. Greek court ceremonial must not be thought of as wholly inflexible, unbending and rigid. If the Greeks wanted to they could charm and flatter their foreign visitors as they did Liudprand himself in 949. The *Legatio* was, even more than the *Historia Ottonis*, a *livre d'occasion* which by itself left no trace and had no known literary afterlife, unlike the *Antapodosis*. It is a text we possess precariously, one of several medieval transmissions resting on no surviving manuscript whatsoever. All the same the sentiments of the *Legatio* had a deep resonance and audible echoes. It is possible that Bishop Dietrich of Metz, a nephew of Queen Mathilda and cousin to Otto I, possessed a copy and we know of his deep indignation with the Empress Theophanu from Alpert of Metz's *Fragment*.[67] [143]

Liudprand in the *Antapodosis*, we have said, became the spokesman of Christianity's hardening attitudes towards Islam, one of the first signs of an incipient counter-offensive. The *Legatio* too marks a divide. As late as 962 Constantinople was almost the centre of gravity of Liudprand's Christian world. It had been that for the Pavese hitherto. In the *Legatio* this centre has shifted to Rome and the itinerant Ottonian court. It was not to move again for three hundred years. Among the makers of Latin Europe Liudprand holds and important place. He was indeed one of the architects of a new, self-centred polarity in the Latin west. It did not rule out gusts of benevolence towards the Greeks and their church but the matter-of-fact, unquestioned solidarity we meet in the *Antapodosis* was now, only six years later, a thing of the past. Efforts, selfconscious efforts, had to be made and sometimes were made to try

---

[64] Notker, *Gesta Karoli* II 6, pp. 55-7.

[65] Ibid., p. 54: 'piscis fluvialis et pigmentis infusus'.

[66] Ibid., pp. 54f. and Widukind, *Res Gestae Saxonicae* III 71, p. 148.

[67] Alpertus Mettensis, *Fragmentum de Deoderico primo episcopo Mettensi*, cc. 2, 4, ed. H. van Rij and A.S. Abulafia, *Alpertus von Metz* (Amsterdam, 1980), pp. 110, 114. The *Legatio* was first edited by H. Canisius, professor of civil and canon law at Ingolstadt. His manuscript was sent to him from Augsburg but it had lain at Trier. Pertz thought that perhaps the Ottos themselves or the empress Adelheid had sent it there: *MGH SS* 3, 269 and 273. What happened to his codex is not known. Canisius's edition is entitled thus: *Chronicon Victoris Episcopi Tunnunensis, Chronicon Ioannis Biclarensis, Episcopi Gerundensis, Legatio Liutprandi Episcopi Cremonensis, ad Nicephorum Phocam . . .Synodus Bauarica sub Tassilone Bavariae Duce Tempore Caroli Magni, Omnia Nunc primum in lucem edita Studio et Opera Henrici Canisi Noviomagi I C et SS Canonum Professoris Ordinarii in Academia Ingolstadiensi* (Inglostadii, 1600).

and regain it, most of them in vain. In the wake of Ottonian policy, as the likely participant in yet another diplomatic mission to Constantinople, Liudprand may not have wished the *Legatio* to be his last word but it became just that. He chose to rouse self-awareness not by pointing to mounting political and religious differences but by dwelling on everyday *habitus* and ingrained responses and whether he knew it or not his means, for all their ease, matched his ends at a much deeper level.

Theophanu Divina Gratia Imperatrix Augusta: Western and Eastern Emperorship in the Later Tenth Century

In the second half of the tenth century the eastern and the western empires confronted one another at a time when neither lacked aggressiveness and self-assurance, though both qualities still had to be tested against crises and setbacks. Their political cultures differed profoundly, and the difference is not best summed up by calling the Byzantine world and its power structures advanced and those of the Saxon Reich barbaric, to use the Greek's own word. True, Byzantine emperorship rested on ancient and, it was felt, divinely willed certainties, while there was as yet something provisional, tentative and looking for a content in that of the west. Yet it too wanted to be seen and understood as being providentially directed by the heavenly architect. As the *arenga* of one of Otto I's diplomata for Hersfeld succinctly expressed it:[1] 'Otto by the ordinance of divine providence august emperor. The power of God advanced us to the pinnacle of the imperial summit so that we should promote the well-being and progress especially of all the places devoted to the service of God, so that by the orisons of his servants, of those who watch and pray there, the prosperity of our Empire should be guided in uninterrupted tranquillity and that after the passing of this temporal life, companionship in eternal felicity shall not be denied to us.' *Contubernium* it was called, like sharing a tent. The historians of the Ottonian Reich and its liturgical practice unceasingly proclaimed it as part of the divine order for the world.

The Byzantine emperor was God's viceroy in this life for the *oikumene*, and by rights his authority stretched over the whole universe, whatever interlopers *de facto* contested, rejected, ignored or denied his lordship.[2] Ottonian emperorship had as yet no such content. It was but an enhanced kingship: rule over

---

[*] Unpublished typescript of a lecture given at a conference on Nimwegen in 1991. The text has been lightly edited; the footnotes are editorial.

[1] D O I 356 (Benevento 15 February 958); the *arenga* recurs essentially unchanged in D O I 373 for Casa Aurea (Pescara), D O I 404 for St Sophia, Benevento, and D O II 17 for Hersfeld.

[2] O. Treitinger, *Die oströmische Kaiser- und Reichsidee nach ihrer Gestaltung im höfischen Zeremoniell* (Jena, 1938), pp. 161-213; F. Dölger, 'Die Familie der Könige im Mittelalter', in idem, *Byzanz und die europäische Staatenwelt* (Ettal, 1953), pp. 34-69; A. Toynbee, *Constantine Porphyrogenitus and his World* (London, 1973), pp. 346-51.

more than one kingdom made manifest and recognised by a rank, a dignity and coronation ritual. When the Italian *dictator* who had drafted the preamble of Otto I's diploma for Hersfeld cited above spoke about the advancement of clerks and monks as the servants of God, he was not only uttering a commonplace repeated in hundreds of such preambles and elsewhere, but he also failed to define a specifically imperial task and duty, for the well-being of churches, their protection and tranquillity, were the first and foremost duty of all kings, not just emperors, and most of them swore to it in their coronation promises.[3] *Arengae* similar to this one also occur in Otto I's diplomata before 2 February 962, when he was crowned emperor by Pope John XII in St Peter's, though they were less frequent. Here is an example, the gift of half the city of Chur to its bishop with all appurtenances and rights of justice:[4] 'If we strive zealously to augment church possessions as they were established by our predecessors, we do not doubt to earn the highest rewards thereby.'

Our task must therefore be to seek out, if possible, and identify those tasks and activities of Otto I's that were specifically imperial and not just royal, and it will soon be found that it is not at all easy to do so. The Byzantine emperor, the *basileus Romaion* commanded a machinery of government and a *lex scripta* to which he could add his own novels as the situation required.[5] Difficult and even fundamental problems, such as the relentless pressure of the *dynatoi* seeking to acquire lands at the expense of the *penetes*, that is of the poor and middling peasant owners,[6] the maintenance of military holdings to keep up the

---

[3] For the *arengae* of Ottonian diplomata see the works cited in n. 93; on coronation promises see P.E. Schramm, *Kaiser, Könige und Päpste: Gesammelte Aufsätze*, 4 vols. in 5 (Stuttgart, 1968-70), especially 'Die Krönung im 9. und 10. Jahrhundert', vol. 2, pp 140-305 and 'Die deutschen Herrscher aus dem sächsischen Hause als Könige (bis 962)', vol. 3, pp. 33-134; J.L. Nelson, *Politics and Ritual in Early Medieval Europe* (London, 1986), especially 'Kingship, Law and Liturgy in the Political Thought of Hincmar of Rheims', pp. 133-71.

[4] D O I 191 (Fritzlar, 16 January 958).

[5] L. Bréhier, *Le Monde byzantin*, 2: *Les Institutions byzantines* (Paris, 1949), especially pp. 89-217; W. Ensslin, 'The Government and Administration of the Byzantine Empire', in *The Cambridge Medieval History*, 4: *The Byzantine Empire*, 2: *Government, Church and Civilisation*, ed. J.M. Hussey (Cambridge, 1967), pp. 1-54; H. Ahrweiler, 'Recherches sur l'administration de l'empire byzantin aux IXe-XIe siècles', in idem, *Études sur les structures administratives et sociales de Byzance* (London, 1971), ch. VIII; reconstructions based on lists of officials in N. Oikonomides, *Listes de préséance byzantines des IXe et Xe siècles* (Paris, 1972), especially pp. 281-363. On law see H.J. Scheltema, 'Byzantine Law', in *Government, Church and Civilisation*, ed. Hussey, pp. 55-78; A.P. Kazhdan and others (ed.), *The Oxford Dictionary of Byzantium* (Oxford, 1991), pp. 1497-8 and P.E. Pieler, 'Rechtsliteratur', in H. Hunger, *Die hochsprachliche profane Literatur der Byzantiner*, 2 (Byzantinisches Handbuch 5/2, Müchen, 1978), pp. 343-480, especially pp. 445-72.

[6] On *dynatoi* and *penetes* see G. Ostrogorsky, 'Agrarian Conditions in the Byzantine Empire in the Middle Ages', in *Cambridge Economic History of Europe*, 1: *The Agrarian Life of the Middle Ages* 2nd edn by M.M. Postan (Cambridge, 1971), pp. 216-22; Toynbee, *Constantine Porphyogenitus* (as n. 2), pp. 145-76. The views there expressed have been subject to some debate in recent decades: R. Morris, 'The Powerful and the Poor in Tenth-century Byzantium Law and Reality', *Past and Present*, 73 (1976), pp. 3-27, argues that the problem is an artificial one; P. Lemerle, *Agrarian History of Byzantium from the Origins to the Twelfth Century: The Sources and Problems* (Galway, 1979), pp. 90-108, sees the issue as essentially one of taxation; A. Harvey, *Economic*

armed forces in as far as they were made up of *stratiotoi* as against the regiments of standing troops,[7] all these things could be and were countered by legislation. Even if these laws did not in the long run arrest, let alone reverse the process, they nonetheless slowed it down and prevented the rapid erosion of what was considered to be a vital resource for both defensive and offensive military operations. The landed aristocracy had no cause to bless the reign of Basil II. His novels and their enforcement and his taxation for once hit them hard, not to mention the punishments for rebellions and the drastic diminution of individual noble fortunes.[8]

It does not follow that the weak, the underdogs, prospered under this regime. They too were taxed, if anything more relentlessly, and governed harshly. The imperial bureaucracy could be directed from the centre. It was literate, it received and could respond to *grammata* and *keleuseis* from the palace, but there was rarely, if ever any attempt to foster attitudes and an atmosphere of loyalty and attachment lower down and among the governed.[9] Army discipline too was harsh and often enough unjust. This must be set against the technical accomplishments of Byzantine warfare in the tenth century, which so greatly impressed those western observers who came to know them. Westerners, not only Italian, were aware of the fast Greek ships with their well-armed troops on board and above all their deadly weapon, Greek fire.[10] Byzantine land forces knew a chain of command, units and sub-

---

Expansion in the Byzantine Empire, 900-1200 (Cambridge, 1989), pp. 37-44, sees the problem as a real one caused by demographic increase and the tenth-century imperial legislation as a response to the strength of the magnates.

[7] Toynbee, *Constantine Porphyrogenitus* (as n. 2), pp. 134-45; Lemerle, *Agarian History* (as n. 6), pp. 115-65; J. Haldon, *Recruitment and Conscription in the Byzantine Empire: A Study in the Origins of the stratiotika ktemata* (Sitzungsberichte der österreichischen Akademie der Wissenschaften zu Wien, phil.-hist. Klasse 357, Vienna 1979), pp. 41-65; G. Dagron and H. Mihăescu (ed.), *Le Traité sur la guerilla (de velitatione) de l'empéreur Nicephore Phocas (963-969)* (Paris, 1986), pp. 266-9, 275-83; D. Gorecki, 'The Strateia of Constantine VII: The Legal Status, Administration and Historical Background', *Byzantinische Zeitschrift*, 82 (1989), pp. 157-76.

[8] Lemerle, *Agrarian History* (as n. 6), p. 107; J.-C. Cheynet, *Pouvoir et contestations à Byzance (963-1210)* (Paris, 1990), pp. 331-6, argues that Basil II did not direct his novels against landlords as a 'class', but rather against specific rival families such as the Phocases. The purges and conflicts with leading noble families are still best followed in G. Ostrogorsky, *History of the Byzantine State*, 3rd revised edn (New Brunswick, 1969), pp. 295-340.

[9] Dagron and Mihăescu, *Le Traité* (as n. 7), pp. 284-7; G. Dagron, 'Byzance et le modèle islamique au Xe siècle: A propos des constitutions tactiques de l'empéreur Leon VI', *Comptes-rendues des séances de l'académie des inscriptions et belles-lettres* (1983), pp. 219-42, especially pp. 237-42 on Byzantine attempts to adapt and exploit Islamic notions of *jihad*; J. Haldon, '"Blood and Ink": Some Observations on Byzantine Attitudes Towards Warfare and Diplomacy', in *Byzantine Diplomacy: Papers from the Twenty-Fourth Spring Symposium of Byzantine Studies, Cambridge, March 1990*, ed. J. Shepard and S. Franklin (London, 1992), pp. 281-94, especially pp. 291-4.

[10] E. Eickhoff, *Seekrieg und Seepolitik zwischen Islam und Abendland bis zum Aufstiege Pisas und Genaus (650-1040)* (Saarbrüken, 1954), pp. 42-98; H. Ahrweiler, *Byzance et la mer: La marine de guerre, la politique et les institutions maritimes de Byzance aux VIIe-XVe siècles* (Bibliothèque Byzantine: Études 5, Paris 1966), especially pp. 93-135. On Greek fire see J. Haldon and M. Byrnes, 'A Possible Solution to the Problem of Greek Fire', *Byzantinische Zeitschrift*, 70

units. They could be marshalled and organised in a way that surpassed the military fluidities of the Ottonians, whose own military capacities were at the same time grossly underrated by Nicephorus Phocas in his conversation with Liudprand of Cremona, if we can trust the bishop's report in the *Legatio*.[11] It is possible that the Greeks, because they seldom, if ever, met the best of the Latin *miles armatus*, heavily armed, shielded, hauberked and mounted warriors, did not follow the military evolution of the west very closely and were thus taken by surprise when they at last came to see it at close quarters during the first crusade.[12]

To identify and discover a programme, an overarching *raison d'être* for Otto I's emperorship other than the vast extent of his overlordship is something that is much harder to do than it is for Charlemagne's, and this for two reasons. In the first place we read in Widukind that he had already been hailed *imperator* by his warriors after the great victory over the Magyars at the battle of the Lech in 955 just as his father's men, according to Widukind again, had called Henry I 'emperor' in 933 after his victory over the Magyars at Riade.[13] This kind of acclamation of a victorious commander, whatever its classical undertones in so well-schooled a writer as the Corvey monk, was not impossible, and even received some support from another source, and that a critical one, the older *Life* of Otto I's mother, Queen Mathilda. The author knew of Otto's Roman coronation, which he believed was by God's command, but he also mentioned and censured what he described as a tumultuous act of Otto I's host, which made him emperor by imposing a diadem that he could not decline or repudiate.[14] Yet the idea of an emperorship that did not owe its beginnings and its rights to a papal coronation had some resonance and appeal, not least, as we

---

(1977), 91-9; E. Pásthory, 'Über das "Griechisches Feuer"', *Zeitschrift für Archäologie und Kunstgeschichte*, 17 (1986), pp. 27-37.

[11] For Byzantine military organisation at this time see Toynbee, *Constantine Porphyrogenitus* (as n. 2), pp. 282-7; G. Dennis (ed.), *Three Byzantine Military Treatises* (Dumbarton Oaks Texts, Washington D.C., 1985); E. McGeer, 'Infantry versus Cavalry: the Byzantine Response', *Revue des Études Byzantines*, 46 (1988), pp. 135-45. For Nicephorus' views on Ottonian soldiers see Liudprand, *Legatio*, c. 11, p. 182.

[12] Anna Comnena, *Alexiad* VIII 3, ed. B. Leib (Paris, 1945), vol. 3, p. 115; cf. also the comments in X 3 5 (vol. 2, p. 197) and XIV 7 2 (vol. 3, p. 173). T. Kolias, *Byzantinische Waffen: ein Beitrag zur byzantinischen Waffenkunde von den Anfängen bis zur lateinischen Eroberung* (Byzantina Vindobonensia, Vienna, 1988), pp. 200-8, especially p. 208 with nn. 129-30, shows that the Byzantines were recruiting mounted warriors from the west from the mid-eleventh century onwards, but the effectiveness of the crusaders was evidently still a shock and a surprise.

[13] Widukind, *Res gestae Saxonicae* III 49, p. 128 (Lechfield); I 39, p. 58 (Riade); see E.E. Stengel, 'Der Heerkaiser (Den Kaiser macht das Heer): Studien zur Geschichte eines politischen Gedankens', in idem, *Abhandlungen und Untersuchungen zur Geschichte des Kaisergedankens im Mittelalter* (Cologne, 1965), pp. 1-169, especially pp. 56-91.

[14] *Vita Mathildis antiquior* c. 16, *MGH SS* 10, p. 81; for commentary see Stengel, 'Heerkaiser' (as n. 13), p. 76.

saw, for Widukind of Corvey.[15] Nevertheless, it could not prevail against the strength of the Carolingian tradition and the papacy's established hold over the act of coronation. It was precisely the frequent papal coronations of local contenders in the struggles for the Italian kingdom during the later ninth and early tenth century, and the occasional imperial unctions of Carolingians from the north like Charles III and Arnulf, that had given the papacy its indefeasible and incontrovertible sanction of crowning or refusing to crown. Wido, Lambert, Louis the Blind and Berengar I had all sought and held emperorships which gave them some standing in Rome without much easing their desperate and treacherous battles for the Italian kingship and its rich assets in Pavia and the Lombard plain.[16] Berengar I of the margraval house of Friuli and through his mother a grandson of Louis the Pious, had been the last to be so crowned, by Pope John X in 915, shortly after the latter's victory over the Saracens at the Garigliano. Berengar had not taken part in this campaign as befitted a king, but a temporary power vacuum in Tuscany had opened the way to Rome for him.[17] It is revealing that entirely local and regional considerations led to the invitation, just as they were to do in the case of Otto I. The house of Theophylact, with its iron grip on Roman society and its very influential friends outside, not least of all in Constantinople, was able to repel at least three assaults by King Hugh, battling at the walls of Rome for an imperial coronation that eluded him. The regime of Alberic, the *princeps Romanus*, may have wanted to dispense with emperorship altogether.[18] When it was unable to do so it turned to an effective and formidable military protector who had already once, in 951-52, subjected the dynasty of the north in the person of Berengar II of the house of Ivrea, who now himself threatened Rome in order to hold together his own following with the magic or poison of success. Otto I's emperorship thus came about because the papacy, the clan of Alberic, now headed by Pope John XII, needed help. It did not need or want what it

---

[15] For a good recent discussion see E. Karpf, *Herrscherlegitmation und Reichsbegriff in der ottonischen Geschichtsschreibung des 10. Jahrhunderts* (Historische Forschungen 10, Stuttgart, 1985), especially pp. 168-75, 196; see also H. Beumann, '*Imperator Romanorum, rex gentium*: Zu Widukind III 76', in idem, *Ausgewählte Aufsätze aus den Jahren 1966-1986* (Sigmaringen, 1987), pp. 324-40.

[16] G. Fasoli, *I re d'Italia (888-962)* (Florence, 1949), pp. 1-96; idem, 'Re, imperatori e sudditi nell'Italia del secolo X', *Studi Medievali*, serie terza, 4 (1963), pp. 52-74; R. Hiestand, *Byzanz und das Regnum Italicum im 10. Jahrhundert* (Geist und Werk der Zeiten 9, Zurich, 1964), pp. 36-137, and, for a brief account in English with a broader context, C. Wickham, *Early Medieval Italy, 400-1000* (London, 1981), pp. 168-81.

[17] Fasoli, *I re d'Italia* (as n. 16), pp. 83-7; Hiestand, *Byzanz* (as. n. 16), pp. 128-37; see most recently R. Savigni, 'Sacerdozio e regno in età post-Carolingia: L'episcopato di Giovanni X, arcivescovo di Ravenna (905-914) e papa (914-928)', *Rivista di storia della chiesa in Italia*, 46 (1992), pp. 1-29, especially p. 4, with further literature.

[18] This seems at least a plausible deduction from Alberic's refusal to grant imperial coronation to Hugo in 933 and (probably) to Otto I in 951/2; on the latter event see the references in Böhmer-Ottenthal, no. 201a, and in general see Hiestand, *Byzanz* (as n. 16), pp. 158-61, 164-9, 177-9 and J. Shepard, 'Byzantium and the West', in *New Cambridge Medieval History*, 3: *900-1024*, ed. T. Reuter (Cambridge, forthcoming).

eventually got, a stark northern military presence, not indeed a permanent occupation but repeated Ottonian expeditions at brief intervals, manned by Saxon, Rhine-Frankish, Suabian and Slav contingents.[19] Otto I's emperorship stemmed from his victories over 'barbarian' peoples, Hungarians and others, so the opening narrative of Pope John XII's privilege authorising the Saxon ruler's most cherished plans, proclaimed. He had come to receive the triumphal crown of victory, 'in inperii culmen' from St Peter, prince of the Apostles 'through us [John XII]'.[20] The formulation of Otto's *arenga* in his diploma for Hersfeld cited above, with its reference to the 'pinnacle of the imperial summit [*imperialis culminis . . . apicem*]', now becomes very clear and significant.[21] John's privilege harnesses the emperorship to the forcible conversion of the Slav peoples under Saxon military rule and envisaged the archbishopric of Magdeburg and suffragan sees as the bastions from which it was to be brought about.[22] The papal privilege entitled the emperor and his successors to allocate and distribute the tributes and the tithes of those baptised or yet to be baptised to the see of Magdeburg, Merseburg and others, together with the converts. But it took some years before Otto's own son, Archbishop William of Mainz, would bow to a diminution of his jurisdiction, and Bishop Bernhard of Halberstadt, for whom it meant ceding some of his parish to the new metropolis, refused to yield as long as he lived, not could Otto coerce him.[23]

---

[19] Fasoli, *I re d'Italia* (as n. 16), pp. 171-204, has a good account of the last days of the Alberician regime in Rome, It should be noted, however, that the theme of the pope appealing to a power north of the Alps for help and getting far more help than he wanted was not confined to the late tenth century but was a leitmotiv of papal history from the eighth through to the twelfth century at least.

[20] John XII for Magdeburg, Rome, 12 February 962: H. Zimmermann, *Papsturkunden, 896-1046*, 1: *896-996*, 2nd edn (Denkschriften der österreichischen Akademie der Wissenschaften, phil.-hist. Klass 174, Vienna, 1988), pp. 281-4 no. 154, here pp. 282-3: 'Otto, devictis barbaris gentibus, Auaribus scilicet ceterisque quam pluribus, ut ad defensionem sanctę Dei ęcclesię triumphalem victorię in inperii culmen per nos a beato Petro apostolorum principe susciperet coronam . . . Otto, qualiter Sclauos, quos ipse devicit, in catholica fide noviter fundaverat, nostrę paternitati innotuit deprecans et obnixe postulans . . . [and receives permission to set up sees at Magdeburg and Merseburg]'.

[21] See above at n. 1.

[22] For an attempt to demonstrate a similar link between Charlemagne's coronation of 800 and Slav mission see H. Löwe, *Die karolingische Reichsgründung und der Südosten: Studien zum Werden des Deutschtums und seiner Auseinandersetzung mit Rom* (Forschungen zur Kirchen- und Geistesgeschichte 13, Stuttgart, 1937), less *zeitbedingt* than the subtitle might suggest.

[23] The resistance put up by William of Mainz and Bernard of Halberstadt (and by others less clearly visible in the sources) to the new ecclesiastical province is best summarised in D. Claude, *Geschichte des Erzbistums Magdeburg bis in das 12, Jahrhundert*, 1: *Die Geschichte der Erzbischöfe bis auf Ruotger (1124)* (Mitteldeutsche Forschungen 67/1, Cologne, 1972), pp. 63-95; see also O. Engels, 'Die Gründung der Kirchenprovinz Magdeburg und die Ravennater "Synode" von 968', *Annuarium Historiae Conciliorum*, 7 (1975), pp. 136-58; G. Tellenbach, *The Western Church from the Tenth to the Early Twelfth Century*, trans. T. Reuter (Cambridge, 1993), pp. 52-4, 58, 72.

Of Charlemagne Einhard had written – in one of his very few anecdotes – that he felt at first so dismayed about his emperorship, the *nomen imperatoris*, that he said he would not have gone to St Peter's, even though it was the holiest of feast days, if he had known what the pope planned to do.[24] In the long debate on the interpretation of this utterance – was it merely a modesty topos or an indignant critique of the coronation's modalities? – we need not here enter.[25] But it is essential to remember that we possess an equally characteristic utterance of Otto I's about his coronation, made just before it. We owe it to Thietmar of Merseburg, who belonged to the Saxon high aristocratic circles where such stories had currency, were remembered and echoed more widespread sentiments. Thietmar, as so often, pauses to recall men whose remembrance he wanted to enjoin on his readers as a pastoral duty, and he lit upon the career of Count Ansfried, late bishop of Utrecht. Ansfried was one of the few nobles who had received both a secular and a clerical education. He had at first been instructed in secular and divine law by his uncle, Archbishop Robert of Trier, and was then placed under the care of Archbishop Brun of Cologne, Otto I's brother, to be trained as a warrior.[26] On the eve of his Roman expedition, in 961, Otto took him into his personal following and made him his swordbearer. On entering Rome he told Ansfried: 'When I pray today at the holy threshold of the Apostles hold your sword always over my head. I know only too well how often our predecessors had reason to worry about the trustworthiness of the Romans. It is wise to be circumspect and guard against all eventualities lest they should get the better of us. Once we are (safely) back you can go and pray as much as you wish.'[27] A note of hard down-to-earthness is sounded here. Otto wanted to be crowned emperor but he had few illusions about the setting and the immediate source of his newly won dignity.

An age-old Carolingian tradition had been refurbished with the Saxon ruler's coronation in 962. It was one his aristocratic warrior and native following could learn to share. Not uncommon Saxon nobles' names like Gunthar, Ricdag and Reding appear among the *signa* of Otto's *pactum confirmationis*, the solemn diploma for St Peter and his vicar, Pope John XII.[28] Kingship over many peoples, such as Otto now possessed, called for some

---

[24] Einhard, *Vita Karoli*, c. 28, p. 32: 'Quod primo in tantum aversatus est, ut adfirmaret se eo die, quamvis praecipua festivitas esset, ecclesiam non intraturum, si pontificis consilium praescire potuisset.'

[25] Summarised in P. Classen, *Karl der Große, das Papsttum und Byzanz: Die Begründung des karolingischen Kaisertums*, revised edn by H. Fuhrmann and C. Märtl (Beiträge zur Geschichte und Quellenkunde des Mittelalters 9, Sigmaringen, 1985), pp. 74-7.

[26] On Ansfried's pre-episcopal career see R. Große, *Das Bistum Utrecht und seine Bischöfe im 10. und frühen 11. Jahrhundert* (Kölner Historische Abhandlungen 33, Cologne, 1987), pp. 115-54.

[27] Thietmar, *Chronicon*, IV, 31, pp. 169/71; see on the passage H. Grundmann, 'Betrachtungen zur Kaiserkrönung Ottos I.', in *Otto der Große*, ed. H. Zimmermann (Wege der Forschung 450, Darmstadt, 1976), pp. 214-17.

[28] D O I 235 (Rome, 13 February 962).

visible expression and recognition, though it was possible without it.[29] Already in the 950s Constantine Porphyrogenitus called Otto I a *megas rex* of 'Francia or Saxony' when he mentioned the 'Belocroats, that is White Croats', in his treatise *De adminstrando imperio*.[30] They were subject to him. Later Skylitzes, writing in the eleventh century but using a late tenth-century source, described Otto as *ton phraggon basileus* not only when he referred to the deposition of Pope John XII in 963 but also when he reported his execution of the *karchas* Bulksu in 955 after the battle at the Lech.[31] What matters here is that they did not see the year of Otto's imperial coronation at Rome as a marker or to present a special challenge such as Charlemagne's had done. For them it changed nothing and made no difference.

Charlemagne, however much he or his *litterati* may have affected to look askance at the imperial dignity, had at once thought to fill it with meaning and content. Again Einhard is one of our chief guides, though by no means the only significant one: *Post susceptum imperiale nomen* he lists his especially imperial activities, attempts which he thought were unsuccessful, to clarify and amend the *leges* of the Franks and to cause the *leges* of the people under his lordship to be collected and written down. This he achieved.[32] Einhard regarded as still more important Charles's efforts to record the *carmina antiquissima*, to have a grammar of the vernacular attempted and to settle the names of the winds and the months again in the vernacular, as imperial acts and for this he could marshal the classical traditions in which he was formidably well schooled.[33] We know of course that Charlemagne did much more: not only had new oaths to be sworn enhancing the obligations of his *fideles*, but historiography was mobilised as a means to propagate a new imperial presence; even the building

---

[29] On this aspect of emperorship see Beumann, '*Imperator Rommanorum, rex gentium*' (as n. 15) and E.E. Stengel, 'Kaisertitel und Suveränitätsidee: Studien und Vorgeschichte des modernen Staatsbegriffs', in *Abhandlungen* (as n. 13), pp. 241-81.

[30] *De Administrando Imperio*, c. 30, lines 73-4, 2nd edn by G. Moravcsik and R. Jenkins (Dumbarton Oaks Texts 1, Washington D.C., 1967), pp. 142-3.

[31] John Skylitzes, *Synopsis Historion*, Constantinus Autokrator cc. 5, 12, ed. H. Thura (Corpus Fontium Historiae Byzantinae: Series Berolinensis 5, Berlin, 1973), pp. 239, 245.

[32] Einhard, *Vita Karoli* c. 29, p. 33, essentially confirmed by modern scholarly work on the *Volksrechte*, summarised most recently by H. Siems, *Handel und Wucher im Spiegel frühmittelalterlicher Rechtsquellen* (Schriften der MGH, Hanover, 1992), pp. 11-157; see also C. Schott, 'Der Stand der Leges-Forschung', *Frümittelalterliche Studien* 13 (1979), pp. 29-55.

[33] Ibid., pp. 33-4; see D. Geuenich, 'Die volkssprachige Überlieferung der Karolingerzeit aus der Sicht des Historikers', *DA*, 39 (1983), pp. 104-30, especially pp. 113-27, for a commentary which significantly relativises Charles's contribution. On Einhard's literary intentions see above all the classic study by H. Beumann, 'Topos und Gedankengefüge bei Einhard', in idem, *Ideengeschichtliche Studien zu Einhard und anderen Geschichtsschreibern des früheren Mittelalters* (Darmstadt, 1962), pp. 1-15, and also H. Löwe, 'Die Entstehungszeit der Vita Karoli Einhards', *DA*, 39 (1983), pp. 85-103.

of a lighthouse could count as an imperial act.[34] There was a ceaseless, almost feverish quest for improvements in all spheres of life, ecclesiastical and lay; a second and almost a third generation of savants and *litterati* were spurred on, and Aachen became a self-consciously imperial centre where Charles would reside and be maintained all the year round allowing the ageing ruler to break out of the rhythm of itineracy halted only by some months of winter residence which had hitherto dominated his use of time.[35]

No such spate of new activities, the quickened opening of new horizons or the enlargement of older ones stemmed from Otto I's emperorship. The presuppositions were simply not there. As king, it is true, he had done something to mend his own education, learning Latin and to read it after the death of his first wife Edith in 946.[36] During the 950s also, as Fleckenstein has shown, the number of *capellani* serving at his court rose.[37] Among them we note two outstanding historians and men of letters: Liudprand, raised to the see of Cremona in 957;[38] and Adalbert, who became the first archbishop of Magdeburg in 968.[39] The number of *capellani* increased again after 965, the year Archbishop Brun of Cologne's death. They now numbered fifteen, and were Otto's literate *comitatus*.[40] From this it would seem that the emperorship did not lead to any startling changes in the composition and make-up of Otto's entourage when he returned from his Italian expedition in 965, although the larger number of *capellani* should not be overlooked. One of them for certain

[34] See F.L. Ganshof, 'Charlemagne's programme of imperial government', in idem, *The Carolingians and Frankish Monarchy*, trans. J. Sondheimer (London, 1971), pp. 55-85. For the lighthouse see *Annales regni Francorum s.a.* 811, p. 135: 'ad Bononiam civitatem maritimam . . . accessit farumque ibi ad navigantium cursus dirigendos antiquitus constitutam restauravit'; *restauravit* has unmistakable imperial overtones, especially as the lighthouse had been built by Caligula (Suetonius, *Caligula*, c. 46).

[35] For this development and its prehistory see D. Bullough, '*Aula Renovata*: The Carolingian Court before the Aachen Palace', in idem, *Carolingian Renewal* (Manchester, 1992), pp. 123-60, especially p. 142 and notes.

[36] Widukind, *Res gestae Saxonicae* II 36, p. 96, no doubt influenced by Einhard, *Vita Karoli*, c. 24-6, pp. 29-31.

[37] J. Fleckenstein, *Die Hofkapelle der deutschen Könige*, 2: *Die Hofkapelle im Rahmen der ottonisch-salischen Reichskirche* (Schriften der MGH 16/2, Stuttgart, 1966), pp. 40-58.

[38] On Liudprand's career and historical writings see K.J. Leyse, 'Ends and Means in Liudprand of Cremona', above pp. 125-42, with full bibliography; see more recently J.N. Sutherland, *Liuprand of Cremona, Bishop, Diplomat, Historian: Studies of the Man and his Age* (Spoleto, 1988 [completed 1977 and published posthumously]).

[39] On Adalbert see Karl Hauck, 'Erzbischof Adalbert von Magdeburg als Geschichtsschreiber', in *Festschrift für Walter Schlesinger*, ed. Helmut Beumann (Köln, 1974), vol. 2, pp. 276-344; Karpf, *Herrscherlegitimation und Reichsbegriff* (as no. 15), pp. 47-62. M. Frase, *Friede und Königsherrschaft: Quellenkritik und Interpretation der Continuatio Reginonis* (Frankfurt, 1990), offers nothing new.

[40] Fleckenstein, *Hofkapelle* (as n. 37), p. 51.

and perhaps others became the patrons of outstanding illuminated manuscripts when they were still serving in Otto's entourage before rising to bishoprics, and they also knew where to commission the wonderful luxury diplomata written in gold on purple which Otto I gave to the Roman Church in 962 and the young Otto II to Theophanu granting her her dower in 972.[41] Here an imperial note was clearly struck, and Byzantine models and their immense attraction stand behind these magnificently executed and decorated texts. But, notaries and *capellani* apart, Otto I did not feel any inner need to foster the cult of letters at his court. He had no programme as emperor to nurture a more expert and homogeneous lay ruling élite side by side with the clerical one. Yet he saw to it that his own son Otto II was well taught and he became indeed a book-lover whose visit to their library the monks of St Gallen feared.[42]

Otto the Great was also an exceptionally restless ruler, more of a migrant than most. Even in the confined of his native Saxony he itinerated ceaselessly whatever the season with but brief pauses in his relatively numerous *palatia*, hunting lodges and *curtes* there, some of them in the religious centres he so zealously built up.[43] Only once can he be found staying for half a year on end in the capital of his Italian kingdom, Pavia. Here he resided from September 962 until April 963, taking stock perhaps of its exceptionally sophisticated services, governmental apparatus and inflow of revenues.[44] There was another stay here of not quite three months from December 969 to March 970.[45] Otto I legislated sparingly, introducing the judicial duel into Italian legal processes over contested land to curtail perjury.[46] He appointed some *missi* and sent out

[41] Ibid., p. 49; H. Hoffmann, *Buchkunst und Königtum im ottonischen und frühsalischen Reich* (Schriften der MGH 30/1, Stuttgart, 1986), pp. 103-26; H. Mayr-Harting, *Ottonian Book Illumination: An Historical Study*, 1: *Themes* (London, 1991), pp. 36-43. Theophanu's dowry diploma is discussed in a number of contributions to A. von Euw and P. Schreiner (ed.) *Kaiserin Theophanu: Begegnung des Ostens und Westens um die Wende des ersten Jahrtausends*, 2 vols. (Cologne, 1991), notably W. Georgi, 'Ottonianum und Heiratsurkunde 962/972', vol. 2, pp. 135-60 and P. Rück, 'Die Urkunde als Kunstwerk', vol. 2, pp. 311-33. See also C. Brühl, 'Purpururkunden', in idem, *Aus Mittelalter und Diplomatik: Gesammelte Aufsätze*, 2: *Studien zur Diplomatik* (Hildesheim, 1989), pp. 601-20.

[42] On the differences in this respect between the 'Ottonian' and the 'Carolingian' renaissances see J. Fleckenstein , 'Königshof und Bischofsschule unter Otto dem Großen', in idem, *Ordnungen und formende Kräfte des Mittelalters: Ausgewählte Beiträge* (Göttingen, 1989), pp. 168-192. For Otto II's education see R. Ahlfeld, *Die Erziehung der sächsischen und salischen Herrscher im Hinblick auf ihre spätere Regierungszeit* (Diss., Greifswald, 1949) [not accessible to me]; Ekkehard IV, *Casus sancti Galli* c. 147, ed. H.F. Haefele (AQDG 10, Darmstadt 1980), p. 284.

[43] Fundamental on this aspect of Ottonian rule is E. Müller-Mertens, *Die Reichsstruktur im Spiegel der Herrschaftspraxis Ottos des Großen: Mit historiographischen Prolegomena zur Frage Feudalstaat auf deutschem Boden, seit wann deutscher Feudalstaat?* (Forschungen zur mittelalterlichen Geschichte 25, Berlin, 1980).

[44] Böhmer-Ottenthal, nos. 329-340a. For the governmental apparatus at Pavia see the *Honorantie Civitatis Papie*, most readily accessible in *MGH SS 30*, pp. 1444-60, also edited by C. Brühl and C. Violante, *Die "Honorantie Civitatis Papie": Transkription, Edition, Kommentar* (Cologne, 1983), with a valuable commentary.

[45] Böhmer-Ottenthal, nos. 505-514.

[46] *MGH Const.* 1, p. 37 no. 16 (971).

written mandates, but very few have come down to us, suggesting that it did not become routine.[47] Verbal orders and messages had to do for the most part.

Only in the realm of historiography did his emperorship seek and find the positive expression that it so badly needed to cope with the new tasks that had to be faced. Liudprand of Cremona in his *Historia Ottonis* furnished a justification of Otto's dealings with the papacy and there is no doubt that the need for such a justification was widely felt.[48] For the same years and incidents particularly, the continuation of Regino of Prüm's *Chronicon* was not the least of the services Adalbert of St Maximin rendered to his lord. Yet its resemblance to the *Annales regni Francorum* should not be pressed too far. As the unwilling plaintive and failed missionary bishop to Kievan Russia, Adalbert pursued at times very personal concerns in his *Chronicon*.[49] His roles and attachments were far too numerous to fit into the year-in-year-out routines of the royal chapel. However close he may have been to the Ottonians during the mid 960s, he was not Otto's first choice for the see of Magdeburg, not was his promotion welcomed by all, as Otto's letter ordering the margraves not to stand in his way shows.[50] Adalbert, moreover, was far from being an unequivocal supporter of the emperor. Yet all the same he had a sense of alignment and ended his chronicle with Otto II's ordination as *imperator* by Pope John XIII before the *Confessio* of St Peter on Christmas Day 967 'to the great joy of our people [*nostratium*] and of the Romans about the most pleasing togetherness of the two *augusti* and the Lord Pope'.[51]

It is Adalbert rather than Liudprand of Cremona who opens for us the theme of the new emperor's relations with Byzantium. It is in fact a more complex story than can be pieced together from the *Legatio* and the *Antapodosis* alone. Like Charlemagne's emperorship, Otto I's needed recognition from the much older empire ruled by the *basileus Romaion*, and as in the case of Charlemagne, Otto's insecure and troubled position at Rome forced him southwards towards the Byzantine possessions in Apulia and her clientele in Capua, Naples and Benevento. However, unlike Charlemagne's eastern contemporaries, the Byzantines, or at least the most potent segments of their society were, whatever the problems of their economic substructure, posed for successful and ongoing offensives both in Asia and, a decade later, also in the north. There was no obvious crisis like the Bulgarian threat of 812 to force

[47] The dividing line between privilege and mandate is not always easy to draw, but there is no doubt that only a few of Otto I's diplomata from the imperial period could be classified as mandates, perhaps D O I 344, 355, 366, 434 (dating uncertain), which represents only a tiny fraction of the *c.* 200 surviving diplomata issued between Otto's imperial coronation in 962 and his death in 973. On *missi* see J. Ficker, *Forschungen zur Reichs- und Rechtsgeschichte Italiens*, vol. 2 (Innsbruck, 1869), pp. 1-6.

[48] Sutherland, *Liudprand* (as no. 38), pp. 86-94; for implicit criticism of Otto's dealings with Benedict V in particular see Thietmar, *Chronicon* II 28; IV 18; VI 88, pp. 72/74, 152, 378.

[49] See the references given above n. 39.

[50] Claude, *Erzbistum Magdeburg* (as n. 23), pp. 114-18; the mandate is D O I 366.

[51] Adalbert, *Continuatio*, p. 179.

them to yield and make concessions over matters of rank and standing.[52] At the same time Ottonian emperorship, just because of its origins and bestowal by the hands of a louche pope from a family of erstwhile Greek clients, urgently needed authentication. There was, as we have said, as yet something provisional about the Ottonian imperial presence. It wanted and was still looking for a larger content, especially south of the Alps where not only its warriors but also its clerics, even its prelates, were predatory and given to plundering cherished relics.[53] The conversion of the heathen Slavs beyond Elbe as set out in John XII's privilege hung fire and did not altogether suffice.[54]

There can be no doubt that Otto I, from an early date, wanted his recognition by the rulers of Byzantium to take the form of a marriage alliance for his son, Otto II, who was already king, having been elected by the *populus*, meaning the military following, at Worms in 961 and then again by the Lotharingians at Aachen where he was sacered.[55] We learn of his plans not only from a letter sent from somewhere near Capua to Duke Hermann Billung and Margrave Dietrich of the northern march, dated 18 January 968, we know it also from Adalbert's *Chronicon*,[56] In April 967 Pope John XIII and Otto I met at Ravenna and here also the emperor's long-cherished wish to see Magdeburg raised to metropolitan status was met by a papal privilege in which the emperor was described as 'omnium augustorum augustissimus' and the third after Constantine; and yet the Pope did not quite venture to call him *imperator Romanorum* as he wanted to do.[57] For at Ravenna an embassy from Nicephorus Phocas arrived with presents seeking peace and friendship. So Adalbert, and we know from him also that the envoys were honourably received.[58] He has not told us how they addressed Otto; there is nothing to compare with the celebrated passage from the *Annales regni Francorum* under the year 812, when Greek envoys from the emperor Michael Rangabe called him *basileus* and emperor with *laudes* 'after their fashion', that is to say in Greek.[59] But whatever the protocol in 967, it did not stand in the way of an Ottonian counter-embassy, asking for nothing less than the hand of Romanos

---

[52] For the situation in 812 see Classen, *Karl der Große* (as n. 25), pp. 93-7; W. Treadgold, *The Byzantine Revival 780-842* (Stanford, 1988), pp. 163-74. 181-3. For the 960s see Ostrogorsky, *History* (as n. 8), pp. 282-95; H. Grégoire, 'The Amorians and Macedonians, 842-1025', in *The Cambridge Medieval History*, 4: *The Byzantine Empire*, 1: *Byzantium and its Neighbours*, ed. J.M. Hussey (Cambridge, 1966), pp. 147-55.

[53] E. Dupré-Theseider, 'La "grande rapina dei corpi santi" dall'Italia al tempo di Ottone I', in *Festschrift Percy Ernst Schramm*, ed. P. Classen and P. Scheibert (Wiesbaden, 1964), vol. 1, pp. 420-32; T. Reuter, *Germany in the Early Middles Ages, c. 800-1056* (London, 1991), pp. 271-2.

[54] See above at n. 3.

[55] Böhmer-Mikoletzky, 574e, 574f; Schramm, 'Deutsche Herrscher' (as n. 3), pp. 110-12.

[56] The mandate, D O I 355, survives only in Widukind, *Res gestae Saconicae* III 70, pp. 146-47, who undoubtedly reworked the text stylistically.

[57] Zimmermann, *Papsturkunden* (as n. 20), pp. 347-9, no. 177. For the question of differences between Otto I and John XIII at this time over 'missionary policy' see most recently the works by Engels and Tellenbach cited above, n. 23.

[58] Adalbert, *Continuatio*, p. 178.

[59] *Annales regni Francorum* (as n. 34), p. 136.

II's daughter for his son, Otto II. Most likely Nicephorus Phocas did not at that time deny a non-Roman imperial title to Otto, the *basileus ton Phraggon* designation which had by now already gathered age and dust about it. That this is so is to some extent confirmed by a passage in Liudprand's *Legatio* where Nicephorus, after complaining about Otto's invasion of Greek possessions in Apulia and wondering why he was waging offensive war, exclaims: 'We were friends and had it in mind to conclude an indissoluble alliance through marriage'.[60]

It was in fact Otto's military operations, his attempt to put pressure on the Greeks, not to say blackmail them, rather than Nicephorus's arrogance, so often denounced by modern Byzantinists,[61] which led to a crisis, and, not least of all to Liudprand's embassy.[62] Its vicissitudes began when Leon Phocas, the *kuropalates*, now denied Otto the *basileus* title, calling him merely *rex*.[63] The hoped-for marriage alliance was of course discussed when Liudprand had a conference with a committee of high-ranking Byzantine dignitaries, first and foremost the *parakoimoumenos* Basil, the only one he named. The price asked for the *porphyrogenita* Anna was nothing less than 'Rome and Ravenna with all the lands from there as far as us' and it was thus unpayable.[64] The impasse was resolved only with the assassination of Nicephorus and the accession of his murderer, John Tsimisces. With characteristic self-centredness and self-importance the Saxon authors – Widukind and following him Thietmar – attributed the warrior-emperor's downfall to the minor defeat of his troops had suffered at the hands of the Saxon counts Gunthar and Siegfried, Otto's commanders in Apulia. They also knew that Nicephorus's wife Theophanu, the mother of the Macedonians Basil and Constantine, was the instigator of the plot, nor did the usurpation of John Tsimisces elude them. For them he was simply 'a certain warrior', *quidam miles*, who carried out the coup and benefited from it.[65] With him Otto I could resume negotiations on recognition in the form of a bride for his son, now himself a crowned emperor, a bride he had spent years negotiating for, like Charlemagne.[66] These negotiations

[60] Liudprand, *Legatio*, c. 6, p. 179.

[61] E.G. R. Jenkins, *Byzantium: the Imperial Centuries, AD 610-1071* (London, 1966), pp. 279-80; Grégoire, 'Amorians and Macedonians' (as in n. 52), pp. 149-51.

[62] On the background to this see P. Lamma, 'Il problema del due imperi e dell'Italia Meridionale nel giudizio delle fonti letterarie nei secoli IX et X', in *Atti del 3. Congresso internazionale di studi sull'alto medioevo* (Spoleto, 1959), pp. 155-254, especially pp. 229-46; W. Ohnsorge, 'Die Anerkennung des Kaisertums Ottos I. durch Byzanz', in idem, *Konstantinopel und der Okzident* (Darmstadt, 1966), pp. 176-207; J.N. Sutherland, 'The Mission to Constantinople in 968 and Liudprand of Cremona', *Traditio* 31 (1975), pp. 55-82; Leyser, 'Ends and Means', above, pp. 135-42.

[63] Liudprand, *Legatio*, c. 2, p. 176.

[64] Liudprand, *Legatio*, c. 15-18, pp. 183-5; on Basil, the *eminence grise* of mid-tenth-century Byzantine politics, see *Oxford Dictionary of Byzantium* (as n. 5), p. 270.

[65] Widukind, *Res gestae Saxonicae* III 73, p. 149-50; Thietmar, *Chronicon* II 15, p. 56.

[66] Classen, *Karl der Große* (as n. 25), pp. 25-42; Treadgold, *Byzantine Revival* (as n. 52), pp. 70-1, 89-91. R. Macrides, 'Dynastic Marriages and Political Kinship', in *Byzantine Diplomacy* (as n. 9), pp. 263-80, is helpful on the Byzantine view of such marriages.

reached their climax with the mission of Archbishop Gero of Cologne and two bishops and allegedly even dukes to Constantinople in 871 in order to come to a conclusion. One of the bishops was most likely Liudprand.[67] To have sent so eminent an embassy was in itself an assurance against failure: the loss of face would have been too much. They brought back Theophanu, and who she was is therefore an essential clue to answering the question of how much and to what extent Byzantium, which at this point was still in the grip of an iron military regime, was willing to acknowledge Otto I's emperorship when all the while it resented his presence in Rome and his invasion of Byzantine spheres of influence in Capua and Benevento and the real threat to Apulia. Who then was Theophanu?

Thietmar of Merseburg gave the fullest answer to this question. She came indeed with a magnificent escort and a breath-taking treasure but she was not the *virgo desiderata*, the purple-born princess the Ottonians wanted. John Tsimisces, the usurper, had sent his niece as the bride to be.[68] All the other and nearest contemporary sources, with the exception of Widukind, confirm and strengthen Thietmar's comment. Widukind evaded the issue altogether; he merely called her *puella*.[69] Not only the *Annales Casinatenses*,[70] but more important the great dower charter Otto II gave to his wife, dated on their wedding day and that of her coronation at Rome on 14 April, described her as the niece, the *neptis clarissima*, of John the Constantinopolitan emperor.[71] On the luxury version of the diploma, the only text that has survived, any reference to the Byzantine as the Roman Empire is carefully avoided.[72] If the Greeks saw it, as they may have done, it was an insult. This too underlined that Theophanu was not a purple-born princess, yet even here a cavil is possible. It has already been mentioned that Widukind and Thietmar fully set out the complicity of the empress Theophanu, the wife of Romanos II and Nicephorus Phocas in her husband's assassination.[73] Had our Theophanu been her child by Romanos II, she would have been the daughter of a murderess. The Ottonians were very sensitive about such things. Altogether they can be credited with an enormous sense of family, much more so than the Carolingians. When Otto II died at Rome on 7 December 983, while his wife was with him and his mother was also in Italy, Henry the Wrangler, his Bavarian cousin and rebel walked free from a kind of detention in Utrecht and very soon not only put forward but fully acted out his claim to the kingship. At this critical moment, moreover, he

[67] Leyser, 'Ends and Means', above, pp. 120-1.

[68] Thietmar, *Chronicon* II 15, p. 56. For recent discussions of the vexed issue of the identity and the family connections of Theophanu see G. Wolf, 'Wer war Theophanu?' and O. Kresten, 'Byzantinische Epilegomena zur Frage: Wer war Theophanu?' in von Euw and Schreiner, *Theophanu* (as n. 41), vol. 2, pp. 385-96 and 403-10 respectively.

[69] Widukind, *Res gestae Saxonicae* III 73, p. 149.

[70] *MGH SS* 3, p. 172.

[71] D O II 21.

[72] Besides the references in n. 41 see also the facsimile edition, D. Matthes, *Die Heiratsurkunde der Kaiserin Theophanu: 972 April 14* (Stuttgart, 1980).

[73] Above, n. 65.

had possession of the young Otto III.[74] Yet he did not attempt to maim, blind or kill him, and no one accused him of having harboured such plans. It was by now unthinkable in the Ottonian house. In Byzantium the Empress Irene had had no such hesitations and the ninth-century Carolingians had few scruples about blinding nephews and even sons.[75]

Theophanu was thus in all likelihood a Byzantine noblewoman, no more, who, if she had any experience of the imperial palace, can only have been there for a relatively short time, after the advent of her uncle John Tsimisces to the purple. It is noteworthy that no Byzantine narrative or documentary source mentioned her or her marriage. Ottonian emperorship, as we have said, needed authentication. That was Theophanu's job and it was for this reason that her imperial descent mattered so much. For this reason also she fulfilled the role for which she was needed in the Ottonian house only in part, being as it were defective in the matter of legitimising imperial origin. Again the Ottonian ambience was well aware of these shortcomings in her titles, so much so that, as Thietmar again tells us, some advised Otto I not to receive her into his family but send her back.[76] He had been deceived. It is just possible that one who counselled against the match and sought to prevent it was Liudprand of Cremona, if only with his dying breath. He knew the social values of the Greeks better than anyone. Having been on the bridal embassy, he reached his native Italy but not his city, Cremona, before he died.[77]

Why then did Otto I ignore this advice and accept Theophanu all the same as his daughter-in-law? It could be argued that even by her most immediate circumstances she was noble enough. The very Thietmar who had questioned her standing and described her as the woman whom they had not wished for later almost contradicted himself and claimed (wrongly) that he had earlier and briefly set out her immense nobility.[78] But above all her bearing and cultural ambience overbore her critics and there were some quite vocal ones, as we shall see. As for Otto I, the reasons why he made do with her were simple and need not be searched for in the parlance of high politics. He had had enough. It was high time to see his house settled, his heir and successor married and so the future, as far as possible, assured. He had been in Italy now for no less than six years. Rule at home *in absentia* had proved troublesome

[74] See most recently J. Laudage, 'Das Problem der Vormundschaft über Otto III.', in von Euw and Schreiner, *Theophanu* (as n. 41), vol. 2, pp. 261-76, with somewhat controversial conclusions and very full references to the earlier literature.

[75] For Irene's blinding of Constatine VI in 796 see Treadgold, *Byzantine Revival* (as n. 52), pp. 108-9; for Carolingian practice see Leyser, *Rule and Conflict*, pp. 85-6.

[76] Thietmar, *Chronicon* II 15, p. 56.

[77] Leyser, 'Ends and Means', above pp. 120-1.

[78] Thietmar, *Chronicon* IV 14, p. 148.

and in Saxony protests were becoming audible and visible.[79] What Theophanu lacked in blood she made up by her sheer presence, nor had she, as has been mentioned, arrived empty-handed. Her enormous treasures, including arte-facts of every kind, many of them hitherto unknown in the north, were spells no Saxon king and his following could resist.[80] It enhanced the awe with which they looked up to him and also aroused their greedy expectations, not least of all those of the bishops. As for the 'politics' of the match, she brought with her the *amicitia* of the emperor John Tsimisces, which Otto needed for security in Italy. It meant also release for numerous Ottonian prisoners in Tsimisces's hands, most important of all for Pandulf Ironhead, the ruler of Capua and Benevento, Otto's chief ally in the south, whom the Greeks had captured in action near Bovino in 969.[81]

Theophanu joined her husband and her new family circle at Rome in April 972. Bishop Dietrich of Metz, a kinsman of the Ottonians, escorted her – he was to be one of her harshest critics later, after the disastrous battle of Cotrone.[82] Here, at Rome, the pope not only joined the pair, he also crowned Theophanu and here also she received her dower.[83] The coronation is of the greatest moment: it was a constitutive act and thanks to it Theophanu could enter into the fullness of rights that gave her rising influence as long as her husband lived and real power when he died and she survived him to face and to negotiate successfully one of the most critical minorities the Reich had to weather.[84] One of her first duties must have been to learn the languages of her new world, both the Latin of the diplomata in which her interventions counted for so much and the vernaculars, the everyday mode of speech of all but the few personal servants she must have taken with her when she left Byzantium.

---

[79] For the incident in Magdeburg in 972 when Hermann Billung, encouraged by Archbishop Adelbert, dined at the emperor's table and slept in the emperor's bed see Thietmar, *Chronicon* II 28, p. 74 and the comments in 'Ritual, Ceremony and Gesture: Ottonian Germany', below, pp. 198-200.

[80] H. Wentzel, 'Das byzantinische Erbe der ottonischen Kaiser: Hypothesen über den Brauts-chatz der Theophanu', *Aachener Kunstblätter*, 40 (1971), pp. 11-84, and 43 (1972), pp. 15-39; idem, 'Alte und altertümliche Kunstwerke der Kaiserin Theophano', *Pantheon*, 30 (1972), pp. 3-18; H. Westermann-Angerhausen, 'Spuren der Theophanu in der ottonischen Schatzkunst?', in von Euw and Schreiner, *Theophanu* (as n. 41), pp. 193-218.

[81] For the 'geopolitical' background see the references given above, n. 62, and also J. Gay, *L'Empire byzantin et l'Italie méridionale depuis l'avénement de Basile Ier jusqu'à la prise de Bari par les Normands (867-1071)* (Bibliothèque des écoles françaises d'Athènes et de Rome 82, Paris, 1904), pp. 289-323 and most recently B.M. Kreutz, *Before the Normans: Southern Italy in the Ninth and Tenth Centuries* (Philadelphia, 1991).

[82] The escort is noted in Sigebert of Gembloux, *Vita Deoderici I episcopi Mettensis* c. 4, *MGH SS* 4, p. 475; the criticism in Alpert of Metz, *Fragmentum de Deoderico primo episcopo Mettensi* c. 2, ed. H. van Rij and A.S. Abulafia (Amsterdam, 1980), p. 110.

[83] N. Gussone, 'Trauung und Krönung: Zur Hochzeit der byzantinischen Prinzessin Theophanu mit Kaiser Otto II.', in von Euw and Schreiner, *Theophanu* (as n. 41), pp. 161-74.

[84] F.-R. Erkens, 'Die Frau als Herrscherin in ottonisch-frühsalischer Zeit', in von Euw and Schreiner, *Theophanu* (as n. 41), pp. 245, especially p. 252, with good bibliography.

Theophanu also had eulogists among the chroniclers and historiographers and one of them described her as *ingenio facundam*.[85] *Facundia* suggests fluency, even eloquence, and was a gift in the vernacular no less than in the languages of literacy.[86] The evidence for her growing influence flows for us mainly out of the sponsorship clauses of imperial diplomata in which she – and it was one of her most habitual functions as empress – intervened. Often we can follow the genesis and preliminaries of a grant to an abbey so some other beneficiary: how the abbot approached her and how she then raised the matter with her husband until the time was ripe for the favour to be granted and a diploma to be engrossed recording it.[87] Altogether she intervened seventy-six times in Otto II's lifetime, and from the wording of the texts it is often clear that the *petitio* or *rogatio*, the request for the grant, stemmed from her.[88] Not infrequently of course she shared intervention with her mother-in-law, the empress Adelheid, Otto II's mother. That the two women were not in accord temperamentally and over house issues is known, but their collaboration in the years of supreme crisis after Otto II's death must be regarded as more important than their estrangements.[89]

As yet Theophanu brought little that can be described as markedly Byzantine to the language of the diplomata, but some striking innovations there were. *Imperatrix Augusta* had been rare before her coming but now it appears

---

[85] *Annales Magdelburgenses s.a.* 972, *MGH SS* 16, p. 152.

[86] For a fuller discussion of this theme see Leyser, 'Ritual, Ceremony and Gesture', below, p. 211 with n. 24.

[87] It is not clear here which diplomata are being referred to; for a list of possibilities see the following note and n. 109.

[88] She appears as intervening in D O II 26, 42*+, 53*, 57*, 66+, 82*, 88, 89+, 90+, 95+, 100+, 104, 106+, 107+, 108+, 110+. 122b+, 127, 130, 131*, 139+, 141, 142, 145, 155+, 157+, 159+, 161, 162, 172, 173, 174+, 175, 176, 179, 183+, 185, 186+, 194, 195, 196, 199, 200+, 201, 206, 207+, 212, 214+, 216, 222, 232, 234, 237+, 241, 242, 258+, 259, 265+, 275+, 280+, 283, 287, 289, 299*, 306*, 307*, 309+; joint interventions with Adelheid are marked with an asterisk, joint interventions with other notables with a cross. See R. Schetter, *Die Intervenienz der weltlichen und geistlichen Fürsten in den deutschen Königsurkunden von 911-1056* (Bottrop, 1935), pp. 11-14 (whose figure of 66 differs from the 68 just listed and from the figure in the text) and M. Uhlirz, 'Studien über Theophano, III: Die Intervention der Kaiserin Theophano zugunsten der Nonnenklöster während der Regierungszeit Ottos II. und ihre Bedeutung', *DA*, 9 (1952), pp. 122-35. The list and the statistics can in any case only be approximate, as the diplomata often make distinctions between *petitio*, *votum*, *rogatus*, *interventus*, etc., which a more detailed investigation might or might not reveal to be significant. At all events it is common for Theophanu's *petitio* or similar word to be distinguished from the *interventus* of others.

[89] W. Glocker, *Die Verwandten der Ottonen und ihre Bedeutung in der Politik: Studien zur Familienpolitik und zur Genealogie des sächsischen Kaiserhauses* (Dissertationen zur mittelalterlichen Geschichte 5, Cologne, 1989), pp. 91-4. For differences over dower issues see below, n. 107; for the infrequency of their joint interventions in Otto II's lifetime (before the reconciliation between Otto II and Adelheid in 980) see the evidence assembled in the previous note, and for Adelheid's role in the decades following Otto I's death P. Corbet, *Les Saints ottoniens: Sainteté dynastique, sainteté royale et sainteté féminine autour de l'an mil* (Beihefte der Francia 15, Sigmaringen 1986), pp. 59-60, 91-2; M. Uhlirz, 'Die rechtliche Stellung der Kaiserinwitwe Adelheid im deutschen und im italienischen Reiche', *Zeitschrift der Savigny-Stiftung für Rechtsgeschichte, germanistische Abteilung*, 74 (1957), pp. 85-97.

much more often, and this for Theophanu rather than her mother-in-law.[90]
Thus we read in a grant to her by Otto II: 'dilectissimae coniugi nostrae
Theophanu coimperatrici nec non imperii regnorumque consorti'.[91] *Reg-
norum* (or *regni*) *consors* had already begun to appear before this, but
coimperatrix is peculiar to Otto II, sometimes coupled also with the *augusta*
title, as in the case of a grant to Memleben of 981.[92] Here the two empires
shared common classical precepts and nursed imperial exaltation from a
common source.

   To study emperorship in the later tenth century, whether eastern or western,
one should perhaps not look chiefly at major political and military crises,
though these were real enough, but at matters of routine, at what was normal
and continuous. Here the *prooimia* of Greek novels and chrysobulls and the
arengae of Latin diplomata invite comparison because it was precisely in these
sonorous commonplaces, these ornate features of official utterance that the
duties, functions and underlying values of rulership were rehearsed and
proclaimed again and again.[93] One feature stands out, however. The *prooimia*
headed the texts of legal enactments; they set out the generalities and reasons
prompting the legislator, and so are part of the magnificent development of
legislative expertise, traditions and practices that remained at the disposal of
the *basileus*. It has already been noted that general legislation was a rarity in
Ottonian government. Instead the *arengae* served as an introduction, a
flourish, expressing the almost uniform sentiment underlying the grant: the
hope of salvation or of the merit accumulated towards it, the hope of blessing
in the hereafter and stability for the Reich in this life, these are the sentiments
usually coupled together by the pious Ottonian grantors. As against this the
prooimion sets out the sum of the *basileus*'s duties and horizons, something
almost like a political theory of Byzantine emperorship.[94] There is the
imitation of God and his omnipresence. Basil II in a *prooimion* counted the
subjugation of the Bulgars as a special gift conferred by God.[95] The emperorship is presented as something almost eternal; the emperor has a special care
and foresight for his subjects, a *pronoia*. He is ever-watchful, a shepherd; he is

[90] Wolf, 'Theophanu' (as n. 68), p. 389 n. 65.

[91] D O II 76 (Mühlhausen, 29 April 974).

[92] D O II 96 (Wallhausen, 21 July 981). For the titles and their significance see Erkens, 'Frau' (as
n. 84); Wolf, 'Theophanu' (as n. 68), pp. 388-9; T. Vogelsang, *Die Frau als Herrscherin im hohen
Mittelalter: Studien zur 'consors regni' Formel* (Göttinger Bausteine zur Geschichtswissenschaft 7,
Göttingen, 1954), pp. 17-39.

[93] On these see H. Fichtenau, *Arenga* (Vienna, 1957); F. Hausmann and A. Gawlik, *Arengen-
verzeichnis zu den Königs- und Kaiserurkunden von den Merowingern bis Heinrich VI.* (MGH
Hilfsmittel 9, Munich, 1987).

[94] H. Hunger, *Prooimion. Elemente der byzantinischen Kaiseridee in den Arengen der Urkunden*
(Wiener Byzantinische Studien 1, Vienna, 1964); see also J. Bompaire, 'A propos des préambules
des actes byzantines des Xe-XIe siècles', in *Prédication et propaganda au moyen âge* (Paris, 1983),
pp. 133-47. H. Ahrweiler, *L'Idéologie politique de l'empire byzantin* (Paris, 1975), has little to say
about imperial *prooimia*.

[95] Hunger, *Prooimion* (as n. 94), p. 72.

a fulfiller of the law, the bringer of measure and harmony, but above all he preaches and dispenses justice. He is the living law, as a *prooimion* of Nicephorus Phocas announced. He, the *basileus*, was also a helper to his subjects, granting grace and favour. He was even a healer. Welfare and philanthropy emanated from him.[96]

Ottonian imperial practice and utterance had nothing so explicit, no such elaborate, permanent and wide-ranging programme. Occasionally the ideas so explicitly set out in a Byzantine *prooimion* occur in the magic that was thought to attend Carolingian and Ottonian kings: that they slept little, were like lions always watchful, had a special penetrating glance, these features hinted at similar cares and values, if only in a far less sophisticated way.[97] Justice stood at the centre here as well, but is was seen mainly as the reward of the good and faithful and the coercion of the wicked and proud. the concept of *dikaiosyne* with its jurisprudential undertones was scarcely there.[98] When Otto I imposed judicial duels in Italy by a written ordinance, he was, paradoxically by latter-day criteria, at one and the same time both advanced in having a text and regressive in what it contained.[99]

Theophanu's moments came when, with the help of a combination of forces, headed or held together by Archbishop Willigis of Mainz, she regained the person of her son, the very young Otto III and became effective sole regent for him until her untimely early death at Nimwegen on 15 June 991, aged less than forty.[100] The situation she had to face was critical. Bad news travelled fast in the tenth century, scarcely less so than today. The report of the battle at Cotrone near Rossano in south Italy in July 982 where Otto II lost the better part of his host, including a good few Saxon nobles, sparked a massive revolt of the Slav tribes east of the Elbe: the Redarii, Wilzi and Liutizi, now all tributaries of the Saxon Reich.[101] The burgwards – the fortress from which Saxon garrisons dominated tribal areas – and the recently built churches were assaulted, fired and destroyed, the left bank of the river was seriously threatened. The whole work of Henry I's and Otto I's conquest, occupation and mission, reaching well beyond Brandenburg, was destroyed and lost. Only

---

[96] Hunger, *Prooimion* (as n. 94), pp. 84-100 (*prontis* and *agrypnia*), 117-21 (living law), 123-54 (*philanthropia*); see also Ahrweiler, *Idéologie* (as n. 94), *passim*, on *philanthropia* as a *Herrschertugend*.

[97] For Charlemagne's and Otto I's short sleeping hours and watchfulness see Einhard, *Vita Karoli* c. 24, p. 29; Widukind, *Res gestae Saxonicae* II 36 and III 75, pp. 96, 153; see K.J. Leyser, 'Some Reflections on Twelfth-Century Kings and Kingship', in idem, *Medieval Germany*, pp. 245-6 and on the king's glance idem, *Rule and Conflict*, p. 83.

[98] For the legislative and judicial content of western diplomata see H. Krause, 'Königtum und Rechtsordnung in der Zeit der sächsischen und salischen Herrscher', *Zeitschrift der Savigny-Stiftung für Rechtsgeschichte, germanistische Abteilung*, 82 (1965), pp. 1-91. Hunger, *Prooimion* (as n. 94), discusses *dikaiosyne* on pp. 114-7.

[99] See above at n. 46.

[100] For the legitimists of 984 see Uhlirz, *Otto III.*, pp. 10-40.

[101] Böhmer-Mikoletzky, 874b.

the southern sector of the occupation, the country between Merseburg and Meissen, seems to have held. Archbishop Giselher of Magdeburg with a number of Saxon margraves and counts succeeded in fighting a victorious defensive action by the River Tanger while Otto II still lived, but Theophanu inherited the results of this catastrophe which had destroyed an uphill, albeit profitable effort of three generations.[102] The year 984 passed with its struggles for the regency and warding off Henry the Wrangler's attempts on the kingship.[103] From 985 onwards there were annual expeditions across the Elbe into Sclavinia to restore the situation and regain, if possible, some of the ground that had been lost, especially Brandenburg with its bishopric founded in 948.[104] Of Theophanu's own attitude towards and experience of war we do not know much, but we must assume that she stood fully behind the Saxon margraves' efforts to counter-attack. Above all the loyalties of Miesco of Poland and Boleslas of Bohemia found a focus in her, and Miesco's armed support in 985 was of crucial importance. In 986 Otto III himself, 'adhuc puerulus' – he was only six years old – took the field so that Miesco could join the host and do homage to him. He brought a camel as an exotic present to please and gratify his young overlord.[105] By 987 the Saxon expeditions into Sclavinia had made it possible to begin rebuilding the destroyed castles by the Elbe.[106] Theophanu's regency, thanks to the vigorous response of the east Saxon warlords, emerged creditably from this crisis. For Theophanu, it might be mentioned, there was no personal interest at stake. Unlike her mother-in-law, Adelheid, she had no direct holdings in the Saxon-Slavonic lands, though the recovery of tribute was also at stake. Her dower, while it included several important Saxon *curtes* like Herford, Tilleda and Nordhausen, included no possessions east of the Elbe. The west and the Rhineland were her favourite regions, not to mention Italy.[107]

---

[102]On 983 and its consequences for the Ottonians' 'Eastern policy' in the 980s and 990s see W.H. Fritze, 'Der slawische Aufstand von 983: Eine Schicksalswende in der Geschichte Mitteleuropas', in *Festschrift der Landesgeschichtlichen Vereinigung für die Mark Brandenburg zu ihrem hundertjährigen Bestehen 1884-1984* (Berlin, 1984), pp. 9-55 and J. Fried, 'Theophanu und die Slawen: Bemerkungen zur Ostpolitik der Kaiserin', in von Euw and Schreiner, *Theophanu* (as n. 41), pp. 361-70.

[103]Uhlirz, *Otto III.*, pp. 10-40; Laudage, 'Vormundschaft' (as n. 74).

[104]See Uhlirz, *Otto III.*, pp. 64-6, 70, 88, 125-6, and Fried, 'Theophanu' (as n. 102).

[105]Thietmar, *Chronicon* IV 9, p. 140.

[106]*Annales Quedlinburgenses*, *MGH SS* 3, p. 67.

[107]For Theophanu's dower see D O II 21, 76, 171, 202a and b; for Adelheid's see D O II 109, renewed in D O III 36 (Allstedt, 21 May 987), in which Theophanu appears as intervenor, thus marking a reconciliation between the two women (see above, n. 89). For Theophanu's itinerary see G. Wolf, 'Itinerar der Prinzessin Theophano/Kaiserin Theophanu', *Archiv für Diplomatik*, 35 (1989), pp. 237-54.

The constitutional formalities of the Reich and its society made little or no allowance for a royal or imperial minority.[108] Diplomata were uttered in the infant Otto III's name as if he were fully able to shoulder them as acts of his own will. They were of course grants and gifts made by his mother, whose intervention now became decisive and habitual. There were few diplomata in which episcopal and lay aristocratic sponsors appeared on their own without her. Yet she was usually not the sole intervenient, and above all Archbishop Willigis of Mainz, who together with Saxon enemies of Henry the Wrangler, and the chancellor, Bishop Hildibald of Worms, had really saved the throne for Otto III in 984, appear together as intervenients many times. They, especially Hildibald, must have been her closest advisers. Only at the beginning did the longevitous empress Adelheid share interventions; then she disappeared leaving the field to her superior rival, who now appears regularly as *imperatrix augusta*.[109]

We possess two diplomata which Theophanu issued wholly in her own name and not in that of her son, the king. In 989 the affairs of the Reich in the north were sufficiently becalmed, despite the intense struggle between the Capetians and the last Carolingian, Duke Charles of lower Lotharingia, during which she was constantly appealed to, for Theophanu to be able to cross the Alps and visit Rome.[110] She went for two reasons: to revisit her husband's tomb and to assert her son's rights. In April 990 we find her at Ravenna, where she responded to a complaint of Abbot John of Farfa with a gift restoring a church, a daughter house, to the abbey. The diploma duly recorded the plea: how, moved by compassion and for the remedy of her soul and that of her lord Otto, she had reinvested the abbot. It is the sanctions clause that invites special attention. Any inhabitant, great or small, 'of our empire' acting against 'our investiture of *mundeburdium*', would be compelled by 'our imperial command' to make composition with 100 pounds of the best gold. Authentication is announced next, the impression of her ring. But what matter above all are the protocol and the dating clause: 'Theophanius, gratia divina imperator augustus'.[111] She appears in full possession as sole emperor even more in the

---

[108]Laudage, 'Vormundschaft' (as n. 74) attempts with some new arguments to maintain the traditional legal historians' view that the rules governing the minority of rulers were the same as those applying in any noble family; for a less legalistic and probably more realistic view of medieval minority arrangements see T. Kölzer, 'Das Königtum Minderjähriger im fränkisch-deutschen Mittelalter: Eine Skizze', *HZ*, 251 (1990), pp. 291-324, who writes (p. 323) of 'de facto regencies which kept up the fiction that [a child king] rules in person'.

[109]She intervenes in DD O III 2+, 3*, 4+, 6*+, 9*+, 11+, 12+, 14+, 15+, 16, 19+, 20, 23+, 29+, 31+, 32+, 33+, 34*+, 35, 37+, 38+, 39, 40, 43+, 44+, 47+, 48+, 49+, 50, 53, 54, 55+, 58+, 65+, 66+, 67, 68+, 69, 70, 71, 107. For further literature and an explanation of the symbols and caveats see above, n. 88; for Theophanu's *intitulatio* see above, n. 90.

[110]For a fuller discussion see '987: The Ottonian Connection', below, pp. 165-79. See also B. Schneidmüller, 'Ottonische Familienpolitik und französische Nationsbildung im Zeitalter der Theophanu', in von Euw and Schreiner, *Theophanu* (as n. 41), pp. 345-60.

[111]D Th. 2 (Ravenna, 1 April 990).

dating clause where we read: 'anno vero imperii domni Theophanii impera-toris XVIII'. Otto III is not mentioned at all here; she has created the impression of eighteen years of full emperorship. It was a revealing moment, and one of singular daring perhaps, because in her earlier grant to S. Vincenzo in the Volturno she styled herself 'Theophanu divina gratia imperatrix augusta' and dated by her son's regnal years.[112]

From these oddities we may conclude that western emperorship was not as coherent, settled and secure as that of the palace of Constantinople. Even during her regency Theophanu had not sought to introduce Byzantine ritual, let alone Byzantine governmental practice. It was too dangerous, and she depended too much on the loyalties of a heterogeneous group of lay nobles who had already set their seal on the styles and forms of western emperorship. It was after all sporadic, with a good many years when there had been no emperor at all. In the last resort an Ottonian emperor remained what he always had been, long before he became that or even king, the leader of a warrior *comitatus*, with friends and *familiares* with whom he closely shared his daily life and marches. Here the encompassing ritual of the Byzantine court, its luxuries and profound elaborations created a wholly different setting and atmosphere. The *palatia* of the Ottonians were not built for the secrecy and intrigues that could be housed so adequately in the east. Neither in his hall nor in his chamber did the Ottonian ruler enjoy or even seek privacy. It was here that Theophanu's son, Otto III, became sole exception. He did indeed cultivate Rome and Aachen as if he were in search of a capital, he surrounded himself at one time with a new court-office, dignitaries and ranks, and he even, to the horror of the onlookers, dined alone.[113] He had moreover the friendship and devotion of some of the most outstanding men of his time. Gerbert of Aurillac was only too anxious to be called for and noticed.[114] As so often in the history of the Reich, Otto did not live long enough for any of this to become permanent. Continuity and endurance in the later tenth century seemed to be on the side of the Byzantines. But let us not forget that the heir to Ottonian emperorship, the Holy Roman Empire of the German nation, lived on until 1806.

[112] D Th. 1 (Rome, 2 January 990).

[113] Thietmar, *Chronicon* IV 47 p. 184; see for Byzantine parallels P.E. Schramm, *Kaiser, Rom und Renovatio*, vol. 1, 2nd edn (Darmstadt, 1957), p. 111 and iden, 'Kaiser Otto III. (*980, +1002): seine Persönlichkeit und sein "byzantinischer Hofstaat"', in idem, *Kaiser, Könige und Päpste* (as n. 3), vol. 3, pp. 277-97 and for comment Leyser, 'Ritual and Ceremony', below, p. 202.

[114] See the letter of Gerbert to the chancellor Heribert, *Die Briefsammlung Gerberts von Reims*, no. 184, *MGH BDK* 2, pp. 217-19, and to Otto III, no. 185, pp. 219-20, both of late 996.

10

987: The Ottonian Connection

By 987 the Capetians were already an old and notably longevitous princely family. The service-lives of Hugh the Great and Hugh Capet between them spanned well over seventy years. 987 is important above all in retrospect. By then the Robertines had already twice given kings to western Francia and for more than two generations their foremost man had been what in tenth-century parlance was called *secundus a rege*[1] To understand the advent of Hugh Capet to kingship we must understand the European setting in which his sacering and the disinheritance of the Carolingian Charles and his family were brought about. Central and western Europe during this decade were dominated by two women, the foremost ladies of the Ottonian house who were its guardians during the minority of Otto III. A mere glance at the addresses of Gerbert's letters suggests that most of the threads of influence, if not of direction, led them. In the collection of his epistolary *oeuvre*, eight letters were intended for Theophanu, eight again for Adelheid, that is more than for any other correspondent with the exceptions of Notker of Liège and Egbert of Trier, who surpasses them all by far.[2] Time and again Gerbert turned to Theophanu for

---

[*] Unpublished English and German typescripts of a lecture first given at Toronto in 1987; the footnotes are editorial.

[1] On the careers of Hugh the Great and Hugh Capet see most recently L. Theis, *LAvènement de Hugues Capet* (Trente Journées qui ont fait la France 4, Paris, 1984); Y. Sassier, *Hugues Capet: Naissance d'une dynastie* (Paris, 1987), pp. 89-198; O. Guillot, 'Formes, fondements et limites de l'organisation politique en France au Xe siècle', in *Il secolo di Ferro: Mito e realtà del secolo X*, 2 vols. (Settimane 38, Spoleto, 1991), vol. 1, pp. 57-116, especially pp. 89-105; K.-F. Werner, 'Les Robertiens' and J. Ehlers, 'Carolingiens, Robertiens, Ottoniens: politique familiale ou relations franco-allemandes', in *Le Roi de France et son royaume autour de l'an mil*, ed. M. Parisse and X. Barral I Altet (Paris, 1992), pp. 15-26 and 39-45 respectively. For *secundus a rege* see P. Lauer (ed.) *Recueil des actes de Louis IV, roi de France* (Paris, 1914), no. 4, p. 10: 'dilectissimus noster et Francorum dux, qui est in omnibus regnis nostris secundus a nobis', and for the ninth-century antecedents of the term 'Nithard and his Rulers', above, p. 21 and n. 12.

[2] *Die Briefsammlung Gerberts von Reims*, ed. F. Weigle (MGH BDK 2, Weimar, 1966), pp. 283-5 (list of recipients).

his orders, and Archbishop Adalbero of Rheims, himself a Lotharingian, was no less swayed by the Ottonian court.[3]

These two exalted figures, both crowned empresses, were supported by a remarkable circle of other ladies, almost as prominent and profiled and close to the possession of authority, respect and lordship: Mathilda, abbess of Quedlinburg and Otto I's daughter;[4] Beatrix, duchess of upper Lotharingia and Hugh Capet's sister;[5] and Emma, the daughter of the empress Adelheid by her first marriage to Lothar of Italy and the wife of the Carolingian Lothar, who together with her son Louis received the paths of fidelity of the French princes in 986.[6] In the letters there is mention of a *colloquium dominarum* which was to be held at Metz in 985 to settle the disputed and confused issues of possession and lordship in Lotharingia which the Ottonian minority had once more unfurled.[7] Kinship and affinity underlay all these tensions and the efforts to contain them. Both Hugh Capet and the Carolingians were of Ottonian descent on their mothers' side. Ottonian names like Brun, Otto, Hathui and Gerberga pervaded Carolingian, Capetian and episcopal nomenclature in tenth-century France.[8] It is not clear that the *colloquium dominarum* ever took place, but the fact that it was seen as a possible way out of the conflicts of Otto III's minority and the Carolingians' efforts to take advantage of them is very significant.[9]

[3]   On the family connections of Adalbero of Rheims see H. Renn, *Das erste Luxemburger Grafenhaus* (Rheinisches Archiv 39, Bonn, 1941), pp. 44-51; M. Parisse, 'Généalogie de la Maison d'Ardenne', in *La Maison d'Ardenne, Xe-XIe siècles* (Luxemburg, 1981), pp. 9-44, here pp. 24-5 and table; W. Glocker, *Die Verwandten der Ottonen und ihre Bedeutung in der Politik: Studien zur Familienpolitik und zur Genealogie des sächsischen Kaiserhauses* (Dissertationen zur mittelalterlichen Geschichte 5, Vienna, 1989), pp. 290, 310-11, 436; M. Bur, 'Adalbéron archevêque de Reims, reconsidéré', in *La Roi de France* (as no. 1), pp. 55-63.

[4]   On Mathilda, abbess of Quedlinburg from 966, see Glocker, *Verwandte* (as n. 3), pp. 201-6.

[5]   Beatrix of Lotharingia, daughter of Otto I's sister Hadwig and Hugh the Great, widow of Duke Frederick I of upper Lotharingia and de facto regent for her son Dietrich; see Glocker, *Verwandte* (as n. 3), p. 288; Renn, *Luxemburger Grafenhaus* (as n. 3), p. 47.

[6]   For the oath-taking of 986 see F. Lot, *Les Derniers Carolingiens: Lothaire, Louis V, Charles de Lorraine (954-991)* (Bibliothèque de l'école des hautes études 47, Paris, 1891), p. 186 and n. 1; P. Hilsch, 'Zur Rolle von Herrscherinnen: Emma regina in Frankreich und in Böhmen', in *Westmitteleuropa - Ostmitteleuropa: Vergleiche und Beziehungen. Festschrift für Ferdinand Seibt*, ed. W. Eberhard and others (Veröffenlichungen des Collegium Carolinum 70, Munich, 1992), pp. 81-9.

[7]   Gerbert, *Epistolae* (as n. 2) nos. 62, 63, 65, 66, pp. 93, 94-5, 95-6, 96-7; the phrase occurs in no. 62, p. 93, and in no. 66, p. 97.

[8]   The genealogical table in Leyser, *Rule and Conflict*, pp. 90-1, provides a convenient guide to the Ottonian names (Brun/Bruno, Otto, Henry, Hathui (Hadwig), Gerberga) in the west Frankish Carolingian and the Capetian families; see also Glocker, *Verwandte* (as n. 3), *passim*, and especially p. 198 on Bishop Bruno of Langres (980-1016). Adalbero of Rheims and Adalbero of Laon were also of Ottonian descent; see the references given above, n. 3.

[9]   Lot, *Derniers Carolingiens* (as n. 6), p. 161 and n. 4 (uncertain); Uhlirz, *Otto III.*, pp. 54-5 with no. 60 (probable); C. Brühl, *Deutschland-Frankreich, Die Gerbut zweier Völker* (Cologne, 1990), p. 588 n. 29 (certain).

For the Carolingian succession crisis in 987 followed close on the heels of an Ottonian one, when Duke Henry of the Bavarian branch of the Liudolfings took possession of his young cousin, Otto III, and found a following to advance himself to the kingship, just as his father had tried to do against Otto I.[10] The fate of Henry's bid was decided not in Lotharingia but in a far corner of southeastern Saxony, where Henry and his forces were trapped by a host of Saxon nobles opposed to him in June 984. It meant that he had to hand over the infant Otto III to his mother and grandmother, though even then the struggle – and the west Frankish interest in it – was far from over.[11] It could be seen to have ended only at the solemn Ottonian Easter-keeping at Quedlinburg in 986 where the dukes served the young king as steward, chamberlain, butler and marshall, with Henry, now once again vested with Bavaria, conspicuously among them.[12] Only a year thus divided the two crises.

Both of them had been precipitated by premature and unexpected deaths, that of Otto II and that of Louis V, but the earlier crisis can explain the later only in so far as Theophanu and her helpers, Archbishop Willigis of Mainz and Bishop Hildibald of Worms, were less able to control events and intervene in France than an adult Ottonian king would have been able to do.[13] Lothar had been unable to wrest the formal cession of Lotharingia, the coveted goal of all the later Carolingians, from the Ottonians' infighting, whatever Henry the Wrangler's promises may have been, but he could exploit the conflict by launching a direct assault on Verdun, taking the town and retaking it after the Lotharingian great, hostile to him, had driven him out.[14] Here the minority government suffered a damaging blow and the enterprise and aggressiveness of the last Carolingians won success, though these were fraught with poisonous dilemmas.

These were inherent in the fundamental situation of the Carolingian house throughout the tenth century. The Carolingians had to contend with the

[10] Uhlirz, *Otto III.*, pp. 10-40, gives the details of Henry's support; for his father's following in 938-41 see Leyser, *Rule and Conflict*, pp. 14-18.

[11] Uhlirz, *Otto III.*, pp. 33-5.

[12] Thietmar, *Chronicon* IV 9, p. 140; for commentary see 'Ritual, Ceremony and Gesture', below p. 202.

[13] For Otto I's ability to intervene in west Francia even during the internal crises of his reign cf. W. Kienast, *Deutschland und Frankreich in der Kaiserzeit (900-1270: Weltkaiser und Einzelkönige* (Monographien zur Geschichte des Mittelalters 9, Stuttgart, 1974), pp. 60-3, 74-6. Brühl, *Deutschland-Frankreich* (as n. 9), pp. 477-9, 489-90, is more sceptical as regards 954, but the arguments against Brun of Cologne's presence at Lothar's coronation are not convincing; cf. Flodoard, *Annales*, p. 139.

[14] Lot, *Derniers Carolingiens* (as n. 6), pp. 144-8; Uhlirz, *Otto III.*, pp. 44-6.

demands of kingship, to master the new intermediate, regional lordships of their princes with an inadequate base of resources and power. This meant in tenth-century terms the means to find *milites* and to reward service.[15] Louis IV and Lothar, being on the whole able men, tried throughout their long reigns to right this imbalance and to tilt the command of resources in their favour by using every opportunity they saw coming their way. They were out for a coup, and this was what made their policies so adventurous and risky. One of these expedients was their continuous and unrelenting attempts to exploit the troubles of their Ottonian neighbours – the early struggles of Otto I and the great rift in the Liudolfing house in 953/54 – within Lotharingia, and to bring this, their homeland, with its economic, political and cultural resources into their ambit and so break the deadlock between themselves and the house of Hugh the Great, *dux Francorum*.[16] Even Louis IV, barely arrived from Wessex, tried to do this in Alsace in 939, entering 'plus hostiliter quam regaliter', as Adalbert of St Maximin indignantly wrote.[17] He had to be expelled by Otto I, himself fighting for his kingship against the *duces* and his own brother. Conversely, only Otto's and King Edmund of Wessex's intervention saved Louis d'Outremer from ending as a prisoner and so sharing the fate of his father. During the 940s Otto and his son-in-law Conrad, now duke of Lotharingia, preserved a modest power-base for the Carolingians against the overwhelming weight of the Capetian, Hugh the Great.[18]

It is widely thought that the Ottonian preponderance in west Francia came to an end when Otto's brother Brun, archbishop of Cologne and *archidux* in Lotharingia, died at Rheims in 965 while once again settling disputes between

---

[15] The best modern account of the politics by the west Frankish Carolingians is K.-F. Werner, 'Westfranken-Frankreich unter den Spätkarolingern und frühen Kapetingern (888-1060)', in *Handbuch der Europäischen Geschichte*, ed. T. Schieder, 1: *Europa im Wandel von der Antike zum Mittelalter*, ed. T. Schieffer (Stuttgart, 1976), pp. 731-83, here pp. 731-55; see also J. Dunbabin, *France in the Making, 843-1180* (Oxford, 1985), pp. 27-37.

[16] West Frankish aspirations in Lotharingia are discussed by B. Schneidmüller, 'Französische Lothringenpolitik im 10. Jahrhundert', *Jahrbuch für westdeutsche Landesgeschichte*, 5 (1979), pp. 1-31. The story of Brun of Cologne's conspiracy with Hugh the Great in 953 (?) told by Thietmar, *Chronicon* II 23, p. 66, may perhaps be an echo of these aspirations.

[17] Adalbert, *Continuatio*, p. 160, with an unconscious echo of the criticism of Conrad I's invasion of Bavaria in 916-7 given by the *Fragmentum de Arnulfo duce, MGH SS 17*, p. 570: 'criminantur, eodem episcopum cum eodem rege et exercitu eius provinciam illam non regaliter sed hostiliter intrasse'.

[18] For Otto I's intervention in west Francia in the 940s see P. Lauer, *Le Règne de Louis IV d'Outre-Mer* (Bibliothèque de l'ecole des hautes études 127, Paris, 1900), pp. 144-202; Kienast, *Deutschland und Frankreich* (as n. 13), pp. 66-71; Brühl, *Deutschland-Frankreich* (as n. 9), pp. 479-83.

Carolingians and Robertines. Henceforth we hear nothing of these hitherto frequent Rhenish and Saxon expeditions into west Francia.[19] Yet a closer look at relations between the Ottonians and west Francia during the 970s does not altogether sustain the view that the Carolingian kingdom could now measure itself as an equal with the Ottonian Reich and turn the proud terminology of its royal diplomata into ruling reality.[20] The stroke of 978 was a bold one and Lothar very nearly succeeded in overrunning and capturing Otto II and Theophanu at Aachen, backed as he was by the Capetian duke and the northern French nobles.[21] If Otto II thought that the Carolingians claims to Lotharingia were satisfied by investing Charles, Lothar's brother, with the *ducatus* of lower Lotharingia, he was mistaken.[22] But the invasion of France by a large Ottonian host later in 978 was massive and purposeful. It struck at and devastated the chief centres of Carolingian lordship, the *palatia* at Attigny, Soissons and Compiègne, and their demesne lands.[23] True, the Compiègne *palatium* must have been restored sufficiently to accommodate a great assembly in 985, a *coventus Francorum*, attended also by Lotharingian princes and an envoy of Henry the Wrangler.[24] Yet the material damage was real enough, however much Richer and eleventh-century French historiography might try to convert the story into one of imperial rout.[25]

Two years later Lothar sought peace, met Otto II at Margut, offered lavish presents, noted with much satisfaction by Saxon writers like Thietmar and the

---

[19] Ruotger, *Vita Brunonis* c. 42, pp. 44-5; Flodoard, *Annales*, p. 157; Adalbert, *Continuatio*, p. 175; Lot, *Derniers Carolingiens* (as n. 6), pp. 49-52. For the interpretation of Brun's death as a turning-point see e.g. ibid., p. 52; Kienast, *Deutschland und Frankreich* (as n. 13), pp. 86-7; T. Reuter, *Germany in the Early Middle Ages, c. 800-1056* (London, 1991), p. 168; Brühl, *Deutschland-Frankreich* (as n. 9), pp. 560-1.

[20] For the imperialising traits in Lothar's diplomata see B. Schneidmüller, *Karolingische Tradition und frühes französisches Königtum: Untersuchungen zur Herrschaftslegitimation der westfränkisch-französischen Monarchie im 10. Jahrhundert* (Frankfurter Historische Abhandlungen 22, Wiesbaden, 1979), pp. 158-62; idem, 'Ottonische Familienpolitik und französische Nationsbildung im Zeitalter der Theophanu', in A. von Euw and P. Schreiner (ed.), *Kaiserin Theophanu: Begegnung des Ostens und Westens um die Wende des ersten Jahrtausends*, 2 vols. (Cologne, 1991), pp. 345-59, here pp. 350-3 and plates; H. Wolfram, 'Lateinische Herrschertitel im neunten und zehnten Jahrhundert', in idem (ed.), *Intitulatio, 2: Lateinische Herrscher- und Fürstentitel im neunten und zehnten Jahrhundert* (Mitteilungen des Instituts für österreichische Geschichtsforschung, Ergänzungsband 24, Vienna, 1973), pp. 19-178, here pp. 145, 148-9.

[21] For Lothar's attack on Aachen see Lot, *Derniers Carolingiens* (as n. 6), pp. 92-7; Kienast, *Deutschland und Frankreich* (as n. 13), pp. 90-2; Brühl, *Deutschland-Frankreich* (as n. 9), pp. 564-6.

[22] Lot, *Derniers Carolingiens* (as n. 6), pp. 89-92; Kienast, *Deutschland und Frankreich* (as n. 13) p. 89; Schneidmüller, 'Lothringenpolitik' (as n. 16), pp. 25-6.

[23] Lot, *Derniers Carolingiens* (as n. 6), pp. 97-106, especially pp. 98-100; Kienast, *Deutschland und Frankreich* (as n. 13) pp. 92-6; Brühl, *Deutschland-Frankreich* (as n. 9), pp. 566-8. For the devastation of the *palatia* and fiscs see Richer, *Historiae* III 74, pp. 90/92.

[24] Described in a letter from Adalbero of Rheims to Adalbero of Metz which can be dated to May or June 985, Gerbert, *Epistolae* (as n. 2) no. 58, pp. 88-90: 'conventum Francorum Compendiaco palatio V id. maii'.

[25] Richer, *Historiae* III 77, pp. 94/96; a contemporary charter for Marmoutier also hails the

Hildesheim annalist, and even Richer admits that *Belgicae pars* (meaning Lotharingia) remained with Otto II.[26] The angry *Historia Francorum Senonensis* described this as an enfeoffment which deeply saddened the Frankish *principes*, perhaps to explain their desertion of the Carolingians later.[27] In doing so Lothar relieved Otto II's flank and enabled him to move to Italy without fears for his western frontiers. What did Lothar hope to gain? If he had tried to solve the Carolingians' perennial problem with one fell blow aimed at Otto II's person in 978, he may now have hoped to redress the balance in his favour in west Francia by enlisting Otto as a friend and ally and having his aid in overturning the Capetian duke. It conjured up the situation of 946, when Otto I had invaded France with an enormous Saxon host at the invitation of his sister Gerberga, Louis IV's wife. The king himself joined him; together they took Rheims and devastated Duke Hugh's lands.[28] Historical memories were long in the tenth century and we can thus understand why Hugh Capet was described as being so deeply indignant and feeling so badly tricked by Lothar's meeting with Otto II at Margut.[29] He matched the Carolingian pact with one of his own and at the emperor's request went all the way to Rome accompanied by the bishop of Orleans and others to pay his respects and make his peace after the 978 clash. Richer has here succeeded brilliantly in misleading his readers and clouding their view, not excluding that of modern historians. He has regaled them with the celebrated anecdote of Otto's sword: how Otto deliberately left his sword by a seat in the chamber where emperor and duke had met, and when their conversation was over (Otto had spoken in Latin,

---

victory, as noted by Werner, 'Westfranken-Frankreich' (as n. 15), p. 751. The eleventh-century west Frankish sources are conveniently assembled in Lot, *Derniers Carolingiens* (as n. 6), p. 103 n. 1, notably Rodulfus Glaber and the *Historia Francorum Senonensis*, both of whom stress the efficacy of Lothar's counter-attack and pursuit; for the importance of the latter source for shaping the view taken by French historiography of the high middle ages see J. Ehlers, 'Die *Historia Francorum Senonensis* und der Aufstieg des Hauses Capet', *Journal of Medieval History* 4 (1978), pp. 1-25, here p. 10. Note that Lot also sees Otto's invasion as a failure although he recognises the panagyric and apologetic tendencies in later historiography.

[26] Thietmar, *Chronicon* III 10, p. 109: 'Lutharius rex cum filio suimet ac muneribus magnificis ad eum venit, et, sibi satisfaciens, amiciciam eius firmiter acquisivit', *Annales Hildesheimenses*, ed. G. Waitz (MGH SRG 8, Hanover, 1878), p. 23: 'Lotharius rex cum magnis muneribus ad imperatorem veniens, sese cum filio suo subicit voluntati imperatoris'; Richer, *Historiae* III 78-81, pp. 96/100; for further sources see Lot, *Derniers Carolingiens* (as n. 6), pp. 118-19 with n. 1.

[27] *MGH SS 9*, p. 367: 'Dedit autem Hlotharius rex Ottoni in beneficio Hlotharium regnum; quae causa magis contristavit corda principum Francorum'; for comment see Ehlers, '*Historiae Francorum Senonensis*' (as n. 25), pp. 11-13.

[28] Lauer, *Louis IV* (as n. 18), pp. 149-53.

[29] Richer, *Historiae* III 81-3, pp. 102/16, especially Hugh's speech to his following, III 82, p. 102: 'Non enim vos latet quanta subtilitate doli Lotharius rex incautum me fefellerit, cum absque me Ottoni reconciliari voluerit feceritque.'

which had to be translated by Bishop Arnulf of Orleans) Otto rose to go and – as if he had forgotten his sword – turned to Hugh who at once went back to fetch it for him. The plan was for him to be seen carrying the emperor's sword, a clear sign of vassalage and client status. In Richer's much-cited tale, the bishop of Orleans, to Otto's admiration, saw through the ruse and with great presence of mind carried the sword to the emperor.[30] By telling this story of honour saved, Richer totally masks and obscures the deference and clientage already manifested clearly and visibly enough in Hugh's journey to Rome itself, even if a pilgrimage *ad limina* was not out of the ordinary for a tenth-century *princeps*.[31]

The *amicitia* of 981 between the duke and the Ottonians – present at Rome were also the two empresses, Mathilda of Quedlinburg 'the metropolitan abbess', and Duke Otto, Liudolf's son – was not allowed to fall into oblivion during the smouldering rift between the Carolingians and the archbishop of Rheims and his family following, both within and without the French kingdom.[32] There is above all (almost certainly) Archbishop Adalbero's letter of 985 to his nephew, Bishop Adalbero of Verdun. It spoke of the former *foedus* between the emperor Otto II and Hugh, who is seen as the real ruler of the Franks, and here plans are broached for Hugh's son Robert to join in an attempt to renew the alliance. This is described as the dying emperor's own wish.[33] In another letter of roughly the same date the archbishop returned to the

---

[30] Ibid., III 84-5, pp. 106/08; for modern interpretations following Richer see e.g. Lot, *Derniers Carolingiens* (as n. 6), pp. 123-4; Theis, *Avènement* (as n. 1), pp. 143-4; Sassier, *Hugues Capet* (as n. 1), pp. 168-9. Kienast, *Deutschland und Frankreich* (as n. 13), pp. 98-9, and Brühl, *Deutschland-Frankreich* (as n. 9), pp. 569-70 dismiss Richer's story as a fable. For Otto II's fluency in Latin see Ekkehard, *Casus sancti Galli* c. 145, ed. H.F. Haefele (AQDG 10, Darmstadt, 1980), pp. 282/84. Richer's claim (p. 108) that Otto II had Hugh escorted from Rome to the Alps is evidently also designed to disguise the nature of his journey; for comment see I. Voss, *Herrschertreffen im frühen und hohen Mittelalter: Untersuchungen zu den Begegnungen der osfränkischen und westfränkischen Herrscher im 9. und 10. Jahrhundert sowie der deutschen und französischen Könige vom 11. bis 13. Jahrhundert* (Beihefte zum Archiv für Kulturgeschichte 26, Cologne, 1987), p. 167.

[31] For an east Frankish/German view of Hugh's journey see the contemporary *Annales Colonienses*, *MGH SS* 1, 98: 'Ugo redit in gratiam imperatoris'. For other tenth-century pilgrimages to Rome by leading *principes*, see for example the two pilgrimages by Margrave Gero of the Saxon marches (Köpke-Dümmler, *Otto I.*, pp. 183, 385), and that by Duke William of Aquitaine in 1010 (Adémar of Chabannes, *Chronicon* III 56, p. 179).

[32] For those present in 981 see *Annales Magdelburgenses, MGH SS* 16, p. 155: 'cum imperatrice Theophanu, presente matre sua Adelheida imperatrice augusta una cum sorore Machtilde, Mertropolitanense abbatissa, convenientibus quoque ex Burgundia regibus, Conrado scilicet et Machthildo, rege Karlingorum Hugone . . .'; the annals themselves are twelfth-century but have good sources. On the feud between the Carolingians and Adalbero of Rheims see Lot, *Derniers Carolingiens* (as n. 6), pp. 142-58; A Dumas, 'L'Église de Reims au temps des luttes entre Carolingiens et Robertiens (888-1027)', *Revue de l'histoire de l'église de France*, 30 (1944), pp. 23-8; Theis, *Avènement* (as n. 1), pp. 150-6; Sassier, *Hugues Capet* (as n. 1), pp. 177-86.

[33] Gerbert, *Epistolae* (as n. 2) no. 41, pp. 71-3, here p. 72: 'Foedus, quod quondam inter se ac inter Ottonem caesarem convenerat, vos velle innovare promisimus adiuncto in foedere filio, quo unico gaudet. Hoc ipsum caesarem morientem expetisse persuasimus per dilectissimum sibi filium

theme: let the bishop of Verdun and Count Hermann, also of the Ardennes comital clan, seek Duke Hugh's friendship and bring him together with Otto III (meaning his minders), and there is no need to fear the *reges Francorum* (meaning the Carolingians).[34] These are indeed the makings of the plot heralding the Carolingians' overthrow. That Lothar should her be called *rex Franciae* only in name, but Hugh not in name but 'actu et opere', is all the more astonishing after the second siege and conquest of Verdun, when Lothar captured the duke of upper Lotharingia, the count of Verdun and his son, and others of note.[35] It raises stark questions about the nature and literary intent of Gerbert's letters.[36] The initiatives for the renewal of these alliances came, it seems, from the archbishop of Rheims, and were part of his search for expedients to escape from the wear and tear of his conflict of loyalties. The Capetian had broken up the *conventus Francorum* at Compiègne with, it was said, 600 *milites*, but shortly afterwards he was once more at peace with Lothar.[37]

All these letters still belong to the struggle for the kingship in the Reich and seek to inform the partisans of the young Otto about their opponents in France and their links with enemies nearer home. When we come to the events of 987 we must note first of all that the great historians of Ottonian Saxony took no notice of Hugh's elevation at all. Neither Thietmar of Merseburg nor the source he frequently used, the Quedlinburg annals, not the Hildesheim yearbooks mention the election and coronation of the Capetian and the exclusion of Charles, Louis V's uncle. There were, it is clear, constant communications between Archbishop Adalbero and the empress Theophanu, and the immediate results of Hugh's advancement were so useful to the Reich and the minority regime that its approval of what had taken place can be assumed, but it is far more difficult to pinpoint the empress's and her circle's

---

Sigefridi.' The letter is transmitted without indication of author or addressee; for the question of authorship see the literature cited ibid., p. 72 n. 1, whose consensus is that the letter was written by Gerbert on behalf of Adalbero of Rheims and addressed to Adalbero of Verdun.

[34] Ibid. no. 48, pp. 77-8: 'Obscuram epistolam et sine nomine paucis absolvimus: Lotharius rex Franciae praelatus est solo nomine, Hugo vero non nomine, sed actu et opere. Eius amicitiam si in commune expetissetis filiumque ipsius cum filio c. [*read* caesaris] coligassetis, iamdudum reges Francorum hostes non sentiretis.' The opening phrase probably indicates that we have here a copy of a summary of a letter, not the letter itself.

[35] See the references given above, no. 14.

[36] For the question of whether the two ancient mss. of Gerbert's letters (one of which is now lost, but known from copies and early editions) represent 'publications' of the letters by Gerbert himself in his own lifetime or are derived from a collection by Gerbert see F. Weigle, 'Studien zur Überlieferung der Briefsammiung Gerberts von Reims', part 3 *DA*, 14 (1958), pp. 149-220 and part 4, ibid., 17 (1961), pp. 385-419, who argues against K.-F. Werner, 'Zur Überlieferung der Briefe Gerberts von Aurillac', ibid., 17 (1961), pp. 91-144, that the letters were *not* intended for publication.

[37] Gerbert, *Epistolae* (as n. 2) nos. 58, 59, pp. 88-91; for discussion see Lot, *Derniers Carolingiens* (as n. 6), p. 158.

direct share in the Capetian enthronement. Gerbert wrote to Archbishop Everger of Cologne in the late summer of 987 that there was now peace between the kings.[38] The first fruits of Hugh's advancement was the restoration of Verdun without bloodshed, hostages or payments.[39] Once again Theophanu seems to be the hub around which everything turns: what she intends to do, her *iter*, where she is to stay and how the Saxon host had fared against recent Slav attacks, these are the things Gerbert most urgently wanted to know, but for what ends?[40] These were the years – and not least of all 987 itself – of intensive warfare on the east Saxon frontiers which absorbed especially the Saxon core of imperial resources and military striking power. The margraves, the archbishop of Magdeburg and even the nobility of the Saxon hinterland were tied down.[41]

The largest and most immediate gainer, though, was Archbishop Adalbero himself. Not only had he been restored to the foremost place, not only had the accusations of treachery been buried, but he also had King Hugh at last order his vassals, Count Odo of Blois and Count Heribert of Troyes, to release Adalbero's brother, Godfrey of Verdun, though only in return for considerable concessions of Verdun lands which he at once wrote to Theophanu not to ratify. Gerbert himself carried this letter, which he had also drafted, to the empress, so that he could convey her orders to the archbishop.[42] That Hugh Capet at this time meditated a marriage alliance with the Macedonian imperial house only underlines his sense of too close a dependence of too many strands of influence and direction leading to the Ottonian court. For once, moreover, the text of this letter addressed to the *basileus*, or its draft, may not have been revealed to the empress and her servants.[43]

[38] Gerbert, *Epistolae* (as n. 2), no 100, pp. 129-30.

[39] Ibid. no. 103, pp. 133-4 (Adalbero of Rheims to Theophanu).

[40] Ibid. no. 100, p. 130: 'Quid domina nostra Th. imperatrix semper augusta in sequenti tempore rerum publicarum sit actura quibusve in locis demoratura, et an Saxonum exercitus victor a consueto hoste redierit, significatum iri nobis plena fide oramus'.

[41] For the Slav campaign of the 980s see Böhmer-Uhlirz, nos. 976a and 978a (985), 983e (986), 995g and 996a (987); a Slav offensive coincided with the election of Hugh Capet. See J. Fried, 'Theophanu und die Slawen. Bemerkungen zur Ostpolitik der Kaiserin', in *Theophanu*, ed. van Euw and Schreiner (as n. 20), pp. 361-70, especially pp. 367-8.

[42] Gerbert, *Epistolae* (as no. 2) no. 103, pp. 133-4.

[43] Ibid., no. 111, pp. 139-40. Weigle gives (p. 139 n. 4) a comprehensive bibliography for discussions of this letter's status (unrealised draft or draft of a letter actually sent) up to 1966: of more recent authors, Kienast, *Deutschland und Frankreich* (as n. 13), p. 120 and n. 278, is uncertain; Sassier, *Hugues Capet* (as no. 1), p. 211, assumes that the letter has a background of real negotiations; Schneidmüller, 'Familienpolitik' (as n. 20), p. 358, follows Vasiliev in being sceptical. It may at least be assumed that the draft, even if never sent, was put together by Gerbert on the instructions of Hugh; it was kept secret by being written in shorthand and was not included in the collection of Gerbert's letters probably destined for Otto III; cf. Böhmer-Uhlirz, no. 998e.

We come now to the most difficult problem the exclusion of Charles of lower Lotharingia. Charles's position was at once formidable and anomalous. He had standing and a place in both kingdoms. As a Carolingian he could not help being a *persona regni*, however much his brother Lothar denied him any *honor* in west Francia. His presence is mentioned at great occasions throughout his brother's reign: he was at Cologne in 965, with Gerberga in Lotharingia in 968, at Compiègne in 985.[44] In 978 he apparently seized Laon and tried his luck as a rival king to his brother, perhaps under duress and certainly in vain.[45] Yet when Richer has Charles declaim to Archbishop Adalbero that he served under his brother no less faithfully than others he was not wholly blazing a trail of rhetoric.[46] Slightly later authors like Aimo of Fleury have misled us when they wrote of him baldly: 'privatis aedibus senuit'.[47] Even this phrase suggests that he had some landed possessions but lacked an *honor* in the kingdom, and we know that he had vassals even before Otto II in 977 took the dangerous step of making him duke of lower Lotharingia. In 976 Charles emerged as a formidable warrior marching with the exiled and disinherited sons of Reginar Longneck to attack Mons, their former seat in Hainault. In a battle against Counts Godfrey and Arnulf a certain Hetdo, one of Charles's *fideles*, fell.[48] As duke of lower Lotharingia Charles protected Cambrai against his brother when the bishopric was vacant in 979.[49] That he thoroughly exploited the situation and made very free with the riches of the see, and that he called his wife to join him and to sleep with him in the bishop's bed is retold with indignant relish by the author of the *Gesta Episcoporum Cameracensium*. Yet it should be remembered that Duke Hermann Billung had done no less in Otto I's time only a few years before as *procurator* of Saxony when he entered

---

[44] Lot, *Derniers Carolingiens* (as n. 6), pp. 48 (965), 61 (968); Gerbert, *Epistolae* (as n. 2) no 58, p. 89 (985). On the family meeting of 965 see now J. Laudage, "Liudolfingisches Hausbewuß-tsein"; zu den Hintergründen eines Kölner Hoftages von 965', in *Köln – Stadt und Bistum in Kirche und Reich des Mittelalters: Festschrift für Odilo Engels zum 65. Geburtstag*, ed. H. Vollrath and S. Weinfurter (Kölner Historische Abhandlungen 39, Cologne, 1993), pp. 23-59.

[45] Known only from the polemical letter of Dietrich of Metz, Gerbert, *Epistolae* (as n. 2) no. 31, pp. 55-6: 'Et quid mirum, si in nepotem pestem tui sordidissimi cordis evomis, qui cruenta manu et ad omne scelus semper promtissima cum latronum grege et furum manipulo, dum fratri tuo nobili Francorum regi Laudunum civitatem suam – inquam suam, nunquam utique tuam – dolo malo subriperes eumque regno fraudares et imperatoriam sororem regnique sui consortem infamares tuisque mendatiis commaculares'; see ibid., p. 56 n. 4, for discussion and also the sceptical comments of Brühl, *Deutschland-Frankreich* (as no. 9), p. 567. The incident evidently did not lead much trace, and was not even brought up against Charles in the debates of 987.

[46] Richer, *Historiae* IV 9, p. 156: ' "Ego fratri subditus, fideliter non minus aliis militavi." '

[47] Aimo of Fleury, *Miracula sancti Benedicti* II (I) 5, ed. E. de Certain (Paris, 1858), p. 104; cf. also III (II) 1, p. 127.

[48] Lot, *Derneirs Carolingiens* (as n. 6), pp. 83-4.

[49] *Gesta Episcoporum Cameracensium* I 101, *MGH SS* 7, pp. 442-3.

Magdeburg solemnly, dined at Otto's table and slept in his bed.[50] As a Carolingian Charles was entitled, if anything, to more than a Saxon frontier *praeses*. Protection and lordship went hand in hand.

Richer, who stood closely behind Archbishop Adalbero of Rheims, has left us in oratorical form the reasons for Charles's exclusion from the succession. There were allegedly four of these, intensively debated since by historians. Charles claimed by heredity and ancestral right, although, so Adalbero now maintained, the kingdom could not be acquired *jure hereditario*;[51] he lacked *idoneitas*, in other words he was untrustworthy and indolent;[52] he served an external king, meaning the emperor;[53] and lastly he was married to a woman not his equal, of vassalic descent ('de militari ordine').[54] These were all debatable points, and Charles himself claimed – again in Richer's rhetoric – to be not only of sound body but to possess also that essential for kingship: *virtus*.[55] There was in fact a fifth reason for Charles's exclusion, much more important than these purported four. This seems to me to have been over-looked by the majority of scholars, although Richer urged it upon his readers no less than the other four and independent evidence exists for it. Richer's method of dramatising *rationes* by shaping them into dialogue and oratory does not make them invalid. After he had Charles plead his case to Adalbero he makes the archbishop reply that Charles had always been surrounded and followed by perjurors, sacrilegious and other evil men 'nor do you want to part

[50] See 'Ritual, Ceremony and Gesture', below pp. 198-200.

[51] Richer, *Historiae* IV 11, pp. 158/62: ' "Non ignoramus K[arolum] fautores suos habere, qui eum dignum regno ex parentum collatione contendant. Sed si de hoc agitur, nec regnum jure hereditario adquiritur, nec in regnum promovendus est, nisi quem non solum corporis nobilitas, sed et animi sapientia illustrat, fides munit, magnanumitas firmat." ' On Richer's analysis of the change of dynasty in 987 and his rhetorical techniques see W. Giese, *'Genus' und 'Virtus': Studien zum Geschichtswerk des Richer von St. Remi* (Augsburg, 1969), pp. 61-80; H.H. Kortüm, *Richer von Saint-Rémi: Studien zu einem Geschichtsschreiber des 10, Jahrhunderts* (Historische Forschungen 8, Stuttgart, 1985), pp. 46-9, 79-112.

[52] Ibid.: ' "Sed quid dignum K[arolo] conferri potest, quem fides non regit, torpor enervat . . . ?" '

[53] Ibid.:' " . . . qui tanta capitis imminutione hebuit ut externo regi servire non horruerit . . . ?" ', a reference to his appointment as duke of lower Lotharingia by Otto II (see above at n. 22); Brühl, *Deutschland-Frankreich* (as n. 9), pp. 590-1, is sceptical that this claim could have been made in view of Hugh's own connections with the Ottonian court.

[54] Ibid.: ' "qui . . . uxorum de militari ordine sibi imparem duxerit? Quomodo ergo magnus dux patietur de suis militibus feminam sumptam reginam fieri sibique dominari? Quomodo capiti suo praeponet, cujus pares et etiam majores genus flectunt, pedibusque manus supponunt?" ' On this charge see J.M. van Winter, 'Uxorem de militari ordine sibi imparem', in *Miscellanea Mediaevalia in memoriam Jan Frederick Niermeyer* (Groningen, 1967), pp. 113-24, and Brühl, *Deutschland-Frankreich* (as n. 9), pp. 591-3, who argues that the *mésalliance* is a figment of Richer's imagination.

[55] Richer, *Historiae* IV 9, p. 156: ' "Omnibus notum est . . . jure hereditario debere fratri et nepoti me succedere. Licet enim a fratre de regno pulsus sim, tamen natura nihil humanitatis mihi derogavit; cum omnibus membris natus sum, sine quibus quivis ad dignitatem quamlibet promoveri non potuit. His etiam non careo quae in regnaturis quibuslibet plurimum queri solent, genere et, ut audeam, virtute." ' On Charles see C. Carozzi, 'Le Dernier des Carolingiens: de l'histoire au mythe', *Le Moyan âge*, 82 (1976), pp. 453-76.

from them.' So how could Charles think of attaining kingship, *principatum*, with such people?[56] Charles's reply to this is one that any good lord in the tenth century would have given. It was not fitting for him to forsake and abandon his men, he would rather strive to acquire the services and loyalties of more and new ones.[57] The archbishop's final reflections upon this are then given, and they contain the key to understanding one of the motives of Hugh's electors. If Charles, who had no *dignitas*, no *honor* in the *regnum Francorum*, associated with evil men whose company he did not want to do without, how disastrous would this be for good men if he were chosen for the kingship![58] The same charge is made against Charles in Bishop Dietrich of Metz's letter denouncing him. He had, so the bishop alleged, seized Laon in 978 with a gang of robbers and a band of thieves. The biblical phrase here only enhances the point.[59]

The sources hostile to him were thus anxious to depict Charles as a man of the margin. What lay behind their denigrations of his followers (whose names, with the exception of Hetdo, we do not know) and this very characteristic juxtaposition of good and evil men? It meant only that if Charles came to kingship he would have to reward and advance his followers and this could only be done at the expense of those at present in possession of *honores* and fiefs. The emergence of a group of *primores* in late Carolingian France was too recent and as yet still far too unstable and subject to the hazards of survival and warfare to have legitimated the new intermediate and regional lordships and so rendered them secure. The second rank of vassals, even Lothar's former followers, could not count on their places, lands and fortunes. It is for this reason that the great, not to mention his own vassals, stood so solidly behind Hugh, though there were exceptions.[60] Charles's elevation would have entailed dispossessions and the downfall of existing tenants. Carolingian governing traditions, moreover, upheld this insecurity. To be able to raise and to disgrace men whom they had advanced (and others) was a deeply rooted principle and an unforgotten part of the Carolingian past, however little freedom of movement a Louis IV and Lothar may have had. Historical memories were, as we said, long. The west Frankish aristocracy never recovered from the trauma of Louis the Pious's palace revolution of 828/29.[61] All the nobility's efforts were henceforth directed towards gaining security of

---

[56] Richer, *Historiae* IV 10, p. 158: ' "Cum" ', inquiens, ' "perjuris et sacrilegis, aliisque nefariis hominibus ipse semper deditus fueris, nec ab eis adhuc discedere velis, quomodo per tales et cum talibus ad principatum venire moliris?" '

[57] Ibid.: 'Ad haec K[arolo] respondente non oportere sese suos deserere, sed potius alios adquirere'. For a similar difficulty, see Leyser, *Rule and Conflict*, p. 29, on Liudolf in 954.

[58] Ibid.: 'episcopus intra se recogitabat: "Cum", inquiens, "omnium dignitatum nunc egens, pravis quibusque annexus est quorum sotietate nullo modo carere vult, in quantam pernitiem bonorum esset si electus procederet in fasces." '

[59] See above, n. 45.

[60] Including Seguin, archbishop of Sens, Albert, count of Vermandois, and of course Charles himself; for details see Lot, *Derniers Carolingiens* (as n. 6), pp. 215-16.

[61] On this see F.L. Ganshof, 'Am Vorabend der ersten Krise der Regierung Ludwigs des Frommen: Die Jahre 828 und 829', *Frühmittelalterliche Studien*, 6 (1972), pp. 39-54.

tenure in its *honores* and fiefs. That was what the treaty of Coulaines in 843 had been about. It was a veritable contract of government, one of the earliest and clearest we have. It became the foundation charter of the new kingdom and the whole reign of Charles the Bald was a commentary on it.[62] The regime of Charles III and the rise of Hagano were more recent reminders of what could happen if a Carolingian king turned the corner of disadvantage and regained effective landed and ruling sources.[63]

For the Ottonians, the secure possession of Lotharingia was culturally, economically, and in every other way essential and here the coming of the Capetians gave them, at least for the time being, relief and ideological control. Otto III's cult of Aachen, of Charlemagne's saving presence vouched for by his remains, was not troubled by sudden raids, and it gained in exclusiveness and uniqueness by the advent of a new *stirps regia* in west Francia and the downfall of the Carolingian there. Their survival as vassals and *fideles* of Otto in lower Lotharingia only underlined the reversal of traditions.[64]

In the struggle that now broke, Charles fought as much for his *patrimonium*, the Carolingian house inheritance, as for the kingship. His having been passed over for the latter posed the problem, always a difficult one, of distinguishing between house and fiscal lands. So limited was the Carolingians substance that the distinction could not really be made: the possession of one necessarily entailed that of the other.[65] Whatever Charles had held before – and we have seen that he must have held something – he was now Louis V's heir. This may explain why he sought first of all to gain control of strongholds and centres of late Carolingian lordship. It is odd that he does not seem to have tried to be crowned and anointed by either or both of the two bishops he succeeded in capturing.[66] He certainly turned to the Ottonian court, in effect to Theophanu, to seek support in his quest for his inheritance. He can be found at the Easter court in Ingelheim in 988, where he met Gerbert and obtained promises from

[62] On Coulaines see 'Nithard and his Rulers', above p. 25 with n. 34.

[63] On Charles III and Hagano see Schneidmüller, *Karolingische Tradition* (as n. 20), pp. 134-8; Kortüm, *Richer* (as n. 51), pp. 50-4.

[64] For Otto's succession as duke in lower Lotharingia in 991 (?) see Sigebert of Gembloux, *Chronicon, MGH SS* 6, p. 353. For Otto III's cultivation of Charlemagne and the links between this and the elimination of the Carolingian dynasty in west Francia see R. Folz, *Le Souvenir et la légende de Charlemagne dans l'Émpire germanique médiéval* (Publications de l'université de Dijon 7, Paris, 1950), 70-93.

[65] W.M. Newman, *Le Domaine royal sous les premiers Capétiens (987-1180)* (Paris, 1937), is so reluctant to take any continuities for granted or make deductions (see his methodological premisses, pp. 87-9) as to be of little help for the question here raised; see also D. Hägermann, 'Die wirtschaftlichen Grundlagen der ersten Kapetinger (987-1108)', in *Pouvoirs et Libertés au temps des premiers Capétiens*, ed. E. Magnou-Nortier (n.p., 1992), pp. 111-23. On the question of the distinction between house lands and royal lands, closely linked with that of the indivisibility of the kingdom, see the discussion in Brühl *Deutschland-Frankreich* (as n. 9), pp. 331-41, and also the comments in Leyser, *Rule and Conflict*, pp. 15-19.

[66] Ascelin of Laon and Arnulf of Rheims: cf. Richer, *Hostoriae* IV 16, 35, pp. 172, 196/98, and the *Historia Francorum Senonensis MGH SS 9*, p. 368: 'Nondum autem ipse Karolus erat unctus in regem, resistente Hugone duce'. See Brühl, *Deutschland-Frankreich* (as no. 9), p. 599.

him too, 'de pace inter reges'.[67] Theophanu and her circle were not willing to see him wholly disinherited, but we do not know what the terms of a settlement were to be. Hugh Capet was anxious to suggest that it was Charles who had rejected her mediation, while he promised to abandon the siege of Laon in return for hostages and above all wished to push for the most faithful alliance and sacred friendship between himself and the empress.[68] He also sought to bring about a meeting between his wife Adelheid and Theophanu, another *colloquium dominarum*.[69] There is no doubt that such a meeting, especially if it had taken place on the banks of the Meuse, the frontier, would have been an invaluable and visible authentication of Hugh's new kingship. Twice at least he sought to bring about such an encounter but the empress did not respond or deign to comply with his request, which denoted equality.[70] It was also fortunate for him that Theophanu died shortly after the betrayal and capture of Charles of Lorraine.[71] The regency and guardianship over Otto III, still barely twelve years old, now fell to the much older and less agile Empress Adelheid. Whether she and the young king met Hugh at Neuville on the Meuse in 992 must remain uncertain.[72] Would not Richer have mentioned it? Instead he treats us to another treason plot by Bishop Adalbero of Laon and Count Odo of Chartres, namely to hand over the kingdom to Otto III. But the minority government would never have embarked on such a hazardous enterprise and it is very unlikely that Adalbero and his partner did not know this. After the events of 991 the bishop was and remained vulnerable to accusations of treachery throughout his long tenure of his see.[73]

To conclude: whatever the problems of Gerbert's letters, they do point to a dense network of communication between the chief actors of 987 and the Ottonian court as it then was. Theophanu cannot have been a stranger to the engendering of the Capetian's accession. Charles's kingship posed problems

---

[67] See the reference in Gerber's letter to him of early June 988, *Epistolae* (as n. 2), no. 115, p. 143.

[68] Ibid. no. 120, pp. 147-8.

[69] Ibid., p. 148, proposed for 22 August 988 at Stenay on the Meuse. On the significance of meetings at the border rather than at, say, Cologne, see Voss, *Herrschertreffen* (as n. 30), pp. 38-87 and Brühl, *Deutschland-Frankreich* (as n. 9), index s.v. *Herrschertreffen*.

[70] Ibid. no. 120 (as previous note) and 138, p. 165, proposing a meeting 'in confinio nostrę Francię Lothariensis regni' in the first half of February (989).

[71] The capture of Charles took place on Palm Sunday (29 March 991): Richer, *Historiae* IV 47, p. 216. Theophanu died on 18 June at Nimwegen: Böhmer-Uhlirz, no. 1035b.

[72] For the meeting cf, Böhmer-Uhlirz, nos. 1058, 1058a, 1059, 1059a, 1059b, 1060, and Uhlirz, *Otto III.*, pp. 154-6, 464-7. It is in the last resort a mere deduction, though a very plausible one, from the place at which D O III 93 was issued on 19 May and the fact that Otto left Aachen after Easter for Saxony and then returned there, to be found in May and June in Lotharingia; see Brühl, *Deutschland-Frankreich* (as n. 9), p. 588 and n. 258.

[73] Richer, *Historiae* IV 96-7, p. 304-8. R.T. Coolidge, 'Adalbero, Bishop of Laon', *Studies in Medieval and Renaissance History*, 2 (1965), pp. 3-114, here p. 55-60, argues not very convincingly that Richer's 'Otto r.' is a reference to Charles's brother, the 'last Carolingian' Otto, duke of lower Lotharingia. On Adalbero of Laon's reputation see Lot, *Derniers Carolingiens* (as n. 6), p. 277 n. 1; Coolidge, 'Adalbero', pp. 43-51, 112-14; Carozzi, 'Le Dernier des Carolingiens' (as n. 55).

and was unwelcome in east Francia as well, but if Hugh had hoped for a visible mark of recognition, an interview at the frontier, he was to be disappointed. Yet this very aloofness and distance also had advantages for him; it suggested his independence, more of it than he actually had. It ushered in those relations of parity and peaceful coexistence which Rodulf Glaber later noted with so much satisfaction.[74] Moreover, the new Capetian regime was closely sustained not only by west Frankish princely solidarities but also by outstanding writers like Abbo of Fleury, Adalbero of Laon and Helgaud. Between them, they furnished Hugh and Robert with a suprapersonal conception of their royalty centred on the *res publica*.[75] Hugh's wife Adelheid was of Carolingian descent, but kinship was now less important than the continuity of a *regnum Francorum* which needed its rulers.[76] Such notions gained further strength precisely because of the wrong committed against Charles of lower Lotharingia, who was and remained stripped of the remaining Carolingian possessions: Laon, Soissons and Attigny. They were treated as fiscs rather than Carolingian houselands; only in this way could the Capetians incorporate them into their kingship. Charles's imprisonment and disinheritance were visible wrongs, which could be concealed only by making the most of kingship's public functions. This more objective view of the institution was something which the Capetians had from the start, something which the Ottonians lacked and might almost envy.[77]

---

[74] See 'Concepts of Europe', above, pp. 17-18 with n. 70; for a similar sense of the equality of the two kingdoms in other late tenth- and early eleventh-century west Frankish writers see Schneidmüller, *Karolingische Tradition* (as n. 20), pp. 72-3.

[75] See on these authors ibid., pp. 69-78, and for the concepts of *patria* and *regnum* B. Schneidmüller, *Nomen Patriae: Die Entstehung Frankreichs in der politisch-geographischen Terminologie (10.-13. Jahrhundert)* (Nationes 7, Sigmaringen, 1987), pp. 53-61. On Abbo see further M. Mostert, *The Political Theology of Abbo of Fleury: A Study of The Ideas about Society and Law of the Tenth-Century Monastic Reform Movement* (Middeleeuwse Studies en Bronnen 2, Hilversum, 1987); on Adalbero see C. Carozzi (ed.) *Adalbéron de Laon: Poême au Roi Robert* (Les Classiques de l'histoire de France au moyen âge 32, Paris, 1979), pp. xcviii-cxix; on Richer see Giese, *Richer* (as n. 51) and Kortüm, *Richer* (as no. 51).

[76] On Adelheids's Carolingian descent see ibid., pp. 73-4, and on claims to the throne through women in France in general H. Schneider, *Die französische Thronfolge (987-1500): Der Ausschluß der Frauen und das salische Gesetz* (Bonn, 1976). It was not mentioned in the debates of the next decades about Carolingian and Capetian legitimacy, on which see, apart from Ehlers, 'Historia Francorum senonensis' (as n. 25), K.-F. Werner, 'Die Legitimität der Kapetinger und die Entstehung des "Reditus regni Francorum ad stirpem Karoli" ', *Welt als Geschichte*, 9 (1952), pp. 203-25, especially pp. 206-13. Election was a more important aspect of Capetian legitimacy: see R.-H. Bautier, 'L'Avènement d'Hugues Capet et le sacre de Robert le Pieux', in *Le Roi de France* (as n. 1), pp. 27-37.

[77] The east Frankish/German contemporaries of the west Frankish/French authors mentioned above, Thietmar and the Lotharingian authors of the *Gesta* and *Vitae episcoporum* either hardly use the terms *res publica* and *patria* at all, or else (as with the Lotharingian authors) use them to refer to a diocese or region. For 'transpersonal' notions of the state in the rather later writings of Wipo see H. Beumann, 'Zur Entwicklung transpersonaler Staatsvorstellungen', in *Das Königtum: Seine geistigen und rechtlichen Grundlagen* (Vorträge und Forschungen 3, Constance, 1956), pp. 185-224.

11

Maternal Kin in Early Medieval Germany

Edmund Burke once wrote: 'A very great part of the mischiefs that vex the world arises from words'. Professor Bullough might have borne this in mind when he chose to make two passages of my article on the German aristocracy from the ninth to the early twelfth century the quarry of his observations on early medieval social groupings.† In doing so he broke, as it were, into the middle of a discussion, an attempt to weigh and qualify the strikingly original analysis of early medieval aristocratic family structures, the work of Karl Schmid. The noble kins of the Carolingian and post-Carolingian world had a fluidity and present to the historian an oddly horizontal rather than vertical aspect, very different from the later dynasties of counts, castellans and, by the twelfth century, even knights, whose emergence in northern France, for example, Georges Duby has so well set out.[1] In the aristocratic clans of the eighth and ninth centuries filiation and agnatic lineages seemingly did not yet form the backbone of family cohesion. Kinsmen gathered round and sought to stand as near as possible to their most successful relatives, bishops and counts, on whichever side, so that the centre of gravity and even the sense of identity of these large families could shift, sometimes within very few generations. Some of the fluidity can be explained by the importance of maternal relatives and descent. They ranked as high as and even higher than paternal kin, if they were thought to be nobler and have better things to offer. The biographers of great men occasionally appear to reflect these attitudes when they recorded only the maternal ancestry of their hero. To give an unused example: the biographer of

* First published in *Past and Present*, 49 (1970), pp. 126-34. World Copyright: The Past and Present Society, Corpus Christi College, Oxford, England. A few additions have been made to the footnotes.

† D.A. Bullough, 'Early Medieval Social Groupings: The Terminology of Kinship', *Past and Present*, 45 (1969), pp. 3-18. For my article see 'The German Aristocracy from the Ninth to the Early Twelfth Century: a Social and Cultural Sketch', *Past and Present*, 41 (1968), pp. 25-53 (Leyser, *Medieval Germany*, pp. 161-89).

[1] G. Duby 'Structures familiales aristocratiques en France du XIe siècle en rapport avec les structures de l'état', in *L'Europe aux IXe-XIe siècles: Aux origines des états nationaux,* ed. T. Manteuffel and A. Gieysztor (Warsaw, 1968), pp. 57ff. and 'Structures de parenté et noblesse, France du Nord Xe-XIIe siècles', in *Miscellanea Mediaevalia in memoriam J.F. Niermeyer* (Groningen, 1967), pp. 149f.

Bishop Bernward of [127] Hildesheim began his work thus: 'The gifted young Bernward sprang from the noble blood of our people, the daughter of Count Palatine Adalbero and he was placed in the care of Osdag, our bishop, by his maternal uncle the deacon Folkmar, later bishop of Utrecht.'[2] Nothing was said about Bernward's father. The two exalted forbears with whom the author wanted his readers to associate Bernward were Otto I's count palatine in Saxony and Bishop Folkmar and they could be reached only through his mother. Karl Schmid, when he explained the frequent pre-eminence of maternal kin, drew attention to what Einhard and Thegan had to say about the ancestry of Hildegard, the short-lived but most important of Charlemagne's wives and the mother of Louis the Pious.[3] Only her mother's blood relations, the Suabian ducal family were mentioned and extolled. Now Professor Bullough objects to the use of the term *cognatio* to denote, in this case Hildegard's maternal kin.[4] It was the way in which Karl Schmid had used it and it seemed to me that it was difficult to be always sure when the word was employed in the wider sense of just 'kinship' or 'a kin' and when it was used in contrast to *agnatio*, a patrilineal descent group.[5]

The question is important for the light it may or may not throw on quite another problem, which seems to have escaped Professor Bullough. In one of his earliest diplomata, only five weeks after his solemn enthronisation at Aachen, Otto I settled the endowment and secular governance of his family's newly founded nunnery at Quedlinburg (13 September 936). He laid down that if someone of his own *generatio* (line) came to be king after him then the abbey and its inmates were to be under his lordship and protection (*defensio*), but if the people were to elect someone else as their king then at least the advocacy over the house was to remain with the most powerful member of the Ottonian *cognatio*.[6] This pronouncement on the [128] succession made in Otto I's name so shortly after his elevation has always been called in evidence for the elective character of the German kingship at its very beginning and if *cognatio* was used here as a blanket substitute for *generatio* then Otto I can indeed be detected to have felt uncertain about his family's chances to become or to continue as the *stirps regia*, the royal stock. On the other hand if *cognatio* was employed here in contrast to *generatio* and meant blood relations through females, mothers and daughters, then it is tempting to think that Otto I perhaps saw the future of his house differently. His diploma for Quedlinburg despite its 'ifs' hinted that

---

[2]   Thangmar, *Vita Bernwardi Episcopi* c. 1, *MGH SS* 4, p. 758. Bernward was entrusted to the care of Bishop Otwin (954-84) rather than Bishop Osdag, his successor. This part of the *vita* was retouched or put together in the twelfth century. See K. Algermissen (ed.), *Bernward und Godehard von Hildesheim* (Hildesheim, 1960), pp. 17f., 20, 21 and n. 6; K. Görich and H. H. Kortüm, 'Otto III., Thangmar und die Vita Bernwardi', *MIÖG*, 98 (1990), pp. 1-58, here pp. 25-7.

[3]   K. Schmid, 'Zur Problematik von Familie, Sippe und Geschlecht, Haus und Dynastie beim mittelalterlichen Adel', *Zeitschrift für die Geschichte des Oberrheins*, 105 (1957), pp. 11, 23f.

[4]   Bullough, 'Social Groupings' (as n. 1), pp. 5ff.

[5]   Schmid, 'Problematik' (as n. 3), pp. 22ff.

[6]   D O I 1, and K. Schmid, 'Die Thronfolge Ottos des Großen', *Zeitschrift der Savigny-Stiftung für Rechtsgeschichte, germanistische Abteilung*, 81 (1964), pp. 126-36.

only when the Ottonian *generatio*, the male line, failed would the people elect someone else, leaving the advocacy as of right to descendants of daughters or of Queen Mathilda's, Henry I's wife's, sisters.

We must return to Hildegard. Professor Bullough seems to me to have been rushing his fences when he asserts sweepingly that any discussion of her maternal kin, my argument on this and much else besides which he does not specify, rested on mistaken terminology.[7] In his paper in *Past and Present* he did not in fact broach the argument at all but in a later review article he claims more boldly that my comments were 'to some extent vitiated by a misunderstanding of the terms *cognatio* and *agnatio* and of the concepts of paternal and maternal kin'.[8] This is of course nonsense for even if I had used the wrong word when speaking of Hildegard's maternal descent it was still her maternal descent I talked about. My suggestion was that Einhard and Thegan did not necessarily wish to laud her Suabian maternal ancestry at the expense of her Frankish father Gerold.[9] What prompted them to do this was perhaps the wish to banish the harassing memory of the savage treatment meted out to Hildegard's maternal kin by Carlmann, Charlemagne's uncle, at Cannstatt in 746. Professor Bullough calls this 'interesting' and then falls back on his own explanation for Einhard's and Thegan's exclusive interest in the queen's descent from the Suabian princes through her mother. To him Hildegard's father was a *homo novus* whose marriage to the Alemannic noblewoman raised him.[10] Be that as it may it cannot [129] be proved, if only because it was after all Hildegard's own, much greater match which really made the Geroldings. The older Gerold however had rights of his own in Suabia unconnected with his wife's. His family belonged to a group of nobles from one of the heartlands of the Carolingian ruling strata, the Mainz, Worms and Lorsch region.[11] There is at least one other, small piece of evidence for the idea that Einhard and Thegan wanted to propitiate the memory of the killings. It comes from an earlier layer of Carolingian family history, the *Annales Mettenses priores* of c.

---

[7] Bullough, 'Social Groupings' (as n. 1), p. 5.

[8] D.A. Bullough, '*Europae Pater*: Charlemagne and his achievement in the light of recent scholarship', *EHR*, 85 (1970), p. 79 n. 2.

[9] Leyser, 'German Aristocracy' (as n. 1), p. 35 (*Medieval Germany*, p. 171). Einhard called Hildegard 'de gente Suaborum praecipuae nobilitatis feminam', a woman of distinguished Suabian nobility: *Vita Karoli* c. 18, p. 22. For Thegan see his *Vita Hludowici imperatoris* c. 2, *MGH SS* 2, pp. 590f., and below at n. 23.

[10] Bullough, '*Europae Pater*' (as n. 8), p. 79 n. 2 and *The Age of Charlemagne* (London, 1965), p. 45. It may well be asked what bearing the terminology of kinship has on this reasoning.

[11] M. Mitterauer, *Karolingische Markgrafen im Südosten* (Archiv für österreichische Geschichte 123, Vienna, 1963), p. 10, and K. F. Werner, 'Bedeutende Adelsfamilien im Reich Karls des Großen', in *Karl der Große: Lebenswerk und Nachleben*, 1: *Persönlichkeit und Geschichte*, ed. H. Beumann (Düsseldorf, 1965), p. 111 (English translation as 'Important Noble Families in the Reign of Charlemagne', in T. Reuter (ed.), *The Medieval Nobility* (Amsterdam, 1978), pp. 165-6) would even relate the Gerolds to the Bavarian ducal family, the Agilolfings, who are now thought to have been of Frankish origin by some scholars (ibid, n. 100).

805. Here the treacherous seizure of the Suabian lords is likened to the miraculous and their execution glossed over and concealed.[12]

But what of *cognatio* and 'cognatic' for maternal kin? If I have sinned I have at least done so in good company for not only Karl Schmid and other German scholars but also Guy Fourquin in his recent synthesis *Seigneurie et féodalité au moyen âge* have interpreted and used the terms in this way.[13] Professor Bullough reasons as follows. After a badly mistaken account of the classical Roman *agnatio* he cites three later Roman legal texts of the second and third centuries, Gaius, Ulpian and Modestinus, and two passages from Isidore of Seville where the words *agnatus, cognatus* and *affinis* are explained.[14] Then he seeks to show, with a liberal scattering of 'semantic shifts', how their meanings varied and changed during the early middle ages. For this scholars will be in his debt, yet before he has proceeded very far on his journey – and we may ask whether this part of it was really necessary – he states categorically that *cognatio* could never mean 'maternal kin' in contrast to *agnatio*, descendants through the male line.[15] Now of the original definitions, Professor Bullough's starting point, the one that really mattered [130] comes from Isidore of Seville's *Etymologiae*, IX vi, which however owed much to Gaius. Isidore's encyclopaedia was the general work of reference for the educated and, what is perhaps as important, for the half-educated throughout the Carolingian and post-Carolingian West. Its normative influence over writers in search of clarity and authority in a world usually threatened by disorder and too much autonomy, cannot be gainsaid. This is what, according to Professor Bullough, Isidore in his *Etymologiae* had to say about *agnati* and *cognati*:

> *agnati* are so called because they are added to the family when sons [al. children] are otherwise (*sic*) lacking...*cognati* are so called because they are linked by the tie of blood relationship.[16]

These quotations are incomplete and Professor Bullough has withheld from his readers an important part of Isidore's (and Gaius's) definitions of *agnati* and *cognati*. 'They', the *agnati*, Isidore said,

> are reckoned to be the first in a family because they arise through persons of the male sex, like a brother born of the same father, or a brother's son or grandson; it is the same with a paternal uncle.

---

[12] *Annales Mettenses priores, s.a.* 746, ed. B. von Simson (MGH SRG 10, Hanover, 1905), p. 37. On the problems of this work and its intent see Wattenbach-Levison-Löwe, vol. 2, pp. 260ff.; O.G. Oexle, 'Die Karolinger und die Stadt des heiligen Arnulf', *Frühmittelalterliche Studien*, 1 (1967), pp. 276ff.; I. Haselbach, *Aufstieg und Herrschaft der Karlinger in der Darstellung der sogenannten Annales Mettenses priores: ein Beitrag zur Geschichte der politischen Ideen im Reiche Karls des Großen* (Historische Studien 412, Lübeck, 1970).

[13] Schmid, 'Problematik' (as n. 3), and 'Thronfolge' (as n. 6), p. 132, and H. Planitz, *Deutsche Rechtsgeschichte*, 2nd edn by K.A. Eckhardt (Graz, 1961), p. 54, independent of Schmid and G. Fourquin, *Seigneurie et féodalité au moyen âge* (Paris, 1970), pp. 54f.

[14] Bullough, 'Social Groupings' (as n. 1), p. 7.

[15] Ibid., p. 9.

[16] Ibid.

Of *cognati* Isidore wrote:

> They are placed behind the *agnati* because they arise [the relationship comes about] through persons of the female sex; they are not agnates but only by natural law blood relations.[17]

Does the female sex exclude mothers? Nor is this all. Sometime between 842 and 846 Hrabanus Maurus, abbot of Fulda (822-842) and archbishop of Mainz (847-56), compiled an encyclopaedia in twenty-two books. As a writer and teacher he did much to propagate the knowledge stored in the *Etymologiae* on new soil for he sent a copy of his work not only to Louis the German but also to a former fellow-student, now bishop of Halberstadt amongst the neophyte east Saxons. Hrabanus wanted his presents to be of use, as he [131] himself wrote in the letters which accompanied them. A chapter on the appellations of kinship duly found its place in his *de rerum naturis* and here Isidore's definitions were simply repeated.[18] The question is how they applied or what they meant to peoples with partly bilateral modes of descent such as the German stems east of the Rhine were.

Now it is true of course that under Isidore's explanations *cognatio* also embraced kinship through the female sex on the father's side, like the descendants of a paternal aunt or of a sister and if Professor Bullough had confined himself to pointing this out his fault-finding would have been less captious than it is.[19] Yet it is also clear that in a society much given to the cult of noble wives' ancestry, and in which fortunes could be owed to mothers as much as to fathers, *cognatio* was heavily weighted on the maternal side. There it included not only descendants but also forbears and therefore more senior blood relations, especially such important personages as a mother's brothers and indeed her whole kin, whereas on the paternal side the most important rôles and key positions necessarily belonged to members of the *agnatio*.

---

[17] Isidore of Seville, *Etymologiarum sive originum libri XX*, IX.vi.1 and 2, ed. W.M. Lindsay (Oxford, 1911), no pagination: 'Qui [the *agnati*] ideo prius in gente agnoscuntur quia veniunt per virilis sexus personas, veluti frater eodem patre natus, vel fratris filius nepoosve ex eo; item patruus', and of *cognati*: 'Qui inde post agnatos habentur, quia per feminini sexus personas veniunt, nec sunt agnati, sed alias naturali iure cognati'. For Isidore's influence on medieval descriptions of age see A. Hofmeister, *'Puer, iuvenis, senex*. Zum Verständnis der mittelalterlichen Altersbezeichnungen', in *Papsttum und Kaisertum: Forschungen zur politischen Geschichte und Geisteskultur des Mittelalters Paul Kehr zum 65. Geburstag dargebracht*, ed. A. Brackmann (Munich, 1926), pp. 287ff. For the relevant passages in Gaius's *Institutes* see F. de Zulueta. *The Institutes of Gaius* 1. 156 (Oxford, 1946), vol. 1, p. 50, especially: 'at hi qui per feminini sexus personas cognatione coniunguntur, non sunt agnati, sed alias naturali iure cognati', i.e. 'those connected through persons of the female sex are not agnates, but cognates related only by natural law' (ibid., p. 51), followed by examples.

[18] Hrabanus Maurus, *De Universo* VII 4, Migne *PL* 111, col. 189. For the letters to Louis the German and Bishop Heimo of Halberstadt see *MGH Epp.* 5, pp. 470f. no. 36 and 472f. no. 37. On Hrabanus see M. Manitius, *Geschichte der lateinischen Literatur des Mittelalters* (Munich, 1911), vol. 1, pp. 288ff. and P. Lehmann, 'Zu Hrabans geistiger Bedeutung', *St Bonifatius: Gedenkgabe zum zwölfhundertjährigen Todestag* (Fulda, 1954), pp. 473ff.

[19] Conversely, of course, for these descendants their mother's kin was again *cognatio*.

Already Marc Bloch had drawn attention to the close bonds between nephews and maternal uncles in *chansons de geste* and in medieval German epics.[20] Thietmar of Merseburg cannot regale his readers enough with the doings of his mother's kin, the counts of Stade. A good example comes also from Sigebert of Gembloux's *Life* of Bishop Dietrich of Metz. Sigebert praised his subject's nobility no less than his devoutness, both imparted to him by his exalted *cognati* and *affines*, the foremost men of Lotharingia and Germany east of the Rhine. Sigebert was not slow in telling his readers who these *cognati* and their affinity were. Dietrich's mother Amalrada was the sister of Queen Mathilda, the wife of Henry I. One of the *primates* was Archbishop Brun of Cologne, [132] Mathilda's and Henry's son so that Sigebert could rightly speak of Dietrich's 'imperial consanguinity'. The other, not mentioned by name, was Archbishop Robert of Trier, the queen's brother. Her uncles, including Reginbern, a renowned victor against the Danes, were not forgotten though Sigebert mistook them for brothers.[22] In Thegan's famous and not quite accurate genealogy of Hildegard: 'Duke Gottfried begat Huoching, Huoching begat Nebi, Nebi begat Imma', it is the last link in the chain, her mother Imma, that must be heeded here.[23] The Suabian princes, including those who became the victims of Carloman's wrath, were her maternal kin, they were *cognatio*. Isidore's and Hrabanus's 'quia per feminini sexus personas veniunt', that is the cognatic relationship arises through persons of the female sex, cannot be ignored.

There is no need to inspect every soldier at Professor Bullough's parade of learning. He goes astray when he defines the classical Roman *agnatio* exclusively by the legal powers of the *paterfamilias*, the head of the family, as if all agnation ceased between brothers when their *paterfamilias* died.[24] On p. 16 he discusses a use of *cognatio* in a ninth-century St Gallen charter where it evidently stood for *agnatio*, people of agnatic descent, though when I say so in the case of Hildegundis, abbess of Geseke, I am, according to him, 'confusing the issue'. Hildegundis moreover was not, as Professor Bullough calls her, a 'Rhineland abbess'.[25] Geseke, her house, lay in Westfalia which in the tenth century was very much part of Saxony. Her ancestors Wicburga had made her gifts 'secundum legem Saxonicam', according to Saxon law, and the *Lex Saxonum* of 802/3 had much to say about Westfalian custom in the matter of dower and property acquired by a man and his wife together during their

---

[20] M. Bloch, *Feudal Society*, trans. C. Postan (London, 1961), p. 137 and n. 1.

[21] *Vita Annonis archiepiscopi Coloniensis* c. 1, *MGH SS* 11, pp. 467f.

[22] Sigebert of Gembloux, *Vita Deoderici prioris Mettensis episcopi* c. 1, *MGH SS* 4, p. 464. Dietrich died in 984 and his *Life* was written about eighty years later. Sigebert took the passage about Reginbert from Widukind I 31, p. 44. Dietrich attached himself to Archbishop Brun, his cousin on the mother's side, who brought about his advancement.

[23] Thegan (as n. 9) c. 2, pp. 590-1: 'Gotefridus dux genuit Huochingum, Huochingus genuit Nebi; Nebe genuit Immam; Imma vero genuit Hiltigardam'.

[24] Bullough, 'Social Groupings' (as n. 1), p. 6 and see W.W. Buckland, *A Textbook of Roman Law*, 3rd edn (Cambridge, 1963), p. 105.

[25] Bullough, 'Social Groupings' (as n. 1), p. 5.

marriage, and does not Professor Bullough himself remind us[26] that the circle of kinsmen varied not only from people to people but locally.[27] His article ends on a note of tart admonition: 'in those few [133] aspects of medieval history where precision is possible we should be precise'.[28] How precise are Professor Bullough's semantic shifts? How precise indeed can they be? When kinship itself was so fluid and often expressed in a welter of blending or ambiguous terms there is a contradiction even here.

As against this vagueness and its vernacular background, what Isidore had to say about *agnatio* and *cognatio* and other relationships was definite and clear. There remains the question whether and how the learning and teaching of the church helped to move early medieval aristocratic society towards a more patrilineal complexion and attitude. It is not one that can be answered here but it would be rash to assume that it was only the interest of hereditary office-holders, counts, castellans and advocates west and east of the Rhine which led to a more marked stress on lineage. The Isidorian tables of kinship informed bishops and influential abbots, anxious to prevent uncanonical marriages, but these again became harder to avoid when in the course of the tenth and the first half of the eleventh century a relatively small number of royal and princely families, already connected by marriage ties in the past, emerged and ruled in most of western and central Europe. When the Salian king, Henry III, wanted to marry Agnes of Poitou in 1043, Abbot Siegfried of Gorze wrote a letter to his like-minded colleague, Poppo of Stavelot, expounding the sinfulness and dangers of this match. It was accompanied by a family tree and contained a detailed account of the bride and bridegroom's descent and consanguinity. Since meeting Poppo earlier in the year the abbot of Gorze had made further inquiries into this *cognatio* and, it may be said in passing, the context here points to a set of relationships wholly on the distaff side.[29]

It remains true however that the development of a more restricted, 'dynastic' kind of family in the Reich was not as whole-hearted as in the west and it is even possible that for all its size, wealth and organised strength the later Ottonian and Salian church did little to advance the process. Its institutions with their expanding resources and superior management provided shelter and support mainly for the kindreds of the nobility in all their local diversity and nuances of standing and power. The many new proprietary sanctuaries were as a rule meant to serve the lay and religious members of the founders' kin. The cathedrals with their large clerical communities, the rising number of collegiate churches near and about them and the [134] reviving older monasteries could and did accommodate whole families of nobles as prelates, *fratres* (brethren) or vassals. At Aschaffenburg (diocese of Mainz), founded sometime

---

[26] Ibid., p. 15.

[27] D O I 158 (26 October 952) and *Lex Saxonum* c. 47 and 48, *Leges Saxonum et Lex Thuringorum*, ed. C. von Schwerin (MGH Fontes iuris Germanici antiqui . . . separatim editi, Hanover, 1918), pp. 29f.

[28] Bullough, 'Social Groupings' (as n. 1), p. 18.

[29] For the text of the letter see W. von Giesebrecht, *Geschichte der deutschen Kaiserzeit*, 2: *Blüthe des Kaiserthums*, 5th edn (Leipzig, 1885), pp. 714-18.

before 974, it was laid down after an ugly feud that no more than three members of a *cognatio* (here 'a kindred'), within the sixth degree of proximity, should be admitted and that sons should not become canons together with their fathers.[30] A very large kin, promoted in or through the church, benefited from the career of Archbishop Anno of Cologne, a reformer and nepotist on a truly regal scale.[31] Anno, like Wolfgang of Regensburg, came from comparatively modest Suabian stock. Some aristocratic families can be recognised by their clerical and monastic dignitaries far more easily than by any of their members in lay estate. The two brothers, Bishops Franco and Burchard of Worms, Archbishop Heribert of Cologne and his brother Bishop Henry of Würzburg, the Immedings at Hamburg and Paderborn and Gero, later archbishop of Magdeburg (1012-23) who followed his maternal uncle into the imperial chapel, may serve as examples.[32] The church in Germany could help to palliate the effects of partible inheritance customs; it could not end them.

---

[30] For Archbishop Willigis's settlement of the feud and ordinance for Aschaffenburg see *Mainzer Urkundenbuch*, 1, ed. M. Stimming (Darmstadt, 1932), pp. 134ff. no. 219, and K.H. Rexroth, 'Der Stiftsscholaster Herward von Aschaffenburg und das Schulrecht von 976', in *1000 Jahre Stift und Stadt Aschaffenburg* (Aschaffenburger Jahrbuch 4, Aschaffenburg, 1957), pp. 205ff. M. Thiel, *Urkundenbuch des stifts St. Peter und Alexander zu Aschaffenburg* 1: *861-1325* (Veröffentlichungen des Geschichts- und Kunstvereins Aschaffenburg e.V.26, Aschaffenburg, 1986), no. 8, pp. 27-39, has argued that the text was in large measure falsified in the twelfth century, but the initial section with the account of the case and the judgement he thinks is based on a genuine tenth-century document.

[31] For a compendious survey of Anno's relations and their careers see F.W. Oediger, *Die Regesten der Erzbischöfe von Köln im Mittelalter* (Publikationen der Gesellschaft für rheinische Geschichtskunde 21, Bonn, 1954-61), vol. 1, no. 839, and also now D. Lück, 'Erzbischof Anno II. von Köln: Standesverhältnisse, verwandtschaftliche Beziehungen und Werdegang bis zur Bischofsweihe', *Annalen des historischen Vereins für den Niederrhein*, 172 (1970), pp. 7-112.

[32] J. Fleckenstein, *Die Hofkapelle der deutschen Könige*, 2: *Die Hofkapelle im Rahmen der ottonisch-salischen Reichskirche* (Schriften der MGH 16, Stuttgart, 1966) pp. 87ff., 113f., 181. The Immedings cannot easily be separated from the so-called *stirps Widukindi*, the posterity of the eighth-century Saxon duke, Widukind. For a list of its clerical dignitaries see K. Schmid, 'Die Nachfahren Widukinds', *DA* 20 (1964), p. 36f. The eleventh-century Immedings are not included, but see p. 38 n. 130, where perhaps Bishop Immad of Paderborn (1051-76) could be added. The most prominent lay figure of this family group in the tenth century was a woman, Queen Mathilda. For other important clerks in Archbishop Heribert's kin see Oediger, *Regesten* (as n. 31), vol. 1, no. 562. Recently, however, G. Althoff, 'Genealogische und andere Fiktionen in mittelalterlicher Historiographie', in *Fälschungen im Mittelalter*, 1: *Kongreßdaten und Festvorträge, Literatur und Fälschungen* (Schriften der MGH 33/1, Hanover, 1988), pp. 417-42, has warned against too readily attributing a self-awareness to such kindreds; see especially pp. 430-4 on the 'Immedings'.

12

Ritual, Ceremony and Gesture: Ottonian Germany

Social anthropologists have done much to illuminate the meanings and functions of ritual, ceremony and habitus in societies with no or only a restricted literacy, not least of all in societies where only a small élite, a priesthood, mastered and at the same time monopolised the written word. In such societies ritual has been see as the key to understanding their make-up, a key that unlocks either all the doors that can be unlocked or at any rate almost as many as can be opened up by literary communications. Analysis of ritual has yielded definitions of its innate character: 'a category of standardised behaviour in which the relationship between means and ends is not intrinsic';[1] 'the rites and rules of conduct in the presence of sacred objects';[2] 'individual life-crisis ceremonials, i.e. rites of passage' and 'means of social communications to re-affirm status differences'.[3] It can be a language in a literal sense to convey 'a conceptual apparatus for intellectual operations at an abstract and metaphysical level'.[4] Often rituals enshrine the most strongly felt values of a society. Classical analysis, moreover, has sometimes sought to pin down ritual as belonging to the category of non-rational acts. For example Durkheim, Radcliffe-Brown and Marcel Mauss assumed that every social action belonged

---

* Unpublished lecture given on a number of occasions in English and German, notably at Münster in 1990. A German version is to appear in *Frühmittelalterliche Studien* 27 (1993). The text is a conflation of the surviving English and German versions with some consequent minor rearrangements; the notes are editorial, but take into account a handful of marginalia in the author's manuscripts.

[1] J. Goody, 'Religion and Ritual: the Definitional Problem', *British Journal of Sociology*, 12 (1961), pp. 142-64, here p. 159, cited by E.R. Leach, 'Ritual', in *International Encyclopedia of the Social Sciences*, ed. D.L. Sills, vol. 13 (New York, 1968), pp. 520-6, here p. 521.

[2] E. Durkheim, *The Elementary Forms of the Religious Life*, trans. J.W. Swain (London, 1915), pp. 51-2; cf. Leach, 'Ritual' (as n. 1), p. 521.

[3] A. van Gennep, *The Rites of Passage*, trans. M.B. Vizedom and G.L. Caffee (London, 1960); cf. Leach, 'Ritual' (as n. 1), p. 521.

[4] Leach, 'Ritual' (as n. 1), 524, paraphrasing C. Lévi-Strauss, *The Savage Mind* (London, 1962).

to one of two kinds: 'mystical, non-utilitarian and sacred, or rational, common-sense, utilitarian and profane'.[5] Yet for the historian of the earlier middle ages this very post-Cartesian distinction raises the haunting question whether, and if so how the participants in a ritual of the past themselves distinguished between rational and irrational acts.[6] In other words, can we understand what they meant except by explaining it from within their own assumptions?

Joined to this must be another question: whether and in what way ritual should be distinguished from ceremony? Here the responses of the social anthropologists have differed a great deal. Some employ these terms indiscriminately, others distinguish rigorously between them.[7] In the latter case it has generally been held that ritual usually transformed, effected a change, and so contained an element of magic, while ceremony reflected and displayed a given state of affairs, social situation or body of ideas: ceremony is conservative. It might thus be said that whereas all rituals are also ceremonies, not all ceremonies are rituals. Here the medievalist may agree. Taking arms at a given age, for example, denoted entry into man's and a warrior's estate and was thus a ritual.[8] Coronation was a ritual because it was deemed to make a new man out of the king but a crown-wearing was only a ceremony which solemnly presented this charismatic *persona* to his followers and *fideles*.[9] But the generalisation has its dangers. When Richard I returned to England in 1194 and wore his crown at Winchester on 17 April, it was to 'wash away the shame

[5] Leach, 'Ritual' (as n. 1), p. 522; Durkheim, *Elementary Forms* (as n. 2); A.R. Radcliffe-Brown, *Structure and Function in Primitive Society* (London, 1952), especially pp. 130, 136-9, 143; M. Mauss, *The Gift* (London, 1960). Goody, 'Religion and Ritual' (as n. 1), offers a good analysis of the distinction, which is ultimately derived from Durkheim's distinction between the sacred and the profane.

[6] See on this the contributions in B. Wilson (ed.), *Rationality* (Oxford, 1970); G. Koziol, *Begging Pardon and Favor: Ritual and Political Order in Early Medieval France* (Ithaca, 1992), ch. 9 'How Does a Ritual Mean?', pp. 289-324.

[7] Leach, 'Ritual' (as n.1), p. 521-2; on the distinction see e.g. J.H.M. Beattie, 'On Understanding Ritual', in Wilson, *Rationality* (as n. 6) pp. 240-68; Koziol, *Begging Pardon and Favor* (as n. 6), p. 316: 'Where there is neither ambiguity nor contradiction, no spiritual or social conflict either within the event or on its edges, there is no longer ritual. There is only ceremony'.

[8] K.J. Leyser, 'Early Medieval Canon Law and the Beginnings of Knighthood', above, pp. 51ff.; J. Flori, 'Les Origines de l'adoubement chevaleresque', *Traditio*, 35 (1979), pp. 209-72, here pp. 214-15, 249-50. Idem *L'Idéologie du glaive: Préhistoire de la chevalerie* (Geneva 1983) is here less helpful; the thesis maintained in idem, *L'Essor de la chevalerie, XIe-XIIe siècles* (Geneva, 1986), pp. 43-9, that the *cingulum militiae* before the eleventh century was used only to confer a public, generally royal office, is very questionable. See now further J.L. Nelson, 'Ninth-century knighthood: the evidence of Nithard', *Studies in Medieval History Presented to R. Allen Brown*, ed. C. Harper-Bill, C. Holdsworth and J.L. Nelson (Woodbridge, 1989), pp. 255-66, especially pp. 263-4.

[9] On royal unction as a rebirth see among others especially W. Ullmann, *The Carolingian Renaissance and the Idea of Kingship* (London, 1970) p. 71-110. On 'festive coronations' see C. Brühl, 'Fränkischer Krönungsbrauch und das Problem der Festkrönungen', in idem, *Aus Mittelalter und Diplomatik: Gesammelte Aufsätze*, 1 (Hildesheim, 1989), pp. 351-412; idem, 'Kronen- und Krönungsbrauch im frühen und hohen Mittelalter', in ibid., pp. 419-43 (first published 1982); K.-U. Jäschke, 'Frühmittelalterliche Festkrönungen. Überlegungen zur Terminologie und Methode', *HZ*, 211 (1970), pp. 556-88.

of his captivity'.[10] The ceremony thus here acquired a much enhanced, indeed a ritualistic function: men expected from a ritual some kind of improvement, some change for the better. However, too severe and narrow a distinction will not be drawn in what follows.

The question I want to look into here and now is whether these modes of anthropological analysis, or perhaps some of them rather than others, can be used to interpret and help us understand ritual and ceremony in the tenth and early eleventh century. The choice of that period is not an accident or the outcome of mere personal predilection. It springs from the discovery in historical literature of a number of occasions, moments of crisis in war, diplomacy, rebellion and submission, where ritual and ceremony focused intentions, aspirations, hopes and fears, in fact were constitutive elements in shaping events, 'expressive or instrumental acts', to use a phrase of E.R. Leach.[11]

It is time to present an example. There is one ritual we still share with the men of the tenth century – we do not know about the women –, and that is giving one's hand.[12] Now the term 'manus dare', to give one's hands, could of course denote the most solemn moment in the ritual of homage where a man placed his folded hands into those of his lord.[13] There are in Widukind some particularly vivid descriptions of the act of homage, but they must be distinguished from acts of hand-giving which stood for an end of hostility, an act of friendship, a pledge of faith or a sign of surrender.[14] Giving one's hand in the aristocratic world of the early middle ages was governed by strict rules and we learn of them above all from Widukind of Corvey, for example in his story of the Saxon stem saga. Thus it was ruled out between masters and servants, even if the latter were of free birth, and a noble should give his hands only to an equal.[15] Now one of Widukind of Corvey's most heroic themes is the story of Count Wichmann, a close kinsman of the Liudolfings through his mother and the nephew of Duke Hermann Billung on his father's side. Count Wichmann waged a life-long feud against Otto I and his uncle whose advancement to the leadership of the east Saxon host and permanent command against the north-

---

[10] K. Norgate, *Richard the Lion Heart* (London, 1924), p. 291, with quotations from Gervase of Canterbury and William of Newburgh (the author cited in the text above).

[11] E.R. Leach, *Political Systems of Highland Burma: a Study of Kachin Social Structures* (London, 1954), *passim*.

[12] A. Erler, 'Handschlag', in *Handwörterbuch zur deutschen Rechtsgeschichte*, ed. A. Erler and E. Kaufmann, vol. 1 (Berlin, 1973), col. 1974.

[13] J. Le Goff, 'Le Rituel symbolique de la vassalité', in idem, *Pour un autre moyen âge* (Paris, 1977), pp. 349-420; W. Kienast, *Die fränkische Vassalität von den Hausmeiern bis zu Ludwig dem Kind und Karl dem Einfältigen*, ed. P. Herde (Frankfurter wissenschaftliche Beiträge, Kulturhistorische Reihe 18, Frankfurt, 1990), pp. 73-123, with rich bibliography on the legal history aspects of the ritual.

[14] Widukind, *Res gestae Saxonicae* III 5, 11 and 76, pp. 64 lines 1-6, 107 lines 18-19, 110 lines 14-18, 153 lines 15-20.

[15] Ibid. I 9, p. 11 lines 19-21: 'Thiadricum vero suum servum tamquam ex concubina natum et ideo indecens fore proprio servo umquam manus dare' (see also ibid., p. 12, lines 11-16); III 46, p. 127 lines 17-18: 'Pudeat iam nunc dominos pene totius Europae inimicis manus dare'.

eastern Slavs riled and gnawed at him because he and his father, the elder Count Wichmann, saw themselves as the senior branch of the Billung family.[16] Although the elder Wichmann had in the end been reconciled to Otto I, his son inherited the original anger and resentment against Hermann Billung's promotion over them. The younger Wichmann had often made peace with Otto and been promised some advancement to foremost command but this was postponed time and again for various reasons, so that he finally rebelled once more.[17] It is characteristic that while Wichmann was the sworn enemy of his uncle Hermann, he had the goodwill and at least partial help of the other great force on the Saxon eastern frontier, Margrave Gero.[18] Gero died in 965, however, and Wichmann, who commanded a sizable military following, was by now once again among the Slavs east of the Elbe waging war against Hermann Billung and other supporters and allies of Otto I, not least of all Miesco I of Poland. Miesco in turn enlisted the help of Boleslas I of Bohemia, and Wichmann's forces were caught between them and he himself forced to a standstill by his own men, who were on foot while he was mounted.[19] After a day's fight and a night's march the exhausted Wichmann was trapped by the Slavs in a farmstead. They asked him to lay down his arms and promised to hand him over safely to their lord.[20] It is Widukind's next phrase that sets forth the act of hand-giving most strikingly as a gesture between equals: 'Although Wichmann', wrote Widukind, 'was in the direst straits, he did not forget his ancient nobility and his *virtus* by giving his hands to such people.'[21] He asked that they inform Miesco of the situation; before him he would lay down his arms and to him he would give his hands. The Slavs promised to do this, but when some went off to find Miesco, a huge crowd surrounded Wichmann and the fighting continued. He killed quite a few, but exhausted he succumbed and handed over his sword with the order to take it to Miesco to send to Otto I. Finally he sank down, turned eastward to pray as best as he could and died.[22] His passing too is ritualised, but what matters most is his refusal to shake hands with the Slav warriors who had surrounded him. It meant that they were not bound, that there was no agreement and therefore that their continuing to fight was no breach of one.

We must now ask why ceremony and ritual appear to be more prominent in the historiography of the Ottonian tenth century than they were in the annals, histories and *Vitae* of the ninth. We hardly meet them in the great Carolingian

---

[16] Leyser, *Rule and Conflict*, pp. 21-2, 28; Widukind, *Res gestae Saxonicae* II 11, III 19, 23-5, 29, 50, 51-2, 55, 60, pp. 75-6, 114, 115-16, 117, 129-30, 135, 136.

[17] Widukind, *Res gestae Saxonicae* III 64, p. 139.

[18] Ibid. III 60, p. 136, III 66 p. 145.

[19] Ibid. III 68-9, pp. 143-4.

[20] Ibid. III 69, p. 145 lines 4-10.

[21] Ibid. III 69, p. 145 lines 10-12: 'Ille, licet in ultima necessitate sit constitutus, non immemor pristinae nobilitatis ac virtutis, dedignatus est talibus manum dare'.

[22] Ibid. III 69, p. 145 lines 12-23.

histories, the *Royal Frankish Annals*, the *Annals of St Bertin*, the *Annals of Fulda* and Region of Prüm's *Chronicle*.[23] They are, however, a striking feature in Widukind of Corvey's *Res gestae Saxonicae*, and notable also in Thietmar of Merseburg's *Chronicon*. The reason for this seems to me to lie in the critical cultural situation of late Carolingian and early Ottonian central and western Europe. The scholars, savants and at the same time men of affairs of the last decade of the ninth and the first of the tenth century, themselves sensed a crisis and felt that their world was tumbling to pieces about them. We have verses written by Bishop Salomon of Constance, one of a race of aristocratic prelates, addressed to Bishop Dado of Verdun during the reign of Louis the Child (900-11). Here he lamented the coming of the Magyars, the devastations, the peaceless, strife-torn and helpless situation of the Reich under the boy king. He ended with the conventional biblical sigh: 'Woe to the kingdom whose ruler is a child'.[24] These verses and letters addressed to Bishop Dado by others, such as Remigius of Auxerre,[25] were almost reminiscent of the correspondence of Gallo-Roman senatorial aristocrats surrounded by barbarians in the fifth century.[26] Their civilised and refined lives were threatened.

This sense of danger and crisis also overtook late-Carolingian historiography in an east Francia and Lotharingia now facing the Hungarian razzias. The *Annals of Fulda* fell silent in 901, Regino of Prüm in 906. He died in 915 at Trier, where the archbishop looked after him once he had had to give up the abbacy of Prüm to a member of a more powerful aristocratic clan in the region.[27] About fifty years lie between the end of these great historical works and the new beginnings of Ottonian historiography with Liudprand of Cremona's *Antapodosis*, which was put in hand in 958.[28] About sixty years sever Regino of Prüm from his continuator, Adalbert, the *capellanus*, notary, monk,

---

[23] For a modification of the view expressed in the text see J.L. Nelson, 'The Lord's Anointed and the People's Choice: Carolingian Royal Ritual', in *Rituals of Royalty. Power and Ceremonial in Traditional Societies*, ed. D. Cannadine and S. Price (Cambridge, 1987), pp. 137-180, especially pp. 166-72 on the secular rituals of the hunt and the banquet.

[24] 'Versus Waldrammi ad Dadonem episcopum a Salomone episcopo missi', *MGH Poetae* 4/1, pp. 297-314, especially book I, verses 51-221, pp. 299-303.

[25] Migne, *PL* 131, cols. 963-70; new edition by R.B.C. Huygens, 'Un Témoin de la crainte de l'an 1000: la lettre sur les Hongrois', *Latomus*, 15 (1956), pp. 225-39, here pp. 229-35. Huygens questions the attribution of the letter to Remigius, pp. 236-7, but his arguments are not compelling.

[26] On the use of Venantius Fortunatus' poems in the *Gesta Episcoporum Virdunensium* written under Dado see M. Manitius, 'Zu Fortunatus, den Annales Quedlinburgenses und Sigeberts Vita Deoderici', *Neues Archiv*, 12 (1887), pp. 591-2.

[27] On the end of the *Annales Fuldenses* see Wattenbach-Levison-Löwe, vol. 6, p. 694 and n. 96 (against the older thesis of a now no longer extant version going as far as 910). For Regino see ibid., pp. 899, 901-4.

[28] Liudprand, *Opera*, p. ix on the date of composition.

missionary bishop, abbot and finally archbishop of Magdeburg.[29] More than sixty years also separate Widukind of Corvey from the *Annals of Fulda*, and at least sixty lie between him and Regino.[30] This chasm, this break is of enormous importance and explains much about the urgency and also the freshness of the Ottonian writers, their distance from Carolingian traditions, not to say their idiosyncracy. It also explains why ritual and ceremony figure much more prominently in them than they had done in ninth-century annals, over and above descriptions they both had in common, like coronation rites and crown-wearings.[31]

Early medieval societies lived in a state of fragile balance between oral transmission and literacy, between expressing ideas and abstractions by acting them out in public and so grasping them visually and their literary incapsulation. The balance tilted decidedly towards literacy in the first half of the ninth century thanks to Charlemagne's determined, not to say wilful, programme of education when even a schooled lay aristocracy became a remote possibility and great men had libraries which they bequeathed to their sons and daughters.[32] Yet with the calamities, internal and external, that overtook Frankish *Christianitas* in the second half of the ninth century, the trend was the other way again and we are moving back towards a more oral society, where communications by ritual gesture and ceremony grew in importance and took on an enhanced functionality. The great surge of intellectual, literary and artistic activity we call the Carolingian renaissance had spent itself by the late ninth century. Beryl Smalley in her *Study of the Bible in the Middle Ages* noted a marked falling off in interpretative biblical scholarship, for instance.[33] What took its place in the tenth century? The reformed monks, at Cluny especially, were above all concerned with liturgy, the enhanced performance of the *opus divinum*; and this meant ceremonial. Their processions, their regimented cult

---

[29] Adalbert, *Continuatio* pp. 154-79; on the date of composition around 966 see K. Hauck, 'Erzbischof Adalbert von Magdeburg als Geschichtsschreiber', in *Festschrift für Walter Schlesinger*, ed. H. Beumann (Köln, 1974), vol. 2, pp. 276-344, here pp. 293-4, 328-9; G. Althoff, *Das Necrolog von Borghost: Edition und Untersuchung* (Veröffentlichungen der Historischen Kommission für Westfalen 40, Westfälische Gedenkbücher und Nekrologien 1, Münster, 1978), pp. 268-83, especially pp. 271-2; E. Karpf, *Herrscherlegitimation und Reichsbegriff in der ottonischen Geschichtsschreibung des 10. Jahrhunderts* (Historishce Forschungen 10, Stuttgart, 1985), pp. 47-62. M. Frase, *Friede und Königsherrschaft: Quellenkritik und Interpretation der Continuatio Reginonis* (Frankfurt, 1990), pp. 14-16, offers nothing new.

[30] On the dating of the various recensions between 967 and 973 see H. Beumann, *Widukind von Korvei: Untersuchungen zur Geschichtsschreibung und Ideengeschichte des 10. Jahrhunderts* (Abhandlungen zur Corveyer Geschichtsschreibung 3, Weimar, 1950), pp. 178-204; addenda and corrigenda: idem, 'Historiographische Konzeption und politische Ziele Widukinds von Corvey', in idem, *Wissenschaft vom Mittelalter* (Köln, 1972), pp. 72-5 (first published 1970); idem, 'Imperator Romanorum, rex gentium. Zu Widukind III 76', in idem, *Ausgewählte Aufsätze aus den Jahren 1966-1986* (Sigmaringen, 1987), pp. 324-40, here p. 329 n. 36; for a summary see Karpf, *Herrscherlegitimation* (as n. 29), p. 144.

[31] Nelson, 'Lord's Anointed' (as n. 23).

[32] R. McKitterick, *The Carolingians and the Written Word* (Cambridge, 1989), pp. 211-70.

[33] B. Smalley, *The Study of the Bible in the Middle Ages*, 3rd edn (Oxford, 1970), p. 44.

of uniformity of gesture and minute bearing became models. They also carried all before them in attracting lay patronage and the wish to be, by means of benefactions and endowments, partakers in and associates of their holiness.[34] This focus on ritual to convey ideas and sentiments and to solemnise crucial events applied *a fortiori* to the nascent and only recently Christianised society of the frontier that was early medieval Saxony.[35] There was no lack of books, far from it. We possess thousands of manuscripts from the ninth century, and so busy had the *scriptoria* been in copying then that the demand for most standard texts – scriptures, *patristica* and commentaries – was more than covered for a long time. In the bleak decades of the first half of the tenth century the *armaria* and *scrinia* of monasteries and cathedrals were full of books, but the schooled élite to read them, the *Nachwuchs* to take them over and use them was in short supply.[36]

It is difficult for us to imagine what happens when oral transmission takes over functions which had at one time been the domain of literacy. As an obvious example, there were the ever more sophisticated Carolingian capitularies in which very complex measures of government and instructions could be communicated to localities and agents like counts who had at least schooled clerks at their side. In the tenth century we have none of this, either in east Francia, where capitularies had already dried up rather early in the ninth century, or – and this is more significant – in west Francia, where they had flourished magnificently up to the time of Charles the Bald's death in 877.[37] There was continuity only in the councils and synods of the church.[38] For the third generation of the Ottonian house, who were by now themselves literate, and for their followers, the growth and possession of a new historical literature was therefore a great step forward, a new anchorage, a better way of giving

[34] B. Rosenwein, 'Feudal War and Monastic Peace: Cluniac Liturgy as Ritual Aggression', *Viator*, 2 (1971) pp. 129-157; eadem, *Rhinoceros Bound. Cluny in the Tenth Century* (Philadelphia, 19820; for good accounts of the ritualism inherent in reform monasticism and its magnetic attraction for the lay world see H. Fichtenau, *Lebensordnungen im 10. Jahrhundert*, 2 vols. paginated as one (Monographien zur Geschichte des Mittelalters 30, Stuttgart, 1984), pp. 334-46 (English translation by P. Geary as *Living in the Tenth Century* (Chicago, 1991), pp. 251-61) and G. Tellenbach, *The Church in Western Europe from the Tenth to the Early Twelfth Century*, trans. T. Reuter (Cambridge, 1993), pp. 101-22.

[35] On the implications of the peripheral position of Saxony see Leyser, *Rule and Conflict*, pp. 110-12; for memories of Christianisation see H. Beumann, 'Die Hagiographie "bewältigt" Unterwerfung und Christianisierung der Sachsen durch Karl den Großen', in idem, *Ausgewählte Aufsätze* (as n. 30), pp. 289-323 (first published 1982) and K.J. Leyser, 'From Saxon Freedoms to the Freedom of Saxony', in *The Gregorian Revolution and Beyond*, pp. 51-67.

[36] C.S. Jaeger, 'Cathedral Schools and Humanist Learning, 950-1150', *Deutsche Vierteljahrsschrift für Literaturwissenschaft und Geistesgeschichte*, 61 (1987), pp. 569-616, here pp. 572-5, on the reconstruction of the cathedral schools in the later tenth century.

[37] F.L. Ganshof, *Was waren die Kapitularien?* (Weimar, 1961), pp. 154-5; J.L. Nelson, *Charles the Bald* (London, 1992), pp. 259-60.

[38] H. Wolter, *Die Synoden im Reichsgebiet und in Reichsitalien von 916 bis 1056* (Konziliengeschichte Reihe A: Darstellungen 5, Paderborn, 1988), pp. 7-66, 477-9. In west Francia the tradition ended with the council of Trosly in 909; see I. Schröder, *Die westfränkischen Synoden von 888-987 und ihre Überlieferung* (MGH Hilfsmittel 5, München, 1980).

voice to problems which troubled them than were ceremonies and rituals.[39] However, the want of capitularies and the rarity of surviving mid tenth-century letter collections were absolute minuses which explains much about the deeper flaws of Ottonian government, the starker divide between its lay and clerical élites which forced rulers to conscript churchmen for services on a still larger scale than had happened before or elsewhere and so enhance tension, on the one hand *crises de conscience* among clerks and on the other hand friction between them and laymen in the competition for rewards.[40]

Altogether Ottonian historiography differed from Carolingian because it echoed, if I may say so, its nearness to an age of oral transmission from which the Reich had only just emerged and hence we read in it much more about rituals and ceremonies as a means to act out ideas and manifest relationships. Here then are the most striking examples. Early in 938 when Otto had to fight for his inheritance and kingship with his own kin, his foremost enemy was at first his half-brother Thangmar, who was allied with the Franconian duke Eberhard. Both of them stormed a fortress, Belecke, where Otto's younger brother Henry, who was shortly to become his most serious rival and contender for the kingship, was staying. Thangmar, Henry I's son by his first wife Hatheburg, naturally hated the offspring of the second marriage to Mathilda among whom the succession lay. It is thus significant that when Henry fell into Thangmar's and Eberhard's hands he was treated not as an exalted prisoner of the highest rank but led away visibly in bonds 'like a vile slave'.[41] Otto soon avenged his brother's humiliation, and Thangmar was trapped by superior forces in the Eresburg, the erstwhile Saxon heathen stronghold, centre of resistance to Charlemagne and conversion. Thangmar fled to the church of St Peter in the fortress and stood by the altar on which he placed his arms and his golden necklace. The latter denoted his rank as a prince, and still more perhaps his membership of what had now become the *stirps regia*.[42] Placing it and the weapons on the altar was a ritual of surrender, of abandoning his claims to contend with Otto for the succession.

---

[39] On the upbringing of Mathilda and of Otto II see Ekkehard, *Casus sancti Galli* c. 145, ed. H.F. Haefele (AQDG 10, Darmstadt, 1980), pp. 282/84 (for Otto II); R. Ahlfeld, *Die Erziehung der sächsischen und salischen Herrscher im Hinblick auf ihre spätere Regierungszeit* (Diss. Greifswald, 1949); W. Glocker, *Die Verwandten der Ottonen und ihre Bedeutung in der Politik: Studien zur Familienpolitik und zur Genealogie des sächsischen Kaiserhauses* (Cologne, 1989), pp. 201-2. On the function of the historiographical boom of the 960s see Karpf, *Herrscherlegitimation* (as n. 29) and G. Althoff, 'Causa scribendi und Darstellungsabsicht: Die Lebensbeschreibungen der Königin Mathilde und andere Beispiele', in *Litterae Medii Aevi: Festschrift für Johanna Autenrieth*, ed. M. Borgolte and H. Spilling (Sigmaringen, 1988), pp. 117-33, both with well-founded scepticism about the conception of an Ottonian 'house' or 'court' historiography.

[40] R. Schieffer, 'Der ottonische Reichsepiskopat zwischen Königtum und Adel', *Frühmittelalterliche Studien*, 23 (1990), pp. 291-301, with bibliography of the recent discussion of the topic; Fichtenau, *Lebensordnungen* (as n. 34) pp. 98-9, 271, 277-84, English translation pp. 68-70, 200, 207-10 (on the twinges of conscience).

[41] Widukind, *Res gestae Saxonicae* II 11 p. 75, lines 1-2: 'quasi vile quoddam mancipium'.

[42] On *armillae* and *torques* see Leyser, 'Early Medieval Warfare', above, p. 35.

There is in fact a whole cluster of ritualistic practices, of rituals shaping events early in Otto I's reign, both in Saxony and its Slav neighbourhood. We read of a judicial duel between champions to decide an important legal issue, whether grandsons should share inheritances with their uncles if their own father had predeceased their grandfather.[43] We hear also, for the first time it seems, of ritualistic punishment for acts of rebellion.[44] The early feuds and disturbances of Otto's young rule forced the king to proceed against Duke Eberhard of Franconia and the leaders of his following in 937. Eberhard had to pay 100 marks in horses as a fine, and his chief followers each had to carry a dog from a certain point to Magdeburg, far distant from the scene of their crimes on the Franco-Saxon border, as a penance for their feud accompanied by arson.[45] It is characteristic that Otto afterwards took these men visibly back into his grace by giving them presents.[46] The ritual was a piece of theatre designed to strengthen Otto's lordship in Saxony and to impress, perhaps to warn the Saxon nobles. How did those who were punished take it? Perhaps not as badly as we might expect. They had won identity as a result, set themselves off from the mass of unknown warriors. Their poor reputation might even have earned respect, for they had performed the deeds for which they were now being punished out of loyalty and service to their lord. Elsewhere also the dog played a ritualised role in making shame and insult visible. When the Daleminzi, a nearby Slav tribe, refused to continue to pay tribute to the Magyars on the eve of the Riade campaign of 933, they did so by throwing a fat dog at them.[47] Warfare itself, as Widukind described it, and especially battle were highly ritualised, without losing any of their ferocity and violence. On the eve of all the great Ottonian engagements, at Lenzen in 929, at Riade in 933 and at the Lech in 955, Ottonian warriors promised and swore to help each other in action by raising their right hands. We may wonder at this as something to be taken for granted, but in feud-ridden societies, such as this one was, it was no idle precaution but an essential one.[48] At Riade Henry I's mounted warriors seem to have sung, so Liudprand tells us, a 'kyrie eleison'.[49] Of fasting before battle we shall hear later.[50]

---

[43] Widukind, *Res gestae Saxonicae* II 10, pp. 73-4.

[44] G. Waitz, *Deutsche Verfassungsgeschichte*, 6: *Die Deutsche Reichsverfassung von der Mitte des neunten bis zur Mitte des 12. Jahrhunderts*, 3rd edn by G. Seeliger (Berlin, 1896), p. 605 with n. 5 and 6; B. Schwenk, 'Das Hundetragen. Ein Rechtsbrauch im Mittelalter', *HJb*, 110 (1990), pp. 289-308.

[45] Widukind, *Res gestae Saxonicae* II 6, p. 72 lines 3-5.

[46] Ibid. II 7, p. 72 lines 7-10.

[47] Ibid. I 38, p. 56 lines 5-7.

[48] Ibid. I 36 (929), I 38 (933), III 44 (955), pp. 52 line 21, 55 lines 22-5, 124 lines 10-11. For the risks see Leyser, 'Early Medieval Warfare', above, pp. 36-7; and for the use of prayer-confraternities to cement such alliances in the face of the Magyar threat see now G. Althoff, *Amicitiae und Pacta: Bündnis, Einung, Politik und Gebetsgedenken im beginnenden 10. Jahrhundert* (Schriften der MGH 37, Hanover, 1992), pp. 69-87.

[49] Liudprand, *Antapodosis* II 30, p. 51.

[50] See below at n. 89

Otto's struggle for his rule, challenged by his son Liudolf and his son-in-law Conrad in 953, took the form of a struggle for the royal ritual of keeping Easter with all its solemnities. Already in Mainz, late in March, Archbishop Frederick, an opponent, had ministered but grudgingly to the king and his following.[51] When Otto I, unwilling to keep the feast in the midst of his enemies at Ingelheim, approached Aachen to celebrate it there, he found that nothing had been prepared for him: Aachen lay in the sphere of lordship of his son-in-law, Duke Conrad of Lotharingia. Otto then had to go to Dortmund where he was and remained master, and there in his Saxon homeland, as Widukind magnificently expressed it, 'he found the king again whom he had nearly lost in Francia'.[52] What this meant was revealed at once by the Corvey historian. Otto now repudiated the agreements he had entered into with his opponents at Mainz and claimed they had been made under duress. Liudolf and Conrad were ordered to hand over their accomplices or be deemed enemies. The Easter-keeping in Saxony became the springboard of stern justice and threats of punishment.[53]

Ritual could also become the vehicle of protest, dissent and even the threat of rebellion. Of this there is a famous instance from the year 972, not long before Otto I's return to Saxony after six years absence in Italy. It was one of the largest, most heralded and historically cherished ritual incidents in the whole Ottonian century, and it has been much commented upon by historians, myself not excluded.[54] During Otto's absence Duke Hermann Billung was in charge of Saxony as the king's procurator, with an authority now extending over the whole stem-land, no longer confined to his ducal frontier command pivoted on his family seat and monastery at Lüneburg and the north-east.[55] There was an assembly at Magdeburg and Archbishop Adalbert received Hermann, led him by the hand into the new cathedral where all the lamps had been lit and all the bells were rung. Later, Hermann dined in the midst of the bishops who had come to the meeting and this at the imperial table, where he sat in the emperor's seat; when the feasting was over he slept in the imperial bed. He had in fact at the archbishop's invitation usurped Otto's place and his

---

[51] Widukind, *Res gestae Saxonicae* III 13, p. 111; Adalbert, *Continuatio*, p. 166.

[52] Ibid. III 14, p. 111, lines 16-19; Adalbert, *Continuatio*, p. 166.

[53] Ibid. III 15, p. 112, lines 1-3, though the meeting with Mathilda and the Saxon magnates took place somewhat later in Quedlinburg, cf. E. Müller-Mertems, *Die Reichsstruktur im Spiegel der Herrschaftspraxis Ottos des Großen* (Forschungen zur mittelalterlichen Geschichte 25, Berlin 1980), p. 130. For the rejection of the *pacta* see H. Naumann, 'Rätsel des letzten Aufstandes gegen Otto I. (953-954)', in *Otto der Große*, ed. Harald Zimmermann (Wege der Forschung 440, Darmstadt, 1976), pp. 97-115 (first published 1964); G. Althoff, *Verwandte, Freunde und Getreue* (Darmstadt, 1990), p. 171 with n. 73; G. Wolf, 'De pactis Ottonis I.', *Archiv für Diplomatik*, 37 (1991), pp. 33-47; Althoff, *Amicitiae und Pacta* (as n. 48), pp. 94-5.

[54] Leyser, *Rule and Conflict*, pp. 25, 94; G. Althoff, 'Das Bett des Königs in Magdeburg. Zu Thietmar II, 28', in *Festschrift für Berent Schwineköper zu seinem siebzigsten Geburtstag*, ed. H. Maurer and H. Patze (Sigmaringen, 1982), pp. 141-53.

[55] G. Althoff, 'Die Billunger in der Salierzeit', in *Die Salier und das Reich*, 1: *Salier, Adel und Reichsverfassung*, ed. S. Weinfurter (Sigmaringen, 1991), pp. 309-29, here pp. 311-14.

reception ritual down to the last detail.[56] Gerd Althoff has shown that this act of *superbia*, as our source Thietmar of Merseburg called it, was meant to express the deep dissatisfaction about Otto's prolonged absence, a hostile comment on his Italian policies.[57] As such, then, the ritual might be classed as one of protest, almost as one of rebellion. It could also have been meant as a statement about the nature of Hermann's *ducatus*. This had hitherto been seen as an exceptionally large and important frontier command in an important area but it did not cover the whole of Saxony, nor could it compare with the fullness of powers which dukes even after Otto's great wars from 937-39 and 952-54 enjoyed in the southern duchies, his brother Henry not least of all in Bavaria.[58] The great reception and entry seemed to proclaim that with Archbishop Adalbert's and many Saxon nobles' consent Duke Hermann was to hold a similar position in Saxony, notwithstanding the Liudolfings' patrimony and royal fisc there. Althoff rejected this interpretation, but could it not be a case of not only but also?[59] Precisely because Otto had got bogged down in Italy the Billung 'duchy' could have taken on a new importance and additional functions. It is in the nature of ritual that it can express more than one transformation at the same time. This is where the rebellious challenge of the ceremony really lay, prompted by Saxon needs and Otto's long absence and hence failure to meet them. The most important aspect of this ritual demonstration of resistance was its tenacious hold on memories, greater than that of almost any other event in the Ottonian age. Memories of it were still present when in 1135 Lothar of Süpplingenburg – once again, a Saxon emperor – ordered a liturgical reception in Magdeburg for Duke Boleslas of Poland. Contemporary Saxon historiographers, the *Annalista Saxo* and the author of the *Annales Magdeburgenses*, expressed their distaste – which may not have been theirs alone – for the granting of honours to a Slav foreigner which, when the first archbishop of Magdeburg Adalbert had once shown them to Hermann Billung, had called down the wrath of Otto the Great.[60] We have referred to the transforming

---

[56] P. Willmes, *Der Herrscher-'Adventus' im Kloster des Frühmittelalters* (Münstersche Mittelalter-Schriften 22, München, 1976); T. Kölzer, 'Adventus regis', in *Lexikon des Mittelalters*, vol. 1 (München, 1977-83), pp. 170-1; M. McCormich, *Eternal Victory: Triumphal Rulership in Late Antiquity, Byzantium, and the Early Medieval West* (Cambridge, 1986), pp. 365, 372-4.

[57] Althoff, 'Bett' (as n. 54), pp. 150-2.

[58] On Henry's quasi-regal standing in Bavaria see K.J. Leyser, 'The Tenth Century in Byzantine-Western Relationships', in Leyser, *Medieval Germany*, p. 109. On the fundamental differences between the south German duchies and those in Lotharingia and Saxony see the classic analysis by G. Tellenbach, 'Vom karolingischen Reichsadel zum deutschen Reichsfürstenstand', in idem, *Ausgewählte Abhandlungen und Aufsätze*, vol. 3 (Stuttgart, 1988), pp. 912-19 (first published 1943; English translation in T. Reuter, *The Medieval Nobility* (Amsterdam, 1978), pp. 214-18), and now H.-W. Goetz, 'Herzog, Herzogtum', in *Lexikon des Mittelalters*, vol. 4 (Munich, 1989), cols. 2189-93, with a good bibliography.

[59] Althoff, 'Bett' (as n. 54), p. 151, arguing primarily against the view that Hermann was here usurping a royal position.

[60] Annalista Saxo, *MGH SS* 6, p. 770 lines 1-5; derived from this is *Annales Magdeburgenses*, *MGH SS* 6, 185 lines 44-51 (see also p. 152 *s.a.* 972).

function of ritual, and here we can see how it became a pillar of Saxon criticism of kingship.

Only one noble had protested against this ritual marker of criticism, arrogation and unrest in the Saxon aristocracy. That was the Billungs' neighbour and, not surprisingly, chief rival in the north east, Count Henry of Stade, Thietmar of Merseburg's maternal grandfather. Duke Hermann Billung had wanted to arrest him but Count Henry had taken care to come to Magdeburg with a large throng of *milites* – it would be premature to call them knights – and so he could not be crushed.[61] Hermann, seeing his authority in Saxony now threatened, wanted to get rid of him and so ordered him to seek out Otto I at Rome, meaning that he should join his expedition as others had done. Henry did so gladly. His first encounter with the emperor was rich in ritual language. He prostrated himself on the ground before Otto, who was astonished – proskynesis as such was not yet part of western ceremonial – and wanted to know the reason for this.[62] The count replied that he feared that he had been accused – Hermann could have sent letters though apparently he did not – and that he had lost Otto's *gratia*, his grace.[63] The royal grace, as well as its opposite, disgrace and the royal anger, were themselves highly ritualised institutions, not only in the Ottonian Reich:[64] one need only think of Berengar II of Italy's appearance at the assembly at Magdeburg in 952, where Otto I had demonstratively refused to receive him.[65] The emperor then, when Henry had risen, kissed him and began to investigate what lay behind all this. He now heard the story of Hermann Billung's regal reception in Magdeburg. His response was what might have been expected: furious. Hermann Billung's deed was all the more resented, it should be noted, because Otto I himself had not yet entered Magdeburg solemnly as an archbishop's seat and cathedral city.[66] Archbishop Adalbert, but not Hermann Billung, was fined heavily in horses, which corresponded in number to the numbers of bells rung and lights lit in his ritual offence, and did what he could to excuse himself by envoys.[67] It is the final act in this series of rituals, not least of all the kiss, which brings us back to the role of golden necklaces. The emperor gave him one and we hear, again from Thietmar, of what the effect of such a gesture of favour was, its repercussions far beyond the circule of bystanders who actually saw the act of

---

[61] Thietmar, *Chronicon* II 28, p. 74 lines 6-9.

[62] Fichtenau, *Lebensordnungen* (as n. 34), pp. 55-6 (English translation pp. 36-8); Koziol, *Begging Pardon and Favor* (as n. 6), pp. 11-12, 66, 95: proskynesis was unknown in the west as a ritual to be used when entering the ruler's presence, except for occasional imitations of Byzantine ceremony, though Koziol argues that it came to be a standard ritual of submission in west Francia in the tenth century; it is possible that his definition of proskynesis is here too broad.

[63] Thietmar, *Chronicon* II 28, p. 74, lines 10-14.

[64] G. Althoff, 'Huld: Überlegungen zu einem Zentralbegriff der mittelalterlichen Herrschaftsordnung', *Frühmittelalterliche Studien*, 25 (1991), pp. 259-82; J.E.A. Jolliffe, *Angevin Kingship*, 2nd edn (London, 1963), chapter 4, 'ira et malevolentia', pp. 87-109.

[65] Widukind, *Res gestae Saxonicae* III 10, pp. 109-110; Adalbert, *Continuatio*, pp. 165-6.

[66] Althoff, 'Bett des Königs' (as n. 54), p. 148.

[67] Thietmar, *Chronicon* II 28, p. 74 lines 21-3.

conferment. It saddened the count's enemies – meaning Hermann Billung – and cheered his *familiares*, meaning not just his following but any fellow nobles who were attached to him in the hope of patronage, rewards and future favours.[68] Thietmar was not, of course, a detached commentator. The gift of the necklace by Otto also helped him to buttress other claims made for his grandfather, notably that he was the emperor's blood-relation and possessed the almost magical gift of being able to calm Otto's anger.[69] The golden necklace was also a princely token, something which was not to fall into impure hands. The warrior who had struck down Thangmar and seized the golden necklace from the altar had committed a double pollution.[70]

It will have been noticed that a meal, a banquet, played a large and very visible part in Archbishop Adalbert's and Duke Hermann's invasion and usurpation of royal ritual. This was by no means the only occasion; on the contrary, meals could be immensely potent rituals both to herald claims and to promote them, to manifest friendship, real or pretended, and acts of reconciliation.[71] As Gerd Althoff has shown, they were the stuff of which noble conspiracies were made, the places where permanent associations of nobles met.[72] When Henry, Otto I's brother, himself entered the lists against him in 938/39 he prepared a famous banquet at Saalfeld in Thuringia where he rallied and feasted his supporters.[73] Saalfeld thus came to be at once and permanently linked with the notion of rebellion and so became part of a ritual of rebellion. For when Liudolf, Otto I's son by his marriage with Edith of Wessex, left his father in Italy in 952, angered and saddened by his father's second marriage to Adelheid with her rich Burgundian and Italian claims, he at once went to Saalfeld to stay there for some time and rally supporters for a rising soon. Widukind called it the 'place of dark counsels'.[74]

[68] Ibid. II 28, p. 74, lines 26-8.

[69] Ibid., lines 24-6. On the genealogical issue see R. Hucke, *Die Grafen von Stade, 900-1144: Genealogie, politische Stellung, Comitat und Allodialbesitz der sächsischen Udonen* (Stade, 1956), pp. 9-15.

[70] See above at n. 42; Widukind, *Res gestae Saxonicae* II, 11, p. 77 lines 5-10; Leyser, *Rule and Conflict*, p. 87; idem, 'The German Aristocracy in the Early Middle Ages: A Historical Sketch', in Leyser, *Medieval Germany*, p. 177.

[71] G. Althoff, 'Der friedens-, bündnis und gemeinschaftsstiftende Charakter des Mahles im früheren Mittelalter', in *Essen und Trinken in Mittelalter und Neuzeit*, ed. I. Bitsch and others (Sigmaringen, 1987), pp. 13-26; idem, 'Fest und Bündnis', in *Feste und Feiern im Mittelalter: Paderborner Symposion des Mediävistenverbandes*, ed. D. Altenburg, J. Jarnut and H.-H. Steinhoff (Sigmaringen, 1991), pp. 29-38.

[72] G. Althoff, 'Zur Frage nach der Organisation von sächsischen *coniurationes*', *Frühmittelalterliche Studien*, 16 (1982), pp. 129-42; idem, *Amicitiae* (as n. 48), p. 94.

[73] Widukind, *Res gestae Saxonicae* II 15, p. 79 lines 18-22.

[74] Ibid. III 9, p. 109 line 14: 'loco consiliis funesto'. See Althoff, 'Zur Frage' (as n. 72), p. 136, and on the ritualised role of another such place idem, 'Breisach — ein Refugium für Rebellen im früheren Mittelalter', in *Archäologie und Geschichte des ersten Jahrtausends in Südwestdeutschland*, ed. H.U. Nuber, K. Schmid, H. Steuer and T. Zotz (Archäologie und Geschichte 1, Sigmaringen, 1990), pp. 457-71.

This by no means exhausts the theme of meals as rituals. We defined ceremonies at the beginning as procedures which made visible a social situation. The Easter-keepings of the Ottonians were just such a procedure, with their divine service and banquet in Quedlinburg.[75] When Henry the Wrangler for his part challenged the kingship of Otto III, a minor, he solemnly manifested his claims at Quedlinburg with what was as nearly as possible a royal Easter-keeping, and here he not only assembled and feasted his formidable following among the Saxon nobility but he also learned who opposed his bid. This happened in 984.[76] Two years later, after his ambitions had been defeated, the vindication of the infant Otto III's regality purposefully took the form of a royal Easter feast at the traditional place for Ottonian Easters, Quedlinburg. Here, Thietmar tells us, the dukes ministered, and it was not without irony and probably also no coincidence that Henry, now once again duke of Bavaria like his father, was in charge of the royal table.[77] It must of course be stressed that royal meals on the great feasts when the king wore his crown were always part of a ritual. When the ruler returned from church in procession with his *comitatus* of bishops, priests, dukes, counts and their dignitaries, they brought him back to his chamber or to the feast which they then shared.[78] It was just here that the ritual ways and means which Otto III used to create and project a novel, more exalted, aloof and monarchical style of emperorship, shocked his Saxon followers and other onlookers the most. For he could be seen sitting alone at a semi-circular table which stood on a higher level than all the rest. Otto's new court offices and ranks, like the patriciate, Thietmar mentioned only in passing, but this startling departure from companionable and gregarious usage struck home and was remembered almost with horror.[79]

Meals as manifestations of kingship and its dignity were thus powerful agents of visual magic, whether to flourish a novel programme or age-old, accustomed right. Here Thietmar has another well-known story, which shows again how intensely public life and political conflict were lived through ritual.

---

[75] C. Brühl, *Fodrum, gistum, servitium regis*, 2 vols. paginated as one (Cologne, 1968), pp. 125-6; Müller-Mertens, *Reichsstruktur* (as n. 53), table on pp. 267-8 with the commentary pp. 96-7; G. Althoff, 'Gandersheim und Quedlinburg: Ottonische Frauenklöster als Herrschafts-und Überlieferungszentren', *Frühmittelalterliche Studien*, 25 (1991), pp. 123-44, here pp. 127-9; W. Huschner, 'Kirchenfest und Herrschaftspraxis: Die Regierungszeiten der ersten beiden Kaiser aus liudolfingischem Hause, Teil I: Otto I. (936-973)', *Zeitschrift für Geschichtswissenschaft*, 41 (1993) pp. 24-55 and 'Teil II: Otto II. (973-983)', ibid., pp. 117-34, especially the tables on pp. 48-55 and 131-4.

[76] Thietmar, *Chronicon* IV 2, pp. 132/134; *Annales Quedlinburgenses, MGH SS* 3, p. 66.

[77] Thietmar, *Chronicon* IV 9, p. 140.

[78] So for example Otto III following his return from the pilgrimage to Gnesen: *Annales Quedlinburgenses, MGH SS* 3, p. 77.

[79] Thietmar, *Chronicon* IV 44, p. 182 line 13: 'comitantibus secum Ziazone tunc patricio et Robberto oblacionario', and IV 47 p. 184 lines 31-3: 'multa faciebat, quae diversi diverse sentiebant. Solus ad mensam quasi semicirculus factam loco caeteris eminenciori sedebat'. See on this and its Byzantine parallels P.E. Schramm, *Kaiser, Rom und Renovatio*, vol. 1, 2nd edn (Darmstadt, 1957), p. 111.

The place is the royal palace and Saxon meeting-place Werla, the year 1002, probably early in April. Here the Saxon great assembled to deliberate on the succession to the kingship, now that Otto III was no more. Duke Henry of Bavaria, the son of the Wrangler, was as near an Ottonian agnatic male descendant as could be found, but a Saxon noble came forward to be elected, if possible by his peers.[80] This was a leading magnate and warrior, Margrave Ekkehard I of Meissen, who had been much advanced under the last of the Ottos. He had, however, powerful enemies, not least Thietmar of Merseburg's uncle, Margrave Liuthar of the northern march, whose family Margrave Ekkehard had wanted to insult mortally by reneging on a marriage that had been negotiated between the two families for Werner of Walbeck and Ekkehard's daughter Liutgard.[81] Liuthar therefore backed Henry of Bavaria. Present at Werla were also the nearest Ottonian blood relations, Otto II's daughters and Otto III's sisters, Adelheid of Quedlinburg and Sophia, soon to become abbess of Gandersheim.[82] These two ladies had gained, now that there was no surviving brother, an enhanced sacral place and role. Their approval was deemed to be necessary, whichever remoter kinsman succeeded and entered upon the Liudolfing inheritance. It is characteristic of their exalted standing that when in 1025 Conrad II, the first Salian, came to the kingship and was about to enter Saxony, these two ladies met him by arrangement at the frontier in Westfalia, at Vreden, a nunnery, and it was their friendly greeting which secured for him, a stranger in Saxony, a fairly ready recognition there.[83] Now at Werla in 1002 a table had been set for Adelheid's and Sophia's dinner, and the food was already there when Margrave Ekkehard of Meissen and his supporters, including Bishop Arnulf of Halberstadt and Duke Bernard Billung simply seized it ahead of the two sisters and sat down to the meal.[84] It was the

[80] Henry II's claim was 'iure hereditario': Thietmar, *Chronicon* V 3, p. 224 lines 6-7; for the controversies about the constitutional significance of the election of 1002 see W. Schlesinger, 'Erbfolge und Wahl bei der Königserhebung Heinrichs II. 1002' and idem, 'Die sogenannte Nachwahl Heinrichs II. in Merseburg', both in idem, *Ausgewählte Aufsätze von Walter Schlesinger, 1965-1979*, ed. H. Patze and F. Schwind (Vorträge und Forschungen 34, Sigmaringen, 1987) pp. 221-53 and 255-71 respectively; H. Keller, 'Schwäbische Herzöge als Thronbewerber: Hermann II. (1002), Rudolf von Rheinfelden (1077), Friedrich von Schwaben (1125). Zur Entwicklung von Reichsidee und Fürstenverantwortung, Wahlverständnis und Wahlverfahren im 11. und 12. Jahrhundert', *Zeitschrift für die Geschichte des Oberrheins*, neue Folge 92 (1983), pp. 123-62, here pp. 133-9. See also the literature cited below, n. 85.

[81] Thietmar, *Chronicon* IV 52 und V 7, pp. 190, 224, on Ekkehard's position, and ibid. IV 39-40, pp. 176/178 for the marriage plans.

[82] Glocker, *Verwandten der Ottonen* (as n. 39), pp. 206-10. For the significance of Werla as a centre of Ottonian lordship in this connection see W. Berges, 'Zur Geschichte des Werla-Goslarer Reichsbezirks vom neunten bis zum elften Jahrhundert', in *Deutsche Königspfalzen*, 1 (Veröffentlichungen des Max-Planck-Instituts für Geschichte 11/1, Göttingen, 1963), pp. 113-57; H.-J. Rieckenberg, 'Zur Geschichte der Pfalz Werla nach der schriftlichen Überlieferung', in *Deutsche Königspfalzen*, 2 (Veröffentlichungen des Max-Planck-Instituts für Geschichte 11/2, Göttingen, 1965), pp. 174-209.

[83] *Annales Quedlinburgenses, MGH SS* 3, p. 90 lines 5-9.

[84] Thietmar, *Chronicon* V 4, p. 224 lines 11-15. See Althoff, 'Bett des Königs' (as n. 54), pp. 145-6.

most obvious, public and visible way to strike at and repudiate the old dynasty. During earlier negotiations in which Ekkehard had not succeeded in carrying the day he had called out to Margrave Liuthar of Walbeck: 'Why are you against me?' To this Liuthar had replied: 'Don't you see that the fourth wheel of your waggon is missing?' This has often been interpreted to mean that Ekkehard lacked royal blood, that he did not belong to the *stirps regia*, although this is now disputed, some thinking that he did.[85] But in seizing the princesses' table and pre-empting its rightful occupants, Margrave Ekkehard and his followers seemed rather to be saying that this did not matter or no longer mattered. Once again it was the ritual of a meal which drove home the point and the insult to the two Ottonian princesses became at least one of the reasons for Ekkehard's murder by the counts of Katlenburg shortly afterwards.[86]

Let it be mentioned in passing that after his absolution by Pope Gregory VII, Henry IV had a meal with him at Canossa as a visible ritual of reconciliation; his appetite is thought to have been poor, according to an unfriendly source, a no less viable sign of not being reconciled.[87] Again, when Frederick Barbarossa submitted at last to Pope Alexander III at Venice in 1177, the pontiff sent him a fattened calf for his dinner to remind him and others that he was the returned prodigal son.[88] Laymen knew enough of the bible to understand this language of signs. Conversely, if meals were ritual modes to express relationships, so often enough were fasts, even secular fasts. It was not uncommon for warriors, whole hosts, to fast on the eve of battles. This for instance happened on the day before the battle at the Lech on 10 August 955.[89] If ritual is an

---

[85] Thietmar, *Chronicon* (as n. 61) IV 52, p. 190 lines 29-31: ' "O Liuthari comes", inquiens, "quid adversaris"? Et ille: "Num", inquid, "currui tuo quartam deesse non sentis rotam?" ' On the question of whether this was a reference to Ekkehard's missing royal descent see E. Hlawitschka, ' "Merkst du nicht, das dir das vierte Rad am Wagen fehlt?" Zur Thronkandidatur Ekkehards von Meißen (1002) nach Thietmar, Chronicon IV c. 52', in *Geschichtsschreibung und geistiges Leben im Mittelalter: Festschrift für Heinz Löwe*, ed. K. Hauck and H. Mordek (Köln, 1978), pp. 281-311, who interprets it rather as a reference to Ekkehard's deficiency in the cardinal virtue of moderation and attempts to show that Ekkehard was related to the Ottonians. For the controversy which followed this see most recently G. Althoff, 'Die Thronbewerber von 1002 und ihre Verwandtschaft mit den Ottonen: Bemerkungen zu einem neuen Buch', *Zeitschrift für die Geschichte des Oberrheins*, 137 (1989), pp. 453-9 (with references to the earlier contributions to the debate) and the reply by Hlawitschka, 'Nochmals zu den Thronbewerbern des Jahres 1002', ibid., pp. 460-7.

[86] For a discussion of the motivation of the feud see Thietmar, *Chronicon* V 6-7, pp. 226/228, especially p. 228 lines 8-10: 'Alii autumant, sicut predixi, in Werlu ob contumeliam consororibus illatam, quia isti libenter his serviebant, ac per convivia minasque ab ipso sibi manifestatas haec eos increpisse.'

[87] Rangerius von Lucca, *Vita metrica p. Anselmi Luccensis episcopi*, verses 3205-8, *MGH SS* 30, p. 1224; on the value of the source see T. Struve, 'Johannes Haller und das Versöhnungsmahl auf Canossa: Eine Korrektur', *Historisches Jahrbuch*, 110 (1990), pp. 110-16.

[88] *Relatio de pace Veneta*, *MGH SS* 19, p. 463; see on this K.J. Leyser, 'Frederick Barbarossa: Court and Country' in Leyser, *The Gregorian Revolution and Beyond*, p. 144.

[89] Widukind, *Res gestae Saxonicae* III 43, p. 124 lines 8-9. Cf. also the behaviour of Arnulf's army before Rome in 896, *Annales Fuldenses*, p. 127.

action not to be justified on rational grounds it could here be seen as a propitiatory deed, almost a kind of prayer, in other words as one of the standardised forms of behaviour in which, as Goody put it, the relationship between ends and means was not intrinsic.[90] And yet it was also a rational one. Fasting did not mean that the warriors ate and drank nothing, it meant in fact only that they did not eat and drink too much, as was all too often their habit. They were thus fitter for action. Drunkenness could have helped to overcome fear and anxiety but it also incapacitated or at least reduced fighting skills (as I know from a horrendous case in the last war which lay within my experience during an action).

More important for emboldening warriors and overcoming anxiety were two other military rituals of which we read often on the eve or the morning or just before the beginning of battles. First of all the boast. It is astonishingly frequent in the histories of the tenth century and must have been very common to raise morale, wish away adverse factors or simply cope with the sheer chanciness of all military operations. Hugh the Great is reported as boasting through an envoy sent to Otto I that he had a larger army than the king had ever seen, that the Saxons in any case were unwarlike, and that he could swallow seven Saxon missiles in one gulp. To this Otto I is reported to have replied that he would soon see more straw hats than he or his father had ever seen before.[91] This meant that most of the huge army which in 946 invaded west Francia under Otto's command wore straw hats (i.e. had no helmets) except, so Widukind wrote, Abbot Bovo of Corvey with his three followers.[92] It could of course also mean that those who had helmets did not wear them all the time on the march (just as in the last war we did not wear steel helmets except in action). The boast here is of course entirely on the Saxon side. Hugh the Great's insult is needed to set it off. Widukind's description of the 946 campaign also uncovers another ritual which might almost be called a rite of impotence. The Ottonian army was able to enter Rheims but it could not take Laon or Rouen. It then made a gesture of besieging Paris, where Hugh the Great had taken his station. This Otto I and Louis IV could take even less and their assaults were beaten back with losses, but they held a special service in honour of St Denis outside the walls. If the Saxon king could not take Paris by storm, he could as it were appropriate the region's foremost patron saint.[93] In 978, during Otto II's retaliatory invasion of France when he was also unable to take Paris, his army held a field service on the Montmartre, where his clerics sang the Alleluia so loudly that they deafened the ears of Hugh Capet and the

---

[90] Goody, 'Religion and Ritual' (as n. 1).

[91] Widukind, *Res gestae Saxonicae* III 2, pp. 104-6. For a further discussion of boasting see 'Early Medieval Warfare', above, pp. 42-3.

[92] Ibid. III 2, p. 105-6 (B text).

[93] Ibid. III 3, p. 107; on the chronology see however P. Lauer, *Le Règne de Louis IV d'Outre-Mer* (Bibliothèque de l'école des hautes études 127, Paris, 1900), pp. 148-9.

Parisians, according to the *Gesta Episcoporum Cameracensium*.[94] In this way too war could be boastfully announced.

Boasting by Otto I to prop up the confidence of his host during the awesome encounter with the Magyars at the Lech is reported by Widukind.[95] In a speech to his warriors, at a moment of crisis during the action, Otto is thought to have reminded his men that they made up for inferior numbers by their great superiority in armament, weaponry and *virtus*. The Magyars, so it was set forth, were naked as far as most arms went – they relied in fact on archery and fast manoeuvre. It would be shameful if the masters of *nearly* all Europe – and Widukind was fond of the European dimension – should give their hands in surrender to their enemies, the Hungarians.[96] The exaggeration of east Frankish power is startling. The king's very advance into battle was enhanced by ritual, for he carried the Holy Lance as his weapon into action.[97] Boasting also mattered in the battle against the Slavs at the Recknitz later in 955, where the Ottonian host was in a very difficult and dangerous situation and Margrave Gero's threats and boasts sought to cover up the crisis.[98] The Slav chieftain with whom he talked across a swamp knew this and heaped abuse on the margrave, the king and his host. Boasting itself could not turn the situation. What did was Gero's Slav alliances, the clientage of the men of Rügen who conducted him on a flank march that gave the Saxons the chance to approach their enemies.[99] It could however be a brave front and so undermine the other side's confidence. Mention has already been made of the second widely practised rite before fighting in a pitched encounter, the promises and oaths of mutual aid.[100] All these rituals served to transform the situation for the better: they aroused hopes and expectations of success.

We must now turn to another role of ritual which anthropologists have categorised; its uses to re-affirm status differences. Here, above all, dress can be seen as an essential ingredient in some tenth-century sources, strongly supporting anthropological norms. Thietmar is again the best guide but not the only one. He himself before his promotion was a clerk of the Magdeburg *familia* and later of his own family's collegiate church at Walbeck.[101] In 994 disaster struck at his maternal kin when the Vikings came up the Elbe and engaged in battle with the counts of Stade. They captured several of Thietmar's uncles, and negotiations opened for them to be ransomed. The families clubbed together and Otto III helped, but even so the raising of large amounts

---

[94] *Gesta Episcoporum Cameracensium* I 97, MGH SS 7, p. 441 lines 4-9, especially line 5: 'ad pompandam victoriae suae gloriam'.

[95] Widukind, *Res gestae Saxonicae* III 46, p. 127 lines 13-18.

[96] K.J. Leyser, 'Concepts of Europe in the Early and High Middle Ages', above, pp. 43-4, and also pp. 7, 9, 15 on the rhetorical function of *paene* in such contexts.

[97] Widukind, *Res gestae Saxonicae* III 46, p. 127, line 24.

[98] Ibid. III 54, p. 133, line 20 to p. 134 line 6.

[99] Ibid. III 54, p. 134 lines 15-22.

[100] See above at n. 48.

[101] Thietmar, *Chronicon* IV 16, VI 44-45, pp. 150, 328/30.

of cash was a slow business in the tenth century.[102] The Northmen were willing to release their prisoners before every penny came in, provided they were given hostages. In their anxiety the Stade counts turned to Thietmar's mother. One of his brothers, Siegfried, was already under a monastic regime but his abbot, when approached, absolutely refused to hand him over. Thietmar, however, lived and studied at the Magdeburg cathedral school and his master released him. He went home to prepare being a hostage and describes how he set out in lay clothes, though he wore his clerical dress beneath, to go to the Vikings. In the meantime however one of his uncles, Count Siegfried, escaped and got home. The enraged Vikings mutilated the hostages they already had and Thietmar was lucky not to have been among them. It is the lay clothes that were deemed to be appropriate for his role that matter here.[103]

Still more did clothes bespeak rank and status in what we might almost call international relations. Thietmar in his *Chronicon* bitterly complained about the rise of Boleslas Chrobry of Poland and his successful seizure of lands up to the River Elster which had once been under Saxon control. Saxons submitted to his deceitful words and so, Thietmar grumbled, lost their honour and became subordinates. 'How different were things in the days of our ancestors! When Margrave Hodo of the Eastern March [*ob.* 993] was still alive, the father of this man [Miesco I] would never have dared to enter a house wearing furs when he knew Hodo would be there, nor would he ever have ventured to remain seated in Hodo's presence when the latter rose.'[104] Furs were very much a garb of the aristocracy, a hallmark almost. Adam of Bremen wrote that for a good fur some nobles would gladly stake their salvation.[105] The implication here is that Miesco was a barbarian chieftain who cold barely be the equal of a Saxon margrave.

Clothes also announced claims to rank and status when they were not altogether secure in other ways. Mathilda, Henry I's wife of the *stirps Widukindi*, is sanctified in her two *vitae* for her massive charities but it is also pointed out, even stressed, that she always were very rich and precious clothes so that her queenly rank should never be for a moment forgotten. As it was a new rank and as she, like her husband, had not been anointed, she evidently

---

[102]Ibid. IV 23, p. 158. For similar difficulties in putting a ransom together, on this occasion dealt with by robbing a monastery, see Adémar, *Chronicon* III 44, p. 166.

[103]Thietmar, *Chronicon* IV 24-5, pp. 158/60, especially p. 160 lines 14-16: 'Veni et cum laicali habitu, quo apud piratus debui obses conversari, prioribus adhuc indutus vestimentis, V. feria profectus sum'.

[104]Ibid. V 10, p. 232 lines 8-26; the quotation above is lines 18-26: 'Quam inique comparandi sunt antecessores nostri et contemporales! Vivente egregio Hodone pater istius Miseco domum, qua eum esse sciebat, crusinatus intrare vel eo assurgente numquam presumpsit sedere'.

[105] Adam of Bremen, *Gesta* IV 18, p. 245 line 15 to p. 246 line 1 '[nos], qui per fas et nefas ad marturinam vestem anhelamus, quasi ad summam beatitudinem'. See on the socio-economic role of furs F. Irsigler, 'Divites aund pauperes in der Vita Meinwerci', *Vierteljahrsschrift für Sozial- und Wirtschaftsgeschichte*, 57 (1970), pp. 449-98, here pp. 466-71.

felt a need to manifest it and would not allow her devotional practice to come into conflict with her anxiety to appear in state.[106]

There is another sphere where ritual, gesture, sign, even facial expression were crucial to deal with what were in any case almost insoluble problems for east Frankish, especially Saxon society, given its paucity of governmental and legislative apparatus and literate skills. This was the realm of law and legal procedures. Here we may refer to the work of Ruth Schmidt-Wiegand, but an example is also in place.[107] In 996 at Nimwegen Otto III tried to settle a dispute over the inheritance of another Count Wichmann, a close follower of Otto I, who, lacking sons, had used much of his patrimony and *proprietas* to endow a nunnery at Elten on the lower Rhine where his daughter Liudgard ruled as abbess. He had, however, a second daughter, the famous and notorious Adela, the Lady Macbeth of the lower Rhine in the early eleventh century, who challenged the whole endowment her father had made without her full consent and together with her second husband, Count Balderich, who alone could appear in court, threatened to undermine it. A settlement was arrived at under imperial pressure: in return for the grant of four *curtes* out of abbey's lands, Adela and Balderich promised peace and security of possession to the nuns. We are specifically told in the diploma that Balderich received the four estates *hilari fronte*, 'with a glad face'.[108] The detail mattered.

Not only settlements but also quarrels and enmity had their rituals. During the great rising of Liudolf, Otto I's son and Conrad, his son-in-law, Liudolf appeared before his father and his uncle, Henry Duke of Bavaria outside Mainz to negotiate. Liudolf's enmity was directed at Henry in the first instance rather than the king and Henry, well aware of this, challenged him to lead his forces against him. And he, according to Widukind, who described if he did not invent this scene, bent down and picked up a stalk from the ground: 'You won't be able to deprive me of even this much worth of all my power'.[109] Now the *festuca* often served as a token used for investitures and land transfers: Count Balderich and Adela, for example, had publicly placed the Elten estates

---

[106]*Vita Mathildis antiquior* c. 11, *MGH SS* 10, p. 579 lines 25-7: 'virginalem...adquisierat palmam, nisi tantum secularibus vestium floresceret ornamentis'; Widukind, *Res gestae Saxonicae* III 74, p. 151 (for the implicit criticism of the *Vita Mathildis* expressed here see Beumann, Widukind [as n. 30] pp. 256-7); *Vita Mathildis altera* c. 16, *MGH SS* 4, p. 294 lines 23-6 (only after the death of her son Henry in 955 did she adopt widows' weeds). On this topic see D. Elliott, 'Dress as Mediator between Inner and Outer Self: the Pious Matron of the High and Later Middle Ages', *Mediaeval Studies*, 53 (1991), pp. 279-307.

[107]R. Schmidt-Wiegand, 'Gebärden', in; *Handwörterbuch* (as n. 12), vol. 1, pp. 1411-19; eadem, 'Gebärdensprache im mittelalterlichen Recht', *Frühmittelalterliche Studien*, 16 (1982), pp. 363-79; eadem, 'Mit Hand und Mund: Sprachgebärden aus dem mittelalterlichen Rechtsleben', ibid., 25 (1991), pp. 289-99. See now further Koziol, *Begging Pardon and Favour* (as n. 6).

[108]D O III 235 (18 December 996); for the background to the settlement, which is by no means fully described in the diploma, see F.W. Oediger, 'Adelas Kampf um Elten (996-1002)', in idem, *Vom Leben am Niederrhein: Aufsätze aus dem Bereich des alten Erzbistums Köln* (Düsseldorf, 1973), pp. 217-35.

[109]Widukind, *Res gestae Saxonicae* III 18, p. 114 lines 14-23; the quotation is lines 18-19: 'et festucam de terra sumens: "Huius", inquit, "pretii a me meaque potestae rapere non poteris..." '.

into Otto III's hands and protection with a stalk 'as is the custom of laymen'.[110] Henry's taunt thus may have had a deeper meaning. It was probably Widukind's way of exposing its hollowness, for almost overnight Henry's Bavarian counts deserted him and his capital, Regensburg his family and his treasure fell into Liudolf's hands.[111] Henry's gesture was thus ironically almost an *exfestucatio*, an act of handing over, the opposite of what he intended.[112]

Gestures thus had a dimension of their own. They enhanced and influenced speech but they could also serve as a means of communication in their own right. They were not only indispensable in legal proceedings but also in expressing inclinations and aversions in the atmosphere of conflict and intrigue that dominated courts and many noble households. A mere glance at the Bayeux Tapestry suffices to demonstrate this.[113] Men could be presented showing their feelings by gesture as much as by words. Once Widukind of Corvey described a scene of seemingly spontaneous bearing but it served, as always, a purpose. He used it to set aside for a moment the iron mould in which he had cast the image of Otto's kingship. When in 939 it was reported to the king, as he lay on the right bank of the lower Rhine opposite Xanten, that his disaffected brother Henry was advancing with full might against a small royal detachment that had already crossed the river, Otto did not conceal his anguish but showed it in motion and gesture. The *constantia* with which Widukind elsewhere endowed him, his unshakableness, is here made to fail the king. Otto was after all human, so Widukind wanted to tell his readers, only to impress them all the more with the forthrightness and power of the king's prayers and the strength of the bonds between the suppliant ruler and his divine protector Otto's greatly outnumbered detachment triumphed over Henry and his Lotharingian backers.[114]

Ritual that reveals much of its purpose and character attended also the judicial duel in the Ottonian world. Here is an example not treated by Robert Bartlett in his book on ordeals.[115] In 979 a certain Waldo accused Count Gero of Alsleben, belonging to the family of the great, deceased Margrave Gero, of an offence. He was arrested and handed over to Thietmar of Merseburg's father and uncle, Margrave Liuthar, for custody. Archbishop Adalbert of Magdeburg and Margrave Dietrich of the northern march, an enemy of the Gero-clan, seem to have been behind all this. The princes of the Reich, summoned to Magdeburg, found a judgement that Count Gero was to fight his accuser in single combat. This took place on an island in the River Elbe. The

[110] As n. 108.

[111] Widukind, *Res gestae Saxonicae* III 20, p. 115.

[112] W. Ogris, 'Festuca', in *Handwörterbuch* (as n. 12), vol. 1, cols. 1111-14, gives a survey of the range of meaning in legal contexts.

[113] H.E.J. Cowdrey, 'Towards an Interpretation of the Bayeux Tapestry', *Anglo-Norman Studies*, 10 (1987), pp. 49-65, stresses the importance of the gestures for understanding the tapestry.

[114] Widukind, *Res gestae Saxonicae* II 17, p. 82 lines 5-6, 11-24.

[115] R. Bartlett, *Trial by Fire and Water: the Early Medieval Judicial Ordeal* (Oxford, 1986), index s.v. 'battle, trial by'.

fight was savage: Waldo, himself severely wounded on the neck, struck Gero down by a blow on the head. Gero, when asked whether he could go on, had to say that he was unable to do so. Waldo himself collapsed and died but Gero was deemed to have been worsted and, by the emperor's and the judges' sentence, beheaded.[116] What matters here is the site of the judicial duel: an island in the Elbe where the two combatants were alone, severed from the outside world and its possible pulls.[117] Their only link was with heaven above and in this way the outcome of their battle became, or could be seen to become, a divine judgement. It did not convince all, for both Duke Otto of Suabia and Bavaria, Liudolf's son, and Count Berthold of Schweinfurt, who happened to arrive at court that day, bitterly blamed the emperor that such a man should ever have been condemned for so wretched a reason.[118] We don't know the charge, but they do not seem to have been able to stop the execution, which took place at sunset. It too was thus enfolded in ritual.

There is a remarkable parallel to the choice of an island as the site for Count Gero's and Waldo's duel so that they fought unattended under the eye of the just God above.[119] In 1073 King Henry IV was accused by one Reginher, a man of his own close following, of having plotted to murder Rudolf of Rheinfelden and Berthold of Zähringen at Würzburg. Reginher offered to prove his accusation by waging a duel. Eventually another of Henry's men, Udalrich of Cosheim, who had been named as an accessory, came forward to refute the charge and defend his master, and was ready to fight. The princes, according to Lampert of Hersfeld, our source, were already in revolt and made their future loyalty to the king dependant on the outcome of the duel. Henry accepted this and ordered that the allegations of both parties should be tried by the just judgement of God, that is that battle should be joined between Reginher and Udalrich after the octave of Epiphany on an island – Marsaue – in the Rhine (near Ingelheim). So once again we have an island site which was to sever the combatants from all contact with the partisan world and its pressures, to bring them face to face with the just Lord above. The duel was never fought in the end because Reginher died in madness.

Comparison with yet a third judicial combat reveals even more the awesome significance of fighting alone on an island. Ermoldus Nigellus in his *Carmen in honorem Hludovici* recorded a combat between two Visigoths, Bero and Sanilo, the latter having accused the former of treason.[120] Here the setting was

[116]Thietmar, *Chronicon* IV 9, pp. 106/108. On Gero's family connections R. Schölkopf, *Die sächsischen Grafen (919-1024)* (Studien und Vorarbeiten zum historischen Atlas Niedersachsens 22, Göttingen, 1957), p. 52. The relationship with Margrave Gero is not explicitly recorded, but seems very probable taking into consideration the name and the location of the lands of the two men.

[117]For Nordic parallels see O. Holzapfel, 'Hólmgangr', in *Handwörterbuch* (as n. 12), vol. 2, col. 219; Bartlett, *Trial by Fire and Water* (as n. 115), pp. 105, 114.

[118]Thietmar, *Chronicon*, IV 9, p. 108, lines 4-9.

[119]Lampert, *Annales* pp. 166-8, 170, 174.

[120]Ermold, *Carmen*, verses 1796-1875, pp. 136-42. The parallel accounts in the *Annales regni Francorum* and in the Astronomer's *Vita Hludowici* add nothing for our purposes.

quite different. The two men fought in a walled park near Aachen on horseback, but a troop was admitted with the duellers to save the defeated from death. The emperor himself watched from a high seat and gave the signal to begin. On a more macabre note, a certain Gundold had been admitted to the enclosure too with a *feretrum*, a bier, should it be needed. The contrast to the Ottonian duel of 978 could not be more marked. The encounter between Bero and Sanilo in the presence of a large throng had none of the eerie solitude of the Ottonian fight on an island or, for that matter, of the grimness of Tristam's duel with Morolt on the islet in the sea in Gottfried of Strasbourg's epos. The choice of an island had a heathen element; it was intended to exclude the possibility of sorcery.[121] The duel between Bero and Sanilo by contrast was an almost purely secular affair of a man seeking to defend his honour against a shameful reproach, in part resembling a duel between two nineteenth-century officers fighting over a slight or an insult.[122] Bero was defeated and therefore guilty, but Louis pardoned him. In Ermoldus Nigellus' account it was the emperor's piety and love of God which moved him to ask each man to confess, promising them his indulgence before they fought. He would have preferred them not to, but was, as so often, fettered by Frankish custom. There is no divine presence during the duel but it was to have effected a peaceful outcome of the anger-laden conflict.[123]

We must survey and sum up. The secular rituals we meet so markedly in Ottonian sources had a very special task to perform in a society where literary communications, at best confined and especially in Saxony a *novum*, had recently suffered renewed setbacks against an always massive and almost impenetrable orality. Even that may have been precarious: *facundia*, it must be remembered, was a gift, in the vernacular no less than in Latin.[124] Only through ritual was clarity achieved, an idea made intelligible and communicated to participants and onlookers alike. Visibility spelt understanding and so it pleaded for 'public' consent or at least acquiescence. The supernatural was needed badly but it had to be tangible, for only then could it be grasped and help to buttress belief. But with the rise of the Ottonian cathedral schools, the ubiquity and strength of Ottonian monasticism the later Saxon and Salian Reich soon recovered much of the ground that had been lost. Royal and princely ceremonial always mattered but with the rich historiography of the

---

[121]The *hólmgangr* was forbidden as a pagan custom in Iceland and elsewhere; cf. Holzapfel, 'hólmgangr' (as n. 117).

[122]U. Frevert, *Ehrenmänner: Das Duel in der bürgerlichen Gesellschaft* (München, 1991).

[123]Ermold, *Carmen*, verses 1873-4, p. 142.

[124]*Facundia* is often stressed in early and high medieval personality descriptions. For contemporary praise of Barbarossa's eloquence in his own language see K. J. Leyser, 'Frederick Barbarossa and the Hohenstaufen Polity', in idem, *The Gregorian Revolution and Beyond*, pp. 115-16 and n. 2; for the empress Theophanu cf. *Annales Magdeburgenses, MGH SS* 16, p. 152 line 27: 'ingenio facundam'; for Wigbert of Merseburg cf. Thietmar, *Chronicon* VI 36, p. 318 line 20; for Mathilda of Tuscany see P. E. Schramm, 'Eine wichtige Gestalt der späten Salierzeit: Die Gräfin Mathilde von Tuszien (†1115): Edition der "Notae de Mathilda Comitissa" ', in idem, *Kaiser Könige und Päpste*, vol. 3 (Stuttgart, 1969), p. 418: 'sermone erat facundissima.

eleventh century, ritual of the kind here encompassed can only have lost something of its special relevance. But even so we must not forget the vividness of gesture, of pleading hands and pointing fingers and their sheer visual power in late Ottonian art, for example the great gospel books of the later tenth and early eleventh century. That is, at first sight, the most memorable feature about them.[125] With the long gestation and the outbreak of the conflict over reform, a whole new genre and range of literacy and literature were born. The struggle spawned a volume, vehemence and tempo of polemics such as Carolingian Europe had never known. Lay investiture too was a ritual but it was assaulted and defended by a flood of writing that soon drowned and submerged the very cause that had brought it forth.[126] The losers in this conflict lost precisely because they could not forego a ritual that made power and its conferment visible and understandable as against those who could. In Norman England bishops still did homage (before consecration) but they received their temporalities by royal writ.[127]

It is time to return to our anthropological theorems and the question of their relevance to our attempts to understand the special role and meanings of the rituals in Ottonian society we have surveyed. It is clear that they performed all the functions postulated by the masters: they were a means of communicating and affirming status differences; they attended, summed up and dramatised rites of passage; and occasionally they expressed abstractions, and were thus a form of political thought, as in the case of Hermann Billung's regal entry in Magdeburg. They also performed tasks which the masters did not envisage but which were essential to the struggles and traumas of the Ottonian ambience, regal, regional and local. I have focused on secular rather than religious rites, if only to show how important they were, how vast a range of relationships they covered outside the church, for instance outside the exaltation of kingship by unction, coronation and crown-wearings, with which we normally associate so much Ottonian ceremonial. Widely and profoundly Ottonian society needed this secular magic. Ritual was the flashpoint of perception and response to situations that could not be managed without it, often the only way of being articulate. It was a 'language' in Lévi-Strauss's sense,[128] which nobles and

---

[125]H. Mayr-Harting, *Ottonian Book Illumination: An Historical Study*, 2 vols. (London, 1991), especially vol. 1, pp. 107-9, 117. See in general F. Garnier, *Le Langage de l'image au moyen âge: Signification et symbolique*, 2 vols. (Paris, 1982-1989).

[126]K.J. Leyser, 'The Polemics of the Papal Revolution', in idem, *Medieval Germany*, pp. 138-61.

[127]Cf. the classical evaluation of the English compromise by Hugh the Chantor, *History of the Church of York*, 2nd edn by C. Johnson, M. Brett, C. Brooke and M. Winterbottom (Oxford Medieval Texts, Oxford, 1990), p. 22: 'rex tandem inuestituras dimisit, dimissione quidem qua nichil aut parum amisit, parum, quidem regie dignitas, nichil prorsus potestatis quem uellet intronizandi'. For the transformation of episcopal installation from a symbolic to an administrative act in twelfth- and thirteenth-century England see M. Brett, *The English Church under Henry I* (Oxford, 1975), pp. 104 with n. 2 and 114; M. Howell *Regalian Right in Medieval England* (University of London Historical Studies 9, London, 1962), pp. 95-7; K.J. Leyser, 'The Anglo-Norman Succession, 1120-25', in idem, *The Gregorian Revolution and Beyond*, p. 105.

[128]As n. 4.

those about them understood and which filled out their thinking and horizons in ways that written instruments were as yet unable to match but could only imitate by their own solemnity. This may help to explain the grandeur and sumptuous finish of diplomata which could be recited and expounded like a sermon.[129] Ritual, like royal sacrality, could not prevent deviance and revolts, in fact these developed their own rituals, as we saw. Its role was thus to give voice and authority to attitudes and values, to make them felt, lived and shared. The acts we have surveyed on the whole contradict Durkheim's, Radcliffe-Brown's and Marcel Mauss's distinction between mystical, non-utilitarian and sacral as against common-sense and rational social action, for expositions of these rituals in terms of political rationality do not help us here.[130] Ritual, ceremony and gesture, if anything, proclaimed, transmitted and warranted the reasonableness of what was being done. They provided the magical component, the symbolic boundary of the comprehensible. They were the deep structures of consciousness which were what really held this society together, an archaic society it is true, but for all that one which perhaps mastered its conflicts more successfully than the incipient rationality of the eleventh century. The loss of the language of ritual might indeed be said to have been a further symptom of the deep irreconcilability of the many conflicts within the Salian Reich.[131]

[129]On the magical and ritual component in diplomata see H. Fichtenau, 'Bermerkungen zur rezitativischen Prosa des Hochmittelalters', in idem, *Beiträge zur Mediävistik: Ausgewählte Aufsätze*, 1 (Stuttgart, 1975), pp. 145-62; C. Brühl, 'Purpururkunden', in idem, *Aus Mittelalter* (as n. 9), pp. 601-19, and most recently Koziol, *Begging Pardon and Favor* (as n. 6), pp. 87-90.

[130]This as against Althoff, e.g. 'Bett des Königs' (as n. 54) p. 151: 'a purposeful and planned political action carried out quite deliberately' and 'Organisation' (as n. 72) p. 142: 'protection and assistance . . . were probably . . . the main aims of the *Vereinigung*'. See most recently his 'Demonstration und Inszenierung: Spielregeln der Kommunikation in mittelalterlicher Öffentlichkeit', *Frühmittelalterliche Studien*, 27 (1993).

[131]K.J. Leyser, 'The Crisis of Medieval Germany', in idem, *The Gregorian Revolution and Beyond*, p. 44: 'What had been relationships of gift and mutual obligation between the Liudolfings and their Saxon followers became attributes of kingship as such, impersonal and enforcible rules, menacing staging-posts almost on the way to statehood or at least institutionalised and legally concrete dealings as against the face-to-face arrangements between princely givers and their military *comitatus*. The Saxon nobles could not fathom this development and it goes far to explain their deep-seated and lasting estrangement'. See also G. Althoff, 'Königsherrschaft und Konfliktbewältigung im 10. and 11. Jahrhundert', *Frühmittelalterliche Studien*, 23 (1989), pp. 265-90 and T. Reuter, 'Unruhestiftung, Fehde, Rebellion, Widerstand: Gewalt und Frieden in der Politik der Salierzeit', in *Die Salier und das Reich*, 3: *Gesellschaftlicher und ideengeschichtlicher Wandel im Reich der Salier*, ed. S. Weinfurter (Sigmaringen, 1991), pp. 297-325, for the decline in the use of ritualised resolution of conflict in the later Salian period.

13

The Ascent of Latin Europe

My task tonight has not been made easier by the resplendent examples I must follow. Yet am I wholly fortunate and privileged to have Sir Richard Southern and Michael Wallce-Hadrill as my predecessors and judges. My indebtedness to them both is huge and continuous and it goes back many years, to the days when Richard Southern was in charge of Sir Maurice Powicke's seminar in 1947 and then, when Michael Wallace-Hadrill from Merton and in his his writings, taught me my first faltering steps in early medieval historiography. I acknowledge it gladly and I should also recall here the impulse I owe to Geoffrey Barraclough's *Mediaeval Germany*. Strictly speaking – and I say this without effrontery – I have no predecessors at all. A Chichele Chair of Medieval History did not exist until very recently indeed and I am its first occupants. I take this designation to mean no more than that I have spoken prose all my working life. It was the Regius Professor who recently, in a review, well defined the business of an inaugural lecture: it should crystallise thought.[1] It can, however, do a number of other things as well. It can survey and take stock of the situation of its subject. Where has the study of medieval Europe and England got to and in which direction is it moving? Are these the right marching goals? Furthermore, it can pause and dwell on the favourite authors and foremost sources the speaker is most deeply engaged with and what they tell us about the world he most wishes to evoke and illuminate. These are the two beacon-lights Sir Richard and Michael have lit and I shall try to steer by both of them and hope to present a crystal or two of my thinking at the same time. [2]

My title may sound strange but it was not chosen casually. Rises can be soaring and meteoric, an ascent always suggests effort, labour, and trouble, and occasional halts to fetch breath. It is one of these or, as I hope to show, but the semblance of a pause, I would like to dwell on today, the first half of the eleventh century before the turmoil and shrillness of what we sometimes call the age of Gregorian reform. Now anyone wishing to reflect on Latin Europe

* First published as *The Ascent of Latin Europe: An Inaugural Lecture Delivered before the University of Oxford on 7 November 1984*, Oxford: Clarendon Press, 1986, pp. 28. Thanks are due to the Syndics of Oxford University Press for permission to republish here.

[1] M. Howard, *The Times Literary Supplement*, no. 4253, 5 October 1984, p. 114.

must of course at once resort to the works of two outstanding scholars who, well over thirty years ago, re-charted our way into this topic, Ernst Curtius and Erich Auerbach. Yet Curtius, in his *European Literature and the Latin Middle Ages*, rather ignored what lay between the Carolingian and the twelfth-century renaissance as an intermediate period and in his *Mimesis* at least, Auerbach gave this moment of Latin writing and thought a miss too.[2] Later he dwelt on some tenth-century authors but their styles and expressive devices appealed to him more than the substance of what they had to say.[3] Curtius went further and in a lecture appended to the English version of his great book he considered that medieval thought and expression became creative only around the year 1050.[4] This is a very challengeable verdict and it shall be challenged here. However, the historian of Europe on the eve of the turmoil, taking stock, the historian who wishes to know how, when, and why Latin Europe began its climb to military, economic, and cultural dominance, how, when, and why it took the shape and shell it lived in until 1939, must above all face and come to terms with the commanding heights of recent and current French scholarship.

Its inspiration and aims lay in a new relationship between the pursuit of history and the social sciences which was proclaimed in a celebrated paper by Ferdinand Braudel published in the *Annales* in 1958.[5] It gave short shrift to Curtius, whose magisterial theme is characterised thus: the study of a cultural system which prolonged and, by its own [3] preferences, disfigured the civilisation of the later Roman empire which was itself weighed down by an oppressive heritage. More damning still was his view of the human sciences in crisis: They remained 'in the grip of a retrograde and insidious humanism which can no longer serve as their framework'.[6] The construction of a new framework, almost a new language – Braudel used the word – thus became the urgent and foremost task realised by, among others, a band of French medievalists. It was led by Georges Duby whose study of the Mâconnais, largely based on the charters of Cluny appeared some five years before Braudel's article and the statement of his aims can be taken as programmatic: 'To approach human beings directly without isolating them from their milieu, to follow the history of families and fortunes closely, to carry on simultaneously the study of activities and diverse institutions and to seize upon the bonds which united them.'[7] This alone can prepare the great syntheses and the search for them

---

[2]   E.R. Curtius, *European Literature and the Latin Middle Ages*, translated by W.R. Trask (Princeton, 1953) and E. Auerbach, *Mimesis: The Representation of Reality in Western Literature*, translated by W.R. Trask (Princeton, 1953).

[3]   E. Auerbach, *Literary Language and its Public in Late Latin Antiquity and in the Middle Ages*, translated by R. Manheim (London, 1965), ch. 2. See for example his comments on Rather of Verona and Liudprand of Cremona, pp. 133-56.

[4]   Curtius, *European Literature* (as n. 2), p. 589, Appendix, 'The Medieval Bases of Western Thought'.

[5]   F. Braudel, 'Histoire et sciences sociales à longue durée, *Annales ESC* 13 (1958), pp. 725-53.

[6]   Ibid., pp. 732, 725.

[7]   G. Duby, *La Société aux XIe et XIIe siècles dans la région mâconnaise* (Bibliothèque générale de l'école pratique des hautes études, VIe section, Paris, 1953), p. ix.

became, one can say, a consuming purpose. An undercurrent of scientific certainty, of geographical, ethnological, and economic model-making, of thinking in terms of structures, carried all before it. Georges Duby's Mâconnais was followed by Fossier's Picardy, Chédeville's Chartrain, Magnou-Nortier's south-west, Toubert's Latium and Bonassie's justly acclaimed Catalonia.[8] The most characteristic product of this band of scholars is thus the microcosmic and all-embracing regional study. The headlines for this were written some twenty years ago by Jacques Le Goff in the preface to his collection of papers, *Pour un autre moyen âge: Temps, travail et culture en Occident* translated under the title, *Time, Work and Culture in the Middle Ages*. The aim here was a historical anthropology of the pre-industrial west and it should be mentioned that Le Goff's middle ages stretch from the later Roman empire until the industrial revolution of the eighteenth and nineteenth centuries. They were to him the primordial past in which our collective identity acquired certain of its essential [4] characteristics. Le Goff has, of course, endorsed 'l'histoire à longue durée', as Braudel prescribed it. 'Vulgar' Marxism is rejected but 'material civilisation and culture must interpenetrate one another within a socio-economic analysis.'[9] It might be said that in this post-Marxist analysis we have a kind of historical materialism without the eschatology, without the immediate, unacceptable consequences for the present, just like a puritanism that has outlived the religious beliefs that had once given birth to it.

And the result? Here we have a grandiose recent synthesis, the work of Robert Fossier, two volumes in the *Nouvelle Clio* series entitled *Enfance de l'Europe*. It is a magisterial survey of the struggles of early medieval societies to break through their poverty trap, to enlarge and enrich themselves without doing so only at the expense of one another. Here again we encounter the restless and ceaseless search for *syntheses* and *structures* and, in particular, Fossier wishes to unfold three closely joined developments: first, the population increase – the insistently swelling wave of people, the greatest, he thinks, in the whole history of the continent. With it arose the settlements and villages as they are still today, on the whole, together with the more immediate phenomenology of new enterprise and expansion: religious, military and mercantile. Next comes, as a consequence, a loosening of familial bonds and their enrichment by other horizontal and vertical forms of association. Lastly Fossier presents, and here he is most emphatic not to say dogmatic, a process

---

[8] R. Fossier, *La Terre et les hommes en Picardie jusqu'à la fin du XIIIe siècle*, 2 vols. (Paris, 1968); A. Chédeville, *Chartres et ses campagnes, XIe-XIIIe siècles* (Paris, 1973); E. Magnou-Nortier, *La Société laique et l'église dans la province ecclésiastique de Narbonne de la fin du VIIIe à la fin du XIe siècle* (Toulouse, 1974); P. Toubert, *Les Structures du Latium médiéval*, 2 vols. (Bibliothèque des écoles françaises d'Athènes et de Rome 221, Rome, 1973); P. Bonnassie, *La Catalogne du milieu du Xe à la fin du XIe siècle: Croissance et mutations d'une société*, 2 vols. (Toulouse, 1975-76).

[9] J. Le Goff, *Time, Work and Culture in the Middle Ages*, translated by A. Goldhammer (Chicago, 1980), pp. ix-xiii. The quotation, from Maurice Lombard, is on p. xiii.

he calls 'encellulement', 'cellularisation' in the seignorial mould which left all initiatives in the hands of a few clerks and warriors.[10] The lives of most men, he points out, were dominated by the exploitive routines applied by these masters, the harsh institutions of local justice and labour services, and the *châteaux* on which they depended. There seems to be a remarkable unanimity about the all-importance of the ban, the rights and powers of coercion as a dominant theme of the eleventh century. A man was either [5] under it and subject to its humiliating burdens and sanctions, and most men were, or he escaped it, that is to say he belonged to the handful of *potentes* who enforced it or was one of the *milites* and clerks who helped them.

Yet however important these institutions became as modes of life, as the cast-iron order of economic and social concentration, *encellulement* did not, it seems to me, destroy all larger identities across the boundaries of castellany and lordship and must not become a sole dominant theme. It is here that the historiography of the tenth and early eleventh centuries comes to our help. Its horizons were scaled by latinity and Latin *christianitas*. History in the tenth and early eleventh century was the temporal framework of divine purpose manifesting itself. Through it, fallible human beings might fitfully apprehend what that purpose was. For men who had lived for generations through anxious seasons of war, heathen invastions, plunder and *depopulatio* and also the self-lacerations of *christianitas*, it is not surprising that history became one of their first preoccupations when the clouds began to life and conditions became a little easier to comprehend and reflect upon. Historiography was the most creative and also the most enduring achievement of later Ottonian and early eleventh-century Europe, much more so than Curtius and Auerbach allowed. It was also the way of bringing about a new and larger cohesion both among lay and clerical elites. Above all it had the critical task of integrating newcomers like the Polish, Magyar and Scandinavian aristocracies into Latin Christianity and it succeeded in performing it.

The Roman empire eventually collapsed because it was no longer able to absorb wave after wave of barbarians into its fabric. The Latin west and centre in the early eleventh century were able to do just that, to resist militarily and to impose culturally, not least of all through the agency of historical writing. Where military resistance failed, as in [6] Æthelred II's England, the cultural ascendency nonetheless triumphed. It was only as a *rex christianus*, seen in the company of the emperor Conrad II at his coronation in Rome that Cnut could hope to stabilise, rule, and transmit his conquests.[11] The empire too was now ringed by Christian eastern and south-eastern neighbours. These converts, whether they liked it or not, had to merge their own oral memories into a larger christological and eschatological context. For their symbiosis with

---

[10] R. Fossier, *Enfance de l'Europe, Xe-XIIe siècles: Aspects économiques et sociaux*, 1: *L'Homme et son espace* (Nouvelle Clio 17, Paris, 1982), pp. 71-2, 288, 290, 301, 364-422.

[11] Wipo, *Gesta Chuonradi II. Imperatoris* c. 16 in *Die Werke Wipos* ed. H. Bresslau (MGH SRG 61, 3rd edn Hanover, 1915), p. 36; *Florentii Wigorniensis Monachi Chronicon ex Chonicis*, ed. B. Thorpe (English Historical Society, London, 1848), vol. 1, pp. 185-9.

Christian Latin neighbours they had to find a place for themselves in a much larger past than they had known hitherto. For this process they often depended on teachers borrowed from their patrons and godfathers. Dudo of Saint-Quentin, the first historian of the Normans, was a clerk from Vermandois. The first historian of Poland, the Gallus Anonymous, seems to have come from Flanders.[12]

The historians of the late tenth and early eleventh century not only masked and documented a process of expansion which thus gives them their special place in the ascent of Latin Europe, they also unfold new forms of self-awareness, new ways of portraying both themselves and social relations. There was a new breadth as well as intimacy such as we do not quite find in the historical writings of the Carolingian world. Let us begin with Adémar of Chabannes.[13] Adémar was a monk at St Cybard in Angoulême but through his uncles he had close links with, and often stayed in, St Martial, at Limoges. Born in 988 he enjoyed an excellent education at St Martial and wrote first of all a history of its abbots, albeit as a monk of another house. His *Chronique*, in three books, is much the most essential historical work bearing on Aquitaine in the tenth and early eleventh centuries. There is scarcely another. To begin with a history of the Franks under the Merovingians and Carolingians based on sources like the *Liber Historiae Francorum*, the *Continuation of Fredegarius* and the *Annales regni Francorum*, from chapter xvi of the third book, the *Chronique* becomes Adémar's own. But this is not all. The all-consuming [7] business and interest of Adémar's life was his passionate attempt to prove that St Martial of Limoges had been one of Christ's disciples and one of the apostles. To this end he wrote a celebrated *Letter* which he sought to porpagate widely, and on this topic he addressed councils, in particular one in 1028, when he preached and disputed on his hobby-horse of a subject. Though of noble birth, Adémar was not a man particularly close to any court. He described the ambience of Duke William the Great of Aquitaine (993/4-1030) but there is almost nothing atypical in his account: the pilgrimages, the presents exchanged with other princes and the emperor Henry II, the constant attendance of bishops near his person, the pious patronage of monasteries, the advice of monks in the *administratio regni*, and the efforts to have the goodwill of Abbot

---

[12] On Dudo see now E. Searle, 'Fact and Pattern in Heroic History: Dudo of St. Quentin', *Viator*, 15 (1984), pp. 119-37, and his editor, J. Lair (below, n. 21). The origins of the Gallus Anonymus remain disputed. See Wattenbach-Hotzmann-Schmale, vol. 2, pp. 812-13 and in particular vol. 3, pp. 228*-30*.

[13] On Adémar see the two articles by L. Halphen in his *A travers l'histoire du moyen âge* (Paris, 1950), and also K.-F. Werner, 'Adémar von Chabannes und die Historia pontificum et comitum Engolimensium', *DA*, 19 (1963), pp. 297-325; Wattenbach-Holtzmann-Schmale, vol. 1, pp. 310-11, vol. 3, pp. 99*-100*; M. Manitius, *Geschichte der lateinischen Literatur des Mittelalters*, vol. 2 (Munich, 1923), pp. 284-94. For an incisive critique of Adémar as a source for Charles the Bald's reign, see J. Gillingham, 'Adémar of Chabannes and the History of Aquitaine in the Reign of Charles the Bald', in *Charles the Bald: Court and Kingdom*, ed M. Gibson and J.L. Nelson, 2nd edn (British Archaeological Reports, International Series 101, Aldershot 1990), pp. 41-51.

Odilo of Cluny: they are all part of a quasi-regal repertoire.[14] We hear much also about the counts of Angoulême in the *Chronique*, but if Adémar was an occasional visitor of their court he did not belong to it. Nor does he ever seem to have held an abbey and yet he was an important and prominent man. His numerous sermons at gatherings to propagate the peace movement, and its oaths, have survived. He accumulated and possessed a splendid library and was an industrious copier of manuscripts whose autographs have survived and been identified. He bequeathed his books to St Martial before setting out on a pilgrimage to Jerusalem from which he did not return and perhaps had not wanted to. He died in 1034. Altogether it is striking how influential and eminent a literate and erudite monk could be in early eleventh-century France and we shall meet other examples. In his obit notice it is set down that he commanded a *Life* of St Martial to be written in golden letters and many other books.[15] He had a large noble kin and was evidently a man of means.

Adémar's *Letter about the Apostolate of St Martial* was addressed not only to a number of local clerical notables, like [8] the bishop of Limoges, canons, monks, an architect, all at Limoges, learned men in the vicinity and various abbots, but it was also meant for the bishop of Rodez, for Bishop Dietrich II of Metz, the empress Cunigunde, Henry II's widow, the emperor Conrad II, and Duke William, 'grammatico, orthodoxo et potentissimo Aquitanorum duci'.[16] Adémar seems to have liked to use *grammaticus* for 'literate'. It was finally meant also for Pope John XIX. For the assessment of the emperor's place at the peak of the worldly hierarchy the inscription is worth remembering. His notice and approval were regarded as important and it was deemed right to try and gain them and not only the goodwill of Adémar's own prince, the duke of Aquitaine. Here, as elsewhere, it is apparent that the world before the investiture conflict had an inner cohesion which did not survive that upheaval into the twelfth century. Adémar's horizons were large and he knew, if in a somewhat blurred way, about men and events in the later Ottonian Reich. He knew, for instance, that Duke Henry of Bavaria, struggling for the kingship in 1002 had gained possession of the *insignia* by some determined arm-twisting, forcing Archbishop Heribert of Cologne to surrender them. He wrote about the foundation of Bamberg and the pope's consecration of it and that Henry II too cultivated Odilo of Cluny, listing his presents to the abbey. His report of Conrad II's election and succession is elaborate if confused. Here the bishops and *proceres* who elevated him were not called 'Saxons' as west Frankish writers sometimes described all their eastern neighbours. Once, at least, Adémar spoke of the *terra Theodisca*.[17]

---

[14] Adémar of Chabannes, *Chronicon* III 41, pp. 163-5.
[15] Ibid. preface, p. x n.3.
[16] Adémar of Chabannes, *Epistola de Apostolatu Martialis*, Migne, *PL* 141, col. 89.
[17] Adémar of Chabannes, *Chronicon* III 33, pp. 155-6; iii. 37, p. 160; iii. 62, pp. 187-8.

Most of what he wrote about Duke William V, we have said, belonged to a well-rehearsed genre of panegyric. Yet in one respect he enlarged on this and hit upon a theme that is central in his vision. William, he wrote, had been taught letters from boyhood and possesed a good knowledge of scriptures. He kept a fine library in his palace and when he took a break from the hubbub of ruling he applied himself to [9] reading for nights on end until sleep overtook him. Not content with this, Adémar linked his hero with a tradition of princely literacy. This is what Louis (the Pious) and his father Charlemagne used to do. More still, Theodosius 'victor Augustus' in the hall of his *palatium* not only read but even wrote with great zeal. Adémar concluded this reflection with a mention of Caesar: 'Octavianus Caesar Augustus' he called him who after his *lectio* wrote of his battles, Roman history, and other things with his own hand. Lupus of Ferrières had occasionally exhorted Charles the Bald to study and imitate the deeds of Trajan and Theodosius. Here a duke is praised for following and aligning himself with the examples from both Christian and pagan Antiquity. Evidently Adémar deeply approved of the continuity he thought he saw.[18]

In his very next chapter he described the Irish and Ireland. The island, he wrote, had twelve *civitates* with ample bishoprics and one king. It had its own language but Latin letters, 'propriam linguam, sed latinas litteras'. St Patrick, a Roman, had converted it. The importance Adémar attached to the latinity of the Irish is heightened by the context in which he mentioned it, a massive Norse attack. The Northmen, according to him, suffered a crushing defeat, none of them escaped.[19] It is not clear whether our Aquitanian author knew much about Ireland's religious past. For him it was a rather remote outpost of Latin Europe and *Christianitas* but is successful defence mattered to the whole of which it formed part. In an earlier chapter Adémar had described how William Longue-Epée succeeded Rollo in Normandy. He had been baptised as a boy and the whole body of Normans who lived close to *Francia* accepted the faith. They forsook their heathen speech and got used to Latin, *sermo latinus*.[20] This must not be taken literally. Nothing could show more clearly how much an observant Latin writer of the early eleventh century was aware of the shifting and uncertain frontiers of Christianity and latinity and there is his note of evident [10] satisfaction about the internal reconquest, as he saw it. Conversely Dudo of Saint-Quentin, in verses addressed to his patron (1014-15), Count Rudolf, made him the heir of Roman heroic *virtus*. Scipio, Pompey and

---

[18] Ibid. III 54, pp. 176-7.
[19] Ibid. III 55, p. 177.
[20] Ibid. III 27, p. 148: 'omnisque eorum Normannorum, qui juxta Frantiam inhabitaverunt, multitudo fidem Christi suscepit, et gentilem linguam obmittens, latino sermone assuefacta est'.

Cato, when they were consuls, Rome was aglow, now the Normans are on top and the *culmen honoris* belongs to Duke Richard I. Whether Dudo succeeded in flattering his Norman hosts by naturalising them in a Roman past we don't know. His work was after all dedicated to so deep-dyed an old fox as Bishop Adalbero of Laon, but at least he tried.[21]

Adémar's sensitivity to speech has left other marks in his *Chronicon*. Not long after the year 1000 the Moors of Cordoba attacked Narbonne suddenly and hoped to take it by sorcery. The Christians inside took the sacraments – Adémar's counterpoint – prepared for death and assaulted the enemy. They won and took many prisoners whom they enslaved and sold. Twenty huge Moors, however, they gave to St Martial at Limoges. The abbot of Gosfred kept two and Adémar remarked that their language was not that of the Saracens but they seemed to bark like dogs. Perhaps this meant they did not speak Arabic but some North-African Berber dialect.[22]

It would be quite wrong to ignore Adémar as the splendid source that he is for some of the processes so well analysed by Georges Duby and Robert Fossier. He tells us much about the peace movement with the relics of saints brought to huge assemblies where peace was preached but also intensive prayer against rampant disease offered. There are throngs of knights holding *beneficia* from a powerful abbot.[23] In a mid-winter campaign between Jordan of Chabanais and Bishop Alduin of Limoges, the former was suddenly attacked and struck down by an unknown *miles* when he was already victoriously on his way back with many prisoners. Characteristically the construction of a castle lay behind the war. Castles again were the key to lordship and the objects of savage warfare elsewhere in the area under Adémar's purview. [11] There was much blinding, even of a choirbishop, and revenge. Duke William when he could not hurt the real culprit maimed his brother instead.[24] Yet there was also an example of Christian forgiveness. When Count William of Angoulême fell ill less than a year after his joyful return from a Jerusalem pilgrimage a woman was accused of having procured his disease by *malefica*. The case was tried by a judicial duel in which the champion of the accusation defeated the defence. Nonetheless the count refused to let the woman, who had not confessed, be tortured again. He died of his illness on 6 April 1028. His son and successor proved to be less forbearing and according to another version of the *Chronique*

---

[21] *De moribus et actis primorum Normanniae ducum auctore Dudone Sancti Quintini decano* II 1-10, ed. J. Lair (Caen, 1865), p. 125: 'Versus ad comitem Rodulfum, hujus operis relatorem'.

[22] Adémar of Chabannes, *Chronicon*, III 52, p. 175: 'more catulorum loquentes, glatire videbantur'.

[23] Ibid. III 45, p. 168.

[24] Ibid. III 42, p. 166: 'Casu ab ignoto milite impetitus . . . interit.' On the blinding see III 25, p. 147; III 28, p. 150.

had the woman and the accomplices burnt.[25] Adémar ends his *Chronique* with the story of a successful military operation against Saracens in Spain whence the Gascon participants return with much booty. The northwards flow of wealth from the Taifa kingdoms had begun.[26] The process of *encellulement* did not bar a larger framework of action and vision.

Adémar of Chabannes had a contemporary whose historical writings even more than his own proclaim awareness of a new order, the birth of a new *ensemble* of peoples in a Christian *orbis Romanus*. That historian was Rodulf Glaber, 'the bald'.[27] What is more he seems to welcome this new order, to stress its discontinuity rather than bonds with the ancient Roman world and to approve of its political pluralism. Instead of one empire there were now two kingdoms and rulers, those of the Franks (west Francia) and the Saxons. Under their new kings the world began to flourish once more and thanks to their mutual peace the kingdom of Christ began to subject tyrants everywhere by the baptismal font. Glaber here celebrated above all the conversion of the Magyars, as elsewhere he was jubilant about the reopening of the land-route to Constantinople and Jerusalem which led necessarily through their settlements. He welcomed also the massive upsurge of the pilgrimage movement even though he did not conceal from himself or his [12] readers the conceit and boasting of many who had made the journey chiefly to be admired by their neighbours. To those who thought that the mass pilgrimage heralded the coming of Anti-Christ he replied calmly that, all the same, the devoted labour of the faithful who went would receive its reward from a just judge.[28]

Rodulf Glaber was born about 983, almost certainly of noble parents though he may have been illegitimate. In his great historical work, the *Historiarum Libri Quinque* which he wrote between 1026 and 1045, he is much more

[25] Ibid III 66, pp. 190-2. For the other version see G. Waitz's edition of Adémar in *MGH SS* 4, pp. 146 n. 2, 147 n. 2, and in J. Boussard (ed.), *Historia Pontificum et Comitum Engolismensium* (Bibliothèque elzévirienne, nouvelle série: Études et Documents, Paris, 1957), pp. 19-20. On the incident, a very early witchcraft trial, see M. Blöcker, 'Ein Zauberprozess im Jahre 1028', *Schweizerische Zeitschrift für Geschichte*, 19 (1979), pp. 533-55. The sources stress that the count had hitherto enjoyed rude good health: 'solebat enim robusto et sano corpore vigere' (Adémar of Chabannes, *Chronicon* p. 191). It was precisely this that roused the need to account for his languishing illness and so prompted the charges of witchcraft. The parallel with the situations described by E.E. Evans-Pritchard, *Witchcraft, Oracles and Magic among the Azande* (Oxford, 1937), pt I. iv.; pt. IV. v, is very striking. See now R. Landes, 'Between Aristocracy and Heresy: Popular Participation in the Limousin Peace of God, 994-1033', in *The Peace of God: Social Violence and Religious Response in France around the Year 1000* ed. T. Head and R. Landes (Ithaca, 1992), pp. 165-83.

[26] Adémar of Chabannes, *Chronicon*, III 70, pp. 194-5.

[27] On Rodulf, see Manitius, *Geschichte* (as n. 13), pp. 347-53; Wattenbach-Hotzmann-Schmale, vol. 1, p. 302-4, vol. 3, pp. 92*-3*; and the two recent editions, *Rodulfi Glabri Historiarum Libri Quinque* ed. J. France (Oxford Medieval Texts, Oxford 1989) and *Rodolfo il Glabro: Cronache dell'anno mille*, 3rd edn by G. Cavallo and G. Orlandi (Milan, 1991), both with bibliographies. On Rodulf's theodicy, proclaimed through the created world, see J. France, 'The Divine Quaternity of Rodulfus Glaber', *Studia Monastica*, 17 (1975), pp. 283-94. I have not discussed this here.

[28] Rodulf Glaber, *Historiae*, I v 22, p. 38; III i 2, p. 96; IV vi 18, pp. 198/200; IV vi 21, p. 204.

autobiographical than was Adémar. At the age of twelve, he related in Book V, a maternal uncle (and one cannot stress the importance of that relationship for the early middle ages enough) placed him in a monastery, St Leger-de-Champeaux, which was, however, subject to St Germain d'Auxerre. As a monk his life is more notable for constant movement, travel and migration than *stabilitas*. He is found at Moutiers, Bèze, at, above all, St Bénigne, Dijon, at Cluny, and at Rome. He knew and stood close to St William of Dijon, whose *Life* he wrote shortly after 1031, and also Odilo of Cluny to whom he dedicated his *Historiae*. He also knew Bishop Odalrich of Orléans who told him events and incidents, things he had experienced on his pilgrimage to Jerusalem. Once again, then, here is a monk who never rose to any prelacy but, nevertheless, was a man of importance whose company was sought after by his superiors who entrusted him with weighty tasks. He tells us how and why. In his early years Rudolf had been anything but a willing recruit to the regular life and while at St Germain or St Leger, he wrote, he exasperated his betters, his equals, and his juniors. Eventually they expelled him but they had no qualms about his future because he was a man of letters, he possessed what he called *litteratoriam notionem*, and those who drove him out felt that he would never want a roof over his head and a place to stay, on that account. Rodulf, moreover, nodded assent: it was the general experience.[29] [13] Men of letters in the west would not always be so confident.

Rodulf's *Histories* had of course many themes in common with Adémar's *Chronique* and this in itself is valuable evidence for what mattered to the *cognoscenti* of the early eleventh century. There again was the peace movement with its assemblies from near and far to which the relics and bodies of the saints were carried by their guardians, monks and clerks, to overawe the lay warriors and instil into them a sense of fear and sacrilege and so make them swear the oaths. Both writers shared the shock and concern about the discovery of heresy among a clerical élite in Orléans. Its very existence and luxuriant self-assurance can be read as a sign of well-being rather than crisis. Rodulf, like Adémar, mentioned the flow of booty from Spain, this time to the altars of Cluny, and he too told the tale of a count killed by a humble *miles* in action. Again there is much fighting round castles.[30]

Rodulf's *Histories*, all the same, differ profoundly from Adémar's *Chronique* in that they explore inwards as well as outwards. The demons that frightened him as he lay in his little bed were a part of himself with which he

[29] Ibid. V i 3, pp. 218/20.
[30] Compare Adémar of Chabannes, *Chronicon* III 35, p. 158; III 69, p. 194, and Rodulf Glaber, *Historiae*, IV v 14-16, pp. 194/96. Both authors, and in particular Adémar numerous sermons bearing on the peace movement, are discussed by H. Hoffmann, *Gottesfriede und Treuga Dei* (Schriften der MGH, 20, Stuttgart, 1964), pp. 27-31, 33-40, 54-6, 81-7, (Treuga Dei), 257-9, and now by the various contributors to Head and Landes, *The Peace of God* (as n. 25). On the Orléans heretics, compare Adémar of Chabannes, *Chronicon* III 59, pp. 184-5, and Rodulf Glaber, *Historiae*, III viii 26-31, pp. 138/50. On booty from Spain, see ibid. IV vii 22, pp. 206/08. On Count Reinald of Autun being killed by a *miles* 'generis infimi', see ibid., IV ix 26, p. 212.

struggled.[31] Their power was, like that of the heretics, all too real and fearsome. Adémar had revealed a society in which the saints sometimes had to do duty for the want of effective government. His *Chronicon* is also a great monument to Aquitaine and its links with *Latinitas* at large. Rodulf addressed himself chiefly to another, and perhaps more profound, function of medieval historiography of which mention has already been made: it was to give a secure temporal framework to the succession of events, to place them in a christologi-cal and eschatological context. Through it men could identify themselves with a larger scheme, and escaped from the chaos of accidents, from a succession of violent happenings, into a divine plan bounded at one end by the Old and the New Testament, and the struggles of the early church and martyrs, and at the other by the second coming. Rodulf achieved this in his very preface [14] when he announced that there had not been anyone for two hundred years who would tell future generations of the things that had come to pass in the churches of God and in the people, not since Bede and Paul the Deacon.[32] The imposing Frankish historiography in between he ignored, and his *Historiae* were dominated and orientated by the year 1000, and the thousandth anniver-sary of the Passion. These dates did not portend for him any imminent disasters; rather they pointed to a hopeful future. Rodulf was sparing with dates but he was deeply aware of differing reckonings of time. Some of his critics have blamed him for chronological vagueness but he did indeed see and write 'histoire à longue durée'.

Rodulf also wrote reflective history. He wanted to ponder over the many things and the men who had been renowned in the *orbis Romanus* from the year 900, but particularly round the year 1000. He also wanted to think about events and contingencies beyond and outside the *orbis Romanus*, overseas and in barbarious regions. Rodulf, too, is well aware of Latin Europe's frontiers and also, as we shall see, of frontiers within it. As a Burgundian he wanted to record what he had heard and lived to see 'in sacris ecclesiis et utroque populo', i.e. what befell the churches and both peoples, the Saxons and the western Franks (these were his words for Germans and French).[33] Their rulers, the emperor Henry II and Robert the Pious, he regarded as equals and the foremost in this part of the world. The Anglo-Saxons entered his horizons later, and like Adémar he knew of Cnut's conquest, but little more. Rodulf, as I have already said, welcomed the end of Carolingian rule because he thought the Carolingians' disappearance had brought peace between the royal families of East and West and so made possible Christianity's advance. His optimism lives through a famous passage when he described how, around the year 1002, in Italy and Gaul churches were being built and rebuilt like new white clothes for the whole world, not only cathedrals and monasteries but [15] also village chapels. This served only to introduce two munificent builders and

---

[31] Ibid. V i 2, p. 218.
[32] Rodulf to Abbot Odilo of Cluny, *Historiae*, pp. 2/4.
[33] Ibid. I i 4, pp. 8/10.

donors, Hervey, the treasurer of Tours who rebuilt St Martins, and William of Dijon.[34] But Rodulf's optimism and confidence went further still. In Book V of his *Histories* he explained: Christ when walking on the waters had allowed St Peter, whom he had set over his church, to walk with him, and by this he signified to the faithful that when all peoples had been subdued, but not altogether destroyed and extirpated, his kingdom would be estalished and endure for all times. The sea stood for the secular world. Here a programme of limitless aggression, of conquest and (forcible?) conversion emerges from the scriptural exposition, and already in Book IV Rodulf has reported a major Christian victory over the Saracens and Conrad II's successful campaign against the Slav and heathen Liutizi (1036). In Rodulf then the ascent of the *orbis Romanus* has already begun, and so he told his readers.[35]

This does not mean that he was silent about the calamities and disasters of his time, men's backslidings and the church's situation in the midst of them. A terrible and prolonged famine preceeded the thousandth anniversary of the Passion when the harvests recovered and there was plenty. The outbreak seems to have been confined to Burgundy but for Rodulf there was nothing accidental about it. He describes the manifestations and horrors of the catastrophe, no less vividly than do our television cameras today. The liquidation of church treasures did not always help the starving crowds because the food, bought at enormous cost, often reached them too late so that it killed rather than saved. Rodulf ended his account of the famine with a stark observation. He noted that this arcane misfortune of divine wrath did not lead men to contrition or pious supplication. Too much suffering dulled rather than roused religious sensibilities.[36] The church was thus not always master of the situation and men in despair did not always turn first to its ministrations for comfort. Rodulf [16] had peace and plenty follow these years of climatic disaster and mortality, to teach his readers the lesson of their creator's *magnanimitas*. We take belief in the populace and in the higher echelons of eleventh-century society for granted. In reality it was a struggle and insecure, something that had to be fought for constantly.

In Book V of his *Histories* Rodulf turned to man's links with the supernatural and in these spheres monks were the expert interpreters, almost the scientists. Here also he looked at the monastic condition and experience and we can learn from him better than from any other source I know of what it was like to be a monk in the early eleventh century. Here also the demon of self-doubt came to the fore with his insinuations: Why do you monks bother so with vigils, fasts, psalmodies and humiliations 'beyond the common usages of other men'? Are not countless laymen, steeped in disgraceful deeds up to the end of their days to receive the same rest as you? One day, one hour (of repentance) could suffice to earn the rewards, the eternal bliss of your justice. So why do

---

[34] Ibid. III iv-v 13-16, pp. 114/22.

[35] Ibid. V i 10, pp.228/30 and see IV vii-viii 22-3, pp. 206/10 (victories over the Saracens and the Liutizi).

[36] For the famine of 1031-2 Rodulf is the principal source: ibid. IV iv 10-13, pp. 186/92.

you trouble to rise at the sound of the bell when you might go on sleeping?' The demon addressing his victim – it is usually another monk, not Rodulf himself – continues: 'I'll tell you a secret though it is damaging to our, the devil's side. Each year on the day of his Resurrection Christ spoils all hell and leads his own back to the better world [*ad supera*]. So you have nothing to fear and can indulge what you fancy by way of carnal pleasure and desires.'[37] Rodulf here reveals a remarkable body of beliefs: that the harrowing of hell was a continuous process. The author is thus voicing gnawing doubts, whether monastic asceticism and intercession were essential in the scheme of salvation either for the living or the dead. He hastened to refute these doubts by the Gospels: not all were so brought back but Rodulf did not slam the door altogether on such insinuations. The falsest demons sometimes uttered things that were not wholly wrong. These apparitions could even [17] lead to self-improvement, but in general those to whom prodigies are shown, either by good or by evil spirits, don't live very long.

It is noticeable how many of these spasms of anguish, the encounters with the demon, occur in Rodulf's test when the bells rang for Matins, the time for rising at dawn or before. It seems to have been the critical moment in the monk's day when devotion most often threatened to break down. Rodulf also tells his readers how his communities dealt with coarse human habits, like spitting and how monks occasionally ran away to spend a few weeks in the world.[38] In his *Vita domni Willelmi* Rodulf was a fervent advocate of reform and its demand for strict and rigorous uniformity. All the more remarkable is his frank avowal of the strains and, for some, the almost unbearable tensions which communal disciplines, old and new, could impose.

The apex of Rodulf Glaber's *orbis Romanus* was the papacy rather than any secular ruler and its casing the church. In another celebrated passage the Roman coronation of the emperor was not a matter of course or of ritual only, but of papal choice and even examination, and this two centuries before Innocent III. The candidate had to be worthy of it. The criterion of *idoneiltas* is more than implied. The pope would not crown any tyrant who thrust himself forward, as had happened formerly. The orb with the cross, which Pope Benedict VIII gave Henry II in 1014, taught a lesson of service and obligation. Henry II, according to Rodulf, learned it respectfully and sent the *sphaira*, like so many other good things, to Cluny.[39] Rodulf almost certainly saw it there and was gratified. Equally firm was he in the rejection of Byzantine attempts to vindicate a certain ecclesiastical autonomy. Without his *Histoires* nothing would be known about the Greeks' approach to Pope John XIX in 1024 asking him to allow their church to be called universal within its own sphere. If Rome was compliant, corruptible or politic, the [18] zealots from the camp of monastic renewal were not and insisted on the *magisterium Petri*, the supreme power to

---

[37] Ibid. V i 1, pp. 216/18.
[38] Ibid. V i 7, p.224.
[39] Ibid. I v 23, pp. 38/40.

bind and loose. Here attitudes were hardening and Byzantium's exclusion and separateness lay already firmly embedded in Rodulf's world picture.[40]

Lastly, he was not merely aware of but, if anything, helped to propagate cultural frontiers within the *orbis Romanus*. It was precisely the plurality of rulers and *regna* that appealed to him and where again he pointed to the future. When Robert the Pious married his queen Constance, between 1001 and 1003 she brought with her a large following from Aquitaine and the Auvergne. Their levity of manners, clothes, weapons, horseharness, hair-styles and shoes were greeted with deep dismay and bitterly denounced by William of Dijon and his mouthpiece, Rodulf. Burgundians, hitherto decent folk, were infected and tarnished by these satanic fashions. Abbot William stood fast and declared that if anyone who had adopted them died, he could only with difficulty be saved.[41] Rodulf ended Book III with a poem where vestiary and moral turpitude went hand in hand. He was, moreover, not alone in his censures for a letter of exactly the same tenor has survived which Abbot Siegfried of Gorze addressed to Poppo of Stavelot damning Henry III's forthcoming match with Agnes of Poitou in 1043. The *honestas regni* in arms and horsemanship was at stake with the advent of French fashions, even before the marriage – besides the tonsure of beards, indecent clothes, and other things unheard of in the days of the Ottos and Henry II.[42] Here too dress and styles stood for a change of *mores* for the worse. Rigorists like William, Siegfried, and Poppo not only ruled their monks with a rod of iron, they also sought to control and to police the bearing of the lay aristocracy. But even here the preachers' horizons were regional rather than local.

So far we have seen the early eleventh century through the eyes of an Aquitanian and a Burgundian monk. It is significant that Rheims and the Île de France were for the [19] moment silent There was so far no Abbot Suger, no Guibert of Nogent, though we must not overlook Fulbert of Chartres. Even the *Life* of Robert the Pious, however, was written by a monk from the Loire valley, Helgaud of Fleury. The centres of gravity were all somewhere different from where they were going to be in the high middle ages. Further east they lay not yet in the Rhine valley but in the marches of Saxony, along the Elbe and the Saale. Here in the homeland of the Ottonians there had been a massive build-up of wealth, material culture and display resting on military strength and success which now, however, were no longer unequivocal and unchallenged. Eastern Saxony too was a land covered with recently built and dedicated, magnificent churches: cathedrals and monasteries, with markets, mints, and the beginnings of towns. There were rich silver mines, and the capacity to work in iron and make things, even to export some of them. There was now a Latin literature in which history once again stood to the fore. It flourished in monastic foyers, but there were also schools of wider learning in

[40] Ibid. IV i 2-4, pp. 172/76; and compare I iv 16, p. 30.

[41] Ibid. III ix 40, pp. 164/68.

[42] For the text of Abbot Siegfried's letter see W. von Giesebrecht, *Geschichte der deutschen Kaiserzeit, 2: Blüthe des Kaiserthums*, 5th edn (Leipzig, 1885), pp. 714-18, in particular p. 718.

Magdeburg, Hildesheim and Halberstadt. Here in east Saxony we meet a morose *esprit* who has confided in us, consciously addressing a posthumous audience with passion, deeply-grounded beliefs, and also a style of their own: I mean of course Thietmar of Merseburg.

Writers like Widukind of Corvey and Liudprand of Cremona achieve a rare literary stature. Relatively little known and rarely read as they are they belong, all the same, to a timeless category that transcends its own contingencies, so vivid a picture they convey of their worlds, their societies, and values. The same is true of that great and sombre memorial, the *Chronicon* of Thietmar of Merseburg.[43] Thietmar defies all the generalisations which have been advanced about the evolution of medieval historiography. He is individual and idosyncratic and reveals himself in all his quirks, his remorses and, at the same time, his deep concern for the salvation of others, friends, and acquaintances. Yet, according to current rules [20] and generalisations, he should echo models and be typecast. He is also intimate about himself, his family, his rulers, and archbishops where he should, under the canons of criticism in vogue, wear a mask of iron. Thietmar's sense of society is very infectious and his was already a complex society. Take, for instance, his own career. It had been intended by his father, Siegfried of Walbeck, that he should be a monk at Berge, the Magdeburg monastery, but in the end the count could not place him there and he joined the cathedral community instead. The canons were given a feast, lasting two days, when he entered.[44] One wonders what stood in the way at Berge where a younger brother, Siegfried, to whom he dedicated the *Chronicon*, later served. It is easy to see why Thietmar was to have become a monk. He was physically a little handicapped and rather a sight. The Ottonians liked good-looking bishops in the secular church – men of stature, literally, who stood out over the shoulders of the crown as rulers should. Thietmar was small, he had a facial swelling and a broken nose that had never healed properly. The last was caused by an accident in his boyhood but he has not told us how it happened.[45] He had, however, an indefatigable memory, and an irresistible urge to record and write about himself, his kin, his contemporaries, and the Ottonian Reich at large. His prompting stemmed from a restless conscience, a vivd capacity for self-reproach which, in his case, could not be assuaged by acts of penance but only by writing about it, an so we are the gainers.

Thietmar's panorama is *christianitas*. He had, however, inherited from Widukind an ethos which marked barbarians off from Christians, and even newly-coverted ones could not always at once and automatically bridge the gap in his esteem. A distinction between us and them underlay his judgement, not only between his aristocratic milieu and the *plebs* but also his Saxon stem-pride towards Poles, Czechs, not to mention Elbe Slavs and others. For their

---

[43] On Thietmar see H. Lippelt, *Thietmar von Merseburg: Reichsbischof und Chronist* (Mitteldeutsche Forschungen 72, Cologne, 1973); Leyser, *Medieval Germany*, p. 246; above, 'Three Historians', pp. 27-8.

[44] Thietmar, *Chronicon* IV 16, p. 150.

[45] Ibid. IV 75, p. 218.

heathen sanctuaries and religion, [21] however, he is by far the most acute observer, who mastered a Slavonic dialect and commanded much personal knowledge of the Sorabian and Liutizi tribes. Seen in this light Thietmar can be regarded as one of the first of the ethnological experts who later became so characteristic of the expanding Latin west. Adam of Bremen in the eleventh century is another. Organised geographical and historical knowledge and a growing body of historical and ethnological literature became thus essential tools and presuppositions for practical measures and the employment of men, arms, and resources in the eastwards enlargement of the Reich. And Thietmar's work was not forgotten but entered and soon belonged to a swirling current of Saxon historiography, a current which became a broad stream in the twelfth century. Nor must his knowledge of Anglo-Saxon England under Danish assault, of the troubles and feuds of the lower Rhenish region, his occasional news of France, his excellent news of the Burgundian kingdom, his interest in Byzantine shipping, and Italian astuteness, be ignored when we seek to put together his horizons.[46]

He was, all the same, not unique for he shared with Rodulf Glaber the autobiographical vein, and the penchant for self-reproach, and Adémar of Chabannes, the historian of Aquitaine, captured the same episodical and personally-linked form of treating recent and contemporary events. Unlike Thietmar, Adémar, as we saw, had a bee under his bonnet, the apostolate of St Martial to which he devoted so much time and attention. To prove his point he would stop at very little in his writings and sermons. Thietmar, more modestly, only misdealt some of the cards, i.e. he tampered with charters on behalf of his beloved and only recently-revived see, the bishopric of Merseburg. All three men had more profound things in common: their historiography rested on the belief that the historical process was divinely directed and that men, if they acted rightly, would experience God's mercy and gifts. Conversely, if they sinned, they must endure [22] setbacks and catastrophes. These were divine punishments. This meant, however, that just as men could strive for their personal salvation so they could by collective good conduct avert misfortunes, starvation, heathen raids, or whatever. In this roundabout way then, as well as by the employment of their *virtus*, men made their own history and were by no means subject to blind chance or incomprehensible forces. The idea that man made his own history, as Vico taught it, may have been secularised but that does not make it any less a legacy from the Latin middle ages.[47]

The characteristics of this early eleventh-century historiography must be looked for in both its treatment of social relations, and individuality. Medievalists are, perhaps understandably, inclined to illuminate their themes through

---

[46] Ibid. VII 36-7, 39-43, VIII 7, pp. 442-3, 446-50, 502, on England; VII 47-9, pp. 456-8, on the lower Rhine; VII 27-30, pp. 430-4, on the kingdom of Burgundy; III 23, p. 126, on Byzantine ships; VII 2, p. 400 on Italian guile.

[47] I. Berlin, 'Vico's Concept of Knowledge', in *Against the Current*, ed. H. Hardy (Oxford, 1981), pp. 11-19, and cf. p. 95.

climaxes. The growth of self was a slower and perhaps more varied process, with more markers, than the great presence of, say, a Lupus of Ferrières or an Abelard might suggest. Here the early eleventh century with Adémar might suggest. Here the early eleventh century with Adémar, Rodulf Glaber, and Thietmar once again heaves into sight. The political world of Thietmar was imposing, well-ordered, and magnificent, that of the two other men at any rate improving. Their decades were a moment of balance, relative calm, and cultural cohesion, before the great crisis of Gregorian reform in the secular church and the investiture conflict. For the south of France that was damaging and the prelude to heresy. In the Reich it proved a tragedy, dividing Germany, forming lasting fronts, associations and aversions within it, such as had not existed before. It also violated Germany from its western neighbours, an isolation that became almost permanent. The voluminous writings about the right relations between *ecclesia* and *regnum* were in the Reich for local audiences only. They did not ring the changes in France or in England. Here lay perhaps another tragedy. The Anglo-Norman coalescence heightened the acuteness of the Franco-German frontier even [23] if Anglo-Norman kings sometimes allied with Salian emperors.

In a fundamental way then the early eleventh century mattered for the configuration of Latin Europe. Its new pluralistic self-awareness, growing confidence, and capacity to reshape the horizons of newcomers, however violent, now began to form a groundwork of attitudes that proved to be remarkably resilient and enduring. Ascent was not just a matter of increasing resources, well deployed, of new military skills, well marshalled. It was, as I hope to have shown, also the work of a society exceptionally well served and well instructed by its historians who were really (forgive the military metaphor) the 'intelligence-officers' of its aims and directions. Here lay one of the Latins' special strengths. Byzantine historiography had above all the task of preserving and safeguarding a past, and to defend it against all comers.

To conclude, I'd like to remind you of an Oxford tradition in medieval historical studies. It goes back to Sir Maurice Powicke and is very alive in the work of Sir Richard Southern and Michael Wallace-Hadrill. It is the intuitive practice of allowing imagination and literary sensibilities to open up direct lines of communication between the historian and his subjects, not least of all his medieval forebears. While they must be understood and interpreted with the help of all the arsenal of critical and philological scholarship, they can and should be also encountered directly, and enjoyed, like any great literature, immediately. Cultural history is therefore not only a reflection of material conditions and predicaments. It is also a timeless dialogue in which, without mystification, we can and must join. The words, images and conceptual moulds of these three, and many other, early- and high-medieval historians are still related to our inner selves, our modes of speech, imagination and feeling. They, like the survivors of the visual arts, are part of our roots and should be cultivated. The humanism still needed to do so, if I may contradict [24]

Ferdinand Braudel, is neither retrograde nor insidious. This is not polemic against the search for new and more bridges between history and the social sciences but a passionate reminder not to neglect or forsake, but to look after and share, this awesome and wonderful legacy.

Index

Aachen 22, 30, 47, 48, 81, 164, 169, 198, 211
—, as second Rome 8
—, Henry I and 81
—, Ottonians and 177
—, *sedes regni* 23
Abbo of Fleury, on three orders 55
—, political theories of 179
Abd ar-Rahman III, caliph of Cordova 14, 131-3
Abelard 231
Abraham, bishop of Freising 16, 113-14, 129
—, and Liudprand 113
Adalbero, archbishop of Rheims 166, 173
—, letter to Adalbero of Verdun 171
—, links with Theophanu 172
—, on Charles' claims to kingship 175-6
Adalbero, bishop of Laon 178, 222
—, on three orders 55
—, political theories of 179
Adalbero, bishop of Verdun 171-2
Adalbero, count palatine of Saxony 182
Adalbert, *dux Austrasiorum* 24
Adalbert II, margrave of Tuscany 10
Adalbert of St Maximin, archbishop of Magdeburg 112, 151, 168, 193-4, 198-9, 201, 209
—, on imperial problem 153
—, purpose of *Chronicon* 30, 153
Adam of Bremen, historian 230
—, on pagan northern Europe 17
Adela of Elten, plots against rival Wichmann 40-1
—, settlement with Elten 208-9
Adelheid, abbess of Quedlinburg 203
Adelheid, empress 97, 128, 135, 165-6, 166, 171, 178, 201
—, lands of 162
—, rivalry with Theophanu 89
Adelheid, wife of Hugh Capet 178-9
Adémar of Chabannes, historian, and cult of St Martial 220
—, career of 219

—, on Irish 221
—, on Northmen 221
—, world view of 219-20, 223
Ælfgifu, sister of Edith 83
—, husband's identity 84
Ælfheah, archbishop of Canterbury, martyred 95
Ælfric, homilist 124
Ælfthryth, wife of Edgar, coronation as queen 97
Ælfwold, bishop of Crediton 107
ætheling 84-5
Æthelred II, king of England 109-10, 218
Æthelweard, ealdorman and historian 78
—, knowledge of Ottonian affairs 98
—, letter to Mathilda of Essen 74
—, on Ælfgifu's marriage 85
Africa, continent 2, 7, 12, 14
Agenor, father of Europe 2, 5, 10
Agobard, archbishop of Lyons, on Louis the Pious's deposition 63
Aistulf, penance imposed on for murdering wife 60
Alberic, *princeps Romanus* 147
Albgis, condemned for wife-abduction 63
Alcuin, on Charlemagne's successes 6-7
—, conception of Europe 7
Alduin, bishop of Limoges 222
Alexander III, pope, sends Frederick Barbarossa fatted calf 204
Alexis Comnenus, Byzantine emperor, and crusaders 52
Andernach, battle at (876) 46-7
—, (939) 90, 123
Angli 74 and n.2
Anglo-Saxons, sense of kinship with Old Saxons 74-5
Annalista Saxo 87, 199
Annals of Fulda 193-4
—, on Arnulf's kingship 11
Anno, archbishop of Cologne 64
—, kindred of 188

Anselm, St, on atonement 117
Ansfried, bishop of Utrecht, as sword-bearer to Otto I at coronation 149
—, lays down sword on becoming bishop 66 and n. 70
Aquitaine, customs of disapproved of 228
arengae as source for Ottonian emperorship 160
Aripert, Lombard king 3
aristocracy, itineracy of 35
—, literacy of 4, 19
armies, Byzantine 145-6
—, command of 36
—, concerted attacks by 38
—, effect on of deaths of leaders 39ff
—, indiscipline among 37
—, subdivisions of 36
—, vulnerability of after victory 46
armillae, as sign of rank 35, 55
Arnulf, bishop of Halberstadt, knights of 38
—, supports Ekkehard of Meissen 203
Arnulf, bishop of Orleans 170-1
Arnulf, duke of Bavaria 77
Arnulf of Carinthia 85, 130 and n. 21, 147
—, allies with Magyars 14
—, becomes king 11
—, defeats vikings 74
arson, in warfare 32
Aschaffenburg, feud at 187-8
Asia, continent 2, 7, 14
Asser, historian 106
Athelstan, king 77
—, and Danes 102
—, and manuscripts 82-3
—, and Ottonians 76, 82
—, backs Louis IV's restoration 94
—, commemorated in Suabian monasteries 81, 84
—, royal styles of 82
—, stories about low birth of 76-7
Attigny 179
—, sack of Carolingian palace at 169
Atto, bishop of Vercelli 111-12, 119, 124
Auerbach, Erich 216
Augustine, St, on Europe 1-2
—, on Europe-myth 5
Avars, Frankish losses against 39
—, war against 7, 30, 138

B, author of Life of St Dunstan, identity of 92 and n. 97, 94
Balderich, husband of Adela of Elten 40, 208-9
Baldwin, count of Flanders, joint attack on by Henry III and Edward the Confessor 99
Bamberg, foundation of bishopric at 220
Basil II, Byzantine emperor 145, 160, 173

basileus ton phraggon, title 155
Bayeux tapestry 109, 209
—, depiction of armour on 68
—, Odo of Bayeux comforts 'boys' 52
Beatrix, duchess of upper Lotharingia 166
Bede 106, 225
—, bequeaths pepper 101
—, on Europe 1
beds, ritual function of 174
belts 41, 55ff
—, assumption and laying down as rite of passage 59
—, *cingulum militare* as equivalent of public office 61
—, *cingulum militare* in Roman legal texts 60-1
—, in Anglo-Saxon wills 56
—, military ones unsuitable for clerics 56
—, penitents to forego use of 57ff
—, stolen 55
—, symbols of military status 57-8
Benedict V, pope, deposition of 128
Benedict VIII, pope 227
Benevento, campaign against (867) 44
Berengar I, king of Italy 147
Berengar II, king of Italy 31, 126-8, 132-3, 147
—, Otto I keeps waiting at Magdeburg 200
—, submits to Otto I at Augsburg 62
Bernard, king of Italy, blinding and killing of 63
Bernard I Billung, duke of Saxony, supports Ekkehard of Meissen 203
Bernard II Billung, duke of Saxony 38
—, comforts Wichmann's followers 41
Bernard of Septimania 21
—, and empress Judith 63, 65
Bernhard, bishop of Halberstadt, opposes archbishopric at Magdeburg 148
Bernward, bishop of Hildesheim, confirms Gandersheim's possessions 82
—, kin of 182
Bertha, daughter of Lothar II 10
Bertha of Turin, wife of Henry IV 64, 91
Berthold, margrave of the northern march 16
Berthold of Zähringen, duke of Carinthia 210
Bible, study of in tenth century 111, 194
Billungs, family feud of 37
Birten, battle at 122-3
blinding, Carolingian and Ottonian attitudes to 24, 156, 222
boasting, importance of in warfare 42
—, ritual of 205
Boleslas I, duke of Bohemia 192
Boleslas II, duke of Bohemia 17, 162
Boleslas Chrobry, duke of Poland, allows Saxon leaders' bodies to be recovered 39

—, and Margrave Hodo 207
—, Henry II's campaigns against 37-8
Boniface, St, makes gift of pepper 101
—, and conversion of Saxons 74-5
Boniface IV, pope 5
Bouvines, campaign of 38
Bovino 158
Breisach, place for rebellions 201 and n. 74
—, siege of 90-1, 123
Brenta, battle of 37
Bretons, Louis the Pious's campaign against 8
Brun, archbishop of Cologne 33, 80, 92, 112, 149, 151
—, kindred of 186
—, role in west Francia 103, 168
Bruno, bishop of Langres 166 and n. 8
Burchard, bishop of Worms 65, 188
—, on restrictions on penitens 59ff
Burchard III, duke of Suabia, campaigns in Italy 32
Burchard the Venerable, on knighthood 71 and n. 86
Byrhtnoth, earl 42
Byzantium, importance of Europe to 12
—, western embassies separated at, 139
—, see also, Constantine Porphyrogenitus; Liudprand; Nicephorus Phocas; Theophanu

Caesar, Julius, on 'soliciting' followers 26
camel 162
Cannstatt, battle of 183
Canossa 65
Canterbury, Christ Church 82
Capetians 165
capitularies 195
Carloman, Frankish king 183, 186
Carolingian culture, crisis of 193
Carolingians, and Lotharingia in tenth century 168, 177
—, marriage-practices of 77
—, 'solicit' their magnates 26
castles, and lordship 222
—, and warfare 31, 224
cattle 45-6
Cathwulf 8
—, homily to Charlemagne 6
chapel, imperial 151-2
Charlemagne, emperor 62, 140
—, acknowledged as emperor by Byzantines 153-4
—, as Caesar 9
—, coronation of 149
—, educational programme of 194
—, gifts to 'Lybians'
—, imperial activities of 150-1
—, imperial rank of 7
—, 'lighthouse of Europe' 8

—, model of rulership 20, 26, 221
Charles, duke of lower Lotharingia 165, 169, 172, 178
—, and bishopric of Cambrai 174-5
—, denounced by Dietrich of Metz 176
—, disinheritance of 179
—, excluded from west Frankish succession 174
—, family lands of 174, 177
—, followers of 175-6
—, marriage of 175
—, possible antikingship of 174
—, relations with Lothar 174
—, seeks Theophanu's support 177-8
Charles III the Fat, emperor 147
—, deposition of 11
—, lays down *cingulum militare* in 873 66-7
Charles III the Simple, king of west Francia 93, 177
Charles Martel, defeats Arabs 15
Charles the Bald 20, 195
—, and Louis the German 23
—, as 'Europe's glory' 9
—, at Fontenoy 42
—, birth 19
—, campaigns against Vikings 44
—, girded with sword on reaching manhood 56
—, relations with magnates 177
—, tactics in early 840s 22
Christian attitudes to Muslims in tenth century 130, 134, 141
Christians, bad ones equivalent to pagans 32-3
Chur 144
cingulum militare, see belts
Clausewitz, Karl von, definition of war 29, 49
clothing, clerical dress inappropriate for hostage 207
—, symbolic aspects of 206
Cluny 224, 227
—, appeal of to lay nobility 194
Cnut, king of England and Denmark 225
—, and house of Wessex 99
—, as *rex christianus* 218
—, empire of 102
Coenwald, bishop of Worcester 82
—, embassy to Henry I 81
—, makes gifts to Continent 96
colloquium dominarum 166, 178
Columba, St, joke about 79
—, letters to popes 5
Compiègne, meeting at (985) 169, 172
—, sack of Carolingian palace at 169
Conrad, king of Burgundy, wives of 84
—, Otto I and 85
Conrad I, king 36, 42

Conrad II, emperor 220
—, campaigns against Slavs 226
—, coronation of 218
—, succession of 203
Conrad the Red, duke of Lotharingia 103, 168
—, corpse stripped by Slavs 55
—, husband of Liutgard 76, 98-9, 103
—, rebels against Otto I 89, 198, 208
consors regni, title of queens 102, 160
Constantine Porphyrogenitus, Byzantine emperor 14, 124, 128, 137
—, on Otto I's kingship 150
Constantine, relics of 73, 74 n. 2
Cordoba 127, 131-4
Cotrone, battle 98, 161
Coulaines, treaty of 25 and n. 34, 177
councils, Merovingian, on incompatibility of penance and military activity 61
Croats 150
crown-wearing 190, 194
crusade, first 18, 69, 146
Cunigunde, wife of Henry II 77, 220
—, kindred of 32
cunning, valued in military leaders 42
Curtius, Ernst 216

Dado, bishop of Verdun 193
Daleminzi, Slav tribe 197
devil 226-7
Dietrich, bishop of Münster, buries and avenges Wichmann 41
Dietrich, bishop of Metz 174 n. 47, 220
—, escorts Theophanu from Byzantium 158
—, hostility to Theophanu 141, 158
—, kindred of 186
dikaiosyne 161
diplomata, ritual aspects of 213
disease, problems of in campaigning 44-5
dog, carrying of as punishment 197
—, used to insult, 197
Dortmund 198
Doubting Thomas, story of 122
Drogo of Paris 111
Dudo of Saint-Quentin, historian 219, 221, 222
duel, island as site of 210-11
—, judicial 222
—, ritualised 209ff
Dunstan, St, archbishop of Canterbury 79
—, and Edmund's death 94
—, relations with King Edmund 92-3
Dyle, battle of 47, 74
dynatoi 144

Ealdred, archbishop of Worcester and York, embassy to Germany and Hungary 99

east Frankish kingdom, formation of 24-5
Eadred, king of England 95
Easter-keepings, Ottonian 198, 202
Eberhard, duke of Franconia 81, 196-7
—, Eresburg campaign against Henry I 42-3
—, rebellion of 90
—, receives Henry I in Franconia 78
—, Widukind depicts as unsuited to kingship 43-4
Edgar, king of England, and Otto I 103
—, coronation at Bath 96-7
—, embassy to Otto I 95ff
—, excessive favour shown to foreigners by 99-100
—, *pactum pacis* with Otto I 95-6
Edith, wife of Otto I, and Magdeburg 91, 104
—, at Lorsch during uprising of 939 90-1
—, death of 88, 91, 93-4, 151
—, dowry of 82
—, following of 92
—, Hrosvitha on descent of 78
—, intercedes for the sins of Otto I 91
—, interventions of in diplomata 88-9
—, marriage to Otto I 76ff
—, piety of 91
—, possible coronation of 87
—, reconciles Mathilda with Otto I 90
—, role of in Ottonian polity 102-3
—, sanctity of descent 78
Edmund, king of England 76, 168
—, backs Louis IV 94
—, commemorated at Pfäfers 84
—, death of 94
—, factions at court of 93
—, near escape in Cheddar Gorge 92
Edmund Ironside, king of England 54
Edward the Elder, king of England 76, 98
Edward the Confessor, king of England, kinship with Henry III 99
—, laws of 74 and n. 2
Egbert, archbishop of Trier 165
Eid, bishop of Meissen 39
Einhard, influence on Widukind 27
—, on Charlemagne 20
—, on Charlemagne and foreigners 131
—, on Charlemagne's imperial coronation 149
—, on Frankish expansion 6
—, on Franks and Saxons 10, 75
—, on Hildegard's kindred 182-3
—, on Spanish campaign of 778 39
—, on subject peoples 29
—, source for Poeta Saxo 10
Ekkard, Saxon warrior 37-8
Ekkehard of Meissen, bids for kingship in 1002 203
—, murdered 204
—, possible Ottonian affinity of 204

—, usurps royal meal in 1002 203
Elster, battle of 34, 41, 68
Emma, daughter of Adelheid 89, 166
emperorship, Byzantine 144-5
—, Byzantine and Ottonian 143, 164
—, 'non-Roman' 146
—, Ottonian 148, 154
encellulement 217-18, 223
Erchanger, Suabian noble, condemned at Hohenaltheim 64
Eresburg 195
Erfurt, assembly at 85-6
Ermenrich, abbot of Ellwangen 9
Ermoldus Nigellus, panegyric on Louis the Pious 8-9, 210-11
Essen, cross of 98
Eugenius Vulgarius, Neapolitan historian 11-12
Europe, and papacy 5-6, 12-13
—, defensive term in late ninth and tenth centuries 13-14
—, expansion of in late eleventh century 18, 68-70
—, geographical limits of in antiquity 2
—, 'in nearly all Europe' rhetoric 9, 15
—, knowledge of concept in early middle ages 3-4
—, Latin 215ff
—, medieval conceptions of 1ff
—, shift in Carolingian conception of 8
Europe, daughter of Agenor 10
Everger, archbishop of Cologne 173
Evracher, bishop of Liège 92
exercitus, equivalent of assembly 62
exfestucatio 209

facundia, see fluency
famine 226
fasting, before battle 204-5
Fatimids, embassies to Otto I 15, 96, 132
festuca, ritual role of in legal proceedings 208
feudalism, instability of 26
fideles sancti Petri 69
fish-sauce 136, 141
Flarchheim, battle of 34
Florence of Worcester, historian 54
fluency (*facundia*) 159, 211
Folkmar, bishop of Utrecht 182
Fontenoy, battle of 22-4
—, as judgement of God 42
Fossier, Robert, view of post-Carolingian age 217
Franco, bishop of Worms 188
Franks, supposed Trojan origins of 4-5
—, peoples subject to 7ff, 29
fraternitas, royal 23
Fraxinetum, Saracen base 130-2, 134-5

Fredegarius, on Europe 1
—, on Franks 4
Frederick, archbishop of Mainz 112
—, hostility to Otto I 62, 198
Frederick I, duke of Suabia 34
Frederick Barbarossa, emperor
—, regulates conferral of *cingulum* 66
—, rewards warriors at siege of Tortona 70
Fulbert, bishop of Chartres 111, 228
Fulcher of Chartres, on *armigeri* 69 and n. 83
furs, mark of nobility 207

Gaius, on affines and cognates 184
Gallus Anonymous, historian of Poland 219
Gandersheim 82
—, Gospels 82 and n. 40
Garigliano, battle of 147
Gerard, bishop of Cambrai, on three orders 55
Gerberga, sister of Otto I, marries Giselbert of Lotharingia 93
—, marries Louis IV 94, 170
Gerbert of Aurillac 165-6, 177
—, and Otto III 164
—, letters 165, 172, 178
—, links with regency government 173
Germanic peoples, not originally part of Europe 3
Gero, archbishop of Cologne 79, 126, 156
Gero, archbishop of Magdeburg 41, 188
Gero, margrave of northern march, ambushed and killed 38-9, 41
—, ravaging of lands of 46
Gero, margrave under Otto I 41
—, and Abodrites 42
—, boasting-match with Slav chieftain 206
—, cunning of 42
—, support for Wichmann Billung 192
Gero of Alsleben, accused of treason 209
—, fights duel and loses 210
Gerold, father of Hildegard, family of 183
Gertrude, St, *Life* of, 3
gestures, as means of communication 209
—, in art 212
gifts, exchange of 83, 103, 132
—, giving 96, 128, 162
Gilbert Crispin, abbot of Westminster 117
girding, manhood ceremony 56
Gisela, wife of Conrad II 77
Giselbert, duke of Lotharingia, 81, 90, 93, 122
—, corpse stripped 55 and n. 19
grace, royal, ritualised nature of 200
Greek fire 145
Gregory I, pope 5
Gregory V, pope 16
Gregory VII, and *militia Christi* 43, 52, 69

Grimald, archchaplain of Louis the German 9
Grone, siege of 36
Guntbald, monk 21

Hagano, Lotharingian noble 177
hands, giving of 191
Harold, king of England, as warrior 54
—, corpse's mutilator punished by William
the Conqueror 66
Harun al-Rashid 11
hats, straw 205
Heito, bishop of Basle 140
Helgaud of Fleury 228
—, political theories of 179
Heliand 75
Henry, bishop of Würzburg 188
Henry, count, killed by Northmen 48-9
Henry, count of Stade, protests against
Hermann Billung's usurpation 200
Henry, count palatine of Lotharingia 34
Henry, duke of Bavaria, brother of Otto I,
54, 80, 196, 199
—, rivalry with Liudolf 89
—, claim to kingship 86ff 122, 201
Henry I, king of Germany 27-8
—, acquisition of Holy Lance 73-4, 122
—, army reforms of 30
—, campaigns of 30
—, designates Otto I as successor 85
—, gifts to Athelstan 82
—, 'house-ordering' of 79-80
—, not in command at Lenzen 36
—, plans expedition to Rome 86
—, progress through Franconia and Suabia
77-8, 80, 84
—, refusal of unction criticised 86
—, standing of in 930 80
Henry II, emperor 219, 225
—, and Europe 16
—, and orb 227
—, campaigns against Boleslas Chrobry 37-8
—, relations with Cnut 95
—, succession of in 1002 203, 220
Henry III, emperor, marriage with Agnes of
Poitou 187, 228
Henry IV, emperor, accused of plotting
magnates' deaths 210
—, and William the Conqueror 74
—, campaigns of 34, 69
—, deserted in 1076 21
—, meal with Gregory VII after Canossa 204
—, purpose of accusations of sexual
misconduct against 64-5
—, rewards warriors at siege of Rome 70 and
n. 84
Henry V, emperor, and Mathilda's Norman
entourage 92

Henry the Wrangler, duke of Bavaria 169
—, rebellion of 16-17, 113
—, bid for succession 156-7, 162-3, 167, 169,
202
heresy 231
Heribert, count of Troyes 173
Heribert, archbishop of Cologne 112, 188, 220
Heriger, archbishop of Mainz 86
Hermann, Lotharingian count 172
Hermann Billung 36, 53-4, 154, 201
—, as Saxon leader 191-2
—, *ducatus* of 198-9
—, reception in Magdeburg 174-5, 198ff, 212
Hersfeld 143-4, 148
Hetdo, follower of Charles of lower
Lotharingia 175-6
Higbald, bishop of Lindisfarne 7
Hildegard, wife of Charlemagne, kindred of
182-3, 186
Hildibald, bishop of Worms 163, 167
Hincmar, archbishop of Rheims, as legislator
60
—, on Lothar II's marriage 59
—, seeks to direct rulers 33
historiography, absence of in early tenth
century 193
—, as means of cultural domination 218
—, Ottonian 153, 195, 211-12
—, socio-political function of 231
Hohenaltheim, synod of (916) 64
Holy Lance 74 and n. 2, 206
homage 191
honores, uncertain tenure of by tenth-century
magnates 176
honour of arms 51, 70-71 and n. 86
—, precedes chivalry 41
Hoolf, Saxon count 79, 82
horse-breeding 107
horses 24, 34, 46-7
Hosed, Saxon warrior 68
Hrabanus Maurus, archbishop of Mainz 9, 57,
63
—, as legislator 60
—, on distinction between agnates and
cognates 185-6
Hrotsvitha of Gandersheim, *Pelagius* 134
—, on Edith 76-7, 81, 83
Hugh Capet, king of France 80, 165-6, 205
—, and Theophanu 178
—, anger at meeting at Margut 170
—, election of 173ff
—, journey to Rome in 981 170-1
—, kingship of 172, 179
—, plans Byzantine marriage alliance 173
—, supporters of 176
Hugh of Arles, king of Italy 126, 130 and n.
21, 132

—, seeks imperial coronation 147
Hugh the Great, duke of Francia 93, 94, 165, 168, 170
—, boasting-match with Otto I in 946 205
Hugh Timidus, count of Tours 67, 140
Hugo, margrave of Tuscany 16

Ibrahim-ibn-Jacub 101
Ignatius, patriarch of Constantinople 12
Immedings 188
imperial church 17
inheritance, partible 187-8
interventions in diplomata 88-9 and n. 77, 159
investiture, as ritual 212
investiture conflict 212-13, 231
Isidore, bishop of Seville, St, on distinction between agnates and cognates 184-7
—, on Europe myth 1-2, 5

John X, pope 147
John XII, pope 128, 144, 147, 148, 149, 150
John XIII, pope 97, 153
—, embassy to Byzantium 136
John XIX, pope 220, 227
John of Gorze, embassy to Abd ar-Rahman III 126-7, 131-5
John Tsimisces, Byzantine emperor 136
—, usurpation of 155-156
Jonas of Orléans 25
Judith, daughter of Charles the Bald, coronation of 87
Judith, empress 63, 83
—, and Charles the Bald 22-3
Jumne, *see* Wolin

Kherboga, emir of Mosul, on diet of Frankish warriors 46
killing, church's attitude to 43
kings, watchfulness of 161
kingship, Anglo-Saxon 108-9
—, clerical view of 33
—, indivisibility of 88
kinship, agnatic versus cognatic 102, 181ff
—, maternal 185-6
—, Roman legists' view of 184-5
—, structures of 181
knighthood, development of 51ff
—, church and 66
—, social status and 69
—, spreads from above, not below 71

Lampert of Hersfeld, historian 54
—, on false motives 21
Lanfranc, archbishop of Canterbury 111
Laon 178, 179, 205
Latinity, significance of in tenth and eleventh centuries 125, 218ff
Lausanne, annals of 80

lay nobility, few civilians among 67
Lecapenoi, Byzantine imperial family, attempted coup of (944) 14
Lech, battle of 15, 30, 32, 37, 103, 150, 197, 204
—, forces engaged at 36
—, Otto I hailed as emperor after 146-7
—, Otto I's role at 54
legatus, term for commander 36
legislation, Byzantine 144
Lenzen, battle at 36, 53, 76, 197
Leo I, pope, on incompatibility of penance and military activity 61
Leo III, pope, meets Charlemagne at Paderborn 7-8
Leo IV, pope, writes to Patriarch Ignatius 12
Leo VI, emperor, as conqueror of Europe 12
Leon Phocas, *kuropalates* 155
Lévi-Strauss, Claude, on ritual as a language 189
Limoges, St Martial 219
Lindisfarne, sack of 7
lineage, sense of 187
literacy, as means of support 224
—, of Frankish lay elite 194
Liudgard, daughter of Otto I 89, 103
—, references to 98
Liudolf, son of Otto I 75, 76
—, burial at St Alban's, Mainz 98
—, campaign in Italy 30
—, dispute with Henry of Bavaria 89, 208
—, isolated after mother's death 89
—, rebellion of 31, 89, 198, 201
Liudolfings, *see* Ottonians
Liudprand of Cremona, aims at historian 130
—, and Recemund of Elvira, 14, 133
—, *Antapodosis* 193
—, anti-Jewish polemics by 114ff, 129
—, apologist for Otto I 121, 125, 153
—, comparison with Notker the Stammerer 138-9
—, condemns Arnulf 14
—, describes Byzantine court 14, 136-7
—, embassies to Constantinople 126, 156
—, 'European' 1, 141-2
—, family of 126, 127
—, homilist 112ff, 129-30
—, in Otto I's *familia* 113-14, 126, 127, 151
—, *Legatio* as traveller's tale 137
—, literary rank of 229
—, mission of 968 135ff
—, modern historians on 120-1
—, negotiations with Byzantines 155
—, on Byzantine Easter-gifts 124, 128
—, on Christians and their enemies 130
—, on divine intervention in human affairs 122

—, on incarnation 115-16
—, on Magyars and Italians 37
—, on rich and poor 118-19, 124
—, opposes marriage of Otto II and Theophanu? 157
—, purpose of *Antapodosis* 121, 133
—, textual transmission of works 135, 141
—, use of Greek 121
Liutfrid, Mainz merchant 126
Liuthar, margrave 203, 209
Lobbes, evangeliary of 82 and n. 42
London 95
—, German merchants trading at 100
Lorsch, and Otto I 90-1, 123
Lothar, king of Italy 166
Lothar, king of west Francia 166, 168
—, attacks Aachen 169
—, kingship of questioned 172
—, meets Otto II at Margut 169-70
Lothar I, emperor 21ff, 176
—, loses support in 842 23
Lothar II, king of Lotharingia 44, 59
Lothar of Süpplingenburg, allows Boleslas of Poland royal reception 199
Lotharingia, rivalry over 167-8
Louis, brother of Rudolf II of Burgundy, marries Edith's sister 84
Louis II, emperor, polemics against Basil I 137
—, anointed by Pope Sergius II 56
Louis IV d'Outremer, king of west Francia 94, 168, 170, 176, 205
Louis V, king of west Francia 166-7, 172, 177
Louis the German, king of east Francia 19ff
—, and Charles the Bald 23
—, as 'star of Europe' 9-10
—, at Fontenoy 42
—, forms east Frankish kingdom 24-5
—, Slav campaigns of 9-10, 44
Louis the Pious, emperor 62, 221
—, abjuration of arms in 833 63, 65
—, and Europe 8
—, arms restored in 834 22, 64
—, chooses second wife 83
—, coup of 828 177
—, duel under 210-11
—, Easter gifts of 55-6, 57
—, girded with sword on reaching manhood 56
—, weakness in last years 22
—, succession problems of 19
—, Louis the Younger, king of east Francia 45
Lupus, abbot of Ferrières 231
—, advice to Charles the Bald 221

Mâconnais, Georges Duby on 216

Magdeburg, erection of archbishopric at 148, 154
—, St Maurice 91-2, 104
Magyars 80, 193, 197
—, boasting by 42
—, invasions by 13-14
—, Saxon tribute-payments to 81
Mainz, bridge over Rhine at 11
—, centre of German spice-trade 101
—, council of (847) 57
—, council of (852) 63
Manegold of Lautenbach 65
manuscripts, availability of in tenth century 195
—, court production of 83 and n. 45
Margut, meeting (980) 169-70
Martin, St, European saint 4-5
—, Sulpicius Severus on 5
Mathilda, abbess of Essen 74, 78, 103
—, correspondence with Æthelweard 98
Mathilda, abbess of Quedlinburg 15, 27, 166, 171
Mathilda, daughter of Henry I of England 92
Mathilda, wife of Henry I 27, 183, 195
—, and Otto I 87-88, 90
—, clothing of compensates status anxiety 207-8
—, conflicts with sons after Henry's death 89-90
—, dower of 79-80
—, family of 86
—, interventions of in diplomata 88-89
—, queenship 86
—, rivalry with Adelheid 89
—, rivalry with Edith 86ff
Maurice, St, relics of 73, 74 n. 2
Mauss, Marcel, on gifts 189, 213
meals, ritual importance of 201-4
meat, importance of to western warriors 45-6
Mediterranean 2, 125, 132-3
Meissen 162
merchants 95, 100
—, as diplomats 126-7
Merseburg 162
—, assembly at (1021) 16
—, see founded at 148
Metz, assembly at (985) 166
Michael Rangabe, Byzantine emperor 154-5
Miesco I, duke of Poland 16-17, 192
—, marriage of 53
—, supports Otto III 162
miles, synonym for *nobilis* 53
—, *gregarius* 52, 68
military organisation, Byzantine 145
—, Ottonian 146
ministeriales 53, 68
minorities, imperial 163

Monumenta Germaniae Historica 105-7
Moravia 47
Mozarabs 132

Narbonne, attacked by Saracens 222
necklace, sign of princely rank 195, 200-1
Nennius 5
Nicephorus Phocas, Byzantine emperor 125, 127
—, and Otto I's imperial title 154, 155
—, exchanges with Liudprand of Cremona 136ff
—, murdered 136, 156
—, on emperor as living law 161
—, on gluttony of western warriors 45, 146
Nicholas I, pope 13
Nithard 19ff
—, criticises Lothar 20
—, deprived of lands by Lothar 25-6
—, follower of Charles the Bald 20
—, on Charlemagne 20, 26
—, on Charles the Bald and Louis the German 23
—, on Charles the Bald 25
—, on false motives 21
—, on justice 26
—, on kings and their magnates 26
—, on Louis the Pious 22
—, on loyalty 25-6
—, on res publica 21
—, on rulers 20, 25
—, on *utilitas* 20-1, 26
—, positive view of Louis the German 24
Noah, sons of, peoples descended from 5
Northmen, besieged in Angers (873) 44
—, besieged in Asselt (882) 44-5
—, campaigns against 39-40
—, military techniques of 46ff
—, *see also*, Vikings
Notker, bishop of Liège 165
Notker the Stammerer, on Franco-Byzantine diplomacy 138-41
—, on Frankish empire as Europe 11
—, on warfare and status 67-8
Nymwegen, palace, used by Northmen as a base 48

Oda, archbishop of Canterbury, commemorated at Pfäfers 84
Odalrich, bishop of Orléans 224
Odilo, abbot of Cluny 220, 224
Odo, abbot of Cluny 111, 124
Odo, bishop of Bayeux, comforts *pueri* 52
Odo, chamberlain, deprived of arms 63
Odo, count of Blois and Chartres 170, 173, 178
Orléans, heresy at (1028) 224

Orosius, on Europe 1ff
Osdag, bishop of Hildesheim 182
Oswald, archbishop of York, embassy to Rome 95ff
—, gifts on continent 96
Oswald, St, cult of 78-9, 103
Otto, bishop of Freising, on Europe 2-3
—, on Italian society 70
Otto, duke of Suabia and Bavaria 98, 171, 210
Otto I, emperor 27-8, 131
—, acclaimed emperor after battle at Lech 146-7
—, and Byzantium 157
—, and judicial duel in Italy 152, 161
—, and kingdom of Burgundy 85
—, and manuscripts 83
—, and Slavs 30-1
—, and southern Italy 135-6, 153
—, at battle of Lech 15
—, backs Louis IV 94
—, boasting at Lech in 955 206
—, campaigns of 30-1
—, career before kingship 77, 80, 85
—, death 27
—, designated king before 936? 80
—, diploma for Quedlinberg 87, 182
—, diploma for Roman church 149, 152
—, early rebellions against 195-6, 209
—, emotion in crisis 209
—, great assembly at Quedlinburg (973) 96
—, imperial coronation of 128
—, imperial title of 154
—, invades west Francia in 946 170
—, marriage to Edith 76ff
—, meets John XIII at Ravenna 154
—, nature of empire of 144
—, no new programme as emperor 151
—, potential refuge for Anglo-Saxon exiles 93
—, punishes Adalbert of Magdeburg 200
—, rebellion of 953/4 168, 198
—, reign as golden age 28
—, rewards Henry of Stade with necklace 200-1
—, rule in Italy 152-3
—, seeks marriage-alliance with Edmund? 94
—, succession to 182
Otto II, emperor 128
—, at Rome (981) 170-1
—, campaign in France (978) 168-9, 205
—, crowned emperor by John XIII 153
—, education of 152
—, election as king 154
—, meets Lothar at Margut 169-70
—, marriage to Theophanu 152
Otto III, emperor 16, 206, 208
—, Byzantinising practices of 164
—, dines alone 164, 202

—, minority of 166-7, 172, 178, 202
—, succession to 203
—, supporters of in 984-5 161, 167
Otto of Northeim, duke of Bavaria 34
Ottonians, campaigning by 14-15
—, continental marriage-connections of 93, 102
—, hegemony in west Francia 168-9
—, kin in west Francia 166
—, kingship authenticated by Anglo-Saxon marriage 78
—, legislation of 161
—, marriage-practices of 77
—, nature of empire 14
—, purpose of Italian expeditions 34

pallium 12
Pandulf of Capua, captured at Bovino 136
—, released from Byzantine captivity 158
papacy, conception of Europe 12-13
Paul the Deacon, historian 7, 225
—, on Lombard migration 3
Paulinus, patriarch of Aquileia 60
Pavia, capital of Italian kingdom 126, 152
—, council of (850) 58
—, tolls exacted by court at 101
peace movement 222
penetes 144
penitents, not to bear arms except against pagans 58ff, 62-3
pepper, form of wealth 34, 100-1
pilgrimages 220, 223
—, eleventh-century 18
—, to Rome in tenth century 171
Pippin I, king of Aquitaine 9, 19, 21
Pippin II, king of Aquitaine 22, 42
Pippin the Hunchback, conspiracy by 57
plunder, of defeated after battle 34-5
Poeta Saxo, on Charlemagne's conquests 8, 10-11, 75
Poitiers, battle of 15
Poles, military tactics of 38
porphyrogenesis 88
pre-Gregorian era, significance of for Latin Europe 215
preaching, by tenth-century bishops 112
Priamus, Trojan king 4-5
prooimia, source for Byzantine emperorship 160
provinces, depicted as females in Ottonian iconography 16 and n. 66
pueri 52

Quedlinburg 87-8, 90, 182-3
—, annals of 15-16, 96
—, source for Thietmar of Merseburg, 28
—, assembly (973) 96

—, banquet and assembly (986) 167, 202
—, Easter-keeping (991) 16
queenship 102, 158

Radbod, bishop of Utrecht, and Ottonian kingship 77
Rather, bishop of Verona 111, 119, 124, 129
Recemund of Elvira, addressed in text of *Antapodosis* 133, 134
—, dedicatee of *Antapodosis* 14, 121, 127, 131, 135
—, meets Liudprand in 956 131-2
Recknitz, battle of 206
Reginar Longneck, sons of 174
Regino of Prüm, on Arnulf's kingship 11
—, *Chronicle* 193-4
—, on restrictions on penitents 59
Reichenau, Ottonians commemorated at 80
—, Wessex ecclesiastics commemorated at 81
relics, collected by tenth-century rulers 34, 73, 74 n. 2
Remigius of Auxerre 193
res publica 21ff, 179
Rheims 205
Riade, battle at 146, 197
Richard I, crown-wearing of (1194) 190
Richer of St Rémi, conception of Europe 2-3
—, misrepresents meeting at Rome 170-1
—, on campaigns of 978 169
—, on election of 987 175ff
—, on meeting at Margut 170
ritual, and conflict-resolution 213 and n. 131
—, and warfare 38, 197
—, differences between Byzantine and Western courts 140-1
—, distinguished from ceremony 190 and n. 7
—, importance of in Saxony 195
—, in legal proceedings 208
—, judicial duel as 209
—, language 212-13
—, more important in tenth than in ninth century 191ff
—, multiple meanings of 199
—, political functions of 212-13
—, rationality of 189-90, 205, 213
—, secular 211
—, social anthropologists' views of 189ff
—, substitute for literacy 189, 195-6
Robert, archbishop of Trier 149, 186
Robert II, king of France 171, 179, 225
—, designated successor 80
—, marries Constance of Aquitaine 228
Robert the Strong, death of 39, 43
Robertines 165; *see also* Capetians
Rodulf Glaber, career of 223-4
—, eschatology of 225-6
—, instrospectiveness of 224-5

—, on devil 227
—, on human suffering 226
—, on papacy 227-8
—, on pilgrimages 223
—, on post-Carolingian Europe 17-18, 179, 223
—, on value of monastic life 226-7
—, world view of 223
Rolls Series 106
Romanus Lecapenus, Byzantine emperor 14, 127
Roncevaux, Frankish losses at 39
Rouen 205
Rudolf II, king of Burgundy 84
—, sends relics to Otto I 92
Rudolf of Rheinfelden, king of Germany 210
—, campaigns against Henry IV 34
—, death of 41, 68 and n. 79

Saalfeld, as place to begin rebellion 201
Sallust 28, 50
Salomon III, bishop of Constance 64
—, on Carolingian crisis 193
Saucourt, battle 49
Saxons, and Gregory VII 65
—, as mercenaries with foreign rulers 100
—, campaigns against Slavs 15, 30, 33, 45, 162
—, conversion of 6-7, 10
—, growth of power of 75-6
—, law 186
—, resist Frankish conquest 7, 30
—, revolt of (1073) 64
—, stem saga 191
scara 36
Schmid, Karl, on medieval nobility 181-2, 184
Sclavinia 17
secundas a rege 21, 165
Sedulius Scottus 9
Sherston, battle of (1016) 54
shield-sellers 47
siege warfare, place for low-ranking experts in 69-70
Siegfried, abbot of Gorze, letter to Poppo of Stavelot, 187, 228
Siegfried, archbishop of Mainz 64
silver mines, Saxon 228
Siricius, on incompatibility of penance and military activity 61
Slavs, conversion of 148, 154
—, Saxon domination of 15, 33, 148, 229-30
—, new kingdoms of 17, 97, 218
—, uprising of 983 161-2
Soissons 179
—, sack of Carolingian palace at 169
Sophia, abbess of Gandersheim 82, 203
Spain, Gascon campaigns in 223-4
St Gallen, Ottonians commemorated at 80

—, Wessex ecclesiastics commemorated at 81
Stein, Freiherr von 105-6
Stephanus, Lombard panegyrist 3
Stephen, count of Blois, unknightly behaviour of 50, 52
Stephen IV, pope 8
Strasbourg, assembly at (842) 23
Suabia, peaceful in tenth century 32
Suger, abbot of Saint-Denis, on Thomas of Marle's misconduct 65
supplies, disruption of in warfare 47
Sviatopluk, duke of Moravia 14
Svein, Danish king 28
sword-bearing, sign of client status 171
sword, clerical approval of 33

Tagino, archbishop of Magdeburg, recommends Thietmar for Merseburg 28
Tanger, battle 162
Tassilo, duke of Bavaria, charged with desertion by Charlemagne 37
—, defeated by Charlemagne 38
taxation 109
Thangmar, brother of Otto I 54
—, bid for kingship 196
—, excesses condemned by Widukind 66
Thegan, historian, on Hildegard's kindred 182-3
Theodosius, as model of literate kingship 221
Theodulf, bishop of Orléans 8
—, as legislator 60
Theophanu 16, 126, 165-6, 171, 173
—, and Adelheid 159, 163
—, and west Frankish succession 172-3, 177-8
—, as Theophanius imperator 163-4
—, coronation of 97, 158
—, death 178
—, diplomata in name of 163-4
—, does not introduce Byzantine practice into Ottonian court life 164
—, dower charter 152, 156
—, dowry of 158, 162
—, eastern campaigns of 162
—, family of 156-7
—, interventions of in diplomata 159, 163
—, outmanoeuvres Henry the Wrangler in 984-5 161-2
—, titles of 159-60
Theophylact, house of 147
Thiedbern, Saxon warrior 37-8
Thiel, emporium 102
Thietmar, bishop of Merseburg 27-8, 112
—, and family foundation at Walbeck 28, 206, 229
—, as forger 230
—, biography of 27-8, 229
—, *Chronicon* as memoirs 28, 229

—, early career and education of 28, 206
—, family of 186
—, ignores Capetian succession 172
—, introspectiveness of 230
—, kinsmen captured by Vikings 206-7
—, knowledge of English affairs 28, 95, 230
—, manuscript of *Chronicon* 28
—, on armies 36
—, on Otto I's imperial coronation 149
—, on Slav heathenism 230
—, use of Widukind 28
—, uses *miles* to denote nobles 53
—, world-view of 229
Thomas of Marle, deprived of *cingulum militare* 65-6
three orders, theory of 55 and n. 17
Tours, rebuilding of 226
Translatio sancti Alexandri 75
treasures, used to denote aristocratic status 35
Tribur, council of (895) 56
tribute 33-4
Trier, episcopal schism at (1008) 32

Ulpian 184
Unstrut, Otto of Northeim's role at battle of 54
Urban II, pope, preaches first crusade 18 and n. 71
Ursula, St, *passio* of as source for Otto I's marriage to Edith 76, 79
utilitas, political concept 20ff

vassals, insecurity of after deaths of lords 40
Venice, trade links of with Germany 101, 126
Verdun, slave-trade from 137
—, west Frankish rulers and 167, 173
Vikings 32, 58, 206-7
—, boasting by 42
—, seen as extra-European and barbarian by Franks 13 and n. 48
—, *see also*, Northmen
Vreden, nunnery 41, 203

Wala, exchanges weapons with peasant 57
Walafrid Strabo 9
Walbeck, foundation of Thietmar's family 28
warfare, annual campaigning 30
—, aristocratisation of 41
—, Byzantine 145
—, church's attitude to 43, 49, 66, 70
—, frequency of in tenth century 31
—, incautious conduct of 43
—, logistic aspects of 47
—, lower orders and 49, 52
—, means of acquiring wealth 33, 49
—, mounted 54-5

—, place in Frankish society 29-30
—, relationship to feud 33, 37, 40-1, 50
—, risks of other than battle 44
—, scale of in late eleventh century 68
—, sinfulness of 43
—, supply problems in 45
—, *see also* ritual
warriors, low-ranking 67-8, 69
Welf, Bavarian count 83
Werla, assembly at (1002) 203
Werner, bishop of Strasbourg, embassy to Constantinople 45
Werner, count of Walbeck 203
Wessex, compared with Ottonian Reich 73
west Francia, tenth-century kings of 168
Wichmann Billung, feud with Otto I and Hermann Billung 31, 37, 191-2
—, refuses to give hand to Slavs 192
—, ritualised death of 192
Wichmann, Saxon count, murder of 40-1
Widukind of Corvey, and Sallust 27
—, biography of 27
—, literary rank of 229
—, on armies 36
—, on Europe 15
—, on *exercitus* 62
—, on Franks and Saxons 75
—, on Lechfeld 54
—, on warfare 29
—, *res gestae Saxonicae* 27
—, uses *miles* for nobles 53-4
William, archbishop of Mainz 77
—, opposes archbishopric at Magdeburg 148
William Longsword, duke of Normandy 221
William of Dijon, St 224, 226-8
William the Conqueror, king of England 66
William Rufus, king of England, struck down by *miles gregarius* 68
William the Great, duke of Aquitaine 219, 220, 222
—, literacy of 221
Willigis, archbishop of Mainz 32-3, 112, 161, 163, 167
witchcraft 223 and n. 25
Wolfgang, bishop of Regensburg 112, 188
Wolin, emporium 17
Worms, assembly of (829) 59
—, council of (868) 58
Wulfhere of Mercia, residence at Thane 107
Wulfhelm, archbishop of Canterbury 81

Xanten, as second Troy 4

Zeus, abducts Europe 2, 10

GEORGE SIGERSON

POET, PATRIOT, SCIENTIST AND SCHOLAR

Sigerson family coat of arms: see Appendix 6

DEDICATION

To my wife, Helen,
and children,
Jacqueline, Siobhan, Fiona,
Declan and Ciaran.

GEORGE SIGERSON

POET, PATRIOT, SCIENTIST AND SCHOLAR

KEN McGILLOWAY

Stair Uladh

Ulster Historical Foundation is please to extend thanks to the following groups/organisations for the financial support they provided towards the publication of this book:

Ard Chomhairle CLG
Comhairle Uladh CLG
Comhairle Ardoideachais CLG
Coiste Tír Eoghain CLG
Cumann Mhic Sioghair CLG, Strabane
O'Neill's Sportswear
Strabane History Society

All contributions are gratefully acknowledged.

First Published 2011
by Stair Uladh
(an imprint of Ulster Historical Foundation)
Charity Ref. No. XN48460
E-mail: enquiry@uhf.org.uk
Web: www.ancestryireland.com
www.booksireland.org.uk

Printed by MPG Biddles
Design by Cheah Design

CONTENTS

Acknowledgements   vi
Preface   viii
Introduction   x

1   The Sigersons of Derry and Tyrone   1
2   Student years   8
3   Early poetry and politics   15
4   Sigerson the doctor   25
5   The Mansion House Relief Committee   32
6   The National Literary Society   42
7   *Bards of the Gael and Gall*   51
8   Family and friends   57
9   Sigerson's later life, 1900–25   67
10   The Sigerson Cup   80

Select bibliography   86
References and notes   89

Appendix 1:   Tributes and appreciations   96
Appendix 2:   Honours and distinctions   104
Appendix 3:   Sigerson's publications – a select list   105
Appendix 4:   Popular songs and poems by George Sigerson   109
Appendix 5:   Introduction to *Songs and poems by George Sigerson* (1927) 121
              Padraic Colum
Appendix 6:   'A Pale family'   126
Appendix 7:   Memorial preface to *Bards of the Gael and Gall* (3rd ed.) 132
              Douglas Hyde
Appendix 8:   Extracts from a lecture by Dr George Sigerson at the   139
              inauguration of the National Literary Society in Dublin,
              August, 1892
Appendix 9:   'The Holocaust' written by Dr Sigerson in Dec. 1867
              following the execution of the Manchester Martyrs   148
Appendix 10: Dedication to *Love songs of Connacht*   150
              Douglas Hyde

Index   152

ACKNOWLEDGEMENTS

There are many people I want to thank for the help and assistance I received in seeing this book reach completion. I earnestly hope that I have adequately acknowledged their generosity in sharing their time and knowledge with me.

My wife, Helen, provided the original inspiration for the book and has given constant support and encouragement over the years to help me complete the journey.

Eibhlin Humphreys gave me access to her grandfather's and her mother's unpublished manuscripts and other important related material, including photographs and letters; I made a promise to her that her grandfather's name would be properly remembered. Dermot Humphreys, her grandson, provided me with additional valuable family photographs and other important information.

From the moment I first shared the story of George Sigerson with him, my late brother Olly gave me his enthusiastic support and encouragement, set me the task of producing 20 pages of text every week and then spent long hours working on a word processor trying to arrange and make sense of my scribble. To him I am eternally grateful.

Joe Martin played a pivotal role in seeing the book reach publication. In 1990, on learning that I was doing research into the life of George Sigerson, he wrote to me, urging me to 'preserve the memory of this great man'. When he eventually had the opportunity to see my work, his response was positive and encouraging, and for this and for the practical help and advice he has given me I offer my sincere thanks.

John Dooher has embraced this project and supported it with enthusiasm since we first met almost two years ago. His extensive knowledge of Irish history, an area in which my knowledge is sadly limited, has proved invaluable and has added much to this story. His role in editing the text has been particularly crucial in the last few months and he has also helped smooth my journey through the publishing process.

Without hesitation, Dónal McAnallen generously provided a very comprehensive and valuable chapter on the history of the Sigerson Cup and has been a tireless worker in promoting the memory of George Sigerson.

I wish to thank the following, who were of particular help in the publication process: Fintan Mullan of the Ulster Historical Foundation for the Foundation's support in agreeing to publish the book; Alicia McAuley, who edited the manuscript with thoroughness and with much patience; Jill Morrison, Cheah Design, for her valued contribution on the design of the book; and John McCandless for his excellent work on the cover and photographs.

I am also indebted to the following people, some of whom, sadly, are no longer with us but who have contributed in no small way to the telling of this story: Eddie McIntyre, former county librarian, Lifford; Michael G. Kennedy of Strabane

Historical Society; Jacqueline McIntyre of Belfast; Professor Robert Welch of the University of Ulster at Coleraine; Dr Billy Kelly of the University of Ulster at Magee College, Derry; Dr Éamonn Ó Cíardha of the University of Ulster at Magee College, Derry; Dr Norman Chestnutt of Altnagelvin Hospital, Derry; Tadhg MacConnell of Buncrana; Betty Caffrey of Dublin; Elizabeth Bell of Kent; Michael Harron of Strabane; Bernadette McGilloway of Derry; Charles McGarrigle of Kent; Fr John Walsh of Buncrana; Charles Gallagher of Derry; Nuala Cassidy of Derry; the staff of Derry Central Library, Belfast Central Library and Downpatrick Library; James Roche of University College, Dublin; and the librarian of the National Library of Ireland, Dublin.

If I have omitted anyone from these acknowledgements, it has been done unknowingly and I offer my sincere apologies.

PREFACE

It was in a second-hand bookshop in Dublin many years ago that I first encountered the name Sigerson. I overheard my wife, Helen, enquiring of the bookseller if he had any books by a Dr Sigerson. Curious, I asked her who he was. She informed me that he was a relative, the brother of her great-grandmother, Jane McGinnis. She said he was famous in his day but that was all she knew about him. My interest was immediately aroused. I wanted to find out who this man was. I did not know it at the time, but that simple question marked the beginning of a fascinating and compelling journey of discovery which would eventually result in this book.

Early on in my research, I was fortunate enough to be introduced to Eibhlin Humphreys, the daughter of Hester Sigerson Piatt and granddaughter of George Sigerson himself. At the age of three, Eibhlin and her brother, Donn, had moved in to live with their grandfather, after the sudden death of their father, also named Donn Piatt, who had been the American vice-consul in Ireland. I spent many enjoyable hours in her company listening to her memories of her mother and grandfather and of the comings and goings in Clare Street, where the Sigerson family lived from 1877 to 1925. Eibhlin gave me access to her mother's unpublished manuscripts,[1] to letters, photographs and other primary sources which have been invaluable in piecing together the story of George Sigerson's life.[2]

The more I learned about Sigerson, the more intrigued I became. His influence was wide ranging, especially regarding the revival of Irish language and culture, medical research and political journalism. Yet many people had never heard of him. There is no doubt of his importance in Irish history – contemporary sources prove this – but researchers and writers have not yet attempted to document his life or his work. I was determined that the story of this exceptional man's life should be told.

This book has assumed many forms since my interest was first aroused in George Sigerson. It began as an attempt to describe in a straightforward way the more obvious facts about Sigerson's life. It became clear at quite an early stage, however, that his story was much more complex – that many of his attitudes, ambitions, achievements and activities had been greatly influenced by the events of the past and by concern for the future. Sigerson lived for 89 years. In that time he was active in helping to establish an independent university, teaching there, caring for the sick, translating Irish poems and songs into English verse, carrying out medical, scientific, political and social research, challenging the understanding of current affairs and helping to promote reform in a wide range of areas.

I have adopted a largely, though not entirely, chronological approach, beginning with Sigerson's journey from his birthplace in Artigarvan near Strabane in County Tyrone to his death in Dublin. He lived through some of the most pivotal events in

Irish history, including the Famine and the Easter Rising. As I describe his life, his achievements are set against the backdrop of the literary, social and political conditions of the time, and of course the characters and personalities of his immediate family and close friends. For parts of the story of Sigerson's life, information was scarce. He was always reluctant to talk about his own life and, although he had spent many years researching the history of the Sigerson family in Ireland, he resisted all requests to write his own memoirs. It was said that because of his Nordic reserve his personality was seldom revealed, even to family and close friends.

This publication is intended to stimulate interest in one of the great figures of nineteenth- and early twentieth-century Ireland and to encourage scholarly research into the life of a man whose influence on many aspects of Irish cultural and political history was significant. Lord Acton (1834–1902), an English historian, considered one of the most learned people of his time, said that George Sigerson was the greatest Irishman he had known. Douglas Hyde (1860–1949), an Irish scholar, founder of the Gaelic League and first president of Ireland, said shortly after Sigerson's death, 'Ireland will not forget him and cannot replace him.'[3] Sadly, Ireland does appear to have forgotten him.

While I have managed to collect much information about the man and his work, I would be the first to acknowledge that I have merely scratched the surface. I must leave it to others to analyse Sigerson's writings, his contribution to medicine and to Irish cultural, literary and political life. My earnest hope is that this account might encourage other, better-qualified writers to take a renewed interest in Sigerson's life and achievements and that it might ultimately help to restore him to his rightful place in Irish history.

INTRODUCTION

For the students who thronged the corridors of Dublin's National University in the spring of 1923, the appearance of their professor of zoology must have been a source of amusement. Although in his eighty-seventh year, frail and slightly stooped, he stood out from the crowd. Resplendent in his long black frock coat and top hat, his white flowing shoulder-length hair and pointed imperial beard gave George Sigerson, MD an appearance that was 40 years out of date.

Old Sigerson was clever and he was a good teacher. He taught anatomy and physiology but his pursuits crossed many disciplines. All through his adult career George Sigerson carried a twofold loyalty: an allegiance divided between the world of science and the world of the humanities. As Douglas Hyde put it:

> his mind was so broad and his genius so varied, and the elements so kindly mixed, that science, economics, history, and poetry all through his life appealed to him with almost equal force, though I have a suspicion that the appeal of poetry was strongest.[1]

Qualified in medicine, Sigerson pursued postgraduate studies in France under the most eminent professors. In later life he would translate Jean-Martin Charcot's book, *Lectures on the diseases of the nervous system*, adding important notes of his own.[2] In his medical practice he specialised in recognising and treating stress and psychosocial illnesses. Scholarly research work earned him membership of many learned societies; Charles Darwin was his proposer for fellowship of the Linnean Society of London. Despite this international recognition, however, he failed to obtain a hospital appointment in Ireland – perhaps because of his involvement in political journalism.

Besides publishing professional and scientific papers, Sigerson became involved in attempting to revive the Irish language and publicising the beautiful songs and stories of old Irish folklore. With the increasing anglicisation of Ireland, much of this material was beginning to disappear. Under the pseudonym 'Erionnach' he contributed numerous poems and essays in Irish periodicals and journals such as the *Harp* and *The Nation*. However, his main claim to distinction lies in the field of translation. Sigerson's first and lasting contribution to literature was the second series of *The poets and poetry of Munster* (1860).[3] Sigerson's role as one of the dominant figures in the formation of an Anglo-Irish literature began at this time. His scholarly work on the Munster poets was to be followed almost 40 years later by what is considered his finest work, *Bards of the Gael and Gall*, which was published in 1897.[4]

Meanwhile, he had become involved in politics. In 1860 he was a member of a deputation that presented a sword of honour to General Patrice de MacMahon, a marshal of France who was destined to become the first president of the Third Republic (1875–9).

From 1860 on, Sigerson was invited to write editorials for the foremost Irish journals and periodicals of the day. One of the most famous of these editorials, entitled 'The Holocaust', referred to the execution of William Philip Allen, Michael Larkin and Michael O'Brien on 23 November 1867.[5] It was during this period, when writing for the Irish Republican Brotherhood's paper, the *Irish People*, that Sigerson met that organisation's leaders. The prominent Fenian John O'Leary, in his book on the Fenians, referred to George Sigerson as 'the chief of literary staff'.[6]

Sigerson also began to write for some of the more liberal English journals. A collection of his articles – which first appeared in the *Daily Chronicle* – was eventually published as *Modern Ireland: its vital questions, secret societies and government* in 1868.[7] When introducing his Irish land legislation, William Gladstone used Sigerson's work on the land question in *History of the land tenures and land classes of Ireland* (1871).[8] Sigerson had in-depth knowledge of Irish political history and wrote an important chapter in R. Barry O'Brien's *Two centuries of Irish history, 1691–1870* (1888).[9] Sigerson later expanded this very considerably into a book – *The last independent parliament of Ireland*, published in 1918.[10]

The Dublin Mansion House Relief Committee appointed him to the post of medical commissioner in 1879–80, when the country was threatened with another famine and when typhus was affecting County Mayo. Following his experiences, Sigerson wrote a paper entitled 'On the need and use of village hospitals in Ireland'.[11] In the early 1880s he was appointed to the Royal Commission on Prisons and was responsible for bringing about improvements in the health and social management of different categories of inmates. His work on the treatment of political prisoners – *Political prisoners at home and abroad* – was subsequently used by the suffragette movement to highlight the uses and abuses of force feeding.[12]

With the founding of the National Literary Society in the summer of 1892, Sigerson's passion for Irish language and culture gained fresh impetus. Douglas Hyde was the first president of the society but, after a few months, he resigned and became president of the newly formed Gaelic League.[13] Sigerson then became president of the National Literary Society and held office until the society ceased to exist in 1924. During the society's existence, he and many others worked hard to encourage and foster an interest in all things Irish. It embraced every aspect of Irish life and from it sprang the Gaelic League, a new Irish theatre and the annual Feis Ceoil.

This all-embracing love of Ireland included its national sports. Sigerson presented a cup for intercollegiate football in 1911. The Sigerson Cup has remained one of the most important competitions in the GAA calendar since that time.

One of Sigerson's great ambitions was to save the Irish language from what seemed a slow but certain death. It was this aspect of his life that led Douglas Hyde to describe him as the outstanding force in the revival movement. In Hyde's eyes, no living Irishman had done more to preserve the oral tradition than Sigerson.

In *Bards of the Gael and Gall* Sigerson offered translations of 139 Irish poems. This anthology of translated Irish song, which included poems from the earliest beginnings of Irish literature, revealed a fascinating and splendid ancient heritage which prompted Ernest Boyd to comment, 'It substantiated the claim of ancient Ireland to be the mother of literature.'[14] It was on one of these pieces, 'The fate of the Children of Lir', that Sigerson based *The saga of King Lir*, which was published in 1913.[15]

An enthusiastic and tireless worker in promoting the cause of the National University, Sigerson chaired many meetings and gave numerous lectures to enlist support. In a lecture delivered in 1906, he told students that the age-old passion the Irish nation had for learning had helped it to thwart the many attempts that had been made over the centuries to destroy Irish education.[16] NUI became a reality as a result of the Irish Universities Act, 1908.

In 1922, Sigerson completed his final book, *The Easter song*, which contains translations from Latin into English verse of long sections of Sedulius's original fifth-century Christian epic.[17]

Appointed by William T. Cosgrave to membership of Seanad Éireann, he chaired its first meeting in September 1922, pending the election of officers.[18] He retired from university teaching in the spring of 1923 and died in Dublin on 17 February 1925, at the age of 89. He is buried in Glasnevin Cemetery, Dublin.

1

The Sigersons of Derry and Tyrone

We begin our story with an extract from the final chapter of George Sigerson's unpublished manuscript, 'A Pale family'.

The Sigersons and the Williamite Wars

When in April, 1689, King James went to join his army before Derry, in the hope that the city would acknowledge him as its lawful sovereign, a Captain John Segerson marched northwards from the family homeland of Kerry with his regiment hoping to join in the battle. His wife, a near kinswoman of Col. Patrick Sarsfield, with a young son and younger daughter, accompanied him. As Sir Maurice Eustace's regiment was there, they had many kindred and friends. When, owing to the inefficiency of its commander, the unsuccessful and dispirited army returned in August, menaced with the approaching invasion by Schomberg and a prolonged campaign, Captain Segerson considered it best to leave his wife and young children under the charge of an old and friendly priest, the Rev Mac Ardle, in the historic town of Benburb. This town, though close by his line of march from Derry to Dublin, was not likely to be approached again, and did remain in peace, the trail of war keeping along the eastern coastline from Carrickfergus to Dublin. Captain Segerson is stated to have fallen in battle with many of his kinsmen; his daughter died young; of his wife's fate there is no account. 'The boy, it appears', writes the Rev Mr McCay, 'was exceedingly handsome and promising, deeply loved by the priest. The priest took great care of the lad, giving him a high education, teaching him Latin and Irish. His Christian name was John. After some years the priest died'. John Segerson married and had off-spring who, in a country emptied by war, succeeded in acquiring land and setting up iron manufacturing in Derry and Tyrone.[1]

The Sigersons in Derry

In the early 1800s, McCormack's Forge along the banks of the Berryburn at Ardmore in County Derry was operated by a descendant of John Segerson, whose name had by now been altered to Sigerson. William Sigerson worked the forge with the help of his family. In time, two of his sons, Richard and James, emigrated to North America; another son, George, went to Australia.[2] Of the remaining members of the family we know little except that the youngest son, William, continued working with his father and grew into adulthood at the Berryburn. This stream separated the townlands of Ardkill and Glenkeen, an area of great natural beauty about seven miles from Derry City, and provided enough power to work several small mills. It is possible, however, that at least one other son or a close relative of the same name was in the area at this time – there were still Sigersons living in the district in the 1950s.

In the early 1800s the majority of rural dwellers were employed on the land and in looking for work it was an advantage if a man had his own spade. A large portion of the Sigersons' income came from providing spades and shovels to farmers and farm labourers. William Sigerson was convinced that the best spades came from Neilson's spade foundry in Artigarvan. Although there was an established spade mill not far from the Berryburn in the townland of Ardkill, he was still prepared to have one of his sons make the tiresome and sometimes arduous journey to Artigarvan. From 1820 on it fell to the young William to make the 20-mile journey.

Neilson's spade mill in Artigarvan

The small village of Artigarvan, four miles from Strabane, was sheltered at its back and sides by the Sperrin Mountains and fronted by the River Foyle. Nestling at the mouth of the Glenmornan Valley, it escaped many of the hardships, natural and otherwise, that troubled much of the rest of the country through the centuries. One narrow escape is recorded, however. In August 1689, retreating from Derry, followers of James II made preparations to burn Holy Hill, the residence of John Sinclair, a Church of Ireland minister. Fortunately, a messenger swam across the Foyle with an order that the house was to be spared. This incident apart, the village was untouched by conflict.

In 1820, when William Sigerson began to travel from the Berryburn to Artigarvan, his first call was always with James Neilson, the spade manufacturer, who lived in a solid two-storey building standing in beautiful surroundings. This house was known to the locals as Holyhill House, possibly because of its proximity to a small rise called the Holy Hill. The Neilsons had lived in the area for generations and were highly respected. They were staunch, hard-working Presbyterians, loyal to earlier Neilsons who had suffered for the right to practise their faith and who, according to tradition, had been prepared to risk their own lives to care for a Catholic priest, hiding him from death. According to Hester Sigerson Piatt, the Neilsons of Artigarvan were related to Samuel Neilson, a founder member of the Society of United Irishmen.[3]

James Neilson was a skilled metalworker and a good businessman. His foundry, one of the first of its kind in Ulster, was famous for the manufacture of spades, shovels and other agricultural implements. Several members of his family had emigrated. The oldest son, Samuel, had died by accidental drowning somewhere in the West Indies but the youngest daughter, Nancy, had remained at home with her mother and father. Over a period of time she had become friendly with William Sigerson and this friendship developed into a wish to get married. When Nancy and William made known their plans to marry, both the Neilson and Sigerson families objected. Nancy was a Protestant, William a Catholic. For everybody's sake, their parents forbade them from marrying.

ADVERTISEMENTS.   93

WILLIAM SIGERSON & CO.,
Spades, Shovels,
— AND —
Scrap Iron Manufacturers,
HOLYHILL, STRABANE.

William Sigerson & Co., Spade Mill, Artigarvan, *c.* 1860

George Sigerson's parents

However, in Strabane in October 1823, against the advice of their parents, Nancy Neilson and William Sigerson did marry. In the first few months of married life there was little contact between their respective families but gradually relations improved. With Mrs Neilson's help they rented a small house 'up the glen', some distance from Artigarvan. Soon afterwards, William, who was an experienced metalworker, found employment in the spade mill. The birth of their first child, James, two years later, prompted Nancy's parents to invite the young family to come and live with them. William continued working in the spade factory and was promoted to a position of responsibility. In 1828, when John, their second child, was born, Nancy and William moved into Holyhill House. Soon afterwards James Neilson retired. By 1833 he had transferred ownership of his foundry business, its buildings and grounds to his daughter and son-in-law.[4]

William Sigerson was a young man of initiative and drive. He immediately started to carry out improvements to the spade mill. He enlarged the foundry buildings, installed more efficient equipment and built new holding sheds nearer the main road. The foundry became more productive and, within six years of taking control of the buildings and grounds, William Sigerson began to expand his property interests in Artigarvan and Strabane. In time, farming became his great interest and he took particular pride in the number of prizes his livestock and farm produce won at county shows.

The Sigerson family had also begun to expand. Ellen was born in 1832 and William in 1833. Just over two years later, on Sunday, 11 January 1836, George was born. Jane arrived in 1838 and, three years later, the birth of Mary Ann completed the family.

William and Nancy successfully reared their family during a period of great distress throughout Ireland – a period when countless others remained destitute and died without dignity. A million Irishmen and Irishwomen lived in workhouses or existed on charity, mainly necessitated by the regular failure of the potato crop, a catastrophe that culminated in the Great Famine of 1845–9. Exactly how many people died will never be known but it is estimated that between 1841 and 1851 a population loss of at least 2.5 million took place through death and emigration.

William Sigerson was very active in giving his support to anything that would help those less fortunate than himself. He became a member of the first Board of Guardians in Strabane, which had been set up to implement the Poor Law legislation of 1838 – in particular, the construction and operation of the Strabane Workhouse.[5] He was also active in the fledgling tenant-right activities in Artigarvan and Strabane and treasurer of the local relief committee, set up to help alleviate destitution in the aftermath of the crop failures. In November 1849, he helped organise a tenant meeting in Artigarvan. This was met with stiff opposition by the bailiff of the local landowner, who reacted by tearing down all notices of the meeting and threatening tenants by name with eviction.[6] William Sigerson responded by having a strongly worded letter published in the *Londonderry Journal* denouncing the activities of the bailiff and rejecting allegations that he was a relative newcomer who had done little for the farmer class and labourers in his own employ.[7]

During his 40 years operating the spade mill, William Sigerson built a very reputable and prosperous business. He was highly respected over a wide area. When he died at home on 8 December 1871, after a short illness, his funeral was attended by clergy and laymen of Catholic and Protestant churches, an unusual occurrence in the 1870s. His wife Nancy died seven years later. Both are buried in the shadow of the little country church at Cloughcor, a few miles from Artigarvan.

Although he was regarded as a shrewd businessman, William Sigerson's generosity and fair-mindedness were well known. On one occasion, when it seemed that his Presbyterian neighbours would have their plan to build a church turned down, he signed a petition and encouraged his Catholic workers to do the same. According to local tradition, he also offered the presbytery a suitable plot of land in Artigarvan village free of charge. A few years later, the church was built on Sigerson's land.

Early years in Tyrone

George Sigerson's earliest recollections of Artigarvan were of happy times spent playing with his brothers and sisters. The natural beauty of the countryside, its glens and rivers, had a lasting effect on him and provided inspiration for many of his poems and ballads. In later years his thoughts often returned to childhood days at Holyhill.

George's daughter, Hester Sigerson Piatt, wrote about the house and the area around it as she remembered it as a child in the 1870s:

William Sigerson,
father of George,
Holyhill, Tyrone *c.* 1865

> Behind it, in those days, was a fairy wood yellow with primroses in the early spring where the ivy had not spread a shining carpet. The murmurous music of the trees, wind stirred and bird haunted, mingled with the never ceasing song of the Glenmornan river which ran behind the house and turned the big wheel of the spade mill. Past the entrance to the house the road wound upwards, dipping and rising and ceaselessly winding towards the heart of the mountains where lies Moorlough, a mountain lake famed in song and story.[8]

In his early childhood, George became friendly with the men who worked in the spade mill. He also knew by sight some of the men who travelled from farm to farm and who often came to the house looking for a day's work. Some of these 'mountainy men' spoke a language he did not understand. They were Irish speakers from the Sperrin foothills and glens – places such as Creggan, Greencastle and Carrickmore – as well as from Gallon, just over the hill towards Newtownstewart. In the early 1800s nearly a third of the people of Tyrone spoke Irish. By a strange coincidence, one of Ulster's most active leaders in the language movement was a Dr William Neilson, a Presbyterian minister. This William Neilson was born in Rademon, County Down, in 1774. In 1808 he published a book entitled *An introduction to the Irish language*.[9] Two years later he published a second book, *Céad leabhar na Gaoidheilge*, which claimed to be 'the first elementary class book, prepared and published in the Irish language'.[10]

In the preface to *An introduction to the Irish language*, Neilson sums up the absolute necessity of saving the Irish language in a few sentences:

> In this language are preserved the remarkable annals of our country … It has been said, indeed, that the use of this language should be abolished and the English prevail universally. It is surely reasonable and desirable that every person should be able to hold converse with his countrymen as well as to taste and admire the beauties of one of the most expressive, philosophically accurate and polished languages that has ever existed.[11]

George Sigerson was fascinated by this language and anxious to learn it, but his family had no knowledge of Irish and suitable books were hard to find in the 1840s. In the beginning he relied on the 'mountainy men' to teach him words and phrases; when his parents did find him a book, they helped him to speak the written words. In time, George Sigerson's persistence and the patience of the spade-mill workers were rewarded.

His daughter, Hester, wrote that a few years later he would walk four miles to Strabane and back to read Archbishop John McHale's Irish translation of Homer's *Iliad*:

> This pale, fair-headed boy with his early passion for reading and study, his indifference to the usual sports and pastimes of the countryside, his strange desire to master the Gaelic tongue – picking up the spoken language from the men who came to the house for a day's work or a meal – soon became the centre of his father's hopes and ambitions.[12]

Early education

When George was six years old, he was sent to the local Glebe school, where he made rapid progress. He was hard working, alert and attentive, a studious pupil who preferred reading to outdoor activities. Yet, away from schoolwork, he loved exploring the countryside around his home and its hills and streams. It would appear that at some stage he received additional tuition from a Fr Hegarty, a native of Burt in County Donegal and a personal friend of his parents. Fr Hegarty was ordained priest in 1844 and appointed as curate in Buncrana before being moved to Ardstraw in 1860 and coming to Strabane as parish priest in 1872.[13] Hester Sigerson Piatt tells that Fr Hegarty was a scholar of the Classics and languages and deeply interested in Irish history and literature. In George Sigerson he found a highly intelligent young boy who was responsive and eager to learn.[14] In time, he advised George's parents to send him to the Academy in Letterkenny – a school whose excellence was mainly due to the ability and energy of its administrator, Dr Crerand. After qualifying as a doctor of medicine, Crerand had lived for many years in Paris, building up an extensive and lucrative practice there, and deciding to leave only because of an increase in revolutionary activity in that city. On coming back to his native Donegal, he immediately established a school for the youth of the area.[15]

In 1850, George Sigerson moved to the Academy, but within a year his parents took him away from it, allegedly because of sectarian trouble in the Letterkenny area. Although he spent only a short time there, Dr Crerand's influence on his young pupil was so profound that it remained with him for the rest of his life. When he was an old man, Sigerson often spoke with pride about his experiences in Letterkenny and his old teacher's scholarship. C.P. Curran recalled Sigerson telling him that his teacher – a Donegal man who had been a tutor to the son of King Louis Philippe of France – saw Wolfe Tone smiling at the walls of Derry Gaol when he was taken there after his capture from the French ship in Lough Swilly.[16]

Once again it was necessary to find somewhere for George to continue his education. His parents had considered a reputable school in Derry, run by brothers called Simpson, but for personal reasons decided against it. It seems likely that during this period he attended the celebrated classical seminary of Master McCloskey at Tergarvil, near Maghera. This famous hedge school produced 137 priests, and George Sigerson is said to have been one of the most illustrious of all the laymen who graduated from Tergarvil Academy.[17]

There had long been a tradition of prosperous Irish families sending their offspring to Europe to complete their education. The Sigerson family had already taken the first step in this direction when George's older brother, William, went to the continent a short while earlier, possibly to a Catholic seminary to train for the priesthood. It was a time of conflicting opinions and views on the best options for higher education at home in Ireland. The Catholic hierarchy and many leading nationalists in the Daniel O'Connell-led Repeal Association had wanted an end to the domination of Trinity College with its strongly Protestant ethos. The government had offered the Queen's Colleges of Cork, Galway and Belfast as an alternative to stripping Trinity of its predominant position but the Catholic bishops rejected this British reform. They argued that the new colleges were designed to weaken Catholicism and perpetuate the stranglehold of the Ascendancy. From 1850 on attempts were made to establish a Catholic University. The redoubtable Dr (later Cardinal) John Henry Newman was appointed its first rector. The Queen's Colleges, meanwhile, were up and running. Higher education in Ireland must have appeared somewhat confusing, especially since some of the more liberal Catholic opinion seemed to favour the new non-denominational colleges. William and Nancy Sigerson may have decided to wait and see what might happen. In the meantime, the young George was sent to France to continue his pre-university education.

2

Student years

Paris

George Sigerson went to St Joseph's College, Paris in 1852, the year that ushered in the Second French Empire and saw Louis-Napoléon Bonaparte become Emperor Napoleon III. France had long been a favourite choice for Irish Catholic students, and during the emergence of Louis-Napoléon as president and later emperor of the new France following the overthrow of the monarchy in 1848, new legislation had restored a greater role for the Church in the French educational system. The young George was already familiar with the story of France, and at the Academy in Letterkenny Dr Crerand had told him about that country's great culture – its artists, poets and writers.

St Joseph's College in the Rue de l'Enfer, in the heart of the Latin Quarter, was once the home of François-René de Chateaubriand, one of the most important writers in French Romantic literature. For George Sigerson, however, memories of the school were not pleasant – it was a spartan place 'where boys in winter broke ice in their wash basins, and their thin red wine was called "Abondance" from its plenitude of water.'[1] The principal of the school, Abbé Jolicler, was a distinguished scholar and a strict disciplinarian. Total commitment to studies and loyalty to the school were expected. Any pupil who broke the rules received severe punishment.

Sigerson's closest friend at the school was a boy called Cavaignac, the grandson of the *conventionnel* who had voted for the execution of Louis XVI, and the son of General Cavaignac, who had mercilessly suppressed the Red Rising against the new assembly following the Revolution of 1848, and who had been runner-up in the election against Louis-Napoléon for the presidency of the short-lived French Republic. According to C.P. Curran, it was at St Joseph's College, with colleagues like the boy Cavaignac, that the seeds that Dr Crerand had already sown in Letterkenny were to grow into an undying affection for France.[2]

There is a daguerreotype of Sigerson, taken around the time when he attended the Academy, where he appears a sturdy round-faced boy of about fourteen. The next daguerreotype, taken in Paris a few years later, is very different. In it he has grown pale and slender and wears a student's uniform. He often commented that his school carried the rule of plain living to excess. The few and plain meals began with a *petit déjeuner* consisting of a portion of bread and a drink of water at six o'clock. The strong, growing boy, who had been accustomed to the good and abundant food of his home, often had to tighten the leather belt of his uniform to stifle pangs of hunger which the sparse meals scarcely more than excited. However, his country upbringing stood him in good stead. He grew thin indeed, but the excellent health he enjoyed all his life was not impaired. He forgot this and other troubles in the exactions of hard work along with, no doubt, a desire to please his father and a natural ambition to succeed.

Two certificates of St Joseph's College, dated August 1854, show that – in a class of more than 40 learners – the 'élève Sigerson, Georges' won first prize in drawing, religious knowledge and German, second in history, geography, mathematics and French composition, and fourth in Latin theme, Latin verse and Greek theme.

On 6 January 1855, Sigerson wrote to his father:

> My Dear Father,
> I cannot better commence my letter than by wishing you a happy new year and many many happy returns of the same. I would have written for Christmas but the Quarterly examinations were a few days after it and I wished to let you know that I passed it. The examiners gave me much praise and good notes. Here is a list of my places in the weekly competitions … In the last competitions I was first in the whole college as it was a competition of the first and highest division of the students in which there were 42 collegians.
>
> John and James' unexpected illness has much afflicted me and it was with great sorrow that I learned it from William. But I hope they will soon have recovered their good health. I trust in God their illness will have entirely gone before your next letter. I'd greatly wish to be at home now to help you in their cares or at least to relieve you of a part of your fatigue. I hope Dr Crerand has been to see them for he is a better doctor than those in Strabane.
>
> My dearest father, the weather here is extremely mild with occasional falls of rain. Last year at Christmas the ground was covered with ice and snow and the river was frozen from side to side at Paris. But this year there was but a light fall of snow before Christmas for two or three days. If it continues there will be a prospect of a bad summer; it is likely that the winter will arrive in spring.
>
> I am glad that my dearest mother is in good health. To her as well as John, James, Ellen, Mary Anne, and Jane I send love and best wishes for a happy new year.[3]

On the back of this letter his brother, William, who, it seems, was studying for the priesthood at the Irish College in Paris, wrote an affectionate note. In reply, his father congratulated George on his success and hoped 'that health and perseverance would enable him to gain distinguished fame and honour'. He encouraged William not to lag behind his brother and hoped that the days would not be far distant when he would be 'gratified by the cheering and heart stirring news of his success'.[4] However, it would appear that the priesthood was not for William, as we hear no more of his time in France. Eventually he emigrated to Australia, lived in Sydney and finally settled in New Zealand. From a reference in his father's will of 1868, we can deduce that William incurred the displeasure of his father, who bequeathed to him the sum of 'one shilling and no more'.[5] George's daughter, Hester, added nothing more about this matter and we are left to wonder what had occurred.

In 1855, his last year at St Joseph's College, George won first prize in Latin, German and Greek; second prize in literary analysis and French composition; and third prize in geometry and German. He also won a prize for Latin translation of 'The exile of Erin'. For his first prizes he was awarded three *couronnes*, or wreaths. The *couronnes* were placed on the heads of successful students by the *aumônier* (or chaplain) of Napoleon III. At the same prizegiving, Sigerson's friend, Cavaignac, refused to accept his awards 'from the hands of the usurper's deputy'.[6] Rather surprisingly in light of his later advocacy for the downtrodden, George does not appear to have supported his friend in his principled stance against the tyranny of the Bonaparte dynasty.

Galway and Cork

George Sigerson returned home in the summer of 1855 and shortly afterwards commenced studies at Queen's College, Galway. It was during this brief period at home, surrounded by the hills, glens and streams of Artigarvan in County Tyrone, that he started writing what he called his 'little pastoral ballads'.

In the autumn of that same year he became ill with typhoid fever. Although unwell for most of his time in Galway, he still managed to win a scholarship to study medicine at Queen's College, Cork. He moved to Cork in 1856 and, after obtaining a further scholarship, remained there for three years. He lost no time in recruiting the support of some of his fellow students to join him in petitioning the college authorities to inaugurate lectures in Irish. These were accordingly arranged for and delivered by the professor of Gaelic, Owen O'Connellan.

Sigerson completed his medical studies in Dublin in 1859, having attended surgery lectures at the Catholic University School of Medicine, Cecilia Street, and graduated during the summer of 1859. In a special examination there he also gained first-class honours in Celtic and Sanskrit. Sigerson continued to pursue his medical studies in the years that followed, and from 1860 onwards he was a frequent visitor to France, where he specialised in the study of neurology.

The Young Ireland movement

During his time in Cork, Sigerson also became interested in journalism. He had scientific papers published in *Atlantis*, the university magazine, and under the pseudonym 'Erionnach' his prose and verse about Ireland and its culture began to appear in many Irish periodicals, including the *Harp* and *The Nation*, the latter being the paper associated with the Young Ireland movement.

Young Ireland had started off as an intellectual faction within the O'Connellite Repeal Association. Many of the leaders of this group were Protestants and politically more liberal that the majority of the Repeal Association. Initially all sides were in agreement over the repeal campaign; there was general approval as well as disappointment at O'Connell's decision to call off the Clontarf meeting in 1843 when it was banned by the government. O'Connell's subsequent imprisonment on fabricated charges by a packed jury demonstrated the determination of the Ascendancy to reject any move towards constitutional change and helped to open the search for alternative methods of gaining self-government.

A split between the Repeal Association and the Young Ireland movement arose in 1844 over Robert Peel's proposals to establish the Queen's Colleges in an attempt to win over moderate Irish opinion. The scheme, which was firmly non-denominational in character, was bitterly denounced by the Catholic hierarchy, who had envisaged a scheme similar to the national education system of 1831. However, it was broadly welcomed by the Young Ireland movement, who strongly favoured the concept of all Irishmen being educated together. The impasse over repeal of the Act of Union and the apparent paralysis of the movement led to disillusionment. In January 1847 the formation of the Irish Confederation embodied the open breach between Young Ireland and the centralised Repeal Association.

The worsening impact of the Famine and the example of the revolutions that had broken out in Europe in 1848 pushed the Young Ireland leadership towards militant action, but their subsequent rising was a desperate failure and led directly to the arrest and exile of most of the active leadership. The subsequent writings of John Mitchel, Charles Gavan Duffy and Michael Doheny kept their memories alive, however, and their brand of Romantic nationalism lived on through the Fenian period and informed the idealism of 1916 and the War of Independence.[7]

In Cork in the late 1850s, Sigerson was one of a group of young people who were influenced by the ideals of the Young Irelanders. The group included scientists, artists, poets and writers. He enjoyed the city of Cork and the friends he met there. Years later, in an article written about his friend, Robert Dwyer Joyce, who was also a poet and writer (he authored *The wind that shakes the barley*), Sigerson described the city of his student days as he remembered it:

> He [Joyce] came into a cultured and congenial society in the city by the pleasant waters of the Lee which had a native atmosphere of elegance, art and letters that might have merited the Violet Crown. In that work of classic wit, 'Father Prout's Reliques' by Father O'Mahoney who made the 'Bells of Shandon' ring around the world, honourable mention is made of Richard Dowden and he still happily flourished with the men of '48 such as Ralph Varian, a man of fine artistic temperament, a lover of Shelly [*sic*] and the best Wordsworthian I have known, whose love of Irish literature gave us two collections of ballad poetry. With this cultured and charming society were literature loving students … and others, so that Joyce found himself at home and in happy surroundings.[8]

The Varians of Cork

Among George Sigerson's company of friends in Cork were Isaac Varian and his youngest sister, Hester, who was to become Sigerson's wife. Isaac Varian, a poet and patriot, had been active in the Young Ireland movement and had suffered imprisonment during the 1840s for his beliefs. Hester's daughter, Hester Sigerson Piatt, wrote about her mother's memories of that time in Cork:

> My mother loved to tell stories of the Cork life of her girlhood, its humours, pleasures and friendships among these. On fine summer evenings the green, shady walks of the Mardyke knew the laughing groups of youths and maidens engaged in badinage, arguments or their favourite sport of 'capping' or improvising rhymes. Sometimes a couple or two would stray apart for the more private interchange of thoughts and feelings and among these would often be Hester Varian and George Sigerson.[9]

The Varians had long been settled in Cork. It is believed that they were originally a Huguenot family, but by this time they were Unitarian in faith, whereas the Sigersons were an old Catholic family. Thus the course of true love was held up early in its career, but not for long. Hester Varian became a Catholic from conviction and remained all her life a devout believer.

Meanwhile, lodging at 31 Ebenezer Terrace, Sunday's Well, Sigerson was sharing accommodation with Colm O'Keefe, whom he found a congenial roommate. O'Keefe was an accomplished chemist and deeply versed in Gaelic lore. He would afterwards become a Land Commissioner. During this time Sigerson was writing prose and verse, translating Gaelic poetry for his first book, beginning scientific researches and writing articles.

At other times he wrote letters to Hester Varian. During a few days' holiday at home with his parents in Tyrone, he wrote:

> I have finished two verses of a little pastoral ballad, 'The Cailin deas cruidhe na mbo' which is to represent you in brunette beauty and other qualifications. I don't

think I'll show it to you until you see it in *The Nation*. … There is a loch upon the mountains here (don't pronounce that word Lok – it's quite un-Irish.) Well this loch, not lok, took it into its head to punch a hole in its side (a fact) for fear of hydrocephalus, or water on the brain. But the oddity of the earth – no one has heard of it burst out anywhere yet. A great dread and heavy fear has seized upon the mountaineers of Tyrone, more especially as the lake is under druidic spell and magic enchantment along with two others. All three were formerly young damsels changed by a wicked magician and when I have heard more of them I will tell you and maybe wed it into an immortal verse.

Have you read in *The Nation* a review of 'Atlantis'? Well, the review of the medical part is by me. It is written for doctors and would take a terrible deal of talk to make unprofessional people know about it, but I think you will be able to get an idea of the case.[10]

Another letter to Hester Varian gives the first hint of the book he was working on:

I wish you not to tell anybody that I am translating a collection; they are not marvellous bursts of magnificent song as Mangan writes but puny ghosts shivering in the light of day.[11]

In yet another letter to Hester, in 1859, he told her that he was having difficulty with John O'Daly, collector of the original manuscripts, and publisher of the first series of *The poets and poetry of Munster*, which had been translated by James Clarence Mangan ten years earlier.[12] O'Daly, founder of the Ossianic Society and a noted collector of old Irish manuscripts, had contacted Sigerson in 1857 and asked him to translate a second series for publication for £200 or even £300. But after some delay on Sigerson's part in forwarding the translations, O'Daly threatened not to publish the book and warned against anybody else publishing the material. It would appear that O'Daly thought – quite wrongly – that Sigerson's motivation was mainly financial. Sigerson was very offended and he repudiated these 'low suspicions'.[13] The difficulties between the two men were eventually resolved, and the second series of *The poets and poetry of Munster* was published in 1860.

In 1865, Ralph Varian – a cousin of Sigerson's wife, Hester – published a book of poems called *Ballads, popular poetry and household songs of Ireland*.[14] The book contained poems by leading Irish writers. It included 13 poems by George Sigerson, two poems by Hester Varian Sigerson and two poems by Hester's brother, Isaac. This book and a later volume entitled *The harp of Erin* feature some of Sigerson's earliest original work.[15] Many of his compositions are about the hills and valleys of his native Tyrone, and his songs, 'The heather glen', 'On the Mountains of Pomeroy' and 'The Enniskillen Dragoon', have found their way into popular balladry. A collection of Irish melodies, which included a number of Sigerson's songs and ballads, was arranged by Michele Esposito, the renowned Italian-born composer, pianist and professor at the Royal Irish Academy of Music, and published by Pigott's in Dublin in the first decade of the twentieth century.[16]

Sheet music, Pigott & Co., 112 Grafton Street, Dublin

3

Early poetry and politics

The early years of the 1860s were of particular significance for George Sigerson. They marked the publication of his first book, *The poets and poetry of Munster*, his increasing involvement in political journalism, and his marriage to Hester Varian.

The poets and poetry of Munster, 1860

In this book of translations, which he dedicated to his father, Sigerson used the pseudonym 'Erionnach'. According to Douglas Hyde, it was not surprising that he did not use his own name. The book, with its outspoken preface, would not have been an appropriate recommendation for a professional man about to set up in the Dublin of the 1860s. Hyde asserted that the publication of both series of *The poets and poetry of Munster* was 'an act of national importance, which at the time no one even suspected'.[1] For Sigerson, it marked the beginning of his efforts to try and save the Irish language, which he compared to 'a patriarch sinking to rest'.[2]

The American critic, Ernest Boyd (1887–1946), in his work *Ireland's literary renaissance*, in which he devotes a chapter to the translation work of Sigerson and Douglas Hyde, stated that *The poets and poetry of Munster* marked 'the beginning of the Celtic Revival which subsequently made such headway under the leadership of Douglas Hyde'. He added that this publication, which contained the text of about fifty very beautiful Irish poems, with those metrical translations which were to become the special study of the author, was the first effective contribution to the Gaelic movement. Boyd went on to say that, had it not been for Sigerson and John O'Daly, 'the later vigour which the language movement attained would certainly have been retarded, if not rendered absolutely impossible'.[3] He described them as the link between the precursors of the Celtic Revival and its initiators, 'joining up the age of Mangan and Ferguson with that of the new literature whose seed was germinating in their work'.[4] He added that 'for many years these two fought alone against the indifference of the public towards Gaelic literature' and asserted:

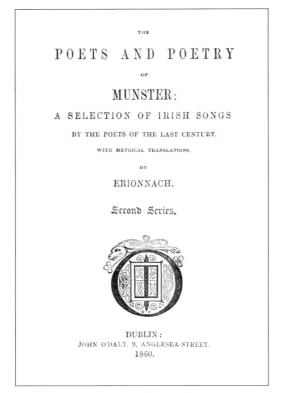

THE

POETS AND POETRY

OF

MUNSTER:

A SELECTION OF IRISH SONGS

BY THE POETS OF THE LAST CENTURY,

WITH METRICAL TRANSLATIONS,

BY

ERIONNACH.

Second Series.

DUBLIN:
JOHN O'DALY, 9, ANGLESEA-STREET.
1860.

Title page of *The poets and poetry of Munster*, 1860

In the field of translation George Sigerson may be said to occupy a position somewhat similar to that of Standish O'Grady in the history of Anglo-Irish literature proper, and to share the honours with him as doyen of the Revival. … The work of the translators and folklorists who collected, transcribed and translated these folk tales and songs, in which the old Celtic traditions still lived, was an important element in the forces that went to the formation of modern Anglo-Irish literature.[5]

France: Marshal (later President) Patrice de MacMahon

Ireland during the 1850s was a country where many people lived in abject poverty and political activity was almost non-existent. The weather added to the misery. Following several wet seasons, the wet summer of 1860 greatly impeded recovery from the years of famine. Unemployment was widespread and emigration, which had slowed down, began to accelerate again. According to Hester Sigerson Piatt, 'those of the western Gael who had survived the Famine seemed now to be swept away by the wholesale evictions and the reeking emigrant ships'.[6]

Living year after year in these conditions, with feelings of degradation and almost despair, many Irish people looked elsewhere to find hope and restore some faith in themselves. To do this, they found encouragement in the successes of Irish people or people of Irish descent in other lands. In 1860, they shared in the success of General Patrice de MacMahon, who had led the French army in defeating the Austrians at Magenta, Italy, the previous year. MacMahon was later to serve as president of the Third Republic (1873–9). Named 'the hero of Magenta', he was made a marshal of France by the Emperor Napoleon III and given the title duke of Magenta.

In Ireland the news of MacMahon's honour in 1860 was greeted largely with enthusiasm and, in response to a demand for information on MacMahon, an elaborate genealogy was published. This quickly led to a surge in public support, and a committee was formed to decide a fitting tribute to honour a man who had brought so much credit and pride to Ireland. It can be argued that the real purpose of all this patriotic fervour was to whip up anti-establishment tension and to direct international interest towards the plight of Ireland.

The committee decided to press ahead and present Marshal MacMahon with a symbol of his profession – a sword of honour and scabbard. An Irish artist, Edmund Fitzpatrick from Kilkenny, was commissioned to design the sword. The deputation to convey it to France included George Sigerson, the exiled Fenian John Mitchel, an Irish priest called Fr Dempsey, and Chevalier J.P. Leonard, a distinguished Irishman living in France who was MacMahon's close friend. Sigerson was already a frequent contributor to *The Irishman* newspaper and, being a fluent French speaker, was the ideal choice to act as the paper's correspondent. The other three members of the deputation lived in France.

Arrangements were made for the presentation in Châlons-sur-Marne, where MacMahon had his headquarters. On the way, at every stop, the presentation party was met by crowds eager to see the Irish sword for the hero of Magenta. Sigerson's first report to *The Irishman* gives a vivid account of the warmth of the reception:

> Through an avenue of white tents, past the high altar with its lofty canopy, where Mass had been celebrated that morning, our carriage advanced. Our arrival was duly notified and an aide-de-camp met us. We were conducted to the headquarters of His Excellence, Patrice de MacMahon, Marshal of France and Duke of Magenta. There he stood before us with his staff, taller than most men, soldierly and erect, giving each of us, as we were presented, a warm and most friendly welcome.[7]

As the presentation took place, an illuminated address, composed by Eugene O'Curry, the great Irish philologist and antiquarian, was read in French by J.P. Leonard. It stressed the reason for the presentation, the national pride felt by the people of Ireland at the high honour bestowed on one of its sons and how it had helped lift the spirit of the country at a time of great hardship. Marshal MacMahon invited the deputation to a celebration banquet that evening at which John Mitchel had a place of honour.

During the course of this visit, Sigerson became friendly with John Mitchel. A barrister by profession, Mitchel was also an experienced journalist. In 1843, he had begun to contribute articles to *The Nation*, eventually becoming its assistant editor. In 1848, he founded and edited the *United Irishman*. In the same year, after openly calling for an uprising as part of the Young Ireland Rebellion, he was tried, convicted of sedition and transported to Australia. He escaped to the United States in 1853 and eventually made his way back to Europe. Soon after his meeting with Sigerson in

1860, Mitchel accepted an invitation to become Paris correspondent for the *United Irishman*. On Sigerson's return to Ireland, he immediately began to make arrangements to have Mitchel's letters published. They appeared the following year as *The last conquest of Ireland (perhaps)*, published in serial form in *The Irishman*.[8]

Marriage and family

George Sigerson and Hester Varian were married in the Church of the Immaculate Conception, Marlborough Street, Dublin, on 11 December 1861. They moved into their first home in Synge Street shortly afterwards, where George set about establishing his medical practice. Their eldest son, William Ralph, was born here but sadly died before he had reached two years of age. Hester recalled her mother describing their first born as an exceptionally intelligent and beautiful child, closely resembling his father, with the same broad forehead. She herself remembered seeing a faded photograph of the dead baby in his cot beside his sorrowful parents. The following lines, taken from Sigerson's *The saga of King Lir*, refer to their first born son:

> The sunbright boy, the flower of all the flock
> And he who tells it knew of one as fair
> For earth too fair, for whom the skies bent down
> Which left one glad in woe.[9]

Soon after his death, the Sigersons moved to 17 Richmond Hill, where the rest of the family, George Patrick, Dora and Hester, were born, and where they lived until 1877. The move to Richmond Hill brought a period of great productivity. Sigerson wrote for many of the leading newspapers and periodicals, including the *Irish People*, *The Nation*, *The Irishman*, *Hibernian Magazine*, *The Shamrock* and the *Harp*. He offered original poetry and translations, articles on patriotic and political subjects, and short stories. He never used his real name but a variety of pseudonyms of which 'Erionnach' was his favourite. Others included 'Snorro', 'Paddy Henry' and 'An Ulsterman'. At one time he edited both *The Irishman* and *The Shamrock* and attracted contributions from many distinguished writers such as John Mitchel, William Carleton, T.C. Irwin, John Augustus O'Shea and Denis Holland.

Hester Sigerson Piatt remembered this time, when she was a young child, very well:

> Always he wrote a weekly leader for *The Irishman* and these occasions are one of my earliest memories. Often in the summer he used to sit in our back garden in Richmond Hill in a sort of bower formed by drooping willows. I recollect his appearance as he sat writing at a little table, pale, with a slight beard, his hair long and fair. We had to be very quiet on these occasions, a matter of so much difficulty in early childhood that it probably fixed the scene in my mind.[10]

Political writings

Sigerson also began writing for English journals early in the 1860s. A representative selection of widely quoted articles which he had written for the *Daily Chronicle* was published as *Modern Ireland: its vital questions, secret societies and government* in 1868 under the pseudonym 'An Ulsterman'. The book included articles on Irish education, the Orange Order, Celtic land tenure and Fenianism. They attracted the attention of politicians and scholars in England and abroad, who quickly recognised Sigerson as a reliable, informed source of information on Ireland. Given his in-depth knowledge of Irish history and the condition and needs of the country, English politicians easily understood his straightforward views. The historian Lord Acton, an adviser to Prime Minister Gladstone and a regular correspondent with Sigerson, wrote:

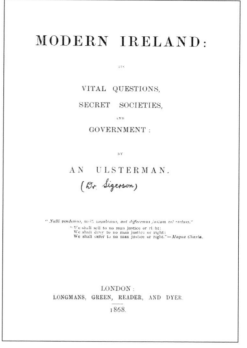

Title page of *Modern Ireland*, 1868

> You must accept the penalty of being the best and soundest authority in my judgement on Irish affairs and I trust you will accept it cheerfully and forgive the trouble I want to give you by my letter.[11]

The land question, which was the most important Irish issue at the time, had already claimed Sigerson's attention, and he had spent many years studying 'with all possible accuracy the relative as well as the absolute position of the Irish land-classes. To accomplish this,' he had said, 'it was necessary to trace out those ancient laws, customs, and usages from which the people had long been separated. … The history of the past showed both what to revive and what to avoid.'[12] A series of his articles on the subject was published in the *North British Review* and the *Home and Foreign Review*, prior to the introduction of the Irish Land Bill of 1870. Greatly expanded and augmented, it was published in 1871 as *History of the land tenures and land classes of Ireland, with an account of the various secret agrarian confederacies*. When Gladstone was preparing his Irish land legislation, he had publicly acknowledged the material on

Irish land tenure which Sigerson had written, and in Ireland the liberal unionist historian Edward Lecky quoted Sigerson's work with approval.

Theodor Mommsen, the German historian and classical scholar who won the Nobel prize for literature in 1902, studied Sigerson's articles before he agreed to send material to T.F. Wetherell for the *North British Review* and the *Home and Foreign Review*. Mommsen's great interest was Roman law but he was also a prominent German politician and he asked Sigerson to be his colleague 'in an enterprise sympathetic to both'.[13] Sadly there is no record as to whether this ever happened.

The Manchester Martyrs

During its brief period of existence (1863–5), Sigerson wrote articles for the *Irish People*, the Fenian newspaper that openly advocated the doctrine of physical force. He became friendly with two of the leaders of Fenianism, John O'Leary and Charles Kickham. According to C.P. Curran:

> Sigerson, although not a Fenian himself, placed himself by their side. It is not easy in our day to realize how much courage and tenacity it meant in 1862 to take the stand he then took and unswervingly held.[14]

The term 'Fenians' was commonly applied to members of the Irish Republican Brotherhood and the Fenian Brotherhood, which had started in 1858 during the political vacuum created by the collapse of the Tenant Right League. Many of the important figures in the movement had been connected with the Young Ireland Rebellion of ten years earlier. In 1865, with many thousands of young men having taken the oath of the Fenian Brotherhood in Ireland, Britain and the United States, plans were hatched for another armed uprising. However, acting on information supplied by an informer who had been planted in the offices of the *Irish People* that an uprising was imminent, the police raided the paper, seized all incriminating documents and arrested anyone suspected of being involved with the Fenians. The failures of the attempted invasions of Canada in 1866 and 1870 and the botched 'insurrection' in Ireland in 1867, however, were essentially token rebellions – little more than staged publicity coups. The subsequent arrests, trials, speeches from the dock, imprisonments and occasional daring rescues were the real successes. Fenianism remained a mystical movement, capable of winning popular approval at a sentimental level but having only indirect impact on life and politics in Ireland. Among those subsequently convicted of treason and felony and sentenced to penal servitude were Sigerson's close friends, John O'Leary and Charles Kickham.

How did Sigerson himself avoid arrest? Although undoubtedly a sympathiser, he had published his work anonymously, so his identity would have been known to very few people. According to O'Leary:

Sigerson was not a Fenian; a nationalist – yes, as his vigorous and numerous prose and verse proved, but knowing little more about our plans than could be gathered from Irish and American papers.[15]

Although the Fenian Rising proved to be a dismal failure, its influence would remain strong in Britain and America for many years. In 1867 an incident occurred in England that sent shockwaves throughout Ireland. During an attempted rescue of two Fenians from a prison van in Manchester, a policeman was killed. Three of those involved in the rescue were captured and, after a short trial, hanged for murder. They became known as the Manchester Martyrs. The executions of William Philip Allen, Michael Larkin and Michael O'Brien caused mass resentment and bitterness throughout Ireland. Great efforts to seek an appeal, even a reprieve, for what many regarded as an accidental killing had failed. Irish newspapers were highly critical of the government's handling of the affair. The executions were denounced as 'judicial murder'. Newspapers, full of passion and invective, risked libel. The jailer and the hangman were declared the 'twin guardians of British rule in Ireland'.[16] Mock funerals were held in different parts of the country, the largest being in Dublin, when over 60,000 mourners followed three coffinless hearses to Glasnevin Cemetery. The well known song 'God save Ireland', which was written by the journalist, T.D. Sullivan, and adopted by the Fenian movement as their anthem, was inspired by Edward O'Meagher Condon's speech from the dock when he stood trial along with Allen, Larkin and O'Brien.

Sigerson, who was editor of *The Irishman* at this time, was incensed by the executions and anonymously wrote a famous article for the newspaper entitled 'The Holocaust'. In it he vehemently denounced the government, comparing its treatment of the Irish to the Egyptians' treatment of the Israelites of old. The opening sentences set the tone for a sustained attack on the workings of England's justice in the conviction and condemnation of the three young Irishmen:

Deaf to all warnings, however ominous, spurning alike the argument of the Just and the prayer of the Merciful, the Government has this day done a deed of blood which shall overshadow its name before the whole world. Nothing can account for its perpetration against all the urgings of statesmanship and humanity save only the blindness which falls from Heaven on overweening pride.[17]

Referring to what he saw as 'a vitiated verdict, on tainted testimony, on evidence which has been admitted to be that of false swearers and perjurers – on a verdict allowed to be flawed with error', he continued, 'There indeed, written large and deep, written in letters indelible, written in letters of BLOOD, read the mercy and justice of England.'[18]

In language which was to be echoed by Pearse at the grave of O'Donovan Rossa, he thundered:

> DEAD! DEAD! DEAD! But there are those who think that in death they will be more powerful than in life. There are those who will read on their Tomb the prayer for an Avenger to spring from their bones ... and we foresee trouble and trepidations which might have been averted by a humane policy ... they shall yet be remembered in their native land along with those who have gone before them; nor shall their deaths shake her desire for a legislative independence, nor her trust in a speedy consummation.[19]

The article caused an immediate sensation and resulted in the paper's owner, Richard Pigott, who refused to disclose its authorship, being imprisoned for 'seditious and unlawful libel'. T.P. O'Connor remembered attending the trial of Pigott and A.M. Sullivan, the owner of the *Weekly News*, another nationalist paper that had published an article about the Manchester Martyrs. In his autobiography, *Memoirs of an old parliamentarian*, he wrote:

> They were convicted of course. Pigott was sentenced to twelve months and Sullivan to six months. The chief article in evidence against Pigott was that in *The Irishman* by Sigerson; it was one of the most powerful articles I ever read; its power was so great that the Attorney General, who was prosecuting, paid a tribute to its effectiveness, coupling that with the statement that the more effective it was, the guiltier it was and the greater the necessity for the punishment of the newspaper proprietor who had published it. This accounted for the longer sentence of imprisonment given to Pigott than to Sullivan.[20]

In *Recollections of an Irish national journalist*, Pigott himself referred to the comments of the prosecution:

> The original article included in the indictment against me was published in a special edition of *The Irishman* on the 25th November, immediately after the news of the executions reached Dublin. It had been greatly praised as a literary work. The Attorney General was good enough to tell the jury that it was written by no ordinary pen, and by a man of high ability. He also said: 'Perhaps you may live many years – you may drink deep of the stream of literature, but I believe you will seldom meet in your reading an article of power, of more vigour, of more stirring eloquence, than the article called The Holocaust'. Rumour ascribed its authorship to my dear lamented friend, Isaac Butt, but I am, I think, in a position to say that he was not the writer.[21]

However, in a letter to Chief Secretary Forster in 1880, Pigott, who would gain notoriety in the late 1880s as the forger of letters which appeared to implicate Parnell in the Phoenix Park murders, had no hesitation in condemning Sigerson, his former editor, as 'a man who, to my own knowledge has written more treason, treason-felony, sedition and incitements to murder and outrage than any other living man in Ireland at least'.[22]

Sigerson and the early Home Rule movement

While focusing on furthering his professional career, Sigerson nevertheless continued with his literary activities and his weekly columns. He remained editor of *The Irishman* and in this capacity received a letter from Isaac Butt, founder of the Home Rule League. Sigerson had met Butt at the Fenian trials nearly ten years earlier, when Butt, a barrister, had defended many of the prisoners. There was at this stage a renewed vigour about the nationalist movement in Ireland. Butt was elected in 1874 and pledged to seek a form of self-government for Ireland. The Liberal Party in Britain, under the leadership of William Gladstone, appeared to be ready to address Irish grievances and some of the more radical Irish members were willing to accept a wait-and-see policy towards the possible benefits of constitutional agitation. The British political elite and much of the press bitterly denounced the unparliamentary conduct of the Home Rule members in the House of Commons, especially the obstructionist tactics of people like Joseph Biggar and Charles Stewart Parnell, suggesting that the Home Rule movement might achieve something worthwhile from the British connection. Isaac Butt, however, was becoming increasingly frustrated at the direction being taken by some of these members of the Home Rule League. This may be reflected in his correspondence with Sigerson.

One of his letters, concerning 'Irish and Irishman politics', reads as follows:

> It occurs to me that the last debate on Ireland is the most wretched confession of impotence ever given by an Assembly. From beginning to end there is not an idea put forward worthy of a statesman, or a sentence uttered there showing an appreciation of the real Irish question. If it will suit the arrangement of the paper, I will send you tomorrow an article on the debate. I am thinking of calling the first article 'The Grand Parliamentary Gabble' – this would be a denunciation of the whole thing. The other two would be – one on the Land question, the other on the Education question, as they were mangled in the debate. … I would be very glad, whenever you have a disengaged hour, to have a long talk with you over 'Irish and Irishman' politics. I would like to make [*sic*] any help I can and give as much help to you as I can.[23]

This letter is quoted in Hester Sigerson Piatt's manuscript but it is undated and difficult to place in context. There were apparently other letters from Butt in the family collection but these have not survived. Thus it is difficult to know if there was ever any meaningful exchange of opinions or ideas between the two men.

For Isaac Butt, however, time had run out. The younger members of the Home Rule League had become impatient with his moderate claims. His lack of fire and passion and his failure to make progress in parliament frustrated them. For them, Charles Stewart Parnell – 'the chief' – was now their real leader. Parnell was elected chairman of the Home Rule Confederation of Great Britain in 1877 and, in the following year, chairman of the Irish Party in the House of Commons. A disappointed man, Isaac Butt died in 1879. He is buried in Stranorlar, County Donegal. It is unlikely that Sigerson developed a close relationship with Butt. The latter's very moderation in politics – he was originally elected to parliament as a Conservative – and his unwillingness to challenge the British connection would have been anathema to the radical nationalism of Sigerson's circle and readership. Parnell and his followers were much more in touch with the ideals of the Fenians and in tune with the growing agrarian expectations of nationalist Ireland in the 1880s.

4

Sigerson the doctor

Science and medicine

Although he continued to be deeply involved in political writing about the key issues of the day, Sigerson nevertheless devoted considerable time to developing his medical skills and pursing medical research. According to his daughter, Hester, 'in the ten years succeeding 1870, he crossed to France yearly in pursuit of his studies'.[1] This was a period of rapid advancement of knowledge in the field of medical science and, in the space of five decades, France had become the centre of this new learning.

Sigerson was a member of the Linnean Society of London – the world's premier society for the study and dissemination of taxonomy and natural history – the Royal Irish Academy and other societies. His scientific papers attracted the attention of scientists such as Charles Darwin, the physicist John Tyndall and the biologist, Thomas Henry Huxley. Following the publication of a paper entitled 'Some remarks on a protomorphic phyllotype' which appeared in the university review, *Atlantis,*[2] Sigerson received a letter from Charles Darwin. In it Darwin made reference to his own work on phyllotaxy and problems he was having with one aspect of it. He wrote that he 'had signally failed in his attempt to explain this phenomenon'. Sigerson in reply sought to clarify a part of his paper in *Atlantis*, which might help Darwin with his problem. As to Darwin's suggestion that he might undertake further research on this subject, Sigerson stated that he was not in a position at that time to pursue the matter but hoped to do so soon.[3]

Throughout the 1860s, Sigerson made numerous journeys to France to continue postgraduate medical studies under the most eminent doctors and scientists and of course to take the opportunity to meet old friends again. In mental and nervous diseases he studied under Jean-Martin Charcot and Duchenne de Boulogne, in histology under Louis-Antoine Ranvier and in physiology with Claude Bernard. One of his oldest and closest friends was Benjamin Ball, professor and examiner at the École de Médicine, Paris. He would also take the opportunity to meet up with former

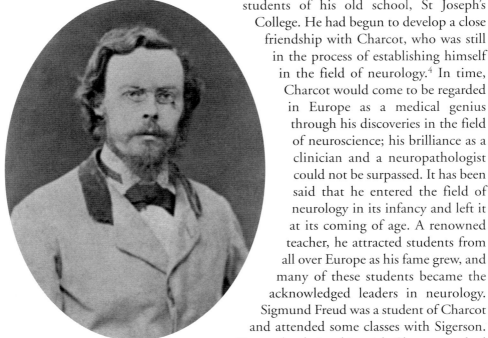

Dr George Sigerson,
Paris 1870

students of his old school, St Joseph's College. He had begun to develop a close friendship with Charcot, who was still in the process of establishing himself in the field of neurology.[4] In time, Charcot would come to be regarded in Europe as a medical genius through his discoveries in the field of neuroscience; his brilliance as a clinician and a neuropathologist could not be surpassed. It has been said that he entered the field of neurology in its infancy and left it at its coming of age. A renowned teacher, he attracted students from all over Europe as his fame grew, and many of these students became the acknowledged leaders in neurology. Sigmund Freud was a student of Charcot and attended some classes with Sigerson. Sigerson's relationship with Charcot resulted in his translation of Charcot's *Lectures on the diseases of the nervous system* into English in 1877.[5]

At home Sigerson's medical practice had begun to expand. His reputation as someone who could successfully treat people with nervous disorders and stress-related problems was becoming well known and resulted in patients attending his surgery from all over Ireland. He was regarded as the first neurologist in Dublin.

In 1865, he received the degree of Master of Surgery at the Queen's University of Ireland. His first academic appointment, in April of that year, was in the Catholic University of Ireland, where he was given a lectureship in botany. His relationship with the Catholic University Medical School was to last for 55 years.

In 1873 Sigerson received a letter from W.K. Sullivan, former professor of chemistry at the Catholic University Medical School and the Royal College of Surgeons, who wrote to him from Cork, where he had now become president of Queen's College:

> I hope the report that you have been made Professor of Natural History in the Catholic University is true, and also that it is not an empty honour and that you get a proper salary. I will not say that I congratulate you, because you know how ardently I had long wished to see justice done to you and an opportunity given to you to devote yourself to science. But I will now tell you that the refusal to make

you professor two or three years since had something to do with my leaving the Catholic University.[6]

Sigerson, however, had to wait some more years before he was appointed to a chair in the university and, despite Sullivan's wish to see him concentrate on his scientific career, was obliged to depend on his medical practice for his livelihood. As suggested earlier, Sigerson appears to have suffered from his high profile as newspaper columnist, editor and outspoken critic of government policies towards Ireland. Clearly his peers had full confidence in his medical competency and leadership potential but the higher echelons of academia were not quite convinced.

By 1874 his research findings had begun to appear in French medical journals. One paper, entitled 'Note sur la paralysie vasomotrice, généralisée des membres supérieurs', which appeared in *Le Progrès Médical* (1874) gained Sigerson much praise. Other papers which he published during the 1870s included 'Heat as a factor in vital action' (1875), 'Contributions to the study of nerve-action in connection with the sense of taste' (1877), and 'On alternate paralyses' (1878).

Always keen to visit France, he accepted an invitation to speak at the St Patrick's Day celebration banquet in the Paris Royale in 1875, at which his fellow speaker was Fr (later Cardinal) Michael Logue. The guests included John O'Leary, J.P. Leonard and Jean-Martin Charcot.

In 1877, Charcot entrusted to Sigerson the translation of his book, *Lectures on the diseases of the nervous system*, and invited him to add original and valuable notes of his own. In the *Dublin Journal of Medical Science*, a review of the book states:

> It is almost needless to call attention to this volume which, under the auspices of the 'New Sydenham Society', is introduced to a wide circle of readers, for its own intrinsic merits will assuredly place it in the foremost ranks of medical literature.[7]

The two friends corresponded frequently, consulting with each other over a variety of neurological problems. In one letter, Charcot announced that he was sending an American patient to Sigerson for treatment of neurasthenia. In 1879, the British Medical Congress was held in Cork and Charcot was invited to speak. In a letter to Sigerson, he wrote that he would only attend the congress if Sigerson accompanied him, adding: 'It will not be for the medicine but to enjoy the fresh air and scenery and to meet nice people.'[8] Having heard much about their beauty, he expressed an interest in visiting the lakes of Killarney and Glengariff, and this was arranged.

In later years Sigerson took his daughters, Dora and Hester, to France and they dined at Charcot's home near Neuilly with his wife and son. This son was later to gain fame as Commander Jean-Baptiste Charcot, world-renowned organiser of two expeditions to the Antarctic, who tragically perished in 1936 when his ship went down off Iceland in a storm.

Clare Street: medical practice

In 1877, the family moved from Richmond Hill to a tall old house in Clare Street, Dublin. This would be George Sigerson's home for the remainder of his life. Writing in the *Sunday Independent*, journalist T.P. O'Hanlon gave an account of Sigerson at this time:

> It was in 3 Clare Street that George Sigerson began to seriously practise his profession – soon gaining a reputation for successfully treating apparently hopeless conditions. This brings me to a phase of the career of Dr Sigerson of which the public knew little or nothing – the extraordinary devotion with which he attended to the sufferers brought to him from all over the country, from England and the United States, and even Australia. For six or seven hours a day, he sat in his study treating all manner of nervous afflictions and often with results which were little short of miraculous – often too, without any other reward than the prayers of the patient. Many who came to him were difficult to deal with, due to the nature of the ailments, mental affliction and the like. His homely, fatherly manner broke down the barrier of their reserve; after a little while in his company his dry humour and warm hearted sympathy won their esteem, confidence and love.[9]

As a further indication of the esteem in which Sigerson was held, O'Hanlon told a story about an elderly Jewish woman who attended his surgery two or three days a week. One day, Sigerson was annoyed with her. The day was bitterly cold because of an east wind. Having told her not to venture out when the weather was harsh, he remonstrated with her. She told him she did not know an east wind was blowing, or from which direction an east wind came. 'Where does the sun rise?' he asked. 'I would not know for certain,' she replied, 'but my own belief is that it rises in Clare Street. And you, Dr Sigerson, remind me of Moses, the law giver, who did good works until the Lord kissed him and took him to heaven.'[10]

In his chosen specialism, the treatment of people suffering diseases of the nervous system, Sigerson enjoyed an international reputation. According to O'Hanlon, who knew him extremely well, all his patients were treated with firmness but also with great compassion. As the years went by, most of the country's leading political and literary figures came to regard Sigerson as their personal physician, though no exceptions were made for reputation or standing. If he made domiciliary visits, he required strict adherence to his instructions. On one occasion, while attending Maud Gonne, he incurred the wrath of W.B. Yeats. Having prescribed complete rest for his patient, Sigerson sent a few visitors away and advised others – including Yeats – not to bother her. Although Yeats believed that Sigerson was being hostile and unnecessarily obstructive, he nevertheless obeyed his instruction and stayed away.

The poet Austin Clarke received Sigerson's medical care following a chance meeting at the university. Sigerson took one look at him, and said, 'Come and see me next

Tuesday at four o'clock.' Clarke attended the surgery for one month, and remembered that 'neither the pins and needles of the galvanic battery nor the black puddings – which were prescribed for their wholesomeness – could compensate for the "folly of youth".'[11]

James Joyce, who attended Sigerson's lectures, advised Nora Barnacle, a chambermaid at Finn's Hotel, quite close to Clare Street, to seek Sigerson's help. He wrote, 'Dear Nora, I hope you haven't that horrible pain this morning. Go out and see old Dr Sigerson and get him to prescribe for you.' There is no record as to whether she followed his advice.[12]

Sir Charles Gavan Duffy, the founder and editor of *The Nation*, wrote to Sigerson from Nice about his insomnia, which only allowed him three hours' sleep at night:

> Is there any remedy but abandoning my work, which would be odious, or taking a sleeping draught which would be worse[?] I want to steal an opinion from you as there is no doctor here in whom I have any confidence.[13]

Even in the early 1920s, when Sigerson was well past retirement age – although he had at last begun to cut back drastically on his workload – he still resisted his daughter Hester's pleas that he should stop practising medicine. His loyalty to his patients remained strong and he was not prepared to abandon them.

Surprisingly, Sigerson never succeeded in securing a hospital appointment in spite of all his high honours, his awards from the greatest medical authorities in Europe and his own medical triumphs, especially in the fields of nervous and mental diseases. It is not unreasonable to conclude that his association with men like the Fenians, Kickham and O'Leary, and his political journalism made him an unacceptable figure and labelled him an extremist.

Absurd stories were told about him. His daughter, Hester, recalled one of the most bizarre. She was asked by a dentist who lived no more than a stone's throw away from Clare Street if it was true that her father had a mat in his hall in the design and colours of the Union Jack and that all visitors and patients were obliged to wipe their feet on it before entering. This particular story caused Sigerson great amusement whenever it was repeated to him.[14]

Rather belatedly, the Royal College of Physicians conferred on him an honorary fellowship in 1918, when he was 82 years of age. He had held a licentiate from the college since 1875 and had delivered his first contribution to medical literature in the college hall in that year. Sigerson graciously thanked the college for the honorary fellowship, though he may have felt rather intrigued by the belated timing of the award. In accepting the honour, however, Sigerson was as unapologetic as ever about his wider role in Irish affairs and strongly implied that many of his fellow medical practitioners might look more fully at what the country needed. If he had diverged a

St George and The Dragon (Dr George Sigerson).
Cartoon by Grace Gifford.
Courtesy of the National Library of Ireland

little from medical work, he continued, it was on principles that derived from their great brotherhood. Nations sometimes suffer from diseases and require remedies less by the surgeon's knife than by the mental or intellectual aid of the physician. Sigerson said that when that great patient, one's country, suffered, it should not be deemed odd that the physician took part in what he considered his duty to relieve pain, to heal wounds, to cultivate hope and assure her of a happier future. It is true, said Sigerson, that in his leisure hours he had trodden the lighter paths of literature, but a change of work was often the best recreation.[15]

Several mornings a week he lectured at the Catholic University Medical School, and the afternoons were used to deal with the ever-increasing numbers of patients. The ante-room seldom emptied and he was prepared to remain on duty until the last patient of the day had been attended to. His dinner, which during the week might be shared with a few close friends, could occur any time between eight o'clock and midnight, depending on the number of patients to be treated. Apart from his undoubted ability as a physician, which would have been enough to guarantee him a large clientele, his reputation for being generous was well known and was often carried to excess. On many occasions he forfeited his fee and prescribed free of charge; moreover, if he felt that a patient's general need was great, he would give a donation of some kind. Douglas Hyde recalled sending him a cheque which as far as he could see was never cashed and he heard other people say the same thing. After Sigerson died and his home in Clare Street was being cleared out, a drawer in his study was found to be full of uncashed cheques.

Because of the pressure of medical work, Sigerson had no option but to do his literary work at night. Hester Sigerson tells us that this was a habit he had developed when his children were young and had gone to bed, but it persisted long after they had married and left home.[16] He admitted that he enjoyed the peace and solitude of the sleeping house, often working through the long hours to complete an article. One project on which he had begun to work in the mid-1870s was a second book of translations – a book that would cover the whole range of Irish poetry and in which all the great epochs would be represented. It would take almost another 20 years to complete.[17]

The Mansion House Relief Committee

The famine of 1879

The ominous signs that had preceded the Great Famine a generation earlier began to appear again in 1879. For the third year in succession there had been a cold, wet summer – the temperature for July being 3.9 degrees below the average – with rain falling on two out of every three days. The previous two years had exhausted any reserves of food or fuel and the population was depending on the autumn harvest. Unfortunately, the harvest of 1879 turned out to be the worst harvest since the Famine: the potato crop was almost totally destroyed, especially in the western counties of Ireland, and many people faced starvation.

On 16 December 1879, a letter from the duchess of Marlborough in *The Times* of London appealed for 'English benevolence, for the relief of distress in Ireland'. It continued:

> There will be extreme misery and suffering among the poor, owing to the want of employment, loss of turf, loss of cattle and failure of the potato, unless a vigorous effort of private charity is got up to supplement the ordinary system of Poor Law relief.[1]

Her letter concluded with an impassioned plea to help alleviate what was, in effect, a famine of food and fuel. A few months earlier, the English press had stressed that, contrary to reports circulating in Ireland, the crops were growing luxuriantly and the potatoes were blight free. The press had proclaimed the same thing in the early autumn of 1845.

Despite adequate warnings and appeals from priests, Protestant clergymen, doctors and landowners, the government would not listen. A deputation of Irish bishops went to Dublin Castle to express their anxiety and concerns, but were met with indifference. The prime minister, Lord Beaconsfield, refused to meet 75 Irish members of parliament to discuss the crisis. The matter was played down to such an extent that, during question time in the House of Commons, James Lowther, the chief secretary for Ireland, when asked if the government proposed to take any steps to alleviate the existing distress in Ireland, replied, 'It is a matter of satisfaction to the Irish Government that we have reason to believe the distress has not been so acutely felt in Ireland as in other parts of the United Kingdom.' Therefore, they did not intend to discuss the matter.[2]

Genuine as all those appeals were, no one – not even those who issued them – would have been prepared to accept that a recurrence of the Great Famine was possible. The circumstances of the late 1870s were very different. The population, which had been decimated by the Famine and subsequent years of emigration, was much smaller and less dependent on the potato. Thus it was hoped that, providing that the grain harvest was successful, there would still be enough food to meet the needs of the people.

But this was not to be. The winds and rain of 1879 almost totally destroyed the grain harvest and turnips lay rotting and wasting in the fields. During the next few months the situation quickly deteriorated, particularly in the west of Ireland, and the bishop of Achonry was forced to make an impassioned plea to an apparently cynical and unsympathetic government:

> We, Irish priests and bishops, are custodians of morality and order. It is our duty to counsel peace and preach loyalty. But it is hard to instil loyalty or promote peace when there is a question of empty stomachs and an unsympathetic Government.[3]

The Mansion House Relief Committee

On Christmas Eve, the bishop's house had been surrounded by some 300 starving people, and stories of similar incidents were becoming commonplace. In Clifden, 1,500 destitute people besieged the local Relief Committee for food. As the crisis became more serious, Sir John Barrington, the lord mayor of Dublin, called together a number of Dublin's leading citizens – people from every walk of life, including church leaders and political figures. It was decided that, since the government was not prepared to take action, the people themselves must act.

They agreed to form a committee whose first aim would be to launch an appeal for funds. At their first meeting they resolved:

> That the poorer classes in many parts of Ireland must, during the coming season, suffer great distress, involving absolute destitution, if extraneous aid be not liberally and promptly supplied, and that, without interfering with the beneficent efforts for a similar purpose already instituted, a Fund be now opened for the relief of distress in Ireland to be called The Dublin Mansion House Relief Fund.[4]

THE IRISH CRISIS OF 1879–80.

PROCEEDINGS

OF THE

DUBLIN MANSION HOUSE

RELIEF COMMITTEE,

1880.

DUBLIN:
BROWNE & NOLAN, NASSAU-STREET.
1881.

Title page of *The Irish crisis of 1879–80*

George Sigerson was a founder member of this committee and would play a very important role in its activities – initially as publicity officer and later, when the famine developed into a fever epidemic, as medical officer.

Following the formation of the committee, a subscription fund was begun and an appeal was telegraphed around the world. The response from Irish exiles and friends in many distant places was immediate. Donations arrived from America, Canada, Australia, India and Europe. A sum of £181,000 was contributed within a period of months, allowing the committee to begin their relief work and distribute aid.

Throughout the early months of 1880 the donations from the Mansion House Committee kept starvation at bay and a change of government meant that the officials in Dublin Castle were more favourable to famine relief. Thus a donation of £50 from the new chief secretary, William Edward Forster, and £500 from Earl Cowper, the incoming lord lieutenant, demonstrated a changed view on official relief just as the funds of the Mansion House Committee were running low. The committee put pressure on the Local Government Board to augment the public works programme launched earlier in the year and the changes in the Poor Law administration that allowed relief to be given outside the workhouse.

The Mansion House Committee had been discussing in May how they could continue to operate and Sigerson had been deputed to draw up a powerful statement for distribution abroad, showing the continuing need for charitable donations. The problems of continuing famine in many places was being added to by the emergence of the new danger, widespread fever.[5]

Just as in 1846, when the Famine was followed by a serious epidemic of fever, reports of outbreaks of famine fever began to reach the committee's headquarters in Dublin in the early summer of 1880. They were isolated at first, but became more numerous by the day. Already 60 homesteads were affected at Garumna in County Mayo and 105 in the district of Kilmaine. The fact that most of the reported illnesses bore the signs of malignant typhus caused the authorities to claim that the epidemic was not caused by destitution – that typhus and famine fever were different diseases with different aetiologies. According to the government, a more likely reason for the outbreaks was insanitary conditions in the homes of the poorer classes. The Mansion House Committee challenged this assumption. It referred to the 1851 census to argue that not only were the typhus and fever directly attributable to the famine, but the famine was to blame for the large number of people who suffered a variety of deformities through years of poverty and deprivation. Despite this – and the census of 1871, which supported the committee's findings – the government held on to the notion that poor sanitation was the reason for the outbreaks of fever.[6]

The Medical Commission

On 28 June 1880, the committee asked Sigerson to form a medical commission to test the government's assumptions and to investigate the actual character and origins of the fevers. He had already been involved in organising relief and, in his voluminous correspondence, his daughter found two interesting letters from Bishop Michael Logue of Raphoe, later to be cardinal and archbishop of Armagh. Both dealt with the bishop's ideas on how relief could best be distributed. He had a firm preference for a diocesan organisation that would not be so susceptible to local pressures when deciding who should be worthy of relief:

> I also believe your Committee shall find in the end that their funds will be more judiciously distributed through a central body that knows the state of the country intimately than if you dealt directly with Parochial committees.[7]

Logue believed that those who shouted loudest could generally control matters at local level and that, since the original scheme had envisaged all interests being included in the relief committees, such committees might have limited the potential influence of the local Catholic clergy.

The second letter was critical of some members of the Mansion House Committee over their readiness to cooperate with the Duchess of Marlborough Relief Fund and with the existing Boards of Guardians. Logue was adamant that such association with the failed property classes could only be detrimental to the interests of the poorer classes throughout the country:

> I have suspected from reading the reports of your meetings, that there are some members of your Committee whose bodies are at the Mansion House, but whose hearts are at the Castle.[8]

There is no record of how closely Sigerson worked with the bishop in the relief schemes but the letters certainly suggest that Logue believed he had a strong ally in the person of the young doctor.

Sigerson requested the assistance of Dr Joseph Kenny, a very experienced and respected Dublin physician. Kenny had gained much knowledge of the effects of poverty at the North City Dispensary. They travelled throughout the west of Ireland, seeing the appalling conditions that prevailed and taking evidence. Sigerson and Kenny found that deficient nutrition was the principal cause, and in many cases the only cause, of the fever problem of 1880. J.A. Fox, who had carried out an investigation into the extent of distress in Mayo, had highlighted the growing incidence of fever in the area and prompted the committee to investigate the matter more thoroughly.[9]

The General Report of the committee concluded that:

> the task was performed in a manner which gained the applause of high medical authorities and which, to a great extent, shaped the course of the Government into a resolute subjugation of the epidemics and in every respect confirmed the Committee's estimate of Dr Sigerson's high scientific and professional reputation.[10]

It found that its own recorded experiences among the sufferers firmly established that:

> deficient nutrition was invariably the principal, and in many cases unquestionably the only cause, of the production of the prevalent disease. A few of the scenes which came under their notice are conclusive upon this point, as well as pitiful beyond the power of words to express.[11]

The report includes extracts from the special investigations carried out by Sigerson and Kenny. The following refer to the Charlestown district of County Mayo, submitted to the Mansion House Committee on 12 July 1880:

Entering one house, fairly circumstanced, we were received by the mother, pale, feeble, scarcely able to move about after a severe attack of fever. Two or three children, convalescents, were sitting in the kitchen, and in the inner room lay, far advanced in emasculated typhus, her father in law, husband, and two grown up daughters. Until a few days ago she had to attend to all. Even now, though an old woman had been got as a nurse, the sick son had been obliged to take the sicker father into his bed in order to restrain him whilst delirious. This house is worse than a fever ward; it is a fever furnace. The family throughout this terrible time of illnesses have been dependent for every life upon the support of the Local Relief Committee.

At Ballintadder, in a musty, dark room, two children were tossing in fever on some straw on the floor, and another ailing on the poor bed. In an adjoining cabin five children had been ailing together; two were up when we entered and three lying in fever, 'heads and points', on an old bedstead, covered with a couple of potato sacks. In the midst of their affliction the father gives refuge to an infirm and aged sister. It may be mentioned, as adding to the sombre character of the scene, that these people are under notice of ejectment.

We had to leave the car on the high road and follow a rugged way, made through the bog by the tenants, for a distance of about three quarters of an English mile, in order to reach their habitations. Those two are the only fever smitten families who have as yet received outdoor relief, so far as we could ascertain.[12]

Regarding this family's notice of ejectment, action was deferred because the Swineford Assizes were postponed on account of the prevalence of fever; but the evictions were subsequently carried out.

Sigerson and Kenny, in their report, described another case as follows:

After a drive of three miles from Charlestown to Upper Lurga, over a most uneven road, we came within sight of a lonely cabin on a bleak moor, of which a few acres had been reclaimed. Descending at some distance, we made our way into the place on foot. All was darkness within the house whence came moans of pain and invocations. Hearing the voice of the owner, D—, saluting us, we requested the window to be opened. There was no window – nothing but a shutter. When this was thrown back we found the earthen floor covered with victims of the destitution fever. At the entrance, their feet near the door way, lay side by side two grown young women, aged respectively 21 and 19; beyond, with her head almost touching theirs, was a younger girl aged 14, recovering but unable to move. On the left hand side, on the floor, lay the mother of the family in her day clothes. There was scarcely straw enough to keep them off the ground, not enough to hide its hardness, doubly hard to the aching backs of fever patients. What scanty covering they had could not be called bed clothes. The only person to nurse or attend on all was a worn and wretched parent, aged 50, trembling with weakness from want and watching as he stood, and expecting every hour to be stricken down, when all would be left to die within the walls. It was impossible to find that they had been exposed to any source of infection. There was no-one ill of all they knew. 'And why the strange disease should have come to us on this wild moor,' exclaimed the mother, 'we cannot know; God alone knows.' They had been passed over in the first six or seven food distributions and had to sell a little calf to buy Indian meal, their cow had run dry, but they had got for a little time some small quantity of milk from one lent by a brother. For months they had nothing but Indian meal to eat, and brownish bog water to drink. These are cases of famine fever if ever famine fever existed.

Only the father and the youngest daughter survived; the mother and the other daughters died.[13]

On a visit to Swineford, Sigerson took the opportunity to repudiate the government's allegations that the insanitary habits of the peasantry were the cause of the fever:

If disrespect for sanitary precepts sufficed of itself to cause the production of emasculated typhus, that disease should be endemic in Faheens. This hamlet, which is within a few miles of the town of Swineford, is unique of its kind. No road or lane leads to it, nor any streets to be found within it. On leaving the highway, we had to get over two or three fences, follow the course of a stream, traverse a field path, and finally we crossed the wall of a mire-pit, trod along its margin, and were at once in the centre of an irregular group of cabins. Each cabin has its midden-stead or manure-pit, the narrow borders of which serves as paths. There are about forty habitations, some huddled together, others straggling apart. Now contrary to all preconceived theories, this hamlet has been remarkably free from fever for a number of years.[14]

To emphasise his point Sigerson referred to the condition of some cottages in the town of Swineford:

There are some cabins here whose insanitary condition[s] rival, if they do not exceed, those of the houses of Faheens. Some are sunken under the level of the street, green and grimy externally; dark, dirty and smokey within, whilst a few feet from their doors stretches a decomposing dung heap. There has been no fever in these. Neither has there been fever in others, small, over crowded and foul to look at, which are to be observed in another direction. The inmates, though poor, of these town cabins, have not had to suffer the extreme privations of their rural compeers and have thus escaped the inroads of fever although the insanitary conditions of the cabins were equal in all.[15]

Sigerson and Kenny showed clearly that the fever, in its different forms, was directly attributable to the extreme destitution of the country. In every case they examined while travelling many hundreds of miles throughout the west of Ireland, the families in which the disease had first shown itself had had to live on the Indian meal allocated by the local relief committee. The only exceptions to this pattern were the cases of medical officers and a few others, who had developed febrile illness through contact.

With every report submitted to the Mansion House Committee, Sigerson and Kenny offered suggestions on how to combat the epidemic and 'remedy the barbarous inefficiency of the Poor Law system of relief'.[16] They also offered suggestions of a practical kind – for example, the provision of cottage hospitals in remote areas. They believed that cottage hospitals, or small hospital-homes, would make the people familiar with proper medical aid and supply nurses when necessary; they would also allay the fears that many people had of the distant workhouse hospital.

Another suggestion concerned the need to provide light, well-sprung conveyances to serve as ambulances for the sick. Sigerson felt that it was inexcusable that very ill patients should be transported to hospital in open cars. To illustrate the problem, he quoted from an article that appeared in the *Freeman's Journal*:

> On Saturday I passed one of these carts on its way to Swineford. A woman lay moaning in fever in it, her burning head resting on her daughter's lap. The cart jumped and jolted over every stone and ruggedness, and such a piteous thing I never do remember as the girl crying out to the driver at every shudder that went through the mother's fevered frame. 'Oh Tom, Tom, drive easy. For God's sake, drive easy.'[17]

Other suggestions included providing byroads to link main roads to remote villages, and admitting clergy to the Boards of Guardians. The ability of the clergy to organise the distribution of relief aid, and the way in which they helped the sick, greatly impressed Sigerson and he saw their membership of the boards as an asset to those bodies.[18]

At a meeting of the Mansion House Committee, on 14 August 1880, when George Sigerson's final report was read and accepted, the meeting resolved 'that the entire series of reports should be printed in book form and distributed amongst the members of the House of Commons'. The meeting also noted that, in a discussion that took place during the previous evening in the House of Commons, W.E. Forster, the chief secretary, had recognised the value of the reports and explained that, in many instances, their recommendations had already been implemented.[19]

In his later years, Sigerson seldom referred to the famine of 1879–80, but on one occasion, in a lecture delivered to the National Literary Society, he concluded with the following:

> On all my travels through leagues of suffering in towns or lonely regions I met no beggar, saw no man drunk. They bore their sorrows with fortitude and deserve the prosperity which comes to them with the dawn of a new day.[20]

Prison reform

Since the time of the Fenian trials, Sigerson had been actively campaigning through the newspapers for better prison conditions for political prisoners. With his appointment to the Royal Prisons Commission in 1884, he had the opportunity to observe and investigate prison conditions at first hand. Using his medical knowledge, he immediately set about trying to improve the treatment and diet of prisoners.

When William O'Brien was imprisoned in 1886 for agitation in his campaign against exorbitant rents, he refused to wear prison uniform or carry out menial tasks. His example was followed by another political offender, John Mandeville, a farmer from Tipperary. O'Brien was widely known in Ireland and abroad and was constantly in the news; he managed to avoid harsh treatment largely because the government were afraid of his possible death in prison. Although Mandeville was chairman of the Mitchelstown Board of Guardians and leader of the Land League in his area, he was less fortunate. When he entered Tullamore Gaol, he was a man of good physique and in perfect health; when he left it, he was in a wretched condition. At his death, which followed shortly after his release, an inquest was held at which the jury found a verdict of murder against the prison governor and doctor.[21] In a letter to Sigerson while he was in prison, the unfortunate Mandeville had told of the effects of the punishment meted out to those prisoners who refused to conform. The letter reached Sigerson a short time before he was released. The letter reads:

> I beg to state that political prisoners in Tullamore Goal sentenced by the Governor to undergo punishment for such offences as refusing to wear prison clothes or do menial work are always confined to their cells, for terms varying from one to three days, without getting a moment to air themselves. From my experience of prison punishment, I think close confinement very severe on a person's health and spirits, and small as is the allowance of bread, after I had been locked up for one day I was unable to consume it. The Resident Magistrate also sentences prisoners to various terms in punishment cells. They get no exercise, very little air and very little daylight; when evening comes the cell is pitch dark until late the following morning. I have always been considered a fairly strong healthy man accustomed to all kinds of outdoor exercise, but I found close confinement and bread and water made me ill in 24 hours. It was no use protesting; the doctor certified I was healthy and no other form of punishment seemed provided by prison rules.[22]

The name Mandeville became one of the battle cries of the Land War, and Mandeville was the first martyr in the cause of distinctive treatment for political prisoners. Sigerson's study of the treatment of political prisoners and a series of letters to the press on behalf of political offenders were eventually published as *Political prisoners at home and abroad*. This book became an acknowledged primary source for anyone concerned with the matter of prison reform for political offenders.

Many years later, Sigerson responded to appeals from the suffragettes, who were seeking political treatment during imprisonment, by allowing them to use one of his letters, entitled 'Custodia honesta', which they published in pamphlet form in 1913. Thanking Sigerson for allowing the movement to use his article, Evelyn Sharp, editor of the suffragette organ *Votes for Women*, wrote, 'It is a real help to have so able a position of our case for political treatment, put by so well known an advocate of the rights of political offenders.[23]

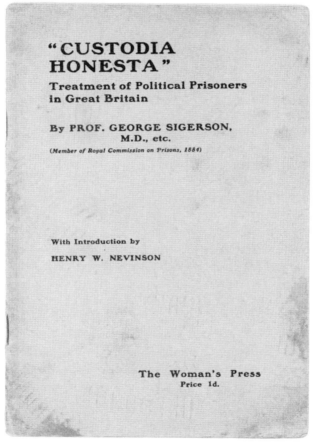

Front cover of 'Custodia honesta': the suffragette movement.
The Woman's Press, 1913

6

The National Literary Society

Clare Street: a centre for the Irish Literary Revival

After 1877, Sigerson's home in 3 Clare Street had become a centre of literary and artistic activity, frequented by many of the leading figures in the world of Irish culture and politics. Although constantly under pressure from his family to moderate his routine, Sigerson paid little attention to such advice, usually going to bed at three or four o'clock in the morning. Among the guests at the weekly dinners he held, John O'Leary and his sister Ellen could usually be found. Douglas Hyde also dined regularly at Clare Street. Hyde used to say that it was Sigerson's translations in *The poets and poetry of Munster* that prompted him to collect songs for his first book, *The love songs of Connacht*.[1]

John B. Yeats (1839–1922), renowned artist, father of W.B. and Jack B. Yeats and another firm friend of Sigerson's, spent many evenings sketching members of the gatherings, although he often complained about the uncertain, flickering light of the candelabrum. Yeats sometimes brought his son, William, with him. Hester Sigerson Piatt described the young W.B. Yeats as 'a slim dark fellow, with a bit of a beard, who used to read many of his early poems'.[2] Rose Kavanagh, a young poet from Tyrone, started visiting as a friend of one of the Sigersons' daughters, and soon found herself staying to listen to the scholarly and stimulating after-dinner gatherings. Other regular visitors to Clare Street included Charles A. Oldham, Charles Kickham, J.F. Taylor, Charles Gavan Duffy, Katharine Tynan, John Todhunter, Maud Gonne, J.P. Leonard, Sir Rowland Blennerhassett and Edmund O'Donovan. They in turn gathered around them a circle of literary and patriotic young people who became the nucleus of the Irish Literary Revival.

When Sigerson's children were young, a visit downstairs to meet the guests was always an exciting occasion. Hester recalled:

Dimly I remember those early Sunday evenings when we were brought in as children to meet the guests reassembling in the drawing room after dinner. It was a large room but it was too full even when there was nobody in it. My father's hobby of collecting pictures and furniture and his complete lack of order with regard to papers and books had left the room crowded, the pictures and engravings covering not only the walls but overflowing onto the chairs and floor. Yet a surprising number of people managed to find seats on the red and gilt Empire chairs. The room was lit by an array of old Sheffield candelabras, giving it a picturesque if slightly smoky appearance. My father was the most courteous of hosts but he led the conversation, never monopolising it, but guiding it on to subjects of general and intellectual interest.[3]

The Sigerson children, growing up in this atmosphere and educated at home, adopted many of their parents' interests and became identified with the Irish Literary Revival. Dora, especially, showed a flair for poetry and sculpture.

Padraic Colum, a popular visitor to Clare Street in later years, recalled:

The Doctor's house was, as Mr Curran has said – again so aptly – like some Balzac interior. 'French furniture of all the Louis and Empires, French paintings and pastels, French miniatures and engravings.' On Sunday evenings his friends would come to dinner to this house that was always lighted with candles. At tea in the drawing-room afterwards the gathering became a salon. ... The sonorous voice of 'the Doctor,' his deliberate utterance, his wit that had its setting in courtesy, moderated all bitterly-held opinions. 'We must not plagiarise from ourselves,' I heard him say once, and people who wanted to repeat items out of a controversy that was going on had to think of something fresher to say.[4]

The National Literary Society

Sigerson became deeply involved in the beginning of a new phase in the literary evolution of Ireland, which gathered momentum in the early 1890s after the Parnellite split and the disillusionment with mainstream nationalist politics that followed. In 1892, Douglas Hyde, W.B. Yeats and others founded the Irish Literary Society in London. In the same year, the National Literary Society was founded in Dublin. Douglas Hyde was the first president of the Dublin society; Charles Gavan Duffy was president of the London society. The main purpose of both societies was to foster the growth of Irish literature through lectures on Irish subjects and the publication of the works of writers who had hitherto been neglected, as well as of the younger writers who were beginning to emerge.

The first meeting of the National Literary Society was held at the Rotunda, Dublin in June 1892, with Sigerson in the chair. In a statement, the organising committee gave details of their hopes and aspirations for the new society. They pointed out that every Irish movement of recent years had drawn a great portion of its power from the literary movement that Thomas Davis, a Young Irelander, had started many years earlier. That movement was now gone and it was not possible to live forever upon the past. A living Ireland must have a living literature.

In August 1892, Sigerson gave the society's inaugural lecture. Entitled 'Irish literature: its origin, environment, and influence' this much-acclaimed lecture emphasised the different traditions that combined to form Ireland's literary past. Sigerson was to develop the theme later in *Bards of the Gael and Gall*:

> Irish literature resembles the great oriel of some ancient cathedral, an illumination of many beautiful colours, some of which can never be reproduced, because the art is lost. We possess an unique treasure in that ancient literature which grew up from a cultured people, self-centred, independent of Roman discipline. ... The knowledge of our old literature ... takes us into the homes and minds of one of those great nations uncomprehended of the Romans, and through that one, enables us to see the great, passionate, pathetic, wild, and generous humanity of all.[5]

He made an impassioned plea to his listeners:

> If our nation is to live, it must live by the energy of intellect, and be prepared to take its place in competition with all other peoples. Therefore must we work, with earnest hearts and high ideals for the sake of our own repute, for the benefit of mankind, in vindication of this old land which genius has made luminous. And remember that whilst wealth of thought is a country's treasure, literature is its articulate voice, by which it commands the reverence or calls for the contempt of the living and of the coming Nations of the Earth.[6]

Conscious of the differences of opinion within the society's membership (which were soon to lead to sharp divisions) regarding the emphasis to be given to various elements of Irish literature, he said, 'Irish Literature is of many blends, not the product of one race but of several.' He confessed dismay:

> some of my patriotic young friends were ready to decide what is and what is not the Irish style in prose and poetry; ... as in other countries, there are not one but many styles, differing with the subject, the writer, and the age.[7]

Unfortunately, the National Literary Society experienced a very troubled beginning and almost failed, mainly owing to the differing perspectives of Charles Gavan Duffy and William B. Yeats, two of its most important members. It was a classic case of a difference of opinion between two generations. Yeats was the spokesman of a new generation that was looking to the future. Duffy, a friend of Thomas Davis and an exponent of the ideas of *The Nation*, spoke for an earlier generation and, in the words of Ernest Boyd, 'his standards were those of the politico-literary groups of his youth'.[8] While Duffy stressed the importance of reviving the material of past Irish writers, Yeats stressed the need to promote contemporary writers. As president, Hyde had his own problems dealing with the argument, complicated by his vision of the socio-political and cultural importance of Irish literature. He had little sympathy for the anti-imperial struggle or propagandist Anglo-Irish literature which O'Leary introduced to Yeats and others. Hyde, like Sigerson, wanted to save the language and its stories and songs. As president, he also realised that Gavan Duffy was a man of great respectability, experience and substance, whereas Yeats had much to learn and prove. Sigerson specifically associated a certain kind of militant patriotism with a narrow, exclusionist reading of the Irish tradition, and argued that such a position betrayed the actual diversity and richness of that tradition.

In 1892, Duffy planned to open an Irish publishing house; and, as a member of the National Literary Society, he intended to promote out-of-print material, especially the material of the Young Ireland movement. Yeats had other ideas. He wanted to publish his own work and the work of up-and-coming writers. Yeats was determined to make available a new spread of literature and he was prepared to antagonise the older members of the society in order to achieve his aims. The unhappy outcome of this major difference of opinion was that the newer writers had their work published elsewhere and neither the Irish Literary Society in London nor the Irish National Literary Society in Dublin provided the coherent leadership that might otherwise been possible.

It has been suggested that Yeats invited Sigerson and John O'Leary to arbitrate between himself and Duffy. If this is the case, something went very wrong. Entries in Hyde's diaries give some indication of how in the beginning the society suffered disagreements between two schools of thought. He wrote, 'In the persons of Duffy and Yeats, the two schools, the two eras, met and clashed.' Time after time, we read of the continuing arguments:

> On January 27 1893, to a meeting of the committee of the National Literary Society. There was a terrible row between Taylor [John F. Taylor, barrister and acting Dublin correspondent for the *Manchester Guardian*] and Yeats, between O'Leary and Sigerson. We broke up at about 11pm. I never saw anything like it, but I escaped without a blow, Thank God. Afterwards I retired to Corless with Yeats and Coffey and we had a few badly need[ed] drinks.[9]

Hyde's biographer Dominic Daly writes, 'In effect it was Yeats and O'Leary against Taylor and Sigerson.'[10] Three weeks afterwards, Duffy and Yeats agreed to merge their ideas. But neither of them was wholly satisfied with the material the society planned to issue. Yeats was especially sensitive. He firmly believed that, if Duffy had his way, using the literature of 50 years before, the society would fail to recruit the kind of talent it needed.

The first volume published by the new Irish Literary Society was a series of articles by Thomas Davis. The series, first published in the *Dublin Monthly Magazine* in 1843, now reprinted, entitled *The patriot parliament of 1689: with its statutes, votes and proceedings* and edited by Duffy, caused Yeats to write a letter to the editor of the *United Ireland*, in which he denounced Duffy's choice of literature as that of a pamphleteer and an amateur.[11]

Yeats never forgave Sigerson and Taylor for not accepting his line of thinking; he was convinced his arguments were right. Years later, however, he could see that his attitude towards Sigerson and Taylor was overconfident and disrespectful. In his letters, quoted by Dominic Daly, he wrote, 'When I look back upon my Irish propaganda of those years I can see little but its bitterness.' He admitted that his emotions were partly fuelled by his feelings for Maud Gonne and her attitude towards the quarrels of the movement. While he saw the intellectual future of Ireland at risk, she dismissed the quarrels as mere disagreements among friends. He wrote:

> I took it all with the seriousness that amazes my more tolerant years, believing as I did years before at the school debating society that I stood with Plato. To Taylor, to Sigerson perhaps, I was an over confident who had interrupted a charming compliment to an old statesman at the end of his career.[12]

Daly adds:

> How deep the bitterness was on his side may be gauged from his petulant description of Dr Sigerson as 'learned, artificial, unscholarly, a typical provincial celebrity, but a friendly man,' and his description of John F. Taylor: 'like a man under a curse, compelled to hide his genius, and compelled to show in conspicuous places his ill judgement and his temper.'[13]

Yet again, in *W.B. Yeats: man and poet* by A. Norman Jeffares, this depth of feeling towards Sigerson is all too apparent:

> Dr Sigerson, a friend of O'Leary's, was another patriot. At first he impressed Yeats, for he spoke with a curious accent and gave the impression of having played the part before ignorant men of a great savant, a great foreign scientist. He fenced with all of Yeats' arguments, avoiding their thrust and after a while Yeats found that Sigerson never revealed any convictions of his own, but adds: 'he was kind and generous'.[14]

For his part, Sigerson seemed incapable of bearing malice and treated Yeats's behaviour with amused toleration. He never failed to recognise Yeats's genius and was a strong supporter of the Irish Literary Theatre. Just before *The Countess Cathleen* was about to have its first performance, a newspaper controversy had been stirred up about the play by Frank Hugh O'Donnell, a virulent opponent of Yeats. O'Donnell had published a bitter personal attack on Yeats and a violent criticism of the play in London. Sigerson immediately sprang to the defence of Yeats and of other Irish pioneer groups who suffered similar obstacles. At a meeting of the National Literary Society, in a florid passage laced with classical references, Sigerson spoke in defence of the new writers:

> These have triumphed not without difficulties. When the Celtic soldiers of Brennus climbed the Tarpeian Rock the alarm was given to the Capitol by the ever-vigilant geese. Since that time there has been enmity between the geese and the Gael. Whenever the Celts raise their heads the hiss of the geese arises also. … There are some writers who take their quills from the wings of the Capitoline geese, some also from the active and fretful porcupine. … But that is availing no longer. We should rather dread the one great defect of the Celts, their hyper-critical faculty; Gallicus Gallico Lupus, said the old observer.[15]

Sigerson was not averse, however, to poking fun at Yeats's interest in the occult and mysticism, as illustrated by the following incident. In *A penny in the clouds*, Austin Clarke related an occasion in Sigerson's surgery when Yeats attempted an act of clairvoyance. It was a sunny Saturday morning. Gazing into a large piece of crystal, which he had placed on a small table near the window, Yeats chanted, 'I see a cloud. It is parting slowly. And now I can see a stately figure … in white robes waving his arms. He is wearing a gold crown. Beyond him are other figures in purple, green and gold …' Sigerson listened, and then remarked, 'If you look out the window you will notice a Medical Hall on the opposite side of the street. A man in white overalls is cleaning the brasses and on the top shelf of the shop window are large glass vessels with purple, green, and yellow liquids in them – pharmaceutical emblems.'[16]

Despite his support for the newer writers, Sigerson was always concerned about preserving the true nature of the past. He expressed strong views on Synge's *Playboy of the western world* when it was first performed in 1907. The *United Irishman* of 17 February of that year carried a report on Sigerson's lecture at the meeting of the National Literary Society on the topic 'The Irish peasantry and the stage: a question of psychopathy'. It is unlikely that the timing of the lecture was coincidental – there had been three weeks of disturbances and outright condemnations following the production of *Playboy* on the Dublin stage.

In his paper Sigerson defended the real Irish peasant and condemned the portrayal of the character in recent plays, claiming:

> The new Irish stage peasant is sordid or silly, or both. He is but the squalid skeleton of a man whom none would like to know, except perhaps an anatomist. Certainly the general impression of the Irish peasantry which one receives from such plays is not a correct one, nor is it faithful to the facts of the present, nor loyal to history.[17]

Lest he be labelled as being too stuck in the past, Sigerson went on to praise the new literature:

> Irish dramatists whose enterprise, originality and genius we are glad to applaud, in order that, being more true to Nature, they shall be more in touch with their Nation. There need be no limit to their study except what is drawn by truth and taste.[18]

Yet there was no doubt that he was displeased with Synge's work and its alleged denigration of the western peasantry. Such highly public views may have provided further arguments for Yeats and his circle to question the fitness of Sigerson and the old brigade in leading the Irish literary movement.

At the end of the National Literary Society's first year, in 1893, Douglas Hyde, whose principal concern was to preserve Irish as a spoken language, resigned as president to help found the Gaelic League (Conradh na Gaeilge) with Eoin MacNeill. Sigerson accepted the role of president of the society at this time on the understanding that it would adhere to its original objectives. The members agreed with him and the society enjoyed comparative harmony and success from that time on. It is widely accepted that the survival and success of the National Literary Society was due to Sigerson's experience, scholarship and credibility. Of her father's presidency, Hester Sigerson Piatt wrote:

> It is no exaggeration to say that its long and harmonious existence was due to my father's influence, to his unflagging interest and energy, his banishing of controversial subjects and to his equally strong resolve that it should never deviate from its original and purely Irish objects.[19]

Sigerson was president for 31 years. A feature of his presidency was the many outstanding lectures he gave, the main thrust of which always centred on the affairs of Ireland. Douglas Hyde said of Sigerson's lectures:

> He poured forth a stream of interesting knowledge upon the most varied subjects, which when we look back, it almost takes our breath away. His minute knowledge

Invitation to a concert in the Mansion House, Feis Ceoil, 1919

of the most out of the way facts and the most abstruse problems of history was marvellous. He seemed to know everything.[20]

C.P. Curran, in an article entitled 'Oisín after the Fianna' in the *Irish Statesman*, also referred to Sigerson's lectures:

> Nor can I dwell on the long series of inaugural lectures at the National Literary Society in which the most diverse subjects of Irish interest, historic, literary, economic, geologic, medical and social were treated with what originality and charm. Hardly less remarkable were the brief addresses which closed each evening's proceedings, infinitely relished by his audience, for their deft wit and French precision and grace. How eagerly in that audience did we wait for the glancing irony which shot through the elaborate folds of his deliberate, ceremonious speech. In public speech Sigerson had a style of his own. His massive speech advanced in the fashion of the classic phalanx, bristling with bright spears, and the rapid shafts of his wit lost nothing in effect from the contrast of his humorous, twinkling eyes, with the sonorous voice and the grave courteous dignity of his bearing. It was the French *éloge* allied to Irish wit.[21]

Writing in *Studies*, Hyde described Sigerson's knowledge of history as an inspiration to those who were fortunate enough to hear him speak. He wrote that Sigerson was able to instil a feeling, not only of reverence, but also 'of the affection shown by children for a wise man who had told them a charming fairy tale'.[22] On a number of occasions, Sigerson was urged to put his lectures in book form, but he always had other things to do.

In 1912, in recognition of his services to Irish literature, the National Literary Society, prompted by Agnes O'Farrelly, commissioned the eminent Ulster artist Sir John Lavery to paint Sigerson's portrait. The painting hangs in the Hugh Lane Gallery, Parnell Square, Dublin.

Dr George Sigerson and D.J. O'Donoghue in St Stephen's Green,
looking for a suitable site for the Mangan monument.
Image courtesy of the IVRLA, from an original in UCD Special Collections.
© Helen Solterer

7

Bards of the Gael and Gall

Sigerson's great literary work, *Bards of the Gael and Gall*, was published in 1897, thirty-seven years after his first book of translations. Conditions now were very different from those that had obtained in 1860; this was no longer the offering of an enthusiastic young student to an apathetic public, but the contribution of a ripe scholar to a subject for which an appreciative audience had developed. By this time, Douglas Hyde had published his *Love songs of Connacht* (1893), and Kuno Meyer and others had begun to edit the older Irish texts with accuracy and understanding. In these thirty-seven years Sigerson had become a highly successful physician and had written well and authoritatively on Irish land tenure and Irish history. Translation from the Irish had continued to interest him and his *Bards of the Gael and Gall* came out of years of attentiveness and study and steady contact with the growing volume of Irish studies. It was addressed to both the Gaelic and the Anglo-Irish sections of the literary revival. To the first, it offered a skilful and faithful translation of the original texts; and to the second, it presented an imposing anthology of Irish poetic literature, enhanced by a scholarly history of Gaelic verse and a vindication of the greatness of Irish culture.

Sigerson, who was now president of the National Literary Society, dedicated his book to Charles Gavan Duffy, president of the Irish Literary Society in London, a representative of the 'Gael', and to Douglas Hyde, president of the Gaelic League and a descendant of the 'Gall'. This was a concise expression of Sigerson's view of Irish culture, which, according to Gregory Schirmer in his history of Irish poetry in English, consisted of 'a blend of interdependent traditions, rather than of an irreconcilable difference between two principal traditions or … the oppression of one tradition by another'.[1]

BARDS
OF THE
GAEL AND GALL

EXAMPLES OF THE
POETIC LITERATURE OF ERINN

DONE INTO ENGLISH AFTER THE METRES AND
MODES OF THE GAEL

BY

GEORGE SIGERSON, M.D., F.R.U.I.

President of the National Literary Society of Ireland, Corresponding Member
of La Société D'Anthropologie, La Société Clinique, and
La Société de Psychologie Physiologique
de Paris, etc.

THIRD EDITION

WITH MEMORIAL PREFACE BY

DR. DOUGLAS HYDE

DUBLIN | LONDON
TALBOT PRESS, LTD. | T. FISHER UNWIN
85 TALBOT STREET | ADELPHI TERRACE
1925

Title page of *Bards of the Gael and Gall*,
1925 edition

The book was breathtaking in its scope, extending over a period of two thousand years and covering all the great epochs of Irish history, from the earliest lays of the Milesian invaders, through the Cúchulainn period, the dawn of Christianity, the Gaelic-Norse and Norman periods to folk songs of the seventeenth and eighteenth centuries. Divided into fourteen sections, each corresponding to a different phase in the development of Gaelic poetry, it constitutes an almost unparalleled lineage of Irish poetry. It contained the translations of 139 poems from old, middle and early modern Irish texts – eight times as many as were contained in *The poets and poetry of Munster*.

Sigerson began his introduction to *Bards of the Gael and Gall* by eulogizing the contribution of early Irish literature to the world:

May not a buried literature have claims upon our attentions? If it be of interest to delve and discover a statue or a city, long concealed, should it not be more attractive to come upon a Kingdom, where long forgotten peoples live, love and act? What a stir there would be, could some delver declare that he had, in his researches underground, discovered a lost literature of Gaul or of Germany, and in it the song, story and music of nations speaking for themselves, whom now we know but by the description of alien foes. Such a treasure trove is beyond hope. The Romans went over the areas they subjugated, like the sands of the Sahara over meadow, destroying all that was of native growth. Of the Bards they preserved nothing but the name. It was fortunate indeed that one island on the western verge of Europe escaped the Roman eagles. … As it is, we have, in her ancient literature, the noblest monument which witnesses to the intellect of the Ultra-Roman world. … It does not only reveal the inner natures of the inhabitants of the island at different epochs, before the coming of the Christian faith, during its progress, and since, but it also enables us to gain some glimpse into the homes of other nations – Teutons as well as Celts – whose lamps were extinguished.[2]

Sigerson wrote in particular of the special qualities of the old Irish poetry:

> We know what ingenuity the ancient Irish displayed in their ornaments of gold
> and silver, which command the admiration of all workers in the precious metals,
> as well as of all artists. Those who have seen the illuminated initials of the Book
> of Kells know the wonderful grace of form shown in the interwoven lines, and
> the exquisite taste displayed in the tints which still freshly adorn them. A similar
> ingenuity, grace, artistic power, delicacy, and taste, were employed in the service
> of poetry.[3]

He dwelt on the closeness of the Irish to the things of nature:

> There have been love-songs and war-odes in other ancient languages, but the Gael
> were the first to recognise the picturesque in scenery and give us nature-songs, to tell
> of sorrow, to depict the exile's pang, and to sing the calm and the tumult of ocean.[4]

According to the literary historian, Robert Welch:

> One of the historical interests of this collection lies in the fact that Sigerson
> devoted nine of these sections to areas of Irish poetry which, up till then, had
> received but scant attention. Until *Bards of the Gael and Gall*, most Irish poetry
> translated into English verse went back no further than the seventeenth century.
> This neglect has a simple explanation. Only in the nineties were the philological
> tools necessary for the understanding of the older Gaelic poetry slowly becoming
> available, through the work of such scholars as Johann Caspar Zeuss, Ernst
> Windisch, Whitley Stokes and Heinrich Zimmer.[5]

Sigerson, in his introduction, referred to this neglect and paid tribute to the work of
these recent European scholars:

> Unhappily for history, that literature was long buried in neglect. Then, for a time,
> it lay locked in an archaic language. … For years, however, the keen and capable
> minds of scholars have been at work and have rendered into the modern languages
> the contents of many most ancient and interesting documents. Now at last, these
> are accessible … though sometimes not readily, for they must often be sought for
> in the pages of foreign periodicals.[6]

In assessing Sigerson's achievement, Welch asserts:

> his anthology constituted a kind of statement; it asserted that there was such a
> thing as a Gaelic poetic tradition, and that that tradition had a long and dignified
> ancestry, reaching back to the time when Ireland, after the fall of Rome, 'held the

literary sceptre of Europe for three centuries'. Sigerson's versions brought some of the best examples of that early literature to the attention of the Irish reading public not long after the scholars had first discovered them.[7]

Ernest Boyd, in *Ireland's literary renaissance*, comments on the remarkable achievement of Sigerson in rendering in English verse both the music and the spirit of the original Irish version and his success in reproducing in his translations the elaborate Gaelic verse structure, 'with its internal rhymes and alliterations, its consonant and assonant rhymes'. He adds that 'these admirable translations reproduce the numerous metrical characteristics of Gaelic literature, whose diversity indicates how highly developed was the art of versification in ancient Ireland'.[8]

Brooke and Rolleston in *A treasury of Irish poetry in the English tongue*, asserted that *Bards of the Gael and Gall* was a contribution to the so-called Celtic Revival, 'the importance of which it would be difficult to over-estimate'. They described his work as 'the result of a subtle fusion of scholar and poet', and regarded this publication as 'essential to all who would form for themselves an idea of the Irish literary past and of Irish versification'.[9]

The Field Day anthology of Irish writing emphasises the inclusiveness of Sigerson's work:

> Sigerson's *Bards of the Gael and Gall* … was important not merely because of the quality of some of the translations themselves, but also for its inclusiveness, its refusal to identify an 'Irish note' in poetry that was peculiar to any one group or that was susceptible to any racial claim. Sigerson, [W.P.] Ryan, [Eoin] MacNeill and others emphasized the mixture of races that constituted the Irish people and derided any notion of an exclusively 'Celtic' spirit. [Thomas] MacDonagh dedicated his book of essays to Sigerson. This is appropriate in many ways … His essays … indicate the continuity of the attempt to see the inter-connexions as well as the contrasts between the developments since the Elizabethan period, in English and Irish verse, and to offer, as a conclusion, the hope that Irish poetry in English might bear witness to its dual heritage.[10]

According to Robert Welch, *Bards of the Gael and Gall* 'had an extensive influence on the course of Irish verse in English' and Austin Clarke agreed that Sigerson taught him a good deal about 'the subtle art of our formal poetry'.[11] Welch asserts that *Bards of the Gael and Gall* provided Clarke with examples of how English could be enriched with the divided echoes and meshed flow of Gaelic metre:

> Clarke's closely-textured re-enactments of the techniques of Gaelic verse are much more elegant and much more successful than Sigerson's efforts; … however, the woven tracery of consonants and the rich chording of vowels which characterise so much of Clarke's verse owe much to the labours of the older man.[12]

Robert Farren, Irish poet and critic, was lavish in his praise of *Bards of the Gael and Gall*. Writing in 1937, he spoke with enthusiasm about 'its sweep through the centuries; its delicacy of choice and insight; its sustained accuracy and poetry; its double power of stimulating and satisfying the appetite for knowledge,' and added:

> Aodh de Blácam believes that those of Sigerson's generation largely owed their knowledge of Gaelic literary tradition to this book; today only those who have cultivated study in Irish with unusual assiduity, perhaps not even those, can dispense with it.[13]

The distinguished historian, F.S.L. Lyons, called it 'an astonishing feat of exact, yet musical, translation from Irish into English'.[14] C.P. Curran said that 'in the nineties it stood alone, and for combined range and discriminating choice of fine poetry this … prospect of our poetic literature has hardly been bettered'.[15] Douglas Hyde said that the English reader could better rely on Sigerson's translations for their accuracy than those of any other person who has ever attempted to turn Irish into English verse:

Dr George Sigerson, cartoon by Frank Leah. Courtesy of the National Library of Ireland

> it was a splendid thought to take the reader by the hand and conduct him along a road the like of which could scarcely be travelled over in any other land in Europe.[16]

He said that the material of Gaelic literature and history was now being released by the magic touch of the translator.

Bards of the Gael and Gall received an enthusiastic welcome when it was published in 1897. The *Irish Monthly* described it as 'the most important addition that Irish literature has received for many a day … the ripe fruit of the enthusiastic industry of many years'. It went on:

Dr Sigerson's knowledge of the theory and practice of the curiously complicated Celtic metres is marvellous … We have seen the new epithet, 'epoch-making', applied to this work. It will certainly link the name Dr George Sigerson with the *Bards of the Gael and Gall* and with the Celtic literature of Ireland.[17]

The *New Ireland Review* was equally enthusiastic:

The movement for revising the knowledge of Ireland's ancient literature and securing for Eirinn her due place in literary history grows apace. In a short time, we hope, it will be a reproach amongst us not to know something of the thought and language of those, who, for a thousand years before the English invasion, thought and wrote and sang for Ireland. The labours of Dr Sigerson will have done a good deal to hasten the advent of that better time. In the book which he has just given us, he renders conspicuous service to the cause of Irish literature. He makes it distinctly respectable, and when once our native public understand that it is respectable, they may be trusted to restore it to popularity.[18]

8

Family and friends

Family

Much of the later part of George Sigerson's life was marked by the sorrow caused by the loss of those close to him. Within his own family circle, only his daughter Hester survived him. His wife, Hester Varian, died in 1898; his son George Patrick died in 1903 at the age of 36; his sister, Jane, who had come to live in Clare Street in 1897, died in 1913, and his daughter Dora died in 1918 at the age of 52. Another son, William, had died in childhood. Hester's husband, Arthur Donn Piatt, died in 1914.

Hester Varian Sigerson (1828–98), wife

Hester Varian had been active in literary circles in Cork prior to her marriage to George Sigerson in 1861. In 1889, she published her first and only novel, *A ruined race*.[1] Dealing with the sufferings of the peasantry under the old land system, it showed a unique sympathy and understanding for the plight of their position but was considered by some as unduly melancholy. During her earlier years, Hester had contributed poetry and ballads to various magazines, including the *Harp*, *Irish Fireside*, *Cork Examiner*, *Boston Pilot*, the *Gael*, *Young Ireland* and *Irish Monthly*, and appeared in the anthologies of her cousin, Ralph Varian – *The harp of Erin* and *Ballads, popular poetry and household songs of Ireland*. However, as the years passed, it would appear that her devotion to her husband and the children prevented her from developing her many literary and artistic talents. It would seem also that, from this time, Hester played little part in the very active professional and social scene that was an increasing aspect of George's life in Clare Street. It is unlikely that this was due to any reluctance on her part; it was more likely caused by developing health problems. She died in 1898.

George Patrick Sigerson (1867–1903), son

In 1903, after an attack of meningitis, Sigerson's surviving son, George Patrick, died at the age of 36. He had taken an MA degree at the Royal University in 1887, winning a studentship in experimental science. According to Hester Sigerson Piatt, he had been a great reader since childhood and had a deep knowledge of science and literature. With a highly scrupulous, generous and amiable character and a brilliant intellect, he seemed destined for an outstanding career. His untimely death was a great shock to his father and, as in the years immediately following the death of his wife, Sigerson's method of coping with his grief was to immerse himself totally in his work.

Jane Sigerson McGinnis (1838–1913), sister

Sigerson's sister, Jane, came to Dublin in the spring of 1897 to help her brother with running the house in Clare Street and to care for his wife, whose health had been deteriorating and who now needed almost constant care. Jane was the widow of Patrick McGinnis, a prominent businessman in the Strabane area. He had extensive business and property interests but had to retire early from public life in 1881 on health grounds. During this time, and in the period following his death in 1883, his numerous business interests – especially his brick, lime and tile works – went into decline to such an extent that Jane was forced into bankruptcy in 1893. She came to Dublin at a very difficult time in her life but lived happily as a close member of the family circle in Clare Street until her death in 1913. Her remains were returned to Strabane and she is buried in the graveyard at Melmount.

Jane's task in running the tall old house in Clare Street for 16 years, even with the help of two maids, was not made easier by her brother's old-fashioned ideas, his general untidiness and his distrust for modern inventions. Since he did most of his writing after everyone had gone to bed, when the maids came down in the morning they could well be confronted by a chaotic scene – sheets of paper, books and pamphlets strewn haphazardly around the place. W.B. Yeats reputedly made reference to 'Sigersonian' untidiness in a letter to John O'Leary, recalling some old pamphlets getting swallowed in the 'volcano' of Sigerson's study.

Another difficulty arose from Sigerson's reluctance, which persisted until very late in his life, to have electricity installed. He preferred candlelight. Although it gave the rooms a picturesque, if smoky, appearance, the flickering light troubled some of the guests. John B. Yeats loved to spend his evening sketching members of the company on his frequent visits but found the uncertain light annoying and was not slow to point this out to his host.

Hester Sigerson Piatt (1870–1939), daughter

Hester Sigerson, born in Dublin in 1870, was herself a distinguished writer, though overshadowed by her older sister, Dora. She contributed to *Lyceum*, *Irish Fireside*, the *Weekly Register* and other American and English journals, and some of her poems were included in an Irish anthology compiled by Yeats. She succeeded her close friend, Rose Kavanagh, the Tyrone poet, as Uncle Remus on the *Weekly Freeman* after

Photograph of Hester Sigerson
taken in 1888

Kavanagh's death in 1891. She was the author of *The passing years: a book of verses* and *The golden quest and other stories*, both published by the Sign of the Three Candles in 1935 and 1940 respectively. Her unpublished manuscript about her father's life has been an important source of information for this publication. She edited her father's collection, entitled *Songs and poems by George Sigerson*, which was published by Duffy and Co., Dublin, in 1927.

In 1901, Hester married Arthur Donn Piatt, the United States vice-consul in Dublin. He was the eldest son of John James Piatt, an American poet and US consul in Ireland from 1882–93, and the poet, Sarah Morgan Bryan. After their marriage, Hester and her husband went to live in Dún Laoghaire but were regular visitors to Clare Street, where they dined every Sunday. Arthur Donn Piatt died in 1914 at the age of 47, and Hester and her young family, Eibhlin and Donn, returned to live in Clare Street. They remained there until her father's death in 1925.

Eibhlin was three years old when they moved in – too young to appreciate what all the activity in the house meant. Later she recalled that during the day the patients kept coming and going. In the evenings it was no quieter, with invited guests and visitors calling. As the years passed she was gradually promoted to dine downstairs, stay for coffee served in the salon, and later stay until midnight. To her often fell the honour of being escorted to dinner by her grandfather – appropriately, as he had often said before, since she was the youngest of those present and he was the oldest.

Dora Sigerson Shorter (1866–1918), daughter

Like her father, Dora Sigerson was a prolific writer. She was also a highly acclaimed poet. Some of her early poems appeared in the *Irish Monthly* and the *Children's Magazine*. Katharine Tynan (1861–1934), poet, prolific novelist and close friend of both Dora and Hester Sigerson, recalled her first meeting with Dora:

Photograph of Dora Sigerson *c.* 1890

She was like a young muse. She had a beautiful shaped head which she did not conceal by masses of hair. Her dark hair was worn short not cropped. She had a beautiful brow and eyebrows, very fine grey eyes, a short straight nose, firmly moulded features, creamy pale skin and vividly red lips. I remember that my brother said to me: 'Miss Sigerson is very beautiful.' She was. Her face had some curious suggestion of the Greek Hermes.[2]

Much of Dora's output of verse in volumes such as *Ballads and poems* (1899) and *New poems* (1912) was influenced by her father's interest in Irish metrics. She also wrote narrative poems such as the 'The fairy changeling' (1897) and 'Madge Linsey' (1913).

Dora and her husband, Clement Shorter, lived in London after their marriage in 1896. He was an eminent journalist and critic. In 1891 he had become editor of the *Illustrated London News*. In addition to editing, he founded three papers: *Sketch* (1893), the *Sphere* (1900) and the *Tatler* (1903). He was editor of the *Sphere* from 1900 until his death in 1926, each week contributing his controversial column, 'A literary letter'. He became the recognised authority on the Brontës and published a highly acclaimed work on the Brontë family.

Dora's talent was not confined to poetry. Before she turned to writing, she had used most of her spare time painting or sculpting, and she was extremely gifted in these pursuits. Sadly, little of her work remains, apart from one large well-known piece – a group of figures in Glasnevin Cemetery commemorating the executed leaders of the 1916 Easter Rising. Although she lived in England for many years, her loyalty to Ireland remained strong. According to Douglas Hyde, 'her very absence from Ireland had made her – a phenomenon which we may often witness – more Irish than if she had never left it'.[3] After Dora's untimely death in 1918, Katharine Tynan spoke of Dora's love of Ireland as 'a passion. The events of Easter week moved her profoundly,' she wrote. 'She spent herself regally on behalf of her people with brain, pen and fortune and at the expense of her vitality.'[4]

Tynan's tribute to Dora provides an interesting insight into the circle in which they moved in the early 1890s:

> For seven good years [after 1887] my life was inextricably interwoven with hers and Hester's. We had the same friends, the same merry-makings, the same tastes and aims. We were of the circle which revolved around the great old Fenian, John O'Leary, and his not less noble sister; we visited the American poets, Mr and Mrs Piatt, at Queenstown, where Mr Piatt was American Consul … We wrote for the same papers. Presently Dora Sigerson and I were together in politics, both Parnellites when the 'split' came. Together we attended Mr Parnell's meetings; we went to meet him when he returned to Dublin from the country; we lived through all the passionate loyalty of those days. Together we exulted; together we mourned; together we followed our chief to the grave, not thinking upon how she should one day lie near him.[5]

Dora and Clement Shorter travelled to Ireland after the 1916 Rising, as soon as the military authorities allowed civilians to land in Dublin. Not long after her visit to Ireland, Dora suffered a stroke. She died on 6 January 1918. According to her husband, she related her illness to anxiety over the events following the Easter Rising. The unmerciful behaviour of the British had caused her much stress. Katharine Tynan had no doubt that the sudden breakdown in Dora's health was due to 'her intense and isolated suffering … after the events following Easter week, 1916, in Dublin, and the troubles which menaced the country she adored; … she broke her heart over it all.'[6] After the executions, seeking support for the republican movement, Dora wrote a series of poems, bought a hand printing-press, and then sent her poems to churchmen and many other distinguished people throughout Ireland. She wrote some of her most moving poems at this time. One poem in particular, 'Sick I am and sorrowful', written a few weeks before her death, gives some idea of how her longing for home gave effect to her dreadful feeling of hopelessness:

> If I saw the wild geese fly over the dark lakes of Kerry
> Or could hear the secret winds, I could kneel and pray.
> But 'tis sick I am and grieving, how can I be well again
> Here, where fear and sorrow are – my heart too far away?[7]

During the last few weeks of her life, she finished a book of poetry which she called *The tricolour: poems of the Irish revolution*. The poems speak of patriotism, heroism and the martyrdom of the leaders of the Easter Rising of 1916. Her dedication reads:

> Sleep well, nor dream that you have failed; for such
> love as yours holds ever aloft the flag of liberty,
> and of such fine clay as yours is our island made.[8]

Dora specified that any profit from *The tricolour* and all other copyright should be used to commemorate the Easter Rising, that her own sculpture dedicated to the rebel leaders should be erected in Glasnevin Cemetery and that her body should be taken there to rest. On a cold January morning in 1918, Dora Sigerson Shorter was buried near the 1916 leaders.

About Dora, his wife Hester, his son George Patrick, his sister Jane and the many other loved ones and friends who were now gone, Sigerson wrote:

> If at middle age we begin to feel the chill of the passing of friends and relatives and the icy breath of advancing solitude, how much more must that lonely isolation close around us when extreme old age has left none that remember us in youth, all are gone, the old familiar faces.[9]

In his poem, 'The old path by the river', he wrote:

> The one most sorrowful mourner
> In the aisle when all depart,
> And ah – the unspeakable loneliness
> That presses around his heart.[10]

Friends and visitors

George Sigerson's house in 3 Clare Street was the centre of a circle of friends from the literary and political world in Dublin. Sunday evening was the busiest evening of the week. The house became a hive of activity as invited friends and acquaintances and distinguished visitors came to dinner. A feature of these evenings was the procession of guests to the dining room, led by Sigerson himself, with the youngest lady present on his right arm and the most important lady on his left.

Douglas Hyde

A constant visitor, who continued to be Sigerson's close friend, was Douglas Hyde. Both were noted translators; both were heavily involved in the Irish Literary Revival of the late nineteenth century; both worked in the National University. They enjoyed a warm personal relationship for over 40 years. An indication of Hyde's esteem for Sigerson is to be found in the fact that he dedicated *The love songs of Connacht* to Sigerson. Hyde used the pseudonym 'An Craoibhín Aoibhinn' ('The Pleasant Little Branch'), the title of a poem in *The poets and poetry of Munster*, which Sigerson had published in 1860, the year of Hyde's birth. Prior to the publication of *The love songs of Connacht* in 1893, Hyde wrote to Sigerson to seek his approval:

> Dear Sigerson, I am sending you the introduction to my new book. I am sending it for your patronage. I offer the introduction to you to challenge/question, but I would not like to publish it without showing it to you first and without your permission. Give that to me, please, and the best wishes and blessing to you. Respectfully. Your dear friend. An Craoibhín Aoibhinn.[11]

In the dedication, Hyde wrote:

> Allow me to offer you this slight attempt on my part to do for Connacht what you yourself and the late John O'Daly, following in the footsteps of Edward Walsh, to some extent accomplished for Munster, more than thirty years ago … not for its intrinsic worth, if it has any, but as a slight token of gratitude from one who has derived the greatest pleasure from your own early and patriotic labours in the same direction. …[12]

Hyde's regard for Sigerson developed into a deep and lasting personal friendship. Probably the most moving tribute paid to Sigerson after his death was that delivered in the Senate by Hyde, while his memorial preface to the third edition of Sigerson's *Bards of the Gael and Gall* in 1926 remains the most comprehensive summary of the enormous contribution Sigerson made to so many aspects of Irish life.[13]

Thomas MacDonagh; Patrick Pearse

Among the many other visitors to those Sunday gatherings were Sir Roger Casement, Joseph Mary Plunkett and Thomas MacDonagh. MacDonagh (1878–1916), poet and playwright, assistant headmaster in Patrick Pearse's St Enda's School at its foundation in 1908, subsequently a lecturer in English in NUI and a signatory to the 1916 Proclamation, was always a welcome caller and was one of Sigerson's favourites. 'Enthusiastic,

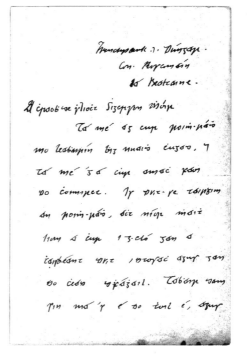

Part of an original letter from
Dr Douglas Hyde to George Sigerson

TO

GEORGE SIGERSON

PATRIOT AND SAGE, BARD OF THE GAEL AND GALL,
TEACHER AND HEALER, OLLAMH OF SUBTLE LORE,
WHOSE WORDS AND WORKS TO IRELAND'S PAST RESTORE
THE GLORY THAT WAS LOST WITH LEARNING'S FALL
IN OUR DARK PASSION, THE IMMEMORIAL
KIND KNOWLEDGE WEARS TO US THE MIEN SHE WORE
TO YOUR YOUNG GAZE ; AND, MASTER, LOOK BEFORE,
SEE WHERE THE CHILDREN WEAVE HER CORONAL.

YOUR HONOUR IS YOUR COUNTRY'S : STILL YOU GIVE
YOUR LIFE'S GREAT SERVICE UNDER GOD TO HER,
AND SHE REPAYS IN FULL, EARLY OR LATE.
SO, THAT SOME WORD OF MINE A WHILE MAY LIVE,
SET WITH YOUR NAME IN HER LOVE'S REGISTER,
THESE TO YOU I INSCRIBE AND DEDICATE.

Dedication of *Literature in Ireland*
by Thomas MacDonagh to George Sigerson,
published posthumously, 1916

exuberant and garrulous, with clear candid eyes,'[14] his love for Ireland and its culture occupied much of his conversation, and in George Sigerson he found a sympathetic ear. Years later, Sigerson reputedly remarked that MacDonagh was totally Irish – in fact, that Irishness was his main attribute. Thomas MacDonagh dedicated his main work, *Literature in Ireland*, which was published in late 1916, following his execution, to George Sigerson.

Although not a regular visitor to Clare Street, Patrick Pearse visited Hester Sigerson Piatt and her husband. Hester remembered Pearse as 'a gentle, thoughtful young man [who] had the look of a young cleric which was emphasised by the fact that he always seemed to dress in black. At first, he seemed absorbed in the question of the Gaelic language and education.' Sigerson assured him that he would help as an external lecturer when St Enda's was founded, if required. 'Soon, however,' according to Hester, 'all the passion of his idealistic nature was caught up in the Sinn Féin and Volunteer movements for the freeing of Ireland.'[15]

John O'Leary

Among Sigerson's closest friends was John O'Leary (1830–1907). Sigerson first met O'Leary in the mid-1860s, when they worked on the Fenian newspaper, the *Irish People*. O'Leary was one of the paper's editors and Sigerson was its leader writer. O'Leary and the other Fenian leaders were sentenced in 1867 to long terms of imprisonment. Nine years later, after giving a commitment never to return to Ireland, he was released. When this condition was dropped in 1889, he returned from exile and settled in Dublin with his sister, Ellen. In his book, *Recollections of Fenians and Fenianism*, O'Leary wrote about his many meetings with Sigerson. The book describes gatherings on Friday evenings at O'Leary's lodgings in the 1860s. Among those present, in addition to Sigerson, were Charles Kickham, Thomas Clarke Luby, Denis Mulcahy, Jeremiah O'Donovan Rossa and James Stephens.

In a footnote to his book, O'Leary wrote:

> The chief of those of whom I have a vivid recollection was Dr Sigerson, for the dialogue between us that began then has been going on ever since, being constant of later years and is pretty sure to last until one or the other of us shall go to join the majority.[16]

O'Leary visited Clare Street every week and the discussion would usually centre on the important political and literary events of the day. On Tuesday, 12 March 1907, a cold wet day, O'Leary made his usual visit. When he was leaving he insisted on walking to his home, a few streets away. His visit to Clare Street was his last outing. Within 48 hours he was dying from pneumonia. Sigerson was at his bedside but could do nothing more than make his old friend as comfortable as possible. John O'Leary died on 16 March 1907.

Charles Kickham

Another visitor to Clare Street was Charles Kickham (1828–82) – novelist, poet, journalist and one of the most prominent members of the Irish Republican Brotherhood, who in 1865 had been charged with high treason and sentenced to fourteen years' penal servitude. Although Hester Sigerson was only twelve years old at the time of Kickham's death, she had very clear recollections of him. Her father had met both Kickham and O'Leary around 1864 and, according to Hester, 'then began the two great friendships of his life which were not to slacken or cease until he stood beside their deathbeds.'[17] Of Kickham she wrote:

> His face bore the marks of the gun-powder explosion which in his youth had destroyed his hearing and injured his sight, but his blue eyes were clear and expressive and they twinkled with humour behind his spectacles. His greying hair was curly and came down on his forehead like a peak. He delighted in talking and telling stories and always had a joke or some humorous remark for us children. He taught us the deaf and dumb alphabet and used to make us spell out replies to his questions on his hand. Settled down for a conversation with my mother or father, he would lie back in his chair and close his eyes, holding out his hand for them to reply on it.[18]

Other visitors

The Sigerson girls had their special favourites. Hester particularly remembered the visits of Stephen McKenna, a Greek and Gaelic scholar and a popular figure in Dublin's literary circle. She recalled how McKenna kept the younger members of the company spellbound with his tales of adventure. He had fought for Greece in the Turkish War, worked in a café in New York and shared a room with John Millington Synge in Paris.

Sigerson's friends clearly enjoyed his company and the intellectual stimulation of the gatherings that took place in his Clare Street home. C.P. Curran described his introduction to Sigerson's company as 'admittance to a lifelong friendship which for me was an inexhaustible illumination'.[19] J.S. Crone, founder and editor of the *Irish Book Lover*, who visited Sigerson in his later years, described him as 'the grand old doyen of Irish literature, as hale and hearty as ever. Age cannot wither his wonderful memory of men and events.'[20] T.P. O'Hanlon, writing in the *Capuchin Annual*, described the hours he spent with Sigerson as 'hours that flew under the spell of his old-world courtliness, his sparkling wit, his good natured banter, his affectionate reminiscences of men like John Mitchel and Charles Kickham who had been his friends'.[21]

Dr Sigerson and John O'Leary (and a third unnamed person).
Pencil sketch by John B. Yeats. Courtesy of the National Library of Ireland

9

Sigerson's later life, 1900–25

Despite the personal tragedies Sigerson experienced, he himself enjoyed excellent health and continued to pursue his literary, political, academic and medical interests with undiminished vigour until the end of his life.

Literary

Although his contributions to newspapers and journals became greatly restricted in his later years, Sigerson was still under pressure to submit material on current affairs. He was a regular contributor to the *Freeman's Journal* and wrote occasional articles for other journals. He published three major works in the last years of his life – *The saga of King Lir*, *The last independent parliament of Ireland* and *The Easter song* of Sedulius.

The saga of King Lir was published in 1913. Thomas MacDonagh described the work as a classic. Urging the public to read it, he wrote:

> Dr Sigerson has laboured all his day for his country. He has written only of Ireland for Ireland. This poem is a portion of his reward. The old spirit of the Irish saga has breathed on him. He has worthily received the inspiration. His utterance has the dignity of Irish literature. His poem is a classic henceforth of our Irish literature in the English tongue.[1]

Unusually, Sigerson's friend, Douglas Hyde, was somewhat critical, being particularly disappointed that the story of the swans was omitted. However, a review in the *Irish Monthly* paid Sigerson a generous tribute:

> At an age when most men are content to rest on their laurels, he has gleaned one of the loveliest legends from the dim grey mists of a shadowy past and wedded it to exquisite modern verse. … With its noble simplicity, its freshness and breadth of treatment, its melting pathos and rich wealth of imagery, Dr Sigerson's work stands alone.[2]

The last independent parliament of Ireland was published in 1918. Thirty years earlier, in 1888, R. Barry O'Brien had published *Two centuries of Irish history*, a series of papers by eminent scholars covering the years 1691–1870. Sigerson had contributed a chapter dealing with the period 1782–1800, from the establishment of legislative independence to the Act of Union. An interesting insight into Sigerson can be gleaned from a letter O'Brien wrote to him after Sigerson had finally given him a manuscript of the chapter:

> All your proofs are to hand. Your work is first rate. … It is a comfort to have you off my hands in spite of the fact that nothing could be better than your work. I now sleep a little and my hair has ceased to turn grey in handfuls. Yours, in a state of complete desperation brought about mainly by you.[3]

Now in 1918, Sigerson had greatly expanded this chapter to form the basis of his book, which he dedicated to his daughter, Dora Sigerson Shorter. It included the origins of the parliament of 1782–1800, its achievements and its relationships with the 'old nation of Ireland'. There was much in Sigerson's book that would give added meaning and justification to the political struggle that was unfolding so dramatically at the time of its publication. A review in the *Irish Ecclesiastical Record* described the contents as:

> a marvellous array of facts which provide a fascinating picture of the most glorious and the most degrading period of Ireland's history. Every page is closely packed with information and reasoning. The subtle and sinister ways of English Ministers and of the Castle junta are analysed and exposed with patience, justice and amazing skill.[4]

Referring to its 'lofty patriotism, sublime diction, keen historical insight', it encouraged the public to study the book carefully, because of its relevance to the events of that time.[5]

Sigerson's last book, *The Easter song*, published in 1922, brought to fruition nearly 30 years of research. It included a rhymed metrical translation of extended passages from the Latin of the *Carmen paschale* of Sedulius, a fifth-century saint who wrote the first Christian epic poem based on the story of the Gospels. It also contained a long preface in which Sigerson set out his theories on metric verse and much interesting historical matter, and appendices in which he attempted to show, among other things, how Milton was indebted to Sedulius. Its publication created a sensation in literary circles, not only because of its original arguments and the beauty of its style, but also because of the allegation that Milton in his *Paradise lost* had extensively plagiarised Sedulius's work.[6]

City Celebrities.—Dr. GEO. SIGERSON, F.L.S., M.D., etc.

George, the son of Siger, made his *debut* "among the green bushes in sweet Tyrone" in the neighbourhood of Strabane in the 'thirties. His ancestors had been in the habit for a considerable time of paying flying visits from the Scandinavian country to Ireland, and on these auspicious occasions they usually "made a collection," having a taste

Sometimes the harmony of the visitations was marred by the natives refusing to part, when arguments ensued, which occasionally resulted in funerals, a typical instance being an episode at Clontarf, in which a certain King Brian Boru entered such an emphatic protest against the Norsemen's levy that several of them died from the damp and many others met with fatal accidents, the King himself being knocked on the head during the discussion. Quite a number of the Danish excursionists having missed the last boat for home on the occasion, settled down and exchanged the somewhat exacting Viking business for the more peaceful if less strenuous occupations of the pastoral description, and of this stock is our hero descended.

At an early age George gave various indications of future greatness by endeavouring to assimilate every document he laid hold of. At this period it is highly probable that a quick lunch consisting of ancient Gaelic MSS. laid the foundation of that appetite for research into Gaelic sayings and doings of the period "beyond the misty space" for which he is now famous. With a view to acquiring, amongst other things, the Munster *blas*, our hero made a descent on the Queen's College, Cork, where having mopped up all the ologies and osculated the Blarney Stone, he came to Dublin and repeated the process at "Old Trinity," and then took a bee-line to Paris, where he added the distinction of Parleyvoo Science to an already long list. The Catholic University, Dublin, having requisitioned him for enlightenment, he was for many years its mentor on matters biological until the advent of the National University, when he switched his light on to that institution, of which he is also a Senator. Literature and Science having both claimed him, it is difficult to say in which he is most distinguished. His published works include books on land tenure, the atmosphere, nervous diseases, botany, heat, Gaelic literature, poetry, the physical geography of Ireland, etc., as well as numerous articles which appeared in *The Nation, Irishman, Dublin Hibernian Magazine,* and others.

Some twenty-one years ago the Irish Literary Society was founded, a body of which George is still President, being, in fact, the "spirit" of the organisation, a preservative which prevents its deteriorating into a log-rollers' club. George has written some good poetry, which possesses the rare advantage nowadays of being easily understood. His addresses, whether of two hours, or two minutes—as when unveiling the Mangan bust in St. Stephen's Green a few years ago—are always interesting, and one of his early articles in *The Irishman,* "The Holocaust," made that paper so popular with the Government of the day that they had the editor arrested and prosecuted. One would think that George's time-table left him no room for hobbies, but the *connoisseur* occasionally breaks out in him, when he may be seen indulging in the artistic dissipation of miniature hunting. He thinks in Gaelic.

for curios and a commendable appreciation of the precious metals. Collection plates and boxes were unknown at that period and cheques being troublesome to negotiate were ignored, the "ready" being only requisitioned, and the contributions being as a rule enclosed in sacks, the term applied to these highly enjoyable excursions was "sacking."

Dr George Sigerson: 'City Celebrities', *The Lepracaun*, May 1913

Political

An analysis of Sigerson's attitude to the political developments of the early years of the twentieth century is outside the scope of this publication and must await the researches of future scholars. Just what was Sigerson's position on the Home Rule and unionism controversies of the first decades of the century? How did he look upon the Ulster Volunteers and the Irish Volunteers, so strongly supported by his friends, Eoin MacNeill, Thomas MacDonagh and Patrick Pearse? How did he look upon the working-class movement in Dublin and the Lockout, so strongly supported by William Martin Murphy? What was his attitude to the Easter Rising and its strong condemnation by Irish political and religious leaders? It is impossible that Sigerson could have escaped being affected by such events and no doubt being canvassed for his support; yet we know little about his views on the period.

Eoin MacNeill, in his unpublished memoir, recalled his involvement in the Irish Volunteer Force in 1913 and mentioned how he had approached his old friend, Dr Sigerson, for his views on how this 'new departure' might be viewed. He claimed that Sigerson neither approved nor disapproved but asked the question, 'Do you think you will be able to control it?' MacNeill argued that he had no desire to control it. His memoir goes on to state that he had hoped to remain outside politics.[7] It is tempting to conclude that this was a typical Sigersonian response – trying to find out how far his questioner had thought out the implications of his actions without revealing anything about his own opinion. It does show, however, that Sigerson was aware of the forces behind the scenes that would take over MacNeill's volunteers in the months leading to Easter 1916.

Sigerson's daughter, Hester, recalled how the immediate outcome of the events of Easter week greatly saddened him. Good and talented friends were dead long before their time, and many others were being hounded and jailed. She spoke of her father's concern for the rebels and their relatives during and after the Easter Rising. While the gunfire and sniping was at its height, Sigerson, who was then 80 years old, kept crossing St Stephen's Green to enquire about missing persons on behalf of their distraught relatives. On the day following the surrender, he called upon the support of the lord mayor of Dublin to save the lives of those who faced execution. The fate of Thomas MacDonagh in particular moved him deeply.[8]

The Easter Rising caused many people to seek medical help. During May and through the early summer of 1916, large numbers of distracted people came to Sigerson for medical care. It is impossible to say how many innocent men, women and children he treated without recompense of any kind. Hester recalled one such occasion:

> I knew a dependent mother whose little girl had become so nervous through repeated raids on their home and the terrific gunfire in the district that it seemed

as if she must die or become insane. When I told him of this case, he immediately arranged to see the child, and happily after some treatment the little girl become quite strong and normal again. He had the prayers of these poor people and of many others. For the raids, arrests, ambushes and gunfire of those days left an aftermath of nervous affections among timid children and delicate people who had otherwise escaped physical injury.[9]

It is tempting to relate the publication of *The last independent parliament* to the emerging Sinn Féin movement and a more aggressive nationalism that was ready to challenge Britain's rule on a number of fronts. Historian Brian Ó Cuív in his chapter in the sixth volume of *A new history of Ireland* suggests that Sigerson had expressed support for abstentionism as far back as February 1868 in an editorial in *The Irishman* under the heading 'To your tents, O Israel'.[10] Sigerson's daughter, Hester, had little doubt that her father had not been a separatist in the same sense that his Fenian friends like Kickham and O'Leary were, but concluded that his sympathies with the executed and imprisoned following the 1916 Rising led him to support the new Sinn Féin movement emerging in those years despite his apparent earlier support for Home Rule. He was prepared to accept the Free State offered by the Anglo-Irish Treaty, but was said to have been very disappointed at partition and the exclusion of his beloved Ulster.[11] His acceptance of the invitation to join Seanad Éireann placed him firmly on the pro-Treaty side in the Civil War and would no doubt help to explain the later threat to his home in the early months of 1923.

The university question

After 1905 the movement to establish an independent university for Ireland had once again begun to gain momentum. In 1906 Sigerson was optimistic enough to conclude a lecture to students with the following words of encouragement:

> The traditions of one country have guided us toward one goal, through sacrifices to success, from repulse to recognition. It is not in nature to cease to advance, or to arrest now, when so much has been gained, that passion for learning which vibrates in every fibre of our people – which has been its honour when prosperous and the ennobling glory of this true liberal land and this indomitable nation.[12]

The university issue had been a controversial one in Ireland and in Anglo-Irish relations from the time of Emancipation in 1829. Equality with Trinity College had been the main demand of Irish nationalists, and British governments had made frequent efforts to go some way towards meeting this ambition. In 1845 Sir Robert Peel had tried to meet the demands of the Catholic leadership for higher education by establishing the non-denominational Queen's Colleges in Belfast, Galway and Cork, but the Catholic hierarchy rejected them and in 1850 attempted to set up

Special order by wire from P.P.P.'s cage.

Pretty Prince Poll

Sometimes I rage
In this lofty cage,
Sometimes I whistle and sing.
Sometimes I hop, flop, and drop,
Sometimes I swagger and swing —
That is my sport,
This is my court,
For I am Poll Parrot the King.
"Eveleen", I call
"Bring me your doll,
I'll give it a dressing, you see.
If you push in your thumb
I'll pretend it's a plum,
And give it a bite
To make you polite,
None must point a finger at me.)
For this is my court,
And that is my sport,
And I am Poll Parrot the King.

over SVP

Fragment of a handwritten poem by George Sigerson
which he presented to his granddaughter
Eibhlin Humphreys on her birthday

their own independent Catholic University under the leadership of the celebrated Dr John Henry Newman. From the beginning, however, it lacked finance and an official charter allowing it to confer degrees, making it a very poor relation in contrast to the well-endowed Trinity and even the Queen's Colleges, which prospered despite the fact that the bishops derisively rejected them as 'godless'.

In the later decades of the nineteenth century, government policies were adapted with the aim of dealing with Irish grievances and thereby reducing support for Home Rule and resolving agrarian unrest. This led to a series of attempts to appease the Catholics. In 1880 the Royal University of Ireland was established as a degree-giving body for the Queen's Colleges and for the Catholic University. That institution now became University College, Dublin. It was under the control of the Jesuits but the Catholic University Medical School remained as a separate college. This move went some way towards meeting Catholic requirements, but in 1897 Cardinal Logue reiterated the bottom line of the hierarchy's demand – one really respectable university equal to Trinity and with episcopal control. This latter point was one that the government found difficult to contemplate and a resolution by the Presbyterian General Assembly in 1903, rejecting the concept of a Catholic university as 'detrimental to university education, as tending to the perpetuation of divisions and animosities amongst the young of different areas and as practically involving in a very objectionable form a state endowment of religion' seemed to postpone the issue to some distant future.[13]

Yet by 1908 the British government had accepted the principle of a university system more in touch with Catholic demands. The sweeping victory of the Liberal Party in the 1906 general election and their close association with the Irish Home Rule movement led Augustine Birrell, the chief secretary for Ireland, to seek agreement on a new measure that became law in 1909. This established the National University of Ireland (NUI), embracing the Queen's Colleges of Cork and Galway, University College, Dublin and Maynooth College, with its management representing the majority student body from each college. In a foretaste of partition a few years later, Queen's College, Belfast became an autonomous university representing the interests of the north-east and possibly reflecting some of the reservations expressed by the 1903 Presbyterian resolution.

In theory NUI was non-denominational but the selection of Archbishop Walsh as chancellor was a clear sign that the Catholic hierarchy saw it as their domain and a hard-won concession from a hostile British political elite. However, the bishops were soon involved in another quarrel, this time with the Gaelic League and the language movement, over the issue of compulsory Irish for matriculation to the new university. The issue had been fought out in Maynooth in 1907, when future leaders like Eoin MacNeill and Patrick Pearse had attacked the downgrading of Irish in the training of priests, and now it arose again. John Dillon, Redmond's deputy leader in the Irish Parliamentary Party, had helped greatly in the act leading to NUI, calling it 'one of the greatest services to the Irish nation which it has ever been given to an English statesman to render'.[14] He fought strongly against this attempt to make Irish compulsory for matriculation, siding with the bishops, but to no avail. The senate of the new institution accepted the argument that it should be both Catholic and Gaelic.[15]

More pertinent was the attempt by people involved with the Gaelic League to have Sigerson appointed as vice-chancellor of NUI, but this had to be dropped when it was seen that the position was to be held in rotation by the presidents of the constituent colleges of the university.[16]

When the National University of Ireland became a reality in 1909, Sigerson was appointed professor of zoology. He continued to work as a professor in NUI until 1923. In his eighties, he still presented a striking figure; with silver-white hair flowing over his black frock coat, he looked private, distinguished and scholarly, and the advancing years increased rather than diminished his striking appearance. In Aodh de Blácam's book, *The black north* (1938), he records the comments of Augustine Birrell, who was visiting NUI and was struck by Sigerson's appearance. Birrell, watching Sigerson from a distance, said, 'It would pay the University just to have him walk the grounds to give it an air of authority and learning.'[17] Joyce briefly mentions his old tutor in *Finnegans wake*, where Joyce's anti-self leans against an ambiguous figure: in part, an ancient pillar-stone awaking ancestral memories, in part a Norseman – 'the butter blond Sigurdson'.[18]

Art collecting

In addition to his many other interests, Sigerson was an avid collector of art, especially French art. According to his daughter, Hester:

his collecting knew no limits. For years he took his brief holidays in Paris or among the old cities of France gathering objects of art which he delighted to display to his friends on Sunday evenings.[19]

Austin Clarke recalled seeing a long, dusty room crammed with ornate tables, sideboards, gilt mirrors and so on, like an auction room or a second-hand shop; but much of the furniture was priceless, and many of the pieces dated back to the time of Louis XIV and Louis XV.[20] Miniatures of the Napoleonic era fascinated Sigerson, and no trip to France was complete and satisfactory without at least a tiny picture to bring back home to Clare Street. C.P. Curran remembered the distinctly French atmosphere of the house:

> The walls were hung with fragments of tapestry, French paintings and pastels. Cabinets were filled with miniatures and there were numerous portfolios stuffed with drawings, engravings, and mezzotints.[21]

His obsession for collecting antiques, especially pictures, remained with him until the end of his long life. Valuable paintings and engravings were stacked in the corners of rooms that were already overcrowded with pieces of furniture, *objets d'art* and books. Thus, many of the rooms were virtually out of bounds for his sister, Jane, and the maids as they went about their duties with only a flickering light to guide them.

Sigerson's wonderful collection of miniatures was exhibited in the National Museum in Dublin. The miniatures, which he had spent a lifetime putting together, consisted mainly of French royalty, soldiers, statesmen and court beauties. It is likely that his daughter, Dora, and her husband, Clement Shorter, took the opportunity to see the collection in the museum when they visited Dublin after the 1916 Rising. Another visitor was Lady Ardilaun, wife of Arthur Guinness and, like Sigerson, an ardent Francophile. In a letter to Sigerson, she wrote, 'Went to the Museum and had a most interesting and delightful time looking at the miniatures. What a collection!'[22]

The Senate
In 1922, the leader of the Free State government, William T. Cosgrave, nominated Sigerson for membership of Seanad Éireann. In September of that year, pending the election of officers, Sir Thomas Esmonde, one of the few people to have served both in the British House of Commons and in the Oireachtas, proposed Sigerson to chair the Senate's first meeting. Alice Stopford Green, historian and author of *The making of Ireland and its undoing* (1908), in seconding the proposal, said, 'It would be to us an honour if so learned and faithful an historian of Ireland would take the chair for this day.'[23] Sigerson thus had the honour, at the age of 86, of presiding at the first meeting of Seanad Éireann. He remained a member of the Senate until his death in 1925.

Dr Sigerson and friend in Grafton Street, Dublin.
Courtesy of the National Library of Ireland

His contributions in the Senate concentrated mainly on the development of agriculture, forestry, fisheries and industry. However, not everyone appreciated his interventions. Among his critics was Lady Augusta Gregory, a close friend of William Butler Yeats. Visiting the Senate on one occasion to listen to Yeats, she unkindly said:

> Then old Sigerson (spoke) – bringing out his words very slowly, and all he said quite wide of the mark, favouring the printing of Ordnance Reports which were not in question at all.[24]

Sigerson's disagreement with Yeats over the aims of the National Literary Society in the 1890s had clearly not been forgotten or forgiven.

Sigerson's membership of the Senate was not without personal sacrifice. On 10 February 1923, a headline in the *Freeman's Journal* read, 'The terror. Dr Sigerson driven out of Senate. Incendiary attack.' The report stated:

> Dr George Sigerson, veteran poet, patriot, scientist and writer has resigned from membership of Seanad Éireann as a result of intimidation. The distinguished man of letters was quite frank as to the cause of his decision when interviewed on Monday evening at his residence, 3 Clare Street. 'Yes', he said, 'I am sorry to say it has become necessary – it is true. I have sent this letter to President Cosgrave saying so. The public will greatly deplore it. Will you be good enough to let them know the reason? Well, I got a communication. I did not mind the threat of shooting, and I attended at the House, as was my duty. But now, with the threat that if I continue to act, my house and property will be burned, I feel that I have no alternative but to resign. I might not care for myself but must have regard for my family and their property.'[25]

The threat was clearly not an idle one, as the home of his fellow senator, Sir Thomas Esmonde, located near Gorey, County Wexford, and dating from the seventeenth century, was later burned by anti-Treaty forces on 9 March 1923. In the event, Cosgrave persuaded Sigerson to ignore the threats, and he continued in Seanad Éireann for another two years. His last visit to the Senate was during early February 1925, when he voted to appoint Douglas Hyde a senator. Speaking with Hyde, he said, 'This is good work you know, careful work, sound work.'[26]

The harp design
In August 1922 the issue of an official symbol for the new Irish state was raised. A number of designs had been submitted for approval but found unsuitable. Further advice was sought. Among those approached were Sigerson and Thomas Sadleir, registrar of the Office of Arms at Dublin Castle. Sigerson had earlier advised the Irish Volunteers on their emblems and, in December 1922, he recommended to the governor of the new state, T.M. Healy, that the harp should be adopted as the symbol of the Free State. He discounted the tricolour since it 'represent[s] division of a country not a United Nation; [… it] is unknown abroad'. He continued:

> There is however a symbol which has been identified with Ireland for ages, which is well-known to other nations, and welcomed in all our provinces. In my youth, it was still frequent on the current coin in many counties, and it still stands in Paris and elsewhere over our exiled colleges. I mean the harp of Ireland. The harp was the common and sacred symbol of the Protestant Volunteer of 1782, of the Presbyterian and Catholic United Irishmen of 1798, of old and Young Ireland and of men of after days – it is in no sense a party or sectional symbol but one

which represents the entire Nation. … It was the only symbol sanctioned by our last Independent Parliament. It is now within the power of an Irish Independent Government to place this emblem of humanizing harmony in its high place of honour, unique and not undistinguished amongst the lions, the leopards, and the single and double headed eagles of the rest of the world.[27]

The enthusiasm of George Sigerson and Thomas Sadleir for the harp clearly influenced those in positions of power, for on 28 December 1922 a meeting of the Executive Council decided that the harp should be adopted. The full weight of academic opinion as represented by Sigerson and Sadleir had thrown itself behind the harp as the outstanding emblem of the nation and a symbol instantly recognised throughout the world as being synonymous with Ireland.

Last years
In the summer of 1923, at the age of 87, Sigerson retired from university teaching and closed his medical practice. In 1924 he was invited to represent Ireland at the Pasteur centenary celebration in Paris. Though it seemed a foolish undertaking to travel alone and so far at his age, he insisted on making the journey. He suffered no ill effects; on the contrary, he came back in very good health and spirits, having been honoured in honourable company. His daughter, Hester, commenting on his visit to Paris, wrote:

> Thus, a very old man, he trod again the streets of that beautiful city, to which he first came as a fresh faced boy from his native Tyrone, with all the world before him and he beheld for the last time the fair land he loved only second to his own.[28]

Except for very poor eyesight, he continued to enjoy surprisingly good health, physically and mentally. His weak eyesight frustrated him, as reading and writing required the assistance of a magnifying glass. Yet he kept on working. After years of researching his own background, a history of the Sigerson family was nearing completion and almost ready for publication. He still found time to entertain old and interesting friends. In *Under the receding wave*, C.P. Curran wrote:

> Once a week we would make our way slowly through dirty ragged portfolios, breaking off at midnight for a bottle of wine and sandwiches, before resuming the task. I learned a great deal from those drawings and prints. Each item was the starting point for a new excursion into French history, or an excuse for reminiscence.[29]

In his introduction to *Songs and poems by George Sigerson*, which was published in 1927, Padraic Colum recalled his last visit to 3 Clare Street. According to Colum, although Sigerson's face was pale and his voice was slower, there was 'no slackness in his intellectual powers'.[30] Through the Christmas season of 1924, a bad chest infection confined him to bed – a most unusual occurrence, as his life was singularly free from illness. During the illness his conversation kept returning to his childhood: his home at Holyhill and the surrounding countryside with its fairy wood and spade mill, the tiny streams, stone bridges and moorlands of heather. On recovering, he remarked that misfortunes often bring benefits, instancing the illness as an event that allowed him to clear his mind and carry out revision on his family history. Donn Piatt, son of Sigerson's daughter, Hester, wrote:

> my grandfather had spent much time over a number of years working on this project and as his death approached he got me to sit by his bedside and read it to him, dictating some corrections which I wrote in.[31]

Surprisingly, shortly after the new year in 1925, his ninetieth year, Sigerson appeared fully recovered and was well enough to visit his friend, T.P. O'Hanlon, on Sunday evenings. His last public outing was a visit to the Senate, where he supported the election of Douglas Hyde.

On Friday, 13 February 1925, he suffered a recurrence of a chest illness and stayed in bed. The following day his condition further deteriorated – so much so that he allowed his daughter, Hester, to send for a doctor and a priest, Fr Aloysius, who was a close friend. During his last days, Sigerson spoke often of the Tyrone of his youth and, in response to a request from his daughter, Hester, he put his own words to the air of 'The foggy dew', his favourite tune. Over the weekend his condition worsened and he died on Tuesday, 17 February, with family and friends gathered around his bed.

Postscript

During the last six months of George Sigerson's life he visited the O'Hanlons most Sunday evenings. Thirty years later, in the *Capuchin Annual*, T.P. O'Hanlon told of a strange occurrence in the weeks approaching Sigerson's death.

One evening he told them that he had just seen a vision. As he had travelled across the city a glowing wheel had appeared in the cab. Before him, resting on the opposite seat, the apparition was fully two feet in diameter. It had seemed so real that he had bent forward to touch it, but the visionary scene had faded. Sigerson himself made little of the wheel and his conversation moved to another topic.

The following Sunday, when Mrs O'Hanlon opened the door, Sigerson said, 'Madam, I saw that wheel again today, exactly the same and in the same position. Curious!' And the following week, he saw the wheel again.

A month after Sigerson's first account of seeing the glowing wheel in a vision, T.P. O'Hanlon received a parcel of books to review. The title of one of the books startled him. The book was called *The flaming wheel*. Stranger still, the title of the book was based on an ancient Norse legend. According to the legend, a flaming wheel symbolises the full circle of a year; and as each year comes full circle, at its close, the mystic wheel rolls into the sea and disappears.

Again, on Sunday, 8 February, Sigerson came with the same story: but this time the wheel had glowed more strongly and lasted longer. It had stayed with him from Trinity College to Phibsborough. The O'Hanlons felt uneasy and decided against mentioning the book, *The flaming wheel*.

The following Sunday came without a visit from Sigerson. Then, two days later, a Capuchin priest called to tell them that Dr Sigerson had died.[32]

10

The Sigerson Cup

Dónal McAnallen

Ironically for a man who had little direct contact with sport in the course of his long life, over the last century the memory of Dr George Sigerson has been preserved primarily by a football trophy. This chapter will examine how Sigerson came to present his famous prize for intervarsity football in 1911, and how his name became a byword for an exceptional and much-celebrated annual festival of Gaelic games.

The Gaelic Athletic Association, founded in 1884, was famously described as sweeping through southern rural Ireland 'like a prairie fire',[1] but its impact on the universities was minimal in its first two decades. The authorities and the relatively small student bodies of both the Royal University of Ireland and Trinity College, Dublin were broadly unionist in outlook and of middle- or upper-class origin. Therefore, they tended to favour rugby union, cricket and hockey as field sports. Although Trinity had a 'hurley' club up until the early 1880s, this game was not as close to hurling as the name suggests and no effort was made to bring it or the club into the ranks of the GAA.[2]

Another major reason for the failure of hurling and Gaelic football to make headway in the universities was the fact that hardly any secondary schools promoted them. St Patrick's College, Drumcondra had successful hurling and football teams in the 1880s,[3] but it was the only higher-education college to become affiliated with the GAA before the turn of the century.

During the decade 1900–1910, hurling and Gaelic football were played intermittently to various extents in each of the university colleges of Dublin, Galway and Cork, and several other higher-education colleges in Dublin.[4] In Queen's College, Galway, for example, students played hurling on an informal basis as far back as 1902. But in the absence of any competition catering specifically for their teams, these colleges depended mainly on school teams or local clubs for opposition. In 1907, a Munster Colleges Council was formed to organise games for various secondary schools and Queen's College, Cork (later UCC).[5] The establishment of the National

University of Ireland in 1908 meant a great deal more than legislative reconfiguration of higher education in Ireland. To Irish nationalists it signified a new opportunity to nurture the revival of Irish culture and pastimes and enhance the general welfare of the country; they campaigned strongly for Irish to be made a compulsory subject for matriculation and they succeeded in this cause in 1910.

George Sigerson, of course, was one of the most enthusiastic supporters of the NUI. As the only surviving professor from the Catholic University still teaching in UCD, Sigerson took great delight in being part of a new university that could provide a 'national' education worthy of its name. He was, accordingly, an avowed advocate of *esprit de corps* within UCD (to which end he wrote a special college song, the idealistic 'Carmen scholare'),[6] and of stimulating camaraderie between the NUI colleges. For such reasons, Sigerson was innately sympathetic to efforts to initiate intercollegiate Gaelic games.

These efforts made quite rapid progress during the 1910/11 academic session. The initiative first arose from the formation of a Leinster Colleges Council at a meeting at the Shelbourne Hotel, Dublin, on 26 November 1910. This council catered primarily for secondary schools (one of whose representatives, Patrick Pearse of St Enda's College, was elected vice-chairman), but also organised hurling and football leagues for the higher-education colleges of Dublin.[7] Commencing in January 1911 (and continuing to the end of the academic year), these leagues comprised teams from UCD, St Patrick's, Drumcondra, Marlborough Street Training College, Albert Agricultural College and the College of Science.[8] In the interim, the students of UCG formed their own GAA club,[9] but the UCG Athletic Union, to which every student compulsorily subscribed, voted against making a grant to the new club.[10] Although at last Gaelic sports were established in all three of the constituent colleges of NUI at once, clearly their promotion and acceptance was not a straightforward matter. In UCC, similarly, Fr Edwin Fitzgibbon, professor of scholastic philosophy, reported that there were 'vigorous hurling and Gaelic football teams', which were to the forefront of efforts to raise 'the flag of nationality' in a college that still chose to fly the Union Jack.[11]

In the spring of 1911, nonetheless, stronger links were forged between the teams of the different university colleges. A hurling game between combined Munster and Leinster colleges (mostly schools) selections on Sunday, 26 March in County Cork – followed by a post-match banquet at which the recent advances of colleges' Gaelic games were acclaimed in speeches – seemed to act as a spur for contests to be held between the three constituent colleges of NUI.[12] A meeting of the Leinster Colleges Council four days later, on 30 March, considered suggestions for a series of games between the NUI colleges. It was intimated that UCC and UCG teams were willing to travel to Dublin, so it was decided to proceed with plans for such matches.[13] As if to prove its desire to join in, the UCG football team travelled to Dublin a couple of days later, and played both the Marlborough Street and Drumcondra training colleges over the weekend of 1–2 April.[14]

On Monday, 3 April, following negotiations between Fr Fitzgibbon of UCC, J.J. McElligott of UCD, Brian Cusack of UCG and David J.P. Burke of the Leinster Colleges Council, arrangements were made for a football competition between their three colleges, to take place in Dublin over three days in May. The newspaper report of these decisions on 7 April, under the sub-heading, 'Sigerson Cup Competition', also revealed news of 'a valuable Silver Cup which has kindly been presented by Dr Sigerson. The competition has already aroused keen interest amongst the students of the different Colleges.'[15]

Up to this point, Sigerson had had little or no direct connection with Gaelic games, and it is not clear whether or not he was approached and asked to donate such a trophy. However, his swift and generous response was an unambiguous demonstration of support for the development of the games at university level. In fact, Sigerson's gesture was almost unprecedented for Gaelic games at national level. Neither the All-Ireland hurling championship nor the football championship, although they had been contested since the 1880s, had a regular trophy until the 1920s. At a time when the GAA struggled to secure patronage for its national competitions, here was a UCD professor donating a cup for an event that had not taken place and was not certain to be repeated, and from which he – unlike the politicians and commercial interests who donated many trophies at county level – did not stand to draw any tangible benefit. The magnitude of the gesture was widely appreciated. A preview of the competition in the *Freeman's Journal*, for example, paid tribute to 'that venerable patriot, Dr Sigerson, who has always shown a keen interest in the doings of the students'.[16]

Early on Tuesday, 9 May, the Cork and Galway college teams arrived in Dublin. At half past four that afternoon, UCC challenged UCD in the maiden game of the Sigerson Cup competition at Jones's Road (later Croke Park). UCC spoiled the hosts' party somewhat by beating UCD, and by defeating UCG on the following day the Cork college secured overall victory in the championship even before the other two teams met on the last day.[17] Between games the teams were treated to an enjoyable programme of social events, namely a visit to the theatre on Tuesday evening and a 'smoker' on Wednesday.[18] Finally, at the close of the competition, the teams were entertained to dinner by the president of UCD, Dr Denis J. Coffey, in the Aberdeen Hall of the Gresham Hotel. Before making the presentation to the UCC captain, John O'Riordan, Sigerson is reputed to have made a speech (although it was not reported at the time) referring to the cup as having risen in the east, veered towards the south, arrived in the west in a short time, before returning to the east.[19]

The Sigerson Cup was designed in the shape of a mether, an ancient drinking urn symbolic of friendship. This suggests that Sigerson had as much affinity for *bon viveur* undergraduates as for diligent students and dedicated sportsmen. The cup had four handles, representing the four provinces of Ireland – aptly so, given that Sigerson himself had spent time living and studying in each province. The Liam MacCarthy Cup for the All-Ireland hurling championship, first presented in 1923, was also modelled on the mether, albeit a much larger version than the Sigerson Cup. Unusually diminutive for a trophy, the Sigerson Cup sat on a small mahogany plinth that incorporated four columns to support its long handles. Around the plinth medals listing the winning teams in full were to be affixed. When the plinth was covered with medals, another tier was built onto it.

It is widely assumed that his presentation of the eponymous trophy was Sigerson's sole contribution to the GAA. That is not the case, however. The doctor's bequest to the intervarsity football scene indicated to the GAA that he was a more enthusiastic supporter than had previously been realised. Thus, when the GAA's Central Council decided to erect a permanent memorial to Dr Thomas Croke, the former archbishop of Cashel and a founding patron of the association, they turned to Sigerson for advice in order to choose the best design for a statue.[20] Sigerson remained in contact with the GAA executive over several years in connection with this problematic project, which dragged into the 1920s.[21]

During the last fourteen years of Sigerson's life, the competition that he had helped to launch became well established as a highlight of the student year and of the Gaelic games calendar. The fact of his trophy being on offer as a perpetual prize did much to ensure the permanence of the competition, while others occasionally went into abeyance. The Sigerson Cup was probably the second most important national Gaelic football competition for over a decade up to the inception of the National League, Railway Cup and inter-county minor championships in the late 1920s. The Sigerson tournament was hosted in rotation between UCD, UCG and UCC, opening typically with fervent receptions and pageantry for the visiting teams at the railway station, and featuring three games spread over three days, with a hectic social schedule and surfeits of revelry throughout. Much the same could be said of the Fitzgibbon Cup competition, which started in 1912 as an intervarsity hurling equivalent to the Sigerson Cup, with a trophy presented by Fr Fitzgibbon of UCC as its prize.

While Sigerson appears not to have attended any games after the initial presentation of his cup in 1911, he was surely aware of its reputation from newspaper reports and word of mouth among excited students.

Since his death in 1925, while his many academic and other achievements have been largely obscured, Dr Sigerson's name has been synonymous with intervarsity Gaelic football. The competition has been quite unique (along with the Fitzgibbon Cup) among national Gaelic games trophies in being named after a trophy-donor throughout this period. Beyond that, though, the name Sigerson also came to embody the epic qualities of the annual event: talented up-and-coming players from different counties playing together and striking up close friendships; cruelly hard training, often in the harshest weather; fiercely contested and unpredictable games in quick succession; and legendary pranks and vigorous celebrations without fail. (Generations of students have put the cup to use as a traditional mether, as Sigerson enabled them to do.)

The fact that intervarsity Gaelic games stayed outside the GAA's ambit of control for decades made them all the more enigmatic, if not precarious. Perhaps more than any other intervarsity competition in Ireland (or the world), the Sigerson Cup competition was perennially afflicted with eligibility controversies – specifically, concerning players' status as *bona fide* full-time students or otherwise. The other anomaly about Sigerson Cup games then, as opposed to football under the GAA's aegis, was the unwritten rule that players would not be sent off, no matter how they behaved, lest the stigma affect their academic careers or future employment. Yet even with these sources of frequent friction, the competition continued to engender the type of amity between the NUI colleges that Sigerson envisaged, and its sheer popularity elevated it to become the supreme Irish intervarsity sporting event.

From 1933 onwards, Queen's University, Belfast became a regular participant (having previously taken part in 1923), and with four teams now involved the competition was restructured to adopt a straight knockout format of semi-finals and final. When Queen's at last won the competition in 1958/9, almost half a century after the cup was first presented, Sigerson's much-vaunted aspiration that it would stay a time in each province was realised.

In the 1960s, with the Irish higher-education sector going through rapid change and growth, the administration of the Sigerson Cup and indeed all Gaelic games in the sector came under more direct control from GAA headquarters at Croke Park. After the admission of Trinity College to the Sigerson Cup competition in 1963 came that of Maynooth College in 1972, the New University of Ulster (Coleraine) in 1976 and the University of Ulster, Jordanstown in 1985. From the mid-1970s, therefore, Sigerson Cup weekend reverted to a three-day format, albeit one in which all the teams played straight knockout from quarter-finals to final over one weekend.

A new departure was reached in 1988, when all colleges playing in the first division of the Comhairle Ardoideachais (Higher Education Council) league, including teacher-training colleges, regional technical colleges and in due course the Garda Training College, were permitted to play in the Sigerson Cup. So much did the field widen that by the late 1990s more than 20 colleges were participating. The fact that many of the newer colleges pressed hard to be admitted to the Sigerson Cup (and Fitzgibbon Cup) ranks, while still being refused entry into the equivalent intervarsity rugby (Dudley Cup) and association football (Collingwood Cup) tournaments, may be seen to speak volumes for the prestige attached to the name and image of the Sigerson Cup.

By a happy coincidence, like the professor himself, the Sigerson Cup spent a total of 89 years travelling the country. This was the longest period that any national Gaelic games trophy has ever been in circulation. The cup's mere survival was a remarkable achievement, considering the many legendary knocks, scrapes and pranks it endured over nine decades. The trophy's plinth – by then several tiers high and dwarfing the cup itself – had suffered somewhat as well, not least in that some of the winners' medals that should have been attached to it were missing. One of the original trophy's last journeys was to Strabane, near George Sigerson's homeplace, where it was taken for one night in March 2000 after Queen's University's victory, before being retired peacefully to the GAA Museum.

A new replica Sigerson Cup was commissioned and presented for the first time at the tournament final in April 2001. The second Sigerson Cup was not as fortunate as its predecessor, however. On the evening of its presentation it went missing and remained so for ten months, during which time another replica trophy (or third Sigerson Cup) was cast at the behest of champion college UUJ. Eventually, however, a high-profile campaign brought the retrieval of the authentic second trophy. It is this second trophy that remains in circulation as the prize for the intervarsity championship and that inspires so many higher-education institutions to ever-greater efforts. In the five years previous to the time of writing, two more colleges recorded their first victories, making a total of 11 colleges on the roll of honour. Whether it still succeeds in achieving Sigerson's dream of bringing colleges closer together is debatable, in the light of recurrent issues over eligibility and an increasingly unbridled pursuit of victory among many colleges, but the Sigerson Cup competition remains one of the most significant of the GAA calendar and a principal social event of the student year.

Más aoibhinn beatha an scoláire, is amhlaidh is fearr í mar gheall ar an Dr Seoirse Mac Síoghair agus Corn Mhic Síoghair.

SELECT BIBLIOGRAPHY

Blaney, Roger, *Presbyterians and the Irish language* (Belfast, 1996).

Boyd, Ernest A., *Ireland's literary renaissance* (New York, 1922).

Brooke, Stopford A. and Rolleston, T.W. (eds), *A treasury of Irish poetry in the English tongue* (London, 1900).

Charcot, J.M. (Sigerson, George, trans.), *Lectures on the diseases of the nervous system* (London, 1877).

Clarke, Austin, *A penny in the clouds: more memories of Ireland and England* (London, 1968).

Crone, J.S., 'Editor's gossip: Dr Crone visits Dublin and sees Dr Sigerson who shows him death mask of Charles Kickham; and Mr Henry Dixon shows him death mask of Fintan Lalor', *Irish Book Lover*, xii (1920), p. 13.

Curran, C.P. *Under the receding wave* (Dublin, 1970).

Daly, Dominic, *The young Douglas Hyde: the dawn of the Irish revolution and renaissance, 1874–1893* (Dublin, 1974).

Davis, Thomas Osborne (Duffy, Charles Gavan, ed.), *The patriot parliament of 1689: with its statutes, votes and proceedings* (Dublin, 1893).

Deane, Seamus (ed.), *The Field Day anthology of Irish writing* (3 vols, Derry, 1990).

De Blácam, Aodh, *The black north: an account of the six counties of unrecover'd Ireland – their people, their treasures and their history* (Dublin, 1938).

De Búrca, Dáithí, 'Irish colleges and Irish pastimes', *Gaelic athletic annual and county directory* (1910), pp. 74–5.

Dublin Mansion House Relief Committee, *The Irish crisis of 1879–80* (Dublin, 1881).

Duffy, Charles Gavan, Hyde, Douglas and Sigerson, George, *The revival of Irish literature* (London, 1894).

Edwards, Ruth Dudley, *Patrick Pearse: The triumph of failure* (London, 1977).

Ellmann, Richard (ed.), *Letters of James Joyce* (3 vols, London, 1957–66).

Esposito, Michele, *Irish melodies for violin with pianoforte accompaniment: op. 56* (Dublin, 1903).

Foster, R.F., *Modern Ireland, 1600–1972* (London, 1988).

Gailey, Alan, *Spade making in Ireland* (Cultra, 1982).

Gamble, John, *Views of society and manners in the north of Ireland, in a series of letters written in the year 1818* (London, 1819).

Garvin, Tom, *The evolution of Irish nationalist politics* (Dublin, 1981).

Gregory, Lady Augusta (Murphy, Daniel J., ed.), *Lady Gregory's journals: books 1 to 29, 10 October 1916 to 24 February 1925* (Oxford, 1978).

Hoppen, K. Theodore, *Ireland since 1800: conflict and conformity* (London and New York, 1989).

Hyde, Douglas, 'George Sigerson', *Studies: An Irish Quarterly Review* xiv, no. 53 (March 1925), pp. 1–18.

— (ed.), *The love songs of Connacht, being the fourth chapter of the songs of Connacht* (Dublin, 1893).

Jeffares, A. Norman, *W.B. Yeats: man and poet* (London and New York, 1949).

Lyons, F.S.L., *Ireland since the Famine* (New York, 1971).

—, *John Dillon: a biography* (Chicago, 1968).

Lyons, J.B., 'George Sigerson: Charcot's translator', *Journal of the History of the Neurosciences*, vi, no. 1 (1997), pp. 50–60.

—, *Brief lives of Irish doctors* (Dublin, 1978).

MacCaffrey, James, *History of the Catholic Church in the nineteenth century (1789–1908)* (2 vols, Dublin, 1909), i.

MacDiarmada, Pádraig, 'Comórtas Sigerson 1911–1963', *Our Games Annual* (1964).

MacDonagh, Thomas, *Literature in Ireland: studies, Irish and Anglo-Irish* (Dublin, 1916).

—, 'Antigone and Lir', *Irish Review*, iv, no. 37 (March 1914), pp. 29–32.

Maguire, Canon, *Letterkenny past and present* (Letterkenny, *c.* 1920).

Mangan, James Clarence (trans.) (O'Daly, John, ed.), *The poets and poetry of Munster: a selection of Irish songs* (1st series, Dublin, 1849).

McCartney, Donal, *UCD, A national idea: the history of University College, Dublin* (Dublin, 1999).

Meenan, Patrick N., *St Patrick's blue and saffron: a miscellany of UCD sport since 1895* (Dublin, 1997).

Mitchel, John, *The last conquest of Ireland (perhaps)* (Dublin, 1861).

Neilson, William, *Céad leabhar na Gaoidheilge* (Dublin, 1810).

—, *An introduction to the Irish language* (Dublin, 1808).

Newman, Cardinal John Henry, *The idea of a university* (London, 1852 and 1858).

O'Brien, Joseph V., *William O'Brien and the course of Irish politics, 1881–1918* (Berkeley, California, 1976).

O'Brien, R. Barry (ed.), *Two centuries of Irish history, 1691–1870* (London, 1888).

O'Connor, Ellen, 'Dr Sigerson's masterpiece', *Irish Monthly*, xlii, no. 487 (January 1914), pp. 30–3.

O'Connor, T.P., *Memoirs of an old parliamentarian* (London, 1929).

O'Farrell, Patrick, *Ireland's English question: Anglo-Irish relations 1534–1970* (London, 1971).

O'Leary, John, *Recollections of Fenians and Fenianism* (Dublin, 1896).

Piatt, Donn, 'A Pale family and Old Dublin, being an account of the Sigerson family', *Dublin Historical Record*, xviii, no. 3 (1962–3), pp. 91–100; no. 4 (1962–3), pp. 112–26.

Piatt, Hester Sigerson, *The golden quest and other stories* (Dublin, 1940).

—, *The passing years: a book of verses* (Dublin, 1935).

Pigott, Richard, *Recollections of an Irish national journalist* (Dublin, 1882).

Power, Patrick C., *The story of Anglo-Irish poetry (1880–1922)* (Cork, 1967).

Schirmer, Gregory A., *Out of what began: a history of Irish poetry in English* (Ithaca, New York, 1998).

Shorter, Dora Sigerson, *The tricolour: poems of the Irish revolution* (Dublin, 1922).

— (Tynan, Katharine, intro.), *The sad years* (3rd ed., London, 1919).

—, *Verses* (London, 1893).

Sigerson, George (Piatt, Hester Sigerson, ed.), *Songs and poems by George Sigerson* (Dublin, 1927).

—, *The Easter song: being the first epic of Christendom by Sedulius, the first scholar-saint of Erinn* (Dublin, 1922).

—, *The last independent parliament of Ireland: with account of the survival of the nation and its lifework* (Dublin, 1918).

—, *The saga of King Lir: a sorrow of story* (Dublin, 1913).

—, *Bards of the Gael and Gall: examples of the poetic literature of Erinn; done into English after the metres and modes of the Gael by George Sigerson* (London, 1897, 2nd ed. 1907, 3rd ed. 1925).

—, *Political prisoners at home and abroad* (London, 1884).

—, 'On the need and use of village hospitals in Ireland', *Journal of the Statistical and Social Inquiry Society of Ireland*, viii, no. 60 (1881–2), pp. 340–9.

—, *History of the land tenures and land classes of Ireland, with an account of the various secret agrarian confederacies* (London and Dublin, 1871).

—, *Modern Ireland: its vital questions, secret societies and government* (London, 1868).

—, 'Some remarks on a protomorphic phyllotype', *Atlantis*, iv, nos 7–8 (1863), pp. 450–8.

— (trans.) (O'Daly, John, ed.), *The poets and poetry of Munster: a selection of Irish songs* (2nd series, Dublin, 1860).

Sigerson, Hester Varian, *A ruined race or, The last MacManus of Drumroosk* (Dublin, 1889).

Sullivan, A.M., *New Ireland: political sketches ad personal reminiscences of thirty years of Irish public life* (London, 1882).

Tierney, Michael (Martin, F.X., ed.), *Eoin MacNeill: scholar and man of action, 1867–1945* (Oxford, 1980).

Unknown, 'Lectures on the diseases of the nervous system by J.M. Charcot, translated by G. Sigerson: reviewed', *Dublin Journal of Medical Science*, lxv, p. 338.

Varian, Ralph (ed.), *The harp of Erin: a book of ballad-poetry and of native song* (Dublin, 1869).

— (ed.), *Ballads, popular poetry and household songs of Ireland* (Dublin, 1865).

Vaughan, W.E. (ed.), *A new history of Ireland, volume 6: Ireland under the union II, 1870–1921* (Oxford, 1996).

Walsh, John R., *A history of the parish of Maghera* (1973).

Welch, Robert, *A history of verse translation from the Irish, 1789–1897* (Gerrard's Cross, Buckinghamshire, 1988).

West, Trevor, *The bold collegians: the development of sport in Trinity College, Dublin* (Dublin, 1991), pp. 33–6.

Woodham-Smith, Cecil, *The great hunger* (London, 1962).

Woodward, George William Otway, *Divided island: conflict, Ireland, 1910–1949* (Auckland, New Zealand, 1976).

Yeats, W.B. (Wade, Allan, ed.), *The letters of W.B. Yeats* (London, 1954).

REFERENCES AND NOTES

Preface
1 Hester Sigerson Piatt, untitled unpublished manuscript (private collection).
2 For example, George Sigerson, 'A Pale family', an unpublished manuscript history of the Sigerson family (private collection).
3 Douglas Hyde, 'George Sigerson', *Studies: An Irish Quarterly Review* xiv, no. 53 (March 1925), p. 18.

Introduction
1 Hyde, 'George Sigerson', p. 6.
2 J.M. Charcot (George Sigerson, trans.), *Lectures on the diseases of the nervous system* (London, 1877).
3 George Sigerson (trans.) (John O'Daly, ed.), *The poets and poetry of Munster: a selection of Irish songs* (2nd series, Dublin, 1860).
4 George Sigerson, *Bards of the Gael and Gall: examples of the poetic literature of Erinn; done into English after the metres and modes of the Gael by George Sigerson* (London, 1897, 2nd ed. 1907, 3rd ed. 1925).
5 Idem, 'The Holocaust', *Irishman* supplement, 30 November 1867; see also Appendix 9.
6 John O'Leary, *Recollections of Fenians and Fenianism* (Dublin, 1896).
7 George Sigerson, *Modern Ireland: its vital questions, secret societies and government* (London, 1868).
8 Idem, *History of the land tenures and land classes of Ireland, with an account of the various secret agrarian confederacies* (London and Dublin, 1871).
9 R. Barry O'Brien (ed.), *Two centuries of Irish history, 1691–1870* (London, 1888).
10 George Sigerson, *The last independent parliament of Ireland: with account of the survival of the nation and its lifework* (Dublin, 1918).
11 Idem, 'On the need and use of village hospitals in Ireland', *Journal of the Statistical and Social Inquiry Society of Ireland*, viii, no. 60 (1881–2), pp. 340–9.
12 Idem, *Political prisoners at home and abroad* (London, 1884).
13 Dominic Daly, *The young Douglas Hyde: the dawn of the Irish revolution and renaissance, 1874–1893* (Dublin, 1974).
14 Ernest A. Boyd, *Ireland's literary renaissance* (New York, 1922), p. 63.
15 George Sigerson, *The saga of King Lir: a sorrow of story* (Dublin, 1913).
16 Idem, 'Irish universities: their historical aspect', *Freeman's Journal*, 11 February 1906.
17 Idem, *The Easter song: being the first epic of Christendom by Sedulius, the first scholar-saint of Erinn* (Dublin, 1922).
18 'Seanad debates/Díospóireachtaí Seanad', i (11 December 1922), *Parliamentary debates/ Díospóireachtaí parlaiminte* (196 vols, http://historical-debates.oireachtas.ie/ en.toc.seanad.html) (16 December 2010).

Chapter one: The Sigersons of Derry and Tyrone
1 Sigerson, 'A Pale family'.
2 James Sigerson, Philadelphia to William Sigerson, McCormack's Forge, 1818 (collection of Eibhlin Humphreys).
3 Piatt, untitled manuscript, Ch. 1, p. 1.
4 Alan Gailey, *Spade making in Ireland* (Cultra, 1982), p. 64.

5   'Board of Guardians (Strabane Workhouse)', *Londonderry Sentinel*, 4 May 1839.

6   'Tenant right activities, Strabane', *Londonderry Journal*, 15 May 1850.

7   *Londonderry Journal*, 9 December 1849.

8   Piatt, untitled manuscript.

9   William Neilson, *An introduction to the Irish language* (Dublin, 1808).

10 See references in Roger Blaney, *Presbyterians and the Irish language* (Belfast, 1996).

11 Neilson, *Introduction to the Irish language*.

12 Piatt, untitled manuscript, Ch. 1, p. 2.

13 It is possible that names have become somewhat mixed up here. The main tutor may have been Fr William Browne, born in Lisdoo near Urney and educated at Maynooth and the Irish College, Paris. Fr Browne returned to Strabane in 1835 and remained in the area until his death in 1863. He was a renowned scholar and well regarded by the leaders of the various Protestant denominations in the district.

14 Piatt, untitled manuscript.

15 Canon Maguire, *Letterkenny past and present* (Letterkenny, *c.* 1920).

16 C.P. Curran, *Under the receding wave* (Dublin, 1970), pp. 83, 84.

17 John R. Walsh, *A history of the parish of Maghera* (1973).

Chapter two: Student years

1   Curran, *Under the receding wave*, p. 85.

2   Ibid.

3   Piatt, untitled manuscript.

4   Ibid., Ch. 1, p. 2.

5   Last will and testament of William Sigerson, 17 December 1871 (PRONI, D3608/16/1).

6   Curran, *Under the receding wave*, p. 85.

7   See Tom Garvin, *The evolution of Irish nationalist politics* (Dublin, 1981); R.F. Foster, *Modern Ireland, 1600–1972* (London, 1988); and K. Theodore Hoppen – *Ireland since 1800: conflict and conformity* (London and New York, 1989).

8   Piatt, untitled manuscript, Ch. 2, p. 3.

9   Ibid., Ch. 2, p. 4.

10 Ibid.

11 Ibid.

12 James Clarence Mangan (trans.) (John O'Daly, ed.), *The poets and poetry of Munster: a selection of Irish songs* (1st series, Dublin, 1849).

13 Piatt, untitled manuscript, Ch. 2, p. 4.

14 Ralph Varian (ed.), *Ballads, popular poetry and household songs of Ireland* (Dublin, 1865).

15 Idem (ed.), *The harp of Erin: a book of ballad-poetry and of native song* (Dublin, 1869).

16 Michele Esposito, *Irish melodies for violin with pianoforte accompaniment: op. 56* (Dublin, 1903). *Songs and poems by George Sigerson*, a complete collection of Sigerson's songs and poems, was published in 1927.

Chapter three: Early poetry and politics

1   Hyde, 'George Sigerson', p. 8.

2   Sigerson, *Poets and poetry of Munster*, p. 10.

3   Boyd, *Ireland's literary renaissance*, pp. 55, 56.

4   Ibid.

5   Ibid.

6   Piatt, untitled manuscript, Ch. 3, p. 18.

7   *The Irishman*, December, 1860

8 John Mitchel, *The last conquest of Ireland (perhaps)* (Dublin, 1861).

9 Sigerson, *Saga of King Lir*, p. 12.

10 Piatt, untitled manuscript, Ch. 4, p. 5.

11 Ibid., p. 27.

12 Sigerson, *Land tenures and land classes*, p. 8.

13 Curran, *Under the receding wave*, p. 88.

14 Ibid., p. 89.

15 O'Leary, *Recollections of Fenians and Fenianism*, p. 17.

16 Piatt, untitled manuscript.

17 Sigerson, 'The Holocaust'; see also Appendix 9.

18 Ibid.

19 Ibid.

20 T.P. O'Connor, *Memoirs of an old parliamentarian* (London, 1929), p. 134.

21 Richard Pigott, *Recollections of an Irish national journalist* (Dublin, 1882).

22 Curran, *Under the receding wave*, p. 90n.

23 Piatt, untitled manuscript.

Chapter four: Sigerson the doctor

1 Piatt, untitled manuscript, Ch. 6, p. 1.

2 George Sigerson, 'Some remarks on a protomorphic phyllotype', *Atlantis*, iv (1863).

3 George Sigerson to Charles Darwin, 8 July 1863 (Darwin Correspondence Project, Letter 4,236) (www.darwinproject.ac.uk/entry-4236) (14 December 2010).

4 J.B. Lyons, 'George Sigerson: Charcot's translator', *Journal of the History of the Neurosciences*, vi, no. 1 (1997), p. 50.

5 Ibid., p. 51.

6 Ibid.

7 Unknown, 'Lectures on the diseases of the nervous system by J.M. Charcot, translated by G. Sigerson: reviewed', *Dublin Journal of Medical Science*, lxv, p. 338.

8 Piatt, untitled manuscript, Ch. 6, p. 2.

9 *Sunday Independent*, 1925.

10 Ibid.

11 Austin Clarke, *A penny in the clouds: more memories of Ireland and England* (London, 1968), pp. 42–3.

12 Richard Ellmann (ed.), *Letters of James Joyce* (3 vols, London, 1957–66), ii (letter dated September 1904), pp. 50–1.

13 Lyons, 'George Sigerson: Charcot's translator', p. 51.

14 Piatt, untitled manuscript, Ch. 6, p. 13.

15 *Irish Times*, 16 March 1918.

16 Piatt, untitled manuscript, Ch. 9, p. 18.

17 Hyde, 'George Sigerson', p. 16.

Chapter five: The Mansion House Relief Committee

1 'Letter from the duchess of Marlborough re. Irish distress', *The Times*, 16 December 1879.

2 Dublin Mansion House Relief Committee, *The Irish crisis of 1879–80* (Dublin, 1881), pp. 3–4.

3 Ibid., p. 13.

4 Ibid., p. 15.

5 Ibid., pp. 56–7.

6 Ibid., p. 62.

7 Bishop Michael Logue to George Sigerson, 10 February 1880 (private collection).

8   Bishop Michael Logue to George Sigerson, n.d. (private collection).
9   Mansion House Committee, *Irish crisis of 1879–80*, pp. 62–7.
10 Ibid., p. 62.
11 Ibid., p. 136.
12 Ibid., p. 136.
13 Ibid., p. 137.
14 Ibid.
15 Ibid., p. 139.
16 Ibid., p. 140.
17 *Freeman's Journal*, 29 June 1880.
18 Mansion House Committee, *Irish crisis of 1879–80*, p. 172.
19 Ibid., p. 198.
20 George Sigerson, 'Connemara' (lecture to National Literary Society, 1890s).
21 Joseph V. O'Brien, *William O'Brien and the course of Irish politics, 1881–1918* (Berkeley, California, 1976), p. 57.
22 Piatt, untitled manuscript, Ch. 5, p. 6.
23 Ibid., Ch. 5, p. 7.

Chapter six: The National Literary Society

1   Douglas Hyde (ed.), *The love songs of Connacht, being the fourth chapter of the songs of Connacht* (Dublin, 1893).
2   Piatt, untitled manuscript, Ch. 2.
3   Ibid., Ch. 9.
4   George Sigerson (Hester Sigerson Piatt, ed.), *Songs and poems by George Sigerson* (Dublin, 1927), p. 5; see also Appendix 5.
5   Idem, 'Irish literature: its origin, environment and influence – inaugural lecture of the National Literary Society' (1892) in Charles Gavan Duffy, Douglas Hyde and George Sigerson, *The revival of Irish literature* (London, 1894).
6   Ibid.
7   Ibid.
8   Boyd, *Ireland's literary renaissance*, p. 90.
9   Daly, *The young Douglas Hyde*, p. 155.
10 Ibid.
11 *United Ireland*, 1 September 1894.
12 Daly, *The young Douglas Hyde*, pp. 219–20.
13 Ibid.
14 A. Norman Jeffares, *W.B. Yeats: man and poet* (London and New York, 1949), p. 86.
15 Curran, *Under the receding wave*, p. 93.
16 Clarke, Austin, *A Penny in the Clouds*, pp. 42–43, 90, 108
17 *United Irishman*, 17 February 1907.
18 Ibid.
19 Piatt, untitled manuscript, Ch. 10.
20 Hyde, 'George Sigerson', p. 13.
21 C.P. Curran, 'Oisín after the Fianna', *Irish Statesman*, 28 February 1925.
22 Hyde, 'George Sigerson'.

Chapter seven: *Bards of the Gael and Gall*

1   Gregory A. Schirmer, *Out of what began: a history of Irish poetry in English* (Ithaca, New York, 1998).

2   Sigerson, *Bards of the Gael and Gall*, p. 22.
3   Ibid., p. 23.
4   Ibid., p. 3.
5   Robert Welch, *A history of verse translation from the Irish, 1789–1897* (Gerrard's Cross, Buckinghamshire, 1988), p. 165.
6   Sigerson, *Bards of the Gael and Gall*, p. 22.
7   Welch, *History of verse translation from the Irish*, p. 168.
8   Boyd, *Ireland's literary renaissance*, pp. 60–1.
9   Stopford A. Brooke and T.W. Rolleston (eds), *A treasury of Irish poetry in the English tongue* (London, 1900). p. 330.
10   Seamus Deane (ed.), *The Field Day anthology of Irish writing* (3 vols, Derry, 1990), ii, p. 723.
11   Welch, *History of verse translation from the Irish*, p. 168.
12   Ibid.
13   Ibid., p. 170.
14   F.S.L. Lyons, *Ireland since the Famine* (New York, 1971), p. 223n.
15   Curran, *Under the receding wave*, p. 91.
16   Sigerson, *Bards of the Gael and Gall* (3rd ed.), p. 12; see also Appendix 7.
17   *Irish Monthly*, xxv (1897).
18   *New Ireland Review*, vii (1897).

Chapter eight: Family and friends

1   Sigerson, Hester Varian, *A ruined race or, The last MacManus of Drumroosk* (Dublin, 1889).
2   Dora Sigerson Shorter (Katharine Tynan, intro.), *The sad years* (3rd ed., London, 1919), pp. 7–12; see also *Observer*, 13 January 1918.
3   Brooke and Rolleston, *A treasury of Irish poetry in the English tongue*.
4   *Observer*, 13 January 1918.
5   Shorter, *The sad years*, pp. 7–12.
6   Ibid.
7   Idem, *The tricolour: poems of the Irish revolution* (Dublin, 1922), p. 10.
8   Ibid., pp. 1–4.
9   Piatt, untitled manuscript, Ch. 8.
10   Sigerson, *Songs and poems*, p. 53.
11   Douglas Hyde to George Sigerson, 15 May 1893 (private collection).
12   Hyde, *Love songs of Connacht*.
13   See Appendixes 1 and 7.
14   Piatt, untitled manuscript, Ch. 8.
15   Ibid.
16   O'Leary, *Recollections of Fenians and Fenianism*, p. 17n.
17   Piatt, untitled manuscript, Ch. 4.
18   Ibid.
19   Curran, *Under the receding wave*, p. 83.
20   J.S. Crone, 'Editor's gossip: Dr Crone visits Dublin and sees Dr Sigerson who shows him death mask of Charles Kickham; and Mr Henry Dixon shows him death mask of Fintan Lalor', *Irish Book Lover*, xii (1920), p. 13.
21   T.P. O'Hanlon, 'George Sigerson', *Capuchin Annual* (1954–5), pp. 95–7.

Chapter nine: Sigerson's later life, 1900–25

1   Thomas MacDonagh, 'Antigone and Lir', *Irish Review*, iv, no. 37 (March 1914), pp. 29–32.

[2]   Ellen O'Connor, 'Dr Sigerson's masterpiece', *Irish Monthly*, xlii, no. 487 (January 1914), pp. 30–3.

[3]   R. Barry O'Brien to George Sigerson, n.d. (collection of Hester Sigerson Piatt).

[4]   *Irish Ecclesiastical Record*, 5th series, xxii (1918).

[5]   Ibid.

[6]   *Catholic Bulletin*, xiii (1923).

[7]   Michael Tierney (F.X. Martin, ed.), *Eoin MacNeill: scholar and man of action, 1867–1945* (Oxford, 1980).

[8]   Piatt, untitled manuscript, Ch. 8.

[9]   Ibid.

[10] W.E. Vaughan (ed.), *A new history of Ireland, volume 6: Ireland under the union II, 1870–1921* (Oxford, 1996).

[11] Piatt, untitled manuscript, Ch. 8.

[12] George Sigerson, 'Irish universities: their historial aspect', *Freeman's Journal*, 11 February 1906.

[13] Patrick O'Farrell, *Ireland's English question: Anglo-Irish relations 1534–1970* (London, 1971), pp. 218–22.

[14] F.S.L. Lyons, *John Dillon: a biography* (Chicago, 1968), pp. 305–6.

[15] For different sides to the issue see: O'Farrell, *Ireland's English question*, p. 223; Tierney, *Eoin MacNeill*, pp. 86–7; and Ruth Dudley Edwards, *Patrick Pearse: The triumph of failure* (London, 1977), pp. 76–9.

[16] Tierney, *Eoin MacNeill*, p. 86.

[17] Aodh de Blácam, *The black north: an account of the six counties of unrecover'd Ireland – their people, their treasures and their history* (Dublin, 1938), pp. 38–40.

[18] James Joyce, *Finnegans wake* (London, 1939).

[19] Piatt, untitled manuscript, Ch. 8.

[20] Clarke, *A penny in the clouds*, p. 108.

[21] Curran, *Under the receding wave*, p. 91.

[22] Lady Ardilaun to George Sigerson, n.d. (private collection).

[23] 'Seanad debates/Díospóireachtaí Seanad', i (11 December 1922), *Parliamentary debates/ Díospóireachtaí parlaiminte* (196 vols, http://historical-debates.oireachtas.ie/en.toc.seanad.html) (16 December 2010).

[24] Lady Augusta Gregory (Daniel J. Murphy, ed.), *Lady Gregory's journals: books 1 to 29, 10 October 1916 to 24 February 1925* (Oxford, 1978), Bk 27, p. 544.

[25] *Freeman's Journal*, 10 February 1923.

[26] Sigerson, *Bards of the Gael and Gall* (3rd ed.), p. 18; see also Appendix 7.

[27] 'Design and change: the Oireachtas harp and an historical heritage', *Design Research Group* (2008) (http://designresearchgroup.wordpress.com/2008/03/28/design-and-change-the-oireachtas-harp-and-an-historical-heritage) (16 December 2010).

[28] Piatt, untitled manuscript, Ch. 8.

[29] Curran, *Under the receding wave*, p. 94.

[30] Sigerson, *Songs and poems*. See also Appendix 5.

[31] Donn Piatt, 'A Pale family and Old Dublin, being an account of the Sigerson family', *Dublin Historical Record*, xviii, no. 3 (1962–3), p. 91.

[32] O'Hanlon, 'George Sigerson'.

Chapter ten: The Sigerson Cup

[1]   *United Irishman*, 11 March 1899.

[2]   Trevor West, *The bold collegians: the development of sport in Trinity College, Dublin* (Dublin, 1991), pp. 33–6.

3   *Celtic Times*, 12 March 1887; ibid., 9 April 1887.
4   Patrick N. Meenan, *St Patrick's blue and saffron: a miscellany of UCD sport since 1895* (Dublin, 1997), pp. 137–8; *Queen's College, Galway: a record of student life*, i, no. 1 (November 1902), p. 26; Patrick Purcell, 'Hurling in college', *National Student*, May 1949, pp. 37–9; *Cork Sportsman*, 12 December 1908; ibid., 23 January 1909.
5   *Irish Independent*, 16 December 1907.
6   *National Student* (1913), pp. 6, 12–13; Donal McCartney, *UCD, A national idea: the history of University College, Dublin* (Dublin, 1999), p. 59.
7   *Freeman's Journal*, 28 November 1910. See also Dáithí de Búrca, 'Irish colleges and Irish pastimes', *Gaelic Athletic Annual and County Directory* (1910), pp. 74–5.
8   See, for example, *Freeman's Journal*, 23 January 1911 and 30 January 1911.
9   *Connacht Tribune*, 17 December 1910.
10 Ibid., 7 January 1911.
11 *Freeman's Journal*, 1 April 1911.
12 Ibid.
13 Ibid., 3 April 1911.
14 Ibid., 4 April 1911; *Connacht Tribune*, 8 April 1911.
15 *Freeman's Journal*, 7 April 1911.
16 Ibid., 6 May 1911.
17 Ibid., 11 May 1911.
18 Ibid., 6 May 1911.
19 Retrospective accounts of the event were recorded by contemporaries and journalists many years later. See, for example, Pádraig Puirséal, 'The Sigerson Cup', *National Student* (Hilary Term 1955), pp. 5–6; 'P. Cavan', 'Sigerson: nursery of classic football', *Sunday Independent*, 27 November 1953; Séamus Ó Ceallaigh, 'How the game "went to school"', *Sunday Independent*, 22 March 1959; Pádraig Mac Diarmada, 'Comórtas Sigerson 1911–1963', *Our Games Annual* (1964), p. 52.
20 GAA Central Council minutes, 23 October 1915, 12 December 1915 (GAA Museum, Croke Park, GAA/CC/01/02).
21 GAA Central Council minutes, 26 May 1918 (GAA Museum, Croke Park, GAA/CC/01/02).

APPENDICES

APPENDIX 1: TRIBUTES AND APPRECIATIONS

Following the death of George Sigerson on 17 February 1925, a large number of tributes were paid in public and in private to this revered figure in the Irish academic and literary world. He had been a colossus in so many fields of Irish life and what follows is a very limited sample of the appreciations that were expressed on his death.

Tributes in Seanad Éireann on the death of Senator Sigerson[1]

An Cathaoirleach
In accordance with my duty under our Standing Orders, I have to announce, with the most sincere sorrow and regret, sorrow and regret which, I am certain, will be shared in every quarter of this House, that since our last meeting Senator Dr George Sigerson has passed away. With the indulgence of the House, I would just like to say a word or two with reference to the loss which the nation and this House has sustained. He was a man of exceptional gifts which he displayed in very many fields of activity in public life, and I may use in regard to him and in respect of those activities the familiar quotation: *Nihil quod tetigit non ornavit.* He lived a life full of years and full of honour, because his great services to his country and his profession were recognised by most of our great learned societies, who conferred upon him the distinction of their Honorary Fellowships.

In contrast to these great gifts, he was one of the most unassuming of men, and here in this House during the time he was with us, we recognised the greatness of his genius as well as his love for his country and his fellow-countrymen. He had strong feelings and convictions on the great political questions of his day, but he wrote of these and he discussed these, always without bitterness or rancour; while in private life, to those who, like myself to a small extent, had knowledge and experience of him, he was a delightful companion and a loyal friend. I hope I may be allowed, in the name of this House and of my colleagues, to convey to those who have been left behind him, an expression of our very deep regret and sorrow for his death.

Dúglas de hÍde
A Chathaoirligh, ní fhéadaim gan focal nó dó do rádh i dtaoibh ár gcarad, sean-ghaisgídheach na h-Éireann, atá, faraoir! anois ar lár, ins an teangaidh sin ba bhinn leis féin. Ba stairidhe, ba fhile, ba fhear ealadhna, ba fhear-státa é, a raibh a chlú go fóir-leathan ar fud na tíre seo; agus thar lear mar an gcéadna. Do bhí aithne agam ar mo shean-charaid ar feadh dhachad bliadhan, agus cara do b'fhearr ná é ní raibh ag éinne riamh. Gach Gaedheal d'fhulaing ar son na hÉireann né no rinne obair mhaith ar son na h-Éireann, bhí teach agus díon agus baile eile aige i dtigh Dochtúir Mac Sigir. Agus níl fhios ag éinne againn cia mhéid oibre rinne sé nach bhfuil clóbhuailte. Chualaidh mé ó n-a bhéal féin dánta chomh maith le h-aon dán do chlóbhuail sé agus, mar shaoil mise, níos fearr ná iad, agus ní fhacaidh na dánta sin an solus riamh. Go mbadh éadtrom an chréafóg ar ár sean-charaid, seanleomhan na tíre agus sean-ghaisgídheach na h-Éireann, an Dochtúir Mac Sigir!

I can't but say a few words about our friend, the old warrior of Ireland who has alas passed away, in the language that was so dear to him. He was an historian, a poet, an artistic man, a statesman who was widely known in this country as well as abroad. I knew my old friend for forty years and one could not have asked for a better friend. Every Irishman who had suffered for the cause of Ireland or who had done good work for Ireland would always have had a welcome at Sigerson's residence and no one knows how much work he has done that has never been published. I have heard from his own lips poems as good as any poem that he had published and in my opinion even better; unfortunately those poems have never been published. May the clay rest easy on our dear friend, the old lion of the nation and the old warrior of Ireland, Dr Sigerson!

Sir Thomas Esmonde

I am sure the Seanad will agree that it is only right and fitting that some expression of the loss we have sustained owing to the death of Senator Dr Sigerson, who was practically the Father of this House, should be made. Senators will agree that some notice is appropriate and desirable. To those of us who knew Dr Sigerson personally, his death comes as the loss of a very deep personal friend. I regret the death of Senator Dr Sigerson more from the point of view of his loss to the country. He was a great outstanding figure; he was known and honoured all over the world, firstly as an eminent practitioner in his profession, and, secondly, for his amazing intellectual capacity, and for the inestimable services which he rendered in the literary sphere, to the country to which he belonged. Most of us have been privileged to read his works. They are marvels of research and erudition. Certainly, our late colleague has left his mark upon the times in which he lived, a mark which will remain for generations to come; and, in mourning the loss of this distinguished man, we must also render tribute to his persistency and courage, and as you very rightly said, the modesty, of his support of the aspirations and interests of his own country. We may take an example from him in how to serve our own country without offending anybody else. I join with you in expressing my deep regret.

'Oisín after the Fianna – George Sigerson, 1836–1925' by C.P. Curran[2]

It is superfluous in this place and at this time to praise the written work of one whom as a scientist Tyndall praised, with whom as a historian Mommsen and Acton consulted and collaborated, and to whose life-long devotion to Irish literature its present credit in the world of letters is largely due. Dr Sigerson is dead –

> The handsome hawk who towered the country o'er
> Top spray of all who sprang from Sigerson Mór

and instead of patiently cataloguing and estimating his achievement I prefer to think of him here as Acton wrote of him in a letter which lies before me, as 'the best Irishman I have known'. Alas for that past tense, and that inexorable time should have at length dealt with him who had so identified himself with history and Ireland as seemingly to be like them, timeless and unageing.

He lived eighty-nine years; he published his first book, translations and study of the 18th century Munster poets, in 1860, and since then, as Douglas Hyde said, he only left down one task for the country in order to take up another. The tasks were manifold, but the spirit single in which he wrought. To him, he once said, it had ever seemed that a man's personal honour was involved in the honour of his nation; if it were exalted he stood the higher, and if it were abased did he not share in the disgrace? With all the energy of intellect and will he dedicated to the honour of his country the three-fold practice of literature, of his profession and of his public and personal action. In literature it was his task to be pioneer in the rescue of Irish letters, to unearth the buried vase and set it in its high place, to discover the rusted sword and place it shining in the hands of another generation. The routine of life and the practice of his noble profession was directed towards a like end. In the evil fever years of 1879 and 1880 he stood between the people and the plague; he brought all the authority of his technical knowledge to bear successfully upon prison reform, and in particular, in the matter of the treatment of political prisoners, whether Irish Nationalists or English suffragettes, he pleaded in a series of publications from 1868 to 1918 for that separate and civilised distinction which, to our shame, is still unrecognized.

But the quiet ways of literature and these apparently side developments of his profession did not sufficiently contain his passion for Ireland. In this he is distinguished from the generation of men of letters immediately following him, and it is this difference which endeared him to the plain people of Ireland. He found other outlets in journalism and in personal association and comradeship. When the Fenians were a reproach and the gentlemen of England who hailed Mazzini and Garibaldi as apostles of liberty stigmatised O'Leary and Kickham as dynamitists and assassins, and when the comrades of these men were vilified by their own countrymen, Sigerson, who had only just passed out of college, quietly took his stand by them and never weakened in his loyalty. When *The Irish People* was suppressed he edited *The Irishman*, which replaced it, and the memory of certain articles of his in that paper is still alive, more than fifty years after they were written. His journalism was literature, purposeful and enduring. His association with *The Shamrock*, of which he was the first editor, is less known, and its first three volumes are worth investigating for his own work, and the contributions of Carleton, T.C. Irwin and other reputable writers. The range of his own articles is significant, chiefly as showing the respect in which he held himself and his popular audience. His contempt was not for the Paudeens, but for a quite different class.

It is not easy for one in our day to realise how much of courage and tenacity it meant in 1862 to take the stand that Sigerson took, and since unswervingly maintained. He came to Dublin with something of a continental reputation, the pupil, associate and friend of Claude Bernard and Charcot, master of the new learning of the Salpetrière. He had unique gifts of personality and a training admirably fitted to display them. His figure was as that of one out of his own *Saga of King Lir*:

> Magnificent he stood: his red-brown locks
> From ample brow and kingly head flowed down,
> A lambent flame.

He did not choose to exploit these gifts for selfish professional advancement in the cabotin fashion, as common in the Dublin professional class then as now. He was like the women distinguished in The Instructions of King Cormac Mac Airt, 'exceeding all bounds in keeping others waiting.' But 'the others' were the wealthy, whose carriages were kept waiting while he attended to his poor. This was madness. But to taint a professional reputation with a tincture of letters was worse, and with Irish letters was stark insanity. To add politics to that – and by politics one always means, naturally, not vice-regal politics – was criminal madness. And so Sigerson went his way. He consorted with, defended, healed Fenians when Fenians were an opprobrium, though indeed he himself, any more than his *anam-chara*, John O'Leary, was never a member of the Brotherhood, and what he lost on the roundabouts he gained, perhaps, in the affectionate respect of the more stable common people. Curiously, too, this line of conduct earned for him friends abroad. It was about this time that he grew intimate with Lord Acton (then Sir John Acton), Wetherell and his friends on *The Chronicle*, *The North British* and *The Home and Foreign Review*, and indeed when they sought the services of the great Mommsen as their correspondent, Mommsen only acceded to their request when he was satisfied, through Sigerson, that they would be colleagues in an enterprise sympathetic to both. It was at this period, at Acton's request, and for Gladstone's use, in view of the impending Land Act of 1870, that he began those studies in Irish land tenures, for *The North British Review*, which were subsequently expanded, read in proof by Gladstone and published as a *History of Irish Land Tenures* in 1871. It will be noticed that a cardinal point in common in the Act and in the articles, is the treatment of the so-called 'Ulster custom', a custom by no means confined to Ulster, which received full and original consideration in these papers. Their merely historical value is fully recognized by Lecky in his history. These historical studies were continued in his contribution to *Two Centuries of Irish History*, edited by Bryce [*sic*] in 1888, and in his *Last Independent Parliament of Ireland* (1918). I pass over these for considerations of space and time, and as well his *Bards of the Gael and Gall*, for the other reason that this, his most important book, is of such fundamental value, that it must be familiar to anyone who cares to read this note. Nor can I dwell on the long series of inaugural lectures at the National Literary Society in which the most diverse subjects of Irish interest, historic, literary, economic, geologic, medical, social, were treated with what originality and charm. Hardly less remarkable were the brief addresses which closed each evening's proceedings, infinitely relished by his audience for their deft wit and French precision and grace. How eagerly in that audience did we wait for the glancing irony which shot through the elaborate folds of his deliberate, ceremonious speech! In public speech Sigerson had an art of his own. Not to him belonged what Mr Healy once styled, 'the untameable squadrons of irrelevant eloquence'. His massive speech advanced in the fashion of the classic phalanx, bristling with bright spears, and the rapid shafts of his wit lost nothing in effect from the contrast of humorous twinkling eyes, with the sonorous voice and the grave, courteous dignity of his bearing. It was the French *éloge* allied to Irish wit.

For where, if anywhere, Sigerson was not Irish he was French. His schooldays were passed in Paris, and there still survives a daguerrotype of a tall, very charming young man in the cap and uniform of a French *lycée*, Georges Sigerson, Irlandais, of 1852, who at the distribution of prizes receives three *couronnes* from the *aumônier* of the Emperor, characteristically for Latin verse, drawing and (I am afraid) good conduct. The French contact, resumed in his post-graduate years, was maintained by annual visits until the War, and fittingly closed when President Cosgrave sent him there a year ago as the representative of Ireland to the centenary commemoration of his friend and teacher, Pasteur. France taught him science and art, and he always strove to repay the debt. He would ill brook any criticism of France and retaliated only less warmly than in defence of his own country. His house was like some Balzac interior;

French furniture of all the Louis and Empires, French paintings and pastels, French miniatures and engravings. The accumulation imperilled even his Spartan ideas of personal comfort. Living simply and labouriously [sic] himself, he was towards others the embodiment of Irish hospitality. And that not merely in the common sense of the word, but with a magnanimity and generosity of mind which forbade mean speech or the belittlement of others, and gave joyful recognition to the most trifling work of Irish value. If around his dinner-table an unguarded word of even deserved criticism was spoken of anyone who had served his country, there came, from that well-stored and tenacious memory, a counter-balancing recital more overwhelming than any rebuke. He had a scorn for small talk out of its proper place, and his contempt for that most lucrative form of bookmaking, which invades and breaks the confidence of private intercourse, makes us the poorer of a valuable record of nineteenth century history from Mitchel to MacDonagh. He held to a more than decent reticence about himself and his contemporaries. He disliked the subjective in life and literature. I have failed here to convey my impression of Dr Sigerson if I have not suggested the idea of a character self-determined, integral in its texture, and very strong-willed. I have failed more signally if that character should appear narrow or prejudiced. A poet is betrayed by his adjectives. I have not reviewed his writings, but if they are read with a divining eye, he will be found to betray his own character in the heroes of his verse and the subjects of his praise. Manful striving, loyal comradeship, truthful living, magnanimity, chivalric courtesy, learning, music and song, these are his themes and his attributes. He said in one address that he had sometimes thought of writing a book to be entitled: 'The Good Deeds of our Enemies'; the picture, he says, would give a true idea of mankind 'for it is surprising how many kind offices were mutually interchanged between foemen – even in this very country – who are always represented as savage, ruthless and exterminating.' This was the stuff of his mind and native always to his thought and action. Irish divisions were the consequences of policy and circumstance. 'Nothing,' he writes in a preface, 'has given the author more gratification than to be able to demonstrate this, and to prove that no inherent forces, no inveterate hostilities of race, or class, or creed, exist to disintegrate the people of Ireland'.

'Death of Dr George Sigerson – Irish poet and scholar', *The Times*[3]

The death occurred, at his residence in Clare Street, Dublin, last night of Dr George Sigerson, a member of the Free State Senate, and the doyen of modern Gaelic scholarship. Dr Sigerson has long been one of the personalities of the Irish capital where he practised, mainly as a specialist in nervous maladies, combining his medical practice with a lectureship in Biology in the National University of Ireland, on the Senate of which he sat. He had studied under the great Charcot in Paris, as well as at the Queen's College, Cork.

Beside these avocations, his activities have been concerned with politics and poetry. He was a strong patriot, and his Fenian friendships and associations must for a long time have left him somewhat solitary among the Dublin doctors. The bent of his mind was largely political, and his personality to the end had something about it of the Liberal young man of the Latin Quarter. Not that he was at all wild. His associates in young manhood were the high-minded and beautiful personalities of the Fenian Movement. The mild and saintly Kickham was one of his friends and patients, and John O'Leary, the old Fenian Chief, was to be found at his fireside till the day of his death. All these people were literary.

Dr Sigerson had married a literary wife in Miss Hester Varian of Cork, so that literature and art were practised, and held in honour, and literary people always found a warm welcome in his hospitable house in Clare Street, Dublin. In the 80s and 90s the meetings at Dr Sigerson's house on Sunday evenings constituted a salon; and there one met the young Irish writers who have become famous since, with many visitors from England, the continent and overseas, all of them noteworthy in one way or another.

As a young man Dr Sigerson had written poetry which is to be found in many anthologies. In later years he produced a notable book in *Ballads of the Gael and Gall*, translations into English verse from the Irish, a very valuable addition to Irish literature. Besides some specialist work, he has written a valuable book on the history of Irish land tenures, and in *Modern Ireland* he had the collaboration of Lord Bryce. It is scarcely to be wondered at that the children of such parents should have been literary, and Dr Sigerson's daughter Dora was well known to the reading public as the poet, Dora Sigerson Shorter.

A man of considerable cultivation, great personal charm, and an unbounded kindness, Dr Sigerson will be sadly missed. He has for many years acted as president of the Irish Literary Society, which has the unique distinction in Ireland of welcoming all classes, creeds, and politics to its membership and its friendship.

Strabane Weekly News[4]
Dr George Sigerson, a distinguished man of letters, has died in Dublin in his 88th year. He was the oldest member of the Free State Senate, but resigned owing to the threat of the republicans to burn his house. Later, Dr Sigerson resumed his seat.

For half a century he has been recognised as one of Ireland's most distinguished men. He was not only an eminent scientist, but was noted for his writings on Irish affairs, as well as for his verse translations from Gaelic poetry. His daughter, Dora, the celebrated poetess, now deceased, was the wife of Mr Clement K. Shorter.

Dr Sigerson wrote for advanced papers in the Fenian days, and has since been associated with every movement towards Irish independence.

Born at Holyhill, close to Strabane, Dr Sigerson was first educated at Letterkenny, and later at Derry and Paris. He was Professor of Biology in the National University, Dublin.

'Obituary', *British Medical Journal*[5]
George Sigerson M.D., F.R.C.P.I., M.R.I.A.
We regret to announce the death of Dr George Sigerson, which took place at his residence in Dublin on February 18th. He was born at Strabane, Co. Tyrone, some ninety years ago, but the exact date of his birth is not known; a younger fellow student of Dr Sigerson at Queen's College, Cork, where he greatly distinguished himself, estimated his age in October 1921 as between 85 and 90 years, and added that in his early manhood Sigerson, a very keen student of Irish, published a translation of the Munster Gaelic poets. On graduating at the Queen's University, Sigerson visited Dublin and went also to Paris, where he pursued his medical studies, devoting special attention to diseases of the nervous system. He took the degrees of M.D., M.Ch., and at a comparatively early age became professor of Botany, and later of Biology, in the Catholic University Medical School, Dublin. As a scholar and writer he won golden opinions from all sorts of people, and his personal charm was such that he was beloved

by the students, who held him in the greatest respect and reverence. When the Royal University of Ireland was founded Sigerson took his place in it, adding steadily to his reputation both in science and literature. Under his aegis the National Literary Society was established in Dublin, and as its president during a long term of years he conferred dignity and distinction upon its discussions. Some seven or eight years ago the members of the society marked their appreciation of his services by presenting him with a portrait of himself by Sir John Lavery, the eminent Irish artist, and many members secured engravings of the portrait. Within recent years the Royal College of Surgeons marked the esteem in which Dr Sigerson was held in his profession by making him an Honorary Fellow. He was the author of several scientific papers which were presented to the Royal Irish Academy, and published in its Transactions. His eminence as a medical man was acknowledged widely, and he was well known as a *littérateur* and a man of science. To the end he enjoyed a large and lucrative practice as a neurologist in Dublin. Among Dr Sigerson's scientific publications were Microscopical Researches on the Atmosphere; Heat as a factor in (so called) Vital Action; Causes of Buoyancy of Bodies of Greater Density than Water; Additions to the Flora of the Tenth Botanical District; Relationship of the Inflorescences; and a translation, with notes, of Professor Charcot's lectures on diseases of the nervous system. Since its foundation, Dr Sigerson has been a Senator of the National University of Ireland. He was a corresponding member of several of the leading literary and scientific societies in Paris. He was married and had one son and three daughters; one of the latter – the late Dora Sigerson Shorter – won some distinction as a writer of verse. In many of his public lectures and addresses Dr Sigerson referred to his descent from the Norsemen, and seemed to take particular pride in it. His massive figure, flowing locks, and long flaxen beard were picturesque corroborations of his claim.

Among Dr Sigerson's attainments, it is probable the majority of his countrymen would give pride of place to his work as an authority on the ancient Gaelic poetry of Ireland. As a young man he was a great friend of the late Dr Sullivan, president of the Queen's College, Cork, and it is more than likely that he met O'Curry, who died in Dublin in 1862. In his explorations in the highways and byways of Gaelic poetry, Sigerson brought into play the vast resources of his learning and intellectual gifts, while his qualities of sympathy and understanding were enlivened by his delicate literary style which lent a charm to everything he wrote. As a lecturer upon those literary subjects that were so dear to him he inspired his hearers with a feeling, not only of reverence, but also of affection. Sigerson surrendered himself entirely to the charm of the music and poetry that captivated the poet Spenser – with this difference, that while the author of the Faerie Queene looked upon Elizabethan Ireland as a stranger looks upon a conquered land, and used the Gaelic gems that he picked up for the adornment of English literature, Sigerson looked upon the English colonial element in his country at the present day as destined to be peacefully absorbed in the revival of a Gaelic Ireland.

Sigerson delved in neglected literature of a period 'where long forgotten peoples lived, loved and acted', and it was his regret that, unhappily for history, that literature was long buried in neglect – 'locked in an archaic language, like some splendid missal claspt in covers of wrought silver, which could not be opened.' Of the Irish literature before the Christian era he says that 'it is, indeed, one of the highest honours of Irish monasticism that, though ascetic and zealous in the extreme, it had a liberal, large-minded respect for the literature of the ancients, and preserved it'. In his introduction to his second edition of *Bards of the Gael and Gaul* [sic] he rejoices that Ireland is the sole representative of that great world which lived and thrived outside the classic camp. The early poems, in which there is no trace of Christian influence, are quoted as evidence that 'when St Patrick came to Ireland, he came, as St Paul to Athens, before a highly cultured audience'.

'Literary musings' by Terence O'Hanlon, *Sunday Independent*[6]

The blood of the Vikings and spirit of the Gael

One of the memories I treasure most is the memory of Dr George Sigerson and the privilege I had of his warm hearted friendship to the end. When he died early in 1925 on the brink of 90 years, Ireland mourned the loss of a man of her few foremost men – a Gall-Gael who prided in his descent from Sigurd who fought on the losing side at the battle of Clontarf.

Big and broad-shouldered and straight as a lance, with forked beard and a wealth of snowy locks 'streaming like a meteor to the troubled air', he showed his Norse origin vividly and, but for the conventional top-hat, frock-coat and pince-nez, might have passed for a Viking of old.

Eloquent on the Norse contribution to Irish culture, he would proudly recall that the first poem in which Dublin is mentioned is a love lyric composed by a Norse king. To him the period when Dublin was a Scandinavian stronghold was a golden age in Ireland, blasted at length by a greedy usurper named Brian Boru. To emphasise this he would parody familiar lines from Tom Moore –:

> With us were the Vikings and virtue,
> With ye, the Gael and the guilt.

For all his romancing in the depths of a noble and chivalrous soul George Sigerson was more Gaelic than the Gael. However proud of his Viking blood, he was prouder still of his native land and through all the years of his long life never ceased to record her sufferings and exalt in her glories.

It was his friend, Charles Gavan Duffy, who, in droll allusion to his Norse-Irish blood, once suggested a final burial of our national feuds, ancient and modern, adding that as a last victim might be required, Dr Sigerson's funeral pyre should be raised on the battlefield of Clontarf.

APPENDIX 2: HONOURS AND DISTINCTIONS

Senator, Irish Free State
Honorary Fellow, Royal College of Physicians, Ireland
Honorary Fellow, Royal College of Surgeons, Ireland
Director of Medical Commission, Dublin Mansion House Relief Committee, 1880
Fellow, Royal University of Ireland
Professor of botany and zoology, Royal University of Ireland
Dean of science, Catholic University of Ireland
Professor of biology/zoology, National University of Ireland
President, National Literary Society of Ireland
Honorary doctor of literature, National University of Ireland
Member, Board of Governors, National University of Ireland
Member, Royal Commission on Prisons, 1884
Fellow, Linnean Society of London
Member, Council, Royal Irish Academy
Member, Royal Dublin Society
Member, Statistical Society of Ireland
Corresponding member, Scientific Society of Brussels
Corresponding member, Clinical Society of Paris
Corresponding member, Anthropological Society of Paris
Corresponding member, Associazione dia Benemeriti Italiani, Palermo. (The title of
corresponding member and a gold medal were awarded to Sigerson by this society for
'scientific and humanitarian distinction')

APPENDIX 3: SIGERSON'S PUBLICATIONS – A SELECT LIST

1857
'Antiquities in Donegal', *Ulster Journal of Archaeology*, series l, v, pp. 253–4.

1860
(trans.) (O'Daly, John, ed.), *The poets and poetry of Munster: a selection of Irish songs* (2nd series, Dublin).

1863
'Some remarks on a protomorphic phyllotype', *Atlantis*, iv, nos 7–8, pp. 450–8.

1865
Thirteen poems and songs in Varian, Ralph (ed.), *Ballads, popular poetry and household songs of Ireland* (Dublin).

1866
'On some relationships in inflorescences, with 2 plates', *Proceedings of the Royal Irish Academy*, series 1, x, pp. 75–82.

1868
Modern Ireland: its vital questions, secret societies and government (London; 2nd ed. 1869).

1869
'Additions to the flora of the tenth botanical district, Ireland, with 1 plate', *Proceedings of the Royal Irish Academy*, science series 2, i, pp. 192–8.
'Anomalous form of corolla in erica tetralix, with 1 plate', *Proceedings of the Royal Irish Academy*, science series 2, i, pp. 191–2.
'Discovery of fish-remains in the alluvial clay of the River Foyle, with observations on the existence and disappearance of an Upper Lough Foyle, and on the former insulation of Derry and of Inishowen', *Proceedings of the Royal Irish Academy*, science series 2, i, pp. 212–24.
'Micro-atmospheric researches, with 7 plates', *Proceedings of the Royal Irish Academy*, science series 2, i, pp. 13–30.
Ten poems and songs in Ralph Varian (ed.), *The harp of Erin: a book of ballad-poetry and of native song* (Dublin).

1870
'Observations on some sepulchral urns and burial monuments in the Co. Tyrone, with remarks on the true site of the Battle of Knockavoe (1522), with 1 plate', *Proceedings of the Royal Irish Academy*, polite literature and antiquities series 2, i, pp. 14–19.

1871

History of the land tenures and land classes of Ireland, with an account of the various secret agrarian confederacies (London and Dublin).

'On heat as a factor in vital action (so called)', *Proceedings of the Royal Irish Academy*, science series 2, ii, pp. 1–6.

1875

'On changes in the physical geography of Ireland,' *Proceedings of the Royal Irish Academy*, science series 2, ii, pp. 6–22.

'On a cause of the buoyancy of bodies of a greater density than water', *Proceedings of the Royal Irish Academy*, science series 2, ii, pp. 22–5.

1877

(trans.) Charcot, J.M., *Lectures on the diseases of the nervous system* (London).

'Contributions to the study of nerve-action in connection with the sense of taste: function of the trigeminus and functions of the chorda tympani', *Proceedings of the Royal Irish Academy*, science series 2, iii, pp. 257–71.

1878

'On alternate paralyses', *Dublin Journal of Medical Science*, lxv, pp. 97–125.

1881

'Report of the Medical Commission of the Mansion House Committee' Dublin Mansion House Relief Committee, *The Irish crisis of 1879–80* (Dublin).

1882

'On the need and use of village hospitals in Ireland', *Journal of the Statistical and Social Inquiry Society of Ireland*, viii, no. 60, pp. 340–9.

1884

Political prisoners at home and abroad (London; 2nd ed. 1890).

'Consideration of the structural and acquisitional elements in dextral pre-eminence, with conclusions as to the ambidexterity of primeval man', *Proceedings of the Royal Irish Academy*, series 2, iv, pp. 38–51.

1886

'The law and the lunatic', *Journal of the Statistical and Social Inquiry Society of Ireland*, ix, pp. 7–30.

1888

'1782–1800: from legislative independence to the Act of Union' in O'Brien, R. Barry (ed.), *Two centuries of Irish history, 1691–1870* (London).

'An excursion in June: a poem beginning "We were a pleasant party, some half-dozen"', *Irish Monthly*, xvi, pp. 473–8.

1890

'Annals of an Hiberno-Norse family, being a note on the Sigerson family', *Journal of the Royal Society of Antiquaries of Ireland*, series 5, i, part 1, p. 113.

'The blessing of Dublin from the Irish of St Benean: a poem beginning "Chill and dead"', *Irish Monthly*, xviii, pp. 215–17.

1894

The revival of Irish literature: addresses by Sir Charles Gavan Duffy, KCMG, Dr George Sigerson and Dr Douglas Hyde (London).

'Genesis and evolution', *New Ireland Review*, i, pp. 18–26.

1897

Bards of the Gael and Gall: examples of the poetic literature of Erinn; done into English after the metres and modes of the Gael by George Sigerson (London; 2nd ed. 1907, 3rd ed. 1925).

1900

'St Patrick as a man of letters', *Journal of the National Literary Society of Ireland*, i, part 1, pp. 1–14.

1902

'O'Curry's great discovery: translation of the ancient laws of Ireland, prefatory note', *Journal of the National Literary Society of Ireland*, i, part 3, pp. 143–6.

1904

'Celtic influence on the evolution of rimed hymns', *Journal of the National Literary Society of Ireland*, i, part 4, pp. 233–48.

1905

'St Patrick as a sun-myth: German scholars at strife', *St Stephen's: a Record of University Life*, ii, no. 7, pp. 151–5.

1907

'Irish fishers of the deep', *New Ireland Review*, xxviii, pp. 1–16.

1912

'The legend of the seven sisters, being a romantic story, contributed by George of Munster (pseud.) to "Notes and Queries", London, May, 1854, from which it was copied', *Kerry Archaeological Magazine*, ii, pp. 48–50.

'The church of the apple tree, in penal times: a poem beginning "Alone within a lonely glen"', *Irish Monthly*, xl, pp. 684–5.

1913

The saga of King Lir: a sorrow of story (Dublin).

'Custodia honesta': treatment of political prisoners in Great Britain … with introduction by Henry W. Nevinson (London).

1916

'The fusing force of ancient friendships in Ireland', *Journal of the National Literary Society of Ireland*, ii, part 1, pp. 1–22.

'At a meeting of the National Literary Society on January 10th Dr George Sigerson lectured on Dr Robert Dwyer Joyce', *Irish Book Lover*, vii, pp. 131–2.

1918

The last independent parliament of Ireland: with account of the survival of the nation and its lifework (Dublin).

1922

The Easter song: being the first epic of Christendom by Sedulius, the first scholar-saint of Erinn (Dublin).

1927

'Two pictures: a poem beginning "The stars send forth a holy light"', *Catholic Bulletin*, xvii, pp. 1,326–7.

Piatt, Hester Sigerson (ed.), *Songs and poems by George Sigerson: with an introduction by Padraic Colum* (Dublin).

1930

'The Abbé Edgeworth de Firmont', *Catholic Bulletin*, xx, pp. 78–81.

APPENDIX 4: POPULAR SONGS AND POEMS BY GEORGE SIGERSON

George Sigerson's many poems and songs include:

'Farewell to Sligo'

'When the swans of Lir come home'

'The guest'

'The lake-meeting'

'Peasant-philosopher'

'The true cavalier'

'The heather glen'

'The Angelus'

'Movourneen mine'

'Consolation'

'The cailín deas'

'The Enniskillen Dragoon'

'O sister dear'

'Far-Away'

'The bonnie brig o' Malezan'

'On the mountain'

'The fragrant dew'

'O hush O!'

'The blackbird'

'Mo chailín donn'

'A snow song'

'The rowan tree'

'The first love-song of Dublin'

'The calling'

'On the Mountains of Pomeroy'

'In the city'

'The exile's return'

'Whence?'

'Sorrow'

'The home rill'

'An invocation'

'The woods of Lisnara'

'The three lamenting lochs'

'The old path by the river'

'The silent abbey'

'The church of the apple tree'

'The leannán sihe'

'The paistín fionn'

'Night'

'An eyrie in Arran'

'Blarney Tower'

'Slán leis an chorrán'

'O'Dwyer of the glen'

'The splendour of all splendours'

Ten popular songs[7]

Farewell to Sligo

(Air: 'I'll drink no more on the roads to Sligo')

I'll drink no more on the roads to Sligo
I will raise my sail from the shelving shore,
Yet here's one toast to my love ere I go
From the dear old island I'll see no more.

Farewell my life 'mid the pleasant flowers
That oped so fair in its morning light,
Farewell my youth 'mid the leafy bowers
That summer showers made ever bright.

Green leaves in spring will deck vale and mountain,
The sun with gold crown yon summit hoar,
and flowers will bloom by the foamy fountain
But joy to me comes again no more.

Farewell my country, with sorrow laden,
Farewell my home high on Knock-na-ree,
And you, farewell, O young fair false maiden!
Who were home and country and life to me.

The heather glen

(Air: 'Up the heather glen')

There blooms a bonnie flower
Up the heather glen,
Though bright in sun – in shower
'Tis just as bright again!
I never can pass by it,
I never dare go nigh it,
My heart it won't be quiet
Up the heather glen!

Sing, O, the blooming heather!
O, the heather glen!
Where fairest fairies gather
To lure in mortal men!
I never can pass by it,
I never dare go nigh it,
My heart it won't be quiet
Up the heather glen!

There sings a bonnie linnet
Up the heather glen,
The voice has magic in it
Too sweet for mortal men!
It brings joy down before us,
With winsome mellow chorus,
But sings far, too far, o'er us
Up the heather glen!

Sing, O, the blooming heather!
O the heather glen!
Where fairest fairies gather
To lure in mortal men!
I never can pass by it,
I never dare go nigh it,
My heart it won't be quiet
Up the heather glen!

O might I pull that flower
Blooming in the glen,
No sorrow that could lower
Would make me sad again!
And might I catch that linnet,
My heart – my hope are in it!
O heaven itself I'd win it
Up the heather glen!

Sing, O, the blooming heather!
O the heather glen!
Where fairest fairies gather
To lure in mortal nen!
I never can pass by it, –
I never dare go nigh it, –
My heart it won't be quiet
Up the heather glen!

Movourneen mine

(Air: 'The wheelwright')

How silent moves the flowing tide
That bears our swift bark on her way;
The clouds with quiet darkness hide
The last soft lingering beam of day.
And now, afar,
One trembling star
Looks down, our guide, above the brine:
One thought of thee
Comes thus to me
From some celestial height divine!

For now, no more, on sea or shore,
Thine eyes will smile, Movourneen mine!

Sometimes a lonely fisher sees,
When laying down his lines at night,
A boat approach against the breeze,
A radiant form that proffers light!
If his heart fail,
The veering sail
Will swiftly into dark decline;
If true and brave,
Then o'er the wave
'Twill lead where Isles of Beauty shine.

Ah! thou no more, on sea or shore,
My life shalt light, Movourneen mine!

Away, away, through storm and strain,
The streaming sea still draws our keel;
We bear our message o'er the main,
And must not fail, howe'er we feel.
Though heart should break,
Our course we take,
While yon fair star shall o'er us shine;
With banner high
Against the sky,
And souls too steadfast to repine.

For evermore, on sea and shore,
Thy love abides, Movourneen, mine!

The Enniskillen Dragoon

(Air: 'The Enniskillen Dragoon')

Farewell, Enniskillen, farewell for a while
To all your fair waters and every green isle,
Your green isles will flourish and your fair waters flow,
And I from old Ireland an exile must go.

Her hair is as brown as the young raven's wing,
Her eyes are as clear as the blue bells of Spring,
And light was her laugh like the sun on the sea,
Till the weight of the world came between her and me.

O what can man do when the world is his foe,
And the looks of her people fall on you like snow?
But bend the brow boldly and fare away far
To follow good fortune and win fame in the War.

They'll tell how we fought on a far foreign shore,
And she'll know that in danger I loved her the more,
When the swords flashed aloft and the swift bullets flew –
I saw your sweet countenance and dear eyes of blue!

If the worst should befall – sure 'tis only to die,
And the true lass that loved me can hold her head high,
Can hold her head high, though the fond heart may break,
For her lover loved bravely and died for her sake.

Then, farewell Enniskillen, farewell for a while
And all around the borders of Erin's green isle,
But, if Fortune do favour, I'll return again soon
And you'll all welcome home the Enniskillen Dragoon.

Far-Away

(Air: 'The Derry air')

As chimes that flow o'er shining seas
When Morn alights on meads of May,
Faint voices fill the western breeze
With whispering songs of Far-Away.
O dear the dell of Doonanore,
A home is odorous Ossory;
But sweet as honey, running o'er,
The Golden Shore of Far-Away!

There grows the Tree whose summer breath,
Perfumes with joy the azure air;
And he who feels it fears not Death,
Nor longer heeds the Hounds of Care.
O soft the skies of Seskinore,
And mild is meadowy Mellary;
But sweet as honey, running o'er,
The Golden Shore of Far-Away!

There sings the Voice whose wond'rous tune
Falls, like a diamond-shower above
That, in the radiant dawn of June
Renews a world of Youth and Love.
O fair the founts of Farranfore,
And bright is billowy Ballintrae;
But sweet as honey, running o'er,
The Golden Shore of Far-Away!

Come, Fragrance of the Flowering Tree,
O sing, sweet Bird, thy magic lay,
Till all the world be young with me,
And Love shall lead us Far Away.
O dear the dells of Doonanore,
A home is odorous Ossory;
But sweet as honey, running o'er,
The Golden Shore of Far-Away!

The fragrant dew

(Air: 'The foggy dew')

Ah sing, Lady fair,
Once more that sweet old air,
Some fairy voice sang it when the world was new:
It falls upon the heart,
All worn with sorrow's smart,
As on sultry flowers at eve falls the fragrant dew.

Again, through the night
The radiant stars give light,
The great sky above them is soft and blue
And near are happy eyes,
And hope on hopes arise
As incense from the flowers greets the fragrant dew.

Old times pass away,
Old friendships decay,
They vanish, the bright hopes, that once seemed true,
But, in that magic strain,
They all take life again,
As the faded flowers revive 'neath the fragrant dew.

Such fortune be mine
That this dear air divine
May recall once my name to the faithful few,
And evoke in memory,
A silent tear from thee –
As on broken flowers at night falls the fragrant dew.

On the Mountains of Pomeroy

(Air: 'The Mountains of Pomeroy')

The morn was breaking bright and fair,
The lark sang in the sky,
When the maid she bound her golden hair,
With a blithe glance in her eye.
For who beyond the gay greenwood
Was waiting her with joy?

Who but her gallant Renardine,
On the Mountains of Pomeroy?
An outlawed man in a land forlorn,
He scorned to turn and fly,
But kept the cause of Freedom safe
Upon the Mountains high.

Full often in the dawning hour,
Full oft in the twilight brown,
He met the maid in the twilight bower,
Where the stream comes foaming down.
For they were faithful in a love
No wars could e'er destroy,
Nor tyrant's law touch Renardine
On the Mountains of Pomeroy,
An outlawed man in a land forlorn,
He scorned to turn and fly,
But kept the cause of Freedom safe
Upon the Mountains high.

'Dear love,' she said, 'I'm sore afraid
For the foeman's force and you;
They've tracked you in the lowland glade,
And all the valley through.
My kinsmen frown when you are named,
Your life they would destroy;
'Beware' they say, 'of Renardine
On the Mountains of Pomeroy.'
An outlawed man in a land forlorn,
He scorned to turn and fly,
But kept the cause of Freedom safe
Upon the Mountains high.

'Fear not, fear not, sweetheart,' he said,
'Fear not the foe for me;
No chains shall fall, whate'er betide,
On the arm which will be free.
O, leave your cruel kin, and come
When the lark is in the sky;
And 'tis with my gun I'll guard you,
On the Mountains of Pomeroy!'
An outlawed man in a land forlorn,
He scorned to turn and fly,
But kept the cause of Freedom safe
Upon the Mountains high.

Mo chailín donn

(Air: 'The River Roe' or 'Irish Molly O')

The blush is on the flower, and the bloom is on the tree,
And the bonnie, bonnie sweet birds are carolling their glee;
And the dews upon the grass are made diamonds by the sun,
All to deck a path of glory for my own Cailín donn!

O, fair she is! O, rare she is! O, dearest still to me!
More welcome than the green leaf to winter-stricken tree,
More welcome than the blossom to the weary, dusty bee,
Is the coming of my true love – my own Cailín donn!

O, Sycamore! O, Sycamore! wave, wave your banners green –
Let all your pennons flutter, O, Beech! before my queen!
Ye fleet and honied breezes, to kiss her hand ye run,
But my heart has past before ye – to my own Cailín donn!

Ring out, ring out, O, Linden! your merry, leafy bells!
Unveil your brilliant torches, O, Chestnut! to the dells;
Strew, strew the glade with splendour, for morn – it cometh on!
O, the morn of all delight to me – my own Cailín donn!

She is coming where we parted, where she wanders every day;
There's a gay surprise before her who thinks me far away!
O, like hearing bugles triumph when the fight of Freedom's won,
Is the joy around your footsteps – my own Cailín donn!

O, fair she is! O, rare she is! O, dearest still to me!
More welcome than the green leaf to winter-stricken tree,
More welcome than the blossom to the weary, dusty bee,
Is your coming, O, my true love – my own Cailín donn!

The blackbird

(Air: 'The blackbird')

O hark to the soaring of clear song outpouring!
The Voice of the lovely green valley, I hear!
Half-craving and crying, half-sobbing and sighing
Triumphing and dying, afar off and near.
Now all the vale over it goes, like a lover,
A-calling and re-calling the years fled away –
Now behold! it comes bringing the Past with its singing
The music of Youth is the Blackbird's sweet lay!

How softly at morning its pure note gave warning,
Awaking all hearts with the lyric of love,
And, making more tender the opening splendour
Illumined all looks with a light from above.
And hear the soft laughter now following after –
The meetings and the greetings, the gay dawn of day!
O what friends flit and dally throughout the glad valley,
Their voices all blend in the Blackbird's soft lay!

Ah, hear the imploring of sad song deploring! –
The wail of the lonely gray valley I hear.
Now craving and crying, now sobbing and sighing
Appealing and dying, afar and a-near,
The glory, the gladness, to sorrow and sadness –
The light unto the night-cloud, all, all fade away!
Ah, how vain the recalling! – to tears slowly falling
The Blackbird at eve sings its lonely sad lay!

O'Dwyer of the glen

(Air: 'Seán O'Duibhir a' ghleanna')

When sings the Birds of Morning,
Welcome is the warning!
Dawn, the Darkness scorning,
Rose-crown'd does appear,
Life is all before us,
Blue the skies are o'er us,
In our hearts a chorus
Of joy-bells we hear!
Blow, huntsman, we will follow,
Stag, now flee the fallow,
Cry, Echo, holloa, holloa,
Repeat the day's delight!
Thereafter cometh quiet,
Laughter dies and riot,
Around us reigns in silence
The great Peace of Night!

How splendid was the Vision,
Flame-like, fair, elysian,
When, for War's decision,
Our bright weapons flash!
Hope showed Erinn's glory,
Fame our place in story;
Gay to combat gory
True comrades we dash!
Crash, cannon, we go onward,
Flag, now flutter sunward,
Let Victory lead vanward,
For Honour holds the field!
Alas, the King who led us,
Failed, forsook, and fled us,
We strove with Patrick Sarsfield,
Men who could not yield!

Now fall on Lim'rick towers
Evening's stormy showers,
Murky midnight lowers
Round each breaking heart.
Vain was all the daring,
Exiles, far we're faring,
From you – from you, Erinn!
Farewell, we do part.
Break, billow, we are cleaving,
Crag, behold us leaving!
If we return not, grieving
Till death, beyond the foam.
'Farewell!' – we hear you calling,
Farewell! – the clouds are falling,
Ah, Shaun O'Deer a Glanna!
You now have no Home.

One bird sings at even
To the soul bereaven,
Still one star in heaven
Will shine through the night.
Life is all behind us,
Dark the skies that bind us,
Bitter tears do blind us –
But, we stand upright!
Fly, fortune, who will follow?
Brag, Foe, your Treaty hollow,
All story still shall hallow
The men to Honour true.
And this be our upbearing,
For you, – for you! – Erinn!
To strike, with Patrick Sarsfield,
One more blow for you.

APPENDIX 5:
INTRODUCTION TO *SONGS AND POEMS BY GEORGE SIGERSON* (1927)[8]
Padraic Colum

Were it not that it has been given already to another book, the title 'Songs and Poems of Irish Chivalry' would be a fitting one for this collection. For in the poems there is something high-minded and magnanimous; there is something soldierly combined with something human: it is this note of chivalry that makes George Sigerson's poetry distinctive in Irish literature.

If anyone in Irish letters was heir to the humane tradition it was George Sigerson. He belonged to an epoch when a good Irishman might also be a good European. His university years were passed abroad, and Paris was always the metropolis of his world. Charcot was his master – Charcot the master of the new learning – and he was also his associate and friend. He had a correspondent in Germany in the great Mommsen, and correspondents in England in Lord Acton and Matthew Arnold. His profession was the most humane of professions – medicine. He was a scholar in what related to his profession; he was a scholar in literature – especially in Irish and Latin literature. And he took a helpful and reconciling part in the public life of his country: the poet-scholar of '*Bards of the Gael and Gall*' and '*The Poets and Poetry of Munster*,' was also the writer of a report upon the treatment of political prisoners and of a '*History of Land Tenures in Ireland*' – a history written at Lord Acton's request and for Gladstone's use. A man of human culture through all this, he was soldierly through his soldierly forefathers.

As we go through this collection of his occasional poems we constantly come upon some living part of our history. Here is a poem that was made on the bringing back to Ireland of the body of an exiled soldier –

> And the shroud of our nation's glory
> Her last brave hero's pall.

And as we read it we know that the famine is not twenty years in the background, and we know that loneliness lies on the land and the shadows of ruined homes; we recognize the bravery that is in the voice that can still speak of a living Ireland. Nearly thirty years more go by, and, in 1898, the ever-varying symbolism of Irish deliverance is receiving from this poet its most romantic embodiment in 'The Swans of Lir' –

> Now some go east, and some go west,
> And some to feuds have gone,
> And men forget their lofty quest
> But still, the Swans live on:
> And still their song is in our souls
> O'er seas of freezing foam
> We'll see the bright glad glowing light
> When the Swans of Lir come home.

And then there is the song that was sung in many gatherings: the young men who sang it never thought that its writer was living amongst them – 'The Mountains of Pomeroy' – it carries down from the past the gallantry of resistance.

Like Roger Casement's, like T.M. Kettle's, George Sigerson's name is there to show us how Scandinavian we are in our racial make-up. The Sigurd in his name shows that his stock was 'Norse and noble.' His forefathers must have been in Ireland from the time of the battle of Clontarf, and yet he remained a miracle of atavism – a distinctly Norse type. He was proud of his ancestry, and proud of the Norse contribution to Irish culture. He would point out that the first poem in which Dublin is mentioned is a love song made by a Norse King. He would remark that the epoch of the Norse Kingdom in Dublin was a golden age in Ireland, and that it was disrupted by a usurper named Brian Boru.

> 'With us are Vikings and virtue,
> With them the Gael and the guilt,'

a friend, parodying Moore, remarked after 'the Doctor' had discoursed on this subject. He delighted in translating Norse poems that showed an intimacy with Irish life, and Irish poems that showed friendship for the Norse. But not only in his translations has he made this Northern element felt – it is in his original poems –indeed it is most striking in certain of his original poems. There is a Northern note that is very thrilling in the dramatic 'O Sister Dear'; the Northern note, too, is in –

> Two friends he hath – two only,
> Good hammer and sweet bird,
> O sorrowful eyes! You tell not
> Who may have been the third,
> Or whether the thrush is singing
> Of summers that bore no gloom,
> Or whether it promiseth sweetly,
> A green bough o'er a tomb.
> When still shall be the hammer,
> Silent all within,
> Hushed the weary clamour
> And the noisy din.

It is in –

> The old path by the river,
> That once was all bright with flowers,
> The mournful pines have o'er-arched it
> With dusk, like living hours.

There is not in this collection any poem as poignant as 'O'Curnain's Lament,' or as brilliant as 'Cuchulainn's Lament over Ferdiad,' to name two of the famous poems of 'Bards of the Gael and Gall'. But there are certain beautiful poems here – poems that are an addition to Irish literature. All are the utterance of a man who has had rapture come to him from the hills and the lakes, from the music, the ruins, and the tradition of Ireland.

As we read 'Songs and Poems' we think of someone moving through lofty halls and looking on possessions still left him – swords and steeds and the tokens of some recognized nobility. There is the memory of a day of arms when the horsemen returned with word of defeat. The woods and the acres outside have been alienated; the Abbey has fallen into decay. Abbey and fields and woods have become storied. Old music rings out in the hall sometimes, and gay and solemn words are blended with it. The warder tells of some hopeful thing glimpsed, and his words bring back flashes of ardour. Not yet is the turmoil and the trouble, the letting-in and the letting-down, of new preparation. All that is said has the memory of a stately background –

> The Splendour of all Splendours with her goes
> The ocean at her footfall thrills and glows!
> Low music fills the wide air with delight,
> For now Wonder strikes the myriad chords of Night!
> O speed, Love! through the shadows from afar,
> Thy coming is the coming of a star!
> O speak, Love, and the night-storm flees away,
> For thy smile is the sunshine of the day!

The poet of such stately words had, when he spoke them, a delivery that was at once ceremonious and precise, slow-moving and sonorous.

'In public speech, Sigerson had an art of his own,' says Mr C.P. Curran, in a memoir which he has aptly entitled 'Oisín after the Fianna'. Mr Curran's is an admirable description of Dr Sigerson's method – it describes him as he presided at the Monday evening meetings of the National Literary Society. 'How eagerly in that audience did we wait for the glancing irony which shot through the folds of his deliberate, ceremonious speech! ... His massive speech advanced in the fashion of the classic phalanx, bristling with bright spears; and the rapid shafts of his wit lost nothing in effect from the contrast of humorous, twinkling eyes with the sonorous voice and the grave, courteous dignity of his bearing.' His wit and his courtesy come back to me from a little picture that I carry in my memory.

A very young writer has come from a house opposite 'the Doctor's' in Clare Street. A meeting is being held there, but no provision was made for lighting the meeting, and the very young writer, leaving his colleagues in semi-darkness, has come across the street to ask for the loan of lights. 'The Doctor' stands upon the steps of his house; a silver candelabra in which there are wax lights is in his hands, and, as he passes on the lights, he says in that sonorous, rolling voice, and with the breathing-pauses which made his delivery so effective, 'Mr —, this is to have the sun borrow light from the moon.' Thus he made his wit the courtesy of a kingly mind.

The Doctor's house was, as Mr Curran has said – again so aptly – like some Balzac interior. ... 'French furniture of all the Louis and Empires, French paintings and pastels, French miniatures and engravings.' On Sunday evenings his friends would come to dinner to this house that was always lighted with candles. At tea in the drawing-room afterwards the gathering became a salon. It was a house in which one would not look to see Bricru's Feast enacted. The sonorous voice of 'the Doctor,' his deliberate utterance, his wit that had its setting in courtesy, moderated all bitterly-held opinions. 'We must not plagiarise from ourselves,' I heard him say once, and people who wanted to repeat items out of a controversy that was going on had to think of something fresher to say.

It was his humour to be partisan about some odd issue. He would maintain, for instance, that people who were of Norse extraction had a better sense of humour than people who were purely Irish. 'But you must admit, Doctor, that the Irish have a fine sense of humour,' O'Neill Russell cried out when that thesis was once advanced at the dinner table. 'I just heard a teacher in Malahide say to a boy, "It's no wonder you're thick-headed, coming from Lambay." Now, wasn't that very witty?' 'Which will see the joke first – the Norse side of the table or the Irish side?' remarked 'the Doctor.' There was silence at the table, while the two sides sat, heads upon hands, trying to see the point. O'Neill Russell went on eating his dinner. And then he looked up and said, 'That's not it at all. What he said was, "It's no wonder you are mutton-headed, coming from Lambay." Now, wasn't that very witty?' 'Pass the red wine, Mr O'Neill Russell,' said 'the Doctor.'

Once – it was at my leave-taking of him in the Autumn of 1924 – I had to tell him that my stay in Paris would be a short one, as I wanted to go on to Rome. I knew, of course, that he would give me reproof for not staying on in Paris, and, thinking of something that might be supposed to make Rome paramount, I said that I wanted to see the Catacombs. 'There are better Catacombs in Paris.' The remark was so right coming from 'the Doctor' that it was to be treasured.

He was near the span of three score of years and ten when I first had the good fortune to be asked to his house; he was nearly ninety when I took leave of him for the last time. His face had pallor, his voice was slower, but there was no slackness in his intellectual powers on the last occasions on which I was with him. Indeed, at no time could I think of him as one whose vigour, wit, or understanding was abated, or the range of whose interest was in any way diminished. At eighty he was working on his translation of Sedulius, making those elaborate notes and writing that scholarly introduction in which he establishes the fact that the writer of the first Christian epic was an Irishman. He had lost no touch with the world.

When I remember that I would meet John O'Leary at his house in the early days, that I would meet Padraic Pearse there later, and that the last time I saw Roger Casement in Ireland was at 'the Doctor's', I am impressed by the thought of how much of Ireland was included in his life – even in the segment of it known to one of my generation. With his broad shoulders and his silvery flowing hair, with his composed speech and his voice that had a tidal movement in it, he seemed like a survivor from some heroic prime. But he was not one to think of himself as a survival; he was in unison with every generation he lived amongst. Where now shall we turn to find so bountiful a mind, such unobtrusive loyalty to an unforgotten, lofty quest, such kindness and such courtesy? The Gaelic poet who praised an ancestor of his wrote words that have an image of him in them –

The handsome hawk who tower'd the country o'er,
Top spray of all who sprang from Sigerson Mór.

Dedicatory Poem – by Padraic Colum[9]
To George Sigerson, Poet and Scholar.

Two men of art, they say, were with the sons
Of Mile, – a poet and a harp player,
When Mile, having taken Ireland, left
The land to his sons' rule; the poet was
Cir, and fair Cendfind was the harp player.

The sons of Mile for the kingship fought –
(Blithely, with merry sounds, the old poem says)
Eber and Eremon, the sons of Mile
And when division of the land was made
They drew a lot for the two men of art.

When Eber had won the northern half
The Harper Cendfind went, and with Eremon
The Northerner, Cir the poet stayed;
And so, the old Book of the Conquests says,
The South has music and the North has lore.

To you who are both of the North and South,
To you who have the music and the lore,
To you in whom Cir and Cendfind are met,
To you I bring the tale of poetry
Left by the sons of Eber and Eremon.

A leabhráin, gabh amach fá'n saoghal,
Is do gach n-aon dá mbuaileann leat
Aithris cruinn go maireann Gaedhil,
T'réis cleasa claon nan Gall ar fad.

APPENDIX 6: 'A PALE FAMILY'

Shortly before his death, George Sigerson was revising new material on the Sigerson family, after much research throughout Britain and Ireland. Beginning with Viking royalty, especially the Sigurds, earls of Orkney, Sigerson researched his own family from AD 800 until the 1690s. This is a synopsis of the opening chapters of the unpublished work.[10]

A Pale family: a history of the Sigerson family

> The history of a nation may be likened to a piece of tapestry. As a single thread in that great tapestry, is the story of a family which may have interest as it passes through scenes of adventure, war, glory and gloom, tinged by hues, the lights and the shadows of that nation's fortunes.

With these words George Sigerson began the foreword to a history of the Sigerson family, which he was revising on his deathbed. Sadly the work was not completed and never published. Donn Piatt, who had helped his grandfather with the corrections, had intended to complete it by including the story of his grandfather's life, but his own early death prevented this from happening. Unfortunately some parts of the original manuscript have now been lost. In a reading to the Old Dublin Society in 1962, Donn Piatt provided an account of Sigerson's manuscript, paying particular attention to the parts of it dealing with old Dublin, since the Sigerson family had been connected with the city over many centuries.

They claimed connection with Sigurd, earl of Orkney, and with certain Gaelic families in Ireland and Scotland who had a strong Norse element in their population. The five sons of Sigurd took part in Viking landings in Ireland and one of them died at the battle of Clontarf. Later the chief branch of the family settled in the south-west of Ireland. There was an old Kerry saying: 'O'Mahoney was, Sigerson is, and O'Connell will be,' showing the family in the ascendant at one time. These three great families intermarried.

The following extracts deal mainly with the Norse connections.[11] George Sigerson was proud of his Norse ancestry and of the influence of the Vikings in Ireland. He was certain that Sigerson was Sigar's or Sigurd's son, and that his family had never changed the 'son' to 'Mac' to make out of Sigurd's son the name MacSigurd.

Sigerson claimed that Norse-Vikings were no newcomers to Ireland in the ninth century and that the fair race of the Tuatha Dé Danaan came to Ireland from Norway. He claimed that the Gael and the Gall had close connections in ancient times and that the annals of Ireland record several intermarriages.

Concerning this, Sigerson wrote:

> Thus, in the second century King Tuatal the Legitimate married a Norse princess, Scal's daughter, and their son also espoused a Norland princess. King Cormac MacArt, in the third century, was grandson of a Norsewoman. There were two Norse ancestresses in the lineage of Ossian, the last great pagan bard – whilst Secundinus, the first Irish hymn-writer in Erinn, was the son of one of the Longobards who are supposed to have then recently left Norway.

The first major invasions of Ireland by the Norsemen happened about A.D. 800. The name 'Viking' was used, in a general way, to describe a member of the Nordic peoples – Norwegians, Swedes and Danes – who attacked and raided England, France, Germany, Ireland, Italy, Spain (and other countries) between the 700s and 1100s. The word Viking may have come from the Norse word 'vik' meaning a bay or inlet. The Vikings in Ireland came from Norway.

Like all Vikings, the men from Norway were a seafaring people and they were the most successful ship-builders in Europe. The Norsemen attacked such places as the Faroe Islands, Greenland, the Hebrides, Iceland, Scotland, the Orkney Islands and Ireland. At first they killed, stole, and destroyed property wherever they landed; they accomplished this with ferocious and insane-like thoroughness. But, in many places, they established important settlements and quickly learned from the people they plundered. They quickly abandoned the Norse gods – such as Odin and Thor – and followed the ways of Christianity. They abandoned piracy and destruction to learn new skills.

Although it is accepted that the Vikings destroyed very many and established ways of life, by becoming traders they helped to develop commerce in their host countries. About A.D. 800 they founded Dyflin – Dublin – and developed it to become a city of great importance, to be rivalled only by London and Bristol as the commercial capital of Europe's western islands. By A.D. 853 the Vikings had established the cities of Wicklow, Wexford, Waterford, Cork and Limerick; and they rapidly extended control of territories throughout Ireland. Dublin was the centre of Viking power in Ireland; that is, until the arrival of the Normans during the twelfth century.

In 1014, Sigurd the Stout, Earl of the Orkneys, came to 'do battle' with King Brian Boru in what was to be the last great Viking battle in Ireland. Sigurd had been invited by Gormliath, the former queen of Brian Boru, who promised him her hand in marriage should he be successful in his quest for the overall sovereignty of Ireland. Gormliath had separated from the usurping Emperor Brian, and she sought to redeem the independence of Leinster.

The two armies met at the weir of Clontarf on Good Friday, 1014. As the battle raged, and as one Viking standard bearer after another fell to the ground, the mighty Sigurd grasped the 'banner' – which had led him to many victories – and, as he hoisted it aloft, he was struck and mortally wounded; thus fulfilling the prophesy of his mother (Audna) who had warned 'victory before whom it is borne, death to the bearer.'

The Vikings were defeated at Clontarf and – apart from King Magnus who fought in alliance with the southern against the northern Irish, about 1100 – the Norsemen took no further major part in Irish wars. But Brian Borumha was also killed at Clontarf, and unity ended among the chiefs under his command.

George Sigerson frequently argued that, contrary to generally held beliefs, the great Hiberno-Norse period was a time of continuing scholarship and learning. He writes:

The Irish annals declare that the wars in Erinn were more frequent and sanguinary in the centuries which preceded the establishment of the empire [Hiberno-Norse Empire], than in those which followed. The Norse Sagas show that the power of the Hiberno-Norse kings immediately after Clontarf was greater than before it. In the Catalogue of Irish Writers, nine are named for the century preceding the empire; seven of more distinction flourished in the century following; in the next eight, and in the next eighteen.

The Annals of the Four Masters mention forty bishops in the eighth century, and eighty in the tenth; they mention thirty learned men of distinction in the eighth and sixty three in the tenth. These statistics are fully borne out by the fact that important manuscripts, such as Book of Leinster and the Lebar na hUidre, date from this period, and by the evidence of many works. It was a period of great intellectual activity, when minds were quickened.

In the years following Clontarf and through the Anglo-Norman period, the descendants of Sigurd settled down to a life of comparative peace with their old and new neighbours. They concentrated on extending their commercial interests. According to George Sigerson, these descendants of Sigurd were named Segerson, Seckerstone, Segarstone, and so on. Sigerson claimed connection with Sigurd through them.

He traced the name Sigurd through such corruptions as Siward and Siurd, and found the name Sigarus – otherwise written Segarus and misspelt Sidgar – in the *Domesday Book* of AD 1086. He found the name in one of the earliest vellum municipal membranes of Dublin:

On 'the most ancient roll' extant, in the archive of the municipality of Dublin, is found the name of Segerson, in its latinised form Filius Segeri; the hard sound of the 'g' has been traditionally retained notwithstanding the analogy of English words. The municipal manuscript in question dates from the 12th century, and its first membranes may have been submitted to the Anglo-Norman monarch when he held his court outside the walls of Dublin in 1172. The names appear in the following form:

> *Ricardus filius Segeri de Swoinesea (Membrane I. col. b)*
> *Robertus cognatus Segeri (Membrane II. col. b)*
> *Henricus filius Segari de Glocestria (Membrane VI. col .b)*

On this roll also are inscribed the names of Sigar dives or Sigar the wealthy, and Segarus de Suthamptune one of whom probably was the benefactor who bestowed his burgage on Christ Church and [is] mentioned in an Inspeximus of King John as Segar the Aged. All were Norsemen.

Having found the 'Filii Segeri', the Segersons in Dublin, when the Normans arrived there, Sigerson referred back to the name Sigurd in the sagas of Norway and the Orkneys. He noted:

In those countries as in Ireland the patronymic was not fitted – but when settled amongst strangers, the names remained constant. Here then are some of the earliest bearers of the name:

860–930 Harald Fairhair, for the sake of the princess Gyda, made himself King over all Norway, introduced feudal forms and established earls over regions previously ruled by petty kings. He offered the Earldom of the Orkneys to his chief Rognvald who, with the sanction of the Kings declined in favour of his brother Sigurd.

Sigurd, first Earl of the Orkneys, enlarged his dominions, conquering the north of Scotland, namely Caithness, Sutherland, Moray and Ross. He built a burg on the southern shore of the Moray firth, and slew the Scottish or Gaelic Earl Maelbrigda (Tooth).

Guttorm Sigurdson, his son, ruled as Earl for about a year and died without children. His first cousin, Rolf the Ganger, expected the succession but, being outlawed, became a powerful Viking and conquered Normandy. Rolf is the ancestor of the Earls of Normandy and King Edward, King Athelfead, William the Conqueror … Baptised in 912, he died in 931. His stepbrothers Hallad and Einar ruled the Orkneys. Einar's son, Thorfin, married Grelanga, daughter of Duncan (Doncad) the Gaelic Earl of Caithness; and his celebrated grandson, of royal Gaelic blood, was Sigurd the Stout who died at Clontarf.

975 Sigurd the Stout, Earl of the Orkneys, restored their feudal rights to the people and recovered Moray from Maelbrigda's nephew Findlaec, son of Ruaidri. Findlaec, the father of Maelbeth (MacBeth) ruled as sovereign over the north of Scotland.

988 Surprised at sea by the fleet of King Olaf Tryggveson Sigurd was offered Christianity or the death of his son, Hundi. Sigurd loved his son (more than he loved Odin.) He accepted baptism and did homage. Kept hostage, Hundi was taken to Norway by Olaf and died a few years later. Then Sigurd paid no further allegiances to Olaf.

Sigurd had three other sons by his first wife. The sons were called Somerlad, Brusse, and Einar. After the death of his wife, Sigurd married the daughter of Malcolm, Gaelic King of the Scots, and Thorfin was born.

1014 Sigurd was killed at the battle of the weir of Clontarf.

Sigerson related that Thorfin Sigurdson was five years old when his father (Sigurd) died, and that the boy's grandfather (Malcolm) made him earl of Caithness and gave him Malcolm's own share of the Orkneys. Thorfin began his Viking career at 14 years old.

According to Sigerson, when Malcolm died, Duncan – who had married Malcolm's eldest daughter – claimed the kingdom. South Scotland accepted Duncan, but Thorfin Sigurdson refused tribute to his aunt's husband. Duncan thereupon made his own nephew, Moddan, earl of Caithness and sent him north with an army to take possession. Earl Thorfin chased Moddan and secured the Moray Firth. Enraged, King Duncan gathered all his own forces, with troops that came from Ireland at Moddan's call, and with Moddan, the Pretender of Caithness and MacBeth, the claimant of Moray, he advanced by sea and land against the independent earl. Land armies and sea fleets met, the latter at Duncansby Head. Thorfin was victorious.

MacBeth deserted his routed monarch and submitted to Thorfin. MacBeth ultimately murdered Duncan and usurped the southern kingship. Thorfin Sigurdson held the north.

George Sigerson also researched the Sigurdsons and England, Sigurdson's intermarriage with royalty of Scotland, and the death of Magnus in Ulster:

1064 Earl Thorfin Sigurdson, the greatest of the Northern Earls died. His rule extended along the Western Isles to Dublin.

1066 King Harald Sigurdson of Norway – Hardrada the Resolute – invaded England to help Earl Tostig in his fight with Tostig's brother, Saxon Harold Godwinson, the King of England. Harold Sigurdson and Tostig were killed at the battle of Stamford Bridge. Nineteen days later, at the Battle of Hastings, William of Normandy (descendant of Rolf the Ganger) defeated King Harold and established the Northern race on the throne of England.

1066 Ingibiorg, widow of Thorfin Sigurdson, married the Gaelic King Malcolm Canmore (son of Duncan murdered by MacBeth). Their son was Duncan, King of the Scots, a Norse-Gael.

1093 Hacon and Magnus, grandsons of Harald Sigurdson, became Kings of Norway. Hacon soon died. Magnus (Barelegs) undertook a great expedition; he established his son Sigurd as Earl of the Orkneys; conquered all the western isles of Scotland, sparing the 'Holy Isle' of Iona; he captured Man and the isle of Anglesey; and he killed Hugo, the Earl of Chester. On his homeward way he seized Cantire. Before arriving home he made a treaty with Malcolm III (King of Scots) in which the dominion of Norway over all the isles was acknowledged. He also contracted his son, Earl Sigurd, in marriage with Byadmynia, daughter of Myrkiartan (King of Kunnaktir), son of Muirceartach (King of Thomond).

1100 In Ireland, uniting forces with Muirceartach, Magnus and Muirceartach conquered Dublin and then made a triumphant march to Inishowen. Ambushed by Ulstermen, Magnus was killed. Sigurd returned home leaving Byadmynia behind. Sigurd was thirteen years old.

Sigerson argued that the Segersons of the Irish seas probably descended from the 'Orkney line'. Earl Thorfin Sigurdson controlled Orkney, Shetland and the Hebrides, and he had 'great possessions' in Scotland and Ireland. Thorfin's grandchildren – described as noblemen and great chiefs – probably retained the possessions in Ireland. Sigerson closed his account of Orkney lineage with the historical romance, 'The seven sons of Siger':

> In ancient Irish Historical Romance, we may discover a distinct reference to the Orkney chiefs of the name. The 'Battle of Moyleana' was transcribed by MacFirbis in 1391; it was composed a considerable time before then – some centuries at least. Now, in this historical romance the seven sons of Siger are given remarkable prominence. They are described as 'foreigners' and 'oversea champions' who came as allies in support of Eoghan Mór against Conn. These two kings had divided Erinn between them, a parting ridge (the Eiscir riada) which runs from Dublin to Galway forming the frontier of Conn's northern half, and Eoghan's southern share. The latter, deeming Conn to have acted unfairly, made war against him, and in Eoghan's army were his oversea champions, the seven sons of Siger ... 'they left home those seven warriors battered dismembered trunks, after having cut their heads off their bodies.'

Sigerson believed that this story with its 'seven sons of Sigar' was written around the year 1100, when the Norse King Magnus came to Ireland, betrothed his son Sigurd to Byadmynia, and advanced in alliance with the southern army against the northern king.

According to Sigerson, the circumstances are similar and the death of the overseas ally is alike in both cases. The sons of Siger referred to were apparently the four Sigurdsons, who had been earls of Orkney (some having possessions in Dublin), 'whose number and period are treated with all an historical novelist's freedom'.

It appears that George Sigerson traced his family to Chester in the Tudor period. One Rauff Sekerston apparently left Chester and set up base in Liverpool, where he became mayor and also represented the town in parliament. One of his sons moved to Ireland in the mid-sixteenth century. Sigerson found record of an Edmund Segerston, son of Rauff of Liverpool, having received a pardon in Dublin in the year 1558. Five years later, Edmund received a lease at Cooke Street in Dublin from the dean of Christ Church. Problems arose over the lease but in 1585 Edmund's executors were confirmed in possession of the property. The family appeared to have prospered and two sons of Edmund, Thomas and Ralph, were recorded as knights and holders of property in Dublin, Wicklow, Wexford and Kildare.

Sigerson was descended from the Kerry branch of the family, which intermarried with the O'Connells and the O'Mahoneys and engaged with these families in the smuggling trade with France. They smuggled out Wild Geese and scholars; they smuggled in French wines and 'wine from the Royal Pope' in the form of young priests.

Another connection is with the English Spensers. A Roger Seckerson is said to have married the widow of Edmund Spenser following the Englishman's early death in 1599 and added land in Cork to his other possessions in Dublin and Kildare. A son, Richard, was born of this marriage, and had the misfortune to remain faithful to the royalist side in the wars of the 1640s. Richard was forced to flee to Connacht in the Cromwellian Plantation of the 1650s. His cousin Christopher also lost his lands in Ballinskelligs and his son, John, played a role in the Williamite Wars on the Jacobite side. At the battle of Aughrim, a number of Sigersons from Ballinskelligs fought in the Jacobite army, and were all killed but one, a boy of 12. This boy, after the battle, was taken care of by a parish priest, who was a native of County Tyrone. The priest sent the boy back to his own parents' family in Tyrone. The dead soldiers' horses are said to have found their way back to Ballinskelligs, and this incident formed the subject of one of Sigerson's own poems: 'They come, great God, all riderless, the horses of the dead'.

The wars and confiscations of the seventeenth century effectively ended the Sigerson power base in both Leinster and Munster and the family joined the long list of the dispossessed of that era. The name lived on in Kerry and the escape of the young boy to Tyrone following the battle of Aughrim provided the opportunity for the re-emergence of that branch of the Sigerson family that traced its ancestry to the Vikings and gloried in their contributions in peace and war to the development of their country and its peoples. George Sigerson took immense pride in the family traditions and his own career was very much in line with the proud family involvement that he so meticulously researched. His lifetime of service to his country represented the best traditions of his forebears and it was perhaps fitting that most of his life was spent in Dublin where he became a leader in so many avenues of Irish life and epitomised the long history of the Sigerson family in preserving the spirit of the past while contributing to a better future. His death in 1925 brought that branch of the family name to an end but in the words of his friend and fellow Gaelic scholar, Douglas Hyde, Ireland 'will not forget him and cannot replace him'.

APPENDIX 7:
MEMORIAL PREFACE TO *BARDS OF THE GAEL AND GALL* (3rd ed.)[12]
Douglas Hyde

GEORGE SIGERSON
Born on January 11, 1836 – Died on February 17, 1925
By Professor Douglas Hyde, LL.D., D.Litt. [An Craoibhín]

The remarkable man who passed away from amongst us on the 17th of February has left a gap in our midst that cannot be filled. He was as it were a giant oak which had seen generations of lesser trees grow around it and pass away, and its own fall in the fulness of years has left vacant the space which had been adorned by its stately presence. The most notable link that connected the Ireland of to-day almost with the Ireland of the Penal times, and certainly with the Ireland of nearly three quarters of a century ago, has been at last snapped. Full of old age and well-deserved honours and reverence and love this outstanding figure has departed from amongst us.

So many were his attainments and so various his interests that it is difficult to properly appraise them; but the most striking thing about him, taken as a whole, was his own career, during which he worked incessantly, never wavering in his affection for things Irish, never halting in giving his allegiance and best service to the cause of mankind and of his own country. As an Irish scholar he was the last link that connected us with the era of O'Donovan and O'Curry, and one of the last that connected us with the men of '48, with Kickham and with Mitchel. He had known them all, shared their counsels and aspirations, befriended and sheltered many of them, and could tell of them from the intimacy of close association in a way that was the privilege of no other living person.

He was not the child of any one province; he was all-Ireland, and one might even say cosmopolitan. Born and reared near Strabane, but with a Kerry ancestry, educated partly in Galway, partly in Cork, and later on in Paris (in close touch with the Irish there), he typified all that was best and broadest and sanest in our race. He always boasted that he came from the old Norse. He often told the present writer that Sigerson was only Sicar's or Sigurd's son, and that though his people had been in Ireland for many hundreds of years they had never changed, as most other families had done, the 'son' for 'mac,' or made out of Sigurd's son Mac Sigir. His northern upbringing was betrayed in his speech, which was deliberate and rather slow, never by any accident outrunning his thought, as so often happens amongst our Milesians, but rather labouring behind it; a characteristic which had at least the effect of imparting to what he said an air of considered conviction.

The following are the chief facts of his life so far as can be ascertained, and for them, especially the medical ones, I am largely indebted to the kindness of the President of University College, Dublin.

He was born at Holyhill near Strabane on the 11th of January, 1836. His family was of Kerry origin. They were settled at Ballinskelligs, where their graves are to be seen in the old Abbey, and where the remains of their ruined castle still stand out gaunt and grey against the western sea. One Christopher Sigerson appears amongst the list of the transplanted Irish in 1654, and Dr Sigerson was probably of the same family. If so, heredity would sufficiently account for his strong national sympathies.

He received his early schooling in Strabane. After that we find him at Auteuil in France in the first years of Napoleon III, probably in 1852–1853. He there gained a school prize for Latin verse, and it is an interesting coincidence, showing already what was the drift of his mind, that it was for a translation of 'The Exile of Erin' he won it. Few careers are more striking in their continuity than his, for he was thinking of or working for his country all the time. The prize was presented to him, as he well remembered, by the grand *aumônier* of the Emperor, and he had a vivid recollection of his travelling home from France in the blue uniform of a scholar worn at that period.

He matriculated in the Queen's University in 1855, when he was eighteen years old, and studied in the Faculty of Medicine in Queen's College, Galway. He continued there for about two years, winning a first year scholarship in medicine. In his third medical year he removed to Cork and studied there in '57 and '58. At that time a medical course only lasted for four years. In Cork he won a further scholarship, in the third year. In '59 we find him attending surgery lectures of the final year in the Catholic University School of Medicine in Cecilia Street, Dublin. In this year also he gained First Honours in Celtic, apparently in a special examination held *ad hoc*. There appears to have been at that time an Honours prize in Celtic and another in Sanscrit [*sic*]. Sigerson got First Honours in Celtic and another man First Honours in Sanscrit, and in the Calendar they are bracketed *ex aequo*. These awards in Celtic and Sanscrit appear to have been introduced in 1852 and not to have been continued beyond 1864.

In 1859, after taking his M.D. in Queen's University, Sigerson appears to have gone to France, probably to do post-graduate work for a couple of years. In after times he dedicated some of his medical work to his beloved master Duchenne (de Boulogne), under whom he must at this time have been studying. He was also, either then or later on, in close touch with Charcot at La Salpêtrière; but as Charcot, born in 1825, was at this time a comparatively young man, it is probable that Sigerson studied diseases of the nervous system under him at a somewhat later period. In advanced life he used to refer to Charcot more than to any of his teachers, and he paid back his debt to his master by translating his book on Nervous Diseases, with valuable notes of his own, in the New Sydenham Society Series. At this time the famous French zoologist, Milne Edwards, took a leading place in Natural Science, and the still more famous Claude Bernard in physiology, and Sigerson was deeply imbued with the spirit of their work. His studies in science and in medicine were conducted along the lines of these great masters. His outlook on Science was a French outlook; his attitude towards medicine was a French attitude. In other words he blended theory with actual practice, and applied theory to actual practice in a manner very different from that of the English or the Germans, who tend to dissociate the two things. It is almost certain that had Sigerson been attached – which he never was – to a large hospital, he would have been one of the outstanding physicians of these islands.

In 1865, after he had been for six years an M.D., he took his degree of M.Ch. in the Queen's University. His first appointment was in the Catholic University of Ireland. The minutes of the Medical Faculty show that his appointment to be lecturer in Botany was made in April, 1865, and his first lectures were delivered in the summer of that year. This was the beginning of his connection with the medical school of the University, which was to last in one way or another without a break for fifty-eight years.

In 1881 the Royal University was founded, and in the following year most of the first appointments of Fellows and Examiners were made. These included the then teaching staffs of the Catholic University College, that is, the Arts College in Stephen's Green and the Medical School in Cecilia Street. Sigerson was first appointed Examiner in Natural Science, and two years later, in 1884, he became Fellow and was made one of the special examiners for the Diploma in Mental Diseases. He remained a Fellow of the Royal University until that institution was replaced by the National University of Ireland in 1909, when he became Professor of Zoology, a post which he continued to fill until his retirement in 1923.

All through his career he must have been conscious of a divided allegiance between Science and Literature. As he lived and worked, he grew from strength to strength; and Ireland, which was never out of his thoughts, became ever more and more his debtor. He was an early and continuous worker in the cause of an Irish National University. An article of his in the *North British Review* was quoted by Gladstone, and Dr Coffey told me that the late President of Maynooth was convinced that another very able article of his in the same Review must have been written by Lord Acton. His research work in physiology and pathology was known and quoted by men like Professor Senator of Vienna and Dr Nothnagel of Berlin; the latter in his book on Gehirnkrankheiten adopts Dr Sigerson's classification. But he was better known in France, where Paul Bert, the physiologist, proposed him for the membership of the Clinical Society, Paris, and Charcot for the membership of the Society of Physiology and Psychology, and Henri Martin, the historian, for the membership of the Anthropological Society. Tyndall said that his researches revealed the true nature of organisms in the atmosphere whose presence he himself had detected, and Darwin proposed him for election as a Fellow of the Linnean Society.

But deeply interested as he was in science, his early love, I think, was literature, and he never neglected it to the day of his death. Nor can it be said of him that pure literature had more attraction for him at one period of his life than at another. In him his mind was so broad and his genius so varied, and the elements so kindly mixed, that Science, Economics, History, and Poetry all through his life appealed to him with almost equal force, though I have a suspicion that the appeal of poetry was the strongest.

As far back as 1860 we find him engaged upon his first literary effort and one that appealed to him with peculiar force. A dozen years previously John O'Daly had published a volume called *The Poets and Poetry of Munster*, for which Clarence Mangan wrote the English translations in verse. Sigerson now proposed to take up the work of Mangan, O'Daly no doubt supplying the texts. O'Daly was a fine Irish scholar of the old traditional type, and had acquired as a result of ceaseless searching a great number of Irish MSS. He had made an excellent collection of poetry out of these for Mangan. He now laid his collection before Sigerson, and between them they produced the 'Second Series' of *The Poets and Poetry of Munster*. Sigerson wrote his own preface and many of the notes, all interesting, and translations into English verse of 46 poems. …

It is probable that Sigerson from this time forward kept in view the publication of further translations from the Irish. I made his acquaintance when I was a student, and he used sometimes to read me a poem. I had the pleasure of dedicating my *Love Songs of Connacht* to him in 1894, thirty-four years after his own work had appeared, no translated book of Irish poetry having been published during that long interval. Three years later he produced his magnum opus, the *Bards of the Gael and Gall*, which – *parvis componere magna* – he dedicated to Gavan Duffy and to myself as representing the Gael and Gall respectively. In this new book he gave us translations of 139 Irish poems, a long vista of bardic compositions, leading back and ever back, from the present into the dim remote almost mythological past. It was a splendid thought to take the reader by the hand and conduct him along a road the like of which could scarcely be travelled over in any other land in Europe. He begins with three lays of the Milesian Invaders and then goes on to the Cuchulainn period (about the time of Christ), then to the Finn period (about three centuries later), then to the Ossianic poems, then to poems of the 'Christian Dawn' and the 'Early Christian' pieces, then to poems of the Gael and Norse (this is perhaps the best section in the book), and after that to the 'Gael and Norman', thence into the 17th century, the 18th century, songs of the emotions, folk songs, and finally two paraphrases from the Gaelic. …

Between science and pure literature lay the great field of philanthropy and politics, and in this domain Sigerson was no less distinguished. He had, as quite a young man, been chosen along with T.D. Sullivan to present a magnificent sword of honour to General Patrick MacMahon, destined to become the first President of the French Republic. This was in 1860, and we may read about it in Mitchel's *Jail Journal*. Sigerson had a great admiration for Mitchel, made him Paris correspondent of *The Irishman*, and arranged for the publication of his *Last Conquest (Perhaps)* in serial form in the same paper. This was the weekly journal to which Sigerson contributed so many excellent leading articles. The famous article 'The Holocaust', written on the execution of Allen, Larkin, and O'Brien, and published on November 23, 1867, immediately after the news reached Dublin, created something of a sensation. At this time and for some years before, he used to contribute poems and essays to many Irish publications, *The Nation*, *The Shamrock*, Duffy's *Hibernian Magazine*, and the *Irish People*, which last was the organ of the Irish Republican Brotherhood. I think the *Irishman*, before Pigott the forger got hold of it, was the paper to which he most contributed. I was told that at one time he was writing nearly all the leading articles for it.

I suppose that, with an ever-growing clientele and the pressure of his University work, he gradually gave up ephemeral writing and interested himself in the bigger things of literature. He was appointed Medical Commissioner to the Dublin Mansion House Committee when Ireland was threatened with a famine, and typhus broke out over the West in 1879–80. He and the late Dr Kenny made a minute tour of the districts affected, chiefly Mayo. One incident of his procedure I heard which will show the common-sense, if rather rough-and-ready way in which he met difficult situations. A young man was lying a helpless cripple on a bed which he had not left for six years. Sigerson immediately suspected that it was a case of nerves. The house was full of people, and a big fire blazed on the hearth. In this fire, with much ceremony and to the great amazement of the company, he heated a plough-share that he found lying on the floor until it became white-hot. He then caused the young man to be laid face downward on the bed and all the bed-clothes taken off. He next drove every one out of the house, seized the white-hot coulter from the fire, and with furious air and gesture ran at the young man, and before he could move, inflicted as quick as lightning half a dozen pricks of the hot iron up his spine. The patient uttered one frantic howl, leapt off the bed, burst out through the door, and tore away at full speed. Sigerson came back to the same place some years afterwards and found him happily married with a large family. His diagnosis had been correct. It was as a result of his experiences on this tour that he wrote his tract on 'The Need and Use of Village Hospitals'.

Three years later he was appointed a member of Lord Spencer's Royal Commission on Prisons. As a result of his labours many improvements were made in the dietary and treatment of prisoners of weak intellect. Reforms inaugurated by him were afterwards, I have been told, adopted largely in England. It was, no doubt, his experiences on this Commission which prompted him to compose his valuable work on political prisoners which appeared in 1890. In this volume he compares the different treatment of different classes of prisoners in the various European countries, and shows that England stood alone in her savage treatment of political misdemeanants.

The land question which, to many at the time, seemed *the* Irish question, had already claimed his attention, and he had, as early as 1871, published the *History of Land Tenures and Land Classes in Ireland*, the proofs of which were read by Mr Gladstone, and that statesman found the knowledge he derived from them very useful when introducing his Irish Land legislation; Lecky also quoted it with approval.

In 1891 or 1892 the National Literary Society was founded. The present writer was the first President of it, and his opening lecture was on the necessity of De-anglicisation. But he resigned when the Gaelic League was founded in 1893, and Dr Sigerson became President and presided over its fortunes until his death. During these many years he poured forth in his presidential addresses a stream of interesting knowledge upon the most varied subjects – all however connected with Ireland – which when we look back upon it almost takes our breath away. His minute knowledge of the most out-of-the-way facts and the most abstruse problems of history was marvellous. Where did he get it all? He never had many books about him; I hardly ever saw him reading, and yet he knew or seemed to know everything – at least everything connected with Ireland. He was often urged to put the erudition contained in these lectures into a book or books, and I imagine that he intended to do so, if he had lived longer. A friend told me he had seen a letter from Lord Acton, in which he described Sigerson as 'the best Irishman I have ever known,' and I believe he pressed him to collaborate with him in his *Cambridge Modern History.* It was Sigerson who wrote for Barry O'Brien's *Two Centuries of Irish History* the chapter (110 close pages) which deals with the eighteen years which elapsed between the grant of Legislative Independence in 1782 and the Act of Union in 1800, and his presentation of the story is masterly. The first edition of this book appeared in 1888. Thirty years afterwards he elaborated this chapter in the volume called *The Last Independent Parliament of Ireland*, and his Appendix contains many interesting facts relative to the condition of our fisheries, kelp-making, the bounty system, the curing of fish, the export of fish, the probity of Irish merchants, their enterprise, the Irish salt duties and salt policy, and other matters, all well documented and showing the amazing advances made under a native parliament.

His poem of King Lir written in blank verse, which he published in 1913 as a separate slender volume, is not, in my opinion, a success. There are in it some fine lines, but a great deal that is unequal, and the whole story of the life of the Swans themselves is omitted. His next poem, the translation of Sedulius, is a very ambitious work. For years he was taken up with the thought of it, and its completion gave him great satisfaction. A long preface sets forth the author's theories on metric to which I have already alluded, but contains also much interesting historical matter. Then follows, on a unique principle which I do not remember to have seen carried out before, a rhymed metrical translation of the best passages in the Easter

Hymn, none being longer than a couple of pages, while he compresses into a prose résumé in smaller print the long stretches of rather blank hexameters that connect one chosen passage with another. He comments freely and in entertaining manner on his text, as he goes, showing how Sedulius must have had a medical training, must have been familiar with fly-fishing, etc. The poem itself as versified and compressed into prose fills only 60 pages; the rest of the volume (210 pages) is taken up with the preface and the appendices, in which, amongst other things, he shows how much Milton was indebted to his hero.

My personal recollections of Dr Sigerson date back to my college days. I first saw him with old John O'Leary, to whom he was exceedingly kind, as he was to all who had worked or suffered for Ireland. On the strength of having seen him with O'Leary I plucked up courage and spoke to him one day. He looked hard at me in a very chilling, in fact intimidating manner, and said: 'You have the advantage of me'; but when I told him I had met him with O'Leary he at once thawed and became friendly, and I flatter myself that I never lost his friendship. Not only was he interested in the Irish language, but also in Irish music. He was one of the founders of the Feis Ceoil. He was interested enough in athletics to give a cup for inter-collegiate competition. His chief relaxation and hobby seemed to be the search for miniatures. His extraordinary and unique collection of Napoleonic and other French miniatures was exhibited for a long time in the National Museum and attracted great attention. Pictures of French *grandes dames* and French *objets d'art* appealed to him strongly. He used to go to the continent almost every summer and never came back without something new. His house was full up of valuable antiques. He was very sociable and loved to have people to dinner on Sundays. Goethe's words,

> *Tages Arbeit, Abends Gäste,*
> *Saure Wochen frohe Feste,*

seemed to have been his *Zauberwort* also. He certainly worked hard throughout the week. His ante-room was always full of patients, and he continued seeing them until a late hour.

I have heard of many wonderful cures he performed on patients affected with nerve-trouble. He was not in the least desirous of money. I think he never accepted it from many of his poorer clients. I imagine that he was very careless about it. I once sent him a cheque; but it was, so far as I could see, never cashed. I heard other people say the same thing. He was always only too willing and even eager to prescribe gratis for his friends, if he thought he could do them any good. In this generosity of his he was perhaps following a family tradition, for Francis Sigerson of Kerry is still locally referred to as 'Proinsias Críona do dhfolach déirc in a thigh,' and a well-known poem still repeated near Ballinskelligs refers to him as a 'Biatach' or hospitaller whose fame was sufficient for the whole of Munster, to whose house the Earl (of Kenmare?) used to resort.

I think he must have done all his literary work late at night, and that he seldom went to bed until near morning. It is fascinating to contemplate his long life as a continuous whole and to think of all the immense changes that have taken place, in almost every one of which he himself bore a hand; the settling of the land question, the establishment of a National University, the recognition of Irish as the National language, the withdrawal of the English. All these things he worked for, and he saw all of them come to pass. It must have seemed to him almost a miracle when he looked back on the days of his youth and thought of the time when it was wise to refrain from putting his name on the title-page of an Irish book of national tendency.

He either was, or pretended to be, inordinately proud of his Norse ancestry. I think that even his best friends did not quite know how far he was in jest about this or how far he was in earnest. He always resented or pretended to resent any implied slur upon the Norsemen, whom he credited with all the virtues. He certainly looked, himself, like an ancient Viking from a Norwegian fiord, and I have been told that in his youth his hair was really red, though it was not so in my time. He had a very keen sense of humour, but was never unkind. Having once heard me deliver what I suppose must have been an indiscreet lecture, sometime after the Parnell split, when it was difficult not to say something to offend somebody, he told me that I reminded him of a little boy running round a garden and shaking each several beehive as I passed along – just to see how many bees would come out and buzz!

As a poet he was best as a lyrist. When the late T.W. Rolleston and his father-in-law, Stopford Brooke, brought out their *Treasury of Irish Poetry in the English Tongue*, they commissioned me to get some poems from Sigerson. It was then I discovered for the first time how sweet and how original a lyrist he was. I sat up with him one night until four o'clock, and he read me a great number of original lyrics, four or five of which entranced me. I picked out three original songs for Rolleston's book, 'The Swans of Lir,' 'The Rowan Tree,' and 'Far-away,' but the editors preferred translations from the Irish and only printed the last one. Where are the others, where are all the poems he read to me that night? I hope sincerely that they are not lost. Lest I be accused of exaggerating his lyric gift, I shall conclude this article by quoting just two verses from the only one of all those pieces that was, so far as I know, saved and printed.

FAR AWAY
As chimes that flow o'er shining seas
When Morn alights on meads of May,
Faint voices fill the Western breeze
With whisp'ring songs from far-away.
Oh, dear the dells of Dunanore,
And bright is billowy Ballintrae;
But sweet as honey, running o'er,
The Golden Shore of Far-Away.

There grows the tree whose summer breath
Perfumes with Joy the azure air;
And he who feels it fears not Death,
Nor longer heeds the hounds of care.
Oh, soft the skies of Seskinore,
And mild is meadowy Melleray;
But sweet as honey, running o'er,
The Golden Shore of Far-Away.

He came to see me take my seat in the Senate about ten days before his death, and his last words to me, after listening to the discussion for a while, were 'This is good work, you know, careful work, sound work.' He died in his ninetieth year in the full enjoyment of his faculties, and Ireland will not forget him and cannot replace him.

An Craoibhín

APPENDIX 8: EXTRACTS FROM A LECTURE BY DR GEORGE SIGERSON AT THE INAUGURATION OF THE NATIONAL LITERARY SOCIETY IN DUBLIN, AUGUST, 1892[13]

Irish literature: its origins, environment, and influence

In the early part of his lecture, Sigerson described pre-Christian and early Christian Ireland, from which sprang 'the treasure of our ancient literature … the lightning-flash of ideas in the darkness of the dawn'. Having referred to the early settlers who made their way from Europe to Ireland, he continued:

> The land must have appeared very beautiful to those first comers who had traversed the desolate wastes and shaggy forests of the continent, but its aspect was not altogether that of to-day. Green pastures there were, where the wild deer browsed, and a wonderful profusion of flowers, and mountain moors that seemed mantled in purple and gold. But there were also the mysteries of dark forests of somber yew, balsamic pine, and immemorial oak, where lurked the fierce wild bull, lean wolf, and other foes of life, now, like them, extinct. We dwell above their remains, for the Book of Nature is a palimpsest where the record of a new life is written over the dead letter of the old.
>
> Men coming to a new home bring with them a stock of ideas, some ancestral, some acquired on the way. They obtain others from the suggestions of their surroundings after arrival. In the excitement of change, in the presence of novel phenomena and new experience, the eye is made keen, the senses are quickened, and the brain is stimulated to the utmost. The rapid climatic variations of their insular abode must have affected those accustomed to more constant continental atmospheres. The earliest remnants of our literature reveal a people who were, or as I think, who had become in these conditions, very sensitive to the things of nature, to whom fair objects of heaven and earth gave joy, and whose exalted imagination saw mystery in new phenomena. These (common things to us) contradicted their experience, and the unknown causes were identified with unseen beings. What wonder if sudden gusts unaccountable, light twirling eddies, mists marching through ravines and gorges, should mask the invisible powers! Man was face to face with nature, vibrating with every change, affected by every influence. His weapons had a secret life within, and the shield of the champion sounded when one of the Three Waves of Erin rose roaring in foam.
>
> The aspect of the living waters was ever present, in the surging seas, the full rivers in all the plains, the liquid voice of streams in every glen, and the silent, mystical lakes among the mountains. Sometimes the waters were troubled, and they saw therein the struggles of gigantic serpents, ancestral memories of extinct animals, or reminiscences of experience in other regions. Sometimes the waters sank, or, suddenly rushing up, overwhelmed the abodes of men, owing, they fancied, to some pledge broken to the invisible deities. These strange phenomena, which have given cause for so many weird legends, I have correlated with those that precede or accompany earthquake action. It has seemed to me probable that there were, of old, beyond our western coasts, islands, which, owing to the same seismical cause, have sunk beneath the ocean level. The memory of their existence, and the fact of their absence, might well give rise to those strange and beautiful traditions of the Lands of Youth, of Life, of Virtues, their mystical appearance and disappearance which for ages inspired the imagination of the poets. When successive waves of invaders had flowed over the land, the earliest driven into the woods, mountains and remote isles assumed mythical

proportions in the minds of the later comers, and, in the haze of knowledge, the land and all its far islands became peopled with a population of phantoms.

Sigerson spoke in particular of the reverence for learning that characterised that early period:

Unquestionably no nation ever so revered its men of learning. They rewarded that reverence by giving immortal life to its heroes, and by winning for that people the respect of modern scholarship I wish I could say of modern Ireland. But our people, generally, drink no more at the high head-fountains of their island-thought. This is one of the greatest losses which can befall a nation, for it loses thus its birthright, that central core of ideas round which new ideas would develop naturally, grow and flourish, as they never can on alien soil. There is a tone of sincerity in the ancient narratives which cannot exist in imported thought, and we are apt to lose inspiring examples of manful striving, loyal comradeship, truthful lives, chivalric courtesy, and great-minded heroism. It is true that so we escape some crude conceptions and improbable wonders. But, as in the physical order, each man seems to pass through various phases of racial development, so the individual in youth has tastes similar to those manifested by the race in its youth. Every people has at first its ideals, simple, sincere, and great, mingled with myths that stimulate the imagination. Every young generation has similar wants, and will seek to satisfy them, if not here, then elsewhere, in a literature that debases the germing ideals, dwarfs the mind, and soils the imagination.

With roots deep struck in the soil, the literature of the Irish Gael and commingled races grew vigorously from its own stock and threw out luxuriant branches and fair blooms. From the first, it exhibited characters peculiarly its own. But these were not what are considered Irish, in latter days: and here let me say that I am taken with dismay when I find some of my patriotic young friends deciding what is and what is not the Irish style in prose and the Irish note in poetry. We all know what is meant. But it is scarcely too much to say that you may search through all the Gaelic literature of the nation, and find many styles, but not this. If it ever existed, it existed outside of our classic literature, in a rustic or plebeian dialect. It must be counted, but to make it exclusive would be to impose fatal fetters on literary expression. As in other countries, there were not one but many styles, differing with the subject, the writer, and the age.

Having dealt at length with the intricacies of Irish metre and with the influence of Irish poetry on other European countries, Sigerson reflected on the relationship between literature and social mechanisms and how these mechanisms found expression in the development of learning in the monastic foundations in Ireland and in the genius of Irish scholars who brought their learning to other parts of Europe:

It occurs to me that from the mechanism of a people's literature, the composition of its metric especially, we can deduce conclusions as to the qualities and capacities in social and governmental matters. Building up verse may be correlated with the building up of a State, for it is an index of constructive power. The rhythmical tramp of the hexameter of Hellas and Rome, and the sustained strength of their great epics, re-appear in the disciplined tread of phalanx and legion, and the long-continued control of their rule. In the ancient Irish metric there was less of the rhythmic tread, and probably, as a consequence, much less sustained power exhibited, whilst there is a great capacity for detail, a special aptitude for fine arrangements and nice distinctions. Our ancient laws and history reveal the existence of great capacity for complex social mechanism with a minor grasp of dominating and sustained control. The character of our metric might have changed had the race developed a strong central authority. In support of this speculation, I think it may be said that in France and England the classic form, borrowed from Rome, ruled with autocracy and disappeared with the theory of the right divine. The Revolution revolutionised poetry as well as politics.

It was a splendid idea of the bards to conjure back Oisín from the land of Youth, and present him and St Patrick – types of Paganism and Christianity – in dramatic debate. The great passionate character of Oisín, his vivid love of battle and the chase, his generous spirit, his pathetic regret for lost kin and comrades, with his fiery flashes of revolt, constitute a creation in literature. No wonder that, even though amplified and altered in the garb of another language, the great conception left its impress on a later age. But I cite it here for a special reason, because it may also be taken as typifying the meeting and interaction of ancient Irish and Roman literatures. Christianity gave the Irish that cohesive organisation which their political system lacked, and the great schools took new vigour and vitality. Their rapid and wide-extended reputation shows that this must have been a pre-cultured people who could thus throw themselves so alertly into new study and so quickly conquer fame. The island became the University of Europe, whither students came from many foreign lands, and where they were warmly welcomed, supplied with food and books, and all gratuitously. But never in any land had learning such an explosive power upon a people as upon the Irish. Elsewhere it merely gave limited impulses. Here, no sooner had scholars trained themselves in academic studies than all the old adventurous spirit of the nation revived, and, ignoring minor ambitions, they swarmed off, like bees from a full hive, carrying with them the honey of knowledge and the ability to create other centres that should be celebrated for all times. …

Whilst some of the early Christians deprecated the study of the pagan classics, the Irish held large and more liberal views. This was peculiarly true of St Columbanus. Authoritative, inflexible, a daring missionary, his royal mind embraced the wide domain of letters. His eloquence is confessed. His monastic maxims are described as fit for a brotherhood of philosophers, whilst his wit is shown in his lighter poems, his culture in the adoption of old Greek metre, and his Irish training in the terminal rhymes in the alliteration of many of his verses. … His national characteristics were impressed on the great School of Bobbio, which he created, in which he died, and whence his influence long radiated over Italy and the North.

Entering the old Cathedral of Aachen, or Aix-la-Chapelle, you will be shown the great marble chair in which, cold as the marble, Charlemagne sat enthroned, sceptre in hand, robed in imperial purple, and with diadem on brow, dead. So he sate when, a century and a half later, Otho and his riotous courtiers broke open the vault and stood sobered and appalled before the majesty of death. On that same chair he sate, in similar apparel, but with the light of life in his eyes, the new Augustus of a new Empire, when two Irish wanderers were brought before him. In the streets of the city in which he hoped to revive the glory of Athens and the greatness of Rome, they had been heard to cry out: 'Who so wants wisdom, let him come to us and receive it, for we have it for sale.' Their terms were not onerous – food and raiment. Their claims stood the test. One, Albinus, was sped to Pavia in Italy; the other, Clement, had the high honour of superseding the learned Anglo-Saxon Alcuin in the Palatine school of the Imperial city. Here he taught the trivium and quadrivium – grammar, rhetoric, dialectic, and arithmetic, music, geometry, and astronomy – the seven arts. In his school sate Charlemagne under the school name of David, the members of his family each under an academic name, and with these the members of the cortege, the Palatins or Paladins, destined to power and feats of fame. The teaching of the Irish professors here must have had considerable influence on the literature (e.g., the Chansons de Geste) which afterwards took its heroes from their scholars. Their authority was enhanced by the fact that Charlemagne himself worked with his Irish professors at a revision of the Gospels on the Greek and on the Syriac text.

In the crash and chaos which followed soon after his death, when feudal vassals, strong as their nominal suzerain, lived an isolated warlike life and forgot letters, in the confusion caused by the shifting about of nations from the east and north, partly a rebound from imperial coercion, certain Irish names shine with especial splendour. The first is that of Johannes Scotus Erigena. Of unquestioned learning, versed in Greek, he was the founder of Scholastic Philosophy. This affects us still, for in Scholasticism, as in a forge, the intellect of the Middle Ages was fired, tempered, and made supple, keen, and trenchant. Hence, with all its powers awakened and under alert control, it was rendered fit for the production of the new sciences of modern times. Nor should it be forgotten that Fearghal the Geometer had but recently died, whose daring scientific speculations as to the Antipodes had shocked the stiff-minded Saxon Boniface. Dicuil brought exact science to bear on a cognate subject, in his work on the measurement of the earth, a work which has been republished in several foreign countries, but never in his native land.

The multitudes of students who flocked to Paris to hear Erigena, contented with couches of straw in the Rue de la Fouarre and old halls of the University, were not the last who invaded it to hear an eloquent Irishman. Four hundred years later, in the very beginning of the fourteenth century, another, and perhaps a still more illustrious, representative of Irish thought, in the person of Duns Scotus, the Subtle Doctor, throned it over the minds of men. So great was his renown that when in 1308 he came to Cologne the city accorded him a triumphal entry, more splendid than a king's.

Far, in every sense, from such ovations that desolate island off the Scotch coast, where, in the sixth century, 'a grey eye turned ever in vain' towards that Ireland 'where the songs of the birds are so sweet, where the clerks sing like birds, where the young are so gentle, the old so wise, and the maidens so fair to wed.' The exile charges his parting pupil to bear his blessing, part to Alba, part to Ireland: 'seven times may she be blessed ... My heart is broken in my breast. If death comes to me suddenly, it will be because of the great love I bear the Gael.'

Columba is the first Irish poet of exile, of which our nation has such sad experience since. His poetry, like his life, is instinct with the deepest affection for his native land, whilst his work has been the most fruitful in influence over the intellectual development of Scotland and England. From the island of Iona, chiefly, went forth that persuasive power which carried education over Britain. The majority of the Anglo-Saxon kingdoms, all the North of England, where English learning and literature took its rise, were bathed in an Irish intellectual atmosphere. Caedmon began his song in this environment, and when later, in the eighth century, English Aldhelm first wrote rhymed Latin verse, it was because he had been a pupil of the Irishman Mailduff, the first Abbot of Malmesbury.

Sigerson then turned to the relationship between Ireland and Scandinavia – a subject that was always dear to his heart:

To speak of literary relations between the Irish and the Norse may provoke some derision. Were not these the fierce sea-kings the 'Danes', whose delight was in war, and whose avocation in peace was the plunder of shrines? They were, however, paradoxical enough to build Christ Church, and to richly endow it. And it is also a curious fact that, previous to three great invasions of other countries, for which they are severely blamed, they had been appealingly besought for help by their supposed victims. Earl Hacon went to oppose the aggressions of the Emperor Otho; King Harald Sigurdson to avenge wrongs inflicted by English Harold; and Earl Sigurd of the Orkneys (whose mother was an Irishwoman) could not resist the appeal of Irish beauty in distress in the person of Queen Brian Borumha, who was mother of the Norse king of Dublin.

There were, in fact, many and important matrimonial alliances between the Irish and Norse princes, who often joined forces against foes. This happened at Clontarf, where the Irish of Leinster had the alliance of the Dublin and Orkney Norse, whilst Brian brought up the Danes of Limerick. This battle, let me remark, is described in the literature of both countries, and in both descriptions there are omens and spiritual beings such as signalise the epic of Homer. So great was Norse influence over Ireland that three of our provinces retain the Northern name-endings, and many a headland and bay has a Norse appellation. They delighted in the loveliness of the land. Linnaeus, in latter days, fell on his knees before the splendour of a furze-bush in blossom, and we can readily imagine how tears came into the eyes of the Arctic rovers when they beheld the fresh green of Ovoca or were dazzled by the crimson and gold of Benn Edair, which they called Howth. Irish music charmed them, and even now some of our old airs awake echoes along the Norland fiords.

The latest and most distinguished authorities declare that Irish literature has largely influenced that of the Scandinavians. Their Heroic Age was much later than ours, from the end of the ninth to the eleventh centuries, when the ambition of Harold Haarfagre to imitate the imperial methods of Charlemagne had driven the independent princes to far isles or foreign voyages. They were in close and continuous contact in peace and war with the Irish, 'whose ancient civilisation was superior and therefore stronger.' Bergen, the old Norse capital, possessed a church dedicated to St Columba, and the revered relics of its patron, St Sunniva, an Irish maiden! As you sail into Reykjavik, the capital of Iceland, you pass the Westman Isles, so-called because of the Irish who had visited and dwelt there. Now Iceland, that strange attractive island, where cold white snow covers the hot volcanic heart, is the old home of the Sagas. It had been first peopled by some Irish monks. Another settlement took place when Queen Aud, widow of White Olaf, the Norse King of Dublin, went thither on the death of her son. Norsemen and Irishmen, her kinsfolk and dependents, accompanied her. Mr Vigfusson, himself an Icelander, writes with a generous fairness, characteristic of the race, as follows:

'The bulk of the settlers were men who, at least for one generation, had dwelt among a Keltic population and undergone an influence which an old and strongly marked civilisation invariably exercises among those brought under it, an attraction which in this particular case was of so potent a kind that centuries later it metamorphosed the Norman knights of the foremost European kingdom with startling rapidity into Irish chieftains. Moreover,' he adds, 'we find, among the emigrants of all ranks, men and women of pure Irish and Scottish blood, as also as many sprung from mixed marriages, and traces of this crossing survive in the Irish names borne by some of the foremost characters of the Heroic Age of Iceland, especially the poets, of whom it is also recorded that they were dark men.' He considers that this close intercourse with the Celts had to do with heightening and colouring the strong but somewhat prosaic Teuton imagination into that finer and more artistic spirit manifested in the Icelandic Saga. The classic land of the Saga was in West Iceland, and there also the proportion of Irish blood was greatest. On the Norsemen who still remain there the Irish influence was yet more effective and powerful. Mr Vigfusson makes an observation, which is a touching and keen reproach to those on whom it devolves to publish the manuscript materials of ancient Irish literature. He writes: 'Only when it is possible to judge fairly of the remains of the Keltic literature of the ninth, tenth, and eleventh centuries, can any definite conception of the influence it exerted on Icelandic, Norse, and English literature be properly estimated.' With the great Sagas, the fame of which has spread abroad as their strong dramatic character deserves, Northern literature possesses the no less celebrated Eddas. These Eddic poems 'discover an ideal of beauty,' writes Mr York Powell, 'an aerial unearthly fairy world, and a love of nature which we do not find in the Saga.' They also reveal that those who composed them were familiar with more southern scenes and manners; and the poems are shown to be the mental offspring of the men 'who won Waterford and Limerick and kinged it in York and East England.' 'It is well to remark,' he adds, 'that among the first poets we have any knowledge of, the majority are of mixed blood with an Irish ancestress not far back in the family tree. ... Their physical characteristics, dark hair and black eyes, like Sighvat and Kormack, their reckless passion and wonderful fluency are also non Teutonic and speak of their alien descent.' In Bragi's Eddic poem there is a very manifest introduction of a characteristic Irish rhyme method.

Thus we have it on unquestionable authority that the noble Norse literature, which occupies a position of the greatest importance, dominating as it does the Teutonic world, was itself the offspring, in a certain sense, of our ancient Irish literature. Irish literary training and talent presided over and took part in its composition, gave dramatic vividness to its narrative, grace, method and myths to its poetry.

With this knowledge in mind you will look with better insight into the story of the Norsemen in Ireland, and see them, no longer as a cloud of barbarians, but as brave adventurous knights whose voyages fringed our seas with a murmur of song, and whose cities, in quiet times, were the favourite resort of Irishmen skilled in letters and all the arts of peace and war. 'Why should we think of faring home?' sang King Magnus. 'My heart is in Dublin. I shall not return in autumn to the ladies of Nidaros. Youth makes me love the Irish girl better than myself.'

Considering how often and how constantly the prejudice of the ignorant prevents a good understanding between neighbours, whether these be individuals or nations, I have sometimes thought of writing a book to be entitled: The Good Deeds of our Enemies. Too often do we find writers stopping at nothing to cover the foe with obloquy. By this they put out their own eyes and blind our moral sight. Proceeding on a different principle, I should show enemies, not in their conflicts, but in their concessions, and the picture would give a truer idea of mankind, for it is surprising how many kind offices were mutually interchanged between foemen even in this very country who are always represented as savage, ruthless, and exterminating.

Ireland has been able to act upon the literature of the Continent and of Britain in three ways: first, directly; next, by means of its pupils on the Continent, and finally by means of the Norse literature. The latter affected both Britain and Germany, so that the Irish spirit has had a double influence, be it much or little, upon both. Professor Morley, indeed, admits that 'the story of our literature begins with the Gael'; and pointing out the intermixture of blood, he adds: 'But for early frequent and various contact with the race which in its half barbarous days invented Oisín's dialogues with St Patrick, and that quickened afterwards the Northmen's blood in France and Germany, England would not have produced a Shakespeare.'

In the final part of his lecture, Sigerson reflected on 'the unique treasure' that is Irish literature, and makes a plea to the country to 'live by the energy of intellect':

It is a strange thing to say that Edmund Spenser, who so deprecates their 'rebellious' love of liberty, might well have envied the position and influence of the Irish poets. At the Queen's Court in England he had learned 'what hell it is in suing long to bide', to 'eat the heart in despair,' and all the miseries of dilatory patronage:

'To fawn, to crouch, to wait, to ride, to run, to spend, to give, to want, to be undone.' In Ireland he saw a different state of things. The poets might almost be described as the patrons, for theirs it was to distribute praise or dispraise in poems, 'the which,' says Spenser, 'are held in so high regard and estimation amongst them that none dare displease them, for feare to runne into reproach through their offence, and be made infamous in the mouths of all men.' Their compositions were sung at all feasts and meetings by other persons, and these also, to his surprise, 'receive great rewards and reputation.' Certain it is, though strange, that Edmund Spenser, had he been least bard in the pettiest principality of Ireland, instead of being the first poet of the monarch of Great Britain, would not have died of hunger. Neglected and starving in Westminster, may he not have regretted his political efforts to destroy the one national organism which above all others had ever generously encouraged the representatives of literature?

It is a study full of interest to watch the development of the culture of the Anglo-Irish Pale, and the continuance of that of the Irish nation. In Latin, their men of learning had long a common language, but the vernacular was not neglected. In 1600 the literary organisation was still strong, and its strength was shown in the great Bardic Contention. Thirty-two years later an assemblage of historians, antiquaries, and monks was held to collect and collate materials for the great Annals of the Kingdom. Four years the Four Masters laboured at the work, safe by the far shore of Donegal, and fortunate it was, for soon after there was no safety in the 'Athens of the West', the 'University of Europe', for those of its faithful offspring who loved learning and letters. Teacher and pupil were banned. In the midst of morasses, forests, or mountain glens, they still studied, their bards still sang, and their minstrels played, often with out-posted sentinels on the watch.

What wonder if sadness shadowed the land? But disaster may have some compensating gifts to noble natures. The true laurel when crushed yields all its inner fragrance. Deprived of their princes and deposed from their estate, the bards ceased to be learned in the classic forms of literary technique; but they became poets of the people. The sincere voice of their hearts spoke in their song, which is brimful of passionate feeling and glowing with fair ideals. If in other times they had too often confined their efforts to the eulogy of particular princes, now it was otherwise. At the hearths of the people they sang the songs of a Nation.

Perhaps now the first idea of modern nationhood was conceived. Now, at all events, pathos became a character of Irish literature, distinguishing it deeply from that counterfeit of late grotesque, the authors of which resemble those mutilators of men who carved the mockery of laughter upon the face of grief.

What a subject for a painter would be that meeting between the blind and hoary bard Carolan, and the young, bright-eyed child Oliver Goldsmith! The venerable aspect of the ancient Celtic poet he never forgot. 'His songs,' he says, 'in general may be compared to those of Pindar; they have frequently the same flight of imagination.' He had composed a concerto 'with such spirit and elegance that it may be compared (for we have it still) with the finest compositions of Italy.' This reminds us of the time when an enemy, Giraldus Cambrensis, declared that the skill of the Irish in music 'was incomparably superior to that of any other nation.'

The meeting of Carolan and Goldsmith may fitly typify the meeting of the literatures of the old nation and of the Pale, one venerable by age and glorified by genius, the other young, buoyant, and destined, like it, to be the guardian and the honour of our common country.

Irish literature is of many blends, not the product of one race but of several. It resembles the great oriel of some ancient cathedral, an illumination of many beautiful colours, some of which can never be reproduced, for the art is lost. We possess an unique treasure in that ancient literature which grew up from a cultured people, self-centred, independent of Roman discipline. Were it not for this we should look at the Northern world through Southern eyes, and, taking our viewpoint from the Capitol, see nothing beyond the light of the empire, but wild woods and wastes made horrid by Cimmerian darkness, and shifting hordes of quarrelsome barbarians. Yet these were the ancestors of most of the modern European peoples, and those who so depicted them were their coercive and uncomprehending foes. Our deliverance from this thraldom of an enemy's judgment abides, in the monuments of the ancient Irish.

The magic password of the Arabian bade the rugged mountain open, and admitted him to the midst of glittering jewels. The knowledge of our old literature takes us into the heart of the Cimmerian darkness, and shows it full of glowing light; it takes us into the homes and minds of one of those great nations uncomprehended of the Romans, and through that one, enables us to see the great, passionate, pathetic, wild, and generous humanity of all.

Thus our ancient literature would be invaluable if for this reason alone, that it gives a new view-point and a new vista. Its importance is augmented in this, that its reckless sincerity stands the enduring evidence of a long-vanished stage of social and intellectual development, where the fiercer and finer powers, the softer and sterner emotions of an early mankind strive and commingle with dramatic effect. If such a deposit were not extant, European scholars might well desire to go as pilgrims, like the bereaved bards, to the grave of Fergus, son of Roi, with power to call him again on earth, that he might recite the famous Taín, the lost Epic of a lost World.

It is strange that words, which are such little things, a mere breath trembling for a moment in the air, should survive the mightiest monarch and outlast the lives of empires. The generations who uttered them are silent; the earth has grown over their homesteads, and forests have decayed above their cities. Yet out of the Dead Past speaks still the Living Voice. So, to-day, we may be illumined by the light of a star which perished a thousand years ago.

It has been said that the history of Ireland is dismal, a chronicle of defeats. But that is because writers generally make history a mere record of wars. The shadow of the swordsman obscures all else. The militant monarch or minister is always put in the foremost place and the highest position. The pigmy on a platform looks greater than the giant in his study but only in the eyes of pigmies. Alexander's Empire died with him, and his satraps shared the spoil. Aristotle's sceptre is over us still.

There is a blindness which is worse than colour-blindness in the eyes which see physical, but which cannot perceive intellectual forces and effects: they will record that Roman power conquered Greece, but fail to recognise that Greek intellect conquered the conqueror. Our nation has had its changes of fortune. It has invaded others, and been itself invaded, often part of the penalty it paid for occupying the fairest isle of the old world, a penalty we might still pay had not a new world opened wide its golden gates in the West. But our defeats have not been always disasters. What seemed to have no other end than the plunder of our wealth has resulted in the enrichment of our literature, the dissemination of our ideas, and the capture of the imagination of other nations. The code, which was devised to accomplish what the most ruthless savage never designed, the annihilation of the intellect of a most intelligent nation, studded the Continent with that nation's colleges and gave to its members the glory of being illustrious leaders of men in the greatest kingdoms of the world.

Last came the great dispersal, when the descendants of those who had taught Europe for three centuries, and generously welcomed all scholars, now made ignorant by law, were driven from their hospitable land by famine. They went forth, as it is said, hewers of wood and drawers of water. In other times and places it had meant extinction as slaves under feudal rule. But mark this! they entered into the great family of a new people, whose fundamental principle of Democracy made them equal, and whose generous nature made them welcome. They have thus been brought to the very well-spring of the new forces which have been re-shaping human society and preparing the transformation of the world. In this incomparable enterprise they are themselves a foremost force, taking part in the intellectual work with the revived vitality of a race which has found its Land of Youth.

If we had a past of shame, were we members of a nation that had never risen or had deeply fallen, these should be incentives to brave hearts to achieve work for the credit of their race. It is otherwise with us, and we dare not stand still. The past would be our reproach, the future our disgrace. Not foreign force, but native sloth can do us dishonour. If our nation is to live, it must live by the energy of intellect, and be prepared to take its place in competition with all other peoples. Therefore must we work, with earnest hearts and high ideals for the sake of our own repute, for the benefit of mankind, in vindication of this old land which genius has made luminous. And remember that whilst wealth of thought is a country's treasure, literature is its articulate voice, by which it commands the reverence or calls for the contempt of the living and of the coming Nations of the Earth.

APPENDIX 9: 'THE HOLOCAUST'[14]
WRITTEN BY DR SIGERSON IN DEC. 1867 FOLLOWING THE EXECUTION
OF THE MANCHESTER MARTYRS

Deaf to all warnings, however ominous, spurning alike the argument of the Just and the prayer of the Merciful, the Government has this day done a deed of blood which shall overshadow its name before the whole world. Nothing can account for its perpetration against all the urgings of statesmanship and humanity save only the blindness which falls from Heaven on overweening pride.

Clouds of passion and prejudice have wrapped their councils round; thick, gloomy and terrible as ever fell the black night of darkness upon the Egyptian land. 'Because' saith the Lord God of Israel, 'Ye would not let my people go'.

Hapless people. They have been required to build without stones, to make brick without straw and when their taskmasters have found the task not completed the lash has been laid unsparingly on their backs. For they have been deprived of their lands and punished for being poor; deprived of their liberty and scourged for being serfs; deprived of their teachers and slain alike for learning and ignorance …

Those days, they say, have passed away; we have long desired to govern you wisely and well. Thus they cry out, and when, we may ask, has the change been shown?

Was it in the Relief Act granted merely through fear of Civil War?

Was it in the prosecution of the Tribune who won it?

Was it in the Famine which slew its millions under their flag?

Was it in the exile of those gallant men whose councils would have guided them to avert the peoples' death?

When and where can we behold this beneficent change of policy? Let it not be hid from the nation.

Was it in the mouthings of a Viceroy … who incessantly proclaimed that Ireland was proper only for brute beasts and not for men?

Was it in the exodus of millions fleeing from all parts before his fist, to the uttermost ends of the earth?

Was it in the refusal to this day to change a system of land laws which plunders them of their hard won earnings and drives them out, bare and miserable, sick and dying, in the heat of summer and the icy chills of winter, from the homesteads of their fathers, from the native land of their race?

Let it be shown to us, this change which should make us glad.

Is it to be found in the benignity of rulers whose faces we never see but whose swords we have often felt?

Is it to be found in a denial that we have a right to a voice in our own Government – like Hungary, like Australia, like any colony, however small, provided it be not Ireland?

Finally the wrongs and grievances of this country are admitted. English statesmen have denounced them in the harshest terms. The present Chancellor of the Exchequer has called them sufficient cause for a revolution. When young men know this, when young men hear this, when too, they see these laws allowed to remain in all their venomous vitality; when too, they see these statesmen not only justifying revolution at home but fostering it abroad; when stung to desperation and madness they act on the lessons taught – where is the exoneration, where is the mercy?

On a vitiated verdict, on tainted testimony, on evidence which has been admitted to be that of false swearers and perjurers – on a verdict allowed to be flawed with error, two men and a youth – in the eyes of the law an infant – are done to a cruel death.

Behold England's justice in the conviction and condemnation, behold England's mercy in the sentence and execution of these political prisoners –

ALLEN, LARKIN and O'BRIEN.

There indeed, written large and deep, written in letters indelible, written in letters of BLOOD – read the mercy and justice of England.

They died far from the land they loved, far from the nation they would fain have served, foully slandered by a sanguinary aristocracy that they were enemies against society – but an army had to interfere between them and the people to prevent a rescue. It is said as an excuse that they were non-political prisoners, but they offered their lives to save those of their fellow men and they died with their face to the West and on their lips the patriot cry 'God Save Ireland'.

DEAD! DEAD! DEAD! But there are those who think that in death they will be more powerful than in life. There are those who will read on their Tomb the prayer for an Avenger to spring from their bones – *exoriare aliquis ex ossibus ultor*, and we foresee trouble and trepidations which might have been averted by a humane policy, which we fain would have averted and which we pray, by wise councils, may yet be saved the nations. Mistaken as the martyred men may have been, they shall yet be remembered in their native land along with those who have gone before them; nor shall their deaths shake her desire for a legislative independence, nor her trust in a speedy consummation.

'From morning watch even until night, Israel shall hope in the Lord.

Because with Him there is mercy, with Him there is plentiful redemption.

AND HE SHALL REDEEM ISRAEL FROM ALL WHO WORK IN INIQUITY'.

APPENDIX 10: DEDICATION TO *LOVE SONGS OF CONNACHT*[15]
Douglas Hyde

MY DEAR DR SIGERSON,

Allow me to offer you this slight attempt on my part to do for Connacht what you yourself and the late John O'Daly, following in the footsteps of Edward Walsh, to some extent accomplished for Munster, more than thirty years ago. Since that attempt of yours, down to the present day, scarcely an effort has been made to preserve what you then felt to be one of the most valuable heritages of the Irish race – its Folk Songs. I have, in the following little volume, collected a few of these, the Love-Songs of a single province merely, which I either took down in each county of Connacht from the lips of the Irish-speaking peasantry – a class which is disappearing with most alarming rapidity or extracted from mss. in my own possession, or from some lent to me, made by different scribes during this century, or which I came upon while examining the piles of modern manuscript Gaelic literature that have found their last resting-place on the shelves of the Royal Irish Academy. The little work of mine, of which this is the fourth chapter – the preceding three having been printed in the now extinct *Nation* – was originally all written in Irish, but the exigencies of publication in a weekly newspaper necessitated the translation of it into English. This I do not now wholly regret; for the literal translation of these songs will, I hope, be of some advantage to that at present increasing class of Irishmen who take a just pride in their native language, and to those foreigners who, great philologists and etymologists as they are, find themselves hampered in their pursuits through their unavoidable ignorance of the modern Irish idiom, an idiom which can only be correctly interpreted by native speakers, who are, alas becoming fewer and fewer every day. It has also given me the opportunity of throwing some of these songs into English verse – such as it is – in doing which I have differed somewhat from yourself, Mangan, Ferguson, and other translators, in endeavouring to reproduce the vowel-rhymes as well as the exact metres of the original poems. This may give English readers, if the book ever fall into the hands of any such, some idea of the more ordinary and less intricate metres of the people, and of the system of Irish interlineal rhyming, though I fear that the unaccustomed ear will miss most of it. My English prose translation only aims at being literal, and has courageously, though no doubt ruggedly, reproduced the Irish idioms of the original.

I have, as you will see, carefully abstained from trenching upon anything ever before published, my object merely being to preserve what was in danger of speedy extinction. It is, however, more than time that the best of those gems of lyric song, published by Hardiman, over sixty years ago, in two expensive and now rare volumes, were given to the public in a cheap and accessible form. It is to them the student should first look for the very highest expression of the lyric genius of our race. I have compiled this selection out of many hundreds of songs of the same kind which I have either heard or read, for, indeed, the productiveness of the Irish Muse, as long as we spoke Irish, was unbounded. It is needless to say that I have taken no liberties with my originals, and, though I have inserted conjectural emendations of many passages and words which to me appeared unintelligible, I have, of course, in every case honestly preserved in foot-notes the reading of the original mss., or the words of the viva-voce reciter, no matter how corrupt they may have appeared, and I have spared no trouble in collating manuscripts wherever I could, so as to give the best text possible.

In conclusion, I beg of you to accept this little *dioscán*, not for its intrinsic worth, if it has any, but as a slight token of gratitude from one who has derived the greatest pleasure from your own early and patriotic labours in the same direction, for, as the poet says:

> *'S í an teanga Ghaoidheilge is greannta cló,*
> *Go blasta léightear í mar cheol,*
> *'S í chanas briathra binn-ghuth beoil.*
> *'S is fíor gur mór a h-áille.*

Is mé, le meas mór,
An Craoibhín Aoibhinn

Notes and References to the Appendices

1. Reprinted from 'Seanad debates/Díospóireachtaí Seanad', iv (18 February 1925), *Parliamentary debates/Díospóireachtaí parlaiminte* (196 vols, http://historical-debates.oireachtas.ie/en.toc.seanad.html) (16 December 2010).
2. Reprinted from Curran, 'Oisín after the Fianna'.
3. Reprinted from *The Times*, 18 February 1925.
4. Reprinted from *Strabane Weekly News*, 21 February 1925.
5. Reprinted from *British Medical Journal*, 7 March 1925.
6. Reprinted from T.P. O'Hanlon, 'Literary musings', *Sunday Independent*, 1947.
7. Reprinted from Sigerson, *Songs and poems*.
8. Reprinted from ibid.
9. Poem originally published in Padraic Colum (ed.), *Anthology of Irish verse* (New York, 1922).
10. Sigerson, 'A Pale family'.
11. Anyone interested in a fuller account, particularly the Elizabethan, Cromwellian and Williamite periods, should consult Piatt, 'A Pale family and Old Dublin'.
12. Reprinted from Sigerson, *Bards of the Gael and Gall* (3rd ed., 1925).
13. Extracts reprinted from Duffy, Hyde and Sigerson, *The revival of Irish literature*.
14. Reprinted from Sigerson, 'The Holocaust'.
15. Reprinted from Hyde, *Love songs of Connacht*.

INDEX

Achonry, bishop of, 3
Act of Union, 1801, 11, 68
Acton, Lord, 19
Adelphi Terrace, London, 52
Albert Agricultural College, Dublin, 81
Allen, William Philip, 21
Aloysius, Fr, 78
Anglesea Street, Dublin, 16
Anglo-Irish Treaty, 1921, 71, 76
Antarctica, 27
Ardilaun, Lady, 74
Ardkill, County Derry, 2
Ardmore, County Derry, 1
Ardstraw, County Tyrone, 6
Armagh, archdiocese of, 35
Artigarvan, County Tyrone, 2, 3, 4, 5, 10
Atlantis, 11, 13, 25
Australia, 2, 10, 17, 28
Austria, 16

Ball, Benjamin, 25
Ballintadder, County Mayo, 37
Balzac, Honoré de, 43
Barnacle, Nora, 29
Barrington, Sir John, 33
Beaconsfield, Lord, 32
Benburb, County Tyrone, 1
Bernard, Claude, 25
Berryburn, River, 1
Biggar, Joseph, 23
Birrell, Augustine, 72, 73
Blennerhassett, Sir Rowland, 42
Book of Kells, 53
Boru, Brian, 69
Boston Pilot, 57
Boyd, Ernest, 15–16, 45
Brennus, 47
British Medical Congress, 1879, 27
Brontë family, 60
Brooke, Stopford A., 54
Bryan, Sarah Morgan, 59, 61
Buncrana, County Donegal, 6
Burke, David J.P., 82
Burt, County Donegal, 6
Butt, Isaac, 22, 23–4

Canada, 20, 34
Capitoline Hill, Rome, 47
Capuchin Annual, 66, 78
Carleton, William, 18
Carrickfergus, County Antrim, 1
Carrickmore, County Tyrone, 5
Casement, Sir Roger, 63
Cashel, diocese of, 83
Catholic University Medical School, Dublin, 10, 26, 30, 72

Catholic University of Ireland, 7, 10, 26–7, 69, 72, 81
Cavaignac, General Louis-Eugène, 8
Cavaignac, Jean-Baptiste, 8
Cavaignac, Mr, 8, 10
Cecilia Street, Dublin, 10
Celtic Revival, *see* Irish Literary Revival
Châlons-sur-Marne, France, 16
Charcot, Commander Jean-Baptiste, 27
Charcot, Jean-Martin, 25, 26, 27
Charlestown, County Mayo, 36–7
Chateaubriand, François-René de, 8
Children's Magazine, 59
Church of Ireland, 2
Church of the Immaculate Conception, Dublin, 18
Clare Street, Dublin, 28–29, 31, 42–3, 57, 58, 59, 62, 64, 65, 66, 74, 75, 77
Clarke, Austin, 28–9, 47, 54, 74
Clifden, County Galway, 33
Clontarf, Dublin, 11, 69
Cloughcor, County Tyrone, 4
Cobh, County Cork, 61
Coffey, Dr Denis J., 82
Coffey, George, 45
Coleraine, County Derry, 84
College of Science, Dublin, 81
Collingwood Cup, 84
Colum, Padraic, 43, 77–8
Comhairle Ardoideachais league, 84
Condon, Edward O'Meagher, 21
Conradh na Gaeilge, *see* Gaelic League
Cork Examiner, 57
Cork, County, 81
Cork, County Cork, 10, 11–12, 26, 27, 57
Cosgrave, William T., 74, 75
Cowper, Earl, 34
'Craoibhín Aoibhinn, An', *see* Hyde, Douglas
Creggan, County Tyrone, 5
Crerand, Dr, 6–7, 8, 9
Croke Park, Dublin, 82, 84
Croke, Dr Thomas, 83
Crone, J.S., 66
Cúchulainn, 52
Curran, C.P., 7, 8, 20, 43, 49, 55, 66, 74, 77
Cusack, Brian, 82

Daily Chronicle, 19
Daly, Dominic, 45, 46
Darwin, Charles, 25
Davis, Thomas, 44, 45, 46
de Blácam, Aodh, 55, 73
Dempsey, Fr, 16
Derry Gaol, Derry, 7
Derry, County, 1–3
Derry City, 1, 2, 7
Dillon, John, 73
Doheny, Michael, 11

Donegal, County, 7
Dowden, Richard, 12
Dublin, 1, 10, 14, 15, 16, 18, 21, 22, 26, 28, 33, 34,
     35, 36, 43, 45, 47, 49, 50, 52, 58, 59, 61, 62, 64,
     65, 69, 70, 74, 80, 81, 82
Dublin Castle, 32, 34, 36, 68, 76
Dublin Journal of Medical Science, 27
Dublin Lockout, 1913–14, 70
Dublin Mansion House Relief Committee, 33–9
Dublin Monthly Magazine, 46
Duchenne de Boulogne, Guillaume-Benjamin-Amand,
     25
Duchess of Marlborough Relief Fund, 36
Dudley Cup, 84
Duffy & Co., 59
Duffy, Charles Gavan, 11, 29, 42, 43, 44–6, 51
Dún Laoghaire, County Dublin, 59

Easter Rising, 1916, 11, 60–1, 62, 63, 70, 71, 74
Ebenezer Terrace, Cork, 12
École de Médicine, Paris, 25
England, 21, 28, 32, 60
Enniskillen, County Fermanagh, 13
'Erionnach', 11, 15, 18
Esmonde, Sir Thomas, 74, 75
Esposito, Michele, 14
Eustace, Sir Maurice, 1

Faheens, County Mayo, 38
Famine of 1845–9, 4, 11, 16, 32, 33, 35
Famine of 1879–80, 32–9
Farren, Robert, 55
Fenian Brotherhood, 20, *see also* Fenian movement
Fenian movement, 11, 17, 19, 20–1, 23, 24, 40, 61,
     64, 71
Fenian Rising, 1867, 20, 21
Ferguson, Samuel, 15
Finn's Hotel, Dublin, 29
Fitzgibbon Cup, 83, 84
Fitzgibbon, Fr Edwin, 81, 82, 83
Fitzpatrick, Edmund, 16
Forster, William Edward, 22, 34, 39
Fox, J.A., 36
Foyle, River, 2
France, 7–10, 16–17, 25, 27, 73–4
Freeman's Journal, 39, 67, 76, 82
Freud, Sigmund, 25

GAA Museum, Dublin, 85
Gael, the, 57
Gaelic Athletic Association, 80–5
Gaelic League, 48, 51, 73
Gallon, County Tyrone, 5
Galway, County Galway, 10
Garda Training College, Templemore, 84
Garumna, County Mayo, 35
Germany, 20, 52
Gifford, Grace, 30
Gladstone, William, 19–20, 23

Glasnevin Cemetery, Dublin, 21, 60, 62
Glengariff, County Cork, 27
Glenkeen, County Derry, 2
Glenmornan Valley, County Tyrone, 2
Glenmornan, River, 5
Gonne, Maud, 28, 42, 46
Gorey, County Wexford, 76
Grafton Street, Dublin, 14, 75
Greece, 65
Green, Alice Stopford, 74
Greencastle, County Tyrone, 5
Gregory, Lady Augusta, 75
Gresham Hotel, Dublin, 82
Guinness, Arthur, 74

Harp, the, 11, 18, 57
Healy, T.M., 76
Hegarty, Fr, 6
'Henry, Paddy', 18
Hibernian Magazine, 18, 69
Higher Education Council League, 84
Holland, Denis, 18
Holy Hill, Artigarvan, 2
Holyhill House, Artigarvan, 2, 3, 5, 78
Home and Foreign Review, 19, 20
Home Rule Confederation of Great Britain, 24,
     see also Home Rule movement.
Home Rule League, 23–4, *see also* Home Rule
     movement
Home Rule movement, 70, 71, 72
Homer, 6
Hugh Lane Gallery, Dublin, 50
Huguenots, 12
Humphreys, Eibhlin (*née* Piatt), 59, 72
Huxley, Thomas Henry, 25
Hyde, Douglas, 15, 31, 42, 43, 45, 48–9, 51, 52, 55,
     60, 62–3, 67, 76, 78

Iceland, 27
Illustrated London News, 60
India, 34
Irish Book Lover, 66
Irish Civil War, 71
Irish College, Paris, 10
Irish Confederation, 11
Irish Ecclesiastical Record, 68
Irish Fireside, 57, 58
Irish Land Bill, 1870, 19
Irish Literary Revival, 15, 16, 42–3, 51, 54, 62
Irish Literary Society, 43, 45, 46, 51, 69
Irish Literary Theatre, 47
Irish Monthly, 55–6, 57, 59, 67
Irish Parliamentary Party, 24, 73
Irish People, 18, 20, 64
Irish Republican Brotherhood, 20, 65, *see also* Fenian
     movement
Irish Statesman, 49
Irish Virtual Research Library and Archive, 50
Irish Volunteer Force, 64, 70

Irishman, The, 17, 18, 21–2, 23, 69, 71
Irwin, T.C., 18
Italy, 16

James II, 1, 2
Jeffares, A. Norman, 46
Jolicler, Abbé, 8
Jones's Road, Dublin, 82, *see also* Croke Park, Dublin
Joyce, James, 29, 73
Joyce, Robert Dwyer, 11–12

Kavanagh, Rose, 42, 58–9
Kenny, Dr Joseph, 36, 37, 38
Kerry, County, 1, 61
Kickham, Charles, 20, 29, 42, 64, 65, 66, 71
Kilkenny, County Kilkenny, 16
Killarney, County Kerry, 27
Kilmaine, County Mayo, 35

Land League, 40
Land War, 40
Larkin, Michael, 21
Latin Quarter, Paris, 8
Lavery, Sir John, 50
Leah, Frank, 55
Lecky, Edward, 20
Lee, River, 12
Leinster Colleges Council, 81, 82
Leonard, Chevalier J.P., 16, 27, 42
Lepracaun, The, 69
Letterkenny Academy, County Donegal, 6, 7, 8, 9
Letterkenny, County Donegal, 6, 7, 8
Liam MacCarthy Cup, 83
Linnean Society of London, 25
Logue, Cardinal Michael, 27, 35–6, 72
London, 19, 32, 43, 45, 47, 51, 52, 60
Londonderry Journal, 4
Louis Philippe, King, 7
Louis XIV, 74
Louis XV, 74
Louis XVI, 8
Lowther, James, 33
Luby, Thomas Clarke, 64
Lyceum, 58
Lyons, F.S.L., 55

MacArdle, Rev., 1
MacDonagh, Thomas, 54, 63–4, 67, 70
MacMahon, Marshal Patrice de, 16–17
MacNeill, Eoin, 48, 54, 70, 73
Magenta, battle of, 16, 17
Magenta, duke of, *see* MacMahon, Marshal Patrice de
Maghera, County Derry, 7
Manchester, 21
Manchester Guardian, 45
Manchester Martyrs, 20, 21–2
Mandeville, John, 40
Mangan, James Clarence, 13, 15, 50, 69

Mansion House (Relief) Committee, *see* Dublin Mansion House Relief Committee
Mansion House, Dublin, 49
Mardyke, Cork, 12
Marlborough Street Training College, Dublin, 81, 82
Marlborough Street, Dublin, 18
Marlborough, duchess of, 32
Maynooth College, County Kildare, 73, 84
Mayo, County, 36
McAnallen, Dónal, 80
McCay, Rev. Mr, 1
McCloskey, Master, 7
McCormack's Forge, County Derry, 1
McElligott, J.J., 82
McGinnis, Jane Sigerson, 3, 9, 57, 62
McGinnis, Patrick, 58
McHale, Archbishop John, 6
McKenna, Stephen, 65
Melmount, County Tyrone, 58
Meyer, Kuno, 51
Milton, John, 68
Mitchel, John, 11, 16, 17–18, 66
Mitchelstown, County Cork, 40
Mommsen, Theodor, 20
Moorlough, County Tyrone, 5
Mulcahy, Denis, 64
Munster Colleges Council, 80
Murphy, William Martin, 70

Napoleon I, 74
Napoleon III, 8, 10, 16
Nassau Street, Dublin, 34
Nation, The, 11, 13, 17, 18, 29, 45, 69
National League, 83
National Library of Ireland, 30, 66, 75
National Literary Society, 39, 42, 43–5, 47, 48–50, 51, 52, 69, 75
National Museum, Dublin, 74
National University of Ireland (NUI), 62, 63, 69, 73, 80–1, 84
Neilson family, 2–3
Neilson, Dr William, 5–6
Neilson, James, 2
Neilson, Mrs, 3
Neilson, Nancy (Sigerson), *see* Sigerson, Nancy (*née* Neilson)
Neilson, Samuel (founder of United Irish Society), 2
Neilson, Samuel (son of James), 3
Neuilly, France, 27
Nevinson, Henry W., 41
New Ireland Review, 56
New Sydenham Society, 27
New University of Ulster, Coleraine, 84
New York, USA, 65
New Zealand, 10
Newman, Cardinal John Henry, 7, 72
Newtownstewart, County Tyrone, 5
Nice, France, 29

Norsemen, *see* Vikings
North America, 2
North British Review, 19, 20
North City Dispensary, Dublin, 36

Ó Cuív, Brian, 71
O'Brien, Michael, 21
O'Brien, R. Barry, 68
O'Brien, William, 40
O'Connell Street, Dublin, 49
O'Connell, Daniel, 7, 11
O'Connellan, Professor Owen, 10
O'Connor, T.P., 22
O'Curry, Eugene, 16
O'Daly, John, 13, 15, 16, 63
O'Donnell, Frank Hugh, 47
O'Donoghue, D.J., 50
O'Donovan, Edmund, 42
O'Farrelly, Agnes, 50
O'Grady, Standish, 15
O'Hanlon, Mrs, 78–9
O'Hanlon, T.P., 28, 66, 78–9
O'Keefe, Colm, 12
O'Leary, Ellen, 42, 61, 64
O'Leary, John, 20–1, 27, 29, 42, 45, 46, 58, 61, 64–5,
    66, 71
O'Mahoney, Fr, 12
O'Riordan, John, 82
O'Shea, John Augustus, 18
Oldham, Charles A., 42
Orange Order, 19
Ossianic Society, 13

Paris Royale, Paris, 27
Paris, France, 7–10, 18, 25, 52, 65, 69, 74, 76, 77
Parnell Square, Dublin, 50
Parnell, Charles Stewart, 22, 23, 24, 43, 61
Pasteur, Louis, 77
Pearse, Patrick, 22, 63, 64, 70, 73, 81
Peel, Sir Robert, 11, 71
Phibsborough, Dublin, 79
Phoenix Park murders, 1882, 23
Piatt, Arthur Donn, 57, 59, 64
Piatt, Donn, 59, 78
Piatt, Eibhlin (Humphreys), *see* Humphreys, Eibhlin
    (*née* Piatt)
Piatt, Hester Sigerson, 2, 5, 6, 10, 12, 16, 18, 23, 25,
    27, 29, 31, 42–3, 48, 57, 58–9, 61, 64, 65, 70–1,
    73–4, 77, 78
Piatt, John James, 59, 61
Pigott & Co., 14
Pigott, Richard, 22–3
Plato, 46
Plunkett, Joseph Mary, 63
Pomeroy, County Tyrone, 13
Poor Law system, 4, 32, 35, 39
Presbyterians, 2, 4, 5, 72, 73, 76
Progrès Médical, Le, 27

Queen's College, Belfast, 7, 11, 71, 72, 73, *see also*
    Queen's University, Belfast
Queen's College, Cork, 7, 10, 11, 26, 69, 71, 72, 73,
    80, *see also* University College, Cork
Queen's College, Galway, 7, 10, 11, 71, 72, 73, 80,
    see also University College, Galway
Queen's University of Ireland, 26
Queen's University, Belfast, 84, 85, *see also* Queen's
    College, Belfast
Queenstown, County Cork, 61

Rademon, County Down, 5
Railway Cup, 83
Ranvier, Louis-Antoine, 25
Raphoe, County Donegal, 35
Redmond, John, 73
Repeal Association, 7, 11
Revolution of 1848 (French), 8
Richmond Hill, Dublin, 18, 28
Rolleston, T.W., 54
Roman Empire, 44, 47, 52
Rossa, Jeremiah O'Donovan, 22, 64
Rotunda, Dublin, 43
Royal College of Physicians, Dublin, 29
Royal College of Surgeons, Dublin, 26
Royal Irish Academy, Dublin, 25
Royal Irish Academy of Music, Dublin, 14
Royal Prisons Commission, 40
Royal University of Ireland, 57, 72, 80, *see also*
    University College, Dublin
Rue de l'Enfer, Paris, 8
Ryan, W.P., 54

Sadleir, Thomas, 76, 77
Sarsfield, Col. Patrick, 1
Schirmer, Gregory, 51
Schomberg, Frederick, first duke of Schomberg, 1
Seanad Éireann, 63, 71, 74–6, 78
Sedulius, 67, 68
Segerson, Captain John, 1
Segerson, John, 1
Segerson, Mrs, 1
Shamrock, The, 18
Sharp, Evelyn, 41
Shelbourne Hotel, Dublin, 81
Shelley, Percy Bysshe, 12
Shorter, Clement, 60, 61, 74
Shorter, Dora Sigerson, 18, 27, 43, 57, 58, 59–62, 68,
    74
Sigerson Cup, 80, 82–5
Sigerson, Dora (Shorter), *see* Shorter, Dora Sigerson
Sigerson, Ellen, 3, 9
Sigerson, George (I), 2
Sigerson, George (II), 3
Sigerson, George Patrick, 18, 57–8, 62
Sigerson, George
    Bards of the Gael and Gall, 44, 51–6, 63
    'Custodia honesta', 41

History of the land tenures and land classes of Ireland, 19–20
Modern Ireland, 19
Political prisoners at home and abroad, 40
Songs and poems by George Sigerson, 59, 77–8
The Easter song, 67, 68
'The Holocaust', 21–2, 69
The last independent parliament of Ireland, 67, 68, 71
The poets and poetry of Munster, 13, 15–16, 42, 51, 52, 62
The saga of King Lir, 18, 67
Sigerson, Hester (*née* Varian), 12–13, 15, 18, 57, 58, 62
Sigerson, Hester (Piatt), *see* Piatt, Hester Sigerson
Sigerson, James (I), 2, 3
Sigerson, James (II), 3, 9
Sigerson, Jane (McGinnis), *see* McGinnis, Jane Sigerson
Sigerson, John, 3, 9
Sigerson, Mary Ann, 3, 9
Sigerson, Nancy (*née* Neilson), 3, 4, 6, 7, 9
Sigerson, Richard, 2
Sigerson, William (I), 2
Sigerson, William (II), 2, 3–4, 5, 6, 7, 9, 10, 15
Sigerson, William (III), 3, 7, 9, 10, 57
Sigerson, William Ralph, 18
Sign of the Three Candles, 59
Simpson brothers, 7
Sinclair, John, 2
Sinn Féin, 64, 71
Sketch, the, 60
'Snorro', 18
Society of Jesus, 72
Solterer, Helen, 50
Sperrin Mountains, 2, 5
Sphere, the, 60
St Enda's School, Dublin, 63, 64, 81
St Joseph's College, Paris, 8–10, 26
St Patrick's College, Drumcondra, 80, 81, 82
St Stephen's Green, Dublin, 50, 69, 70
Stephens, James, 64
Stokes, Whitley, 53
Strabane, County Tyrone, 2, 3, 4, 6, 9, 58, 69, 85
Stranorlar, County Donegal, 24
Suffragette movement, 41
Sullivan, A.M., 22
Sullivan, T.D., 21
Sullivan, W.K., 26, 27
Sunday Independent, 28
Sunday's Well, Cork, 12
Swilly, Lough, 7
Swineford, County Mayo, 37, 38, 39
Sydney, Australia, 10
Synge Street, Dublin, 18
Synge, John Millington, 47–8, 65

Talbot Street, Dublin, 52
Tarpeian Rock, Rome, 47
Tatler, the, 60
Taylor, John F., 42, 45, 46

Tenant Right League, 20
Tergarvil Academy, County Derry, 7
Tergarvil, County Derry, 7
Times, The, 32
Tipperary, County, 40
Todhunter, John, 42
Tone, Wolfe, 7
Trinity College, Dublin, 7, 69, 71, 72, 79, 80, 84
Tullamore Gaol, County Offaly, 40
Tynan, Katharine, 42, 59–60, 60–1
Tyndall, John, 25
Tyrone, County, 1, 5, 12–13, 42, 58, 69, 77, 78

Ulster Volunteer Force, 70
'Ulsterman, An', 18, 19
Unitarians, 12
United Ireland, 46
United Irishman, 17, 47
United Irishmen, 2, 76
United States of America, 17, 20, 21, 27, 28, 34, 59, 61, 65
University College, Cork, 80, 81, 82, 83, *see also* Queen's College, Cork
University College, Dublin, 50, 72, 73, 80, 81, 82, 83
University College, Galway, 81, 82, 83, *see also* Queen's College, Galway
University of Ulster, Jordanstown, 84, 85
Upper Lurga, County Mayo, 37
University of Ulster, Jordanstown (UUJ), 84, 85

Varian, Hester (Sigerson), *see* Sigerson, Hester (*née* Varian)
Varian, Isaac, 12, 13
Varian, Ralph, 12, 13, 57
Vikings, 52, 69, 73, 78
Votes for Women, 41

Walsh, Archbishop William Joseph, 73
Walsh, Edward, 63
War of Independence, 11
Weekly Freeman, 58
Weekly News, 22
Weekly Register, 58
Welch, Robert, 53–4
West Indies, 3
Wetherell, T.F., 20
Williamite Wars, 1
Windisch, Ernst, 53
Wordsworth, William, 12

Yeats, Jack B., 42
Yeats, John B., 42, 58, 66
Yeats, W.B., 28, 42, 43, 44–7, 48, 58, 75
Young Ireland, 57
Young Ireland movement, 11, 12, 44, 45, 76
Young Ireland Rebellion, 1848, 17, 20

Zeuss, Johann Caspar, 53
Zimmer, Heinrich, 53